TExES
CORE SUBJECTS EC–6 291

D0809515

By: Sharon Wynne, M.S.

XAMonline, INC.
Boston

Library of Congress Cataloging-in-Publication Data

Wynne, Sharon A.
    TExES Core Subjects EC–6 291 Essentials Edition / Sharon A. Wynne. 1st ed
    ISBN 978-1-60787-488-1
    1. TExES Core Subjects EC–6 291
    2. Study Guides
    3. TExES
    4. Teachers' Certification & Licensure
    5. Careers

Disclaimer:

The opinions expressed in this publication are the sole works of XAMonline and were created independently from the National Education Association, Educational Testing Service, or any State Department of Education, National Evaluation Systems or other testing affiliates.

Between the time of publication and printing, state specific standards as well as testing formats and Web site information may change and therefore would not be included in part or in whole within this product. Sample test questions are developed by XAMonline and reflect content similar to that on real tests; however, they are not former test questions. XAMonline assembles content that aligns with state standards but makes no claims nor guarantees teacher candidates a passing score. Numerical scores are determined by testing companies such as NES or ETS and then are compared with individual state standards. A passing score varies from state to state.

Printed in the United States of America   œ-1

TExES Core Subjects EC–6 291 Essentials Edition
ISBN: 978-1-60787-488-1

Table of Contents

COMPETENCY 2
PHONOLOGICAL AND PHONEMIC AWARENESS

COMPETENCY 3
ALPHABETIC PRINCIPLE

COMPETENCY 4
LITERACY DEVELOPMENT

COMPETENCY 5
WORD ANALYSIS AND IDENTIFICATION SKILLS

COMPETENCY 6
FLUENCY READING

COMPETENCY 7
READING COMPREHENSION AND APPLICATIONS

COMPETENCY 11
WRITTEN COMMUNICATION

COMPETENCY 12
VIEWING AND REPRESENTING

COMPETENCY 13
ASSESSMENT OF DEVELOPING LITERACY 115

DOMAIN II
MATHEMATICS 127

COMPETENCY 16

COMPETENCY 17

COMPETENCY 18
PROBABILITY AND STATISTICS

COMPETENCY 19
MATHEMATICAL PROCESSES

DOMAIN III
SOCIAL STUDIES 219

COMPETENCY 20
SOCIAL SCIENCE INSTRUCTION 229

COMPETENCY 21
HISTORY 248

COMPETENCY 22
GEOGRAPHY AND CULTURE

COMPETENCY 23
ECONOMICS

COMPETENCY 24
GOVERNMENT AND CITIZENSHIP

DOMAIN IV
SCIENCE 383

COMPETENCY 25
SAFE AND PROPER LABORATORY PROCESS 391

COMPETENCY 26
HISTORY AND NATURE OF SCIENCE..401

COMPETENCY 27
IMPACT ON SCIENCE 416

COMPETENCY 28
CONCEPTS AND PROCESSES 423

COMPETENCY 32

COMPETENCY 33

COMPETENCY 34

COMPETENCY 35

COMPETENCY 44
MUSIC

COMPETENCY 45

COMPETENCY 46

TExES

CORE SUBJECTS
EC–6 291

SECTION 1
ABOUT XAMONLINE

XAMonline—A Specialty Teacher Certification Company

Created in 1996, XAMonline was the first company to publish study guides for state-specific teacher certification examinations. Founder Sharon Wynne found it frustrating that materials were not available for teacher certification preparation and decided to create the first single, state-specific guide. XAMonline has grown into a company of over 1,800 contributors and writers and offers over 300 titles for the entire PRAXIS series and every state examination. No matter what state you plan on teaching in, XAMonline has a unique teacher certification study guide just for you.

XAMonline—Value and Innovation

We are committed to providing value and innovation. Our print-on-demand technology allows us to be the first in the market to reflect changes in test standards and user feedback as they occur. Our guides are written by experienced teachers who are experts in their fields. And our content reflects the highest standards of quality. Comprehensive practice tests with varied levels of rigor means that your study experience will closely match the actual in-test experience.

To date, XAMonline has helped nearly 600,000 teachers pass their certification or licensing exams. Our commitment to preparation exceeds simply providing the proper material for study—it extends to helping teachers **gain mastery** of the subject matter, giving them the **tools** to become the most effective classroom leaders possible, and ushering today's students toward a **successful future**.

SECTION 2
ABOUT THIS STUDY GUIDE

Purpose of This Guide

Is there a little voice inside of you saying, "Am I ready?" Our goal is to replace that little voice and remove all doubt with a new voice that says, "I AM READY. **Bring it on!**" by offering the highest quality of teacher certification study guides.

Organization of Content

You will see that while every test may start with overlapping general topics, each is very unique in the skills they wish to test. Only XAMonline presents custom content that analyzes deeper than a title, a subarea, or an objective. Only XAMonline presents content and sample test assessments along with **focus statements**, the deepest-level rationale and interpretation of the skills that are unique to the exam.

Title and field number of test

→ Each exam has its own name and number. XAMonline's guides are written to give you the content you need to know for the specific exam you are taking. You can be confident when you buy our guide that it contains the information you need to study for the specific test you are taking.

Subareas

→ These are the major content categories found on the exam. XAMonline's guides are written to cover all of the subareas found in the test frameworks developed for the exam.

Objectives

→ These are standards that are unique to the exam and represent the main subcategories of the subareas/content categories. XAMonline's guides are written to address every specific objective required to pass the exam.

Focus statements

→ These are examples and interpretations of the objectives. You find them in parenthesis directly following the objective. They provide detailed examples of the range, type, and level of content that appear on the test questions. **Only XAMonline's guides drill down to this level.**

How Do We Compare with Our Competitors?

XAMonline—drills down to the focus statement level
CliffsNotes and REA—organized at the objective level
Kaplan—provides only links to content
MoMedia—content not specific to the state test

Each subarea is divided into manageable sections that cover the specific skill areas. Explanations are easy to understand and thorough. You'll find that every test answer contains a rejoinder so if you need a refresher or further review after taking the test, you'll know exactly to which section you must return.

How to Use This Book

Our informal polls show that most people begin studying up to eight weeks prior to the test date, so start early. Then ask yourself some questions: How much do you really know? Are you coming to the test straight from your teacher-education program or are you having to review subjects you haven't considered in ten years? Either way, take a **diagnostic or assessment test** first. Also, spend time on sample tests so that you become accustomed to the way the actual test will appear.

Fill out the **Personalized Study Plan** page at the beginning of each chapter. Review the competencies and skills covered in that chapter and check the boxes that apply to your study needs. If there are sections you already know you can skip, check the "skip it" box. Taking this step will give you a study plan for each chapter.

Week	Activity
7 weeks prior to test	Build your Personalized Study Plan for each chapter. Check the "skip it" box for sections you feel you are already strong in. ✖ SKIP IT ☐
6-3 weeks prior to test	For each of these four weeks, choose a content area to study. You don't have to go in the order of the book. It may be that you start with the content that needs the most review. Alternately, you may want to ease yourself into plan by starting with the most familiar material.
2 weeks prior to test	Take the sample test, score it, and create a review plan for the final week before the test.
1 week prior to test	Following your plan (which will likely be aligned with the areas that need the most review) go back and study the sections that align with the questions you may have gotten wrong. Then go back and study the sections related to the questions you answered correctly. If need be, create flashcards and drill yourself on any area that you makes you anxious.

SECTION 3

The TExES Core Subjects EC–6 (291) test is designed to assess whether a test taker has the requisite knowledge and skills that an entry-level educator in Texas public schools must possess. The 267 multiple-choice questions are based on the Core Subjects EC–6 test framework, and range from grades EC–6. The test may contain questions that do not count toward the score.

The test is structured with five Subject Tests:

- English Language Arts and Reading & the Science of Teaching Reading
- Mathematics
- Social Studies
- Science
- Fine Arts, Health and Physical Education

If, upon completion of the entire Core Subjects EC–6 (291) test, a test taker does not pass one to four of the Subject Tests, they are eligible to retake one or more Subject Tests on another date 45 days after taking the initial Core Subjects EC–6 (291) test. The timing for the Core Subjects EC–6 (291) test is by subject test, rather than the total test.

Subject Test	Total Items	Time
English Language Arts and Reading & the Science of Teaching Reading	75 questions	1 hour and 45 minutes
Mathematics	47 questions	60 minutes
Social Studies	41 questions	35 minutes
Science	52 questions	40 minutes
Fine Arts, Health and Physical Education	52 questions	40 minutes
TOTAL	267 questions	4 hours and 40 minutes

Question Types

You're probably thinking, enough already, I want to study! Indulge us a little longer while we explain that there is actually more than one type of multiple-choice question. You can thank us later after you realize how well prepared you are for your exam.

1. **Complete the Statement.** The name says it all. In this question type you'll be asked to choose the correct completion of a given statement. For example:

   > **The Dolch Basic Sight Words consist of a relatively short list of words that children should be able to:**
   >
   > A. Sound out
   >
   > B. Know the meaning of
   >
   > C. Recognize on sight
   >
   > D. Use in a sentence

   The correct answer is C. In order to check your answer, test out the statement by adding the choices to the end of it.

2. **Which of the Following.** One way to test your answer choice for this type of question is to replace the phrase "which of the following" with your selection. Use this example:

   > **Which of the following words is one of the twelve most frequently used in children's reading texts:**
   >
   > A. There
   >
   > B. This
   >
   > C. The
   >
   > D. An

   Don't look! Test your answer. _____ is one of the twelve most frequently used in children's reading texts. Did you guess C? Then you guessed correctly.

3. **Roman Numeral Choices.** This question type is used when there is more than one possible correct answer. For example:

> Which of the following two arguments accurately supports the use of cooperative learning as an effective method of instruction?
> I.   Cooperative learning groups facilitate healthy competition between individuals in the group.
> II. Cooperative learning groups allow academic achievers to carry or cover for academic underachievers.
> III. Cooperative learning groups make each student in the group accountable for the success of the group.
> IV. Cooperative learning groups make it possible for students to reward other group members for achieving.
>
> A. I and II
> B. II and III
> C. I and III
> D. III and IV

Notice that the question states there are **two** possible answers. It's best to read all the possibilities first before looking at the answer choices. In this case, the correct answer is D.

4. **Negative Questions.** This type of question contains words such as "not," "least," and "except." Each correct answer will be the statement that does **not** fit the situation described in the question. Such as:

> Multicultural education is **not**
>
> A. An idea or concept
> B. A "tack-on" to the school curriculum
> C. An educational reform movement
> D. A process

Think to yourself that the statement could be anything but the correct answer. This question form is more open to interpretation than other types, so read carefully and don't forget that you're answering a negative statement.

5. **Questions that Include Graphs, Tables, or Reading Passages.** As always, read the question carefully. It likely asks for a very specific answer and not a broad interpretation of the visual. Here is a simple (though not statistically accurate) example of a graph question:

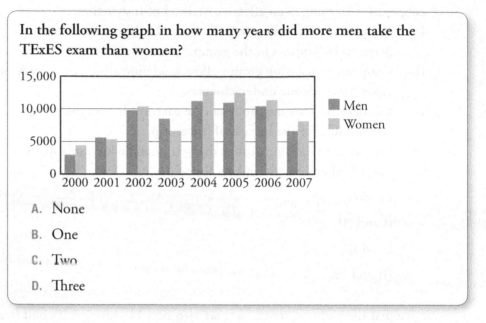

In the following graph in how many years did more men take the TExES exam than women?

A. None

B. One

C. Two

D. Three

It may help you to simply circle the two years that answer the question. Make sure you've read the question thoroughly and once you've made your determination, double check your work. The correct answer is C.

SECTION 4
HELPFUL HINTS

Study Tips

1. **You are what you eat.** Certain foods aid the learning process by releasing natural memory enhancers called CCKs (cholecystokinin) composed of tryptophan, choline, and phenylalanine. All of these chemicals enhance the neurotransmitters associated with memory and certain foods release memory enhancing chemicals. A light meal or snacks of one of the following foods fall into this category:

- Milk
- Rice
- Eggs
- Fish
- Nuts and seeds
- Oats
- Turkey

The better the connections, the more you comprehend!

2. **See the forest for the trees.** In other words, get the concept before you look at the details. One way to do this is to take notes as you read, paraphrasing or summarizing in your own words. Putting the concept in terms that are comfortable and familiar may increase retention.

3. **Question authority.** Ask why, why, why? Pull apart written material paragraph by paragraph and don't forget the captions under the illustrations. For example, if a heading reads *Stream Erosion* put it in the form of a question (Why do streams erode? What is stream erosion?) then find the answer within the material. If you train your mind to think in this manner you will learn more and prepare yourself for answering test questions.

4. **Play mind games.** Using your brain for reading or puzzles keeps it flexible. Even with a limited amount of time your brain can take in data (much like a computer) and store it for later use. In ten minutes you can: read two paragraphs (at least), quiz yourself with flash cards, or review notes. Even if you don't fully understand something on the first pass, your mind stores it for recall, which is why frequent reading or review increases chances of retention and comprehension.

5. **The pen is mightier than the sword.** Learn to take great notes. A by-product of our modern culture is that we have grown accustomed to getting our information in short doses. We've subconsciously trained ourselves to assimilate information into neat little packages. Messy notes fragment the flow of information. Your notes can be much clearer with proper formatting. *The Cornell Method* is one such format. This method was popularized in *How to Study in College*, Ninth Edition, by Walter Pauk. You can benefit from the method without purchasing an additional book by simply looking up the method online. Below is a sample of how *The Cornell Method* can be adapted for use with this guide.

2½" Cue Column	6" Note Taking Column
	1. **Record:** During your reading, use the note-taking column to record important points.
	2. **Questions:** As soon as you finish a section, formulate questions based on the notes in the right-hand column. Writing questions helps to clarify meanings, reveal relationships, establish community, and strengthen memory. Also, the writing of questions sets the state for exam study later.
	3. **Recite:** Cover the note-taking column with a sheet of paper. Then, looking at the questions or cue-words in the question and cue column only, say aloud, in your own words, the answers to the questions, facts, or ideas indicated by the cue words.
	4. **Reflect:** Reflect on the material by asking yourself questions.
	5. **Review:** Spend at least ten minutes every week reviewing all your previous notes. Doing so helps you retain ideas and topics for the exam.
↕ 2"	**Summary** After reading, use this space to summarize the notes from each page.

*Adapted from **How to Study in College**, Ninth Edition, by Walter Pauk, ©2008 Wadsworth*

6. **Place yourself in exile and set the mood.** Set aside a particular place and time to study that best suits your personal needs and biorhythms. If you're a night person, burn the midnight oil. If you're a morning person set yourself up with some coffee and get to it. Make your study time and place as free from distraction as possible and surround yourself with what you need, be it silence or music. Studies have shown that music can aid in concentration, absorption, and retrieval of information. Not all music, though. Classical music is said to work best

7. **Get pointed in the right direction.** Use arrows to point to important passages or pieces of information. It's easier to read than a page full of yellow highlights. Highlighting can be used sparingly, but add an arrow to the margin to call attention to it.

8. **Check your budget.** You should at least review all the content material before your test, but allocate the most amount of time to the areas that need the most refreshing. It sounds obvious, but it's easy to forget. You can use the study rubric above to balance your study budget.

Testing Tips

1. **Get smart, play dumb.** Sometimes a question is just a question. No one is out to trick you, so don't assume that the test writer is looking for something other than what was asked. Stick to the question as written and don't overanalyze.

2. **Do a double take.** Read test questions and answer choices at least twice because it's easy to miss something, to transpose a word or some letters. If you have no idea what the correct answer is, skip it and come back later if there's time. If you're still clueless, it's okay to guess. Remember, you're scored on the number of questions you answer correctly and you're not penalized for wrong answers. The worst case scenario is that you miss a point from a good guess.

3. **Turn it on its ear.** The syntax of a question can often provide a clue, so make things interesting and turn the question into a statement to see if it changes the meaning or relates better (or worse) to the answer choices.

4. **Get out your magnifying glass.** Look for hidden clues in the questions because it's difficult to write a multiple-choice question without giving away part of the answer in the options presented. In most questions you can readily eliminate one or two potential answers, increasing your chances of answering correctly to 50/50, which will help out if you've skipped a question and gone back to it (see tip #2).

5. **Call it intuition.** Often your first instinct is correct. If you've been studying the content you've likely absorbed something and have subconsciously retained the knowledge. On questions you're not sure about trust your instincts because a first impression is usually correct.

6. **Graffiti.** Sometimes it's a good idea to mark your answers directly on the test booklet and go back to fill in the optical scan sheet later. You don't get extra points for perfectly blackened ovals. If you choose to manage your test this way, be sure not to mismark your answers when you transcribe to the scan sheet.

7. **Become a clock-watcher.** You have a set amount of time to answer the questions. Don't get bogged down laboring over a question you're not sure about when there are ten others you could answer more readily. If you choose to follow the advice of tip #6, be sure you leave time near the end to go back and fill in the scan sheet.

> *The proctor will write the start time where it can be seen and then, later, provide the time remaining, typically fifteen minutes before the end of the test.*

Do the Drill

No matter how prepared you feel it's sometimes a good idea to apply Murphy's Law. So the following tips might seem silly, mundane, or obvious, but we're including them anyway.

1. **Remember, you are what you eat, so bring a snack.** Choose from the list of energizing foods that appear earlier in the introduction.

2. **You're not too sexy for your test.** Wear comfortable clothes. You'll be distracted if your belt is too tight or if you're too cold or too hot.

3. **Lie to yourself.** Even if you think you're a prompt person, pretend you're not and leave plenty of time to get to the testing center. Map it out ahead of time and do a dry run if you have to. There's no need to add road rage to your list of anxieties.

4. **No ticket, no test.** Bring your admission ticket as well as **two** forms of identification, including one with a picture and signature. You will not be admitted to the test without these things.

5. **You can't take it with you.** Leave any study aids, dictionaries, notebooks, computers, and the like at home. Certain tests **do** allow a scientific or four-function calculator, so check ahead of time to see if your test does.

6. **Prepare for the desert.** Any time spent on a bathroom break **cannot** be made up later, so use your judgment on the amount you eat or drink.

7. **Quiet, Please!** Keeping your own time is a good idea, but not with a timepiece that has a loud ticker. If you use a watch, take it off and place it nearby but not so that it distracts you. And **silence your cell phone**.

To the best of our ability, we have compiled the content you need to know in this book and in the accompanying online resources. The rest is up to you. You can use the study and testing tips or you can follow your own methods. Either way, you can be confident that there aren't any missing pieces of information and there shouldn't be any surprises in the content on the test.

If you have questions about test fees, registration, electronic testing, or other content verification issues please visit *www.ets.org*.

Good luck!

Sharon Wynne
Founder, XAMonline

DOMAIN I
ENGLISH LANGUAGE ARTS AND READING

PERSONALIZED STUDY PLAN

KNOWN MATERIAL/ SKIP IT

PAGE	COMPETENCY AND SKILL	
13	**1: Oral language**	☐

1.1: Knows and teaches basic linguistic concepts *(e.g., phonemes, segmentation)* and the developmental stages in the acquisition of oral language—including phonology, semantics, syntax (subject-verb agreement and subject-verb inversion), and pragmatics—and recognizes that individual variations occur within and across languages, in accordance with the Science of Teaching Reading (STR). ☐

1.2: Plans and implements systematic oral language instruction based on informal and formal assessment of all students, including English-language learners; fosters oral language development; and addresses students' individual needs, strengths and interests, in accordance with the STR. ☐

1.3: Recognizes when speech or language delays or differences warrant in-depth evaluations and additional help or interventions. ☐

1.4: Designs a variety of one-on-one and group activities *(e.g., meaningful and purposeful conversations, dramatic play, language play, telling stories, singing songs, creating rhymes, playing games, having discussions, questioning, sharing information)* to build on students' current oral language skills. ☐

1.5: Selects and uses instructional materials and strategies that promote students' oral language development; respond to students' individual needs, strengths and interests; reflect cultural diversity; and build on students' cultural, linguistic and home backgrounds to enhance their oral language development, in accordance with the STR. ☐

1.6: Understands relationships between oral language and literacy development and provides instruction that interrelates oral and written language to promote students' reading and writing proficiencies. ☐

1.7: Selects and uses instructional strategies, materials, activities and models to strengthen students' oral vocabulary and narrative skills in spoken language and teaches students to connect spoken and printed language. ☐

1.8: Selects and uses instructional strategies, materials, activities and models to teach students skills for speaking to various audiences for various purposes and for adapting spoken language for various audiences, purposes and occasions. ☐

1.9: Selects and uses instructional strategies, materials, activities and models to teach students listening skills for various purposes *(e.g., critical listening to evaluate a speaker's message, listening to enjoy and appreciate spoken language)* and provides students with opportunities to engage in active, purposeful listening in a variety of contexts. ☐

1.10: Selects and uses instructional strategies, materials, activities and models to teach students to evaluate the content and effectiveness of their own spoken messages and the messages of others. ☐

PERSONALIZED STUDY PLAN

✗ KNOWN MATERIAL/ SKIP IT

PAGE	COMPETENCY AND SKILL	
	1.11:	Recognizes the interrelationships between oral language and the other components of reading, in accordance with the STR.	☐

PAGE		COMPETENCY AND SKILL	KNOWN MATERIAL/ SKIP IT
	1.11:	Recognizes the interrelationships between oral language and the other components of reading, in accordance with the STR.	☐
	1.12:	Selects and uses appropriate technologies to develop students' oral communication skills.	☐
27	2:	**Phonological and phonemic awareness**	☐
	2.1:	Understands the significance of phonological and phonemic awareness for reading, is familiar with typical patterns in the development of phonological and phonemic awareness and recognizes that individual variations occur, in accordance with the STR.	☐
	2.2:	Understands differences in students' development of phonological and phonemic awareness and adjusts instruction to meet the needs of individual students, including English-language learners.	☐
	2.3:	Plans, implements and adjusts instruction based on the continual use of formal and informal assessments of individual students' phonological development, in accordance with the STR.	☐
	2.4:	Knows the age ranges at which the expected stages and patterns of various phonological and phonemic awareness skills should be acquired, the implications of individual variations in the development of phonological and phonemic awareness and ways to accelerate students' phonological and phonemic awareness, in accordance with the STR.	☐
	2.5:	Uses a variety of instructional approaches and materials *(e.g., language games, informal interactions, direct instruction)* to promote students' phonological and phonemic awareness *(e.g., hearing and manipulating beginning, medial and final sounds in spoken words; recognizing spoken alliteration).*	☐
	2.6:	Understands how to foster collaboration with families and with other professionals to promote all students' phonological and phonemic awareness both at school and at home.	☐
	2.7:	Recognizes the interrelationships between phonological and phonemic awareness and the other components of reading (vocabulary, fluency and comprehension), in accordance with the STR.	☐
32	3:	**Alphabetic principle**	☐
	3.1:	Understands the elements of the alphabetic principle *(e.g., letter names, letter sequence, graphophonemic knowledge, the relationship of the letters in printed words to spoken language)* and typical patterns of students' alphabetic skills development, and recognizes that individual variations occur with students.	☐
	3.2:	Understands that not all written languages are alphabetic, that many alphabetic languages are more phonetically regular than English and that students' literacy development in English is affected by these two factors.	☐

PERSONALIZED STUDY PLAN

KNOWN MATERIAL/ SKIP IT

PAGE	COMPETENCY AND SKILL	
	3.3: Selects and uses a variety of instructional materials and strategies, including multisensory techniques, to promote students' understanding of the elements of the alphabetic principle and the relationship between sounds and letters and between letters and words, in accordance with the STR.	☐
	3.4: Uses formal and informal assessments to analyze individual students' alphabetic skills, monitor learning and plan instruction, in accordance with the STR.	☐
	3.5: Understands how to foster collaboration with families and with other professionals to promote all students' development of alphabetic knowledge.	☐
36	**4:** **Literacy development**	☐
	4.1: Selects and uses instructional strategies, materials and activities to assist students in distinguishing letter forms from number forms and text from pictures.	☐
	4.2: Understands that the developing reader has a growing awareness of print in the environment, the sounds in spoken words and the uses of print, in accordance with the STR.	☐
	4.3: Selects and uses instructional strategies, materials and activities to assist students in distinguishing letter forms from number forms and text from pictures.	☐
	4.4: Understands the importance of students being able to differentiate words and spaces, first and last letters, left-right progression, and identification of basic punctuation, in accordance with the STR.	☐
	4.5: Understands that literacy development occurs in multiple contexts through reading, writing and the use of oral language.	☐
	4.6: Selects and uses instructional strategies, materials and activities that focus on functions of print and concepts about print, including concepts involving book handling, parts of a book, orientation, directionality and the relationships between written and spoken words, in accordance with the STR.	☐
	4.7: Demonstrates familiarity with literature and provides multiple opportunities for students to listen to, respond to and independently read literature in various genres and to interact with others about literature.	☐
	4.8 Selects and uses appropriate instructional strategies to inform students about authors, authors' purposes for writing and author's point of view in a variety of texts.	☐
	4.9 Selects and uses appropriate technology to teach students strategies for selecting books for independent reading.	☐
	4.10 Understands how to foster collaboration with families and with other professionals to promote all students' literacy.	☐

PERSONALIZED STUDY PLAN

KNOWN MATERIAL/ SKIP IT

PAGE	COMPETENCY AND SKILL	
42	**5:** **Word analysis and identification skills**	☐
	5.1: Understands that while many students develop word analysis and decoding skills in a predictable sequence, individual variations may occur, in accordance with the STR.	☐
	5.2: Understands the importance of word recognition skills *(e.g., letter-sound correspondences, decoding, blending, structural analysis, sight word vocabulary, contextual analysis)* for reading comprehension and knows a variety of strategies for helping students develop and apply word analysis skills, including identifying, categorizing and using common synonyms, antonyms, homographs, homophones and analogies.	☐
	5.3: Teaches the analysis of phonetically regular words in a simple-to-complex progression *(i.e., phonemes, blending onsets and rimes, short vowels/long vowels, consonant blends, other common vowel and consonant patterns, syllable types),* in accordance with the STR.	☐
	5.4: Selects and uses instructional strategies, materials, activities and models to teach students to recognize high-frequency words, to promote students' ability to decode increasingly complex words and to enhance word identification skills of students reading at varying levels.	☐
	5.5: Knows strategies for decoding increasingly complex words, including the alphabetic principle, vowel-sound combinations, structural cues *(e.g., morphology-prefixes, suffixes, roots, base words, abbreviations, contractions),* and syllable types and for using syntax and semantics to support word identification and confirm word meaning, in accordance with the STR.	☐
	5.6: Understands the value of using dictionaries, glossaries and other sources to determine the meanings, usage, pronunciations, correct spelling, and derivations of unfamiliar words and teaches students to use those sources.	☐
	5.7: Understands how to foster collaboration with families and with other professionals to promote all students' word analysis and decoding skills.	☐
49	**6:** **Fluency reading**	☐
	6.1: Knows the relationship between reading fluency and comprehension, in accordance with the STR.	☐
	6.2: Understands that fluency involves rate, accuracy, prosody and intonation and knows the norms for reading fluency that have been established by the Texas Essential Knowledge and Skills (TEKS) for various age and grade levels, in accordance with the STR.	☐
	6.3: Understands the connection of word identification skills and reading fluency to reading comprehension.	☐

PERSONALIZED STUDY PLAN

PAGE	COMPETENCY AND SKILL	
	6.4:	Understands differences in students' development of word identification skills and reading fluency and knows instructional practices for meeting students' individual needs in those areas, in accordance with the STR.	☐
	6.5:	Selects and uses instructional strategies, materials and activities to develop and improve fluency *(e.g., reading independent-level materials, reading orally from familiar texts, repeated reading, partner reading, silent reading for increasingly longer periods, self-correction)*, in accordance with the STR.	☐
	6.6:	Knows how to teach students strategies for selecting books for independent reading, in accordance with the STR.	☐
	6.7:	Provides students with opportunities to engage in silent reading and extended reading of a wide range of materials, including expository texts and various literary genres.	☐
	6.8:	Uses strategies to encourage reading for pleasure and lifelong learning.	☐
	6.9:	Recognizes the interrelationship between reading fluency and the other components of reading, in accordance with the STR.	☐
	6.10:	Understands how to foster collaboration with families and with other professionals to promote all students' reading fluency.	☐
57	**7:**	**Reading comprehension and applications**	☐
	7.1:	Understands reading comprehension as an active process of constructing meaning, in accordance with the STR.	☐
	7.2:	Understands factors affecting students' reading comprehension *(e.g., oral language development, word analysis skills, prior knowledge, language background/experience, previous reading experiences, fluency, vocabulary development, ability to monitor understanding, characteristics of specific texts)*, in accordance with the STR.	☐
	7.3:	Understands levels of reading comprehension and knows how to model and teach skills for literal comprehension *(e.g., identifying stated main idea, recalling details, identifying point-of-view)*, inferential comprehension *(e.g., inferring cause-and-effect relationships, moral lessons and themes, making predictions)*, and evaluative comprehension *(e.g., analyzing character development and use of language, detecting faulty reasoning, explaining point of view)*.	☐
	7.4:	Provides instruction in comprehension skills that support students' transition from "learning to read" to "reading to learn" *(e.g., recognizing different types of texts, understanding text structure, using textual features such as headings and glossaries, appreciating the different purposes for reading)* to become self directed, critical readers.	☐

PERSONALIZED STUDY PLAN

KNOWN MATERIAL/ SKIP IT

PAGE	COMPETENCY AND SKILL	
	7.5: Uses various instructional strategies to enhance students' reading comprehension *(e.g., linking text content to students' lives and prior knowledge, connecting related ideas across different texts, comparing different versions of the same story, explaining the meaning of common idioms, adages and foreign words and phrases in written English, engaging students in guided and independent reading, guiding students to generate questions and apply knowledge of text topics).*	☐
	7.6: Knows and teaches strategies that facilitate comprehension of different types of text *(e.g., literary, expository, multistep directions, procedural)* before, during and after reading *(e.g., previewing, making predictions, questioning, self-monitoring, rereading, mapping, using reading journals, discussing texts).*	☐
	7.7: Knows and teaches strategies that facilitate making connections between and across multiple texts *(e.g., summarizing and paraphrasing, locating and distinguishing between facts and opinions, and determining whether the text supports or opposes an issue).*	☐
	7.8: Understands metacognitive skills, including self-evaluation and self-monitoring skills, and teaches students to use those skills to enhance their reading comprehension, in accordance with the STR.	☐
	7.9: Knows how to provide students with direct, explicit instruction and reinforcing activities to promote the use of strategies to improve their reading comprehension *(e.g., previewing, self-monitoring, visualizing, recognizing sensory details, re-telling)*, in accordance with the STR.	☐
	7.10: Selects and uses instructional strategies, materials and activities to guide students' understanding of their own culture and the cultures of others through reading, in accordance with the STR.	☐
	7.11: Teaches elements of literary analysis, such as story elements and figurative language, and features of various literary genres, including fables, myths, folktales, legends, drama and poetry.	☐
	7.12: Understands the continuum of reading comprehension skills in the state standards and grade-level expectations for those skills.	☐
	7.13: Knows the difference between guided and independent practice in reading and provides students with frequent opportunities for both.	☐
	7.14: Understands how to foster collaboration with families and with other professionals to promote all students' reading comprehension.	☐
70	**8: Vocabulary development**	☐
	8.1: Knows how to provide explicit, systematic instruction and reinforcing activities to help students increase their vocabulary, in accordance with the STR.	☐
	8.2: Knows how to use direct and indirect methods to effectively teach vocabulary, in accordance with the STR.	☐

PERSONALIZED STUDY PLAN

X
KNOWN MATERIAL/ SKIP IT

PAGE	COMPETENCY AND SKILL	
	8.3: Selects and uses a wide range of instructional materials, strategies and opportunities with rich contextual support for vocabulary development, in accordance with the STR *(e.g., literature, expository texts, content-specific texts, magazines, newspapers, trade books, technology)*.	☐
	8.4: Recognizes the importance of selecting, teaching and modeling a wide range of general and specialized vocabularies.	☐
	8.5: Understands how to assess and monitor students' vocabulary knowledge by providing systematic, age-appropriate instruction and reinforcing activities *(e.g., morphemic analysis, etc.)*.	☐
	8.6: Provides multiple opportunities to listen to, read and respond to various types of literature and expository texts to promote students' vocabulary development.	☐
75	**9: Reading, inquiry, and research**	☐
	9.1: Teaches students how to develop open-ended research questions and a plan *(e.g., timeline)* to locate, retrieve and record information from a range of content-area, narrative and expository texts.	☐
	9.2: Selects and uses instructional strategies to help students comprehend abstract content and ideas in written materials *(e.g., manipulatives, examples, graphic organizers)*.	☐
	9.3: Selects and uses instructional strategies to teach students to interpret information presented in various formats *(e.g., maps, tables, graphs)* and how to locate, retrieve, and record information from technologies, print resources and experts.	☐
	9.4: Selects and uses instructional strategies to help students understand study and inquiry skills across the curriculum *(e.g., brainstorming; generating questions and topics; using text organizers; taking notes; outlining; drawing conclusions; applying critical-thinking skills; previewing; setting purposes for reading; locating, organizing, evaluating and communicating information; summarizing information; selecting relevant sources of information; using multiple sources of information; recognizing identifying features of sources, including primary and secondary sources; interpreting and using graphic sources of information)* and knows the significance of organizing information from multiple sources for student learning and achievement.	☐
	9.5: Knows grade-level expectations for study and inquiry skills in the Texas Essential Knowledge and Skills (TEKS) *(e.g., in kindergarten, use pictures in conjunction with writing to document research; in fifth–sixth grades, refine research through use of secondary questions)*.	☐
	9.6: Provides instruction to develop a topic sentence, summarize findings and use evidence to support conclusions.	☐

X

PERSONALIZED STUDY PLAN

KNOWN MATERIAL/ SKIP IT

PAGE	COMPETENCY AND SKILL	
	9.7: Understands how to foster collaboration with peers, families and with other professionals to promote all students' ability to develop effective research and comprehension skills in the content areas.	☐
82	**10: Writing conventions**	☐
	10.1: Understands that many students go through predictable stages in acquiring writing conventions *(e.g., physical and cognitive processes involved in scribbling, recognition of environmental print, mock letters, letter formation, word writing, sentence construction, spelling, punctuation, grammatical expression)*, and individual students vary in their rates of development of those conventions.	☐
	10.2: Understands the relationship between spelling and phonological and alphabetic awareness and understands the role of conventional spelling in success in reading and writing.	☐
	10.3: Understands the stages of spelling development (precommunicative writing in which the student understands the function of writing but cannot make the forms, prephonemic, phonemic, transitional and conventional) and knows how and when to support students' development from one stage to the next.	☐
	10.4: Provides spelling instruction and gives students opportunities to use and develop spelling skills in the context of meaningful written expression *(e.g., single syllable homophones, commonly used homophones, commonly confused terms, simple and complex contractions)*.	☐
	10.5: Selects and uses instructional strategies, materials and hands-on activities for developing fine motor skills necessary for writing, according to grade-level expectations in the Texas Essential Knowledge and Skills (TEKS).	☐
	10.6: Selects and uses instructional strategies, materials and activities to help students use English writing conventions *(e.g., grammar, capitalization, punctuation)* in connected discourse.	☐
	10.7: Recognizes the similarities and differences between spoken and written English *(e.g., syntax, vocabulary choice, audience)* and uses instructional strategies to help students apply English writing conventions and enhance their own writing.	☐
	10.8: Knows writing conventions and appropriate grammar and usage and provides students with direct instruction and guided practice in those areas.	☐
	10.9: Selects and uses instructional strategies, materials and activities to teach correct pencil grip.	☐

PERSONALIZED STUDY PLAN

X

KNOWN MATERIAL/ SKIP IT

PAGE	COMPETENCY AND SKILL	
96	**11: Written communication**	☐
	11.1: Understands differences between first-draft writing and writing for publication and provides instruction in various stages of writing, including prewriting, drafting, revising (including both self-revision and peer revision) and editing.	☐
	11.2: Knows how to promote students' development of an extensive reading and writing vocabulary by providing students with many opportunities to read and write.	☐
	11.3: Monitors students' writing development and provides motivational instruction that addresses individual students' needs, strengths and interests.	☐
	11.4: Understands differences between first-draft writing and writing for publication and provides instruction in various stages of writing, including prewriting, drafting, revising (including both self-revision and peer revision) and editing.	☐
	11.5: Understands the benefits of technology for teaching basic writing skills and writing for publication and provides instruction in the use of technology to facilitate written communication.	☐
	11.6: Understands writing for a variety of audiences, purposes and settings and provides students with opportunities to write for various audiences, purposes and settings and in various voices and styles.	☐
	11.7: Teaches students to use appropriate conventions to support ideas in writing and to use an appropriate form of documentation to acknowledge sources *(e.g., quotations, bibliographical information, differentiation between paraphrasing and plagiarism).*	☐
	11.8: Knows grade-level expectations in the Texas Essential Knowledge and Skills (TEKS).	☐
	11.9: Understands how to foster collaboration with families and with other professionals to promote students' development of writing skills.	☐
105	**12: Viewing and representing**	☐
	12.1: Knows grade-level expectations for viewing and representing visual images and messages as described in the Texas Essential Knowledge and Skills (TEKS).	☐
	12.2: Understands and teaches the characteristics and functions of different types of media *(e.g., film, print)* and knows how different types of media influence and inform.	☐
	12.3: Teaches students to compare and contrast print, visual and electronic media, including the level of formality of each *(e.g., email, Web-based news article, blogs).*	☐
	12.4: Teaches students to evaluate how visual image makers *(e.g., illustrators, documentary filmmakers, political cartoonists, news photographers)* represent messages and meanings and provides students with opportunities to interpret and evaluate visual images in various media.	☐

X

PERSONALIZED STUDY PLAN

✗ KNOWN MATERIAL/ SKIP IT

PAGE	COMPETENCY AND SKILL	KNOWN MATERIAL/ SKIP IT
	12.5: Knows how to teach students to analyze visual image makers' choices *(e.g., style, elements, media)* and evaluate how those choices help represent or extend meaning.	☐
	12.6: Provides students with opportunities to interpret events and ideas based on information from maps, charts, graphics, video segments and technology presentations and to use media to compare ideas and points of view.	☐
	12.7: Knows steps and procedures for teaching students to produce visual images and messages with various meanings to communicate with others.	☐
	12.8: Teachers students how to select, organize and produce visuals to complement and extend meanings.	☐
	12.9: Provides students with opportunities to use technology for producing various types of communications *(e.g., class newspapers, multimedia reports, video reports)* and helps students analyze how language, medium and presentation contribute to the message.	☐
	12.10: Understands how to foster collaboration with families and with other professionals to promote students' development of media literacy.	☐
115	**13: Assessment of developing literacy**	☐
	13.1: Knows how to select and administer formative and summative assessments and use results to measure literacy acquisition *(e.g., alphabetic skills, literacy development, word analysis and word identification skills, fluency, comprehension, writing conventions, written communications, visual images, study skills)* and address individual students' needs identified in informal and formal assessments.	☐
	13.2: Knows the characteristics of informal and formal reading comprehension assessments *(e.g., criterion-referenced state tests, curriculum-based reading assessments, informal reading inventories, norm-referenced tests).*	☐
	13.3: Analyzes students' reading and writing performance and uses the information as a basis for instruction.	☐
	13.4: Knows the state content and performance standards for reading, writing, listening and speaking that constitute the Texas Essential Knowledge and Skills (TEKS) and recognizes when a student needs additional help or intervention to bring the student's performance up to grade level.	☐
	13.5: Knows how to determine students' independent, instructional and frustration reading levels and uses the information to select appropriate materials for individual students and to guide students' selection of independent reading materials.	☐
	13.6: Uses ongoing assessments to determine when a student may be in need of classroom intervention or specialized reading instruction and to develop appropriate instructional plans.	☐

PERSONALIZED STUDY PLAN

KNOWN MATERIAL/ SKIP IT

PAGE	COMPETENCY AND SKILL	
13.7:	Understands the use of writing in assessment of students and provides opportunities for students to self-assess and peer assess writing *(e.g., for clarity, interest to audience, comprehensiveness)* and ongoing literacy development.	☐
13.8:	Knows how to select, administer and use results from informal and formal assessments of literacy acquisition.	☐
13.9:	Analyzes students' errors in reading and responds to individual students' needs by providing focused instruction to promote literacy acquisition.	☐
13.10:	Knows informal and formal procedures for assessing students' use of writing conventions and uses multiple, ongoing assessments to monitor and evaluate students' development in that area.	☐
13.11:	Uses ongoing assessments of writing conventions to determine when students need additional help or intervention to bring students' performance to grade level based on state content and performance standards for writing in the Texas Essential Knowledge and Skills (TEKS).	☐
13.12:	Analyzes students' errors in applying writing conventions and uses the results of the analysis as a basis for future instruction.	☐
13.13:	Selects and uses a variety of formal and informal procedures for monitoring students' reading comprehension and adjusts instruction to meet the needs of individual students, including English-language learners.	☐

COMPETENCY 1
ORAL LANGUAGE

> **SKILL 1.1** **Knows and teaches basic linguistic concepts** (*e.g., phonemes, segmentation*) **and the developmental stages in the acquisition of oral language—including phonology, semantics, syntax (subject-verb agreement and subject-verb inversion), and pragmatics—and recognizes that individual variations occur within and across languages, in accordance with the Science of Teaching Reading (STR).**

Phonemes

A PHONEME is the smallest contrastive unit in a language system and the representation of a sound. The phoneme has been described as the smallest meaningful psychological unit of sound. The phoneme is said to have mental, physiological, and physical substance: our brains process the sounds; the sounds are produced by the human speech organs; and the sounds are physical entities that can be recorded and measured. Consider the English words *pat* and *sat*, which appear to differ only in their initial consonants. This difference, known as opposition, is adequate to distinguish these words, and therefore the *p* and *s* sounds are said to be different phonemes in English. A pair of words, identical except for such a sound, is known as a minimal pair, and the two sounds are separate phonemes.

> PHONEME: the smallest contrastive unit in a language system and the representation of a sound

Phonemic awareness

PHONEMIC AWARENESS is the acknowledgement of sounds and words; for example, a child's realization that some words rhyme. Onset and rhyme, for example, are skills that might help students learn that the sound of the first letter, *b*, in the word *bad* can be changed with the sound *d* to make it *dad*. The key in phonemic awareness is that when you teach it to children it can be taught with the students' eyes closed. In other words, it's all about sounds, not about ascribing written letters to sounds.

> PHONEMIC AWARENESS: the acknowledgement of sounds and words; for example, a child's realization that some words rhyme

To be phonemically aware means that the reader or listener can recognize and manipulate specific sounds in spoken words. The majority of phonemic awareness tasks, activities, and exercises are oral.

Since the ability to distinguish between individual sounds, or phonemes, within words is a prerequisite to the association of sounds with letters and manipulating sounds to blend words (a fancy way of saying "reading"), the teaching of phonemic awareness is crucial to emergent literacy. Children need a strong background in phonemic awareness in order for phonics instruction to be effective.

Phonics

PHONOLOGICAL AWARENESS: the reader's ability to recognize the sound of spoken language, including how sounds can be blended together, segmented, and manipulated

PHONICS: a method for teaching children to read

PHONOLOGICAL AWARENESS refers to the reader's ability to recognize the sound of spoken language, including how sounds can be blended together, segmented (divided up), and manipulated (switched around). This awareness then leads to PHONICS, a method for teaching children to read. It helps students "sound out words."

Development of phonological skills may begin during pre-K years. Indeed, by the age of 5, a child who has been exposed to rhyme can recognize a rhyme. Such a child can demonstrate phonological awareness by filling in the missing rhyming word in a familiar rhyme or rhymed picture book.

Phonological awareness skills include:

1. Rhyming and syllabification

2. Blending sounds into words—such as *pic-tur-bo-k*

3. Identifying the beginning or starting sounds of words and the ending or closing sounds of words

4. Breaking words down into sounds—also called "segmenting" words

5. Recognizing other smaller words in a big word by removing starting sounds, e.g., *hear* to *ear*

Morphology, Syntax, and Semantics

MORPHOLOGY: the study of word structure

SYNTAX: the rules or patterned relationships that correctly create phrases and sentences from words

SEMANTICS: the meaning expressed when words are arranged in a specific way

MORPHOLOGY is the study of word structure. When readers develop morphemic skills, they are developing an understanding of patterns they see in words. For example, English speakers realize that *cat*, *cats*, and *caterpillar* share some similarities in structure. This understanding helps readers to recognize words at a faster and easier rate, since each word doesn't need individual decoding.

SYNTAX refers to the rules or patterned relationships that correctly create phrases and sentences from words. When readers develop an understanding of syntax, they begin to understand the structure of how sentences are built, and, eventually, the beginning of grammar.

SEMANTICS refers to the meaning expressed when words are arranged in a specific way. This is where connotation and denotation of words eventually has a role with readers.

Pragmatics

Pragmatics is concerned with the difference between the writer's meaning and the literal meaning of the sentence based on social context. When someone is competent in pragmatics, he or she is able to understand the writer's intended meaning. In a simpler sense, pragmatics can be considered the social rules of language.

> **SKILL 1.2** **Plans and implements systematic oral language instruction based on informal and formal assessment of all students, including English-language learners; fosters oral language development; and addresses students' individual needs, strengths and interests, in accordance with the STR.**

Assessment of Oral Language Skills

Assessment information should be used to provide performance-based criteria and academic expectations for all students in evaluating whether students have learned the expected skills and content of the subject area. By analyzing the various types of assessments, teachers can gather more definitive information on projected student academic performance. Instructional strategies for teachers would provide learning targets for student behavior, cognitive thinking skills, and processing skills that can be employed to diversify student learning opportunities.

Assessment drives the instruction. Some of the methods teachers can employ to assess for learning involve both formative and summative evaluation. Formative assessment consists of testing; however, teachers can make summative assessment part of their daily routine by using such measures as:

- Anecdotal records
- Portfolios
- Listening to children read
- Oral presentations
- Checklists
- Running records
- Samples of work
- Self-evaluation

Informal assessment

For informal assessment, teachers can observe students during their everyday classroom activities. Teachers should make a point to evaluate a student multiple times at different times of the day and during different types of tasks. They can keep records, notes, or checklists of the child's oral skills. This type of assessment can include other students, for example, in cooperative learning environments. This type of assessment is often particularly authentic because the student will display typical oral skills while at ease. Students in higher grades can learn how to assess themselves using checklists, journals, portfolios, and other types of self-evaluation.

Formal assessment

Formal assessments take more planning. The teacher typically targets certain oral skills utilizing specific tasks and assessment methods. A formal assessment can be an oral interview that is recorded in some manner; picture-cued description/stories; oral prompts; text retelling; or role playing. There are also formal assessment tests teachers can obtain to formally record a student's oral skill development.

English-Language Learners

The teacher needs to assess the ELL students to determine how cultural, ethnic, and linguistic experiences can affect the students' learning. The teacher should work with students to:

- **Promote cross-cultural understanding:** Providing personal communication with another person from a different cultural environment can help promote understanding.

- **Challenge stereotypes, intolerance, and racism:** Some expressions and behaviors normal or common in the ELL's home culture may be considered unacceptable in an English-language culture.

- **Explain and clarify typical English-language cultural views, morals, and societal norms:** This helps give context to ELL beliefs in English-language culture.

Language development in children develops in an efficient manner, so the focus should be on allowing the child to create his or her own language scenarios in constructing language repertoires.

SKILL 1.3 Recognizes when speech or language delays or differences warrant in-depth evaluations and additional help or interventions.

Speech or Language Delays

Speech or language delays in children can be cause for concern or intervention. Understanding the development of language in young children can provide information on delays or differences. Parents and teachers must understand the difference between developmental speech, word development, and language delays/differences that may prevent oral language acquisition. The ability to differentiate between the natural development of children's language patterns and the delayed development of those patterns should be the focus of the adult caregivers who provide the environmental stimulis and language experiences for children.

Age/language acquisition guidelines

- Children at the age of 2 should have speech patterns that are about 70 percent intelligible.

- Children at the age of 3 should have a speech pattern that is about 80 percent intelligible.

- Children at the age of 4 should have a speech pattern that is about 90 percent intelligible.

- Children at the age of 5 should have a speech pattern that is 100 percent intelligible.

- Children over the age of 5 will develop speech patterns that continue at 100 percent intelligibility with increased vocabulary.

Teachers and parents who have concerns about a child's language development should be proactive in addressing them. Early intervention is critical. Effective steps in addressing language delays or differences include: contacting a speech pathologist to evaluate a child's speech, an auditory specialist to test for hearing disorders, a pediatrician to test for motor-function delays, and utilizing other assessment resources for evaluation.

> **SKILL 1.4** **Designs a variety of one-on-one and group activities** *(e.g., meaningful and purposeful conversations, dramatic play, language play, telling stories, singing songs, creating rhymes, playing games, having discussions, questioning, sharing information)* **to build on students' current oral language skills.**

Stimulating Development of Children's Oral Language Skills

In order to stimulate the development of their oral language skills, children should be exposed to a challenging environment that is rich in opportunities. Teachers should remain focused on oral language skills throughout the day, even while teaching other subjects.

Activities that encourage development of oral language skills

- Encourage meaningful conversation
- Allow dramatic playtime
- Let children share personal stories
- Sing the alphabet song

- Teach the art of questioning
- Read rhyming books
- Play listening games
- Encourage sharing of information

If an educational program is child-centered, it will surely address the developmental abilities and needs of the students because it will take its cues from students' interests, concerns, and questions.

Scaffolding Theory

Most language skills need to have layers of information gathered and stored to ensure a sound basis for continued learning. Scaffolding is a metaphorical term that illustrates the process of gathering knowledge of concepts. Some ingredients of scaffolding are predictability, playfulness, focus on meaning, role reversal, modeling, and nomenclature.

Instructional scaffolding is the provision of sufficient supports to promote learning when concepts and skills are first being introduced to students. These supports may include:

- Resources: The teacher provides supportive materials such as recommended readings, documents, or storyboards.

- A compelling task: The student or group is given an extensive task to perform, which requires them to learn and master successive and continually more difficult facets of a particular language skill.

- Templates and guides: The teacher provides outlines, language-use templates, and study guides. Initially, these supports explain the skill to the student and provide examples to allow the student to model the communicative task.

- Guidance on the development of cognitive and social skills: Each layer of language scaffolding should call for increased development of cognitive thinking. With young students, in particular, activities should include development of progressively more advanced socially acceptable patterns and norms.

> ### SKILL 1.5 Selects and uses instructional materials and strategies that promote students' oral language development; respond to students' individual needs, strengths and interests; reflect cultural diversity; and build on students' cultural, linguistic and home backgrounds to enhance their oral language development, in accordance with the STR.

Strategies for Enhancing Language Development

The act of simulating the sounds and words in his or her environment provides the child with language enhancement and acquisition. The promotion of language development should include repetition and language engagement.

Children's toys, games, and books can be used to further language development. Providing language simulation activities that model how to ask questions or put words into sentences are effective instructional strategies.

Providing children with instructional language cues can facilitate learning and language development. Using strategic tools such as rephrasing sentences (e.g., "dada goed") into questions (e.g., "Is daddy going?") can provide children with correct sentence formats and other ways of looking at oral meaning. When children are given labels for objects, they can use word association in developing language acquisition.

Teachers and evaluators of children's language development must work effectively with families. Fostering collaborative efforts to provide a community approach to promoting children's oral development is both pragmatic and necessary if children are to become effective communicators.

When parents and teachers understand that children have individualized language foundations that are valid communication systems, a child can develop beginning speech patterns without the stereotype of an adult's perception of language delay or differences. Children reflect their environments and their cultural and familial identifications.

Engaging children in conversations with teachers and parents can provide nonverbal and verbal clues about how conversations work and what visual cues or body cues can be used to express nonverbal meaning.

> **SKILL 1.6** Understands relationships between oral language and literacy development and provides instruction that interrelates oral and written language to promote students' reading and writing proficiencies.

Relationship between Oral and Written Language

A "balanced literacy" curriculum focuses on the use of oral and written language skills in various instructional contexts.

- **Independent reading:** Students independently choose books that are at their reading levels.

- **Guided reading:** Teachers work with small groups of students to help them with their particular reading problems.

- **Whole-group reading:** The entire class reads the same text, and the teacher incorporates activities to help students learn phonics, comprehension, fluency, and vocabulary.

In addition to these components of balanced literacy, teachers incorporate writing so that students can learn the structures of communicating through text.

Role of oral development

In 2000, the National Reading Panel released its now well-known report on teaching children to read. The report's "big five" critical areas of reading instruction are:

- **Phonemic awareness:** The acknowledgement of sounds and words

- **Phonics:** The connection between the sounds and letters on a page

- **Fluency:** Reading connected pieces of text

- **Comprehension:** The reader's ability to ascribe meaning to text

- **Content-area vocabulary:** The specific vocabulary related to the particular concepts of various academic disciplines

Role of vocabulary

Teachers need to help students learn strategies to figure out the meanings of difficult words when they encounter them on their own. They can do this by teaching students how to identify the meanings of words in context (usually through activities in which the word is taken out of the sentence and the students have to figure out a way to make sense of the sentence). In addition, dictionary skills must be taught in all subject areas. Teaching vocabulary is not just the teaching of words: it is the teaching of complex concepts, each with histories and connotations.

Explicitly teaching vocabulary works best when teachers connect new words to words, ideas, and experiences with which students are already familiar. Finally, students need plenty of exposure to the new words.

Read alouds

Read alouds can be used to teach the student listener while developing background knowledge, increasing comprehension skills, and fostering critical thinking.

> **SKILL 1.7** Selects and uses instructional strategies, materials, activities and models to strengthen students' oral vocabulary and narrative skills in spoken language and teaches students to connect spoken and printed language.

Teaching Public Speaking Skills

In public speaking, not all speeches require the same type of speaking style. For example, when delivering a humorous speech, it is important to utilize body language to accent humorous points. However, when giving instructions, it is extremely important to speak clearly and slowly, carefully noting the mood of the audience, so that if there is confusion on peoples' faces, the speaker can go back and review something. In group discussions, speakers must be sure to listen to other speakers carefully and tailor their messages to fit the general mood of the discussion at hand. The speaker should focus on covering the content, while also relating to audience members as much as possible.

As students practice these skills, they can receive guidance and modeling by watching videos of speeches similar to those they are giving themselves. Also, the various attributes of each type of oral speaking strategy should be discussed with students so that they clearly hear the differences.

The skills needed to write an essay are helpful when trying to prepare a presentation, participate in a discussion about literature, or orally retell a story. Non-written genres and traditions that include literary elements have systematic organizational structures. Such genres and traditions include, but are not limited to, oral narratives, persuasive rhetoric, research presentations, poetry recitations, and responses to literature.

> **SKILL 1.8** Selects and uses instructional strategies, materials, activities and models to teach students skills for speaking to various audiences for various purposes and for adapting spoken language for various audiences, purposes and occasions.

Persuasive Pieces

When working to persuade an audience about a particular issue, a speaker often presents many scenarios or examples rather than explaining the issue in full detail. This method ensures that people are emotionally and logically persuaded without making it seem as if the speaker's opinion is being forced on people.

Research Presentations

Research presentations often present a thesis or overarching claim or argument. Then they explicate, or explain, the thesis or argument with examples and details. The point of a research presentation is to provide an audience with enough details that they will: (a) remember the presentation, and (b) believe the argument, but not so many details that they will become bored with the presentation.

Poetry

Poetry recitation involves the reading aloud of written poetry. It requires a careful understanding of the poetry before reciting it, as the meaning often changes the way it is read out loud. Good poetry recitation involves drama, persona, and charisma.

Discussion

Responding to literature, particularly in discussions, involves making claims about the literature and then defending those claims with specific details from the text or personal experience.

SKILL 1.9 Selects and uses instructional strategies, materials, activities and models to teach students listening skills for various purposes *(e.g., critical listening to evaluate a speaker's message, listening to enjoy and appreciate spoken language)* and provides students with opportunities to engage in active, purposeful listening in a variety of contexts.

Teaching Listening Skills

For young children, listening discrimination aids their learning and further oral development. Games that encourage students to distinguish between animal sounds or that ask students to match a sound with the picture that makes the sound are two excellent activities teachers can use with students to practice listening discrimination. Phoneme games that, for example, ask students to circle the letter that is the beginning sound or a rhyming sound also aid listening skills. In addition, music games that encourage children to pat a beat, hear a rhyme, or follow an instruction (e.g., Simon Says) all allow children to practice listening in a fun environment.

For older students, two aspects of listening warrant attention:

1. **Comprehension:** Understanding what someone says, the purposes behind the message, and the contexts in which it is said.

2. **Purpose:** When we understand the purpose of listening in various contexts, comprehension becomes much easier. Furthermore, when we know the purpose of listening, we can better adjust our comprehension strategies.

First, when complex or new information is provided to us orally, we must analyze and interpret it. Second, the purpose of listening is often simply enjoyment. We like to listen to stories; we enjoy poetry; we like radio dramas and theater. Listening to literature can also be a great pleasure.

Finally, listening in large- and small-group conversation requires more than just listening. It involves feedback and active involvement. Students need to learn how listening carefully to others in discussions actually promotes better responses on the part of subsequent speakers. One way teachers can encourage this in both large- and small-group discussions is to encourage students to respond *directly* to the previous student's comments before moving ahead with their new comments.

Strategies for Active Listening

As soon as we start listening to something new, we can tap in to our prior knowledge to attach new information to what we already know. This not only helps us understand the new information more quickly, it also assists us in remembering the material.

We can also look for transitions between ideas. Sometimes, in oral speech, the speaker's tone of voice or body language changes when he or she is beginning to talk about a new idea. Listeners should take advantage of this and notice how the speaker changes character and voice in order to signal a transition between ideas.

Listeners can also better comprehend the underlying intent of a speaker when they notice nonverbal cues. The expression on the face of a speaker can do more to signal irony, for example, than actual words.

Other classroom methods can help students learn good listening skills. For example, teachers can have students practice following complex directions. They can also have students orally retell stories or retell (in writing or in oral speech) oral presentations of stories or other materials.

One good way to follow oral speech is to take notes and outline major points.

Effective listening

- **Associate:** Listeners relate ideas to each other.

- **Visualize:** Listeners try to see pictures in their minds as they read.

- **Concentrate:** Listeners have a specific purpose for reading.

- **Repeat:** Listeners keep telling themselves important points and associating details with these points.

> SKILL 1.10 **Selects and uses instructional strategies, materials, activities and models to teach students to evaluate the content and effectiveness of their own spoken messages and the messages of others.**

Evaluating Effectiveness of Spoken Messages

Responding to messages

In addition to the words, messages are transferred by eye contact, physical closeness, tone of voice, visual cues, and overall body language.

In addition to the words, messages are transferred by eye contact, physical closeness, tone of voice, visual cues, and overall body language. Language employs symbols—gestures, visual clues, or spoken sounds—to represent communication between the teacher and the student.

A straight message is one in which words, vocal expression, and body movements are all congruent.

Evaluating messages

Analyzing the speech of others is a good technique for helping students to improve their own public speaking abilities. Video is a useful tool for this purpose.

Students should pay attention to:

- **Volume:** A speaker should use an appropriate volume—not so loud as to be annoying, but not so soft as to be inaudible.

- **Pace:** The rate at which words are spoken should be appropriate—not so fast as to make the speech impossible to understand, but not so slow as to put listeners to sleep.

- **Pronunciation:** A speaker should make sure words are spoken clearly. Listeners do not have a text to go back to so they can reread things they didn't catch.

- **Body language:** While animated body language can help a speech, too much of it can be distracting. Body language should help convey the message but not detract from it.

- **Word choice:** The words speakers choose should be consistent with their intended purpose and the audience.

- **Visual aids:** Visual aids, like body language, should enhance a message. Many visual aids can be distracting and detract from the message.

> **SKILL 1.11** Recognizes the interrelationships between oral language and the other components of reading, in accordance with the STR.

See Skill 1.6 and Skill 1.7

> **SKILL 1.12** Selects and uses appropriate technologies to develop students' oral communication skills.

Technology for Developing Oral Communication Skills

Using technology to create computerized versions of books that emulate oral language patterns can engage children in endless hours of structured learning activities.

Technologies that provide children with tools to practice language patterns can include instructional content that increases vocabulary of high frequency words, irregular words, and age-appropriate words. Tape recorders and educational software can encourage children with opportunities to develop word comprehension and meaning along with automatic recall and usage.

Using technology to create computerized versions of books that emulate oral language patterns can engage children in hours of structured learning activities. Technologies that provide children with tools to practice language patterns include instructional content that increases vocabulary of high-frequency words, irregular words, and age-appropriate words. The following technologies allow for differentiation and can help students connect the content to their daily lives. Common technology tools are as follows:

- Interactive whiteboards

- Computer software

- Web Quests, in which students utilize a predetermined list of websites to explore a topic

- Wikis, in which students contribute content to a webpage

- Video conferencing

- Podcasts, which are published audio recordings

COMPETENCY 2
PHONOLOGICAL AND PHONEMIC AWARENESS

> **SKILL 2.1** Understands the significance of phonological and phonemic awareness for reading, is familiar with typical patterns in the development of phonological and phonemic awareness and recognizes that individual variations occur, in accordance with the STR.

Phonics involves studying the rules and patterns found in language. By age 5 or 6, children can typically begin to use phonics to understand the connections between letters, their patterns, vowel sounds (i.e., short vowels, long vowels), and the collective sounds they all make.

Phonemic awareness is the ability to break down and hear separate and/or different sounds and distinguish between the sounds one hears. Phonemic awareness is required to begin studying phonics, when students will need to be able to break down words into the smalls units of sound, or phonemes, to later identify syllables, blends, and patterns. Phonological awareness is a broader term that includes phonemic awareness.

Instructional Methods

Since the ability to distinguish between individual sounds, or phonemes, within words is a prerequisite to association of sounds with letters and manipulating sounds to blend words (a fancy way of saying "reading"), the teaching of phonemic awareness is crucial to emergent literacy. Children need a strong background in phonemic awareness in order for phonics instruction to be effective.

Methods for teaching phonemic awareness

- Clapping syllables in words

- Distinguishing between a word and a sound

- Using visual cues and movements to help children understand when the speaker goes from one sound to another

- Incorporating oral segmentation activities which focus on easily distinguished syllables rather than sounds

- Singing familiar songs (e.g., "Happy Birthday," "Knick-Knack, Paddy Wack") and replacing key words in them with words with a different ending or middle sound (oral segmentation)

- Dealing children a deck of picture cards and having them sound out the words for the pictures on their cards or calling for a picture by asking for its first and second sound

Five types of phonemic awareness tasks

Theorist Marilyn Jager Adams, who researches early reading, has outlined five basic types of phonemic awareness tasks:

- **Task 1:** The ability to hear rhymes and alliteration

- **Task 2:** The ability to do oddity tasks (recognize the member of a set that is different, or odd, among the group)

- **Task 3:** The ability to orally blend words and split syllables

- **Task 4:** The ability to orally segment words

- **Task 5:** The ability to do phonics manipulation tasks

For English-language learners, the phonology of English is an important component. Phonographemic differences between words in English are a common source of confusion and thus need to be taught explicitly with plenty of learning activities to enable learners to acquire them sufficiently.

> SKILL 2.2 **Understands differences in students' development of phonological and phonemic awareness and adjusts instruction to meet the needs of individual students, including English-language learners.**

Promoting Phonological and Phonemic Awareness

English has approximately forty phonemes. Language games that encourage phonological and phonemic awareness help students understand that language is a series of sounds that form words, and, ultimately, sentences.

- Listening games sharpen a student's ability to hear selective sounds.

- Counting syllables games help students discover that many words are made of smaller chunks.

- Rhyming games draw students' attention to the sound structure of words.

- Word and sentence-building games help students understand that language consists of words connected to form sentences.

Structured computer programs can also help teach or reinforce these skills.

When families are asked to participate in a reading program by reading, discussing stories, and writing with their children, teachers are encouraging the family to reinforce the development of students' reading awareness skills.

Activities that parents can practice with students at home:

- Playing games with words that sound alike as you experience them in everyday home activities

- Demonstrating how sounds blend together in familiar words

- Playing a game in which the goal is to find objects with names that begin with a certain initial sound

- Playing clapping games in which you clap with each distinct sound

> Daily reading sessions with the students (one-on-one or in a group) help develop their understanding of print concepts.

Phonemic Awareness for ELL Classrooms

Some areas of focus for the ELL classroom include:

- **Homonyms:** A general term that describes word forms that have two or more meanings

- **Homographs:** Two or more words that have the same spelling or pronunciation but different meanings, e.g., *stalk* (part of a plant)/*stalk* (follow)

- **Homophones:** Two or more words that have the same pronunciation but different meanings and spelling, e.g., *wood/would, cite/sight*

- **Heteronyms:** Two or more words that have the same spelling but different pronunciation and meaning, e.g., *Polish/polish*

Some useful activities for instruction would be to identify misspelled words, to recognize multiple meanings of words and sentences, to spell words correctly, and to match words with their meanings.

SKILL 2.3 **Plans, implements and adjusts instruction based on the continual use of formal and informal assessments of individual students' phonological development, in accordance with the STR.**

Phonological Assessment

Phonological assessment should focus on a student's ability to listen for, distinguish between, and identify sounds. Assessments that consider rhyme and syllable awareness are key to assessing phonological development. Students should also be able to identify and distinguish beginning (initial), middle, and ending sounds of simple words in the early childhood and elementary classrooms.

Once the basics of phonics are understood, phonological assessments should move on to consider a student's grasp of sound blends and ability to pull apart and manipulate sounds and sound blends. Teachers can evaluate a student's invented spelling to see how he or she understands and identifies sounds. They can also have students match words to the same words or to rhyming words to evaluate this skill. A third possibility is to have students play sound games in which they isolate the sounds they hear, showing they are able to identify them.

> **SKILL 2.4** Knows the age ranges at which the expected stages and patterns of various phonological and phonemic awareness skills should be acquired, the implications of individual variations in the development of phonological and phonemic awareness and ways to accelerate students' phonological and phonemic awareness, in accordance with the STR.

PHONEMIC AWARENESS: the ability to break down and hear separate and/or different sounds and distinguish among the sounds one hears

Phonics involves studying the rules and patterns found in language. By age five or six, children typically can begin to use phonics to understand the connections among letters, their patterns, vowel sounds (i.e., short vowels, long vowels), and the collective sounds they all make. **PHONEMIC AWARENESS** is the ability to break down and hear separate and/or different sounds and distinguish among the sounds one hears. Phonemic awareness is required to begin studying phonics, when students will need to break down words into the smalls units of sound, or phonemes, to later identify syllables, blends, and patterns.

At the beginning of kindergarten, students should be able to tell whether two words rhyme and generate a rhyme for a simple word. By the end of kindergarten, students should be able to isolate and pronounce the beginning sounds in a word and blend the sounds in two-phoneme words. Midway through first grade, students should be able to isolate and pronounce all the sounds in two- and three-phoneme words and to blend the sounds in four-phoneme words containing initial consonant blends. By the end of first grade, students should be able to isolate and pronounce the sounds in four-phoneme words containing initial blends and blend the sounds in four- and five-phoneme words containing initial and final blends. Phonological awareness is a broader term that includes phonemic awareness. Specific methods and teaching strategies to accelerate students' awareness include the following:

- Direct instruction

- Modeling

- Providing leveled readers
- Matching students with "just right" books that are below their frustration level
- Building vocabulary
- Phonics instruction
- Read alouds
- Small-group instruction and activities

SKILL 2.5 Uses a variety of instructional approaches and materials *(e.g., language games, informal interactions, direct instruction)* to promote students' phonological and phonemic awareness *(e.g., hearing and manipulating beginning, medial and final sounds in spoken words; recognizing spoken alliteration)*.

See Skills 2.1 and 2.2

SKILL 2.6 Understands how to foster collaboration with families and with other professionals to promote all students' phonological and phonemic awareness both at school and at home.

See Skill 2.2

SKILL 2.7 Recognizes the interrelationships between phonological and phonemic awareness and the other components of reading (vocabulary, fluency and comprehension), in accordance with the STR.

See Skills 1.6 and 1.7

COMPETENCY 3
ALPHABETIC PRINCIPLE

SKILL 3.1 **Understands the elements of the alphabetic principle** *(e.g., letter names, letter sequence, graphophonemic knowledge, the relationship of the letters in printed words to spoken language)* **and typical patterns of students' alphabetic skills development, and recognizes that individual variations occur with students.**

ALPHABETIC PRINCIPLE: sometimes called graphophonemic awareness, describes the understanding that written words are composed of patterns of letters that represent the sounds of spoken words

The **ALPHABETIC PRINCIPLE**, sometimes called graphophonemic awareness, describes the understanding that written words are composed of patterns of letters that represent the sounds of spoken words.

The alphabetic principle has two parts:

- Words are made up of letters and each letter has a specific sound.
- The correspondence between sounds and letters leads to phonological reading.

Since the English language is dependent on the alphabet, being able to recognize and sound out letters is the first step for beginning readers. Decoding is essential.

Basic features of the alphabetic principle

1. Students need to be able to take spoken words apart and blend different sounds together to make new words.

2. Students need to apply letter sounds to all of their reading.

3. Teachers need to use a systematic, effective program in order to teach children to read.

4. The teaching of the alphabetic principle usually begins in kindergarten.

Patterns of Alphabetic Skill Development
Critical skills that students need to learn are:

- Letter-sound correspondence
- How to sound out words
- How to decode text to make meaning

Students who are first learning to read need appropriate instruction in understanding, learning, and using the correct spelling-sound conventions of the English writing system.

Instruction must be adapted to account for children's differences. For those children with previous knowledge of the alphabetic principle, instruction extends their knowledge as they learn more about the formal features of letters and their sound correspondences. Students with fewer prior experiences have to be taught the beginning alphabetic principle: that a limited set of letters makes up the alphabet and that these letters stand for the sounds that make up spoken words. These students will require more focused and direct instruction.

> **SKILL 3.2** **Understands that not all written languages are alphabetic, that many alphabetic languages are more phonetically regular than English and that students' literacy development in English is affected by these two factors.**

Literacy Development for Children From Non-English-Speaking Cultures

The nasal phonetics of French differ vastly from the sharp, nasal phonetics of Asian languages that are based on a combination of symbols and vowel sounds used both in singular and combination patterns to create meaningful dialogue for the speaker and the person interpreting the meaning of those sounds.

American English oral language consists of phonological components that create rules for combining sounds where words have beginnings and endings, unlike some words in other languages that have long-sounding tones and shorter interpretations. Semantic components are the smallest combination of words and letters to produce different words. The syntactic component uses rules that allow for semantic inclusions into complex sentences.

For English-language learners from a variety of language backgrounds that include cultural and familial inflections and language use, the ability to transcend the foundational boundaries that are imposed by the English standards of language can be insurmountable, both short- and long-term. Effective instructional design should include language constructions that recognize the importance of cultural language acquisition as a more pragmatic approach to teaching children the English alphabet.

> **SKILL 3.3** Selects and uses a variety of instructional materials and strategies, including multisensory techniques, to promote students' understanding of the elements of the alphabetic principle and the relationship between sounds and letters and between letters and words, in accordance with the STR.

Strategies for Teaching the Alphabetic Principle

Multisensory structured language education uses visual, auditory, and kinesthetic cues simultaneously to enhance memory and learning.

Multisensory structured language education uses visual, auditory, and kinesthetic cues simultaneously to enhance memory and learning.

- **Quilt book:** Students can piece together pictures of objects whose names begin with the same letter of the alphabet.
- **Rhyme time:** Students participate in reciting a rhyme and identifying the words that all begin with the same sound.
- **Letter path:** Use masking tape to outline a large letter on the floor. As the students follow the path of the letter, have them name words that begin with that letter.
- **Shape game:** Call out a letter. Have the students arrange themselves to form the shape of that letter.

> **SKILL 3.4** Uses formal and informal assessments to analyze individual students' alphabetic skills, monitor learning and plan instruction, in accordance with the STR.

Formal and Informal Assessments for Alphabetic Skills

Teachers should closely monitor the development of each individual student's language acquisition skills.

Assessment tools

- Checklists
- Observations/surveys
- Portfolio collections

Teachers should monitor the development of each student's language acquisition skills closely. The specific test that can be administered is the Texas Essential Knowledge and Skills (TEKS), which assesses students' alphabetic skills. Teachers can use formal and informal assessments such as the following to gather information on students' learning.

Formal Assessments

- **Running record:** Records of individual students' behaviors or actions over time

- **Curriculum-based tests:** Assessments based on students' performance in the TEKS assessment that are used to gather information about their skills and to make instructional decisions

- **Diagnostic tests:** Assessments used to identify weaknesses in learning, to assess current levels of knowledge, or to identify learning problems

Informal Assessments

- **Observations:** Watching students with a purpose

- **Checklists**

- **Portfolio collections**

> **SKILL 3.5** Understands how to foster collaboration with families and with other professionals to promote all students' development of alphabetic knowledge.

Teachers should promote independent reading outside of school by providing enjoyable and easy-to-implement activities for home use. Teachers should also strive for frequent home-school communication. Parents can also be encouraged to spend time in the classroom observing and helping the teacher.

To foster positive parental and community involvement, teachers can implement a variety of programs:

- Home reading journals

- Telephone calls

- Informal notes

- Parent-teacher meetings

- Literacy newsletters

COMPETENCY 4
LITERACY DEVELOPMENT

SKILL 4.1 Selects and uses instructional strategies, materials and activities to assist students in distinguishing letter forms from number forms and text from pictures.

EMERGENT LITERACY: the concept that young children are emerging into reading and writing with no real beginning or ending point

EMERGENT LITERACY is the concept that young children are emerging into reading and writing with no real beginning or ending point. This stage of reading is when the reader understands that print contains a consistent message.

Characteristics of emerging readers:

1. Can attend to left-to-right directionality and features of print

2. Can identify some initial sounds and ending sounds in words

3. Can recognize some high-frequency words, names, and simple words in context

4. Can use pictures to predict meaning

Areas of Emerging Evidence

1. Experiences with print (through reading and writing) help preschool children develop an understanding of the conventions, purpose, and functions of print.

2. Phonological awareness and letter recognition contribute to initial reading acquisition by helping children develop efficient word recognition strategies.

3. Storybook reading affects children's knowledge about, strategies for, and attitudes toward reading.

Design Principles in Emergent Literacy

Conspicuous strategies can be incorporated in beginning reading instruction to ensure that all learners have basic literacy concepts.

• Conspicuous strategies: A sequence of teaching events and teacher actions used to help students learn new literacy information and relate it to their existing knowledge. Conspicuous strategies can be incorporated in beginning reading instruction to ensure that all learners have basic literacy concepts.

- **Mediated scaffolding:** A systematic transition from fully teacher-directed instruction to more student-directed learning. Teachers can act as scaffolds during storybook-reading activities by adjusting their demands (e.g., asking increasingly complex questions or encouraging children to take on portions of the reading) or by reading more complex text as students gain knowledge of beginning literacy components.

- **Strategic integration:** Many children have difficulty making connections between old and new information. Strategic integration can be applied to help link old and new learning.

- **Primed background knowledge:** Teachers can utilize children's background knowledge to help children link their personal literacy experiences to beginning reading instruction, while also closing the gap between students with rich literacy experiences and those with poorer literacy experiences.

- **Emergent literacy:** Strong support is found in the literature for the important contribution that early childhood exposure to oral and written language makes to the facility with which children learn to read.

> **SKILL 4.2** Understands that the developing reader has a growing awareness of print in the environment, the sounds in spoken words and the uses of print, in accordance with the STR.

Developing Students' Awareness of Print

The structure of the English language consists of rules of grammar, capitalization, and punctuation. For younger children, this means being able to recognize letters and form words. For older children, it means being able to recognize different types of text, such as lists, stories, and signs, and knowing the purpose of each type.

Reid (1988, p. 165) described three metalinguistic abilities that young children acquire through early involvement in reading activities:

1. **Word consciousness:** Children who have access to books can tell the story through the pictures first. Gradually, they begin to realize the connection between the spoken words and the printed words. The beginning of letter and word discrimination begins in the early years.

2. **Language and conventions of print:** During this stage, children learn how to hold a book, where to begin to read, the left-to-right motion, and how to continue from one line to another.

3. **Functions of print:** Children discover that print can be used for a variety of purposes and functions, including entertainment and information.

> **SKILL 4.3** Selects and uses instructional strategies, materials and activities to assist students in distinguishing letter forms from number forms and text from pictures.

Instructional Strategies

- **Big books in the classroom:** Gather the children around you in a group with the big book placed on a stand. As you read, point to each word.

- **A classroom rich in print:** There should be plenty of books in the classroom for children to read on their own or in small groups.

- **Word wall:** Each of the letters of the alphabet is displayed with words under it that begin with that letter.

- **Sounds of the letters:** In addition to learning the letter names, students should learn the corresponding sound of each letter.

- **Book-handling skills**

  - Practicing how to handle a book: How to turn pages, find the top and bottom of pages, and tell the difference between the front and back covers

  - Book organization: Students demonstrate an understanding of the organization of books by being able to identify the title, cover, author, left-to-right progression, top-to-bottom order, and one-to-one correspondence. Students may learn these skills individually as they become more familiar with books.

Distinguishing letters from numbers and text from pictures

Children should understand that pictures show words in action. Pictures can have one or multiple meanings, depending on the reader or the teacher creating the instruction.

SKILL 4.4 Understands the importance of students being able to differentiate words and spaces, first and last letters, left-right progression, and identification of basic punctuation, in accordance with the STR.

To develop awareness of print and reading, in a small-group or individual setting, have students show you the front of book, the title of the book, where you should begin reading, a letter, a word, the first word of a sentence, the last word of a sentence, the first and last word on a page, a punctuation mark, a capital letter, a lowercase letter, and the back of the book.

Ways to promote students' ability to differentiate words and spaces, locate first and last letters, understand left-right progression, and identify basic punctuation include the following:

- Phoneme deletion

- Morning message: Students learn that writing is speech written down and learn proper letter formation, upper- and lowercase letter recognition, associating letters and sounds, and left-to-right progression. They learn to differentiate among a letter, a word, and a sentence; learn to read common sight words; understand spacing and punctuation; and learn to look for patterns within words (word families).

SKILL 4.5 Understands that literacy development occurs in multiple contexts through reading, writing and the use of oral language.

See Skill 1.6 and Skill 1.7

SKILL 4.6 Selects and uses instructional strategies, materials and activities that focus on functions of print and concepts about print, including concepts involving book handling, parts of a book, orientation, directionality and the relationships between written and spoken words, in accordance with the STR.

See Skill 4.3 and Skill 4.7

> **SKILL 4.7** Demonstrates familiarity with literature and provides multiple opportunities for students to listen to, respond to and independently read literature in various genres and to interact with others about literature.

Types of Literature for Different Developmental Stages

From being read to by parents and caregivers from the earliest ages, toddlers can handle board books with sturdy pages. Children ages 2 and 3 enjoy what are called toy books, i.e., those that have flaps to lift up, textures to touch, or holes to peek through. From ages 3 to 7, children enjoy a variety of nonfiction concept books. These books combine language and pictures to show concrete examples of abstract concepts.

Another category of concept books is alphabet books, popular with children from preschool through grade 2.

In grades K–2, when children are becoming early readers, two other genres of literature become salient: wordless picture books and easy-to-read books. Wordless picture books accommodate readers and nonreaders alike because there is no text.

From the preschool years onward, picture books, characterized by illustrations and a plot that are closely interrelated (one usually cannot exist independently of the other), are suitable for children.

Chapter books are appropriate for readers in grades 2, 3, and 4 and beyond. They are characterized by occasional illustrations, relatively short chapters, and interesting plots that appeal to children ages 8 and up.

> **SKILL 4.8** Selects and uses appropriate instructional strategies to inform students about authors, authors' purposes for writing and author's point of view in a variety of texts.

Determining the author's purpose and the point of view of a text can help students deepen their understanding of what they read and read through a critical lens. These are lifelong skills readers need when analyzing text to distinguish different perspectives and/or identify propaganda. The following approaches can help students understand author's purpose:

- Start with *Why?* Discuss the structure of the text. Has the author chosen a structure to make the reader feel a certain way? How does the structure affect the content? Ask students to think about why the author wrote the text in the way he or she did and to connect this to their own writing.

- Students can practice identifying author's purpose and point of view by discussing TV shows, movies, advertisements, campaigns, and speeches.

SKILL 4.9 Selects and uses appropriate technology to teach students strategies for selecting books for independent reading.

The school media specialist and classroom teachers will collaborate to develop, teach, and evaluate building curricular goals with emphasis on promoting inquiry and critical thinking; providing information literacy learning experiences to help students access, evaluate, use, create, and communicate information; and enhancing learning and teaching through technology. Teachers can incorporate technology to allow students to select books for independent reading. During the first five minutes of community reading time, book talks can introduce students to books, magazine articles, websites, and other print or electronic materials from the school or classroom library. Reading online digital books like those found on the International Digital Children's Library website can be very motivating for young readers. In addition, using Scholastic Book Wizard online can also assist children in identifying a just right book; the website provides a guided reading level, Lexile level, grade-level equivalent to the book after typing in the title and author of the book. When students use these resources, they will be able to identify whether the book they have selected is appropriate for their independent reading level.

- International Children's Digital Library

  http://en.childrenslibrary.org. Retrieved Aug. 25, 2015.

- Scholastic Book Wizard

  http://www.scholastic.com/bookwizard/. Retrieved Aug. 25, 2015.

SKILL 4.10 Understands how to foster collaboration with families and with other professionals to promote all students' literacy.

Teachers should communicate with students' families about classroom literacy. Families should be provided information that will engage children in literacy-related activities. Getting to know students' parents can help teachers plan instructional activities that are relevant to the students. Teachers should collaborate with other professionals to promote children's literacy development. Teachers can hold parent-teacher literacy nights to foster and encourage parents to read with their children and ask comprehension questions while reading. Demonstrations can show parents how to read and interact with their children and encourage reading time at home. When teachers and other education professionals meet, they should discuss strategies that work when promoting children's literacy. During this time, teachers can share out what might work for different learning styles.

COMPETENCY 5
WORD ANALYSIS AND IDENTIFICATION SKILLS

SKILL 5.1 **Understands that while many students develop word analysis and decoding skills in a predictable sequence, individual variations may occur, in accordance with the STR.**

Teachers must understand the importance of reading and decoding and basic skills should not be taught in isolation. Vocabulary knowledge is a core component in a child's language proficiency. Vocabulary can be taught in various ways it is up to the educator to find and help develop those variations through observations of the students leaning patterns.

For example, teachers could start with a Words Their Way vocabulary assessment to determine where individual students might struggle with decoding words. Once a teacher analyzes students' patterns, the teacher can provide individualized instruction to students struggling with specific skills.

SKILL 5.2 **Understands the importance of word recognition skills** (e.g., letter-sound correspondences, decoding, blending, structural analysis, sight word vocabulary, contextual analysis) **for reading comprehension and knows a variety of strategies for helping students develop and apply word analysis skills, including identifying, categorizing and using common synonyms, antonyms, homographs, homophones and analogies.**

WORD ANALYSIS: the process readers use to figure out unfamiliar words based on written patterns

WORD RECOGNITION: the process of automatically determining the pronunciation and some degree of the meaning of an unknown word

Word Recognition Skills

WORD ANALYSIS (also called phonics or decoding) is the process readers use to figure out unfamiliar words based on written patterns. WORD RECOGNITION is the process of automatically determining the pronunciation and some degree of the meaning of an unknown word. In other words, fluent readers recognize most written words easily and correctly, without consciously decoding or breaking them down.

DECODING refers to the ability to sound out a word by translating different letters or groups of letters (graphemes) into sounds (phonemes).

Reading comprehension requires the reader to learn the code in which a message is written and to be able to decode it to get the message. ENCODING involves changing a message into symbols.

Tasks for assessing word-analysis and decoding skills can be grouped into three categories:

- Comparing sounds

- Blending phonemes into words

- Segmenting words into phonemes

> **DECODING:** the ability to sound out a word by translating different letters or groups of letters (graphemes) into sounds (phonemes)

> **ENCODING:** changing a message into symbols

Sight-Word Vocabulary

Sight words, or high-frequency words, are words that appear frequently in reading, and are thought to make up approximately 50 percent of elementary textbook reading. For example, some basic sight words for kindergartners include: *the, a, here, to, in, and, is, be, it, go, you, be, he, she, him, her, for,* and *are*. Because these words have little actual meaning on their own, they derive their meaning from the surrounding context, and most students learn to immediately recognize them on sight.

Context clues

When people read, they use four sources of background information to comprehend the meaning behind the literal text (Reid, pp. 166–71):

1. **Word knowledge:** One's knowledge of word meanings is *lexical knowledge*—a sort of dictionary. Knowledge of spelling patterns and pronunciations is *orthographic knowledge*.

2. **Syntax and contextual information:** When children encounter unknown words in a sentence, they rely on their background knowledge to choose a meaning that makes sense.

3. **Semantic knowledge:** This encompasses the reader's background knowledge of a topic, which is combined with information from the text as the reader tries to comprehend the material.

4. **Text organization:** Good readers are able to differentiate types of text structure (e.g., narrative, exposition, compare-contrast, or time sequence). They use their knowledge of text to build expectations and to construct a framework of ideas on which to build meaning.

Contextual redefinition

This strategy supports children in using the context more effectively by presenting them with sufficient context *before* they begin reading. It models the use of contextual clues to make informed guesses about word meanings.

> **SKILL 5.3** **Teaches the analysis of phonetically regular words in a simple-to-complex progression** *(i.e., phonemes, blending onsets and rimes, short vowels/long vowels, consonant blends, other common vowel and consonant patterns, syllable types)***, in accordance with the STR.**

Identification of Vowel Sounds

Applying vowel sounds to syllabic words increases reading ability and word usage. Children who understand and have memorized the vowel-sound essentials increase their decoding of new words by a higher percentage than children who base comprehension on predictable text of known words and usage.

> *Children who understand and have memorized the vowel-sound essentials increase their decoding of new words by a higher percentage than children who base comprehension on predictable text of known words and usage.*

The vowel-sound essentials include the following vowel-letter combinations:

- Short vowels: *a, e, i, o,* and *u*

- Long vowels: *a, e, i, o,* and *u*

- Diagraphs (two letters that produce one sound): *ai, ee, ie, oa, ay, au,* and *aw*

- Diphthongs (two letters with two sounds): *ou, oo*-long/short, *ew, ow*-long/short, *oi*

- R vowels: *ar, er, ir, or, ur*

The phonetics of syllabic words includes a core nucleus of vowel sounds that can be viewed in common words as a "consonant-vowel-consonant" sequence of letters and sounds. Longer syllabic words such as *imagination* have stress and tone on each part of the syllabic segments that includes a phonetic emphasis on the core nucleus of the word.

Examples of the Six Types of Syllables

One of the most useful devices for developing automaticity in young students is the visual pattern provided in the six syllable types.

1. **NOT** (closed)

   <u>Closed</u> in by a consonant—vowel makes its **short** sound

2. **NO** (open)

   <u>Ends</u> in a vowel—vowel makes its **long** sound

3. **NOTE** (silent "e")

   <u>Ends</u> in vowel consonant "*e*"—vowel makes its **long** sound

4. **NAIL** (vowel combination)

   <u>Two vowels together</u> make the sound

5. **BIRD** ("*r*" controlled)

   <u>Contains</u> a vowel followed by the letter r—vowel sound is changed by the r

6. **TABLE** (consonant "*l*"-"*e*")

   <u>Applied</u> at the end of a word

These orthographic (letter) patterns signal vowel pronunciation to the reader. Students must learn to apply their knowledge of these patterns to recognize the syllable types and to see the patterns automatically, and ultimately, to read words as wholes. The move from decoding letter symbols to identifying recognizable terms to automatic word recognition is a substantial move toward fluency.

> *Students must learn to apply their knowledge of these patterns to recognize the syllable types and to see the patterns automatically, and ultimately, to read words as wholes.*

Four Types of Words

English orthography is made up of four basic word types:

1. Regular for reading and spelling (e.g., *cat, print*)

2. Regular for reading but not for spelling (e.g. *float, brain*—could be spelled *flote* or *brane*, respectively)

3. Rule-based (e.g., *canning*—doubling rule, *faking*—drop *e* rule)

4. Irregular (e.g., *beauty*)

Instruction in phonics involves helping beginning readers learn how sounds are linked to letters and letter combinations in the written language. It teaches that there is a predictable pattern to much of our language. A PHONEME is the meaning of a letter or digraph, the "mouth move" signaled by the letter. The spelling of a word (its letter sequence) is a map of the pronunciation—its phoneme sequence.

> **PHONEME:** the meaning of a letter or digraph, the "mouth move" signaled by the letter

To teach students phonics, help them find each phoneme in spoken words. Daily writing opportunities with invented spelling allow children to identify phonemes and practice using correspondences they are learning. Using onsets and rimes also

ONSET: the initial consonant or consonant cluster of a word

RIME: the vowel and consonants that follow the initial consonant or consonant cluster of the word

can be helpful. The ONSET is the initial consonant or consonant cluster of a word, and the RIME is the vowel and consonants that follow the initial consonant or consonant cluster of the word. For example, in the word *bat, b* is the onset and *-at* is the rime. This is an important skill in mastering word families.

Teaching consonant blends is a good idea because they frequently occur together. This shows students common patterns in words. This is taught best through direct instruction in which the teacher provides precise directions. Struggling readers may require additional guided practice in small groups, and instruction must be differentiated to meet individual needs. Vowel and consonant patterns require reviewing CV and CVC patterns. Teachers should explain that looking for patterns of vowels and consonants will help students read and spell words correctly. Review the definitions of *vowel* and *consonant* using student-friendly language. Provide visual cue cards or posters.

> **SKILL 5.4** Selects and uses instructional strategies, materials, activities and models to teach students to recognize high-frequency words, to promote students' ability to decode increasingly complex words and to enhance word identification skills of students reading at varying levels.

Students will be better at comprehension if they have a strong working vocabulary.

Students will be better at comprehension if they have a strong working vocabulary. Research has shown that students learn more vocabulary when it is presented in context, rather than in vocabulary lists, for example.

Teachers should introduce high-frequency words in a meaningful way. Have students connect the words and their meanings to their environment. A personal dictionary is one way in which students can use materials to help them store and refer to words they learn. Making and using flashcards and practicing the words in isolation also are instructional strategies that will help students identify high-frequency words. Writing the words within short phrases or sentences and having students read them aloud will increase the fluency with which students identify the words. Teachers can use flashcards and have students group the words by first letter, last letter, rhymes, and other characteristics.

MORPHOGRAPH: a representation of a specific letter-meaning relationship

Word study activities will help students decode increasingly complex words. Instruction must be explicit, systematic, and scaffolded. Chunking can help students increase the generative, deeper knowledge of English needed to decode and spell words independently. A MORPHOGRAPH is a representation of a specific letter-meaning relationship. Familiarity with morphographs aids in spelling, reading, and making sense of difficult words, increasing students' ability to decode words.

> SKILL 5.5 **Knows strategies for decoding increasingly complex words, including the alphabetic principle, vowel-sound combinations, structural cues** (e.g., morphology-prefixes, suffixes, roots, base words, abbreviations, contractions), **and syllable types and for using syntax and semantics to support word identification and confirm word meaning, in accordance with the STR.**

Identification of Common Morphemes, Prefixes, and Suffixes

Key structural analysis components include:

- **Root words:** Words from which other words are developed.

- **Base words:** Stand-alone linguistic units that cannot be deconstructed or broken down into smaller words. For example, in the word *retell*, the base word is *tell*.

- **Contractions:** Shortened forms of two words in which a letter or letters have been deleted. The deleted letters have been replaced by an apostrophe.

- **Prefixes:** Beginning units of meaning that can be added, or *affixed*, to a base word or root word.

- **Suffixes:** Ending units of meaning that can be *affixed*, or added, to the ends of root or base words.

- **Compound words:** Words that are formed when two or more base words are connected to form a new word. The meaning of the new word is in some way connected with that of the base words.

- **Inflectional endings:** Types of suffixes that impart a new meaning to the base or root word. These endings change the gender, number, tense, or form of the base or root words. Like other suffixes, they are also called "bound morphemes."

SYNTAX refers to the rules or patterned relationships that correctly create phrases and sentences from words. When readers develop an understanding of syntax, they begin to understand the structure of how sentences are built, and, eventually, the beginning of grammar.

SEMANTICS refers to the meaning expressed when words are arranged in a specific way. This is where connotation and denotation of words eventually has a role with readers.

> **SYNTAX:** the rules or patterned relationships that correctly create phrases and sentences from words

> **SEMANTICS:** the meaning expressed when words are arranged in a specific way

SKILL 5.6 Understands the value of using dictionaries, glossaries and other sources to determine the meanings, usage, pronunciations, correct spelling, and derivations of unfamiliar words and teaches students to use those sources.

The Value of Dictionaries, Glossaries, and Other References

Dictionary

The uses of a dictionary include:

- Word spelling
- Word pronunciation
- Syllable breakdown
- Definition or definitions

- Part of speech
- Synonyms/antonyms
- Word origin
- Use in a sentence/context/connotation

Every word in the dictionary is an entry word. The words at the top of each page are called guide words, and they identify the first word on the page (upper left) and the last word on a page (upper right). These words help users find their entry words more efficiently.

Glossary

A glossary is similar to a dictionary in that it provides definitions of words; however, a glossary is typically a collection of difficult, unfamiliar, or new words located in one section of a reading.

Thesaurus

A thesaurus helps people locate synonyms and antonyms of words.

SKILL 5.7 Understands how to foster collaboration with families and with other professionals to promote all students' word analysis and decoding skills.

See Skills 4.10, 7.14, and 11.9

COMPETENCY 6
FLUENCY READING

> ### SKILL 6.1 Knows the relationship between reading fluency and comprehension, in accordance with the STR.

Reading fluency helps students' overall reading comprehension. Fluency strategies such as repeated reading should be a major focus of instruction for students to comprehend what they are reading. Reading fluency creates a bridge to reading comprehension. Implementing fluency strategies into the balanced literacy framework can improve overall reading comprehension for children. The ultimate goal of reading is to make meaning and comprehend what was read, not to read the text as quickly as possible.

See also Skills 6.3 and 7.2

> ### SKILL 6.2 Understands that fluency involves rate, accuracy, prosody and intonation and knows the norms for reading fluency that have been established by the Texas Essential Knowledge and Skills (TEKS) for various age and grade levels, in accordance with the STR.

Reading Rates

One way to evaluate reading fluency is to look at student accuracy, and a good way to do this is to keep running records of students during oral reading.

Results of running record informal assessment can be used for teaching based on text accuracy. If a child's accuracy rate is from 95 to 100 percent, the child is ready for independent reading. If a child's rate is from 92 to 97 percent, the child is ready for guided reading. If a child's rate is below 92 percent, he or she needs a read aloud or shared reading activity.

Reading rate guidelines by grade level

The following general guidelines can be applied for reading lists of words with a speed drill and a one-minute timing:

- 30 correct words per minute (wpm) for first- and second-grade children

- 40 correct wpm for third-grade children

- 60 correct wpm for mid-third-grade children
- 80 wpm for students in fourth grade and higher

Techniques to help students with decoding

- Students listen to text as they follow along with the book
- Students follow the print using their fingers as guides
- Reading materials are used that students would be unable to read independently

Experts recommend that a beginning reading program should incorporate partner reading, practice reading difficult words prior to reading the text, timings for accuracy and rate, opportunities to hear books read, and opportunities to read to others.

Prosody

PROSODY concerns versification of text and involves such matters as which syllable of a word is accented. It is that aspect which translates reading into the same experience as listening in the reader's mind. It involves intonation and rhythm through such devices as syllable accent and punctuation.

> **PROSODY:** concerns versification of text and involves such matters as which syllable of a word is accented

> **SKILL 6.3** Understands the connection of word identification skills and reading fluency to reading comprehension.

Importance of Word Identification Skills and Reading Fluency to Reading Comprehension

Fluency in reading depends on automatic word identification, which assists the student in achieving comprehension. Automatic reading involves the development of strong orthographic representations, which allows fast and accurate identification of whole words made up of specific letter patterns.

See also Skill 6.1

> ### SKILL 6.4
> **Understands differences in students' development of word identification skills and reading fluency and knows instructional practices for meeting students' individual needs in those areas, in accordance with the STR.**

Reading fluency and comprehension depend not only on readers' oral vocabulary and background knowledge, but also on their ability to recognize words in print, their knowledge of letter-sound correspondences and common spelling patterns, their mastery of phonics and word analysis skills, and their development of automatic recognition of many words. Fluent readers do not have to devote energy to decoding words, so they can focus their attention on what the text means. The following are good teaching practices:

Fluent readers do not have to devote energy to decoding words, so they can focus their attention on what the text means.

- Using visual or concrete materials will make learning phonics skills more memorable. Letter cards, cards for word-sorting activities, dry-erase boards, and other concrete resources provide students a visual link to their learning.

- Begin by teaching students to decode words with simple syllable patterns, such as *am* and *mop,* and then incrementally progress to words with more difficult syllable patterns, such as *spot, boat,* and *tape.* As readers progress, add complex phonics patterns and the sounds and spellings of inflectional endings, prefixes, and suffixes.

- Provide students with regular opportunities to practice new learning in phonics by reading decodable texts.

- Provide students with opportunities to transfer skills to a broad range of texts and reading and writing activities that will support their ongoing development of literacy skills and enhance their motivation by promoting their ownership of new learning.

Teachers should be aware of students' prerequisite and component skills of fluency and be able to recognize factors that can disrupt their fluency, such as the reading level of a text or comprehension-related factors.

- Teachers can model fluent reading when reading aloud. Family members or other students who are skilled readers also can serve as good models.

- Teachers can read aloud a big book or another shared text and think aloud about prosodic aspects of the reading performance. Reading at a conversational rate and with good phrasing, intonation, and expression supports reading comprehension.

- Students can benefit from listening to and rereading along with audio-recorded stories while following along in the printed text.

See also Skill 6.5

> **SKILL 6.5** **Selects and uses instructional strategies, materials and activities to develop and improve fluency** *(e.g., reading independent-level materials, reading orally from familiar texts, repeated reading, partner reading, silent reading for increasingly longer periods, self-correction)*, **in accordance with the STR.**

The following are important components of effective fluency instruction:

- **Modeling fluent reading:** Teachers can model fluent reading when reading aloud.

- **Providing explicit instruction in fluency:** Teachers can read aloud a big book or another shared text and think aloud about prosodic aspects of the reading performance. They should stress that reading at a conversational rate and with good phrasing, intonation, and expression supports reading comprehension. Students also can benefit from listening to and rereading along with audio-recorded stories while following along in the printed text.

- **Choral reading:** All students, directed by the teacher or a student, read aloud together.

- **Echo reading:** The teacher or a skilled student partner reads a text aloud sentence by sentence or line by line and has students chorally mimic his or her style.

- **Repeated reading:** Students read a passage several times as their teacher offers suggestions of areas for improvement.

- **Paired reading:** One student reads the text silently and then reads the passage aloud to his or her partner.

- **Buddy reading:** An upper-grade student or a more proficient reader takes turns reading aloud with a less skilled reader or listens to the less skilled reader read aloud and then offers constructive feedback or discusses what is happening in the text.

- **Reader's theater:** Students read a script from appropriate literature. Emphasis is on preparing to read with prosody in a dramatic performance of the text. Repeated practice in rehearsals helps students build fluency in a purposeful, authentic task.

A great deal of practice helps young students develop automaticity and prosody.

SKILL
6.6 **Knows how to teach students strategies for selecting books for independent reading, in accordance with the STR.**

Students should be knowledgeable of their independent reading levels. Classroom libraries should be leveled, which makes it easier for students to select books on their independent reading levels. Scholastic Book Wizard (*http://www.scholastic.com/ bookwizard/*) is a website that can be used to look up individual book levels. The books students choose for independent reading should be at their reading level, meaning accuracy, fluency, and comprehension are all attainable. A just right book is one that provides a little bit of a challenge for the student. It should be a book that the student finds interesting and can be read with a small amount of assistance. Spending time reading just right books during independent reading time will help students become stronger readers. One way of determining independent reading level is to use the "Goldilocks" method: too easy, too hard, and just right. Modeling this strategy for students will help them understand before they have to apply it independently.

Opportunities to Read Various Literary Genres

Reading specialists need to have a large amount of material available to be able to meet the needs of the various students they may encounter. There are various accepted methods of organizing material. In most cases, the texts should be leveled according to some standards. Many people use the Fountas and Pinnell leveling system or the developing readers assessment system. They both provide lists of books and their corresponding levels; in fact, most major publishing companies provide this information for all of their materials.

Fictional genres that may appeal to students in kindergarten through grade 12 include:

- Mystery
- Fantasy
- Drama
- Historical fiction
- Fable
- Mythology
- Fairy tale

- Poetry
- Folklore
- Legends
- Realistic fiction
- Tall tales
- Science fiction

Nonfiction genres include:

- Essays
- Narrative nonfiction
- Biography
- Speech
- Autobiographies

Reference materials include:

- Dictionaries
- Thesauruses
- Encyclopedias
- Almanacs

SKILL 6.7 **Provides students with opportunities to engage in silent reading and extended reading of a wide range of materials, including expository texts and various literary genres.**

When reading for research or reading for pleasure, students have opportunities to engage in silent reading and extended reading of a wide range of expository text, including research books, websites, and nonfiction. Regular practice and frequent opportunities to read a wide range of material are important. Engage students and encourage them to read regularly. All students benefit from reading practice, and books are the tools that provide students with the opportunities to practice. Access to quality books influences how much students read and interact with text. Teachers can set up their reading blocks to include time for students to read independently and give students open library time to become absorbed in a variety of genres.

SKILL 6.8 **Uses strategies to encourage reading for pleasure and lifelong learning.**

Teachers should model a love for reading to encourage reading for pleasure and lifelong learning. Modeling and expressing a personal love for reading in the classroom and sharing with your students that you read for pleasure will make you a positive role model. Discuss reading in a positive light, encourage your students to read, and teach them how to make a connection to the books they are reading.

See also Skill 6.7

| SKILL 6.9 | Recognizes the interrelationship between reading fluency and the other components of reading, in accordance with the STR. |

There are five aspects to the reading process: phonics, phonemic awareness, vocabulary, reading comprehension, and fluency. Fluency is the bridge between decoding and reading comprehension. Fluency is essential to the learning process and directly contributes to student learning outcomes.

| SKILL 6.10 | Understands how to foster collaboration with families and with other professionals to promote all students' reading fluency. |

Fostering Collaboration to Promote Literacy

Regardless of the positive or negative impacts on students' education from outside sources, it is the teacher's responsibility to ensure that all students in the classroom have an equal opportunity for academic success. This begins with the teacher's statement of high expectations for every student, and develops through the planning, delivery, and evaluation of instruction that provides for inclusion and ensures that all students have equal access to the resources necessary to acquire the academic skills being taught and measured in the classroom.

Involvement among families, teachers, libraries, principals, and other school professionals should be viewed as a partnership in which everyone actively strives to create and promote an enriching environment for children to develop their reading skills. Many schools are instituting school-wide computer programs and using other technology to aid in the ongoing reading development of their students.

Schools can collaborate with local libraries to create summer reading programs. Teachers can also form literacy programs to involve the community and families in the students' reading curriculum.

Teachers, family members, and other professionals should utilize the following reading fluency instructional strategies:

- Model fluent oral reading (read aloud) followed by student reading

- Model reading with expression followed by student reading with expression

- Guided oral repeated readings

- Audio-assisted reading

- Partner reading

COMPETENCY 7
READING COMPREHENSION AND APPLICATIONS

SKILL 7.1 **Understands reading comprehension as an active process of constructing meaning, in accordance with the STR.**

Reading comprehension is an intentional, active, interactive process that allows students to construct meaning from a variety of text. Reading comprehension is a process of simultaneously extracting and constructing meaning through interaction and involvement with written texts, students learn how to become self-regulated, active readers who have a variety genres and strategies on how to construct meaning from them.

See also Skills 6.1 and 7.2

SKILL 7.2 **Understands factors affecting students' reading comprehension** *(e.g., oral language development, word analysis skills, prior knowledge, language background/experience, previous reading experiences, fluency, vocabulary development, ability to monitor understanding, characteristics of specific texts),* **in accordance with the STR.**

Several factors affect an individual's ability to read: native intelligence, eyesight, neural processing, and prior knowledge. Elementary school teachers are well acquainted with students who can decode well enough to read a passage aloud, but who cannot restate what has been "read" to demonstrate that they comprehended it. If a student does not see adults and older siblings reading at home, the student may perceive reading as something to be endured rather than enjoyed.

See also Skills 6.1 and 7.1

> **SKILL 7.3** Understands levels of reading comprehension and knows how to model and teach skills for literal comprehension (e.g., identifying stated main idea, recalling details, identifying point-of-view), **inferential comprehension** (e.g., inferring cause-and-effect relationships, moral lessons and themes, making predictions), **and evaluative comprehension** (e.g., analyzing character development and use of language, detecting faulty reasoning, explaining point of view).

Literal Comprehension

The topic of a paragraph or story is what the paragraph or story is about.

The main idea of a paragraph or story states the important idea(s) that the author wants the reader to know about a topic.

The topic sentence indicates what the passage is about. It is the subject of that portion of the narrative.

A paragraph is a group of sentences about one main idea. Paragraphs usually have two types of sentences: a topic sentence, which contains the main idea, and two or more detail sentences, which support, prove, provide more information, explain, or give examples.

Inferential Comprehension

In order to draw inferences and make conclusions, a reader must use prior knowledge and apply it to the current situation. A conclusion or inference is never stated.

Conclusions are drawn as a result of a line of reasoning. Inductive reasoning begins with particulars and reasons to a generality.

Deductive reasoning begins with a generalization, such as "Green apples are sour," and supports that generalization with specifics.

A common fallacy in reasoning is the *post hoc ergo propter hoc* ("after this, therefore because of this"), or the false-cause fallacy. These occur in cause/effect reasoning, which may go either from cause to effect or effect to cause. They occur when an inadequate cause is offered for a particular effect, when the possibility of more than one cause is ignored, or when a connection between a particular cause and a particular effect is not made.

STYLE: the artful adaptation of language to meet various purposes

TONE: the attitude an author takes toward his or her subject

Interpretive and Evaluative Comprehension

STYLE is the artful adaptation of language to meet various purposes. TONE is the attitude an author takes toward his or her subject. The author's choice of words helps the reader determine the overall tone of a statement or passage.

POINT OF VIEW is an author's perspective. While most of us think of point of view in terms of first- or third-person (or even the points of view of various characters in stories), point of view also helps explain a lot of language and the presentation of ideas in nonfiction and fiction.

> **POINT OF VIEW:** an author's perspective

> **SKILL 7.4** Provides instruction in comprehension skills that support students' transition from "learning to read" to "reading to learn" *(e.g., recognizing different types of texts, understanding text structure, using textual features such as headings and glossaries, appreciating the different purposes for reading)* **to become self directed, critical readers.**

Transition from "Learning to Read" to "Reading to Learn"

At points in the learning-to-read process, teachers can help students understand that people read for a variety of reasons. Sometimes people read for pleasure, in which case they can decide whether to skim quickly for the content or read slowly to savor ideas and language. Other times, people simply want to find information quickly, in which case they skim or scan. In some texts, rereading is necessary to fully comprehend information.

Skimming is when readers read quickly while paying little attention to specific words. This is often done when readers want a full picture of a text, but do not want to focus on the details. Skimming can be done as a preview or a review.

Scanning is a bit different from skimming. In scanning, readers go straight to specific ideas, words, sections, or examples. They pick and choose what to read in a text. This is done when the reader does not need to know everything in a text.

In-depth reading is done when readers want to enjoy a text or learn from it thoroughly. For the most part, in this type of reading, readers move forward quickly and do not stop to focus on a specific word or idea, although sometimes this is necessary. The main idea of this type of reading is that readers do not skip over or read quickly to get information. They read everything carefully and thoroughly.

The final type of reading is rereading. Sometimes, whole texts must be reread for the concepts. This is usually the case when the text is difficult. A word, concept, or a few ideas may need to be reviewed before the reader can go on. Another method of rereading is rereading a whole text months or years after reading it the first time.

> **SKILL 7.5** **Uses various instructional strategies to enhance students' reading comprehension** (e.g., linking text content to students' lives and prior knowledge, connecting related ideas across different texts, comparing different versions of the same story, explaining the meaning of common idioms, adages and foreign words and phrases in written English, engaging students in guided and independent reading, guiding students to generate questions and apply knowledge of text topics).

Strategies for Facilitating Comprehension

Making predictions

One theory or approach to the teaching of reading that gained currency in the late sixties and early seventies was the importance of asking inferential and critical-thinking questions that would challenge and engage the reader in the text. This approach went beyond the literal level of what was stated in the text to an inferential level of using text clues to make predictions and then to a critical level of involving the child in evaluating the text. While this approach is still used, it is currently only considered to be one component of the teaching of reading.

Questioning

Although questioning tends to be overused in many classrooms, it is still a valid method of teaching students to comprehend.

As the word implies, students answer questions regarding a text, either out loud, in small groups, or individually on paper. The best questions are those that require students to think about the text (rather than just find an answer in the text).

Graphic organizers

Graphic organizers are graphical representations of content in a text. Graphic organizers solidify a visual relationship among various reading and writing ideas, including: sequence, timelines, character traits, fact and opinion, main idea and details, and differences and similarities (generally done using a Venn diagram of interlocking circles, KWL chart, etc).

KWL charts

KWL charts are exceptionally useful for reading comprehension by outlining what students **K**now, what they **W**ant to know, and what they've **L**earned after reading. Students are asked to activate prior knowledge and further develop their knowledge about a topic using this organizer. Teachers often display and maintain KWL charts throughout the study of a text to continually record pertinent information about students' reading.

> **SKILL 7.6** **Knows and teaches strategies that facilitate comprehension of different types of text** (e.g., *literary, expository, multistep directions, procedural*) **before, during and after reading** (e.g., *previewing, making predictions, questioning, self-monitoring, rereading, mapping, using reading journals, discussing texts*).

The directed reading-thinking activity can be used across all content areas before and during reading. This activity focuses on comprehension strategies:

- Prediction

- Inference

- Reading purpose

It requires students to use their background knowledge, make connections to what they know, make predictions about the text, set their own purpose for reading, use the information in the text, and then make evaluative judgments. The directed reading-thinking activity can be used with nonfiction and fiction texts.

The **question–answer relationship (QAR) strategy** can be used across all content areas. During and after reading, the focus is comprehension and determining importance. Questioning and synthesizing is a strategy that targets the question, "Where is the answer?" The teacher and the students create questions that fit into a four-level thinking guide. The levels of questions require students to use explicit and implicit information in the text.

Another strategy that can be used before, during, and after reading expository text is a **KWL chart** that focuses on the following comprehension strategies:

- Activating background knowledge

- Questioning

- Determining importance

The KWL chart guides students' thinking as they begin reading and involves them in each step of the reading process. Students begin by identifying what they already know about the assigned reading topic, then they identify what they want to know about the topic, and finally, after they have read the material, they identify what they have learned as a result of reading. The strategy requires students to build on past knowledge and is useful in making connections, setting a purpose for reading, and evaluating one's own learning.

Response journals are another powerful learning tool. Students benefit greatly from exploring their thinking through writing. They clarify their ideas, identify confusing points, integrate new information with their background knowledge, and deepen their understanding and memory of the reading. Response journals provide many opportunities for students to use writing as a tool for learning. Teachers can use response journals before students read an assignment, during the reading, and/or after the reading.

See also Skill 7.5

SKILL 7.7 **Knows and teaches strategies that facilitate making connections between and across multiple texts** *(e.g., summarizing and paraphrasing, locating and distinguishing between facts and opinions, and determining whether the text supports or opposes an issue).*

Anticipation guides are useful in all content areas before, during, and after reading. They have the following focus:

- Practicing comprehension strategies
- Activating background knowledge
- Inferring/Predicting

An anticipation guide is a series of statements that require students to use their background knowledge and make predictions. Students are asked to read each statement of the anticipation guide before they read the assignment and decide whether they agree or disagree with the statement. After they have completed the reading assignment, they go back to each statement and again decide whether they agree or disagree, given their new knowledge. Anticipation guides provide connection to prior knowledge, engage students with the topic, and encourage them to explore their thoughts and opinions.

See also Skill 7.6

SKILL 7.8 **Understands metacognitive skills, including self-evaluation and self-monitoring skills, and teaches students to use those skills to enhance their reading comprehension, in accordance with the STR.**

Self-monitoring and self-assessment support reading comprehension. Students who struggle with self-monitoring can benefit from checklists and other support materials that can be teacher created. Sticky-notes can be used as students are reading to jot down information that might need to recalled or support their comprehension. Metacognitive skills, which involve thinking about one's thinking, apply what one believes and what one knows to be true to new information.

Proficient readers use one or more metacognitive strategies to comprehend text. Teachers can provide mini-lessons during which they "think aloud" as they read aloud, demonstrating the interplay between the text and their own thoughts. Then, they allow time for guided practice, and finally, independent practice. This gradual release of responsibility and modeling their thinking helps students' reading comprehension.

> **SKILL 7.9** **Knows how to provide students with direct, explicit instruction and reinforcing activities to promote the use of strategies to improve their reading comprehension** (e.g., previewing, self-monitoring, visualizing, recognizing sensory details, re-telling), **in accordance with the STR.**

The following are examples of specific procedures that you can use to help students improve their comprehension across all texts:

- Ask questions that keep students on track and focus their attention on main ideas and important points in the text.

- Focus attention on parts of a text that require students to make inferences.

- Call on students to summarize key sections or events.

- Encourage students to return to any predictions they have made before reading to see if the text confirms them.

- Check understanding by paraphrasing or restating important and/or difficult sentences and paragraphs.

After reading, the teacher may do the following:

- Guide discussion of the reading.

- Ask students to recall and tell in their own words important parts of the text.

- Offer students opportunities to respond to the reading in various ways, including through writing, dramatic play, music, reader's theatre, videos, debate, or pantomime.

As the teacher uses explicit instruction, explaining why retelling is useful, modeling the procedure, giving students opportunities to practice, and providing feedback, students' retellings should become more detailed as they become better readers. Have students do the following:

- Identify and retell a sequence of actions or events.

- Make inferences to account for events or actions.

- Offer an evaluation of the story.

In addition to retelling, story maps, story frames, KWL charts, questioning the author, and reciprocal teaching are ways a teacher can provide students with direct, explicit instruction and reinforcing activities to improve their reading comprehension.

SKILL 7.10 Selects and uses instructional strategies, materials and activities to guide students' understanding of their own culture and the cultures of others through reading, in accordance with the STR.

Building curriculum around personal narratives and incorporating identity-based responses into the study of texts are good ways to guide students' understanding of their own culture and the cultures of others through reading. At the community level, it is important to understand neighborhood demographics, strengths, concerns, conflicts, and challenges. The classroom environment must provide safe spaces where students are seen, valued, cared for, and respected. It also is important that students have opportunities to learn from one another's experiences and perspectives.

Classroom-reflective texts coupled with nonjudgmental dialogue is another instructional strategy. Choosing texts that reflect classroom demographics and following the readings with discussions or reflective writing assignments can provide teachers with powerful information about their students' hopes, concerns, strengths, and life circumstances. These practices also open channels of understanding among students. Successful conversations about issues of identity frequently lead to deeper dialogue about students' backgrounds and the experiences of others.

SKILL 7.11 Teaches elements of literary analysis, such as story elements and figurative language, and features of various literary genres, including fables, myths, folktales, legends, drama and poetry.

Elements of Literary Analysis

Children's literature is a genre of its own and emerged as a distinct and independent form in the second half of the eighteenth century.

COMMON FORMS OF CHILDREN'S LITERATURE	
Traditional literature	Traditional literature opens up a world in which right wins out over wrong, hard work and perseverance are rewarded, and helpless victims find vindication. Children are introduced to fanciful beings, humans with exaggerated powers, talking animals, and heroes who will inspire them.
Folktales/fairy tales	Adventures of animals or humans and the supernatural characterize these stories. The hero is usually on a quest and is aided by otherworldly helpers. More often than not, the story focuses on good and evil and reward and punishment.
Fables	Animals that act like humans are featured in these stories and usually reveal human foibles or sometimes teach a lesson.
Myths	These stories about events from the earliest times, such as the origin of the world, are often considered true in the societies of their origin.
Legends	These are similar to myths except that they tend to deal with events that happened more recently.
Poems	The only requirement of poetry is rhythm. Subgenres include fixed types of literature such as the sonnet, elegy, ode, pastoral, and villanelle. Unfixed types of literature include blank verse and dramatic monologue.
Tall tales	These are purposely exaggerated accounts of individuals with superhuman strength.
Modern fantasy	The stories start out based in reality, which makes it easier for the reader to suspend disbelief and enter worlds of unreality. These tales often appeal to children's ideals of justice and address issues having to do with good and evil; because children tend to identify with the characters, they are more likely to retain the message in the story.
Science fiction	Robots, spacecraft, mystery, and civilizations from other ages often appear in these stories. Most presume advances in science on other planets or in a future time. Most children like these stories because of their interest in space and the "what if" aspect of the stories.
Modern realistic fiction	These stories are about real problems that real children face. By discovering that their hopes and fears are shared by others, young children can find insight into their own problems.
Historical fiction	Historical fiction tells a story set in the past, often in a significant or notable period of time. The events or backdrop to the story are based on actual historical events but told from the perspective of a fictional character living during the time period being portrayed.
Biography	A biography is the story of a person's life, as written by someone other than that person.

SKILL
7.12 **Understands the continuum of reading comprehension skills in the state standards and grade-level expectations for those skills.**

Reading Comprehension Skills in K–6 Statewide Curriculum and Grade-Level Expectations for Those Skills

Kindergarten

Information in this section is taken from Reading/ Comprehension Skills, Kindergarten–Grade 5, Beginning with School Year 2009–2010 at:

http://ritter.tea.state.tx.us /rules/tac/chapter110 /19_0110_0010-1.pdf

Students use a flexible range of metacognitive reading skills in both assigned and independent reading to understand an author's message. Students will continue to apply earlier standards with greater depth in increasingly more complex texts as they become self-directed, critical readers. The student is expected to: (a) discuss the purposes for reading and listening to various texts (e.g., to become involved in real and imagined events, settings, actions, and to enjoy language), (b) ask and respond to questions about text, (c) monitor and adjust comprehension (e.g., using background knowledge, creating sensory images, rereading a portion aloud), (d) make inferences based on the cover, title, illustrations, and plot, (e) retell or act out important events in stories, and (f) make connections to his or her own experiences, to ideas in other texts, and to the larger community, and discuss textual evidence.

First grade

Students use a flexible range of metacognitive reading skills in both assigned and independent reading to understand an author's message. Students will continue to apply earlier standards with greater depth in increasingly more complex texts as they become self-directed, critical readers. The student is expected to: (a) establish purposes for reading selected texts based upon desired outcome to enhance comprehension, (b) ask literal questions of text, (c) monitor and adjust comprehension (e.g., using background knowledge, creating sensory images, rereading a portion aloud), (d) make inferences about text and use textual evidence to support understanding, (e) retell or act out important events in stories in logical order, and (f) make connections to his or her own experiences, to ideas in other texts, and to the larger community, and discuss textual evidence.

Students use a flexible range of metacognitive reading skills in both assigned and independent reading to understand an author's message. Students will continue to apply earlier standards with greater depth in increasingly more complex texts as they become self-directed, critical readers.

Second grade

Students use a flexible range of metacognitive reading skills in both assigned and independent reading to understand an author's message. Students will continue to apply earlier standards with greater depth in increasingly more complex texts as they become self-directed, critical readers. The student is expected to: (a) establish purposes for reading selected texts based upon content to enhance comprehension, (b) ask literal questions of text, (c) monitor and adjust comprehension (e.g., using background knowledge, creating sensory images, rereading a portion aloud, generating questions), (d) make inferences about text using textual evidence to support understanding, (e) retell important events in stories in logical order, and (f) make connections to his or her own experiences, to ideas in other texts, and to the larger community, and discuss textual evidence.

Third grade

Students use a flexible range of metacognitive reading skills in both assigned and independent reading to understand an author's message. Students will continue to apply earlier standards with greater depth in increasingly more complex texts as they become self-directed, critical readers. The student is expected to: (a) establish purposes for reading selected texts based upon his or her own or others' desired outcome to enhance comprehension, (b) ask literal, interpretive, and evaluative questions of text, (c) monitor and adjust comprehension (e.g., using background knowledge, creating sensory images, rereading a portion aloud, generating questions), (d) make inferences about text and use textual evidence to support understanding, (e) summarize information in text, maintaining meaning and logical order, and (f) make connections (e.g., thematic links, author analysis) between literary and informational texts with similar ideas and provide textual evidence.

Fourth grade

Students use a flexible range of metacognitive reading skills in both assigned and independent reading to understand an author's message. Students will continue to apply earlier standards with greater depth in increasingly more complex texts as they become self-directed, critical readers. The student is expected to: (a) establish purposes for reading selected texts based upon his or her own or others' desired outcome to enhance comprehension, (b) ask literal, interpretive, and evaluative questions of text, (c) monitor and adjust comprehension (e.g., using background knowledge, creating sensory images, rereading a portion aloud, generating questions), (d) make inferences about text and use textual evidence to support understanding, (e) summarize information in text, maintaining meaning and logical order, and (f) make connections (e.g., thematic links, author analysis) between literary and informational texts with similar ideas and provide textual evidence.

Fifth grade

Students use a flexible range of metacognitive reading skills in both assigned and independent reading to understand an author's message. Students will continue to apply earlier standards with greater depth in increasingly more complex texts as they become self-directed, critical readers. The student is expected to: (a) establish purposes for reading selected texts based upon his or her own or others' desired outcome to enhance comprehension, (b) ask literal, interpretive, evaluative, and universal questions of text, (c) monitor and adjust comprehension (e.g., using background knowledge, creating sensory images, rereading a portion aloud, generating questions), (d) make inferences about text and use textual evidence to support understanding, (e) summarize and paraphrase texts in ways that maintain meaning and logical order within a text and across texts, and (f) make connections (e.g., thematic links, author analysis) between and across multiple texts of various genres, and provide textual evidence.

Sixth grade

Students use a flexible range of metacognitive reading skills in both assigned and independent reading to understand an author's message. Students will continue to apply earlier standards with greater depth in increasingly more complex texts as they become self-directed, critical readers. The student is expected to: (a) establish purposes for reading selected texts based upon his or her own or others' desired outcome to enhance comprehension, (b) ask literal, interpretive, evaluative, and universal questions of text, (c) monitor and adjust comprehension (e.g., using background knowledge; creating sensory images; rereading a portion aloud; generating questions), (d) make inferences about text and use textual evidence to support understanding, (e) summarize, paraphrase, and synthesize texts in ways that maintain meaning and logical order within a text and across texts, and (f) make connections (e.g., thematic links, author analysis) between and across multiple texts of various genres, and provide textual evidence.

The following information is taken from Reading/ Comprehension Skills, Grades 6–8, Beginning with School Year 2009–2010 at:

http://ritter.tea.state.tx.us /rules/tac/chapter110 /19_0110_0017-1.pdf

---

> **SKILL 7.13** Knows the difference between guided and independent practice in reading and provides students with frequent opportunities for both.

In **guided reading**, the teacher guides small groups of students in reading short, carefully chosen texts to build independence, fluency, comprehension skills, and problem-solving abilities. The teacher regularly observes and assesses students' changing needs and adjusts groupings accordingly. Guided reading allows a teacher to provide different levels of support, depending on the needs of the students. In **independent reading**, students read books on their own, exploring different kinds of texts and applying new learning. Teachers confer individually with students during independent reading or model their own silent reading. A 90-minute literacy block should include time for both practices. Guided reading typically takes place while other students are engaged in independent reading time.

Guided reading allows a teacher to provide different levels of support, depending on the needs of the students.

SKILL 7.14 Understands how to foster collaboration with families and with other professionals to promote all students' reading comprehension.

Literacy nights and collaborative planning are ways that an educator can foster collaboration with families and with other professionals to promote all students' reading comprehension.

See also Skill 4.10

COMPETENCY 8
VOCABULARY DEVELOPMENT

> **SKILL 8.1** Knows how to provide explicit, systematic instruction and reinforcing activities to help students increase their vocabulary, in accordance with the STR.

National Reading Panel Vocabulary Guidelines

1. There is a need for direct instruction of vocabulary items required for a specific text.

2. Repetition and multiple exposures to vocabulary items are important. Students should be given items that will be likely to appear in many contexts.

3. Learning in rich contexts is valuable for vocabulary learning. Vocabulary words should be those that the learner will find useful in many contexts. When vocabulary items are derived from content learning materials, the learner will be better equipped to deal with specific reading matter in content areas.

4. Vocabulary tasks should be restructured as necessary. It is important to be certain that students fully understand what is asked of them in the context of reading rather than focusing only on the words to be learned.

5. Vocabulary learning is most effective when it entails active engagement in learning tasks.

6. Computer technology can be used effectively to help teach vocabulary.

7. Vocabulary can be acquired through incidental learning. Much of a student's vocabulary will have to be learned in the course of doing things other than explicit vocabulary learning. Repetition, richness of context, and motivation may also add to the efficacy of incidental learning of vocabulary.

8. Dependence on a single vocabulary instruction method does not result in optimal learning. A variety of methods can be used effectively, with emphasis on multimedia, richness of context in which words are to be learned, and the number of exposures to words that learners receive.

Only two or three words should require explicit teaching. If the number is higher than that, the children need guided reading and the text needs to be broken down into smaller sections for teaching. When broken down, each text section should only have two to three words that need explicit teaching.

To develop students' vocabulary, teachers must encourage a curiosity about the meaning and use of unfamiliar words and promote strategies that will help students find the meaning of unfamiliar words. Examples of specific instructional techniques and activities for increasing vocabulary include technology, oral language, graphic organizers, word walls, vocabulary journals, vocabulary in context, and the following.

Using structure:

- Flipbooks
- Making words activities
- Making big words
- Boggle boards
- Word sorts
- Prefix/suffix boxes

Using context:

- Guess the meaning
- Super word web
- Four-part foldables
- Predictable/probable passages
- Word detectives
- Five-box word analysis matrix

STRUCTURAL ANALYSIS, looking at word structure or word parts that students know—a base word, prefix, suffix, or word root—to determine the meaning of an unfamiliar word is another useful strategy. Once students understand how multisyllabic words are constructed and master the meanings of common prefixes and suffixes, they can deconstruct the meaning of an unfamiliar word.

> **STRUCTURAL ANALYSIS:** looking at word structure or word parts that students know—a base word, prefix, suffix, or word root—to determine the meaning of an unfamiliar word

SKILL 8.2 Knows how to use direct and indirect methods to effectively teach vocabulary, in accordance with the STR.

Dictionary Use

Dictionaries are useful for spelling, writing, and reading. It is important to initially expose and habituate students to using the dictionary.

Cooper (2004) suggests that the following be kept in mind as the teacher of grades K–6 introduces and then habituates children to a lifelong fascination with the dictionary and vocabulary acquisition.

Requesting or suggesting that children look up a word in the dictionary should be an invitation to a wonderful exploration, not a punishment or busywork that has no connection to their current reading assignment.

Model the correct way to use the dictionary for children even as late as grades 3–6. Many have never been taught proper dictionary skills. The teacher needs to demonstrate to the children that as an adult reader and writer, he or she routinely uses the dictionary and learns new information that makes him or her better at reading and writing.

Having children work as a whole class or in small groups on a content-specific dictionary for a topic regularly covered in their grade level social studies, science, or mathematics curriculum offers an excellent collaborative opportunity for children to design a dictionary/word resource that can celebrate their own vocabulary learning. Such a resource can then be used with the next year's classes.

Other Strategies

Hierarchical and linear array vocabulary development strategies support struggling learners or English–language learners (ELLs). Using these arrays allows these learners to "see" and diagram word relationships. The diagrams are easy to make, and they can be illustrated. With sufficient support and modeling, many students struggling with vocabulary can do simple linear and hierarchical arrays on their own. The arrays also can be displayed in classrooms as a demonstration of students' ownership of their words.

SKILL 8.3 **Selects and uses a wide range of instructional materials, strategies and opportunities with rich contextual support for vocabulary development, in accordance with the STR** *(e.g., literature, expository texts, content-specific texts, magazines, newspapers, trade books, technology).*

Teachers should select and use a wide range of instructional materials, strategies, and opportunities with rich contextual support for vocabulary development when teaching literature, expository texts, content-specific texts, magazines, newspapers, trade books, technology within the literacy block, word work, or study time. Varied methods of instruction and types of texts provide an opportunity for students to dig deeper into new vocabulary. The more exposure students have to a variety of texts, the more likely they are to encounter new vocabulary and expand their word bank.

See also Skills 5.4 and 8.1

SKILL 8.4 **Recognizes the importance of selecting, teaching and modeling a wide range of general and specialized vocabularies.**

See Skills 8.1 and 8.3

SKILL 8.5 **Understands how to assess and monitor students' vocabulary knowledge by providing systematic, age-appropriate instruction and reinforcing activities** *(e.g., morphemic analysis, etc.).*

Assessing students' vocabulary development can be done through formal and informal assessments. Students can be assessed in the following manners:

Informal assessments:

- Read the word and circle a picture of it.
- Look at a picture and circle the word for it.
- Read the word and circle a definition.
- Read the word and circle a synonym.
- Read the word and circle an antonym.
- Read the word in context and circle a definition, synonym, or antonym.
- Read a sentence and write the missing word.
- Read a sentence and supply the missing word orally.

Formal assessments:

- Anecdotal records

- Student work samples

- Checklists

- Portfolios that include students' goals and their reflection on their learning over time

---

SKILL 8.6 **Provides multiple opportunities to listen to, read and respond to various types of literature and expository texts to promote students' vocabulary development.**

Teachers must provide vocabulary development and address students' needs to promote their development of robust listening, speaking, reading, and writing. Teachers can do this by providing meaningful exposure to and opportunities to use new vocabulary and respond to different types of texts: narrative, nonfiction, expository, content-specific, magazines, newspapers, trade books, and online content. These opportunities promote their development of an extensive reading and writing vocabulary.

See also Skills 8.1 and 8.3

COMPETENCY 9
READING, INQUIRY, AND RESEARCH

> **SKILL 9.1** **Teaches students how to develop open-ended research questions and a plan** (e.g., timeline) **to locate, retrieve and record information from a range of content-area, narrative and expository texts.**

A proper research question will be narrow enough to cover in an assignment but general enough so that students can find and use others' research on the subject. For example, "What are the causes of the Vietnam War?" is too broad for a student research project. A more streamlined version might be, "What were the political causes of the United States' involvement in the Vietnam War?" In this version, the question is more focused and students will have the ability to narrow their research to only political causes and only the perspective of the United States.

Open-ended research questions require more than a yes or no answer; they ask "why" and "how." When teaching students how to create these types of questions, graphic organizers and brainstorming activities can be helpful. Students can brainstorm topics surrounding an event, historical time period, or person that they'd like to know more about. They should ask questions on their graphic organizer, such as "Who is George Washington?" and "What did he accomplish as president?" Next, they could go through a peer review round during which they talk with other students and the instructor to find the question that most intrigues them. Then, they could revise the question to create a well-rounded, easily researchable inquiry. For example, "Who is George Washington?" could become "What were the strengths that George Washington brought to the presidency?" The second version focuses on his strengths during a particular job that he did and during a certain period of time, so it is narrow enough for the student to cover in a research project and still provides opportunity for a large amount of research.

Open-ended research questions require more than a yes or no answer; they ask "why" and "how."

After creating a research question, students need to learn how to create a timeline to locate, retrieve, and record information from a variety of sources. Books (expository texts), reputable Internet sources, and primary sources such as interviews and narrative texts are all options for gathering information, but students must know where to find the information, how to glean the most important information, and how to record and cite the information to avoid plagiarism. The first step is locating the best sources for answering the research question. It's easy to get lost in the search, so elementary and middle school teachers may place a cap on the number of sources a student needs. Teach students to record their sources and the information they find in them on index cards, to take notes on a computer, or to notate a graphic organizer. It's important that they always cite the entire source and write the source in the same place they are transcribing the thought or quote. This way, students know which of their ideas came from which source and can cite them easily.

SKILL 9.2   **Selects and uses instructional strategies to help students comprehend abstract content and ideas in written materials** *(e.g., manipulatives, examples, graphic organizers).*

Often, students will not understand a concept from direct instruction, and teachers will need to create more in-depth lesson plans that address multiple learning styles. For example, elementary teachers often use manipulatives, which are items that a student can touch, to illustrate abstract concepts. A first-grade teacher may explain the difference between odd and even numbers by having students make pairs with small blocks. When the teacher calls out a number, if students can create it by making pairs, it is even. If pairs are impossible, it is odd.

Manipulatives also can be used in spelling and reading. Often, teachers will have letter tiles that include sound combinations such as diagraphs and diphthongs, and students can place these sounds together to create a word. Using sound tiles helps students understand that a sound often can be more than one letter.

Examples also are useful in math, reading, spelling, and writing. Students will better understand a concept if they can see a teacher go through an entire process. Teachers can do more than model the example—they can ask for student participation and even leave out steps to see if the students can figure out which piece of the process is missing.

Students can use charts to distinguish the main idea from the details of the story or to identify literary devices such as similes and metaphors.

Graphic organizers are useful when teaching comprehension and writing. Students can use charts to distinguish the main idea from the details of the story or to identify literary devices such as similes and metaphors. When writing, a graphic organizer can serve as a useful brainstorming tool for choosing topics, narrowing a focus, developing research questions, or even setting the scene or developing characters when writing fiction.

SKILL 9.3 Selects and uses instructional strategies to teach students to interpret information presented in various formats (e.g., maps, tables, graphs) and how to locate, retrieve, and record information from technologies, print resources and experts.

Often, it is necessary to read information from maps, tables, and graphs to get the most up-to-date and relevant data. Reading these sources requires skills in addition to those required for reading text. For example, students need to be familiar with basic descriptive statistics such as mean, median, and mode to read graphs. Students need to be familiar with percentages and decimals to be able to understand the data presented some tables and graphs. Spend time with students explaining the basics of parts of one hundred. Using manipulatives, looking at examples of charts and graphs, and even creating charts, graphs, and maps can help students understand these information sources and how to use them.

Often, visual sources such as maps, graphs, and charts are found at the end of a text, but sometimes they are found below or near an explanation of a concept. Students may look at an atlas or globe to locate a specific place, or they may use a topographical map to discern altitudes and terrains.

Editing work and finding errors through citation scavenger hunts can help students identify the correct way to cite various sources. If a student is speaking with an expert about a topic, she will need to either record the interview or take extensive notes, which she then must cite appropriately in the text and at the end of the paper. Students can practice interviewing each other, taking notes on the conversations, and then summarizing these notes in a written essay to prepare for a research interview.

For more information on citation styles, see Skill 11.7.

> Students can practice interviewing each other, taking notes on the conversations, and then summarizing these notes in a written essay to prepare for a research interview.

> **SKILL 9.4** Selects and uses instructional strategies to help students understand study and inquiry skills across the curriculum *(e.g., brainstorming; generating questions and topics; using text organizers; taking notes; outlining; drawing conclusions; applying critical-thinking skills; previewing; setting purposes for reading; locating, organizing, evaluating and communicating information; summarizing information; selecting relevant sources of information; using multiple sources of information; recognizing identifying features of sources, including primary and secondary sources; interpreting and using graphic sources of information)* **and knows the significance of organizing information from multiple sources for student learning and achievement.**

Interpreting Information in Various Formats

Quantitative data is often easily presented in graphs and charts in many content areas.

Students should be taught to evaluate all of the features of a graph, including the main title, what the horizontal axis represents, and what the vertical axis represents. Also, students should locate and evaluate the graph's key (if there is one) in the event there is more than one variable represented on the graph. For example, line graphs are often used to plot data from a scientific experiment. If more than one variable was used, a key or legend would indicate what each line on the graph represents. Then, once students have evaluated the axes and titles, they can begin to assess the results of the experiment.

Study Skills

Because good comprehension the goal of all reading, teachers can help their students by teaching them specific features of texts that they can use to clarify or enhance their understanding.

Using specific textual features, students can begin to find information more easily, which allows them to create their own schema. Using this schema, they can analyze and organize the information in a manner that ties it directly to their own personal experience and prior knowledge. Once it is connected, it will be easier to recall.

Most texts provide brief introductions, which readers can use to determine if the information they are seeking is located in the passage to be read. By reading a short passage, a student can quickly ascertain whether a complete reading is necessary or if a quick skim will suffice.

When searching for information, students can become much more efficient if they learn to use a glossary and index.

Charts, graphs, maps, diagrams, captions, and photos in text can be as helpful as looking up unknown words in the glossary. They can provide more insight into and clarification of concepts and ideas the author is conveying.

Highlighting is a difficult strategy for students to master. Even at the college level, students seem to have a hard time determining what is important. **Key ideas** and vocabulary are a good place to start with highlighting. Teaching students to highlight less information rather than more is also important.

Outlining is a skill many teachers use to help students understand the important facts.

Mapping involves using graphics, pictures, and words to represent the information in the text. The students can personalize their maps and use colors and pictures that have meaning to them. This provides a natural bridge to prior knowledge and frames the information in a more personal way.

Note-taking skills also require direct instruction.

Test taking is another area in which students sometimes lag in skill development. Teaching students to eliminate automatic wrong answers first, then narrow down the choices is a start. In open-ended questions, students need to be able to restate the question in their answer and understand that they need to answer all parts of the question being asked.

SKILL 9.5 **Knows grade-level expectations for study and inquiry skills in the Texas Essential Knowledge and Skills (TEKS)** *(e.g., in kindergarten, use pictures in conjunction with writing to document research; in fifth–sixth grades, refine research through use of secondary questions).*

As a child grows cognitively, she will be able to handle more complicated research inquiries. A student in the lower elementary grades will draw pictures to convey ideas, and in first and second grade may begin to write words and sentences to match his conclusions. He will be focusing on the lower levels of Bloom's taxonomy. He will be comprehending, remembering, and understanding material on a concrete level. A middle elementary student from grades 4–6 can be expected to begin applying his knowledge to draw more advanced and extensive conclusions. This student may be able to write a paragraph about his thoughts, and although he will be exploring the lower levels of Bloom's taxonomy to guarantee understanding, he will begin to include a basic analysis.

Younger students will begin researching by asking primary questions. Older students will use primary questions as jumping-off points and will then develop secondary questions, which will probe the topic further. For example, a younger study may stop an inquiry with the question, "Why did the woman sell her hair in 'The Gift of the Magi'?" An older student may begin with that question and then, once she found the answer, she may extend her question to "How was she feeling when she sold her hair? How was she feeling when she received the comb as a gift?"

> ### SKILL 9.6
> ### Provides instruction to develop a topic sentence, summarize findings and use evidence to support conclusions.

A strong topic sentence should start every piece of writing. A topic sentence should gain reader interest and give a brief summary of the topic, laying the foundation for a well-organized and informative paragraph. Topic sentences are used most often in nonfiction writing. When students are asked to summarize findings, they should be able to glean the main idea from their work or from the narrative they have read and choose important details to highlight. It's important that students are able to distinguish the main idea from supporting details.

Teaching these skills requires teachers to break down the concepts and have students complete exercises to practice these techniques. Be sure to create exercises that involve multiple learning styles. For example, when teaching how to write topic sentences, teachers may explain situations without using a topic sentence and then have students create a topic sentence to match the situation, which they then can share with the class. Doing this type of exercise shows other students that there are many correct ways to create a topic sentence. Another activity would be to write various paragraphs and then cut out the topic sentences from the papers. Next, pairs of students would be given the paragraphs and topic sentences and would have to match each topic sentence with its respective paragraph.

Teach students that relevant details support the main idea.

When teaching students to summarize findings, begin by having them fill out graphic organizers. Organizers that incorporate a big circle with smaller circles shooting out from the middle will encourage students to write the main idea in the larger circle and the details that connect to it in the smaller circles. Teach students that relevant details support the main idea. Once students understand the concepts of main idea and details, they can be asked to incorporate evidence. For example:

> *As noted on page 96, one of the causes of World War II was economic. (Smith, 2010, p. 96).*

When making assertions in a nonfiction paper or in a paper that analyzes a piece of fiction, it is important that students find a detail in the text that supports the conclusion and cite it using an appropriate in-text citation. To teach this skill, send students on scavenger hunts through the text. For example, ask them to find a place where the author explains the causes of World War II. Or, ask them to find the dates of the beginning and end of the war from two separate sources. When students have located this information, ask them to notate it on paper and teach them how to cite the information correctly.

<table>
<tr><td>SKILL 9.7</td><td>Understands how to foster collaboration with peers, families and with other professionals to promote all students' ability to develop effective research and comprehension skills in the content areas.</td></tr>
</table>

John Dewey and Lev Vygotsky, both social educational theorists, concluded that social interaction and an environment rich with conversation is crucial to learning. Developing research and comprehension skills is no exception.

Peer editing is paramount to the writing process and also can be used for research projects. Students can help one another find appropriate sources, check for citation errors, and discuss alternative ways to research the question. Additionally, allowing students to research with partners and participate in think-pair-share and jigsaw activities can help them develop effective and collaborative research skills.

Research has shown that family support and involvement is critical to student success. Involving families in research projects can motivate the student and encourage family support. Students can conduct interviews with family members, practicing their ability to record and retrieve information from a primary source. Community leaders can be primary sources for students. Open-ended interviews may be too intimidating for students, so in the elementary grades, it may be helpful to provide students with a list of questions to ask the participant. As a child gets older, he can come up with the questions that match his topic and even allow for some open-endedness in the answers, allowing the interview to become less structured.

Students can help one another find appropriate sources, check for citation errors, and discuss alternative ways to research the question.

COMPETENCY 10
WRITING CONVENTIONS

> **SKILL 10.1** **Understands that many students go through predictable stages in acquiring writing conventions** *(e.g., physical and cognitive processes involved in scribbling, recognition of environmental print, mock letters, letter formation, word writing, sentence construction, spelling, punctuation, grammatical expression)*, **and individual students vary in their rates of development of those conventions.**

Stages in Development of Writing Skills

Learning to write is generally a sequential process and can be broken down into five stages:

- **Readiness:** The first stage includes scribbling, showing interest in writing tools, marking paper, enjoying stories, and noticing print and pictures in the environment.

- **Drawing and exploring:** The second stage includes shape and early letter writing, connecting pictures to expressions, associating letters with sounds, and playing with letters, sounds, and pictures.

- **Confident experimentation:** The third stage includes writing more, experimenting with words, print, and pictures more, and shows early conventions of print such as word spacing and punctuation, and attempting longer words.

- **Moving toward independence:** The fourth stage includes keen observation of print in the environment, expanding oral stories, writing words and phrases independently, and increased conventions of print.

- **Expanding and adding detail:** The final, fifth stage includes writing sentences and paragraphs, experiments with sharing writing and journaling, increased details and use of writing conventions, and showing expanding vocabulary and use of writing with pictures.

From *http://www.learningtowrite.ecsd.net/stages percent20of percent20writing.htm*.

SKILL 10.2 Understands the relationship between spelling and phonological and alphabetic awareness and understands the role of conventional spelling in success in reading and writing.

Developmental Stages of Spelling

Like writing, spelling develops in stages. The developmental stages of spelling are:

1. **Pre-phonemic spelling:** Children know that letters stand for a message but they do not know the relationship between spelling and pronunciation.

2. **Early phonemic spelling:** Children are beginning to understand spelling. They usually write the beginning letter correctly but write consonants or long vowels for the rest.

3. **Letter-name spelling:** Some words are consistently spelled correctly. The student is developing a sight vocabulary and a stable understanding of letters as representing sounds. Long vowels are usually used accurately, but silent vowels are omitted. The child spells unknown words by attempting to match the name of the letter to the sound.

4. **Transitional spelling:** This phase is typically entered in late elementary school. Short vowel sounds are mastered and some spelling rules known. Children are developing a sense of which spellings are correct and which are not.

5. **Derivational spelling:** This stage is usually reached between high school and adulthood. This is the stage when spelling rules are being mastered.

SKILL 10.3 Understands the stages of spelling development (precommunicative writing in which the student understands the function of writing but cannot make the forms, prephonemic, phonemic, transitional and conventional) and knows how and when to support students' development from one stage to the next.

See Skill 10.2

SKILL 10.4 **Provides spelling instruction and gives students opportunities to use and develop spelling skills in the context of meaningful written expression** (e.g., single syllable homophones, commonly used homophones, commonly confused terms, simple and complex contractions).

Rules and Conventions of Punctuation, Capitalization, and Spelling

Spelling

Most plurals of nouns that end in hard consonants or hard consonant sounds followed by a silent *e* are made by adding *s*. Some words ending in vowels only add *s*.

> fingers, numerals, banks, bugs, riots, homes, gates, radios, bananas

Nouns that end in soft consonant sounds *s, j, x, z, ch,* and *sh,* add *es*. Some nouns ending in *o* add *es*.

> dresses, waxes, churches, brushes, tomatoes, potatoes

Nouns ending in *y* preceded by a vowel just add *s*.

> boys, alleys

Nouns ending in *y* preceded by a consonant change the *y* to *i* and add *es*.

> babies, corollaries, frugalities, poppies

Some nouns' plurals are formed irregularly or remain the same.

> sheep, deer, children, leaves, oxen

Some nouns derived from foreign words, especially Latin, may make their plurals in two different ways, one of them Anglicized. Sometimes the meanings are the same; other times, the two plurals are used in slightly different contexts. It is always wise to consult the dictionary in these cases.

> appendices, appendixes   criterion, criteria
> indexes, indices   crisis, crises

Make the plurals of closed (solid) compound words in the usual way except for words ending in *ful,* which make their plurals on the root word.

> timelines, hairpins, cupsful

Make the plurals of open or hyphenated compounds by adding the *s* to the word that changes in number.

> *fathers-in-law, courts-martial, masters of art, doctors of medicine*

Make the plurals of letters, numbers, and abbreviations by adding *s*.

> *fives and tens, IBMs, 1990s,* **ps** *and* **qs** *(note that letters are italicized)*

Spelling instruction should be interactive and multisensory. Students should be taught to use their fingers to count the letters, should have an opportunity to say the sounds of each letter, diphthong, or digraph as they write, and should practice writing with various textures such as shaving cream, sand, and rice.

Homophones

HOMOPHONES are words that sound the same but are spelled differently and have different meanings. Examples of single-syllable homophones are *bear* and *bare* and *cent* and *scent*. Examples of commonly used homophones include the following:

I, eye	*Sell, cell*	*Four, for*	*Hour, our*
Bear, bare	*Be, bee*	*Flour, flower*	
Buy, by	*Die, dye*	*Hear, here*	

> **HOMOPHONES:** words that sound the same but are spelled differently and have different meanings

Teachers can use a child's visual strengths to teach homophones. Ask students to draw T-charts and then place one homophone on each side. Next, students can draw pictures of each homophone to help remember the difference. This activity works especially well with homophones such as *I* and *eye*. Children can remember terms if they can see them visually and colorfully. Additionally, students can act out each homophone. This fun exercise will help them remember the differences between words that are easy to confuse.

Commonly Confused Terms

The following are commonly confused terms:

Than, then	*Passed, past*	*To, too, two*
Affect, effect	*Principal, principle*	

Drawing pictures can help students understand the difference between words such as *principal* and *principle,* but other words, like *than* and *then,* have to be memorized. Some drill exercises may be necessary here, but students can also be sleuths and find inappropriate uses of these terms in faux editing worksheets or when they peer edit their classmates' work.

Simple and Complex Contractions

> **CONTRACTION:** when two words are combined by eliminating some of the letters and adding an apostrophe to create one shorter word

A **CONTRACTION** is formed when two words are combined by eliminating some of the letters and adding an apostrophe to create one shorter word. For example, *will not* is shortened to *won't*. Sometimes the contraction looks the two words from which it is made, and sometimes, like in the example above, it does not. Contractions are used in speech and informal writing. In formal writing, contractions are not used. A simple contraction is usually one of the following words: *I, he, we, she, who, what, when, where, how,* plus one of the following words: *be, will, would, have had.* Some examples follow:

I would = I'd	*I am = I'm*
She has = she's	*We will = we'll*

Students can take apart and put together words using tiles or other manipulatives. They can use whiteboards to draw and erase contracted words. They can also search for them in word hunts or incorporate them into writing. For example, a teacher could request that in a paragraph of writing, the student must use three contractions.

- Common Homophones List

  https://www.englishclub.com/pronunciation/homophones-list.htm. Retrieved Aug. 27, 2015.

> **SKILL 10.5** Selects and uses instructional strategies, materials and hands-on activities for developing fine motor skills necessary for writing, according to grade-level expectations in the Texas Essential Knowledge and Skills (TEKS).

Development of Fine-Motor Skills for Writing

In order for children to write correctly, they must first develop their fine-motor skills. These hands-on activities are excellent for practicing fine-motor skills:

- **Tearing:** Tear newspaper into strips and then crumple them into balls. Use the balls to stuff a Halloween pumpkin or other art creation.

- **Cutting:** Cut pictures from magazines. Cut a fringe on the edge of a piece of construction paper.

- **Puzzles:** Have children put together a puzzle with large pieces. This will help to develop proper eye-hand coordination.

- **Clay:** Manipulating playdough into balls strengthens a child's grasp. Let the children explain what they created from their playdough objects.

- **Finger painting:** If a child has not developed fine-motor skills yet, it helps to trace a pattern with the child's finger before he or she tries it with a pencil. Have the child trace a pattern in sand, cornmeal, finger paint, etc.

- **Drawing:** Draw at an easel with a large crayon. Encourage children to practice their name or letters of the alphabet.

Strategies for Teaching Pencil Grip

- **The primary grip:** Beginning writers with undeveloped fine-motor skills should be taught the primary grip. First, have the child join the tips of the thumb and middle finger. Then place the pencil in the space between them. Finally, have the child lay the index finger on top of the pencil. This way, the index finger pushes against the thumb and middle finger. As children grow, the proportions of their hands change. This allows them to hold the pencil or pen differently and write faster.

- **Paper position:** Right-handed children should place the paper directly in front of them and hold it in place with the left hand. The light should come from the left. Otherwise, the child's hand will cast a shadow just where the child needs to see what he or she is writing. With the paper slightly to the right of the writer, the line of vision is clear. Teachers should check to see if students are sitting upright. Make sure they are not gripping the pen too hard, and that the paper is in the right position.

- **Beginning strokes:** A teacher may need to teach a student the direction of the pencil strokes. A good word to practice with is the student's first name. Identify one letter at a time. Show the beginning point right on the top line and the ending point on the bottom line. Slowly write the child's name on one line, one letter at a time, so he or she can clearly see it. Have the child write directly under your sample, not to the side. Write your sample in straight, easy-to-copy letters.

Potential problems

- **Gripping the pencil too tightly:** A common problem for all young children learning to write is gripping the pencil too tightly, which makes writing tiresome. Usually, students learn to relax their grip as their writing skills develop, but teachers can remind students to hold the instrument gently.

- **Holding the pencil incorrectly:** If the child tends to hold the pencil too close to the point, make a mark on the pencil at the correct spot to remind him or her where to grip it.

- **Left-handed writers:** A right-handed student writes away from his or her body and pulls the pencil, while a left-handed student must write toward his or her body and push the pencil. Left-handed students should place the paper at an angle and to the left.

> *In languages that are written from left to right, like English, it is more difficult to write with the left hand.*

> **SKILL 10.6** Selects and uses instructional strategies, materials and activities to help students use English writing conventions *(e.g., grammar, capitalization, punctuation)* in connected discourse.

Capitalization

Capitalize all proper names of persons (including specific organizations or agencies of government); places (countries, states, cities, parks, and specific geographical areas); things (political parties, structures, historical and cultural terms, and calendar and time designations); and religious terms (deities, revered persons or groups, and sacred writings).

Capitalize proper adjectives and titles when they are used with proper names.

> *California gold rush, President John Adams, French fries, Homeric epic, Romanesque architecture, Senator John Glenn*

> **Note:** *Some words that represent titles and offices are not capitalized unless used with a proper name.*

Capitalize all main words in titles of works of literature, art, and music.

Punctuation

In a quoted statement that is either declarative or imperative, place the period inside the closing quotation marks.

> *"The airplane crashed on the runway during takeoff."*

If the quotation is followed by other words in the sentence, place a comma inside the closing quotations marks and a period at the end of the sentence.

> *"The airplane crashed on the runway during takeoff," said the announcer.*

In most instances in which a quoted title or expression occurs at the end of a sentence, the period is placed before either the single or double quotation marks.

> *"The middle-school readers were unprepared to understand Bryant's poem 'Thanatopsis.'"*

> *Early book-length adventure stories like* **Don Quixote** *and* **The Three Musketeers** *were known as "picaresque novels."*

There is an instance in which the final quotation mark would precede the period—if the content of the sentence were about a speech or quote so that the meaning might be obscured by the placement of the period.

> *The first thing out of his mouth was "Hi, I'm home."*

but

> *The first line of his speech began "I arrived home to an empty house".*

In sentences that are interrogatory or exclamatory, the question mark or exclamation point should be positioned outside the closing quotation marks if the quote itself is a statement or command or cited title.

> *Why was Tillie shaking as she began her recitation, "Once upon a midnight dreary..."?*

In declarative sentences that include a quotation that is a question or an exclamation, place the question mark or exclamation point inside the quotation marks.

Commas

Separate two or more coordinate adjectives modifying the same word and three or more nouns, phrases, or clauses in a list.

> *Maggie's hair was dull, dirty, and lice-ridden.*
>
> *Dickens portrayed the Artful Dodger as skillful pickpocket, loyal follower of Fagin, and defender of Oliver Twist.*

Use commas to separate antithetical or complementary expressions from the rest of the sentence.

> *The veterinarian, not his assistant, would perform the delicate surgery.*
>
> *The more he knew about her, the less he wished he had known.*

Semicolons

Use semicolons to separate independent clauses when the second clause is introduced by a transitional adverb. (These clauses can also be written as separate sentences, preferably by placing the adverb within the second sentence.)

> *The Elizabethans modified the rhyme scheme of the sonnet; thus, it was called the English sonnet.*

Use semicolons to separate items in a series that are long and complex or have internal punctuation.

> *The Italian Renaissance produced masters in the fine arts: Dante Alighieri, author of the* **Divine Comedy***; Leonardo da Vinci, painter of* **The Last Supper***; and Donatello, sculptor of the* **Quattro Coronati***, the four saints.*

Colons

Place a colon at the beginning of a list of items.

> *The teacher directed us to compare Faulkner's three symbolic novels:* **Absalom, Absalom***;* **As I Lay Dying***; and* **Light in August***.*

Do not use a colon if the list is preceded by a verb.

> *Three of Faulkner's symbolic novels are* **Absalom, Absalom***;* **As I Lay Dying***, and* **Light in August***.*

Subject-verb agreement

A verb agrees in number with its subject. Making them agree depends on one's ability to properly identify the subject.

> *One of the boys was playing too aggressively.*
>
> *No one in the class, not the teacher or the students, was listening to the message from the intercom.*
>
> *The candidates, including a grandmother and a teenager, are debating some controversial issues.*

If two singular subjects are connected by *and*, the verb must be plural.

> *A man and his dog were jogging on the beach.*

If two singular subjects are connected by *or* or *nor*, a singular verb is required.

> *Neither Dot nor Joyce has missed a day of school this year.*
> *Either Fran or Paul is missing.*

If one singular subject and one plural subject are connected by *or* or *nor*, the verb agrees with the subject nearest to the verb.

> *Neither the coach nor the players were able to sleep on the bus.*

If the subject is a collective noun, its sense of number in the sentence determines the verb. It is singular if the noun represents a group or unit and plural if the noun represents individuals.

> *The House of Representatives has adjourned for the holidays.*
> *The House of Representatives have failed to reach agreement on the subject of adjournment.*

Verbs (tense)

Present tense is used to express that which is currently happening or is always true.

> *Randy is playing the piano.*
> *Randy plays the piano like a pro.*

Past tense is used to express action that occurred in a past time.

> *Randy learned to play the piano when he was six years old.*

Future tense is used to express action or a condition of future time.

> *Randy will probably earn a music scholarship.*

Present perfect tense is used to express action or a condition that started in the past and is continued or completed in the present.

> *Randy has practiced piano every day for the last ten years. Randy has never been bored with practice.*

Past perfect tense expresses action or a condition that occurred as a precedent to some other action or condition.

> *Randy had considered playing clarinet before he discovered the piano.*

Future perfect tense expresses action that started in the past or the present and will conclude at some time in the future.

> *By the time he goes to college, Randy will have been an accomplished pianist for more than half of his life.*

Verbs (mood)

Indicative mood is used to make unconditional statements; subjunctive mood is used for conditional clauses or wish statements that refer to conditions that are possible or wished for but not real.

Indicative mood is used to make unconditional statements; subjunctive mood is used for conditional clauses or wish statements that refer to conditions that are possible or wished for but not real. Verbs in subjunctive mood are plural with both singular and plural subjects.

> *If I were a bird, I would fly.*
>
> *I wish I were as rich as Warren Buffet.*

Verb conjugation

The conjugation of verbs follows the patterns used in the discussion of tense, above. However, the most frequent problems in verb use stem from the improper formation of past and past participial forms.

Regular verbs:	*believe, believed, (have) believed*
Irregular verbs:	*run, ran, run; sit, sat, sat; teach, taught, taught*

Other problems stem from the use of verbs that are the same in some tenses but have different forms and meanings in other tenses.

> *I lie on the ground. I lay on the ground yesterday. I have lain down.*
>
> *I lay the blanket on the bed. I laid the blanket there yesterday. I have laid the blanket there every night.*
>
> *The sun rises. The sun rose. The sun has risen.*
>
> *He raises the flag. He raised the flag. He had raised the flag.*
>
> *I sit on the porch. I sat on the porch. I have sat in the porch swing.*
>
> *I set the plate on the table. I set the plate there yesterday. I had set the table before dinner.*

Pronouns

A pronoun used as a subject of predicate nominative is in nominative case.

A pronoun used as a direct object, indirect object, or object of a preposition is in objective case.

Common pronoun errors occur from misuse of reflexive pronouns:

Singular:	*myself, yourself, herself, himself, itself*
Plural:	*ourselves, yourselves, themselves*
Incorrect:	*Jack cut <u>hisself</u> shaving.*
Correct:	*Jack cut <u>himself</u> shaving.*
Incorrect:	*They backed <u>theirselves</u> into a corner.*
Correct:	*They backed <u>themselves</u> into a corner.*

Adjectives

An adjective should agree with its antecedent in number.

Those apples are rotten. This one is ripe. These peaches are hard.

Comparative adjectives end in *-er* and superlatives in *-est*, with some exceptions like *worse* and *worst*. Adjectives that cannot easily make comparative inflections are preceded by *more* or *most*.

Ms. Carmichael is the <u>better</u> of the two basketball coaches.

That is the <u>hastiest</u> excuse you have ever contrived.

When comparing one thing to others in a group, exclude the thing under comparison from the rest of the group.

Incorrect:	*Joey is larger than <u>any</u> baby I have ever seen. (Since you have seen him, he cannot be larger than himself.)*
Correct:	*Joey is larger than <u>any other</u> baby I have ever seen.*

Include all necessary words to make a comparison clear in meaning.

I am as tall as my mother. I am as tall as she (is).

My cats are better behaved than those of my neighbor.

> **SKILL 10.7** Recognizes the similarities and differences between spoken and written English *(e.g., syntax, vocabulary choice, audience)* and uses instructional strategies to help students apply English writing conventions and enhance their own writing.

Strategies for Promoting Awareness of the Relationship between Spoken and Written Language

- Writing down or encoding what the children say on a language chart.

- Highlighting the uses of print products found in the classroom such as labels, yellow sticky pad notes, labels on shelves and lockers, calendars, signs, and directions.

- Discussing and comparing with children the length, appearance and boundaries of specific words. For example, children can see that the names of Dan and Dora share certain letters and a similar shape.

- Having children match oral words to printed words by forming an echo chorus as the teacher reads poetry or rhymes aloud and they echo the reading.

- Having the children combine, manipulate, switch and move letters to change words.

- Working with letter cards to create messages and respond to the messages that they create.

Both written and spoken English are used for communication, and both have purpose. While both can be formal or informal, as a general rule, written English is more formal than spoken English. Spoken English includes more than just words. Body gestures, tone, and eye contact all contribute to the delivery of the words, and these details are lost in a letter, email, or written paper. Spoken English is useful when the goal is to interact with others because the syntax and vocabulary choice are meant to relate to the audience, to evoke emotion, or to persuade. The audience both listens to the words and observes the person who is speaking to decide if the speaker is relatable.

Written English generally is more formal. The word choice and vocabulary are more deliberate, and essays have a formalized plan. The author has taken a lot of time to prepare a piece of writing. Some spoken English, such as a prepared speech, also takes much preparation, but most spoken English reacts to a moment or question and does not include preparation. In written English, sentence structure follows conventions, and there should be no grammatical errors or dialect unless one is writing a fiction story with dialogue. In this case, dialect can greatly enhance a story and create a more realistic conversation.

Teachers should explicitly teach the difference between spoken and written English so students understand the different expectations for them in class. For example, a student will use spoken English to answer a question posed in class. He may use dialect or incomplete sentences or pause to say "um" as he answers. Because of the informality of spoken English, this behavior is appropriate. However, if the same student were to answer a teacher's question in a short essay, he would think about his answer prior to writing and write complete sentences with minimal errors.

When teaching the difference between written and spoken English, teachers can focus on the syntax and vocabulary differences and on the various spellings and sounds that change whether one is speaking or writing. Often, teachers of ELL students teach these sorts of lessons because there are so many nuances to language. One option is to give students a worksheet with many statements on it, some that are appropriate for the written word and some for the spoken word. Students will have to choose which statements belong where and explain why.

- Bortoluzzi, M. "Blurring the boundary between spoken and written language in EFL." *http://iteslj.org/Lessons/Bortoluzzi-Boundary.html*. Retrieved Aug. 23, 2015.

SKILL 10.8 **Knows writing conventions and appropriate grammar and usage and provides students with direct instruction and guided practice in those areas.**

See Skill 10.6

SKILL 10.9 **Selects and uses instructional strategies, materials and activities to teach correct pencil grip.**

See Skill 10.5

COMPETENCY 11
WRITTEN COMMUNICATION

SKILL 11.1 Understands differences between first-draft writing and writing for publication and provides instruction in various stages of writing, including prewriting, drafting, revising (including both self-revision and peer revision) and editing.

When teaching writing, teachers must provide many opportunities for children to write. Writing should be a daily activity in the classroom, just as reading is.

Stages of Writing

Students must understand that writing is a process and typically involves many steps.

Writing is an iterative process. As students engage in the various stages of writing, they develop and improve not only their writing skills but their thinking skills as well.

Stages of the writing process:

- **Prewriting:** Students gather ideas before writing. Prewriting may include clustering, listing, brainstorming, mapping, free writing, and charting.

- **Drafting:** Students compose the first draft. Students should follow their notes/writing plan from the prewriting stage.

- **Revising and editing:** Revision is probably the most important step in the writing process. In this step, students examine their work and make changes in wording, details, and ideas.

- **Proofreading:** Students proofread the draft for punctuation and mechanical errors.

- **Publishing:** Students may have their work displayed on a bulletin board, read aloud in class, or printed in a literary magazine or school anthology.

SKILL 11.2 Knows how to promote students' development of an extensive reading and writing vocabulary by providing students with many opportunities to read and write.

In a strong literacy classroom, reading and writing opportunities will be abundant. However, these opportunities do not always have to be obvious. Students will read in class, will have a reading nook or library where they can peruse books during centers, and may have a five-minute activity at the beginning of each class that involves some writing. Teachers also can be more creative. For example, give students a chance to journal their thoughts in pictures and in words. Or, develop an interactive bulletin board. For young students, this could mean covering the board with white paper and sectioning off eight to ten blocks. Read a story out loud and then, with the class, document the major events in the story. Split the class into small groups, and allow each group to draw a picture and write a sentence to match one of the major events. Last, each group can tape its event onto the bulletin board in the correct order. Bulletin boards also can be useful for practicing reading sight words, recognizing word families, or gaining vocabulary. Create pockets in the board where students can choose the materials to complete a short game or challenge.

For kinesthetic students, using very large print can be motivating. Place sight words on the floor and play leapfrog, asking students to jump from one word to another without touching the ground. Place letters on the ground ask them to jump from one letter to another as they practice spelling. For example, to spell "lock," the student would jump from L to O to C to K, counting on his fingers as he jumps to remember the letters.

It is important to label items and bins in the classroom and write the students' names on laminated paper on their desks. Having many books, magazines, and posters around the room also will promote literacy.

Older students who already know how to read still need many reading and writing opportunities. Motivate these students by creating treasure hunts around the room, writing song lyrics or poetry, encouraging pleasure reading, and inviting them to develop their own pieces of fiction.

SKILL 11.3 **Monitors students' writing development and provides motivational instruction that addresses individual students' needs, strengths and interests.**

Writing is an individual process, and teachers need to respect that process when designing writing lesson plans. First, instruction should be motivating. To motivate students, connect instruction to students' home and outside interests. In prewriting exercises, students can look at photos and magazine pictures, make collages, or conduct interviews to learn about topics and gain motivation to continue the project. Graphic organizers, completed after the initial prewriting exercise, can help students organize their thoughts.

Because writing is such a unique process, all students will be at different places and will have different needs. It is important to address those needs and help students grow where they need it the most. Developing learning centers that focus on different skills such as organizing thoughts, grammar, sentence structure, and story order can address individual students' needs.

Some children will have difficulty with the writing process, and a teacher must address this. Sometimes, stepping away from the details can be the most useful tactic. Young children can draw pictures to illustrate their story, and older children can tell it without the intimidation of having to write. Once the gestalt of the story has been discussed, writing will be less complicated because there already is an outline. Some students having difficulty may need small-group lessons on specific writing techniques, and teachers can use class time to incorporate mini-lessons into the objectives for the day.

Teachers can monitor writing development through formative and summative assessments. Asking students to journal and then reading these journals can give teachers an idea of how students organize their thoughts. Reading a completed paper after it has been through revisions can help a teacher determine a student's grasp of grammar, spelling, sentence structure, and word choice.

> ### SKILL 11.4 Understands differences between first-draft writing and writing for publication and provides instruction in various stages of writing, including prewriting, drafting, revising (including both self-revision and peer revision) and editing.

A first draft often is a jumble of ideas—the beginning of a story or of a structured essay—without the cohesiveness necessary for a final product. A piece about to be published is error-free, flows well, and has a focused topic and an intriguing story.

Students should not be graded on their final piece of work, but instead graded on their journey through the writing process.

Students should not be graded on their final piece of work, but instead graded on their journey through the writing process. The steps in this process will vary according to students' ages and may take different amounts of time, but whatever their level, students must be taken through the entire process.

To encourage students to prewrite, teachers should give them opportunities to complete writing exercises. Brainstorming with partners, completing graphic organizers, or talking as a class about a topic are effective prewriting exercises. Next, the students will begin their first drafts. This draft will be on-topic, but it may have grammar or spelling errors, may have inappropriate transitions, or may be missing some key material. It is the student's first effort.

Next, the student will move to the revision phase. There are two types of revision: self- and peer-revision. In a self-revision, students fill out a rubric that measures their grammar, spelling, transitions, organization, topic, and synthesis of the material. After making adjustments, they give their papers to a classmate for a peer review. In this peer review, the classmates fill out another rubric that evaluates similar topics. Often, the fresh set of eyes catches most errors. The students should discuss the peer evaluation if possible. The author then revises the paper according to peer suggestions. Sometimes, at this point, a teacher will complete conferences with each student to discuss any revisions or questions about the direction in which to take the final draft.

Finally, students complete the final draft of their papers. After proofreading, the papers will be ready for publication.

> SKILL
> 11.5
> **Understands the benefits of technology for teaching basic writing skills and writing for publication and provides instruction in the use of technology to facilitate written communication.**

Technology, specifically word processing, provides tools for students such as spell check, a dictionary, and a thesaurus that is available at the click of a mouse. These tools can eliminate errors, save time, and develop a new set of skills.

However, before technology can be useful, children have to learn how to use it. This will include a typing class, lessons on Internet safety, and instruction on how to distinguish a reputable from a disreputable source. Once students are efficient in using technology, they can use it to their advantage: to get complicated ideas on paper faster, to communicate, and to do research.

Next, teachers can use motivating and authentic assignments to help students improve their writing skills and enhance their technology skills. For example, students can publish their pieces online on a class website or blog. This authenticity will motivate them to feel strongly about the final product because many people will see it. Additionally, students can communicate with other students or even professionals from across the country or around the world. Writing an email to someone who will respond will motivate students to care more about their final product, and the writing process will be more authentic.

- Using Technology to Enhance Literacy Instruction

    http://www.ncrel.org/sdrs/areas/issues/content/cntareas/reading/li300.htm. Retrieved Aug. 27, 2015.

> **SKILL 11.6** Understands writing for a variety of audiences, purposes and settings and provides students with opportunities to write for various audiences, purposes and settings and in various voices and styles.

Writing for Various Audiences

There are four main forms of discourse: persuasion, exposition, narration, and description.

PERSUASION is a piece of writing—a poem, a play, a speech—the purpose of which is to change the minds of readers or listeners or to get them to do something. This can be achieved in many ways:

- The credibility of the writer/speaker might lead the listeners/readers to a change of mind or a recommended action.

- Reasoning is important in persuasive discourse. No one wants to believe that he or she accepts a new viewpoint or goes out and takes action just because he or she likes and trusts the person who recommended it. Logic comes into play in persuasive reasoning.

- The third and most powerful force that leads to acceptance or action is emotional appeal.

> **PERSUASION:** a piece of writing—a poem, a play, a speech—the purpose of which is to change the minds of readers or listeners or to get them to do something

EXPOSITION is discourse intended to inform. Expository writing is not focused on changing anyone's mind or getting anyone to take a certain action. Its purpose is to give information. Examples include driving directions to a particular place or the instructions for putting together a toy that arrives unassembled.

> **EXPOSITION:** discourse intended to inform

NARRATION is discourse that is presented chronologically—something happened, and then something else happened, and then something else happened. It is also called a story. News reports are often narrative in nature, as are records of trips, etc.

> **NARRATION:** discourse that is presented chronologically

DESCRIPTION is discourse intended to make an experience available through one of the five senses—seeing, smelling, hearing, feeling (as with the fingers), and tasting. Descriptive words allow the reader to "see" with her mind's eye, hear through her mind's ear, smell through her mind's nose, taste with her mind's tongue, and feel with her mind's fingers.

> **DESCRIPTION:** discourse intended to make an experience available through one of the five senses

A paraphrase is the rewording of a piece of writing. The result is not necessarily shorter than the original. It uses different vocabulary and possibly a different arrangement of details.

A summary is a distillation of the elements of a piece of writing or a speech. A summary is much shorter than the original. A summary does not make judgments about the original; it simply reports the original in condensed form.

Letters are often expository in nature—their purpose is to provide information. However, letters are also often persuasive—the writer wants to persuade or get the recipient to do something. They are also sometimes descriptive or narrative—the writer shares an experience or tells about an event.

Research reports are a special kind of expository writing. A topic is researched—explored by searching the literature, interviewing experts, or even conducting experiments—and the findings are written up to convey what was discovered to a particular audience. Research reports can be simple, such as delving into the history of an event, or complex, such as a report on a scientific phenomenon that requires complicated testing and reasoning to explain. A research report often suggests several alternative conclusions but highlights one as the best answer to the question that originally inspired the research, which becomes the thesis of the report.

Clarifying Writing

Writing introductions

It's important to remember that in the writing process, the introduction should be written last. Until the body of the paper has been determined, it's difficult to make strategic decisions regarding the introduction. The basic purpose of the introduction, then, is to lead the audience into the discourse. It lets the reader know the purpose of the discourse and it conditions the audience to be receptive to what the writer wants to say. It can be very brief or it can take up a large percentage of the total word count.

The introduction often ends with the thesis, the point or purpose of the paper. However, this is not set in stone. The thesis may open the body of the discussion, or it may conclude the discourse. The most important thing to remember is that the purpose and structure of the introduction should be deliberate if it is to serve the purpose of "leading the reader into the discussion."

> The most important thing to remember is that the purpose and structure of the introduction should be deliberate if it is to serve the purpose of "leading the reader into the discussion."

Writing conclusions

Aristotle taught that the conclusion of a piece of writing should strive to do five things:

1. Inspire the reader with a favorable opinion of the writer

2. Amplify the force of the points made in the body of the text

3. Reinforce the points made in the body of the text

4. Rouse appropriate emotions in the reader

5. Restate in a summary way what has been said

> **SKILL 11.7** **Teaches students to use appropriate conventions to support ideas in writing and to use an appropriate form of documentation to acknowledge sources** (e.g., quotations, bibliographical information, differentiation between paraphrasing and plagiarism).

Ideas are only opinions until they are backed by a respected source. Students must cite their sources both to give credit to the original author of the idea and to give evidence to support their argument. There are different ways to cite sources and different types of citations. The two common citation styles that students use are APA and MLA. APA is used for most science and analytical papers; MLA is used primarily for literature analysis in English or theatre class. For the purpose of this section, we will discuss APA because it is the most commonly taught.

When a student is quoting a source or taking the exact words from another author, she must put quotation marks around the wording that she has copied. She will put a period at the end of the last sentence and then place the quotation marks after the period. Then she will cite the author, giving the date the piece was published and the page number from the source. For example: "There are only three blue fish left in the world," said O'Donnell. (O'Donnell, 2014, p. 20). If the quote is longer than 40 words, it is necessary to place the quote in its own paragraph, centered, and double spaced, without quotation marks. At the end of her paper, she will include a works cited page, where she will give full details of this source, including the publishing company, date of publication, title, author, and full page numbers, written in the APA style. For example:

> O'Donnell, Mark. (2014). *Blue fish epidemic.* New York: Random House.

Note the capitalization and use of italics.

Sometimes, a student may not use the exact words an author used but wants to convey the same idea. This is called paraphrasing. When a student paraphrases another author, the student weaves the author's ideas into her argument. At the end of the section, she needs to cite the source because the ideas are not all hers. In this case, her in-text citation will look like this:

> (O'Donnell, 2014).

There is no need for a page number here because she is not quoting exact words. However, at the end of the paper, she needs a full citation.

PLAGIARISM: when a writer takes words or ideas from another author and does not give credit to that author

PLAGIARISM is when a writer takes words or ideas from another author and does not give credit to that author. Some schools have very strict penalties for plagiarism, including suspension or even expulsion. In writing, original authors always must be given credit for their ideas.

Sometimes, the source will be online. In that case, the student still needs an in-text and end of document citation. The in-text citation will include the author and date, but the reference list at the end of the paper will include the website and when the information was retrieved.

- Purdue University Online Writing Lab

   https://owl.english.purdue.edu/owl/resource/560/02/. Retrieved Aug. 23, 2015.

SKILL 11.8 Knows grade-level expectations in the Texas Essential Knowledge and Skills (TEKS).

Grade-level expectations increase and become more complicated as a child develops cognitively and is able to handle more abstract thought. In the early grade levels, the focus is on reading and math literacy and concrete understanding. By third grade, students are no longer learning to read; they are reading to learn. Students will no longer be focusing only on reading the words and identifying patterns in the sentences. They will now be looking for metaphoric language, doing analysis, and recognizing the purpose of and audience for each text. Students think increasingly abstractly, and assignments involve more higher-order thinking. By middle school, students will be analyzing and evaluating, rather than just describing. For example, as noted in the TEKS, "in kindergarten, students will use pictures in conjunction with writing to document research, but as fifth graders, they will refine research through the use of secondary questions" (Core Subjects, TEKS).

SKILL 11.9 Understands how to foster collaboration with families and with other professionals to promote students' development of writing skills.

The family is a child's first teacher and must be treated with respect and kindness, even when the family's values and home priorities are different from what the school deems important. It will be helpful to use the family's strengths to building literacy at home. For example, the type and variety of language that a young child hears at home is a precursor to early literacy. It is important for parents to speak to their children, to repeat their sentences, to validate what they say, and to use a variety of vocabulary so children can hear various words and syntax in daily language. Parents can ask young children questions and respond by using active listening techniques and then asking a follow-up question. Parents of older

> The family is a child's first teacher and must be treated with respect and kindness, even when the family's values and home priorities are different from what the school deems important.

children can ask their children to tell stories, to make up characters and settings, or to draw a picture and then explain it. All of these techniques promote early writing skills.

Parents also can foster literacy by reading to their children. This can start at about four months old, when a baby has established strong eye contact. Reading can give a child an inside look at the shape of a story—its beginning, middle, and end—which will prepare her to write one eventually.

Teachers should be aware that some families do not consider books to be a priority. However, these families have other forms of literacy, and those can be used to foster a love of writing. For example, some families may value storytelling instead of reading a book, and other families may value singing songs. Both tell stories. From these family events, students can learn the value of the structure of a story and can apply these skills learned at home to writing in school.

Teachers can learn which types of literacy are present in each home and then encourage parents or guardians to help make the connections between home and school. For example, if a student is from a family that enjoys storytelling, the teacher can ask the child to tell her a story while she writes it down. Once that exercise is complete, the student can see that he just wrote a story, just with a different technique.

Writing is not only about storytelling, but also about writing conventions. Families can be encouraged to write notes to their children before bed, to keep a journal between parent and child, to play word games with their child, or to play storytelling games. These suggestions can be included in a class newsletter, suggested at parent conferences, or available on the class website. It's important for the teacher to encourage participation but not to demand it. Parents and guardians want their children to succeed in school, and most are willing to work with suggestions but will not appreciate an instructor who dictates how they must participate.

COMPETENCY 12
VIEWING AND REPRESENTING

SKILL
12.1 **Knows grade-level expectations for viewing and representing visual images and messages as described in the Texas Essential Knowledge and Skills (TEKS).**

The Texas Essential Knowledge and Skills (TEKS) are the statewide curriculum standards. The State Board of Education (SBOE) revises them regularly. The English Language Arts and Reading aspects of the TEKS include the following strands:

1. **Reading:** Students read and comprehend various literary and informational texts.

2. **Writing:** Students create different genres of written texts with a distinctive main idea, inherent organization, and ample detail.

3. **Research:** Students must locate a variety of relevant sources and then evaluate, synthesize, and present the information.

4. **Listening and Speaking:** Students listen to the ideas of others while giving their own ideas in academically oriented discussions and in groups.

5. **Oral and Written Conventions:** Students use the oral and written conventions of English when both speaking and writing.

Each teacher must understand the grade-level expectations for viewing and representing visual images and messages in accordance with these strands. For example, when a student is addressing a research question or topic, the student must gather evidence from various sources. The student can record the gathered information in basic visual formats, such as charts, tables, and diagrams. Students can view images on websites, in textbooks, and in other forms of media, and they can include these images in their work. They can transfer the images or replicate them in graphic organizers and other visual depictions of information.

This is also true when students are reading literary text with sensory language. Students can demonstrate their understanding by identifying language that evokes imagery. The visual experience the text produces can be recorded in a journal, and pictures may be drawn by the student. Other teachers may ask students to collect images from magazines and create a collage representing an aspect of the book, such as character traits of the main character. Students can not only identify the language that generates images, but also create such images with their own interpretation.

Using visual images and messages means the students are familiar with and prepared for the demands of the digital age. The resources they use should include electronic sources, and they should identify graphic representations of information readily. The insertion of graphic organizers into the curriculum framework also is important for students because they are part of a more global, interconnected, and technology-driven world. In the twenty-first century, we all are inundated with images and messages.

> **SKILL 12.2** Understands and teaches the characteristics and functions of different types of media *(e.g., film, print)* and knows how different types of media influence and inform.

Comparing and Contrasting Print, Visual, and Electronic Media

A print message has positive and negative features. Positive features include longevity and portability. Print messages appeal almost exclusively to the mind, and allow students to recursively read sections that warrant more thought. A negative feature of print messages is that they are not accessible to nonreaders.

A graphic message gives a quick overview of a quantifiable situation. Some learners find that graphic information is easier to understand than print, and many struggling readers find graphic messages more helpful, too. However, compared to print, graphic messages convey a much smaller range of information.

An audio message allows for messages delivered with attention to prosody. Students who can't read can still access the material. Audio messages invite the listener to form mental images consistent with the topic of the audio. Audio messages allow learners to close their eyes for better mental focus. Listening to an audio message is a more passive activity than reading a print message.

An audiovisual message offers the greatest accessibility for learners. It has the advantages of both media, the graphic and the audio. Learners' eyes and ears are engaged. Nonreaders get significant access to content. On the other hand, viewing an audiovisual presentation is an even more passive activity than listening to an audio message because information is coming to learners effortlessly through two senses.

> **SKILL** **Teaches students to compare and contrast print, visual and**
> **12.3** **electronic media, including the level of formality of each** *(e.g., email,*
> *Web-based news article, blogs).*

Today, we have copious ways of gaining information. When students learn how to research material and decide which should be used in a paper or presentation, they must know how to compare and contrast information sources. They also must have a strong understanding of fact versus opinion to tell the difference between a source with reputable data and a source that is an author's unsupported opinion.

A strong print source will have an author and a date of publication and will be from a reputable publication. Most newspapers, books, and magazines are reputable print sources. While newspapers and magazines are useful for recent information and opinions, books are important as a foundation for knowledge and background about the topic. Many books and most newspapers and magazines combine facts with the author's opinions that the facts support.

Visual and electronic media are common ways to receive information. Students can watch the news or television or listen to the radio. Students should keep in mind that a lot of visual and electronic media is biased and contains unsupported opinions.

Electronic media includes news-based Web articles, online encyclopedias, blog posts, and emails. It is important for students to know that anyone can publish anything online, so just because information is online does not mean it is credible. A credible online source will have an author and a date of publication, will be well written, and will be published on a reputable website. Students should learn the difference between a news-based article, which will give them information on recent events, and a blog entry that, although it may be popular, is not a reputable news source. Websites designed for teacher and student news article access include the following:

> *www.timeforkids.com*
>
> *www.dogonews.com*
>
> *www.kids.nationalgeographic.com/explore*

Email is a common method of communication, and if the email is treated like an interview, it can be used as a primary source. However, the writer must have explicit, written permission to use emails as a source in the paper, just as one would when using a interview as a source.

See also Skill 12.2

Many books and most newspapers and magazines combine facts with the author's opinions that the facts support.

> **SKILL 12.4** Teaches students to evaluate how visual image makers *(e.g., illustrators, documentary filmmakers, political cartoonists, news photographers)* represent messages and meanings and provides students with opportunities to interpret and evaluate visual images in various media.

See also Skill 12.2

Interpreting and Evaluating Visual Images

Political cartoons

The political, or editorial, cartoon presents a message or point of view about people, events, or situations using caricature and symbolism to convey the cartoonist's ideas, sometimes subtly, sometimes brashly, but always quickly. A good political cartoon has wit and humor, which is usually obtained by slick exaggeration and not used merely for comic effect. It also has a foundation in truth; that is, the characters must be recognizable to the viewer and the point of the drawing must have some basis in fact even if it has a philosophical bias. The third requirement is a moral purpose.

> *Using political cartoons as a teaching tool enlivens lectures, prompts classroom discussion, promotes critical thinking, develops multiple talents and learning styles, and helps prepare students for standardized tests. It also provides humor.*

Using political cartoons as a teaching tool enlivens lectures, prompts classroom discussion, promotes critical thinking, develops multiple talents and learning styles, and helps prepare students for standardized tests. It also provides humor. However, it may be the most difficult form of literature to teach. Many teachers who choose to include cartoons in their social studies curricula caution that, while students may enjoy them, they may not always understand the cartoonists' messages.

The best strategy for teaching such a unit is through a subskills approach that leads students step by step to higher orders of critical thinking. For example, the teacher can introduce caricature and use cartoons to illustrate the principles. Students are able to identify and interpret symbols if they are given the principles for doing so and get plenty of practice, and cartoons are excellent for this. It can cut down the time it takes for students to develop these skills, and many of the students who might not learn to identify symbols may overcome the roadblocks through the analysis of political cartoons. Many political cartoons exist for the teacher to use in the classroom.

Illustrations provide students with chances to look at visual images. Artists provide our books with pictures, and graphic artists provide images for icons and backgrounds of webpages students may navigate. Graphic artistry can be in the classroom; students can have access to graphic image-making software to make meaning of a theme or unit. For example, students can use images from the media, including Internet sources, to find and understand a symbol in a story.

Filmmaking is also popular. Students can use software to create, direct, and present ideas to the class. Using such programs gives students different venues of expression. Teachers can check for understanding through pictorial means with project-based learning and the use of flexible assessments.

News photographers capture moments that depict aspects of the articles written. Using a photo can provide a lesson starter or opener to introduce a new theme to the class. When students interpret and evaluate photographic and visual images, they are able to connect to a topic prior to reading and writing. The visual source acts as a primer for understanding.

> **SKILL 12.5** **Knows how to teach students to analyze visual image makers' choices** *(e.g., style, elements, media)* **and evaluate how those choices help represent or extend meaning.**

Analyzing Data Presented in Visuals

Visuals are an effective and dynamic way to add meaning to a text. Some possibilities for the analysis of data, whether presented in tables, charts, graphs, maps, or other illustrations, include:

- **Qualitative descriptions:** Would drawing conclusions about the quality of a particular treatment or course of action be revealed by the illustration?

- **Quantitative descriptions:** How much do the results of one particular treatment or course of action differ from another, and is that variation significant?

- **Classification:** Is worthwhile information derived from breaking the information down into classifications?

- **Estimations:** Is it possible to estimate future performance on the basis of the information in the illustration?

- **Comparisons:** Is it useful to make comparisons based on the data?

- **Relationships:** Are relationships between components revealed by scrutiny of the data?

- **Cause-and-effect relationships:** Do the data suggest that there are cause-and-effect relationships that were not previously apparent?

- **Mapping and modeling:** If the data were mapped and a model drawn up, would the point of the document be demonstrated or refuted?

Choosing the appropriate graphic form depends on the type of information and data with which one is working. For example, a pie chart that shows parts of a whole would not be useful for showing trends over time. A line chart, rather than a bar chart, is more effective when showing the interaction of two variables.

- **Tables:** Tables depict exact numbers and other data in rows and columns.

- **Graphs:** Graphs depict trends, movements, distributions, and cycles more clearly than tables. While graphs can present statistics in a more interesting and comprehensible form than tables, they are less accurate.

- **Maps:** While the most obvious use of maps is to locate places geographically, they can also show specific geographic features such as roads, mountains, and rivers. Some maps show information according to geographic distribution such as population, housing, or manufacturing centers.

- **Illustrations:** A wide range of illustrations, such as photographs, drawings, and diagrams, can be used to illuminate the text in a document. Illustrations can also be part of a graphic layout designed to make a page more attractive.

Analyzing an image's style and elements is an integral part of comprehending why the image-maker made specific choices. The style of the image may reveal information about time and place. For example, a photograph of a covered bridge may be rural and calming. Perhaps the photographer picks a landscape layout so many of the environmental elements can be revealed in the picture. He or she includes the babbling brook beneath the bridge, plant life, and so forth. Such elements of nature evoke a specific mood the photographer is looking to convey.

Students may want to incorporate stylistic elements into their work. For example, the time period may call for a black and white drawing or photograph if the unit of study or novel is set in the year 1890. Using color, location of objects, and visual effects allows students to express an understanding of what they are reading and writing by connecting it to imagery.

> **SKILL Provides students with opportunities to interpret events and ideas**
> **12.6 based on information from maps, charts, graphics, video segments**
> **and technology presentations and to use media to compare ideas**
> **and points of view.**

Students must be able to interpret events and ideas by using visual and multi-media information. Information derived from visual sources gives students an extension of content learning. Sources of visual and multimedia information include the following:

- **Maps:** Understanding the location of an event or the origin of an idea gives added dimension to student understanding. The "where" element in reading comprehension can be understood through mapping a location. The map may be as simple as a neighborhood sketch or as complex and detailed as an aerial view of a monument. Noting the location of an event or related idea builds contextual meaning for students.

- **Charts:** Diagrams, charts, and graphs extend knowledge. These pictorial representations of information can convey numerical data, demonstrate trends, and depict structures. The interpretation of information can support the understanding of a text or novel.

- **Graphics:** Pictures are often representative of the words in context. Pictures and graphics that relate to a piece of text allow students to take a meaningful "picture walk" prior to reading.

- **Video segments:** Video segments provide multimedia modes of dissecting information and can enhance the understanding of a text. Showing a short video before, during, or after a lesson can help cement students' understanding. The components of the visual images come together to give students a context to understand, for example, what characters look like, where events take place, and how something was discovered or made.

- **Technology presentations:** Presentations using software such as Prezi or Microsoft PowerPoint allow students to demonstrate comprehension and complete project-based assessments.

Students can select visuals using search engines to find images on the Internet in a safe context. The gathering of images is the selection process. Students can organize elements of a visual project by date order, color, size, or other elements teachers may specify.

SKILL 12.7 Knows steps and procedures for teaching students to produce visual images and messages with various meanings to communicate with others.

Teaching students to produce visual images and messages with various meanings to communicate with others provides a dynamic element to lessons and assessments.

First, the teacher must identify the type of media to be used. Are the students to create short videos to demonstrate understanding? Would they prefer they make a voice recording? Teachers must consider questions like these to narrow the type of media students will use for an assignment or project.

Second, students should sketch a plan. They may draw or make a prototype, write a short description, or outline a plan. They can choose colors, locations, characters, and so forth. Students may also want to make a storyboard or use another graphic organizer for planning, particularly if the media depicts a sequence or flow of events.

Finally, students develop their image. Once students know their media and have a plan, they can convey the information required. Offering a rubric or checklist to students will help shape their creative craft.

See also Skills 12.5 and 12.6

SKILL 12.8 Teachers students how to select, organize and produce visuals to complement and extend meanings.

See Skill 12.7

> **SKILL 12.9** Provides students with opportunities to use technology for producing various types of communications (*e.g., class newspapers, multimedia reports, video reports*) and helps students analyze how language, medium and presentation contribute to the message.

Technology for Producing Teaching Material

MULTIMEDIA refers to a technology for presenting material in both visual and verbal forms. This format is especially conducive to classroom use since it reaches both visual and auditory learners.

> **MULTIMEDIA:** a technology for presenting material in both visual and verbal forms

Software programs for producing teaching material

- Adobe Acrobat
- PC Paintbrush
- Microsoft Word
- Microsoft Excel
- Microsoft Visio
- Microsoft PowerPoint

Technology gives students a venue of creative expression and an opportunity for project-based learning. Creating articles for a class newspaper can be done using word processing software. The class news can also appear on a teacher's webpage or the school website. Links to blogs allow students to convey messages and reports in text and images. Students may post a message on a blog, provide a link for information, and share short video clips.

Students may analyze how language and diction offer a message tone and mood. Students find and express their voices through this process of language analysis and selection. The medium used also gives context to the format students can use to demonstrate an idea most efficiently or effectively.

Students should take advantage of the technology available in the classroom to extend their ideas. Programs such as Prezi, Storyboard, and ThingLink give students the resources to build language through a specific medium, and present such visuals to the class.

SKILL 12.10 Understands how to foster collaboration with families and with other professionals to promote students' development of media literacy.

Collaborating with other teachers, psychologists, therapists, and support service workers in the building promotes a communal sense of literacy. Collaboration among professionals develops media literacy in locations such as the art room and the library, for example. Media literacy can be incorporated into a graphic design project in art class. In the library, literacy can be connected to the book that the media center specialist is reading to students. He or she can incorporate audiovisual components in his or her lesson, such as showing a video, playing an audio clip, or having the students share ideas on a blog.

Collaboration with families also is essential to extending literacy skills. Teachers can create a webpage with links to resources for developing literacy skills, such as games, interactive lists of words, and PDF files. For example, teachers can put helpful links on their webpages or create a reference list for parents.

A helpful link for reading can be found Reading Rockets: *http://www.readingrockets. org/article/25-activities-reading-and-writing-fun*

Several other games can be found on the following link: *http://www.bataviacsd.org/ information_technology.cfm?subpage=3504*

COMPETENCY 13
ASSESSMENT OF DEVELOPING LITERACY

> **SKILL 13.1** **Knows how to select and administer formative and summative assessments and use results to measure literacy acquisition** (e.g., *alphabetic skills, literacy development, word analysis and word identification skills, fluency, comprehension, writing conventions, written communications, visual images, study skills*) **and address individual students' needs identified in informal and formal assessments.**

ASSESSMENT is the practice of collecting information about something from children's responses, and EVALUATION is the process of judging the children's responses to determine how well they are achieving particular goals or demonstrating certain skills.

There are two broad categories of assessment:

- **Informal assessment** utilizes observation and other nonstandardized procedures to compile evidence of children's progress. Informal assessments include but are not limited to: checklists, observations, and performance assessments/tasks.

- **Formal assessment** consists of standardized tests and procedures carried out under circumscribed conditions. Formal assessments include state tests, standardized achievement tests, NAEP tests, etc.

> **ASSESSMENT:** the practice of collecting information about something

> **EVALUATION:** the process of judging the children's responses to determine how well they are achieving particular goals or demonstrating certain skills

Key Terms

- **Formative testing** sets targets for student learning and creates an avenue to provide data on whether students are meeting the targets.

- **Diagnostic testing** is used to determine students' skill levels and current knowledge.

- **Normative testing** establishes rankings and comparatives of student performance against an established norm of achievement.

- **Alternative testing** is a nontraditional method of helping students construct responses to problem solving.

- **Authentic testing** refers to real-life assessments that are relevant and meaningful in a student's life (e.g., calculating a 20 percent discount on an iPod for a student learning math percentages creates a more personalized approach to learning).

- **Performance-based testing** judges students according to pre-established standards.

- **Traditional testing** refers to the variety of teacher assessments that either come with the textbooks or are directly created from the textbooks.

SKILL 13.2 **Knows the characteristics of informal and formal reading comprehension assessments** (e.g., criterion-referenced state tests, curriculum-based reading assessments, informal reading inventories, norm-referenced tests).

Criterion-Referenced and Norm-Referenced Tests

Criterion-referenced tests

CRITERION-REFERENCED TESTS are tests that measure children against criteria or guidelines that are uniform for all of the test takers. Therefore, by definition, no special questions, formats, or considerations are given for the test taker who is either from a different linguistic/cultural background or is already identified as a struggling reader/writer. On a criterion-referenced test, it is possible that a child can score 100 percent if he or she has been exposed to and mastered all of the concepts on the test. A child's score on such a test indicates which of the concepts have already been taught and what the child needs additional review or support in mastering.

> **CRITERION-REFERENCED TESTS:** tests that measure children against criteria or guidelines that are uniform for all of the test takers

Norm-referenced tests

NORM-REFERENCED TESTS are tests that measure children against one another. Scores on these tests are reported in percentiles. Each percentile indicates the percentage of the testing population whose scores were lower than or the same as a particular child's score. Standardized norm-referenced tests are being used in many districts today. They foster unhelpful and invalid comparisons between young readers, which do not help individual readers progress in reading development, but rather track and stigmatize them. Of course, this type of test does not take into account special linguistic, cultural, socioeconomic, or special needs concerns.

> **NORM-REFERENCED TESTS:** tests that measure children against one another

Characteristics of an Effective Assessment

1. Assessment should be an ongoing process, with the teacher making some kind of an informal or formal assessment almost every time the child speaks, listens, reads, writes, or views something in the classroom. The assessment should be a natural part of the instruction and not intrusive.

2. The most effective assessment is integrated into ongoing instruction. Throughout the teaching and learning day, the child's written, spoken, and reading contributions to the class, or lack thereof, need to be continually assessed.

3. Assessment should reflect the actual reading and writing experiences for which classroom learning has prepared the child. The child should be able to show that he or she can read and explain or react to a similar literary or expository work.

4. Assessment needs to be a collaborative and reflective process. Teachers can learn from what the children reveal about their own individual assessments. Children, even as early as grade 2, should be supported by their teacher to continually and routinely ask themselves questions assessing their reading (and other skill) progress. They might ask: "How have I done in understanding what the author wanted to say?", "What can I do to improve my reading?", and "How can I use what I have read to learn more about this topic?" Teachers need to be informed by their own professional observation *and* by children's comments as they assess and customize instruction for children.

> *Assessment needs to be a collaborative and reflective process. Teachers can learn from what the children reveal about their own individual assessments.*

5. High-quality valid assessment is multidimensional and may include, but is not limited to: samples of writings, student retellings, running records, anecdotal teacher observations, self-evaluations, and records of independent reading. From this multidimensional data, the teacher can derive a consistent level of performance and design additional instruction to enhance the level of student performance.

6. Assessment must take into account children's ages and ethnic/cultural patterns of learning.

7. Assessment should be performed in order to teach children from their strengths, not their weaknesses. Teachers should find out what reading behaviors children demonstrate well and then design instruction to support those behaviors.

8. Assessment should be part of children's learning process, and not done *on* them but, rather, *with* them.

Validity, Reliability, and Bias in Testing

VALIDITY is how well a test measures what it is supposed to measure. **RELIABILITY** is the consistency of the test. This is measured by whether the test indicates the same score for the child who takes it twice.

Bias in testing occurs when the information in the test or the information required to respond to a multiple-choice question or constructed response (essay question) is not available to test takers who come from a different cultural, ethnic, linguistic, or socioeconomic background than the majority of the test takers.

VALIDITY: how well a test measures what it is supposed to measure

RELIABILITY: the consistency of the test

Literacy Portfolios

Portfolios should include the following categories of materials:

- **Work samples:** These can include children's story maps, webs, KWL charts, pictures, illustrations, storyboards, and writings about the stories they have read.

- **Records of independent reading and writing:** These can include the children's journals, notebooks, or logs of books read with the names of the authors, titles of the books, date completed, and pieces related to the book completed or in progress.

- **Checklists and surveys:** These include checklists designed by the teacher for reading development, writing development, ownership checklists, and general interest surveys.

- **Self-evaluation forms:** These are the children's own evaluations of their reading and writing process framed in their own words. They can be simple templates with starting sentences such as: "I am really proud of the way I..."

Some teachers and schools advocate having the child include formal test results and questions in the portfolio.

See also Skill 13.1

SKILL 13.3 Analyzes students' reading and writing performance and uses the information as a basis for instruction.

See Skills 13.2, 13.4, 13.5, 13.7, 13.8, and 13.9

> **SKILL 13.4** Knows the state content and performance standards for reading, writing, listening and speaking that constitute the Texas Essential Knowledge and Skills (TEKS) and recognizes when a student needs additional help or intervention to bring the student's performance up to grade level.

The TEKS provides a basis for determining if a student is reading, writing, listening, and speaking below, at, or above grade level. Teachers should use the standards to determine gaps in student learning. Any student who is achieving below grade level is entitled to services if the proper evaluation is performed and recorded according to Texas-specific procedures. The TEKS should be reviewed closely. They can be obtained on the Internet at the following website:

http://ritter.tea.state.tx.us/rules/tac/chapter110/ch110c.html

> **SKILL 13.5** Knows how to determine students' independent, instructional and frustration reading levels and uses the information to select appropriate materials for individual students and to guide students' selection of independent reading materials.

Determining Students' Reading Levels

Reading levels consist of a combination of a word accuracy percentage and a comprehension percentage.

Independent

This is the level at which the child can read text totally on his or her own. When reading books at the independent level, students are able to decode between 95 and 100 percent of the words and comprehend the text with 90 percent or better accuracy. Much of the research indicates that about 98 percent accuracy makes for a good independent reader; however, other research uses figures as low as 95 percent accuracy.

Instructional

This is the level at which the student should be taught. Materials at the instructional level provide enough difficulty to increase the student's reading skills without providing so much that it becomes too cumbersome to finish the selection. Typically, the acceptable range for accuracy is between 85 and 94 percent, with 75 percent or greater comprehension. Some standards rely on the number of errors made instead of the accuracy percentage, with no more than one error out of twenty words read being the acceptable standard.

Frustrational

Books at a student's frustrational level are too difficult for that child and should not be used. The frustrational level is any text with less than 85 percent word accuracy and/or less than 75 percent comprehension.

Reading Stages for English-Language Learners

- **Stage 1 readers:** These readers have developed a phonological awareness of the second language and are becoming familiar with the letter-sound correlations. They are comfortable with the direction of English print and have begun to acquire some basic vocabulary in the language. They recognize a few sight words.

- **Stage 2 readers:** These readers have a good grasp of the phonological aspects of the language and their vocabulary is growing. They are beginning to recognize many of the high-frequency words as sight words, without having to decode the sounds. They are able to understand the main idea of simple text, and they are starting to use meaningful patterns of intonation when they read aloud.

- **Stage 3 readers:** These readers are reading more difficult texts with better fluency. They have developed some reading strategies, such as predicting and using context clues for meaning. They are able to read for information, with less attention to the decoding process. They are able to read for different purposes, such as to find answers to questions or to summarize.

- **Stage 4 readers:** These readers are fluent. They have a well-developed vocabulary and they use all sources of information for interpreting the text, including grammatical and syntactic structures. They are efficient users of reading strategies and they are able to analyze the text and respond to it in different ways. They are able to read for pleasure as well as for practical reasons.

> **SKILL 13.6** Uses ongoing assessments to determine when a student may be in need of classroom intervention or specialized reading instruction and to develop appropriate instructional plans.

Record of Reading Behavior

There are specific steps for taking the record of reading behavior and analyzing its results:

1. **Select a text:** If you want to see if the child is reading on instructional level, choose a book that the child has already read. If the purpose of the test is to see whether the child is ready to advance to the next level, choose a book from that level which the child has not yet seen.

2. **Introduce the text:** If the book is one that has been read, you do not need to introduce the text other than by saying the title. However, if the book is new to the child, you should briefly share the title and tell the child a bit about the plot and style of the book.

3. **Take the record:** Generally with emergent readers in grades 1–2, there are only 100–150 words in a passage used to take a record. Make certain that the child is seated beside you so that you can see the text as the child reads it.

You may want to photocopy the text in advance for yourself so you can make direct notations on your text while the child reads from the book.

After you introduce the text, make certain that the child has the chance to read the text independently. Be certain that you do not "teach" or help the child with it, other than to supply an unknown word that the child requests. The purpose of the record is to see what the child does on his or her own. As the child reads the text, you must be certain to record the reading behaviors the child exhibits.

Comprehension check

A comprehension check should be done by inviting the child to retell the story. This retelling can then be used to ask further questions about characters, plot, setting, and purpose, which allow you to observe and record the child's level of comprehension.

Calculating the Reading Level and the Self-Correction Rate

Calculating the reading level lets you know if the book is at the level the child can read independently, comfortably with guidance, or at a level that frustrates the child.

Generally, an accuracy score of 95–100 percent suggests that the child can read the text and other books or texts on the same level independently.

An accuracy score of 90–94 percent indicates that the text will probably present challenges for the child, but with guidance from you, a tutor, or parent, the child will be able to master these texts and enjoy them. This is instructional level.

However, an accuracy score of 89 percent or less tells you that the material you have selected for the child is too hard for the child to control alone. Material at this level needs to be shared with the child in a shared reading situation or read to the child.

Keeping score on the record

Insertions, omissions, substitutions, and teacher-told responses all count as errors. Repetitions are not scored as errors. Corrected responses are scored as self-corrections.

No penalty is given for a child's attempts at self-correction that result in a finally incorrect response, but the attempts should be noted. Multiple unsuccessful attempts at a word score as one error only.

The lowest score for any page is zero. If a child omits one or more lines, each word omitted is counted as an error. If the child omits a page, deduct the number of words omitted from the total number of words that you have used for the record.

Calculating the reading level

Note the number of errors made on each line on the Record of Reading Behavior in the column marked E (for Error).

Total the number of errors in the text and divide this number into the number of words that the child has read. This will give you the error rate.

If a child read a passage of 100 words and made 10 errors, the error rate would be 1 in 10. Convert this to an accuracy percentage, or 90 percent.

Calculating the self-correction rate

Total the number of self-corrections.

Next, add the number of errors to the number of self-corrections and divide by the number of self-corrections.

A self-correction rate of 1 in 3 to 1 in 5 is considered good. This rate indicates that the child is able to help him- or herself as problems are encountered in reading.

This record should assist the educator in developing a detailed, date-specific picture of the child's progress in reading behavior. It should be used to help the educator individualize instruction for the specific child.

Analyzing the record

As you review the errors, consider whether the child made an error because of semantics (cues from meaning), syntactics (language structure), or visual information difficulties.

As you analyze self-corrections, consider what led the child to make that self-correction. Consider which cues the child uses effectively and which ones the child does not use well.

Understands the use of writing in assessment of students and provides opportunities for students to self-assess and peer assess writing (e.g., for clarity, interest to audience, comprehensiveness) **and ongoing literacy development.**

Writing skills are not restricted to grammar rules and spelling conventions. The holistic assessment of student writing allows teachers to assess understanding of a topic or theme. The creation of a rubric or list can help assessment and allow for qualitative and quantitative data gathering. An example of a specific rubric for a fact sheet assignment can be seen below:

Assessment Rubric: Fact Sheet Assignment

Criteria	Exemplary	Mature	Developing	Formative	Out-Comes
Purpose/Context/Audience	• readers can identify purpose and context easily	• reader can identify purpose and context	• reader can identify purpose and context with effort	• reader cannot identify purpose and context	1.1
	• text /visual elements coordinated with purpose and clear to reader	• text/visual elements coordinated with purpose	• several text and visual elements don't support unified purpose	• text/visual elements element unconnected to purpose and unclear to reader	1.5
	• provides audience with context through clear background information	• addresses the needs and interests of the audience	• does not provide the audience with clear information	• does not meet the needs or interests of the audience	1.4
Orderly Line of Thought	• easily identifiable unifying theme(s); wide range of appropriate textual and visual features ensure unity, cohesion, and continuity	• identifiable unifying theme(s); sufficient number of textual and visual features that ensure unity, cohesion and continuity;	• some difficulty identifying unifying theme(s); insufficient number and/or some inadequate use of textual and visual features that ensure unity, cohesion and continuity	• lack of unifying theme(s), continuity and cohesion; data pieces randomly arranged	1.3
	• all individual parts help reader follow the line of thought	• for the most part, individual pieces relevant and help reader see main focus of the document	• some digression from/ disruptions in line of thought	• major digressions from/disruptions of the line of thought	1.5
	• each paragraph focuses on the same thing, has an introductory device clarifying focus, connects w/ other paragraphs	• for the most part, paragraphs are unified and help the reader move smoothly through the document	• some paragraph issues (poor unity within paragraphs, weak connections b/w ¶s) slow down the reader	• major paragraph issues (e.g., lack of unity within paragraphs, no logical connections between paragraphs) slow down and/ or confuse the reader	
	• appropriate transitions ensure smooth development of ideas/create connections b/w ideas	• adequate transitional devices allow the reader to move through the document	• few effective transitional devices somewhat slow down the reader	• lack of and/or inappropriate use of transitional devices slows down/ confuses the reader	
	• appropriate visual cues (consistency/ parallelism in typography /spacing; page layout) guide reader and enhance the general	• adequate visual cues guide read reader and contribute to theme	• visual cues are somewhat confusing and/or disrupting to the orderly line of thought	• no effective visual cues that would guide the reader through the document	

Source: http://isucomm.iastate.edu/wrubric

Peer sharing and assessing also can give students insight into their work. Students may swap work and write a reaction or observation. They may converse in regard to the structure of an assignment, or they can utilize a pre-made checklist to guide their feedback and suggest valid points to fellow students.

Knows how to select, administer and use results from informal and formal assessments of literacy acquisition.

See Skills 13.3, 13.4, 13.5, and 13.6

SKILL 13.9 Analyzes students' errors in reading and responds to individual students' needs by providing focused instruction to promote literacy acquisition.

See Skill 13.6

SKILL 13.10 Knows informal and formal procedures for assessing students' use of writing conventions and uses multiple, ongoing assessments to monitor and evaluate students' development in that area.

Informal procedures for assessing students' use of writing conventions can be simple teacher-made rubrics and assessments. Listing what is expected of an assignment or project gives the students a sense of what they need to do to complete an assignment successfully and gives the teacher context for grading and offering structured feedback. The teacher can monitor student development by looking at commentary and points received/not received on structured rubrics and assessment forms. Websites such as *www.scholastic.com* give teachers readymade informal writing assessments and ideas.

Formal procedures often entail a deeper analysis of students' understanding of the underpinnings of writing. Formal assessment tests, such as the TOWL-4 Test of Written Language, provide younger students with an image to analyze and write about. They can reflect on a picture given and then write about it.

SKILL 13.11 Uses ongoing assessments of writing conventions to determine when students need additional help or intervention to bring students' performance to grade level based on state content and performance standards for writing in the Texas Essential Knowledge and Skills (TEKS).

Vocabulary usage, diction, grammar, spelling, organization, and coherence are a few components of writing assessment. Analyzing students' needs and intervening to help bring them to grade level is important for the writing process. Teachers can assess whether students are using elements of the writing process, such as planning, drafting, revising, editing, and publishing, to construct and compose a text.

Students can be assessed not only in the writing process, but also in the type of writing according to genre. Writing literary texts, expository texts, and procedural texts require different rubrics and structural components.

Please refer to the Texas Education Agency for further information specific to the state of Texas:

> http://tea.texas.gov/Curriculum_and_Instructional_Programs/Subject_Areas/
> English_Language_Arts_and_Reading/English_Language_Arts_and_Reading/

SKILL 13.12 **Analyzes students' errors in applying writing conventions and uses the results of the analysis as a basis for future instruction.**

Error analysis in writing enables teachers to identify issues to incorporate into future instruction. Noting common spelling errors gives insight into a student's phonemic knowledge and orthographic abilities. Grammar and punctuation analysis gives insight into a student's knowledge of English language rules. Identifying structural issues, such as sentence fragments and run-on sentences, gives a basis for sentence-building lessons. Transitional phrases, verb tense, and pronoun usage are three of the elements of writing a teacher can analyze.

SKILL 13.13 **Selects and uses a variety of formal and informal procedures for monitoring students' reading comprehension and adjusts instruction to meet the needs of individual students, including English-language learners.**

English–language learners often grapple with writing in English. The order of words in a sentence may perplex the ELL student. There are many writing resources available for ELL teachers, including *http://www.colorincolorado.org/educators/teaching/writing_ells/*.

See also Skills 13.10 and 13.11

DOMAIN II
MATHEMATICS

PERSONALIZED STUDY PLAN

✗
KNOWN MATERIAL/ SKIP IT

PAGE	COMPETENCY AND SKILL	
133	**14: Mathematics instruction**	☐
	14.1: Plans appropriate instructional activities for all students by applying research-based theories and principles of learning mathematics.	☐
	14.2: Employs instructional strategies that build on the linguistic, cultural, and socioeconomic diversity of students and that relate to students' lives and communities.	☐
	14.3: Plans and provides developmentally appropriate instruction that establishes transitions between concrete, symbolic, and abstract representations of mathematical knowledge and that builds on students' strengths and addresses their needs.	☐
	14.4: Understands how manipulatives and technological tools can be used appropriately to assist students in developing, comprehending, and applying mathematical concepts.	☐
	14.5: Creates a learning environment that motivates all students and actively engages them in the learning process by using a variety of interesting, challenging, and worthwhile mathematical tasks in individual, small-group, and large-group settings.	☐
	14.6: Uses a variety of tools *(e.g., counters, standard and nonstandard units of measure, rulers, protractors, scales, stopwatches, measuring containers, money, calculators, software)* to strengthen students' mathematical understanding.	☐
	14.7: Implements a variety of instructional methods and tasks that promote students' ability to do the mathematics described in the Texas Essential Knowledge and Skills (TEKS).	☐
	14.8: Develops clear learning goals to plan, deliver, assess, and reevaluate instruction based on the mathematics in the Texas Essential Knowledge and Skills (TEKS).	☐
	14.9: Helps students make connections between mathematics and the real world, as well as between mathematics and other disciplines such as art, music, science, social science, and business.	☐
	14.10: Uses a variety of questioning strategies to encourage mathematical discourse and to help students analyze and evaluate their mathematical thinking.	☐
	14.11: Uses a variety of formal and informal assessments and scoring procedures to evaluate mathematical understanding, common misconceptions, and error patterns.	☐
	14.12: Understands the relationship between assessment and instruction and knows how to evaluate assessment results to design, monitor and modify instruction to improve mathematical learning for all students, including English-language learners.	☐
	14.13: Understands the purpose, characteristics and uses of various assessments in mathematics, including formative and summative assessments.	☐
	14.14: Understands how mathematics is used in a variety of careers and professions and plans instruction that demonstrates how mathematics is used in the workplace.	☐

PERSONALIZED STUDY PLAN

KNOWN MATERIAL/ SKIP IT

PAGE	COMPETENCY AND SKILL	
142	**15: Number concepts and operations**	☐
	15.1: Analyzes, creates, describes, compares and models relationships between number properties, operations and algorithms for the four basic operations involving integers, rational numbers and real numbers, including real-world situations.	☐
	15.2: Demonstrates an understanding of equivalency among different representations of rational numbers and between mathematical expressions.	☐
	15.3: Selects appropriate representations of real numbers *(e.g., fractions, decimals, percents)* for particular situations.	☐
	15.4: Demonstrates an understanding of ideas from number theory *(e.g., prime factorization, greatest common divisor, divisibility rules)* as they apply to whole numbers, integers, and rational numbers, and uses those ideas in problem situations.	☐
	15.5: Understands the relative magnitude of whole numbers, integers, rational numbers, and real numbers including the use of comparative language and sets of objects.	☐
	15.6: Identifies and demonstrates an understanding of and uses of a variety of models and objects for representing numbers *(e.g., fraction strips, diagrams, patterns, shaded regions, number lines)*.	☐
	15.7: Uses a variety of concrete and visual representations to demonstrate the connections between operations and algorithms.	☐
	15.8: Identifies, demonstrates and applies knowledge of counting techniques, including combinations, to quantify situations and solve math problems *(e.g., to include forward, backward and skip counting, with or without models)*.	☐
	15.9: Identifies, represents and applies knowledge of place value *(e.g., to compose and decompose numbers)*, rounding and other number properties to perform mental mathematics and computational estimation with automaticity.	☐
	15.10: Demonstrates a thorough understanding of fractions, including the use of various representations to teach fractions and operations involving fractions.	☐
	15.11: Uses a variety of strategies to generate and solve problems that involve one or more steps, with fluency.	☐
161	**16: Patterns and algebra**	☐
	16.1: Illustrates relations and functions using concrete models, tables, graphs, and symbolic and verbal representations, including real-world applications.	☐
	16.2: Demonstrates an understanding of the concept of linear function using concrete models, tables, graphs, and symbolic and verbal representations.	☐
	16.3: Understands how to use algebraic concepts and reasoning to investigate patterns, make generalizations, formulate mathematical models, make predictions, and validate results.	☐
	16.4: Formulates implicit and explicit rules to describe and construct sequences verbally, numerically, graphically, and symbolically.	☐

PERSONALIZED STUDY PLAN

KNOWN MATERIAL/ SKIP IT

PAGE	COMPETENCY AND SKILL	
	16.5: Knows how to identify, extend, and create patterns using concrete models, figures, numbers, and algebraic expressions.	☐
	16.6: Uses properties, graphs, linear and nonlinear functions, and applications of relations and functions to analyze, model, and solve problems in mathematical and real-world situations.	☐
	16.7: Translates problem-solving situations into expressions and equations involving variables and unknowns.	☐
	16.8: Models and solves problems, including those involving proportional reasoning, using concrete, numeric, tabular, graphic, and algebraic methods (*e.g., using ratios and percents with fractions and decimals*).	☐
	16.9: Determines the linear function that best models a set of data.	☐
	16.10: Understands and describes the concept of and relationships among variables, expressions, equations, inequalities, and systems in order to analyze, model, and solve problems.	☐
	16.11: Applies algebraic methods to demonstrate an understanding of whole numbers using any of the four basic operations.	☐
175	**17: Geometry and measurement**	☐
	17.1: Applies knowledge of spatial concepts such as direction, shape, and structure.	☐
	17.2: Identifies, uses, and understands and models the development of formulas to find lengths, perimeters, areas, and volumes of geometric figures.	☐
	17.3: Uses the properties of congruent triangles to explore geometric relationships.	☐
	17.4: Identifies, uses and understands concepts and properties of points, lines, planes, angles, lengths, and distances.	☐
	17.5: Analyzes and applies the properties of parallel and perpendicular lines.	☐
	17.6: Uses a variety of representations (*e.g., numeric, verbal, graphic, symbolic*) to analyze and solve problems involving angles and two- and three-dimensional figures such as circles, triangles, polygons, cylinders, prisms, and spheres.	☐
	17.7: Uses symmetry to describe tessellations and shows how they can be used to illustrate geometric concepts, properties, and relationships.	☐
	17.8: Understands measurement concepts and principles, including methods of approximation and estimation, and the effects of error on measurement.	☐
	17.9: Explains, illustrates, selects, and uses appropriate units of measurement to quantify and compare time, temperature, money, mass, weight, area, capacity, volume, percent, speed, and degrees of an angle.	☐
	17.10: Uses translations, rotations and reflections to illustrate similarities, congruencies and symmetries of figures.	☐
	17.11: Develops, justifies and uses conversions within and between measurement systems.	☐

PERSONALIZED STUDY PLAN

KNOWN MATERIAL/ SKIP IT

PAGE	COMPETENCY AND SKILL	KNOWN MATERIAL/ SKIP IT
	17.12: Understands logical reasoning, justification, and proof in relation to the axiomatic structure of geometry and uses reasoning to develop, generalize, justify, and prove geometric relationships	☐
	17.13: Understands attributes of various polygons, including names and how sides and angles of the polygon affect its attributes.	☐
	17.14: Partitions or decomposes polygons to express areas as fractions of a whole or to find areas of nonstandard polygons.	☐
	17.15: Demonstrates the value and relationships of United States coins and bills and uses appropriate symbols to name the value of a collection.	☐
	17.16: Identifies, uses and understands the concepts and properties of geometric figures and their relationships.	☐
	17.17: Describes the key attributes of the coordinate plane and models the process of graphing ordered pairs.	☐
197	**18: Probability and statistics**	☐
	18.1: Investigates and answers questions by collecting, organizing and displaying data in a variety of formats as described in the Texas Essential Knowledge and Skills (TEKS) and draws conclusions from any data graph.	☐
	18.2: Demonstrates an understanding of measures of central tendency (e.g., mean, median, mode) and range and uses those measures to describe a set of data.	☐
	18.3: Explores concepts of probability through data collection, experiments, and simulations.	☐
	18.4: Uses the concepts and principles of probability to describe the outcome of simple and compound events.	☐
	18.5: Determines probabilities by constructing sample spaces to model situations.	☐
	18.6: Applies deep knowledge of the use of probability, in different scenarios, to make observations, draw conclusions, and create relationships.	☐
	18.7: Solves a variety of probability problems using combinations and geometric probability (e.g., probability as the ratio of two areas).	☐
	18.8: Supports arguments, makes predictions, and draws conclusions using summary statistics and graphs to analyze and interpret one-variable data.	☐
	18.9: Applies knowledge of designing, conducting, analyzing, and interpreting statistical experiments to investigate real-world problems.	☐
	18.10: Generates, simulates, and uses probability models to represent situations.	☐
	18.11: Uses the graph of the normal distribution as a basis for making inferences about a population.	☐
206	**19: Mathematical processes**	☐
	19.1: Understands the role of logical reasoning in mathematics and uses formal and informal reasoning to explore, investigate, and justify mathematical ideas.	☐

PERSONALIZED STUDY PLAN

KNOWN MATERIAL/ SKIP IT

PAGE	COMPETENCY AND SKILL	KNOWN MATERIAL/ SKIP IT
19.2:	Applies correct mathematical reasoning to derive valid conclusions from a set of premises.	☐
19.3:	Applies principles of inductive reasoning to make conjectures and uses deductive methods to evaluate the validity of conjectures.	☐
19.4:	Evaluates the reasonableness of a solution to a given problem.	☐
19.5:	Understands connections among concepts, procedures and equivalent representations in areas of mathematics *(e.g., algebra, geometry)*.	☐
19.6:	Recognizes that a mathematical problem can be solved in a variety of ways and selects an appropriate strategy for a given problem.	☐
19.7:	Expresses mathematical statements using developmentally appropriate language, standard English, mathematical language and symbolic mathematics.	☐
19.8:	Communicates mathematical ideas using a variety of representations *(e.g., numeric, verbal, graphic, pictorial, symbolic, concrete)*.	☐
19.9:	Demonstrates an understanding of the use of visual media such as graphs, tables, diagrams and animations to communicate mathematical information.	☐
19.10:	Demonstrates an understanding of estimation, including the use of compatible numbers, and evaluates its appropriate uses.	☐
19.11:	Knows how to use mathematical manipulatives and a wide range of appropriate technological tools to develop and explore mathematical concepts and ideas.	☐
19.12:	Demonstrates knowledge of the history and evolution of mathematical concepts, procedures and ideas.	☐
19.13:	Recognizes the contributions that different cultures have made to the field of mathematics and the impact of mathematics on society and cultures.	☐
19.14:	Demonstrates an understanding of financial literacy concepts and their application as these relate to teaching students *(e.g., describes the basic purpose of financial institutions; distinguishes the difference between gross and net income; identifies various savings options; defines different types of taxes; identifies the advantages and disadvantages of different methods of payments, savings and credit uses and responsibilities)*.	☐
19.15:	Applies mathematics to model and solve problems to manage financial resources effectively for lifetime financial security, as it relates to teaching students *(e.g., distinguishes between fixed and variable expenses, calculates profit in a given situation, develops a system for keeping and using financial records, describes actions that might be taken to develop and balance a budget when expenses exceed income)*.	☐

COMPETENCY 14
MATHEMATICS INSTRUCTION

> **SKILL 14.1** Plans appropriate instructional activities for all students by applying research-based theories and principles of learning mathematics.

Teachers can use theories of learning to plan curriculum and instructional activities. Research indicates that students learn math more easily in an applied, project-based setting.

Many educators believe that the best method of teaching math is situated learning. Proponents of situated learning argue that learning is largely a function of the activity, context, and environment in which it occurs. According to situated learning theory, students learn more easily from instruction involving relevant, real-world situations and applications than abstract concepts. Research or project-based learning is a product of situated learning theory. Open-ended research tasks and projects promote learning by engaging students on multiple levels. Such tasks require the use of multiple skills and reasoning strategies and help keep students focused and attentive. Projects also promote active learning by encouraging the sharing of ideas and teacher-student and student-student interaction.

Another popular theory of math learning is constructivism. Constructivism argues that prior knowledge greatly influences the learning of math and that learning is cumulative and vertically structured. Thus, it is important for teachers to be aware of the knowledge and ideas that students already have about a subject. Instruction must build on students' innate knowledge and address any common misconceptions they may have. Teachers can gain insight into students' prior knowledge by beginning each lesson with open questions that allow students to share their thoughts and ideas on the subject.

SKILL
14.2 **Employs instructional strategies that build on the linguistic, cultural, and socioeconomic diversity of students and that relate to students' lives and communities.**

Instructional Strategies Building on Diversity

The cultural and ethnic background of a student greatly affects his or her approach to learning mathematics. In addition, factors such as socioeconomic status can affect student learning styles.

Students of certain ethnic and racial groups that emphasize expressiveness and communication may benefit from an interactive learning environment. Conversely, students of ethnic groups that emphasize personal learning and discipline may benefit from a more structured, traditional learning environment. As is always the case when considering ethnic differences, however, one must be careful to avoid making inappropriate generalizations.

Low-income students may not have had the same early educational background and exposure to traditional educational reasoning strategies and techniques that other students have. Thus, they may initially require a more application-based curriculum until they develop sufficient abstract reasoning skills.

SKILL
14.3 **Plans and provides developmentally appropriate instruction that establishes transitions between concrete, symbolic, and abstract representations of mathematical knowledge and that builds on students' strengths and addresses their needs.**

Sequence of Instruction

When introducing a new mathematical concept to students, teachers should utilize the concrete-to-representational-to-abstract sequence of instruction. The first step of the progression is the introduction of a concept modeled with concrete materials. The second step is the translation of concrete models into representational diagrams or pictures. The third and final step is the translation of representational models into abstract models using only numbers and symbols.

Teachers should first use concrete models to introduce a mathematical concept because they are the easiest to understand. For example, teachers can allow students to use counting blocks to learn basic arithmetic. Teachers should give students ample time and many opportunities to experiment, practice, and demonstrate mastery with the concrete materials.

The second step in the learning process is the translation of concrete materials to representational models. For example, students can use tally marks or pictures to represent the counting blocks they used in the previous stage. Once again, teachers should give students ample time to master the concept on the representational level.

The final step in the learning process is the translation of representational models into abstract numbers and symbols. For example, students represent the processes carried out in the previous stages using only numbers and arithmetic symbols. To ease the transition, teachers should associate numbers and symbols with the concrete and representational models throughout the learning progression.

SKILL 14.4 **Understands how manipulatives and technological tools can be used appropriately to assist students in developing, comprehending, and applying mathematical concepts.**

Manipulatives and Other Tools

The use of supplementary materials in the classroom can greatly enhance the learning experience by stimulating student interest and satisfying different learning styles. Manipulatives, models, and technology are examples of tools available to teachers.

MANIPULATIVES are materials that students can physically handle and move. They allow students to understand mathematical concepts by allowing them to see concrete examples of abstract processes. MODELS are means of representing mathematical concepts by relating the concepts to real-world situations.

Other tools are available to help students learn math:

- **Counters:** Counters can be used to help students understand number sense, from basic counting to algebra.

- **Rulers:** Rulers help students learn about measurement, the length of an object, or distance. Rulers teach students about fractions, the relationships among the standard units (inch, foot, yard, mile) and between the standard units and metric units (millimeters, centimeters, meters, kilometers). Understanding measurement is critical to understanding perimeter, circumference, and area in geometry.

- **Measuring containers:** Measuring containers teach students about fractions and the relationships among the standard units (pint, quart, gallon) and between the standard units and metric units (milliliter, liter). Students also learn about the volume of available space in different-size containers.

- **Protractors:** Protractors teach students about angles. Protractors measure the opening of an angle. Students will be able to understand some properties of triangles and polygons by knowing the angle measurements.

> **MANIPULATIVES:** materials that students can physically handle and move

> **MODELS:** means of representing mathematical concepts by relating the concepts to real-world situations

- **Scales:** Scales teach students about fractions and the relationships among the standard units (pounds and ounces) and between the standard units and metric units (grams and kilograms).

- **Money:** Students are exposed to money at an early age. Students must understand the value associated with each denomination. Students learn the basic concepts of money management and personal finances using their addition and subtraction skills.

- **Software:** Math programs can enhance the teaching and learning of mathematical concepts. Programs such as tutorials can be individualized so each student has a course tailored to his or her specific needs. Students can strengthen mathematical understanding by playing games that require them to use their math skills to advance.

> **SKILL 14.5** Creates a learning environment that motivates all students and actively engages them in the learning process by using a variety of interesting, challenging, and worthwhile mathematical tasks in individual, small-group, and large-group settings.

Methods of Instruction

Successful teachers select and implement instructional delivery methods that best fit the needs of a particular classroom format. Individual, small-group, and large-group classroom formats require different techniques and methods of instruction.

Individual instruction allows the teacher to interact closely with the student.

Small-group instruction requires the teacher to provide instruction to multiple students at the same time. Because the group is small, instructional methods that encourage student interaction and cooperative learning are particularly effective. For example, group projects, discussion, and question-and-answer sessions promote cooperative learning and maintain student interest. In addition, working problems as a group or in pairs can help students learn problem-solving strategies from each other.

Lecture is a common instructional method for teaching large groups. In addition, demonstrating methods of problem solving and allowing students to ask questions about homework and test problems is an effective strategy for teaching large groups.

It is important to be aware that not all students learn the same way and, therefore, alternative instructional strategies may be appropriate.

Alternative methodologies include the use of:

- Simulations
- Toolkits
- Multimedia
- Storytelling structures

- Strategy and role-playing games
- Peer tutoring
- Learning by design
- Group, cooperative, and collaborative learning

- Coaching and scaffolding
- Case studies
- Encouraging mathematical discourse

SKILL 14.6 **Uses a variety of tools** *(e.g., counters, standard and nonstandard units of measure, rulers, protractors, scales, stopwatches, measuring containers, money, calculators, software)* **to strengthen students' mathematical understanding.**

See Skill 14.4

SKILL 14.7 **Implements a variety of instructional methods and tasks that promote students' ability to do the mathematics described in the Texas Essential Knowledge and Skills (TEKS).**

See Skills 14.4 and 14.5

SKILL 14.8 **Develops clear learning goals to plan, deliver, assess, and reevaluate instruction based on the mathematics in the Texas Essential Knowledge and Skills (TEKS).**

Assessment

State standardized testing is an important tool for curriculum design and modification. Most states have stated curriculum standards that mandate what students should know. Teachers can use the standards to focus their instruction and curriculum planning.

When an assessment does not provide the expected results, the teacher must reflect on the method of instruction and make modifications so the students learn the material. To avoid this, the teacher may want to incorporate informal assessments into the instruction to check students' understanding along the way

Teachers should use a variety of assessment procedures. In addition to the traditional methods of performance assessment like multiple-choice, true/false, and matching tests, many other methods are available to teachers.

Types of assessment

An alternative assessment is any type of assessment in which students create a response rather than choose an answer. This type of assessment is sometimes called formative assessment, due to the emphasis on feedback and the flow of communication between teacher and student. It is the opposite of summative assessment, which occurs periodically and consists of temporary interaction between teacher and student.

Alternative assessment includes:

- Short-response and essay questions

- Student portfolios

- Projects, demonstrations, and oral presentations

One type of alternative assessment is bundled testing, the grouping of different question formats for the same skill or competency. For example, a bundled test of exponential functions may include multiple-choice questions, short-response questions, word problems, and essay questions. The variety of questions tests different levels of reasoning and expression.

Scoring methods

Scoring methods are an important, and often overlooked, part of effective assessment. Teachers can use a simple three-point scale for evaluating student responses. No answer or an inappropriate answer that shows no understanding scores zero points. A partial response showing a lack of understanding, a lack of explanation, or major computational errors scores one point. A somewhat satisfactory answer that answers most of the question correctly but contains simple computational errors or minor flaws in reasoning receives two points. Finally, a satisfactory response displaying full understanding, adequate explanation, and appropriate reasoning receives three points.

> When evaluating student responses, teachers should look for common error patterns and mistakes in computation. Teachers should also incorporate questions and scoring procedures that address common error patterns and misconceptions into their methods of assessment.

Assessment for English-language learners

Mathematic assessments may understate the abilities of English-language learners because poor test scores may stem from difficulty in reading comprehension, not a lack of understanding of mathematic principles. Uncharacteristically poor performance on word problems by English-language learners is a sign that reading comprehension, not mathematic understanding, is the underlying problem.

SKILL
14.9 **Helps students make connections between mathematics and the real world, as well as between mathematics and other disciplines such as art, music, science, social science, and business.**

Math in the Workplace

Teachers can increase students' interest in math by relating mathematical concepts to familiar events in their lives and using real-world examples and data whenever possible. Relating math to various careers and professions shows students why math is relevant and helps them in the career exploration process.

Online Resources

The online resources connect math to the real world.

Using weather concepts to teach math: *http://www.nssl.noaa.gov/education/educators/*

Election math in the classroom: *http://mathforum.org/t2t/faq/election.html*

Math worksheets related to the Iditarod, an annual Alaskan sled dog race: *http://www.educationworld.com/a_lesson/01-1/lp225_01.shtml*

Graphing with real data: *http://www.middleweb.com/2469/creative-graphing-ideas/*

The use of math in various disciplines

Artists, musicians, scientists, social scientists, and business people use mathematical modeling to solve problems in their disciplines. Mathematics is a key aspect of visual art. Artists use the geometric properties of shapes, ratios, and proportions in creating paintings and sculptures. For example, mathematics is essential to the concept of perspective. Artists must determine the appropriate lengths and heights of objects to portray three-dimensional distance in two dimensions.

The uses of mathematics in science are endless. Physical scientists use vectors, functions, derivatives, and integrals to describe and model the movement of objects. Biologists and ecologists use mathematics to model ecosystems and study DNA. Chemists use mathematics to study the interaction of molecules and to determine proper amounts and proportions of reactants.

Many social science disciplines use mathematics to model and solve problems. Economists, for example, use functions, graphs, and matrices to model the activities of producers, consumers, and firms. Political scientists use mathematics to model the behavior and opinions of the electorate. Sociologists use mathematical functions to model the behavior of humans and human populations.

Mathematical problem solving and modeling is also essential to business planning and execution. For example, businesses rely on mathematical projections to plan business strategy. Stock market analysis and accounting also rely on mathematical concepts.

Examples in the classroom

Teachers can be creative in showing how math is used in different professions. Here are just a few examples:

- Learning about math in different professions can begin as early as kindergarten. When teaching the basics of addition and subtraction, teachers can set up a "bank" in the classroom.

- Math is used in the construction industry. Teachers can set up their classrooms as work zones. Students can use measurement and shapes in constructing or designing a building or playground.

- A lesson about tessellations include students designing a floor or wallpaper.

- A lesson on fractions can lead to discussions of how they are used in cooking and baking.

SKILL 14.10 **Uses a variety of questioning strategies to encourage mathematical discourse and to help students analyze and evaluate their mathematical thinking.**

The **questioning technique** is a mathematic process skill in which students devise questions to clarify the problem, eliminate possible solutions, and simplify the problem-solving process. By developing and attempting to answer simple questions, students can tackle difficult and complex problems.

Sometimes, the teacher can guide the discourse by asking questions to generate discussion. Other times, the students can be encouraged to generate their own discussions, sharing their questions and thoughts among themselves. A third type of discourse takes place in small groups when the students work both independently and collaboratively.

Teachers can ask the following types of questions to encourage higher-order thinking:

- Questions that require manipulation of prior knowledge

- Questions that require students to state ideas or definitions in their own words

- Questions that require students to solve a problem

- Questions that require observation and/or description of an object or event

- Questions that call for comparison and contrast

It is also recommended that teachers give a student enough time to attempt to answer a question before calling on another student. When a student is having trouble responding to a question, a teacher should ask probing questions; for example:

- Asking for clarification

- Rephrasing the question

- Asking related questions

- Restating the student's ideas (Ornstein, 1995)

SKILL 14.11 Uses a variety of formal and informal assessments and scoring procedures to evaluate mathematical understanding, common misconceptions, and error patterns.

See Skill 14.8

SKILL 14.12 Understands the relationship between assessment and instruction and knows how to evaluate assessment results to design, monitor and modify instruction to improve mathematical learning for all students, including English-language learners.

See Skill 14.8

SKILL 14.13 Understands the purpose, characteristics and uses of various assessments in mathematics, including formative and summative assessments.

See Skill 14.8

SKILL 14.14 Understands how mathematics is used in a variety of careers and professions and plans instruction that demonstrates how mathematics is used in the workplace.

See Skill 14.9

COMPETENCY 15
NUMBER CONCEPTS AND OPERATIONS

> **SKILL 15.1** Analyzes, creates, describes, compares and models relationships between number properties, operations and algorithms for the four basic operations involving integers, rational numbers and real numbers, including real-world situations.

WHOLE NUMBER: one of the counting numbers

INTEGER: a positive or negative number

RATIONAL NUMBER: the quotient $\frac{a}{b}$ of two integers, where $b \neq 0$

REAL NUMBER: a member of the set of all numbers, rational and irrational

IRRATIONAL NUMBER: any real number that cannot be expressed as the quotient $\frac{a}{b}$ of two integers, where $b \neq 0$

PRIME NUMBER: a number with exactly two factors, itself and one

COMPOSITE: a number with more than two factors

Whole Numbers, Integers, Rational Numbers, and Real Numbers

A WHOLE NUMBER is one of the counting numbers. There are only ten of them:

0, 1, 2, 3, 4, 5, 6, 7, 8, 9

An INTEGER is a positive or negative number.

An odd number is an integer that is not a multiple of two, e.g., –5, –17, 7, 111.

An even number is an integer that is a multiple of two, e.g., –24, –2, 36, 2004.

A RATIONAL NUMBER is the quotient $\frac{a}{b}$ of two integers, where $b \neq 0$. Since an integer can be written as a fraction with a denominator of 1, integers are included in the set of rational numbers. The set of rational numbers is also infinite. Rational numbers include all of the whole numbers, integers, and fractions whose decimal equivalents terminate.

A REAL NUMBER is a member of the set of all numbers, rational and irrational. The set of real numbers is also infinite. An IRRATIONAL NUMBER is any real number that cannot be expressed as the quotient $\frac{a}{b}$ of two integers, where $b \neq 0$.

A PRIME NUMBER has exactly *two* factors, itself and one. A COMPOSITE number has more than two factors. Zero and 1 are *neither* prime nor composite.

Rational- and Real-Number Algorithms

ALGORITHMS are methods or strategies for solving problems. In general, algorithms make use of number properties to simplify mathematical operations.

ALGORITHMS: methods or strategies for solving problems

Addition

The partial sums method of integer addition relies on the associative property of addition. Consider the partial sum algorithm of the addition of 125 and 89. We first sum the columns from left to right and then add the results.

$$
\begin{array}{r}
125 \\
+ \ \ 89 \\
\hline
100 \quad \text{Hundreds column sum} \\
+ \ 100 \quad \text{Tens column sum} \\
+ \ \ \ 14 \quad \text{Ones column sum} \\
\hline
214
\end{array}
$$

The associative property of addition shows why this method works. We can rewrite 125 plus 89 as follows:

$(100 + 20 + 5) + (80 + 9)$

Using the associative property to group the terms:

$(100) + (20 + 80) + (5 + 9) = 100 + 100 + 14 = 214$

Rational number addition relies on the distributive property of multiplication over addition and the understanding that multiplication of any number by one yields the same number. Consider the addition of $\frac{1}{4}$ to $\frac{1}{3}$ by means of common denominator.

$\frac{1}{4} + \frac{1}{3} = \frac{3}{3}(\frac{1}{4}) + \frac{4}{4}(\frac{1}{3}) = (\frac{3}{12}) + (\frac{4}{12}) = \frac{7}{12} \rightarrow$ Recognize that $\frac{3}{3}$ and $\frac{4}{4}$ both equal 1.

A common error in rational number addition is the failure to find a common denominator and adding both numerators and denominators.

Subtraction

The same-change rule of substitution takes advantage of the property of addition of zero. The addition of zero does not change the value of a quantity.

$289 - 97 = 292 - 100$ because

$289 - 97 = (289 + 3) - (97 + 3) = (289 - 97) + (3 - 3)$

$= 289 - 97 + 0$

Note the use of the distributive property of multiplication over addition, the associative property of addition, and the property of addition of zero in proving the accuracy of the same-change algorithm. A common mistake when using the same-change rule is adding from one number and subtracting from the other. This is an error in reasoning resulting from misapplication of the distributive property (e.g., failing to distribute –1).

A common error in rational number addition is the failure to find a common denominator and adding both numerators and denominators.

Multiplication

The partial products algorithm of multiplication decomposes each term into simpler numbers and sums the products of the simpler terms.

$$84 = 80 + 4$$
$$\times\ 26 = 20 + 6$$

$$
\begin{array}{rcl}
80 \times 20 & \rightarrow & 1600 \\
80 \times 6 & \rightarrow & 480 \\
20 \times 4 & \rightarrow & 80 \\
6 \times 4 & \rightarrow & \underline{24} \\
& & 2184
\end{array}
$$

We can justify this algorithm by using the **foil method** of binomial multiplication and the distributive property of multiplication over addition.

$$(80 + 4)(20 + 6) = (80)(20) + (4)(20) + (6)(80) + (6)(4)$$

Common errors in partial product multiplication result from mistakes in binomial multiplication and mistakes in pairing terms of the partial products (e.g., multiplying incorrect terms).

Division

We can justify the partial quotients algorithm for division by using the distributive property of multiplication over division. Because multiplication is the reverse of division, we can check the result by multiplying the divisor by the partial sums.

$$
\begin{array}{r}
18\overline{)1440}\ | \\
-\ \underline{900}\ |\ 50 \\
540\ | \\
-\ \underline{360}\ |\ 20 \\
180\ | \\
-\ \underline{90}\ |\ 5 \\
90\ | \\
-\ \underline{90}\ |\ \underline{5} \\
0 \quad 80 \rightarrow \text{final quotient} = 80 \text{ with no remainder}
\end{array}
$$

Check:

$$18\,(50 + 20 + 5 + 5) = (18)(50) + (18)(20) + (18)(5) + (18)(5) = 1440$$

Common errors in division often result from mistakes in translating words to symbols, for example, misinterpreting 10 divided by 5 as $\frac{5}{10}$. In addition, when using the partial quotients algorithm, errors in subtraction and addition can produce incorrect results.

Example: Jack invited 6 friends to a party and gave each friend 2 cookies. Jack kept 4 cookies for himself. How many cookies were there before the party?

This is solved in two steps. First, decide how many cookies were eaten by multiplying $6 \times 2 = 12$.

In the next step, add the cookies that were eaten to the cookies Jack kept: $12 + 4 = 16$.

There were 16 cookies before the party.

SKILL 15.2 Demonstrates an understanding of equivalency among different representations of rational numbers and between mathematical expressions.

Different Representations of Rational Numbers

Rational numbers can be written using several different representations, including fractions, decimals, percents, and exponents.

In order to express a fraction as a decimal or percentage, convert it into an equivalent fraction with a denominator that is a power of 10 (for example, 10, 100, or 1000).

Example: $\frac{1}{10} = 0.10 = 10\%$

Alternatively, a fraction can be converted into a decimal by dividing the numerator by the denominator.

Example: $\frac{3}{8} = 8\overline{)3.000} = 37.5\%$ with quotient 0.375

A decimal can be converted to a percentage by multiplying by 100, or merely moving the decimal point two places to the right, as shown in the examples above.

A percentage can be converted to a decimal by dividing by 100, or moving the decimal point two places to the left.

A percentage can be converted to a fraction by placing it over 100 and reducing to simplest terms.

The exponent form is a shortcut way of writing repeated multiplication. The base is the factor. The EXPONENT tells how many times that number is multiplied by itself.

> **EXPONENT:** a number that tells how many times the base is multiplied by itself

Example: $3^4 = 3 \times 3 \times 3 \times 3 = 81$

where 3 is the base and 4 is the exponent.

When 10 is raised to any power, the exponent indicates the number of zeroes in the product.

Example: $10^7 = 10,000,000$

A mathematical expression can take on numerous equivalent forms. For instance, some expressions can be in various stages of simplification.

Example

A number property can change the way an expression looks without changing its value. For instance:

$-3x + 7 = 7 - 3x$ by reason of the commutative property of addition.

$5x^2(2x - 3) = 10x^3 - 15x^2$ by applying the distributive property.

Example

The following expressions are equivalent.

$$4x^2 - 2x - 3x^2 - x - 28 = x^2 - 3x - 28 = (x - 7)(x + 4)$$

Any changes are due to simplifying (by collecting like terms) or rewriting (by changing to factored form).

SKILL 15.3 **Selects appropriate representations of real numbers** *(e.g., fractions, decimals, percents)* **for particular situations.**

Real numbers can be represented in a variety of formats. Some of these formats are more amenable to certain problems than others, and it is important to be able to select the proper representation of a real number for a given situation.

For instance, if exact calculations are required, decimal representations (or percent representations, which are the decimal representation multiplied by 100) of irrational numbers are not appropriate. The use of a decimal requires use of a finite representation; thus, the decimal form of an irrational number must be rounded to some digit, leading to inaccuracies in calculations. Thus, irrational numbers such as π and square roots of certain integers should usually be left in their symbolic or square root forms. If inexact calculations are acceptable, then a decimal or approximate fractional representation may be suitable.

If the decimal is repeating (such as 0.1111111...), a fractional representation may be the best approach. A fraction can be manipulated easily, and it is sometimes more conducive to exact calculations than are repeating decimals (or even long, nonrepeating decimals in some cases).

In other cases, such as when calculating with very large or very small numbers, an exponential form such as scientific notation is useful. Exponentials (or their inverses, logarithms) may also be a preferred representation for graphing a set of numbers that spans a wide range.

The simplicity of the calculation is also important when selecting an appropriate representation of a number. For hand/mental calculations, for instance, simplicity may be paramount.

SKILL 15.4 Demonstrates an understanding of ideas from number theory *(e.g., prime factorization, greatest common divisor, divisibility rules)* **as they apply to whole numbers, integers, and rational numbers, and uses those ideas in problem situations.**

Divisibility Rules

- Rule 1: A number is **divisible by 2** if it is an even number (which means the last digit is 0, 2, 4, 6, or 8).

- Rule 2: A number is **divisible by 3** if the sum of its digits is evenly divisible by 3.

- Rule 3: A number is **divisible by 4** if the last two digits of the number are evenly divisible by 4.

Number Properties

The three basic number properties are distributive, commutative, and associative. These number properties are the rules of number operations.

1. **Distributive property of multiplication over addition:** $x(y + z) = xy + xz$.

2. **Commutative property of multiplication and addition:** The order of numbers does not matter. In other words, $a + b = b + a$ and $ab = ba$.

3. **Associative property of addition and multiplication:** The grouping of numbers does not matter. In other words, $(a + b) + c = a + (b + c)$ and $a(bc) = (ab)c$.

> **SKILL 15.5** Understands the relative magnitude of whole numbers, integers, rational numbers, and real numbers including the use of comparative language and sets of objects.

For the definitions of whole numbers, integers, rational numbers, and real numbers, see Skill 15.1.

Every point on a number line is a real number.

Often, sets of numbers are analyzed to determine order from largest to smallest. Comparing integers can be demonstrated on a number line. Moving to the left, numbers get smaller, even as the magnitude grows. For example, $-6 < -2$. Moving to the right, numbers get larger.

$$\leftarrow\ \overset{}{\underset{-7}{|}}\ \overset{}{\underset{-6}{|}}\ \overset{}{\underset{-5}{|}}\ \overset{}{\underset{-4}{|}}\ \overset{}{\underset{-3}{|}}\ \overset{}{\underset{-2}{|}}\ \overset{}{\underset{-1}{|}}\ \overset{}{\underset{0}{|}}\ \overset{}{\underset{1}{|}}\ \overset{}{\underset{2}{|}}\ \overset{}{\underset{3}{|}}\ \overset{}{\underset{4}{|}}\ \overset{}{\underset{5}{|}}\ \overset{}{\underset{6}{|}}\ \overset{}{\underset{7}{|}}\ \overset{}{\underset{8}{|}}\ \rightarrow$$

When comparing the magnitudes of decimals and whole numbers, look at the place value. 2,304 is larger than 2,034 because in the hundreds place, 3 is larger than 0.

Example: Order the following numbers from least to greatest: 2.14, 2.07, 2.1, 2.01

All have 2 in the ones places. 2.14 and 2.1 have the same tenths digit, but 4 is greater than 0. 2.14 is the largest, then 2.1, then 2.07, because the hundredths digit of 7 is greater than the 1 in 2.01.

The ordered list is: 2.14, 2.1, 2.07, 2.01

When comparing fractions to determine order, it's helpful to find a common denominator.

Example: Compare the pair of fractions using $<$, $>$, or $=$.
$$5\tfrac{1}{2} \underline{\hspace{1cm}} \tfrac{11}{12}$$

Make $5\tfrac{1}{2}$ into an improper fraction.
$$\tfrac{11}{2} \underline{\hspace{1cm}} \tfrac{11}{12}$$

The common denominator is 12, so multiply $\tfrac{11}{2}$ by 6.
$$\tfrac{66}{12} > \tfrac{11}{12}$$

Identifies and demonstrates an understanding of and uses of a variety of models and objects for representing numbers (e.g., *fraction strips, diagrams, patterns, shaded regions, number lines*).

Different Representations of Real Numbers

Real numbers can be represented in a variety of formats. Some of these formats are more amenable to certain situations than others, and it is important to be able to select the proper representation of a real number for a given situation.

For instance, if exact calculations are required, decimal representations (or percent representations, which are simply the decimal representation multiplied by 100) of irrational numbers are not appropriate. The use of a decimal necessarily requires use of a finite representation; thus, the decimal form of an irrational number must be rounded to some digit, leading to inaccuracies in calculations. In other cases, such as when calculating with very large or very small numbers, an exponential form such as scientific notation is useful.

The Fundamental Theorem of Arithmetic

Any integer $n > 1$ that is divisible by at least one positive integer that is not equal to one or n is called a composite number. A natural number n that is only divisible by one and n is called a prime number.

According to the fundamental theorem of arithmetic, every integer greater than 1 can be written uniquely in the form:

$$p_1^{e_1} p_2^{e_2} \cdots p_k^{e_k}$$

where the p_i are distinct prime numbers and the e_i are positive integers.

Greatest Common Factor

GCF is the abbreviation for the GREATEST COMMON FACTOR. The GCF is the largest number that is a factor of all of the numbers given in a problem. The GCF can be no larger than the smallest number given in the problem. If no other number is a common factor, then the GCF is the number 1. To find the GCF, list all possible factors of the smallest number given (include the number itself). Starting with the largest factor (which is the number itself), determine whether it is also a factor of all of the other given numbers. If so, that is the GCF. If that factor does not work, try the same method on the next smallest factor. Continue until a common factor is found. This is the GCF.

> **GREATEST COMMON FACTOR:** the largest number that is a factor of all of the numbers given in a problem

> **Note:** There can be other common factors besides the GCF.

Example: Find the GCF of 12, 20, and 36.

The smallest number in the problem is 12. The factors of 12 are 1, 2, 3, 4, 6, and 12. Twelve is the largest factor, but it does not divide evenly into 20. Neither does 6, but 4 will divide into both 20 and 36 evenly. Therefore, 4 is the GCF.

Least Common Multiple

LEAST COMMON MULTIPLE: the smallest number that all of the given numbers will divide into

LCM is the abbreviation for LEAST COMMON MULTIPLE. The least common multiple of a group of numbers is the smallest number that all of the given numbers will divide into. The least common multiple is always the largest of the given numbers or a multiple of the largest number.

Example: Find the LCM of 20, 30, and 40.

The largest number given is 40, but 30 will not divide evenly into 40. The next multiple of 40 is 80 (2 × 40), but 30 will not divide evenly into 80 either. The next multiple of 40 is 120. 120 is divisible by both 20 and 30, so 120 is the LCM (least common multiple).

Visual Representations of Numbers and Algorithms

Numbers need not be represented exclusively as standard Arabic numerals. They can be represented by:

- Shaded regions (to represent either a whole number or a fraction)
- Fraction strips
- Number lines
- Diagrams (one type of diagram involves a particular number of objects of the same type to represent a number)

Concrete and visual representations can help demonstrate the logic behind operational algorithms.

Concrete examples are real-world applications of mathematical concepts. For example, measuring the shadow produced by a tree or building is a real-world application of trigonometric functions; acceleration or velocity of a car is an application of derivatives; and finding the volume or area of a swimming pool is a real-world application of geometric principles.

Blocks or other objects modeled on the base-ten system are useful concrete tools. Base-ten blocks represent ones, tens, and hundreds.

Tiles, blocks, or other countable manipulatives such as beans can also be used to demonstrate numbers in base ten or in other bases. Each stack represents a place, with the number of blocks in the stack showing the place value.

Tiles, pattern blocks, or geoboards can be used to demonstrate geometry algorithms for the calculation of quantities such as area and perimeter.

Stacks of blocks representing numbers are useful for teaching basic statistics concepts such as mean, median, and mode. Rearranging the blocks to make each stack the same height demonstrates the mean or average value of the data set.

Percentage calculations can be visualized using two parallel number lines, one showing the actual numbers, the other showing percentages.

Multiplication can be shown using arrays. For instance, 3×4 can be expressed as 3 rows of 4 each.

□ □ □ □
□ □ □ □
□ □ □ □

Fractions can be represented using pattern blocks, fraction bars, or paper folding.

Diagrams of arithmetic operations can present mathematical data in visual form. For example, a number line can be used to add and subtract, as illustrated below.

This number line represents five added to negative four on the number line, or $-4 + 5 = 1$.

SKILL 15.7 Uses a variety of concrete and visual representations to demonstrate the connections between operations and algorithms.

See also Skill 15.6

Concrete and visual representations can help demonstrate the logic behind operational algorithms. Some examples are given below.

Addition and subtraction of integers can be taught with counters that have different colors on each side. In the example below, the shaded circle represents a red counter, or a negative number. The open circle represents a yellow counter, or a positive number. When a red counter and a yellow counter are added, they cancel to zero.

Example: Use counters to represent the problem −8 + 3.

Since three pairs of counters cancel to zero, there are 5 negative counters left. So, −8 + 3 = -5.

Blocks or other objects modeled on the base-ten system are useful concrete tools. Base-ten blocks represent ones, tens, and hundreds. Modeling the partial sums algorithm with base-ten blocks, for example, helps clarify it.

Consider the sum of 242 and 193: Represent 242 with two one hundred blocks, four ten blocks, and 2 one blocks. Represent 193 with 1 one hundred block, nine ten blocks, and three one blocks. In the partial sums algorithm, manipulate each place value separately and add the results. Thus, we group the hundred blocks, ten blocks, and one blocks and derive a total for each place value. We combine the place values to complete the sum.

Tiles, blocks, or other countable manipulatives such as beans can also be used to demonstrate numbers in base ten or in other bases. Each stack represents a place, with the number of blocks in the stack showing the place value.

An example of a visual representation of an operational algorithm is modeling a two-term multiplication problem as the area of a rectangle. For example, consider the product of 24 and 39: We can represent the product in geometric form. Note that the four sections of the rectangle equate to the four products of the partial products method.

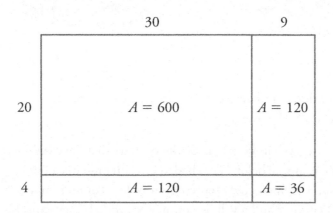

The final product is the sum of the areas, or 600 + 180 + 120 + 36 = 936.

The main algorithm of rational number division is multiplication by the reciprocal. Thus,

$$\frac{\frac{1}{3}}{\frac{1}{4}} = \left(\frac{1}{3}\right)\left(\frac{4}{1}\right) = \frac{4}{3}$$

The definition of multiplication and division as inverse operations justifies the use of reciprocal multiplication.

Tiles, pattern blocks, or geoboards can be used to demonstrate geometry algorithms for the calculation of quantities such as area and perimeter. In the example shown below, twelve tiles are used to form different rectangles.

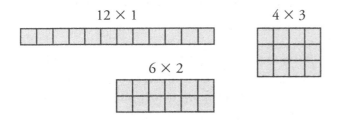

Stacks of blocks representing numbers are useful for teaching basic statistics concepts such as mean, median, and mode. Rearranging the blocks to make each stack the same height would demonstrate the mean, or average, value of the data set. The example below shows a data set represented by stacks of blocks. Rearranging the blocks to make the height of each stack equal to 3 shows that 3 is the mean value.

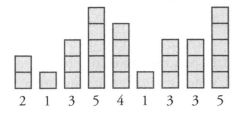

Percentage calculations can be visualized using two parallel number lines, one showing the actual numbers and the other showing percentages.

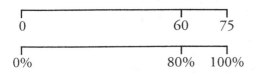

A practical demonstration of percent changes can be made by photocopying a figure using different copier magnifications.

Algeblocks are blocks designed specifically for teaching algebra with manipulatives: *http://www.etacuisenaire.com/algeblocks/algeblocks.jsp*

Identifies, demonstrates and applies knowledge of counting techniques, including combinations, to quantify situations and solve math problems *(e.g., to include forward, backward and skip counting, with or without models).*

Counting Techniques

When experiencing math at an early age, students should learn how numbers represent quantity. Specifically, they must develop an understanding of one-to-one correspondence and be able to link a single number name with one object at a time. For example, a child counts four blocks in a row and says the number as each block is touched. Getting a carton of milk for each of the other children at a table is another example of practicing this concept.

Additionally, children must see that numbers form a counting pattern. A good way to show this is with a number line. The number line can also give students a tactile opportunity to practice the skill of counting on, which mimics addition.

Suppose we want to count 3 on to 6, or show 6 + 3 on a number line.

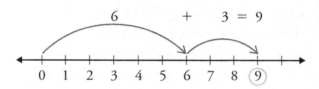

We can think of addition as starting from 0 and counting 6 units to the right on the line in the positive direction and then counting 3 more units to the right. The number line shows that this activity is the same as counting 9 units to the right. The number line can also help students master the patterns of counting backward and skip counting (counting by 2s, by 5s, etc.), which are important foundations for efficiency of counting and for grouping sets of numbers.

As with other subjects, it is important to provide explicit instruction for students about the relationship between the oral numbers and their written form. Typically, this instruction begins by showing students examples of numbers in their written format. Then, provide students with direct instruction in the mechanical formation of the numbers.

As counting skills grow and develop, they can increase in complexity, as seen in the following scenarios.

Counting sequences of numbers

It is easy enough to count a list of numbers that starts with one and increases in increments of one (e.g., 1, 2, 3, ... 18), but how about a list such as 12, 13,

14, … 34 or 4, 8, 12, … 68? How can one determine how many numbers there are in each of those lists without actually counting each one of them?

In the first case, try subtracting 11 from each number in the list:

$$12 - 11, 13 - 11, 14 - 11, … 34 - 11$$

This leads to the list 1, 2, 3, … 23 and it is clear that the number of terms in that list is 23.

In general, for a list of numbers that goes from x to y, subtract $x - 1$ from each number. Thus, the total number of items in the list is $y - (x - 1) = y - x + 1$.

In the second case, try dividing each number in the list by 4. Thus 4, 8, 12, … 68 becomes 1, 2, 3, …17 and it is obvious that there are seventeen numbers in that list.

Counting overlapping lists

The classic method for solving problems with overlapping lists is using Venn diagrams that make it easy to visualize the overlapping and nonoverlapping parts.

The classic method for solving problems with overlapping lists is using Venn diagrams that make it easy to visualize the overlapping and nonoverlapping parts.

Example: The 65 fifth graders in a school all play the flute or the violin. Thirty-five of them play the flute, and 10 of those students also play the violin. How many students play the violin?

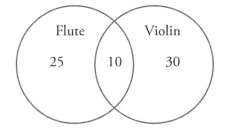

It is clear from the diagram that 25 students play only flute, 10 play both flute and violin, and the remaining 30 play only violin. Thus, 40 students play violin.

Counting multiple independent events

A familiar type of counting problem is one in which the total number of possibilities of combining independent events is counted.

Example: Emma has 7 skirts, 5 tops, and 12 scarves. How many different outfits can she create using combinations of one skirt, one top, and one scarf?
Emma can select a skirt in 7 ways, a top in 5 ways, and a scarf in 12 ways.

Hence, the total number of possible combinations is the product of the possible choices in each category: $7 \times 5 \times 12 = 420$.

Permutations and combinations

A **PERMUTATION** is one of a number of possible selections of items, without repetition, where order of selection is important.

A **COMBINATION** is one of a number of possible selections, without repetition, where order of selection is not important.

> PERMUTATION: one of a number of possible selections of items, without repetition, where order of selection is important

> COMBINATION: one of a number of possible selections, without repetition, where order of selection is not important

Example: If any two numbers are selected from the set {1, 2, 3, 4}, list the possible permutations and combinations.

Combinations

12, 13, 14, 23, 24, 34

(six combinations)

Permutations

12, 21, 13, 31, 14, 41,
23, 32, 24, 42, 34, 43,

(twelve permutations)

The formula for $_nP_r$, the number of possible permutations of r objects selected from n objects, is:

$$_nP_r = n(n-1)(n-2) \dots (n-r+1) = \frac{n!}{(n-r)!}$$

The formula for the number of possible combinations of r objects selected from n, $_nC_r$, is:

$$_nC_r = \frac{_nP_r}{r!} = \frac{n!}{(n-r)!r!}$$

The number of permutations of n objects in a ring is given by $(n-1)!$.

> **SKILL 15.9** Identifies, represents and applies knowledge of place value *(e.g., to compose and decompose numbers)*, **rounding and other number properties to perform mental mathematics and computational estimation with automaticity.**

Place Value

Whole-number place value

Consider the number 792. We can assign a place value to each digit. There are 7 sets of 100, plus 9 sets of 10, plus 2 ones in the number 792.

Decimal place value

More complex numbers have additional place values to both the left and right of the decimal point. Consider the number 374.8. The number after the decimal (8) is in the tenths place and tells us that the number contains 8 tenths.

Place value for older students

Each digit to the left of the decimal point increases progressively in powers of ten. Each digit to the right of the decimal point decreases progressively in powers often.

Example: 12345.6789 occupies the following powers-of-ten positions:

10^4	10^3	10^2	10^1	10^0	0	10^{-1}	10^{-2}	10^{-3}	10^{-4}
1	2	3	4	5	.	6	7	8	9

> *Each digit to the left of the decimal point increases progressively in powers of ten. Each digit to the right of the decimal point decreases progressively in powers of ten.*

Rounding Numbers

Whole numbers

To round whole numbers, first find the place value to which you want to round (the rounding digit) and look at the digit directly to its right. If the digit is less than five, do not change the rounding digit and replace all numbers after the rounding digit with zeroes. If the digit is greater than or equal to five, increase the rounding digit by one and replace all numbers after the rounding digit with zeroes.

Example: Round 517 to the nearest ten.

1 is the rounding digit because it occupies the tens place.
517 rounded to the nearest ten = 520; because 7 > 5, we add one to the rounding digit.

Decimals

Rounding decimals is the same as rounding whole numbers except that you simply drop all of the digits to the right of the rounding digit.

Example: Round 417.3621 to the nearest tenth.

3 is the rounding digit because it occupies the tenths place.
417.3621 rounded to the nearest tenth = 417.4; because 6 > 5, we add one to the rounding digit.

Mental Math

Frequent calculator use can deprive students of a sense of numbers. As a result, they may approach a sequence of multiplications and divisions in an unnecessarily difficult way.

For instance, when asked to calculate $770 \times 36 \div 55$, students may first multiply 770 and 36 and then do long division with the 55. This approach fails to recognize that both 770 and 55 can be divided by 11 and then by 5 to considerably simplify the problem, as follows:

$$\frac{770 \times 36}{55} = \frac{7 \times 11 \times 5 \times 2}{5 \times 11} = 7 \times 2 = 14$$

Similarly, recognizing powers of ten within a calculation can simplify a problem:

$$30 \times 500 \times 7{,}000 = (3 \times 5 \times 7)(10 \times 10^2 \times 10^3)$$
$$= 105 \times 10^6$$
$$= 105{,}000{,}000$$

> **SKILL 15.10** Demonstrates a thorough understanding of fractions, including the use of various representations to teach fractions and operations involving fractions.

Operations with Fractions

Operations involving rational numbers represented as fractions require unique algorithms. Remember that fractions are division problems in which the bottom number is the divisor. The fraction $\frac{2}{5}$ can be written as $2 \div 5$.

When adding and subtracting fractions, use multiplication to convert the fractions and find common denominators. If the denominators are the same, only the numerators are added or subtracted.

Example: $\frac{4}{12} + \frac{6}{12} - \frac{3}{12} = \frac{4 + 6 - 3}{12} = \frac{7}{12}$

Example: $\frac{3}{8} + \frac{2}{3}$

The common denominator is 24. Both the numerator and the denominator of each fraction must be multiplied by the correct factor of 24 to create equivalent fractions with common denominators.

$$\frac{3}{8} \cdot \frac{3}{3} + \frac{2}{3} \cdot \frac{8}{8}$$
$$\frac{9}{24} + \frac{16}{24} = \frac{25}{24} = 1\frac{1}{24}$$

Multiplication of fractions requires no common denominator. Just multiply the numerators together and the denominators together. When dividing, take the reciprocal of the second fraction and multiply the fractions. If there are mixed numbers, turn them into improper fractions before multiplying or dividing.

Example: $2\frac{1}{5} \times \frac{2}{9} = \frac{11}{5} \times \frac{2}{9} = \frac{11 \times 2}{5 \times 9} = \frac{22}{45}$

Example: $3 \div \frac{3}{7} = 3 \times \frac{7}{3}$

Make the whole number a fraction by putting a 1 in the denominator.

$\frac{3}{1} \times \frac{7}{3} = \frac{21}{3} = 7$

Fractions can be applied to rates in real-life problems. This usually involves multiplication of fractions.

Example: A man hikes for $2\frac{1}{2}$ hours up a mountain. If he climbs at a rate of 225 feet per hour, how high will he climb?

Take the rate of 225 feet/hour and multiply by $2\frac{1}{2}$ hours:

$\frac{225}{1} \times \frac{5}{2} = \frac{1,125}{2} = 562\frac{1}{2}$ feet

Representing Fractions

See Skill 15.6 for a discussion of models and representations.

The use of shaded regions can be a helpful way to represent a number (whether a whole number or a fraction). Fraction strips are another method of representing numbers.

Number lines are also a common method for representing fractions. An example of a number line with multiple labeling scales is shown below.

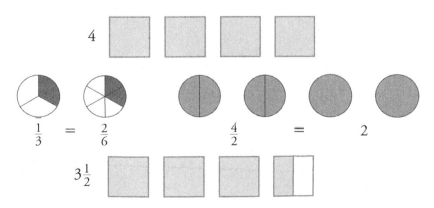

Diagrams are yet another representational method. One type of diagram involves a given number of objects of the same type to represent that number. If each box represents a whole, shading can indicate partial units, or fractions.

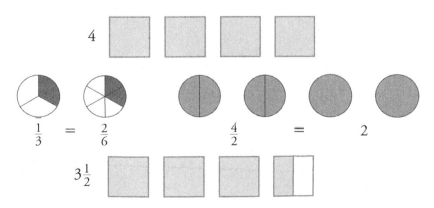

Fraction Equivalency

Teachers should include fraction equivalency relationships in their discussions and examples. For instance:

$$\frac{4}{4} = \frac{7}{7} = \frac{10}{10} = 1 \text{ and } \frac{8}{4} = 2$$

Additionally, students should recognize that dividing the whole into more or fewer pieces will change the value of the fraction. For example, when sharing a cake, if you divide the cake among 4 people, each person gets $\frac{1}{4}$ of the cake. This gives each person a larger portion than if you divided the cake among 20 people, each of whom would get $\frac{1}{20}$ of the cake.

When adding and subtracting fractions, models can be used to represent equivalency. Models can also help with fraction computation.

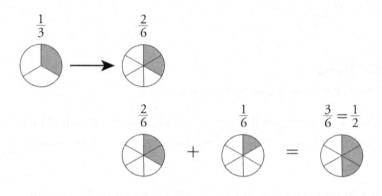

| SKILL 15.11 | Uses a variety of strategies to generate and solve problems that involve one or more steps, with fluency. |

See Skill 15.1

COMPETENCY 16
PATTERNS AND ALGEBRA

SKILL
16.1 **Illustrates relations and functions using concrete models, tables, graphs, and symbolic and verbal representations, including real-world applications.**

Visual Representations of Functions

The relationship between two or more variables can be analyzed using a table, graph, written description, or symbolic rule. The function $y = 2x + 1$ is written as a symbolic rule. The same relationship is also shown in the table below:

x	0	2	3	6	9
y	1	5	7	13	19

A relationship could be written in words by saying the value of y is equal to two times the value of x, plus one. This relationship could be shown on a graph by plotting given points, such as the ones shown in the table above.

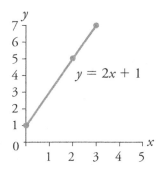

Functions can be written as equations to model real-life situations. When reading the problem, choose the variables and translate the words into mathematical language: y is the dependent variable, and x is the independent variable.

Example: James contributes $85 per month to a retirement account. This $85 is withheld from his earnings. His job pays him $16 per hour. Write an equation that relates m, the money earned in one month, to h, the number of hours worked.
The dependent variable is m, and the independent variable is h. Express the function as $m = 16h - 85$.

Some relations between variables are not functions. If an *x*-value corresponds to more than one *y*-value, the relation is not a function.

FUNCTION	
x	*y*
0	1
2	4
3	1
5	5
7	12

NOT A FUNCTION	
x	*y*
1	1
2	5
2	6
7	15
10	22

SKILL 16.2 Demonstrates an understanding of the concept of linear function using concrete models, tables, graphs, and symbolic and verbal representations.

Representation of a Linear Function

> **LINEAR FUNCTION:** a function defined by the equation $y = mx + b$

A **LINEAR FUNCTION** is a function defined by the equation $y = mx + b$. It is determined by m, the slope of the line, otherwise known as the rate of change. The slope is constant everywhere on the line.

Example: Consider the function $y = 2x + 1$. This function can be represented as a table of values as well as a graph, as shown below.

x	*y*
-2	-3
-1	-1
0	1
1	3
2	5

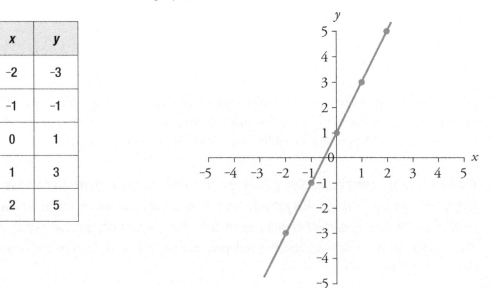

Linear equations can represent a variety of real-life situations. Data can be graphed and then modeled to fit a straight line, or a situation can be modeled with linear equations.

Example: Jerry has only nickels and dimes in his piggy bank, and he knows he has 260 cents. Write an equation that represents the situation. What are possible combinations of nickels and dimes?

Since nickels are worth 5 cents and dimes worth 10 cents, write the equation as: $0.05n + 0.10d = 260$

This equation can be graphed by putting it into slope-intercept form, where n is the independent variable. First, put the variables in a table to determine combinations of nickels and dimes.

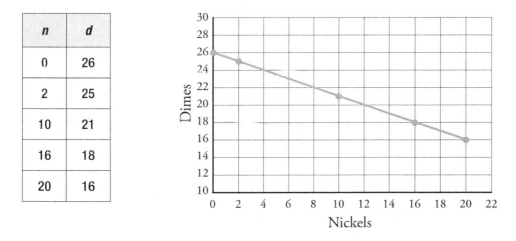

n	d
0	26
2	25
10	21
16	18
20	16

Graph the points and look between values on the line to get other combinations of nickels and dimes.

SKILL 16.3 Understands how to use algebraic concepts and reasoning to investigate patterns, make generalizations, formulate mathematical models, make predictions, and validate results.

Using Algebra to Make Predictions

Algebraic concepts and reasoning can be used to investigate patterns, make generalizations, formulate models, make predictions, and validate results by providing an organized system by which to display the data. The data can be displayed in various formats, such as tables and graphs, to help define the pattern.

Example: The following table represents the number of problems Mr. Rodgers is assigning his math students for homework each day, starting with the first day of class.

Day	1	2	3	4	5	6	7	8	9	10	11
Number of Problems	1	1	2	3	5	8	13				

If Mr. Rodgers continues this pattern, how many problems will he assign on the eleventh day?

Day 2 = 1 + 0 = 1
Day 3 = 1 + 1 = 2
Day 4 = 2 + 1 = 3
Day 5 = 3 + 2 = 5
Day 6 = 5 + 3 = 8
Day 7 = 8 + 5 = 13

Therefore, Day 8 would have 21 problems; Day 9, 34 problems; Day 10, 55 problems; and Day 11, 89 problems.

SKILL 16.4 Formulates implicit and explicit rules to describe and construct sequences verbally, numerically, graphically, and symbolically.

Constructing Sequences

SEQUENCE: a pattern of numbers or symbols arranged in a particular order

A SEQUENCE is a pattern of numbers or symbols arranged in a particular order. Examining a sequence sometimes reveals a particular rule that governs the pattern. For instance, the sequence 1, 4, 9, 16, ... consists of the squares of the natural numbers. Using this rule, the next term in the series, 25, can be found by squaring the next natural number, 5.

Other patterns can be created using algebraic variables. Patterns can also be pictorial. In each case, one can predict subsequent terms or find a missing term by first discovering the rule that governs the pattern.

In sequences defined with implicit governing rules, the rules have not been stated but can be discovered by studying the patterns. The task in each of the examples is to uncover the explicit rule that governs the sequence.

The most common numerical patterns based on explicit rules are arithmetic sequences and geometric sequences. In an arithmetic sequence, each term is separated from the next by a fixed number (e.g., 3, 6, 9, 12, 15, ...). In a geometric sequence, each term in the series is multiplied by a fixed number to get the next term (e.g., 3, 6, 12, 24, 28, ...)

Arithmetic Sequences

An ARITHMETIC SEQUENCE is a set of numbers with a common difference between the terms. Terms and the distance between terms can be calculated using the following formula:

$a_n = a_1 + (n - 1)d$, where

$a_1 =$ the first term

$a_n =$ the nth term (general term)

$n =$ the number of the term in the sequence

$d =$ the common difference

> **ARITHMETIC SEQUENCE:** a set of numbers with a common difference between the terms

Example: Find the eighth term of the arithmetic sequence 5, 8, 11, 14, ...

$a_n = a_1 + (n - 1)d$

$a_1 = 5$ identify the first term

$d = 8 - 5 = 3$ find d

$a_8 = 5 + (8 - 1)3$ substitute

$a_8 = 26$

Geometric Sequences

A GEOMETRIC SEQUENCE is a series of numbers in which a common ratio can be multiplied by a term to yield the next term. The common ratio can be calculated using the formula:

$r = \frac{a_{n+1}}{a_n}$, where $r =$ common ratio and $a_n =$ the nth term

> **GEOMETRIC SEQUENCE:** a series of numbers in which a common ratio can be multiplied by a term to yield the next term

The ratio is then used in the geometric sequence formula:

$a_n = a_1 r^{n-1}$

Example: Find the eighth term of the geometric sequence 2, 8, 32, 128, ...

$r = \frac{a_{n+1}}{a_n}$ use common ratio formula to find the ratio

$r = \frac{8}{2}$ substitute $a_n = 2, a_{n+1} = 8$

$r = 4$

$a_n = a_1 \times r^{n-1}$ use $r = 4$ to solve for the eighth term

$a_8 = 2 \times 4^{8-1}$

$a_8 = 32{,}768$

SKILL 16.5 **Knows how to identify, extend, and create patterns using concrete models, figures, numbers, and algebraic expressions.**

Identifying and Creating Patterns

Models

Models are a means of representing mathematical concepts by relating the concepts to real-world situations.

When introducing a new mathematical concept to students, teachers should utilize the concrete-to-representational-to-abstract sequence of instruction.

When introducing a new mathematical concept to students, teachers should utilize the concrete-to-representational-to-abstract sequence of instruction. The first step is the introduction of a concept modeled with concrete materials. The second step is the translation of concrete models into representational diagrams or pictures. The third and final step is the translation of representational models into abstract models using only numbers and symbols.

Scaled Drawings

Scaled drawings (maps, blueprints, and models) are used in many real-world situations. Architects make blueprints and models of buildings. Contractors use these drawings and models to build the buildings. Engineers make scaled drawings of bridges, machine parts, roads, airplanes, and many other things. Maps of the world, countries, states, and roads are scaled drawings. Landscape designers use scale drawings and models of plants, decks, and other structures to show how they should be placed around a house or other building. Models of cars, boats, and planes made from kits are scaled. Automobile engineers construct models of cars before the actual assembly is done. Many museum exhibits are scaled models because the real size of the items displayed would be too large.

Examples of real-world problems that students might solve using scaled drawings include the following:

- Reading road maps and determining the distance between locations by using the map scale

- Creating a scaled drawing (floor plan) of their classroom to determine the best use of space

- Creating an $8\frac{1}{2}$-by-11-inch representation of a quilt to be pieced together

- Drawing a blueprint of their room and creating a model from it

Example: Kepler discovered a relationship between the average distance of a planet from the Sun and the time it takes the planet to orbit the Sun.

The following table shows the data for the six planets closest to the Sun:

	Mercury	Venus	Earth	Mars	Jupiter	Saturn
Average distance, x	0.387	0.723	1	1.523	5.203	9.541
x^3	0.058	0.378	1	3.533	140.852	868.524
Time, y	0.241	0.615	1	1.881	11.861	29.457
y^2	0.058	0.378	1	3.538	140.683	867.715

Looking at the data in the table, we see that $x^3 = y^2$. We can conjecture the following function for Kepler's relationship: $y = \sqrt{x^3}$.

SKILL 16.6 **Uses properties, graphs, linear and nonlinear functions, and applications of relations and functions to analyze, model, and solve problems in mathematical and real-world situations.**

Using Algebra to Solve Real-World Problems

Many real-world situations involve linear relationships. One example is the relationship between distance and time traveled when a car is moving at a constant speed. The relationship between the price and quantity of a bulk item purchased at a store is also linear, assuming that the unit price remains constant. These relationships can be expressed using the equation of a straight line, and the slope often describes a constant or average rate of change, expressed in miles per hour or dollars per item, for example.

Example: A man drives a car at a speed of 30 mph along a straight road. Express the distance, d, traveled by the man as a function of the time, t, assuming the man's initial position is d_0. The equation relating d and t is expressed by:

$$d = 30t + d_0$$

Notice that this equation is in the familiar slope-intercept form $y = mx + b$. In this case, the time, t (in hours) is the independent variable, and the distance, d (in miles) is the dependent variable. The slope is the rate of change of distance with time, i.e., the speed (in mph). The y-intercept, or intercept on the distance axis, d_0, represents the initial position of the car at the start time, $t = 0$.

The above equation is plotted below with $d_0 = 15$ miles (the point on the graph where the line crosses the *y*-axis).

$$d = 30t + 15$$

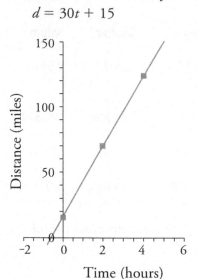

The **x-intercept**, or intercept on the time axis represents the time at which the car would have been at $d = 0$, assuming it was traveling at the same speed before $t = 0$. This value can be found by setting $d = 0$ in the equation:

$$0 = 30t + 15$$
$$30t = -15$$
$$t = \frac{-15}{30} = -\frac{1}{2} \text{ hr}$$

This simply means that if the car was at $d = 15$ miles when we started measuring the time ($t = 0$), it was at $d = 0$ miles half an hour before that.

Example: A cubic container is modified so that its length is increased by 4 inches and its width is shortened by 2 inches. The height of the container remains unchanged. If the volume of the container is 16 cubic inches, what is its height?
Let the side of the original cube be x inches.

The volume of the modified container is given by

$$x(x + 4)(x - 2) = 16$$

Distributing and rearranging, we get

$$x(x^2 + 2x - 8) = 16$$
$$\rightarrow x^3 + 2x^2 - 8x - 16 = 0$$

The third-order polynomial equation above can be grouped and factored as follows:

$$x^2(x + 2) - 8(x + 2) = 0$$
$$\rightarrow (x + 2)(x^2 - 8) = 0$$

The solutions to the equation are, therefore, $x = -2, \pm 2\sqrt{2}$.

Since the height of the box must be a positive number, we choose the positive solution. Thus the height is $2\sqrt{2}$ inches.

SKILL 16.7 **Translates problem-solving situations into expressions and equations involving variables and unknowns.**

See also Skills 16.6, 16.8, and 19.8

SKILL 16.8 **Models and solves problems, including those involving proportional reasoning, using concrete, numeric, tabular, graphic, and algebraic methods** *(e.g., using ratios and percents with fractions and decimals).*

Using Proportions to Solve Problems

A PROPORTION is an equation in which a fraction is set equal to another. To solve the proportion, multiply each numerator by the other fraction's denominator. Set these two products equal to each other and solve the resulting equation. This is called cross-multiplying the proportion.

> **PROPORTION:** an equation in which a fraction is set equal to another

Proportions can be used to solve word problems whenever relationships are compared; for example, in situations involving scale drawings and maps, similar polygons, speed, time and distance, cost, or comparison shopping.

Example: Which is the better buy, six items for $1.29 or eight items for $1.69?
Find the unit cost.

$$\frac{6}{1.29} = \frac{1}{x} \qquad\qquad \frac{8}{1.69} = \frac{1}{x}$$
$$6x = 1.29 \qquad\qquad 8x = 1.69$$
$$x = 0.215 \qquad\qquad x = 0.21125$$

Thus, eight items for $1.69 is the better buy.

Using linear systems of equations and inequalities

Problems with more than one unknown quantity can be modeled and solved using linear systems of equations and inequalities. Some examples are given below.

Example: Farmer Greenjeans bought four cows and six sheep for $1700. Mr. Ziffel bought three cows and twelve sheep for $2400. If all of the cows were the same price and all of the sheep were another price, find the price charged for a cow and the price charged for a sheep.

Let x = price of a cow

Let y = price of a sheep

Farmer Greenjeans's equation would be: $4x + 6y = 1700$

Mr. Ziffel's equation would be: $3x + 12y = 2400$

To solve by addition-subtraction:

Multiply the first equation by -2: $-2(4x + 6y = 1700)$

Keep the other equation the same: $(3x + 12y = 2400)$

By doing this, the equations can be added to each other to eliminate one variable and solve for the other variable.

$$-8x - 12y = -3400$$
$$\underline{3x + 12y = 2400} \qquad \text{Add these equations.}$$
$$-5x \qquad = -1000$$
$$x = 200 \leftarrow \text{the price of a cow was \$200.}$$

Solving for y, $y = 150 \leftarrow$ the price of a sheep was $150

LINEAR PROGRAMMING is the optimization of a linear quantity that is subject to constraints expressed as linear equations or inequalities.

Example: Sharon's Bike Shoppe can assemble a 3-speed bike in 30 minutes and a 10-speed bike in 60 minutes. The profit on each bike sold is $60.00 for a 3-speed bike and $75.00 for a 10-speed bike. How many of each type of bike should the shop assemble during an 8-hour day (480 minutes) to maximize its possible profit? Total daily profit must be at least $300.00.

Let x be the number of 3-speed bikes and y be the number of 10-speed bikes. Since there are only 480 minutes to use each day, the first inequality is the following:

$$30x + 60y \leq 480$$
$$x + 2y \leq 16$$

> **LINEAR PROGRAMMING:** the optimization of a linear quantity that is subject to constraints expressed as linear equations or inequalities

Since the total daily profit must be at least $300.00, then the second inequality can be written as follows, where P is the profit for the day.

$P = \$60x + \$75y \geq \$300$

$4x + 5y \geq 20$

To visualize the problem, plot the two inequalities and show the potential solutions as a shaded region.

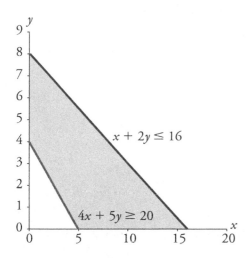

The solution to the problem is the ordered pair of whole numbers in the shaded area that maximizes the daily profit. The profit curve is added as shown below.

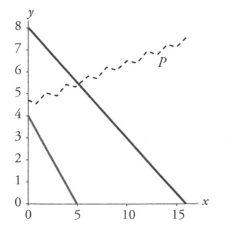

Based on the plot, it is clear that the profit is maximized for the case in which only 3-speed bikes (corresponding to x) are assembled. Thus, the correct solution can be found by solving the first inequality for $y = 0$.

$x + 2(0) \leq 16$

$x \leq 16$

Assembling sixteen 3-speed bikes (and no 10-speed bikes) maximizes profit to $960.00 per day.

Determines the linear function that best models a set of data.

Sets of data give predictions and information about real-life situations. After a set of data is graphed, the graph is analyzed to determine relationships between variables. **CORRELATION OF DATA** is the process of determining relationships from data.

CORRELATION OF DATA: the process of determining relationships from data

If there is no correlation in the data, a graph will look like this:

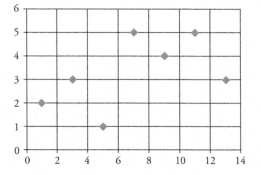

A positive correlation is when variables increase together at a proportional rate. The graph looks like this:

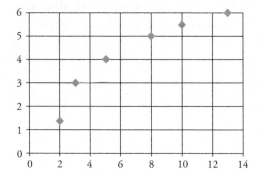

A negative correlation is when one variable decreases as the other variable increases. The graph looks like this:

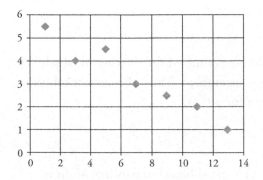

Real-life data can be used to build a model and then can be represented by an equation. This is done by graphing the data, analyzing the correlation, and plotting a **best-fit line**. The line becomes the equation of the model.

Example: Consider the data in the table that relates income to number of hours worked. Determine if there is a correlation in the data, and if so, find the equation of the best fit line.

Hours Worked	Income ($)
1	10
3	35
3	32
5	70
6	74
8	90
8	72

The graph of the data is as follows:

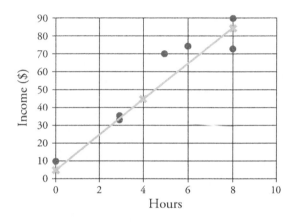

After the line of best fit was drawn, an x was put at the y-intercept $(0, 5)$ and at two ordered pairs on the line so that slope could be determined: $(4, 45)$ and $(8, 85)$.

Calculate slope first: $\frac{y_2 - y_1}{x_2 - x_1} = \frac{85 - 45}{8 - 4} = \frac{40}{4} = 10$.

Using the slope-intercept formula $y = mx + b$, where b is the y-intercept and m is the slope, write the equation of the model as $y = 10x + 5$, where $y =$ income and $x =$ hours.

SKILL 16.10 Understands and describes the concept of and relationships among variables, expressions, equations, inequalities, and systems in order to analyze, model, and solve problems.

See Skill 16.8

Applies algebraic methods to demonstrate an understanding of whole numbers using any of the four basic operations.

See Skills 16.6 and 16.8

COMPETENCY 17
GEOMETRY AND MEASUREMENT

> **SKILL 17.1** Applies knowledge of spatial concepts such as direction, shape, and structure.

Spatial Concepts

The union of all points on a simple closed surface and all points in its interior form a space figure called a **solid**.

A **NET** is a two-dimensional figure that can be cut out and folded up to make a three-dimensional solid.

Cube 6 squares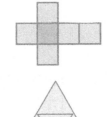

Tetrahedron 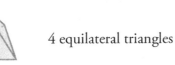 4 equilateral triangles

CONGRUENT FIGURES have the same size and shape. The symbol for congruence is ≅.

Polygons (pentagons) *ABCDE* and *VWXYZ* are congruent. They are exactly the same size and shape.

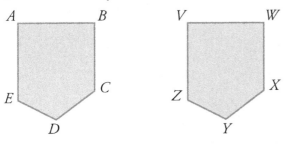

The five regular solids, or polyhedra*, are the cube, tetrahedron, octahedron, icosahedron, and dodecahedron.*

NET: a two-dimensional figure that can be cut out and folded up to make a three-dimensional solid

CONGRUENT FIGURES: figures that have the same size and shape

Identifies, uses, and understands and models the development of formulas to find lengths, perimeters, areas, and volumes of geometric figures.

Perimeter, Area, and Volume

PERIMETER: the sum of the lengths of the sides of the figure

AREA: the number of square units covered by the figure

Perimeter and area

The PERIMETER of any polygon is the sum of the lengths of the sides of the figure. The AREA of a polygon is the number of square units covered by the figure.

Figure	Area Formula	Perimeter Formula
Rectangle	LW	$2(L + W)$
Triangle	$\frac{1}{2}bh$	$a + b + c$
Parallelogram	bh	sum of lengths of sides
Trapezoid	$\frac{1}{2}h(a + b)$	sum of lengths of sides

Example: Find the area of this trapezoid.

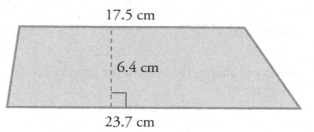

17.5 cm

6.4 cm

23.7 cm

The area of a trapezoid equals one-half the sum of the bases times the altitude.

$$A\,trapezoid = \tfrac{1}{2}h(b_1 + b_2)$$
$$= 0.5(6.4)(17.5 + 23.7)$$
$$= 131.84 \text{ cm}$$

Volume and surface area

Figure	Volume	Total Surface Area
Right cylinder	$\pi r^2 h$	$2\pi rh + 2\pi r^2$
Right cone	$\dfrac{\pi r^2 h}{3}$	$\pi r\sqrt{r^2 + h^2} + \pi r^2$
Sphere	$\frac{4}{3}\pi r^3$	$4\pi r^2$
Rectangular solid	LHW	$2LW + 2WH + 2LH$

Figure	Lateral Area	Total Area	Volume
Regular pyramid	$\frac{1}{2}Pl$	$\frac{1}{2}Pl + B$	$\frac{1}{3}Bh$

$P =$ perimeter, $h =$ height, $B =$ area of base, $l =$ slant height

Example: How much material is needed to make a basketball that has a diameter of 15 inches? How much air is needed to fill the basketball?
Draw and label a sketch:

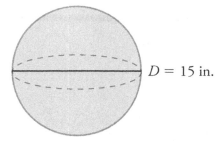

$D = 15$ in.

Total Surface Area	Volume	
$TSA = 4\pi r^2$	$V = \frac{4}{3}\pi r^3$	1. Write formula
$= 4\pi(7.5)^2$	$= \frac{4}{3}\pi(7.5)^3$	2. Substitute
$= 706.8$ in^2	$= 1767.1$ in^3	3. Solve

SKILL 17.3 Uses the properties of congruent triangles to explore geometric relationships.

Properties of Congruent Triangles

Two triangles are congruent if each of the three angles and three sides of one triangle correspond in a one-to-one fashion with the angles and sides of the second triangle.

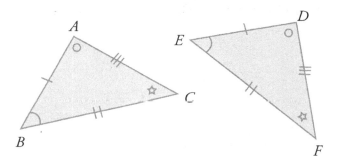

MATHEMATICS

In the example above, the two triangles *ABC* and *DEF* are congruent if these six conditions are met:

1. $\angle A \cong \angle D$ 4. $\overline{AB} \cong \overline{DE}$

2. $\angle B \cong \angle E$ 5. $\overline{BC} \cong \overline{EF}$

3. $\angle C \cong \angle F$ 6. $\overline{AC} \cong \overline{DF}$

SAS Postulate

SAS Postulate (side-angle-side): If two sides and the included angle of one triangle are congruent to two sides and the included angle of another triangle, then the two triangles are congruent.

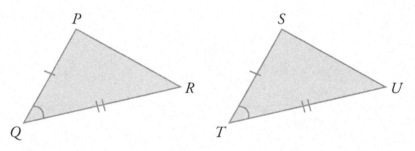

SSS Postulate

SSS Postulate (side-side-side): If three sides of one triangle are congruent to three sides of another triangle, then the two triangles are congruent.

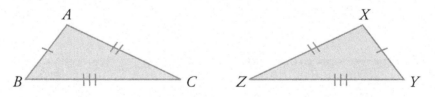

Since $AB \cong XY$, $BC \cong YZ$, and $AC \cong XZ$, then $\triangle ABC \cong \triangle XYZ$.

ASA Postulate

ASA Postulate (angle-side-angle): If two angles and the included side of one triangle are congruent to two angles and the included side of another triangle, the triangles are congruent.

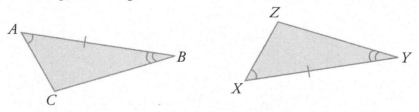

Since $\angle A \cong \angle X$, $\angle B \cong \angle Y$, $AB \cong XY$, then $\triangle ABC \cong \triangle XYZ$.

HL Theorem

HL Theorem (hypotenuse-leg): A congruence shortcut that can only be used with right triangles. According to this theorem, if the hypotenuse and leg of one right triangle are congruent to the hypotenuse and leg of another right triangle, then the two triangles are congruent.

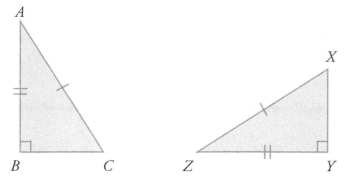

If $\angle B$ and $\angle Y$ are right angles and $AC \cong XZ$ (hypotenuse of each triangle), then $AB \cong YZ$ (corresponding leg of each triangle), and $\triangle ABC \cong \triangle XYZ$.

SKILL 17.4 Identifies, uses and understands concepts and properties of points, lines, planes, angles, lengths, and distances.

Points, Lines, Angles, and Planes

A POINT is a dimensionless location with no length, width, or height.

A LINE connects a series of points and continues "straight" infinitely in two directions.

A LINE SEGMENT is a portion of a line. Because line segments have two end points, they have a defined length or distance.

A RAY is a portion of a line that has only one end point and continues infinitely in one direction.

An angle is formed by the intersection of two rays.

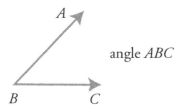

angle ABC

Angles are measured in degrees. $1° = \frac{1}{360}$ of a circle.

> **POINT:** a dimensionless location with no length, width, or height

> **LINE:** connects a series of points and continues "straight" infinitely in two directions

> **LINE SEGMENT:** a portion of a line

> **RAY:** a portion of a line that has only one end point and continues infinitely in one direction

A right angle measures 90°.

An acute angle measures more than 0° and less than 90°. An obtuse angle measures more than 90° and less than 180°. A straight angle measures 180°. A reflexive angle measures more than 180° and less than 360°.

A PLANE is a flat surface defined by three points. Planes extend indefinitely in two dimensions.

> **PLANE:** a flat surface defined by three points; planes extend indefinitely in two dimensions

> | SKILL 17.5 | Analyzes and applies the properties of parallel and perpendicular lines. |

Parallel and Perpendicular Lines

PARALLEL LINES in two dimensions can be defined as lines that do not intersect.

Two lines are PERPENDICULAR in two or three dimensions if they intersect at a point and form 90° angles between them.

> **PARALLEL LINES:** lines that do not intersect

> **PERPENDICULAR LINES:** lines that intersect at a point and form 90° angles

Properties of parallel lines

The parallel postulate in Euclidean planar geometry states that if a line, l, is crossed by two other lines, m and n (where the crossings are not at the same point on l), then m and n intersect on the side of l where the sum of the interior angles α and β is less than 180°.

This implies that if α and β are both 90° and, therefore, $\alpha + \beta = 180°$, then the lines do not intersect on either side. This is illustrated below.

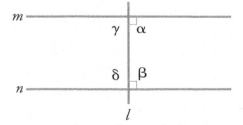

Let the nonintersecting lines *m* and *n* used in the above discussion remain parallel, but adjust *l* such that the interior angles are no longer right angles.

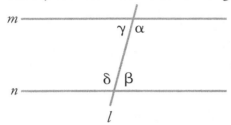

The parallel postulate still applies, and it is therefore still the case that $\alpha + \beta = 180°$ and $\gamma + \delta = 180°$. Combined with the fact that $\alpha + \gamma = 180°$ and $\beta + \delta = 180°$, the alternate interior angle theorem can be justified. This theorem states that if two parallel lines are cut by a transversal, the alternate interior angles are congruent.

One of the consequences of the parallel postulate, in addition to the alternate interior angle theorem, is that corresponding angles are equal. If two parallel lines are cut by a transversal line, then the corresponding angles are equal. The diagram below illustrates one set of corresponding angles (α and β) for the parallel lines *m* and *n* cut by *l*.

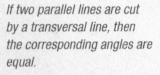

If two parallel lines are cut by a transversal line, then the corresponding angles are equal.

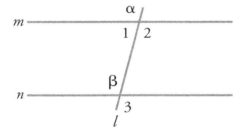

SKILL 17.6 Uses a variety of representations *(e.g., numeric, verbal, graphic, symbolic)* to analyze and solve problems involving angles and two- and three-dimensional figures such as circles, triangles, polygons, cylinders, prisms, and spheres.

Polygons

A POLYGON is a simple closed figure composed of line segments. A regular polygon is one for which all sides are the same length and all interior angles are the same measure.

POLYGON: a simple closed figure composed of line segments

The sum of the measures of the interior angles of a polygon can be determined using the following formula, where *n* represents the number of angles in the polygon.

$$\text{Sum of } \angle s = 180(n - 2)$$

The sum of the measures of the exterior angles of a polygon, taken one angle at each vertex, equals 360°.

> **QUADRILATERAL:** a polygon with four sides

A QUADRILATERAL is a polygon with four sides. The sum of the measures of the angles of a convex quadrilateral is 360°.

A TRAPEZOID is a quadrilateral with *one* pair of parallel sides.

> **TRAPEZOID:** a quadrilateral with *one* pair of parallel sides

The two parallel sides of a trapezoid are called the bases, and the two nonparallel sides are called the legs.

In an isosceles trapezoid, the nonparallel sides are congruent.

> **PARALLELOGRAM:** a quadrilateral with *two* pairs of parallel sides

A PARALLELOGRAM is a quadrilateral with *two* pairs of parallel sides and has the following properties:

1. The diagonals bisect each other.
2. Each diagonal divides the parallelogram into two congruent triangles.
3. Both pairs of opposite sides are congruent.
4. Both pairs of opposite angles are congruent.
5. Two adjacent angles are supplementary.

Circles

> **CIRCUMFERENCE:** The distance around the perimeter of a circle

The distance around the perimeter of a circle is the CIRCUMFERENCE. The ratio of the circumference to the diameter is represented by the Greek letter pi (π), where $\pi \cong 3.14$. The circumference of a circle is expressed by the formula $C = 2\pi r$ or $C = \pi d$, where *r* is the radius of the circle and *d* is the diameter. The area of a circle is expressed by the formula $A = \pi r^2$.

If you draw two radii in a circle, the angle they form with the center as the vertex is a central angle. The measure of an arc is equal to the measure of the central angle that forms the arc.

Given two points on a circle, the two points form two different arcs. The arc that measures less than 180° is a minor arc and the arc that measures more than 180° is a major arc.

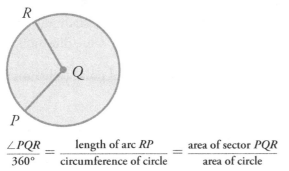

$$\frac{\angle PQR}{360°} = \frac{\text{length of arc } RP}{\text{circumference of circle}} = \frac{\text{area of sector } PQR}{\text{area of circle}}$$

Three-Dimensional Figures

Similar solids share the same shape but are not necessarily the same size. The ratio of any two corresponding measurements of similar solids is the scale factor. For example, the scale factor for two square pyramids, one with a side measuring 2 inches and the other with a side measuring 4 inches, is 2:4.

If the scale factor of two similar solids is a:b, then

    ratio of base perimeters = a:b

    ratio of areas = a^2:b^2

    ratio of volumes = a^3:b^3

> SKILL 17.7 **Uses symmetry to describe tessellations and shows how they can be used to illustrate geometric concepts, properties, and relationships.**

Tessellations

A transformation is a change in the position, shape, or size of a geometric figure. TRANSFORMATIONAL GEOMETRY is the study of manipulating objects by flipping, twisting, turning, and scaling. SYMMETRY is exact correspondence between two parts or halves, as if one were a mirror image of the other.

A TESSELLATION is an arrangement of closed shapes that completely covers a plane without overlapping or leaving gaps. Unlike tilings, tessellations do not require the use of regular polygons. In art, the term *tessellation* is used to refer to pictures or tiles, mostly in the form of animals and other life forms, that cover the surface

TRANSFORMATIONAL GEOMETRY: the study of manipulating objects by flipping, twisting, turning, and scaling

SYMMETRY: exact correspondence between two parts or halves, as if one were a mirror image of the other

TESSELLATION: an arrangement of closed shapes that completely covers a plane without overlapping or leaving gaps

of a plane in a symmetrical way without overlapping or leaving gaps. M.C. Escher is known as the "father" of modern tessellations. Tessellations are used for tiling, mosaics, quilts, and other art forms.

There are four basic transformational symmetries that can be used in tessellations: translation, rotation, reflection, and glide reflection.

A translation is a transformation that "slides" an object a fixed distance in a given direction. An example of a translation in architecture would be stadium seating. The seats are the same size and the same shape and face in the same direction.

A rotation is a transformation that turns a figure around a fixed point called the center of rotation.

An object and its reflection have the same shape and size, but the figures face in opposite directions. The line where a mirror can be placed is called the line of reflection.

A glide reflection is a combination of a reflection and a translation.

Dilation is a transformation that shrinks a figure or makes it bigger.

See Skill 17.10 for more information about transformations.

SKILL 17.8 **Understands measurement concepts and principles, including methods of approximation and estimation, and the effects of error on measurement.**

Estimation and Measurement

One must be familiar with the metric and U.S. customary systems in order to estimate measurements.

COMMON EQUIVALENTS		
ITEM	APPROXIMATELY EQUAL TO	
	Metric	Imperial
Large paper clip	1 gram	1 ounce
1 quart	1 liter	
Average-size man	75 kilograms	170 pounds
1 yard	1 meter	

COMMON EQUIVALENTS		
Math textbook	1 kilogram	2 pounds
1 mile	1.6 kilometers	
1 foot	30 centimeters	
Thickness of a dime	1 millimeter	0.1 inches

Estimating height: The most effective method of estimating height is to compare the height of an object to an object of known height.

Estimating distance: An effective method of estimating short distances is "stepping off," or "pacing."

Estimating perimeter: We can estimate the perimeter of geometric shapes by estimating the length of one portion of the shape (e.g., the side of a polygon).

Any measurement you get with a measuring device is approximate.

Precision and accuracy

PRECISION is an indication of how exact a measurement is, without reference to a true or real value. If a measurement is precise, it can be made again and again with little variation in the result.

ACCURACY is a measure of how close the result of measurement comes to the true value.

If you are throwing darts, the true value is the bull's eye. If all three darts land on the bull's eye, the dart thrower is both precise (all land near the same spot) and accurate (the darts all land on the true value).

PRECISION: an indication of how exact a measurement is, without reference to a true or real value

ACCURACY: a measure of how close the result of measurement comes to the true value

> **SKILL 17.9** Explains, illustrates, selects, and uses appropriate units of measurement to quantify and compare time, temperature, money, mass, weight, area, capacity, volume, percent, speed, and degrees of an angle.

Metric System

The basic unit of **length** is the meter. One meter is approximately one yard.

The basic unit of **weight** or mass is the gram. A paper clip weighs about one gram.

The basic unit of **volume** is the liter. One liter is approximately one quart.

MOST COMMONLY USED UNITS	
1 m = 100 cm	1000 mL = 1 L
1 m = 1000 mm	1 kL = 1000 L
1 cm = 10 mm	1000 mg = 1 g
1000 m = 1 km	1 kg = 1000 g

U.S. System

UNITS OF LENGTH ARE INCHES, FEET, YARDS, AND MILES		
12 inches (in.)	=	1 foot (ft.)
36 in.	=	1 yard (yd.)
3 ft.	=	1 yd.
5,280 ft.	=	1 mile (mi.)
760 yd.	=	1 mi.

To change from a larger unit to a smaller unit, multiply.

To change from a smaller unit to a larger unit, divide.

UNITS OF WEIGHT ARE OUNCES, POUNDS, AND TONS		
16 ounces (oz.)	=	1 pound (lb.)
2,000 lb.	=	1 ton (T.)

UNITS OF CAPACITY ARE FLUID OUNCES, CUPS, PINTS, QUARTS, AND GALLONS		
8 fluid ounces (fl. oz.)	=	1 cup (c.)
2 c.	=	1 pint (pt.)
4 c.	=	1 quart (qt.)
2 pt.	=	1 qt.
4 qt.	=	1 gallon (gal.)

SKILL 17.10 Uses translations, rotations and reflections to illustrate similarities, congruencies and symmetries of figures.

See Skill 17.7 for definitions of the four basic transformations.

There are four basic transformational symmetries that can be used in tessellations: translation, rotation, reflection, and glide reflection.

The tessellation below is a combination of the four types of transformational symmetry:

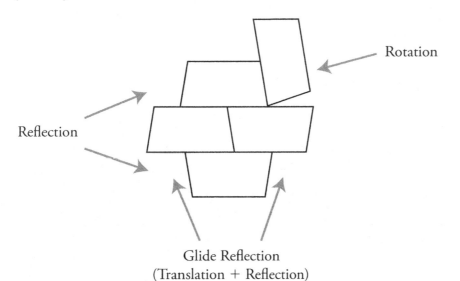

Rotation

Reflection

Glide Reflection
(Translation + Reflection)

A **frieze** is a pattern that repeats in one direction. Friezes are often seen as ornaments in architecture. There are seven different possible frieze patterns: translation, glide reflection, two parallel reflections, two half turns, a reflection and a half turn, horizontal reflection, and three reflections.

Starting with this pattern,

we derive these seven possibilities:

Translation	
Glide Reflection	
Two Parallel Reflections	
Two Half Turns	
Reflection and a Half Turn	
Horizontal Reflection	
Three Reflections	

FRACTAL: an endlessly repeating pattern that varies according to a set formula

A **FRACTAL** is an endlessly repeating pattern that varies according to a set formula, a mixture of art and geometry. A fractal is any pattern that reveals greater complexity as it is enlarged. An example of a fractal is an ice crystal freezing on a glass window.

Fractals are **self-similar** and have **fractional (fractal) dimension**. Self-similar means that a fractal looks the same over all ranges of scale.

Example

Fractional, or fractal, dimension means that the dimension of the figure is a non-integer, or fraction.

Example

Use dilation to transform a diagram.

Starting with a triangle whose center of dilation is point P,

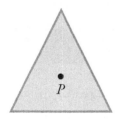

we dilate the lengths of the sides by the same factor to create a new triangle.

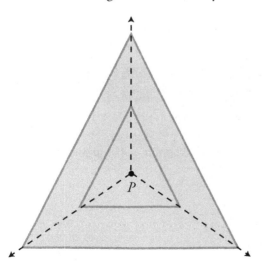

A **CONTRACTION** is the opposite of a dilation. It results from multiplying all dimensions of a figure by a number between zero and one.

Example

The figure on the right is a dilation of the figure on the left because its length and width are one-half those of the figure on the left.

SKILL 17.11 Develops, justifies and uses conversions within and between measurement systems.

Conversions between Measurement Systems

CONVERSION OF LENGTH FROM ENGLISH TO METRIC		
1 inch	≈	2.54 centimeters
1 foot	≈	30 centimeters
1 yard	≈	0.9 meters
1 mile	≈	1.6 kilometers

CONVERSION OF WEIGHT FROM ENGLISH TO METRIC		
1 ounce	≈	28 grams
1 pound	≈	0.45 kilogram ≈ 454 grams

CONVERSION OF VOLUME FROM ENGLISH TO METRIC		
1 teaspoon (tsp.)	≈	5 milliliters
1 fluid ounce	≈	15 milliliters
1 cup	≈	0.24 liters
1 pint	≈	0.47 liters
1 quart	≈	0.95 liters
1 gallon	≈	3.8 liters

Conversions within a System

There are many methods for converting measurements within a system. One method is to multiply the given measurement by a conversion factor. This conversion factor is the ratio of:

$$\frac{\text{new units}}{\text{old units}} \quad \text{OR} \quad \frac{\text{what you want}}{\text{what you have}}$$

Example: Convert 3 miles to yards.

$$\frac{3 \text{ miles}}{1} \times \frac{1,760 \text{ yards}}{1 \text{ mile}} = \underline{\qquad} \text{ yards}$$

5,280 yards

1. Multiply by the conversion factor
2. Cancel the miles units
3. Solve

SKILL 17.12 Understands logical reasoning, justification, and proof in relation to the axiomatic structure of geometry and uses reasoning to develop, generalize, justify, and prove geometric relationships

Proving Geometric Relationships

THEOREMS are mathematical statements that can be proven to be true based on postulates, definitions, algebraic properties, given information, and previously proved theorems.

> **THEOREMS:** mathematical statements that can be proven to be true based on postulates, definitions, algebraic properties, given information, and previously proved theorems

The following algebraic postulates are frequently used as reasons for statements in two-column geometric properties:

Addition Property	If $a = b$ and $c = d$, then $a + c = b + d$.
Subtraction Property	If $a = b$ and $c = d$, then $a - c = b - d$.
Multiplication Property	If $a = b$ and $c \neq 0$, then $ac = bc$.
Division Property	If $a = b$ and $c \neq 0$, then $\frac{a}{c} = \frac{b}{c}$.
Reflexive Property	$a = a$
Symmetric Property	If $a = b$, then $b = a$.
Transitive Property	If $a = b$ and $b = c$, then $a = c$.
Distributive Property	$a(b + c) = ab + ac$
Substitution Property	If $a = b$, then b can be substituted for a in any other expression (a can also be substituted for b).

In a two-column proof, the left side of the proof should be the given information, or statements that could be proved by deductive reasoning. The right side of the proof consists of the reasons used to determine that each statement on the left is true. The right side can identify given information or state theorems, postulates, definitions, or algebraic properties used to prove that particular line of the proof is true.

To write indirect proofs, assume the opposite of the conclusion. Keep your hypothesis and given information the same. Proceed to develop the steps of the proof, looking for a statement that contradicts your original assumption or some other known fact. The contradiction indicates that the assumption you made at the beginning of the proof was incorrect; therefore, the original conclusion has to be true.

SKILL
17.13 **Understands attributes of various polygons, including names and how sides and angles of the polygon affect its attributes.**

See Skill 17.6

Partitions or decomposes polygons to express areas as fractions of a whole or to find areas of nonstandard polygons.

The area of any regular polygon having *n* sides may be expressed as a sum of the areas of *n* congruent triangles. If each side of the polygon is of length *a*, and the APOTHEM (distance from the center of a polygon to one side) is *h*,

area of the polygon $= n \times \frac{1}{2} \times a \times h$ (*n* times the area of one triangle)

Since $n \times a$ is the perimeter of the polygon, we can also write

area of the polygon $= \frac{1}{2} \times$ perimeter $\times$ apothem

> **APOTHEM:** distance from the center of a polygon to one side

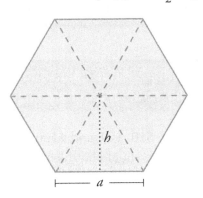

Example: Find the area of a regular hexagon in which the length of each side is 12 and the apothem has a length of $6\sqrt{3}$.

Area $= \frac{1}{2} \times$ *apothem* $\times$ *perimeter* $= \frac{1}{2} \times 6\sqrt{3} \times 6(12) = 216\sqrt{3}$.

In irregular polygons, the area can sometimes be divided up into manageable regions. Then, the areas of the regions can be added to find the polygon's area.

Example: Find the area of the pentagon below, given the side lengths as marked and given angle T and angle P are right angles.

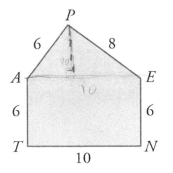

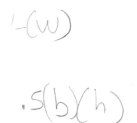

Divide the region into a triangle and a rectangle:

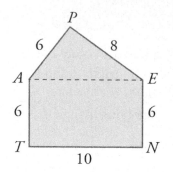

Then, the triangle region's area is found by
$A = \frac{1}{2}bh = \frac{1}{2}(6)(8) = 24$.

The rectangular region's area is
$A = l \times w = 6(10) = 60$. Therefore, the total area of the pentagon is $24 + 60 = 84$.

SKILL 17.15 Demonstrates the value and relationships of United States coins and bills and uses appropriate symbols to name the value of a collection.

United States dollars are in denominations of $1, $2, $5, $10, $50, and $100. Coins are in cents as follows: 1, 5, 10, 25, and 50. Students should be able to compute values and convert amounts as necessary.

Example 1: Find the total of 3 quarters, 5 dimes, and 2 nickels.
A student may begin to work the problem in cents: $3(25) + 5(10) + 2(5) = 135$¢. To convert to dollars: 135¢ (1 $/100¢) = $1.35

Example 2: $15 is to be divided among 4 children. Calculate how much money each child will receive and describe the smallest quantity of coins and/or bills that can deliver the amount.
$15 ÷ 4 = $3.75. The smallest amount of currency for this total would be 3 dollar bills and 3 quarters.

SKILL 17.16 Identifies, uses and understands the concepts and properties of geometric figures and their relationships.

See Skills 17.2, 17.3, and 17.6

Describes the key attributes of the coordinate plane and models the process of graphing ordered pairs.

Students begin their understanding of graphing by plotting points on a number line. This helps them visualize the comparative magnitude of numbers, to see the relationship between positive and negative numbers, to understand betweeness of numbers, and so forth. The next stage of graphical expression expands into two dimensions through coordinate graphing. On the coordinate plane, students see the relationship between sets of pairs of numbers, which often come from mathematical relations and functions. Coordinate graphing follows this standard model:

Ordered pairs are listed (x, y) where x represents the horizontal distance from zero and y represents the vertical distance from zero.

The ORIGIN is the point $(0, 0)$ from where all distances are measured, or counted.

The X-AXIS is the horizontal number line in a coordinate plane, and the Y-AXIS is the vertical number line in a coordinate plane. Positive is right or up; negative is left or down.

The coordinate plane is divided into four regions, or quadrants, by the axes:

Example: Graph point P at (2, 4) and point J at (–5, 3).

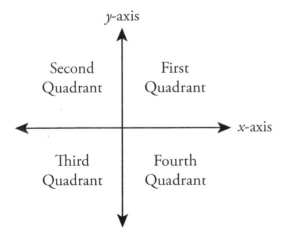

Any ordered pair has one specific location on the coordinate plane.

> *Ordered pairs are listed (x, y) where x represents the horizontal distance from zero and y represents the vertical distance from zero.*

> **ORIGIN:** the point $(0, 0)$

> **X-AXIS:** the horizontal number line in a coordinate plane

> **Y-AXIS:** the vertical number line in a coordinate plane

Students should put their pencil at the origin and count 2 spaces right, followed by 4 spaces up to graph point *P*. Similarly, count 5 spaces left and 3 spaces up for point *J*.

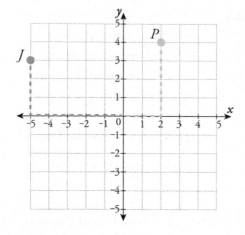

It should be emphasized that even though a number line, or axis, appears to end at a certain number, in reality it extends to infinity.

COMPETENCY 18
PROBABILITY AND STATISTICS

SKILL 18.1 **Investigates and answers questions by collecting, organizing and displaying data in a variety of formats as described in the Texas Essential Knowledge and Skills (TEKS) and draws conclusions from any data graph.**

Displaying Data in Different Formats

Basic statistical concepts can be conveyed without the need for computation. For example, inferences can be drawn from a graph or statistical data.

Example: Graph the following information using a line graph.

The number of National Merit finalists in each school year.

	90–91	91–92	92–93	93–94	94–95	95–96
Central	3	5	1	4	6	8
Wilson	4	2	3	2	3	2

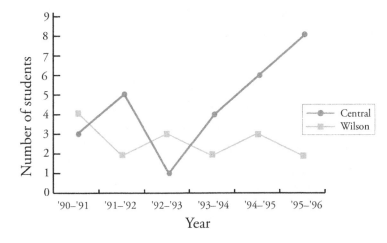

Scatter plots compare two characteristics of the same group of things or people and usually consist of a large body of data. They show how much one variable is affected by another. The relationship between the two variables is their **correlation**. The closer the data points come to making a straight line when plotted, the closer the correlation.

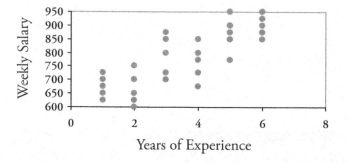

Demonstrates an understanding of measures of central tendency *(e.g., mean, median, mode)* **and range and uses those measures to describe a set of data.**

Measures of Central Tendency and Spread

MEAN: the average value of a data set

MEDIAN: the middle value of a data set

MODE: the value that appears most often in a data set

RANGE: the difference between the highest and lowest values in a data set

VARIANCE: the average squared distance from each value of a data set to the mean

STANDARD DEVIATION: the square root of the variance

Measures of central tendency define the center of a data set, and measures of dispersion define the amount of spread.

The most common measures of central tendency that define the center of a data set are mean, median, and mode. The MEAN is the average value of a data set; the MEDIAN is the middle value of a data set; and the MODE is the value that appears most often in a data set. The mean is the most descriptive value for tightly clustered data with few outliers. Outlier data, values in a data set that are unusually high or low, can greatly distort the mean. The median, on the other hand, may better describe widely dispersed data and data sets with outliers because outliers and dispersion have little effect on the median value.

The most common measures of spread that define the dispersion of a data set are range, variance, standard deviation, and quantiles. The RANGE is the difference between the highest and lowest values in a data set. The VARIANCE is the average squared distance from each value of a data set to the mean. The STANDARD DEVIATION is the square root of the variance. A data set clustered around the center has a small variance and standard deviation, while a dispersed data set with many gaps has a large variance and standard deviation. Quantiles or percentiles divide a data set into equal sections.

SKILL **Explores concepts of probability through data collection,**
18.3 **experiments, and simulations.**

Data Collection, Experiments, and Simulations

SAMPLE STATISTICS are important generalizations about the entire sample, such as mean, median, mode, range, and sampling error (standard deviation).

Sample size is one important factor in the accuracy and reliability of sample statistics. As sample size increases, sampling error (standard deviation) decreases. Sampling error is the main determinant of the size of the confidence interval. Confidence intervals decrease in size as sample size increases. A confidence interval gives an estimated range of values, which is likely to include a particular population parameter.

The law of large numbers states that the larger the sample size, or the more times we measure a variable in a population, the closer the sample mean will be to the population mean.

The central limit theorem states that as the number of samples increases, the distribution of sample means (averages) approaches a normal distribution.

> **SAMPLE STATISTICS:**
> important generalizations about the entire sample, such as mean, median, mode, range, and sampling error (standard deviation)

SKILL **Uses the concepts and principles of probability to describe the**
18.4 **outcome of simple and compound events.**

Basic Principles of Probability

PROBABILITY measures the chance of an event occurring. The probability of an event that must occur, a certain event, is one. When no outcome is favorable, the probability of an impossible event is zero.

$$P(\text{event}) = \frac{\text{number of favorable outcomes}}{\text{number of total outcomes}}$$

A simple event is one that describes a single outcome, whereas a compound event is made up of two or more simple events. The following discussion uses the symbols $\cap$ to mean "and," $\cup$ to mean "or," and $P(x)$ to mean "the probability of x."

> **PROBABILITY:** the chance of an event occurring

Probability of events A and B occurring

If A and B are independent events, then the probability that both A and B will occur is the product of their individual probabilities.

$$P(A \cap B) = P(A)P(B)$$

Example: Given two dice, the probability of tossing a three on each of them simultaneously is the probability of a three on the first die, or $\frac{1}{6}$, times the probability of tossing a three on the second die, also $\frac{1}{6}$.

$$\frac{1}{6} \times \frac{1}{6} = \frac{1}{36}$$

When the outcome of the first event affects the outcome of the second event, the events are **dependent**. Any two events that are not independent are dependent. This is also known as **conditional probability**.

$$P(A \cap B) = P(A)P(B|A)$$

Example: Two cards are drawn from a deck of 52 cards, without replacement; that is, the first card is not returned to the deck before the second card is drawn. What is the probability of drawing a diamond?

$A =$ drawing a diamond first

$B =$ drawing a diamond second

$$P(A) = \frac{13}{52} = \frac{1}{4} \qquad\qquad P(B) = \frac{12}{51} = \frac{4}{17}$$

$$P(A \cap B) = \frac{1}{4} \times \frac{4}{17} = \frac{1}{17}$$

Probability of event A or B occurring

For arbitrary events,

$$P(A \cup B) = P(A) + P(B) - P(A \cap B)$$

For mutually exclusive events,

$$P(A \cup B) = P(A) + P(B)$$

Example: A card is selected from a deck of playing cards. What is the probability that it is a king or a spade?

Since the two outcomes (king or spade) are not mutually exclusive, we use the formula:

$$P(A \cup B) = P(A) + P(B) - P(A \cap B)$$

The probability of selecting a king $= \frac{4}{52} = \frac{1}{13}$.

The probability of selecting a spade $= \frac{13}{52} = \frac{1}{4}$.

The probability of selecting both a king and a spade $= \frac{1}{52}$.

Therefore, the probability that the selected card is a king or a spade is

$$\frac{1}{13} + \frac{1}{4} - \frac{1}{52} = \frac{16}{52} = \frac{4}{13}.$$

Fundamental counting principle

In a sequence of two distinct events in which the first one has n number of outcomes or possibilities and the second has m number of outcomes or possibilities, the total number of possibilities of the sequence will be:

$n \times m$

Example: A car dealership has three Mazda models and each model comes in a choice of four colors. How many different Mazda cars are available at the dealership?

Number of available Mazda cars $= (3)(4) = 12$

The **Addition Principle of Counting** states:

If A and B are events, $n(A \text{ or } B) = n(A) + n(B) - n(A \cap B)$.

The **Addition Principle of Counting for Mutually Exclusive Events** states:

If A and B are mutually exclusive events, $n(A \text{ or } B) = n(A) + n(B)$.

The **Multiplication Principle of Counting for Dependent Events** states:

Let A be a set of outcomes of Stage 1 and B a set of outcomes of Stage 2. Then the number of ways [$n(A \text{ and } B)$], that A and B can occur in a two-stage experiment is given by:

$n(A \text{ and } B) = n(A)n(B|A)$,

where $n(B|A)$ denotes the number of ways B can occur, given that A has already occurred.

The **Multiplication Principle of Counting for Independent Events** states:

Let A be a set of outcomes of Stage 1 and B a set of outcomes of Stage 2. If A and B are independent events, then the number of ways [$n(A \text{ and } B)$], that A and B can occur in a two-stage experiment is given by:

$n(A \text{ and } B) = n(A)n(B)$.

SKILL 18.5 **Determines probabilities by constructing sample spaces to model situations.**

See Skill 18.4

SKILL
18.6 Applies deep knowledge of the use of probability, in different scenarios, to make observations, draw conclusions, and create relationships.

See Skill 18.4

SKILL
18.7 Solves a variety of probability problems using combinations and geometric probability *(e.g., probability as the ratio of two areas).*

Geometric Probability (Probability as the Ratio of Two Areas)

GEOMETRIC PROBABILITY describes situations that involve shapes and measures. For example, given a 10-inch string, we can determine the probability of cutting the string so that one piece is at least 8 inches long.

> **GEOMETRIC PROBABILITY:** describes situations that involve shapes and measures

Other geometric probability problems involve the ratio of areas. For example, to determine the likelihood of randomly hitting a defined area of a dartboard (pictured below), we determine the ratio of the target area to the total area of the board.

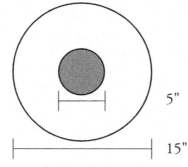

5"

15"

Given that a randomly thrown dart lands somewhere on the board, the probability that it hits the target area is the ratio of the areas of the two circles. Thus, the probability, P, of hitting the target is

$$P = \frac{(2.5)^2\,\pi}{(7.5)^2\,\pi} \times 100 = \frac{6.25}{56.25} \times 100 = 11.1\%$$

> ## SKILL 18.8
> Supports arguments, makes predictions, and draws conclusions using summary statistics and graphs to analyze and interpret one-variable data.

Using Probability to Draw Conclusions

Some probability-related questions to ask about events being observed include:

- Are the events equally likely?

- Are the events independent?

- Are the events mutually exclusive?

The law of large numbers is a useful concept to keep in mind while making observations.

STATISTICAL HYPOTHESIS TESTING is a method of determining, to within a certain confidence level, whether a particular conclusion can be accepted according to a certain set of data.

The first step of hypothesis testing is to formulate the so-called null hypothesis, which is assumed to be true unless sufficient evidence warrants its rejection.

The next step involves computation of a test statistic using the associated sample data. Comparison of this data with a critical value for the test statistic (which is a threshold value for a given confidence) allows one to determine whether to accept or reject the null hypothesis. Common test statistics include the t-test, the z-test, and the x^2 (chi-square) goodness-of-fit test.

> STATISTICAL HYPOTHESIS TESTING: a method of determining, to within a certain confidence level, whether a particular conclusion can be accepted according to a certain set of data

Probability models

There are three common probability distributions or models used to represent situations: the normal distribution, the binomial distribution, and the geometric distribution. The first type, the normal distribution, would be covered in an EC–6 classroom.

> There are three common probability distributions or models used to represent situations: the normal distribution, the binomial distribution, and the geometric distribution.

Applies knowledge of designing, conducting, analyzing, and interpreting statistical experiments to investigate real-world problems.

Statistics in the Real World

Statistical experiments are used to study real-world phenomena that involve a large number of observations with multiple possible outcomes when the outcome of a particular observation depends on chance.

In the classroom, statistical analysis can be done using a variety of real-world examples:

- **Comparing temperature:** Students can use the measures of central tendency, mean, mode, and range to compare temperatures in their area to temperatures in another state or country.

- **Sampling:** Students can create a survey to use with students in different grades. The results can be displayed with a graph, histogram, or line plot.

- **Tracking populations in the wild:** Students can determine the population of an animal, tree, or plant in a region by taking a sampling of a small area and using that to determine the population in a larger area.

- **Sports:** Statistics are widely used in sports. Most of the statistics are centered around the mean, or average.

Generates, simulates, and uses probability models to represent situations.

See Skills 18.4, 18.7, and 18.8

Uses the graph of the normal distribution as a basis for making inferences about a population.

NORMAL DISTRIBUTION: the distribution associated with most sets of real-world data

A **NORMAL DISTRIBUTION** is the distribution associated with most sets of real-world data. It is frequently called a **bell curve**. A normal distribution has a **random variable** X with mean μ and variance σ^2.

Z-SCORE: a measure of the distance in standard deviations of a sample from the mean

Example: Albert's Bagel Shop's morning customer load follows a normal distribution, with mean (average) 50 and standard deviation 10. The standard deviation is the measure of the variation in the distribution. Determine the probability that the number of customers tomorrow will be less than 42.

First, convert the raw score to a **Z-SCORE**. A z-score is a measure of the distance in standard deviations of a sample from the mean.

The z-score $= \dfrac{X_i \times \bar{X}}{s} = \dfrac{42 - 50}{10} = -\dfrac{8}{10} = -0.8$

Next, use a table to find the probability corresponding to the z-score. The table gives us 0.2881. Since our raw score is negative, we subtract the table value from 0.5.

$0.5 - 0.2881 = 0.2119$

We can conclude that $P(x < 42) = 0.2119$. This means that there is about a 21% chance that there will be fewer than 42 customers tomorrow morning.

Percentiles

Percentiles divide data into 100 equal parts. A person whose score falls in the sixty-fifth percentile has outperformed 65% of those who took the test. This does not mean that the score was 65% out of 100, nor does it mean that 65% of the questions answered were correct. It means that the grade was higher than the grades of 65% of the test-takers.

Stanine ("standard nine") scores combine the understandability of percentages with the properties of the normal curve of probability. Stanines divide the bell curve into nine sections, the largest of which stretches from the fortieth to the sixtieth percentile and is the fifth stanine (the average, taking into account the possibility of errors).

> *Stanine ("standard nine") scores combine the understandability of percentages with the properties of the normal curve of probability.*

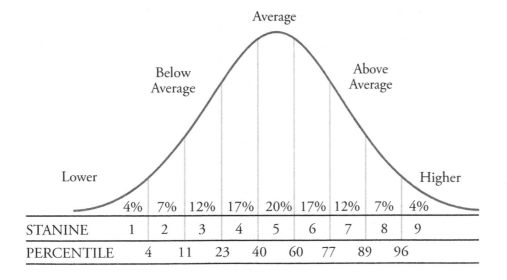

	4%	7%	12%	17%	20%	17%	12%	7%	4%
STANINE	1	2	3	4	5	6	7	8	9
PERCENTILE		4	11	23	40	60	77	89	96

Example: Given the following set of data, find the percentile of the score 104.
70, 72, 82, 83, 84, 87, 100, 104, 108, 109, 110, 115

Solution: Find the percentage of scores below 104.

$\dfrac{7}{12}$ of the scores are less than 104. This is 58.333%; therefore, the score of 104 is in the fifty-eighth percentile.

See also Skill 18.8

COMPETENCY 19
MATHEMATICAL PROCESSES

> **SKILL 19.1** Understands the role of logical reasoning in mathematics and uses formal and informal reasoning to explore, investigate, and justify mathematical ideas.

Deduction and Induction

There are two kinds of logical reasoning that students can use when learning mathematical concepts:

INDUCTION: the process of finding a pattern from a group of examples

DEDUCTION: the process of arriving at a conclusion based on statements that are known to be true

HYPOTHESIS: the information that is assumed to be true

CONCLUSION: what must be proven true

- **INDUCTION** is the process of finding a pattern from a group of examples. The pattern is the conclusion that the set of examples seems to indicate. It may be a correct conclusion or an incorrect conclusion due to the fact that other examples may not follow the predicted pattern.

- **DEDUCTION** is the process of arriving at a conclusion based on statements that are known to be true, such as theorems, axioms, or postulates. Conclusions found using deductive thinking based on true statements will always be true.

Conditional statements are frequently written in **if-then form**. The *if* clause of the statement is known as the **HYPOTHESIS**, and the *then* clause is known as the **CONCLUSION**. In a proof, the hypothesis is the information that is assumed to be true whereas the conclusion is what must be proven true. A conditional is considered to be in the form:

   If p, then q.

P is the hypothesis. Q is the conclusion.

Example: If an angle has a measure of 90 degrees, then it is a right angle.
   In this statement, "an angle has a measure of 90 degrees" is the hypothesis. "It is a right angle" is the conclusion.

Conditional: If p, then q.
   P is the hypothesis. Q is the conclusion.

Inverse: If ~ p, then ~ q.
   Negative of both the hypothesis (if not p, then not q) and the conclusion from the original conditional.

Converse: If q, then p.

> Reverse of the two clauses. The original hypothesis becomes the conclusion. The original conclusion then becomes the new hypothesis.

Contrapositive: If ~ q, then ~ p.

> Reverse the two clauses. The "If not q, then not p" original hypothesis becomes the conclusion. The original conclusion now becomes the new hypothesis. *Then* both the new hypothesis and the new conclusion are negated.

Suppose the following statements were given to you, and you were asked to reach a conclusion:

> All rectangles are parallelograms.
> Quadrilateral *ABCD* is not a parallelogram.

In if-then form, the first statement would be:

> If a figure is a rectangle, then it is also a parallelogram.

Note that the second statement is the negation of the conclusion of the first statement (remember also that the contrapositive is logically equivalent to a given conditional). That is, If ~ q, then ~ p. Since "*ABCD* is *not* a parallelogram" is like saying, "If ~ q," then you can come to the conclusion, "then ~ p."

Therefore, the conclusion is that *ABCD* is not a rectangle.

SKILL 19.2 Applies correct mathematical reasoning to derive valid conclusions from a set of premises.

See Skill 19.1

SKILL 19.3 Applies principles of inductive reasoning to make conjectures and uses deductive methods to evaluate the validity of conjectures.

See Skill 19.1

Evaluates the reasonableness of a solution to a given problem.

It is good practice for students to learn to check the reasonableness of an answer. This not only ensures that they did a problem correctly but also that they understand the mathematical process used to arrive at the answer.

Estimation

Estimation is a good tool for checking the reasonableness of an answer. Here are two examples of checking the answer through estimation.

Add: $56 + 24 + 87 + 71 = 238$

Check using estimation: $60 + 20 + 90 + 70 = 240$

Since the estimate is close to the actual answer, the student can feel secure that his or her answer is correct. If the estimate was not close to the actual answer, the student may have made an error when adding the numbers.

An online bookseller is selling paperback books for $2.25 plus $5.00 shipping. How many books can one purchase for $25.00?

Total cost = cost per book × number of books + shipping cost

$25 = 2.25b + 5$

$b = 8.8$

After doing the calculations, you determine you can buy 8 books.

To determine the reasonableness of the answer, substitute the number 8 for b in the equation, and the result should be less than $25.00.

Since 23 is less than 25, the answer, 8, is reasonable.

Checking for the reasonableness of an answer will help students feel confident about mathematical concepts. For teachers, it is easy to forget to check an answer. This does a disservice to students. Taking a minute or two to talk about the answer and why it is reasonable will help students remember to do this. Students can catch errors in calculations and change answers when they check to make sure their answers are reasonable. Checking the reasonableness of an answer should be part of every mathematical problem.

See also Skill 19.6

SKILL
19.5 **Understands connections among concepts, procedures and equivalent representations in areas of mathematics** *(e.g., algebra, geometry).*

For more information about the coordinate plane, see Skill 17.17.

We can represent any two-dimensional geometric figure in the Cartesian or rectangular coordinate system. The Cartesian or rectangular coordinate system is formed by two perpendicular, or coordinate, axes: the *x*-axis and the *y*-axis. If we know the dimensions of a two-dimensional, or planar, figure, we can use this coordinate system to visualize the shape of the figure.

Example: Represent an isosceles triangle with two sides of length 4.
Draw the two sides along the *x*- and *y*-axes and connect the points (vertices).

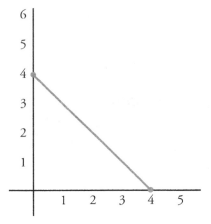

To represent three-dimensional figures, we need three coordinate axes (*x, y,* and *z*), which are mutually perpendicular to one another. Since we cannot draw three mutually perpendicular axes on a two-dimensional surface, we use oblique representations.

Example: Represent a cube with side length of 2.

Once again, we draw three sides along the three axes to make things easier.

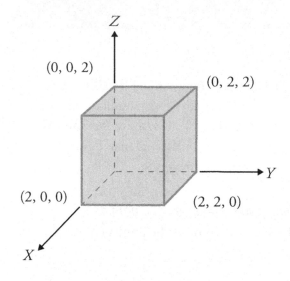

Each point has three coordinates: (x, y, z).

Identify Slope and Intercepts of Graph or Equation

A first-degree equation has an equation of the form, $ax + by = c$. To find the slope of a line, solve the equation for y. This gets the equation into slope-intercept form, $y = mx + b$. In the previous equation, m is the line's slope.

To find the y-intercept, substitute 0 for x and solve for y. This is the y-intercept. The y-intercept is also the value of b in $y = mx + b$.

To find the x-intercept, substitute 0 for y and solve for. This is the x-intercept.

If the equation solves to $x = $ **any number**, then the graph is a vertical line. It only has an x-intercept. Its slope is undefined.

If the equation solves to $y = $ **any number**, then the graph is a horizontal line. It only has a y-intercept. Its slope is 0 (zero).

Example: Find the slope and intercepts of 3x + 2y = 14.

$$3x + 2y = 14$$
$$2y = -3x + 14$$
$$y = -\frac{3}{2}x + 7$$

The slope of the line is $-\frac{3}{2}$, the value of m.

The y-intercept of the line is $(0, 7)$.

The intercepts can also be found by substituting 0 for the other variable in the equation.

To find the y-intercept:

Let $x = 0$; $3(0) + 2y = 14$

$0 + 2y = 14$

$2y = 14$

$y = 7$

$(0, 7)$ is the y-intercept.

To find the x-intercept:

Let $y = 0$; $3x + 2(0) = 14$

$3x + 0 = 14$

$3x = 14$

$x = \frac{14}{3}$

$\left(\frac{14}{3}, 0\right)$ is the x-intercept.

Determine the Equation of a Line, Given Its Graph

The equation of a graph can be found by finding its slope and its y-intercept. To find the slope, find two points on the graph where coordinates are integer values. Using points (x_1, y_1) and (x_2, y_2):

$$\text{slope} = \frac{y_2 - y_1}{x_2 - x_1}$$

The y-intercept is the y-coordinate of the point where the line crosses the y-axis. The equation can be written in slope-intercept form, which is $y = mx + b$, where m is the slope and b is the y-intercept. To rewrite the equation in another form, first multiply each term by the least common denominator of all the fractions. Then rearrange terms as necessary.

> **SKILL 19.6** Recognizes that a mathematical problem can be solved in a variety of ways and selects an appropriate strategy for a given problem.

Selecting a Strategy to Solve a Problem

The process of problem solving in mathematics is similar to problem solving in other areas. One of the first steps is to identify what is known about the problem. Each problem for which a solution can be found should provide enough information to form a starting point from which a valid sequence of reasoning leads to the desired conclusion: a solution to the problem. Between identification of known information and identification of a solution to the problem is a gray area that, depending on the problem, could potentially involve myriad different approaches. Two potential approaches that do not involve a "direct" solution method are discussed below.

The guess-and-check strategy calls for making an initial guess about the solution, checking the answer, and using the outcome of this check to inform the next guess. With each successive guess, one should get closer to the correct answer.

Between identification of known information and identification of a solution to the problem is a somewhat gray area that, depending on the problem, could potentially involve a myriad of different approaches.

Another indirect approach to problem solving is working backwards. If the result of a problem is known (for example, in problems that involve proving a particular result), it is sometimes helpful to begin from the conclusion and attempt to work backwards to a particular known starting point.

Selection of an appropriate problem-solving strategy depends largely on the type of problem being solved and the area of mathematics with which the problem deals. For instance, problems that involve proving a specific result often require different approaches than do problems that involve finding a numerical result.

SKILL 19.7 Expresses mathematical statements using developmentally appropriate language, standard English, mathematical language and symbolic mathematics.

Mathematics often involves symbolic representations, which can help alleviate the ambiguities found in common language.

Mathematics is, in some ways, a formalization of language that concerns such concepts as quantity and organization. Mathematics often involves symbolic representations, which can help alleviate the ambiguities found in common language. Therefore, communication of mathematical ideas requires conversion between verbal and symbolic forms. These two forms can often help elucidate one another.

Mathematical ideas and expressions can sometimes be simple to translate into language; for instance, basic arithmetic operations are usually easy to express in everyday language (although complicated expressions may be less so). In some cases, common language more easily expresses ideas than does symbolic language (and sometimes vice versa). Much of the translation process is learned through practicing expression of mathematical ideas in verbal (or written) form and by translating verbal or written expressions into symbolic form.

The material throughout this guide attempts to present mathematical ideas in both symbolic and written forms. Thus, practicing by carefully following the text and example problems and by attempting to articulate the various concepts both in English and in mathematical symbols should help the student (and teacher) of mathematics gain mastery of this skill.

Throughout this guide, mathematical operations and situations are represented through words, algebraic symbols, geometric diagrams, and graphs. A few commonly used representations are discussed below.

The basic mathematical operations include addition, subtraction, multiplication and division. In word problems, these are represented by the following typical expressions.

Operation	Descriptive Words
Addition	plus, combine, sum, total, put together
Subtraction	minus, less, take away, difference
Multiplication	product, times, groups of
Division	quotient, into, split into equal groups

Some verbal and symbolic representations of basic mathematical operations include the following:

7 added to a number	$n + 7$
a number decreased by 8	$n - 8$
12 times a number divided by 7	$12n \div 7$
28 less than a number	$n - 28$
the ratio of a number to 55	$\frac{n}{55}$
4 times the sum of a number and 21	$4(n + 21)$

Pictorial illustrations of mathematic concepts help clarify difficult ideas and simplify problem solving. The following example illustrates the use of pictures.

Rectangle R represents the 300 students in School A. Circle P represents the 150 students who participated in band. Circle Q represents the 170 students who participated in a sport. Seventy students participated in both band and a sport.

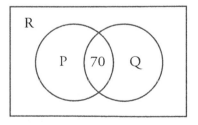

> **SYMBOLIC REPRESENTATION:** the basic language of mathematics

SYMBOLIC REPRESENTATION is the basic language of mathematics. Converting data to symbols allows for easy manipulation and problem solving. Students should be able to recognize what the symbolic notation represents and convert information into symbolic form. For example, from the graph of a line, students should be able to determine the slope and intercepts and derive the line's equation from the observed data. Another possible application of symbolic representation is the formulation of algebraic expressions and relations from data presented in word-problem form.

See also Skill 15.6

> **SKILL 19.9** Demonstrates an understanding of the use of visual media such as graphs, tables, diagrams and animations to communicate mathematical information.

See Skills 15.6, 15.7, 15.10, and 19.8

> **SKILL 19.10** Demonstrates an understanding of estimation, including the use of compatible numbers, and evaluates its appropriate uses.

Estimation

Estimation and approximation can be used to get a rough idea of the result of a calculation or to check the reasonableness of an answer. A simple check for reasonableness is to ask whether the answer expected is more or less than a given number. For instance, when converting 20 km to meters, ask yourself whether you are expecting a number greater or less than 20.

The most common estimation strategies taught in schools involve replacing numbers with numbers that are simpler to manipulate. These methods include rounding off, front-end digit estimation, and compensation. While rounding off is done to a specific place value (e.g., nearest ten or hundred), front-end estimation involves rounding off or truncating to whatever place value the first digit in a number represents.

Compensation involves replacing different numbers in different ways so that one change can more or less compensate for the other.

Example: $32 + 53 = 30 + 55 = 85$

> SKILL 19.11 **Knows how to use mathematical manipulatives and a wide range of appropriate technological tools to develop and explore mathematical concepts and ideas.**

See Skill 14.4

> SKILL 19.12 **Demonstrates knowledge of the history and evolution of mathematical concepts, procedures and ideas.**

Early History of Mathematics

The early history of mathematics is found in Mesopotamia (Sumeria and Babylon), Egypt, Greece, and Rome. Noted mathematicians from these times include Euclid, Pythagoras, Apollonius, Ptolemy, and Archimedes.

Islamic culture from the sixth through the twelfth centuries acquired knowledge of math from areas of the globe ranging from Africa and Spain to India. Contacts in India provided additional influences from China. This mixture of cultures and ideas brought about many developments, including the concept of algebra, our current numbering system, and the concept of zero. India was the primary source of many of these developments. Notable scholars of this era include Omar Khayyam and Muhammad al-Khwarizmi.

Mathematics predates recorded history. Prehistoric cave paintings that use geometrical figures and slash counting have been dated prior to 20,000 BCE in Africa and France.

Important figures in history of math

The growth of mathematics since 1800 has been enormous and has affected nearly every aspect of life. Some names significant in the history of mathematics since 1800 and the work they are most known for include:

- Joseph-Louis Lagrange (theory of functions and of mechanics)
- Pierre-Simon Laplace (celestial mechanics, probability theory)
- Joseph Fourier (number theory)
- Lobachevsky and Bolyai (non-Euclidean geometry)
- Charles Babbage (calculating machines, origin of the computer)
- Lady Ada Lovelace (first known program)
- Florence Nightingale (nursing, statistics of populations)
- Bertrand Russell (logic)
- James Maxwell (differential calculus and analysis)

- John von Neumann (economics, quantum mechanics, and game theory)

- Alan Turing (theoretical foundations of computer science)

- Albert Einstein (theory of relativity)

- Gustav Roch (topology)

> **SKILL 19.13** Recognizes the contributions that different cultures have made to the field of mathematics and the impact of mathematics on society and cultures.

See Skill 19.12

> **SKILL 19.14** Demonstrates an understanding of financial literacy concepts and their application as these relate to teaching students *(e.g., describes the basic purpose of financial institutions; distinguishes the difference between gross and net income; identifies various savings options; defines different types of taxes; identifies the advantages and disadvantages of different methods of payments, savings and credit uses and responsibilities).*

Even young students can learn what math skills they need to be financially cognizant. Any finance preparation offered to a young child promotes the development of an educated, responsible consumer. Everyday examples of personal finance can be covered in simple word problems. Addition and subtraction are used to total expenses or to calculate net income after deductions are taken from gross income. Calculating tax paid or discounts offered gives practice with percent. Math is always better learned and appreciated when real-life applications are offered to students.

Example: The total amount of a shopping bill, before tax, is $75. $50 of this is taxed at 1.5%, and the remaining $25 is taxed at 7%. Determine the final bill after tax is added.

$$50 + (0.015)(50) = 50 + 0.75 = \$50.75 \text{ and}$$
$$25 + (0.07)(25) = 25 + 1.75 = \$26.75.$$

The final amount charged will be $50.75 + 26.75 = \$77.50$.

Responsible money management also requires an understanding of the basic purposes of a financial institution. While details vary from one facility to the next, students should understand that a bank customer can earn money by keeping money in the bank but that it will cost a consumer money to borrow money from a bank or lending institution. The word interest is used in both cases, but consumers earn interest on a savings account, while they are charged interest on a loan.

Example: Using the formula $A = P(1 + r)^t$, determine the balance after 5 years on a savings account opened with an initial deposit of $500 and an interest rate, compounded annually, of 2.2%.

Evaluate the formula: $A = P(1 + r)^t = 500(1.022)^5 = 557.47$. Thus, in 5 years the consumer would have earned $57.47 in interest to reach the final balance of $557.47.

Variations of a problem such as this can show students how increases in the deposit, interest rate, and duration of savings can change the final balance.

Example: A consumer takes out a 3-year, $12,000 loan for a used car. The interest rate charged is 4%. The amortization table for the first 6 months of the loan is as follows:

Month	Payment	Principal	Interest	Balance
1	$354.29	$314.29	$40.00	$11,685.71
2	$354.29	$315.34	$38.95	$11,370.38
3	$354.29	$316.39	$37.90	$11,053.99
4	$354.29	$317.44	$36.85	$10,736.55
5	$354.29	$318.50	$35.79	$10,418.05
6	$354.29	$319.56	$34.73	$10,098.49

After 6 months, how much money has the consumer spent on the car and how much interest has been charged on the loan?

The consumer has spent 6(354.29) or $2,125.74, and $224.22 of that represents the interest charged (the sum of the entries in the Interest column).

Here, students should have the opportunity to experiment with online amortization table calculators (*http://www.bankrate.com*) to see how a shorter loan or a greater down payment can affect the monthly payment and interest charges.

A more intense study of interest charges can be done with credit card interest calculations. Examples and scenarios that show students how large interest charges can become and how long it can take to pay off a balance when making only the minimum payment should be discussed.

- *http://www.consumercredit.com/financial-education/financial-calculators/credit-card-interest-calculator.aspx*

- *http://www.nerdwallet.com/blog/tips/credit-score/how-credit-card-interest-calculated/*

These relatively basic comparisons and calculations will give students a better appreciation of how math is used in their lives while helping them become confident, responsible money managers.

> **SKILL 19.15** **Applies mathematics to model and solve problems to manage financial resources effectively for lifetime financial security, as it relates to teaching students** *(e.g., distinguishes between fixed and variable expenses, calculates profit in a given situation, develops a system for keeping and using financial records, describes actions that might be taken to develop and balance a budget when expenses exceed income).*

Studying real-world examples of math used in consumer situations can help students improve their mathematics appreciation and prepare them to be sound managers of their own money. Consider these additional learning opportunities:

- Have students create and maintain a ledger (either on paper or in an electronic spreadsheet) in class. Each day, spend a few moments adding income or deducting expenses. Each month, analyze the resulting profit or loss.

- Use company annual reports and balance statements as a basis for understanding of how budgets are created and monitored.

- Discuss and analyze realistic family budget scenarios in which a family apportions its known income to cover a list of expenses and determines what, if any, dollar amount can be saved.

- Create a project in which students are given an imaginary allowance and must manage the spending and saving of their funds. A poster board display or class presentation can summarize their plan.

Continued exposure to the mathematics of money can help students develop a growing understanding of and responsibility for their own personal finances.

DOMAIN III
SOCIAL STUDIES

PERSONALIZED STUDY PLAN

KNOWN MATERIAL/ SKIP IT

PAGE	COMPETENCY AND SKILL	
229	**20: Social science instruction**	☐
	20.1: Understands the state social studies content and performance standards that constitute the Texas Essential Knowledge and Skills (TEKS).	☐
	20.2: Understands the vertical alignment of the social sciences in the Texas Essential Knowledge and Skills (TEKS) from grade level to grade level, including prerequisite knowledge and skills.	☐
	20.3: Understands and uses social studies terminology correctly.	☐
	20.4: Understands the implications of stages of student growth and development for designing and implementing effective learning experiences in the social sciences (e.g., knowledge of and respect for self, family, and communities; sharing; following routines; working cooperatively in groups).	☐
	20.5: Selects and applies effective, developmentally appropriate instructional practices, activities, technologies, and materials to promote students' knowledge and skills in the social sciences.	☐
	20.6: Selects and applies currently available technology as a tool for teaching and communicating social studies concepts.	☐
	20.7: Selects and uses effective instructional strategies, activities, technologies, and materials to promote students' knowledge and skills in the social sciences.	☐
	20.8: Understands how to promote students' use of social science skills, vocabulary, and research tools, including currently available technological tools.	☐
	20.9: Applies instruction that relates skills, concepts, and ideas across different social science disciplines.	☐
	20.10: Provides and facilitates instruction that helps students make connections between knowledge and methods in the social sciences and in other content areas.	☐
	20.11: Uses a variety of formal and informal assessments and knowledge of the Texas Essential Knowledge and Skills (TEKS) to determine students' progress and needs and to help plan instruction that addresses the strengths, needs, and interests of all students, including English-language learners and students with special needs.	☐
	20.12: Understands and relates practical applications of social science issues and trends.	☐
	20.13: Creates maps and other graphics to represent geographic, political, historical, economic, and cultural features, distributions, and relationships.	☐
	20.14: Communicates the value of social studies education to students, parents/caregivers, colleagues, and the community.	☐

PERSONALIZED STUDY PLAN

✗
KNOWN MATERIAL/ SKIP IT

PAGE	COMPETENCY AND SKILL	
248	**21: History**	☐
	21.1: Demonstrates an understanding of historical points of reference in the history of Texas, the United States, and the world *(e.g., the Texas Revolution, the Republic of Texas and the annexation of Texas by the United States)*.	☐
	21.2: Analyzes how individuals, events, and issues shaped the history of Texas, the United States and the world.	☐
	21.3: Demonstrates an understanding of similarities and differences among Native American groups in Texas, the United States and the Western Hemisphere before European colonization.	☐
	21.4: Demonstrates an understanding of the causes and effects of European exploration and colonization of Texas, the United States and the Western Hemisphere.	☐
	21.5: Analyzes the influence of various factors *(e.g., geographic contexts, processes of spatial exchange, science, technology)* on the development of societies.	☐
	21.6: Understands common characteristics of communities past and present, including reasons people have formed communities *(e.g., need for security, religious freedom, law and material well-being)*, ways in which different communities meet their needs *(e.g., government, education, communication, transportation, recreation)* and how historical figures, patriots and good citizens helped shape communities, states and nations.	☐
	21.7: Demonstrates an understanding of basic concepts of culture and the processes of cultural adaptation, diffusion and exchange.	☐
	21.8: Applies knowledge and analyzes the effects of scientific, mathematical, and technological innovations on political, economic, social and environmental developments as they relate to daily life in Texas, the United States and the world.	☐
	21.9: Demonstrates an understanding of historical information and ideas in relation to other disciplines.	☐
	21.10: Demonstrates an understanding of how to formulate historical research questions and use appropriate procedures to reach supportable judgments and conclusions in the social sciences.	☐
	21.11: Demonstrates an understanding of historical research and knows how historians locate, gather, organize, analyze and report information by using standard research methodologies.	☐
	21.12: Knows the characteristics and uses of primary and secondary sources used for historical research *(e.g., databases, maps, photographs, media services, the Internet, biographies, interviews, questionnaires, artifacts)*; analyzes historical information from primary and secondary sources; understands and evaluates information in relation to bias, propaganda, point of view and frame of reference.	☐

PERSONALIZED STUDY PLAN

KNOWN MATERIAL/ SKIP IT

PAGE	COMPETENCY AND SKILL	KNOWN MATERIAL/ SKIP IT
	21.13: Applies and evaluates the use of problem-solving processes, gathering of information, listing and considering options, considering advantages and disadvantages, choosing and implementing solutions and assessing the effectiveness of solutions.	☐
	21.14: Applies and evaluates the use of decision-making processes to identify situations that require decisions: by gathering information, identifying options, predicting consequences and taking action to implement the decisions.	☐
	21.15: Communicates and interprets historical information in written, oral and visual forms and translates information from one medium to another *(e.g., written to visual, statistical to written or visual).*	☐
	21.16: Analyzes historical information by categorizing, comparing and contrasting, making generalizations and predictions and drawing inferences and conclusions *(e.g., regarding population statistics, patterns of migration, voting trends and patterns).*	☐
	21.17: Applies knowledge of the concept of chronology and its use in understanding history and historical events.	☐
	21.18: Applies different methods of interpreting the past to understand, evaluate and support multiple points of view, frames of reference and the historical context of events and issues.	☐
	21.19: Demonstrates an understanding of the foundations of representative government in the United States, significant individuals, events and issues of the Revolutionary era and challenges confronting the United States government in the early years of the Republic.	☐
	21.20: Demonstrates an understanding of westward expansion and analyzes its effects on the political, economic and social development of the United States and Texas, including its effects on American Indian life.	☐
	21.21: Analyzes ways that political, economic and social factors led to the growth of sectionalism and the Civil War.	☐
	21.22: Understands individuals, issues and events involved in the Civil War and analyzes the effects of Reconstruction on the political, economic and social life of the United States and Texas.	☐
	21.23: Demonstrates an understanding of major United States and Texas reform movements of the nineteenth and twentieth centuries *(e.g., abolitionism, women's suffrage, civil rights, temperance).*	☐
	21.24: Demonstrates knowledge of boom and bust cycles of leading Texas industries *(e.g., railroads, the cattle industry, oil and gas production, cotton, real estate, banking, computer technology).*	☐
	21.25: Demonstrates an understanding of important individuals, issues and events of the twentieth and twenty-first centuries in Texas, the United States and the world *(e.g., urbanization, Great Depression, the Dust Bowl, the Second World War, growth of the oil and gas industry).*	☐

PERSONALIZED STUDY PLAN

KNOWN MATERIAL/ SKIP IT ✘

PAGE	COMPETENCY AND SKILL	
	21.26: Analyzes ways that particular contemporary societies reflect historical events *(e.g., invasion, conquests, colonization, immigration)*.	☐
302	**22: Geography and culture**	☐
	22.1: Analyzes and applies knowledge of key concepts in geography *(e.g., location, distance, region, grid systems)* and knows the locations and the human and physical characteristics *(e.g., culture, diversity)* of places and regions in Texas, the United States and the world.	☐
	22.2: Analyzes ways that location (absolute and relative) affects people, places and environments *(e.g., the location of renewable and nonrenewable natural resources such as fresh water, fossil fuels, fertile soils and timber)*.	☐
	22.3: Analyzes how geographic factors have influenced the settlement patterns, economic development, political relationships and historical and contemporary societies, including those of Texas, the United States and the world.	☐
	22.4: Demonstrates an understanding of physical processes *(e.g., erosion, deposition, weathering; plate tectonics; sediment transfer; flows and exchanges of energy and matter in the atmosphere that produce weather and climate; weather patterns)* and their effects on environmental patterns.	☐
	22.5: Analyzes how humans adapt to, use, and modify the physical environment and how the physical characteristics of places and human modifications to the environment affect human activities and settlement patterns.	☐
	22.6: Demonstrates an understanding of the physical environmental characteristics of Texas, the United States and the world, past and present, and analyzes how humans have adapted to and modified the environment.	☐
	22.7: Examines how developments in science and technology affect the physical environment; the growth of economies and societies; and definitions of, access to and the use of physical and human resources.	☐
	22.8: Creates and interprets maps of places and regions that contain map elements, draws sketch maps that illustrate various places and regions, and uses the compass rose, grid system and symbols to locate places on maps and globes.	☐
	22.9: Demonstrates an understanding of basic concepts of culture; processes of cultural adaptation, diffusion, and exchange; and positive and negative qualities of a multicultural society.	☐
	22.10: Demonstrates an understanding of the contributions made by people of various racial, ethnic, and religious groups.	☐
	22.11: Analyzes the effects of race, gender, socioeconomic class, status and stratification on ways of life in Texas, in the United States and the world.	☐

✘

PERSONALIZED STUDY PLAN

PAGE	COMPETENCY AND SKILL	
	22.12: Identifies, explains and compares various ethnic and/ or cultural customs, celebrations and traditions.	☐
	22.13: Demonstrates an understanding of relationships among cultures of people from various groups, including racial, ethnic and religious groups, in the United States and throughout the world *(e.g., conflict and cooperation among cultures; factors that influence cultural change, such as improved communication, transportation and economic development)*.	☐
	22.14: Compares and analyzes similarities and differences in the ways various peoples at different times in history have lived and have met basic human needs, including the various roles of men, women, children and families in past and present cultures.	☐
	22.15: Compares similarities and differences among Native American groups in Texas, the United States and the Western Hemisphere before European colonization.	☐
	22.16: Applies knowledge of the role of families in meeting basic human needs and how families and cultures develop and use customs, traditions and beliefs to define themselves.	☐
	22.17: Understands and applies the concept of diversity within unity.	☐
	22.18: Relates geographic and cultural information and ideas to information and ideas in other social sciences and other disciplines.	☐
	22.19: Formulates geographic and cultural research questions and uses appropriate procedures to reach supportable judgments and conclusions.	☐
	22.20: Demonstrates an understanding of research related to geography and culture and knows how social scientists in those fields locate, gather, organize, analyze and report information by using standard research methodologies.	☐
	22.21: Demonstrates an understanding of the characteristics and uses of various primary and secondary sources *(e.g., databases, maps, photographs, media services, the Internet, biographies, interviews, questionnaires, artifacts)*; utilizes information from a variety of sources to acquire social science information; answers social science questions; and evaluates information in relation to bias, propaganda, point of view and frame of reference.	☐
	22.22: Applies evaluative, problem-solving and decision-making skills to geographic and cultural information, ideas and issues by identifying problems, gathering information, listing and considering options, considering advantages and disadvantages, choosing and implementing solutions, and assessing the solutions' effectiveness.	☐
	22.23: Communicates and interprets geographic and cultural information in written, oral, and visual form *(e.g., maps and other graphics)* and translates the information from one medium to another *(e.g., written to visual, statistical to written or visual)*.	☐
	22.24: Analyzes geographic and cultural data using geographical tools and basic mathematical and statistical concepts and analytic methods.	☐

PERSONALIZED STUDY PLAN

KNOWN MATERIAL/ SKIP IT

PAGE	COMPETENCY AND SKILL	
	22.25: Understands and analyzes the characteristics, distribution and migration of populations and the interactions between people and the physical environment, including the effects of those interactions on the development of Texas, the United States and the world.	☐
	22.26: Demonstrates knowledge of the institutions that exist in all societies and how the characteristics of those institutions may vary among societies.	☐
	22.27: Demonstrates an understanding of how people use oral tradition, stories, real and mythical heroes, music, paintings and sculpture to represent culture in communities in Texas, the United States and the world *(e.g., importance of individual writers and artists to the cultural heritage of communities; significant examples of art, music and literature from various periods).*	☐
	22.28: Understands the relationship between the arts and the times and societies in which they are produced, including how past and contemporary issues influence creative expressions, and identifies examples of art, music and literature that have transcended the boundaries of societies and convey universal themes such as religion, justice and the passage of time.	☐
	22.29: Analyzes relationships among religion, philosophy and culture and their effect on ways of life in Texas, the United States and the world.	☐
	22.30: Understands and analyzes how changes in science and technology relate to political, economic, social and cultural issues and events.	☐
344	**23: Economics**	☐
	23.1: Compares and contrasts similarities and differences in how various peoples at different times in history have lived and met basic human needs, including the various roles of men, women, children and families in past and present cultures.	☐
	23.2: Understands and applies knowledge of basic economic concepts *(e.g., economic system, goods and services, free enterprise, interdependence, needs and wants, scarcity, roles of producers and consumers, factors of production, specialization and trade, entrepreneurship);* knows that basic human needs are met in many ways; and understands the value and importance of work and of spending, saving and budgeting money.	☐
	23.3: Demonstrates knowledge of the ways people organize economic systems and of the similarities and differences among various economic systems around the world.	☐
	23.4: Understands and applies the knowledge of the characteristics, benefits and development of the free-enterprise system in Texas and the United States and how businesses operate in the United States free-enterprise system *(e.g., importance of morality and ethics in maintaining a functional free-enterprise system and the impact of past and present entrepreneurs).*	☐
	23.5: Applies knowledge of the effects of supply and demand on consumers and producers in a free-enterprise system.	☐

PERSONALIZED STUDY PLAN

KNOWN MATERIAL/ SKIP IT

PAGE	COMPETENCY AND SKILL	
	23.6: Demonstrates knowledge of patterns of work and economic activities in Texas and the United States, past and present, including the roles of consumers and producers, and the impact of geographic factors, immigration, migration, limited resources, mass production, specialization and division of labor, and American ideas about progress and equal opportunity.	☐
	23.7: Demonstrates knowledge of categories of economic activities, economic indicators and how a society's economic level is measured.	☐
	23.8: Understands the effects of government regulation and taxation on consumers, economic development and business planning.	☐
	23.9: Demonstrates an understanding of major events, trends and issues in economic history *(e.g., factors leading societies to change from rural to urban or agrarian to industrial, economic reasons for exploration and colonization, economic forces leading to the Industrial Revolution, processes of economic development in different areas of the world, factors leading to the emergence of different patterns of economic activity in the various regions of the United States).*	☐
	23.10: Analyzes the interdependence of the Texas economy with those of the United States and the world.	☐
360	**24: Government and citizenship**	☐
	24.1: Demonstrates knowledge of historical origins of democratic forms of government, such as ancient Greece.	☐
	24.2: Understands and applies the purpose of rules and laws; the relationship between rules, rights and responsibilities; the fundamental rights of American citizens guaranteed in the Bill of Rights and other amendments to the U.S. Constitution; and the individual's role in making and enforcing rules and ensuring the welfare of society.	☐
	24.3: Understands the basic structure and functions of the United States government, the Texas government and local governments (including the roles of public officials); the relationships among national, state and local governments; and how local, state and national government services are financed.	☐
	24.4: Demonstrates knowledge of key principles and ideas contained in major political documents of Texas and the United States *(e.g., the Declaration of Independence, United States Constitution, Texas Constitution)* and of relationships among political documents.	☐
	24.5: Demonstrates an understanding of how people organized governments in colonial America and during the early development of Texas.	☐
	24.6: Understands the political processes in the United States and Texas and how the United States political system works.	☐

PERSONALIZED STUDY PLAN

**KNOWN
MATERIAL/
SKIP IT**

PAGE	COMPETENCY AND SKILL	
	24.7: Demonstrates knowledge of types of government *(e.g., democratic, totalitarian, monarchical)* and their respective levels of effectiveness in meeting citizens' needs *(e.g., reasons for limiting the power of government, record of human rights abuses by limited and unlimited governments).*	☐
	24.8: Understands the formal and informal processes of changing the United States and Texas Constitutions and the impact of changes on society.	☐
	24.9: Understands and promotes students' understanding of the impact of landmark Supreme Court cases.	☐
	24.10: Understands the components of the democratic process *(e.g., voluntary individual participation, effective leadership, expression of different points of view, the selection of public officials)* and their significance in a democratic society.	☐
	24.11: Understands the importance of effective leadership in a constitutional republic and identifies past and present leaders in state, local and national governments and their leadership qualities and contributions.	☐
	24.12: Demonstrates knowledge of important customs, symbols, landmarks and celebrations that represent American and Texan beliefs and principles and contribute to national unity.	☐
	24.13: Analyzes the relationships between individual rights, responsibilities and freedoms in democratic societies.	☐
	24.14: Applies knowledge of the rights and responsibilities of citizens and nonprofit and civic groups in Texas and the United States, past and present, and understands characteristics of good citizenship *(e.g., community service)* as exemplified by historical and contemporary figures.	☐
	24.15: Understands how the nature, rights and responsibilities of citizenship vary among societies.	☐

COMPETENCY 20
SOCIAL SCIENCE INSTRUCTION

> **SKILL 20.1** Understands the state social studies content and performance standards that constitute the Texas Essential Knowledge and Skills (TEKS).

The mission of the Texas Education Agency is to provide leadership, guidance, and resources to help schools meet the educational needs of all students. The Texas Essential Knowledge and Skills Web site contains the information needed for each grade level necessary knowledge and skills. See *www.tea.state.tx.us* for further details and *www.tea.state.tx.us/rules/tac/chapter113/index.html* for specific details on social studies.

> **SKILL 20.2** Understands the vertical alignment of the social sciences in the Texas Essential Knowledge and Skills (TEKS) from grade level to grade level, including prerequisite knowledge and skills.

See Chapter 113, TEKS for Social Studies at http://ritter.tea.state.tx.us/rules/tac/chapter113/index.html

> **SKILL 20.3** Understands and uses social studies terminology correctly.

A complete social studies glossary would be too lengthy to include here. Instead, here are two online sources for your reference.

PDF document: *http://www.michigan.gov/documents/10-02Glossary_48851_7.pdf*

HTML Web page: *http://www.whitehall.k12.mi.us/curriculum/socialstudies/glossaryofterms.htm*

— Compiled by Karen R. Todorov, Social Studies Education Consultant for the Michigan Department of Education

SKILL
20.4 **Understands the implications of stages of student growth and development for designing and implementing effective learning experiences in the social sciences** (e.g., knowledge of and respect for self, family, and communities; sharing; following routines; working cooperatively in groups).

SOCIALIZATION: the process by which humans learn the expectations society has for their behavior in order for them to successfully function within that society

SOCIALIZATION is the process by which humans learn the expectations society has for their behavior in order for them to successfully function within that society. Socialization takes place primarily through childhood as children learn the rules and norms of their culture. Children grow up eating the common foods of their culture, and therefore may develop a "taste" for these foods, for example. By observing adults and older children, they learn about gender roles and appropriate ways to interact. The family is the primary influence for this kind of socialization and contributes directly to a person's sense of self-importance and identity.

Through socialization, a person gains a sense of belonging with common ideals and behaviors. When one encounters people affiliated with other groups, one's own group affiliation is reinforced, in contrast, contributing to one's own sense of personal identity.

The teacher has a broad knowledge and thorough understanding of the development that typically occurs during the students' current stage of life. More important, the teacher understands how children learn best during each period of development. The most important premise of child development is that all domains of development (physical, social, and academic) are integrated. Development in each domain is influenced by the other domains. Moreover, today's educator must also have knowledge of exceptionalities and how these exceptionalities affect all domains of a child's development.

Social and behavioral theories examine the social interactions of students in the classroom that affect learning opportunities in the classroom. The psychological approaches behind both types of theories are subject to individual variables that are learned and applied either proactively or negatively in the classroom.

The stimulus of the classroom can promote learning or evoke behavior that is counterproductive for both students and teachers. Students are social beings who normally gravitate to action in the classroom, so teachers must create engaging classroom environments that provide focus and maximize learning opportunities.

Physical Development

It is important for the teacher to be aware of the physical stages of development and how a child's physical growth and development affect his or her learning. Factors determined by the physical stage of development include: ability to sit and attend, the need for activity, the relationship between physical skills and self-esteem, and the degree to which physical involvement in an activity (as opposed to being able to understand an abstract concept) affects learning.

Cognitive (Academic) Development

Children demonstrate patterns of learning beginning with preoperational thought processes and moving to concrete operational thoughts. Eventually they begin to acquire the mental ability to think about and solve problems in their head because they can manipulate objects symbolically. Children of most ages can use symbols such as words and numbers to represent objects and relationships, but they sometimes need concrete reference points. It is essential that children be encouraged to use and develop these thinking skills to solve problems that interest them. The content of the curriculum must be relevant, engaging, and meaningful to them.

Social Development

Children progress through a variety of social stages. Beginning with an awareness of peers but a lack of concern for their presence, young children engage in "parallel" activities (playing alongside their peers without directly interacting with them). During the primary years, children develop an intense interest in peers. They establish productive, positive social and working relationships with one another. This stage of social growth continues to increase in importance throughout the child's school years. The teacher should provide opportunities and support for cooperative small-group projects that not only develop cognitive ability but also promote peer interaction. The ability to work and relate effectively with peers is of major importance and contributes greatly to the child's sense of competence.

In order to develop this sense of competence, children need to be successful in acquiring the knowledge and skills recognized by our culture as important, especially those skills that promote academic achievement.

Elementary-age children face many changes during their early school years. These changes may positively and/or negatively affect how learning occurs. Some cognitive developments (e.g., learning to read) may broaden their areas of interest as students realize the amount of information (e.g., novels, magazines, nonfiction books) that is available.

On the other hand, a young student's limited comprehension may inhibit some of his or her confidence (emotional) or conflict with values taught at home (moral). Joke telling (linguistic) becomes popular with children ages 6–7, who may use this newly discovered "talent" to gain friends or social "stature" in their class (social). Learning in one domain often spills over into other areas for young students.

As previously stated, development occurs in all domains. For example, physical changes take place (e.g., body growth, sexuality); cognitive changes take place (e.g., better ability to reason); linguistic changes take place (e.g., a child's vocabulary develops further); social changes take place (e.g., figuring out identity); emotional changes take place (e.g., changes in ability to be concerned about other people); and moral changes take place (e.g., testing limits).

> **SKILL 20.5** Selects and applies effective, developmentally appropriate instructional practices, activities, technologies, and materials to promote students' knowledge and skills in the social sciences.

It is important for teachers to consider students' development and readiness when making instructional decisions. If an educational program is child-centered, then it will surely address the developmental abilities and needs of the students because it will take its cues from students' interests, concerns, and questions. Making an educational program child-centered involves building on the natural curiosity children bring to school, and asking them what they want to learn.

Teachers help students identify their own questions, puzzles, and goals, and then structure widening circles of experience for them and investigation of those topics. Teachers must infuse all of the skills, knowledge, and concepts that society mandates into a child-driven curriculum. Teachers should also draw on their understanding of children's developmental needs and enthusiasms to design experiences that lead them into areas they might not otherwise choose but that engage them and that they do enjoy. Teachers can also bring their own interests and enthusiasms into the classroom to motivate children.

Implementing such a child-centered curriculum is the result of careful and deliberate planning. Planning serves as a means of organizing instruction and influences classroom teaching. Good planning includes: specifying behavioral objectives, specifying students' entry behavior (knowledge and skills), selecting and sequencing learning activities to move students from entry behavior to objective, and evaluating the outcomes of instruction in order to improve planning.

Students can use just their basic reading skills to understand things such as a reading passage, math word problem, or directions for a project. However, students apply additional thinking skills to fully comprehend how what they read could be applied to their own life or how to make comparisons or choices based on the factual information given. These higher-order thinking skills are called critical thinking skills, as students must think about thinking. Teachers are instrumental in helping students use and develop these skills through everyday activities.

SKILL 20.6 Selects and applies currently available technology as a tool for teaching and communicating social studies concepts.

Teachers need a toolkit of instructional strategies, materials, and technologies to encourage and provide students with problem-solving and critical thinking skills about subject content.

There are many resources available for teaching social science concepts. Teachers should use different kinds of resources in order to make the subject matter more interesting to students and to appeal to different learning styles. First, a good textbook is required. This provides students with something they can refer to and study. Students generally like to have a text. The use of audio/video aids can also be beneficial in the classroom environment. Many students are visual learners and retain information better when it is presented visually. Audiovisual presentations such as movies provide them with the concepts through pictures that they can more easily retain.

Library projects also work well for students. The school library has an abundance of resources students should become familiar with at an early age. There are books and magazines they can look through or read to expand their knowledge beyond the textbooks provided in the classes. Younger children, particularly, like to look at pictures.

The computer also offers abundant opportunities as a teaching tool and resource. The Internet provides a wealth of information on all topics, including material suitable for any age group. Children enjoy playing games so presenting material in a game-like format is also a good teaching tool. Making puzzles for vocabulary, letting students present information in the form of a story or even a play, and using other engaging activities helps the students learn and retain various concepts.

Libraries of all sorts are valuable when conducting research. These days almost all libraries have electronic search systems to assist students in finding information on almost any subject. And, using the Internet, with powerful search engines like Google, students can retrieve information that can be difficult to find in the local library.

High-powered computers have revolutionized the organizing and retrieving of data for research projects. Creating multilevel folders, copying and pasting into the folders, making ongoing additions to the bibliography at the very time a source is consulted, and using search-and-find functions make this stage of the research process go much faster with less frustration and a decrease in the likelihood important data might be overlooked.

Students can utilize spreadsheets, graphing programs, graphic arts programs, and Web design software to present research findings for both small and large projects. Teachers can also set up Web searching "games" such as WebQuests to quiz or reinforce material with students.

> *Field trips, if possible to arrange, are also a good way to expose children to various aspects of social science.*

Field trips, if possible to arrange, are also a good way to expose children to various aspects of social science. Trips to places like the stock exchange or the Federal Reserve are things children enjoy and remember. Teachers could even use technologies for webcasts to perhaps view a place, see a presentation, or interview a source across the state, country or globe! Today's world of technology makes a myriad of resources available to the teacher. The teacher should make use of as many of them as possible to keep the material interesting for the student and to aid in their retention of the material.

See also Skill 20.7

SKILL 20.7 Selects and uses effective instructional strategies, activities, technologies, and materials to promote students' knowledge and skills in the social sciences.

The Internet and other research resources provide a wealth of information on thousands of interesting topics for students preparing presentations or projects. Using search engines like Google, Microsoft, and Infotrac, students are able to search multiple Internet resources or databases with one command. Students should have an outline that includes:

- **Purpose:** Identity the purpose of the research.

- **Objective:** Specifying a clear thesis for a project will allow the students to be specific with Internet searches.

- **Preparation:** When using resources or collecting data, students should create folders for sorting the information. Providing labels for the folders will organize it and make construction of the final project or presentation easier and faster.

- **Procedure:** Organized folders and a procedural list of what the project or presentation needs to include will create A+ work for students and make grading easier for teachers.

- **Visuals or artifacts:** Choose data or visuals that are specific to the subject content or presentation. Make sure that poster boards or PowerPoint presentations can be seen from all areas of the classroom. Teachers can provide laptop computers for PowerPoint presentations.

When a teacher models and instructs students in the proper use of search techniques, he or she minimizes wasted time. In some school districts, students are allowed a maximum number of printed pages per week. Since students have Internet accounts for computer usage, it is easy for the school's librarian and teachers to monitor printing.

Having the school's librarian or technology expert as a guest speaker in the classroom provides another method of sharing and modeling proper presentation preparation using technology. Teachers can also appoint technology experts from the students in a classroom to work with students on projects and presentations. In high schools, technology classes provide students with upper-class teacher assistants who fill the role of technology assistants.

See also Skill 20.6

> *Having the school's librarian or technology expert as a guest speaker in the classroom provides another method of sharing and modeling proper presentation preparation using technology.*

SKILL 20.8 Understands how to promote students' use of social science skills, vocabulary, and research tools, including currently available technological tools.

There are many social science skills required to promote learning in the social science classroom. In summary, these are:

- acquiring information

- organizing and using information

- communicating information

- social participation

- content-area vocabulary development

First, students need to learn how to acquire information, while evaluating its validity and usefulness. Students acquire information through a variety of methods such as reading, study skills, listening skills, research skills, technical skills, and social skills. Teachers should create lessons that require students to utilize higher-order thinking skills for an assignment or project. For example, while watching and listening to an audiovisual presentation on Native American tribes, students must listen to the material, recall what is important, summarize, evaluate the statements, and then later, utilize the material for a purpose. Students should also be coming up with questions about the topic so they can conduct thorough research.

Once the information is acquired, students must make sense of it and organize it for a purpose. As they explore the information on various higher-order levels, teachers should encourage students to explore patterns and themes across topics so that the material is linked to other concepts, and is therefore more easily internalized.

Finally, students must make a decision about what to present from their findings. Teachers typically have students present information in various forms throughout the school year in order to communicate their findings. Students should reflect on what this information means to them, as well as how it has affected people, groups, and entire societies. This social participation ties together the major themes that cross the spectrum of the social sciences.

As students study concepts, themes, and events, they continually encounter content-area vocabulary. Students should be taught and encouraged to use resources such as word walls, glossaries, online resources, KWL charts, textbooks, and teammates to reinforce and internalize terms and concepts relevant to understanding content material. Teachers should vary the methods used to introduce content vocabulary as well as continue to revisit terms taught in the past so that students develop strong, working vocabularies throughout their study of the social sciences. Teachers should also monitor and differentiate this instruction so that no student is left behind when content terms are being introduced, since understanding the terms is part of the vital foundation of learning the higher concepts.

For information on research tools and technologies, see Skills 20.6 and 20.7.

For information on organizing, using, and communicating information, see Skills 20.10 and 20.11.

> **SKILL 20.9** Applies instruction that relates skills, concepts, and ideas across different social science disciplines.

The major disciplines in the social sciences are intertwined and interrelated. Knowledge and expertise in one requires background that involves some or most of the others.

For information about the disciplines that constitute the social sciences, see Skill 21.9.

Social Science Concepts

CAUSE: the reason something happens

- **Causality:** The reason something happens—its cause—is a basic category of human thinking. We want to know the causes of a major event in our lives. In the study of history, causality is the analysis of the reasons for change. The question we ask is why and how a particular society or event developed in the particular way it did given the context in which it occurred.

- **Conflict:** Conflict in history is the opposition of ideas, principles, values, or claims. Conflict may take the form of internal clashes of principles or ideas or claims in a society or group, or it may take the form of opposition between groups or societies.

- **Bias:** Bias is a prejudice or predisposition either toward or against something. In the study of history, bias can refer to the persons or groups studied, in terms of a society's bias toward a particular political system, or it can refer to the historian's predisposition to evaluate events in a particular way.

- **Interdependence:** This is a condition in which two things or groups rely on one another, as opposed to independence, in which each thing or group relies only on itself.

- **Identity:** Identity is the state or perception of being a particular thing or person. Identity can also refer to the understanding or self-understanding of groups or nations.

- **Nation-state:** This is a type of political entity that provides a sovereign territory for a specific nation in which other factors also unite the citizens (e.g., language, race, or ancestry).

- **Culture:** Culture refers to the civilization, achievements, and customs of the people of a particular time and place.

- **Socialization:** This is the process by which humans learn the expectations their society has for their behavior, in order that they might successfully function within that society.

> **CONFLICT:** the opposition of ideas, principles, values, or claims

> **BIAS:** a prejudice or predisposition either toward or against something

---

SKILL 20.10 Provides and facilitates instruction that helps students make connections between knowledge and methods in the social sciences and in other content areas.

The interdisciplinary curriculum planning approach creates a meaningful balance between the depth and breadth of inclusive curriculum. Historically, educational research has shown a strong correlation between the need for interdisciplinary instruction and cognitive learning application. Understanding how students process information and create learning was the goal of earlier educators. Researchers examined how the brain connected pieces of information into meaning and found that learning takes place along intricate neural pathways that formulate processing and meaning from data input into the brain. The implications for student learning are vast in that teachers can work with students to break down subject content area into bits of information to be memorized and applied to a former learning experience and then further processed into integral resources of information.

A critical thinking skill is a skill target teachers use to help students learn in specific subject areas and apply that learning in other subject areas. For example, when a math student is learning algebraic concepts to solve a math word problem about how much fencing material is needed to build a fence around an 8- by 12-foot backyard area, he or she must understand the order of numerical expression in order to simplify algebraic expressions. Teachers can provide instructional strategies that show students how to group the fencing measurements into an algebraic word problem so they are able to use addition, subtraction, and multiplication to produce an answer equal to the amount of fencing materials needed to build the fence.

> **SKILL 20.11** Uses a variety of formal and informal assessments and knowledge of the Texas Essential Knowledge and Skills (TEKS) to determine students' progress and needs and to help plan instruction that addresses the strengths, needs, and interests of all students, including English-language learners and students with special needs.

Assessment methods are always important in teaching. Assessment methods are ways to determine if a student has sufficiently learned the required material. There are many ways of accomplishing this. The test is the usual method, where the student answers questions on the material he or she has studied. Tests, of course, can be written or verbal. Tests for younger children may be game-like. Students can be asked to draw lines connecting various associated symbols or to pick a picture representing a concept. Other methods involve writing essays on various topics. The essays don't have to be long—just long enough for the student to demonstrate he or she has adequate knowledge of a subject. Verbal reports can accomplish the same goal.

In evaluating school-reform improvements for school communities, educators may assess student academic performance using norm-referenced, criterion-referenced, and performance-based assessments. Effective classroom assessment can provide educators with a wealth of information on student performance and teacher instructional practices. Assessment can provide teachers with data to use in planning student learning to increase academic achievement and success for students.

Assessment

The process of collecting, quantifying, and qualifying student performance data using multiple types of assessment of student learning is called ASSESSMENT. A comprehensive assessment system must include a variety of assessment tools such as norm-referenced, criterion-referenced, performance-based, or student-generated alternative assessments that can measure learning outcomes and goals for student achievement.

> **ASSESSMENT:** process of collecting, quantifying, and qualifying student performance data using multiple types of assessment of student learning

Norm-referenced assessments

NORM-REFERENCED TESTS (NRTS) are used to classify student learners in homogenous groupings based on ability level or basic skills into a ranking category. In many school communities, NRTs are used to classify students into Advanced Placement (AP), honors, regular, or remedial classes, which can have a significant impact on the student's future educational opportunities or success. NRTs are also used by national testing companies such as Iowa Test of Basic Skills (Riverside), Florida Achievement Test (McGraw-Hill), Texas Assessment of Knowledge and Skills (TAKS) by the Student Assessment Division and other major test publishers to test a group of students against the norms gathered from a national sample. Stiggins (1994) states, "Norm-referenced tests (NRTs) are designed to: highlight achievement differences between and among students and produce a dependable rank order of students across a continuum of achievement from high achievers to low achievers."

> **NORM-REFERENCED TESTS (NRTS):** used to classify student learners in homogenous groupings based on ability level or basic skills into a ranking category

Educators can use NRTs to compare their students with a larger pool of students in the same grade or who are the same age. There are instructional implications in the scores a student receives on NRTs. NRT ranking ranges from 1–99, with 25 percent of students scoring in the lowest category of 1–25, and 25 percent of students scoring in the highest category of 76–99.

TAKS measures statewide curriculum in reading for grades 3–9; writing for grades 4 and 7; English language arts for grades 10 and 11; mathematics for grades 3–11; science for grades 5, 10, and 11; and social studies for grades 8, 10, and 11. The Spanish TAKS is given to grades 3–6. Satisfactory performance on the TAKS at grade 11 is a prerequisite for a high-school diploma.

Criterion-referenced assessments

CRITERION-REFERENCED ASSESSMENTS look at specific student learning goals and performance compared to a set of specific required learning standards. According to Bond (1996), "Educators or policy makers may choose to use a criterion-referenced test (CRT) when they wish to see how well students have learned the knowledge and skills which they are expected to have mastered." Many school districts and state legislation use CRTs to ascertain whether schools are meeting

> **CRITERION-REFERENCED ASSESSMENTS:** look at specific student learning goals and performance compared to a set of specific required learning standards

national and state learning standards. The latest national educational mandate of No Child Left Behind (NCLB) and Adequate Yearly Progress (AYP) use CRTs to measure student learning, school performance, and school improvement goals as structured accountability expectations in school communities. CRTs are generally used in learning environments to reflect the effectiveness of curriculum implementation and learning outcomes.

Performance-based assessments

Performance-based assessments are currently being used in a number of state testing programs to measure the learning outcomes of individual students in subject content areas. Washington State uses performance-based assessments for the WASL (Washington Assessment of Student Learning) in reading, writing, math, and science to measure student learning performance. Attaching a graduation requirement of passing the required state assessment for the class of 2008 created a high-stakes testing and educational accountability for both students and teachers in meeting the expected skill-based requirements for tenth-grade students taking the test.

In today's classrooms, performance-based assessments in core subject areas must have established and specific performance criteria starting with pretesting in a subject area and maintaining daily or weekly progress monitoring to gauge student learning goals and objectives. To understand a student's learning is to understand how a student processes information. Effective performance assessments highlight the gaps or holes in student learning, which allows for an intense concentration on providing fillers to bridge nonsequential learning gaps. Typical performance assessments include oral and written student work in the form of research papers, oral presentations, class projects, journals, student portfolios, and community service projects.

Summary

Today's emphasis on educational accountability by the public and the legislature is a mandate for effective teaching and assessment of student learning outcomes. Performance-based assessments are being used exclusively for state testing of high school students in ascertaining student learning outcomes based on individual processing and presentation of academic learning. Before a state, district, or school community can determine which type of testing is the most effective, there must be a determination of testing outcome expectation; content learning outcome; and the effectiveness of the assessments in meeting the learning goals and objectives of the students.

English–Language Learners (ELLs)

Teaching students who are learning English poses some unique challenges, particularly in a standards-based environment. The key is realizing that no matter how little English a student knows, the teacher should teach with the student's developmental level in mind. This means that instruction should not be "dumbed-down" for ELL students. Different approaches should be used, however, to ensure that ELLs (a) get multiple opportunities to learn and practice English, and (b) still learn content.

Many ELL approaches are based on social learning methods. When they are placed in mixed-level groups or paired with a student of a different level of ability, students get a chance to practice English in a natural, nonthreatening environment. In these groups students should not be pushed to use complex language or experiment with words that are too difficult. They should simply get a chance to practice with simple words and phrases.

In teacher-directed instructional situations, visual aids such as pictures, objects, and video are particularly effective at helping students make connections between words and items they are already familiar with.

ELLs may need additional accommodation with assessments, assignments, and projects. For example, teachers may that find written tests provide little information about a student's understanding of the content. Therefore, an oral test may be better suited to ELLs. When students are somewhat comfortable and capable with written tests, a shortened test may be preferable to a longer one; note that students may need extra time for translation.

From our high school and college experiences, most of us think that learning a language strictly involves drills, memorization, and tests. While this is a common method (some people call it a structural, grammatical, or linguistic approach) that works for some students, it certainly does not work for all.

Although dozens of methods have been developed to help people learn additional languages, the focus here is on some of the more common approaches used in today's K–12 classrooms. The cognitive approach to language learning focuses on concepts. While words and grammar are important, when teachers use the cognitive approach, they focus on using language for conceptual purposes rather than simply learning new words and grammar. This approach focuses heavily on students' learning styles; it does not have specific techniques but is more a philosophy of instruction.

Many approaches are noted for their motivational purposes. Generally, to motivate students to learn a language, teachers do things to help reduce fear and to help students identify with native speakers of the target language. A common method is often called the functional approach. In this approach, the teacher focuses on communication. For example, a first-grade ELL teacher might help students learn phrases to help them find a restroom, ask for help on the playground, etc. Many functionally based adult ELL programs help learners with travel-related phrases and words.

Another common motivational approach is Total Physical Response. This is a kinesthetic approach that combines language learning and physical movement. In essence, students learn new vocabulary and grammar by responding with physical movement to verbal commands. Some people say it is particularly effective because the physical actions create good brain connections with the words.

The best methods do not treat students as if they have a language deficit. Rather, they build upon what students already know, and they help to instill the target language as a communicative process rather than a list of vocabulary words that have to be memorized.

For further details, refer to www.tea.state.tx.us, and for specifics on social studies, see www.tea.state.tx.us/rules/tac/chapter113/index.html

SKILL 20.12 Understands and relates practical applications of social science issues and trends.

Current research shows ten trends in social studies:

1. **Study more history:** Curriculum studies have shown the need for a stronger emphasis on history, including social history, which focuses on the day-to-day lives of people. In addition to studying political, military, and diplomatic history, students should be taught a wider view of world history in which they examine the many cultures and nations that contributed to the growth and development of the United States. Rather than merely acquiring and memorizing facts, students should examine wider themes from multiple perspectives to determine cause and effect and to separate fact from fiction.

2. **Study more geography:** Geography has reappeared in school curriculums, often as a separate course rather than a subtopic of history or other social studies courses. As with history, the focus has shifted away from memorizing rote facts and figures to the study of human geography. Students are taught a sense of place and use of locational skills; they are learning to connect themselves to their environment; they study the reasons and effects of migration; and they examine the interrelatedness and interdependence of their lives to the world.

3. **Use literature:** Research has shown that student interest increases when literature is incorporated into the social studies curriculum. By using both fiction and nonfiction in the classroom, teachers can make concepts and themes come alive for students.

4. **Focus on multiculturalism:** The number of immigrants in this country today is even greater than it was in the early 1900s, and people are arriving from all over the world. Because this influx represents a change to our culture and our society, an effective social studies curriculum will study this diversity openly and accurately. Students should examine multiculturalism as an example of this country's philosophy of pluralism: *e pluribus unum* (from many, one).

5. **Renew attention to Western civilization:** Balanced with the study of multiculturalism is the need to examine America's debt to Western Europe for its political and economic heritage. Students should understand that the foundation for America's beliefs and principles make this country unique.

6. **Emphasize ethics and values:** Like a pendulum swinging back and forth, the social studies curriculum is now arcing toward the study of specific ethics and values. While students in the 1950s and 1960s were taught about honesty and punctuality and students in the 1970s and 1980s were open to setting their own standards, today's students are encouraged to examine their roles in society. Civic virtues such as fair play and respect and tolerance for others are encouraged.

7. **Renew attention to religion:** Although a controversial subject, religion is reappearing in the classroom so that students can study its role and significance in history and in today's global society. Besides learning about the beginnings and development of various faiths, students are taught the effects religion has on values and attitudes. Religion is an integral part of multicultural studies.

8. **Study contemporary and controversial issues:** Although some educators, parents, and textbook publishers shy away from problematic areas, research is showing that students should examine contemporary and controversial issues to develop critical thinking and decision-making skills. One way to facilitate this is to provide a wide assortment of materials representing diverse perspectives.

9. **Cover issues in depth:** If students are to study contemporary and controversial issues, they must do so in depth. A surface examination defeats the purpose of developing students to be effective participants in a democracy. While time and money can be short to do this effectively, many states and

schools are reorganizing curriculum so that fewer topics can be covered more thoroughly.

10. **Write, write, write:** Research proves that students who write more achieve more. With well-developed individual or group social studies assignments, students can develop an in-depth appreciation of the materials. Writing encourages thoughtful deliberation and enhances creativity.

—From "Trends in K–12 Social Studies: Educational Resources: ADD, ADHD, Literacy, ESL, Special"

> **SKILL 20.13** Creates maps and other graphics to represent geographic, political, historical, economic, and cultural features, distributions, and relationships.

An idea presented visually is always easier to understand than an idea presented verbally, that one hears or reads. Among the more common illustrations used are various types of maps and graphs.

Photographs and globes are useful as well, but because they are limited in the kind of information they can show, they are rarely used. An exception to this would be the case of a photograph of a particular political figure or a time that one wishes to visualize.

Properties of Maps

Although maps have advantages over globes and photographs, they do have one major disadvantage: most maps are flat and the Earth is a sphere. It is impossible to reproduce exactly on a flat surface an object shaped like a sphere. In order to put the Earth's features onto a map they must be stretched in some way. This stretching is called **distortion**.

Distortion does not mean that maps are wrong; it simply means that they are not perfect representations of the Earth or its parts. **Cartographers**, or mapmakers, understand the problems of distortion. They try to design them so that there is as little distortion as possible in the maps.

> **PROJECTION:** the process of putting the features of the Earth onto a flat surface

The process of putting the features of the Earth onto a flat surface is called **PROJECTION**. All maps are really map projections. To properly analyze a given map, one must be familiar with the various parts and symbols that most modern maps use. For the most part, this is standardized, with different maps using similar parts and symbols, which include:

- **The title:** All maps should have a title, just as all books should. The title tells you what information is on the map.

- **The legend:** Most maps have a legend. A legend tells the reader about the various symbols used on the map and what the symbols represent (also called a **map key**).

- **The grid:** A grid is a series of lines that are used to find exact places and locations on the map. There are several different kinds of grid systems in use; however, most maps use the longitude and latitude system, known as the **geographic grid system**.

- **Directions:** Most maps have a directional system to show which way the map is being presented. Often there is a small compass on a map, with arrows showing the four basic directions: north, south, east, and west.

- **The scale:** The scale shows the relationship between a unit of measurement on the map and the real-world measure on the Earth. Maps are drawn to different scales. Some maps show a lot of detail for a small area. Others show a greater span of distance. One should always be aware of the scale being used. For instance, the scale might be something like 1 inch = 10 miles for a small area or 1 inch = 1,000 miles for a map of the world.

Types of Maps

Relief maps

Maps that show the physical features of an area often show information about the elevation, or **relief**, of the land. Elevation is the distance above or below sea level. The elevation is usually shown with colors, for example, all areas on a map that are at a certain level are shown in the same color. Relief maps usually give more detail than simply showing the overall elevation of the land's surface: They show the shape of the land surface, indicating whether it is flat, rugged, or steep.

Thematic maps

Thematic maps are used to show more specific information, often on a single **theme**, or topic. Thematic maps show the distribution or amount of something over a certain given area. For example, topics such as population density; climate; or economic, cultural, or political information would be visually comprehensive on a thematic map.

A map can provide information that might take hundreds of words to explain. Maps can be used to convey a wide variety of information and can be made in many different ways.

Political maps show lines defining countries, states, or territories. Unlike geographical maps that show borders, political maps also include information pertaining to which areas of the world belong to a particular country or state.

Historical maps illustrate history. They depict information pertaining to a specific period in history and show events from the past. Examples include maps of boundaries of the thirteen colonies, where battles were fought during the French Revolution, or which areas were covered by each Chinese dynasty.

Economic maps illustrate the trade, commerce, transport of goods, and/or the general economic conditions of an area. In an elementary classroom, an example of an economic map might include the primary crops/goods developed in each area of the United States. Cultural maps illustrate the culture of a region and include information about the area's religion, traditions, land use, government, trades, language, jobs, and common pastimes.

> ### SKILL 20.14 Communicates the value of social studies education to students, parents/caregivers, colleagues, and the community.

Teachers need to communicate to parents, colleagues, and the community that the field of social studies education is shifting in order to meet the challenges of today's complex world. Students no longer only need to memorize dates or locations on a map but must learn to apply critical thinking skills to the challenges and global issues in our nation and world.

There are several strategies that can be implemented by teachers to communicate the value of a social studies education:

For Students

- Invite a foreign exchange student to speak to your class to discuss his or her country and culture.

- Design a history project in which students learn about the history/culture of the community.

- Invite speakers involved in various social studies fields to visit your class.

For Parents

- Invite parents to special events in the social studies classroom.

- Create a calendar of social studies activities that families can complete during the summer.

- Tell parents what students are learning in your social studies classroom.

For the Community

- Invite the community to a History Day.

- Speak to leading groups in your community about the importance of a social studies education.

- Organize an outreach program in a senior citizen center so students can work with senior members of the community.

COMPETENCY 21
HISTORY

> **SKILL 21.1** **Demonstrates an understanding of historical points of reference in the history of Texas, the United States, and the world** (e.g., the Texas Revolution, the Republic of Texas and the annexation of Texas by the United States).

Key points of reference in the history of Texas include:

- Settlement and culture of Native American tribes before European contact

- 1528–1534: Alvar Nunez Cabeza de Vaca (Spanish explorer) explores Texas for trade

- 1529: Spanish explorer Alonso Alvarez de Pineda maps the Texas coast

- 1685: French explorer Sieur de La Salle establishes Fort St. Louis at Matagorda Bay, providing the basis of the French claim to Texas territory

- 1688: The French colony is massacred

- 1689: The French continue to claim Texas but no longer physically occupy any part of the territory

- 1690: Alonso de Leon establishes San Francisco de los Tejas Mission in East Texas, opening the Old San Antonio Road portion of the Camino Real

- 1700–1799: Spain establishes Catholic missions throughout Texas

- 1762: The French give up their claims to Texas and cede Louisiana to Spain until 1800

- 1800: Much of north Texas is returned to France and later sold to the U.S. in the Louisiana Purchase

- 1823: Stephen Austin begins a colony known as the Old Three Hundred along the Brazos River

- 1832: Battle of Velasco—first casualties of the Texas Revolution

- 1832–1833: The Conventions respond to unrest over the policies of the Mexican government

- 1835: The Texas Revolution officially begins in an effort to obtain freedom from Mexico

- 1836: The Convention of 1836 signs the Texas Declaration of Independence

- The Battle of the Alamo

- Santa Anna executes nearly 400 Texans in the massacre at Goliad

- Santa Anna is believed to have ended the Texas rebellion

- Sam Houston leads an army of 800 to victory by capturing the entire Mexican army at the Battle of San Jacinto

- The Treaty of Velasco is signed by Santa Anna and Republic of Texas officials

- 1837: Sam Houston moves the capital of Texas five times, ending in Houston in 1837

- 1839: Austin becomes the capital of the Republic of Texas

- 1842: Mexican forces twice capture San Antonio and retreat

- 1845: Texas admitted to the Union as a state

- 1850: The Compromise of 1850 adjusts the state boundary and assumes Texas's debts

- 1861: Texas secedes from the Union and joins the Confederacy

- 1861: A government is organized, replacing Houston because of his refusal to swear allegiance to the Confederacy

- 1865: Union troops land in Galveston and put the Emancipation Proclamation into effect in Texas, thus ending slavery

- 1870: Texas is readmitted to the Union

- 1900: Galveston is destroyed, and 8,000 people are killed by a category 4 hurricane

- 1901: The Lucas Gusher comes in, starting the Texas oil boom

The Texas Revolution

The issue of whether Texas would become independent or remain loyal to Mexico resulted in the Texas Revolution. The first battle of the revolution was the Battle of Gonzales, which took place in October 1835. Santa Anna led the Mexican troops during the Revolution, and Sam Houston led the Texan troops. Houston's troops surprised Santa Anna's troops at San Jacinto, causing the Mexican army to retreat south of the Rio Grande River. The Texans declared their independence from Mexico in March 1836.

The Republic of Texas

The Republic of Texas came into existence in March 1836 and lasted approximately two weeks less than ten years. It encompassed an area that includes present-day states of Texas, Oklahoma, Kansas, Colorado, Wyoming, and New Mexico. Mexico had continued to refuse to recognize the independence of Texas and continued raiding the republic's borders. Texas, as a separate nation, continued to attract settlers and on December 29, 1845, Congress approved annexation of the area as a state. Sam Houston served as the republic's president. The continued border disputes with Mexico led to the Mexican–American War, which lasted from 1846 to 1848.

The Annexation of Texas by the United States

Texas was admitted to the United States as the 28th state. President John Tyler promoted the annexation of Texas, and the election of 1844 focused on the republic's admission. James Polk, the Democrat candidate, favored annexation while Henry Clay, the Whig candidate, opposed annexation. Slavery was one of the issues surrounding the republic's admission. The annexation of Texas was approved by Congress on December 29, 1845. The republic relinquished sovereignty to the United States and was admitted to the Union as a slave state in February 1846.

Territorial Expansion in the United States

In the United States, territorial expansion occurred in the expansion westward under the banner of Manifest Destiny. The United States was also involved in the War with Mexico, the Spanish–American War, and support of the Latin American colonies of Spain in their revolt for independence. In Latin America, the Spanish colonies were successful in their fight for independence and self-government.

For information on the twentieth and twenty-first centuries, see Skill 21.26.

SKILL 21.2 **Analyzes how individuals, events, and issues shaped the history of Texas, the United States and the world.**

For information on Native American civilization in Texas prior to early colonization, see Skill 21.3.

For information about the history of Texas, see Skill 21.1.

Spanish Control in Early Days

In 1529, the Spanish explorer Alonso Alvarez de Pineda first mapped the coast of Texas, while Alvar Nunez Cabeza de Vaca explored inland for potential trade opportunities. It was the French, over 150 years later, who first attempted to establish a colony in the Texas territory.

Fort St. Louis was founded by Sieur de La Salle at Matagorda Bay in 1685, establishing France's claim on the region. Through mutiny and massacre at the hands of natives, the colony was eventually destroyed in 1688. France continued to claim Texas for decades following the massacre, even though they had no physical presence in the region.

For more information on early colonization, see Skill 21.4.

Meanwhile, the Spanish began to build missions throughout Texas, beginning in 1690 with the San Francisco de los Tejas Mission in East Texas, founded by Alonso de Leon. Spain continued to populate the area with missions through the eighteenth century. France relinquished its claim on Texas in 1762, turning it over to Spain. France also turned over Louisiana, which included northern Texas, until 1800, when it was given back to France and sold to the United States in the Louisiana Purchase.

Spain's effective control over Texas lasted from 1690 until 1821, when Mexico gained independence from Spain. During this time, Texas had mainly been a thinly populated buffer region between the territories claimed by France and Spain. Mexico, wanting to encourage settlement in the area, invited European and American settlers to the region. In 1823, Stephen Austin began a colony called the Old Three Hundred on the Brazos River, opening the way for further settlement.

Conflict with Mexico

As the young nation of Mexico sought to establish its influence over Texas and the new settlers, unrest developed over government policies. Mexico was officially a Catholic country and expected its citizens to be Catholic. Many of the white settlers were Protestant, however. Mexico also banned slavery, which was widespread in the southern United States at the time. Unrest eventually erupted into conflict in 1832 at the Battle of Velasco between a small Mexican force and a militia of Texas colonists. Following the battle, Texans held conventions to outline their disagreement with Mexican policies, culminating in the signing of a Texas Declaration of Independence on March 2, 1836. Four days later, a Mexican force of 4,000 to 5,000 besieged a small force of Texans at the Alamo in San Antonio. All of the Texan defenders were killed, and the Alamo defeat became a battle cry for Texan independence.

Texas continued to battle against Mexican General Santa Anna and his forces. They suffered more setbacks, but eventually emerged victorious at the Battle of San Jacinto, where Texan troops led by Sam Houston captured the entire Mexican army, including Santa Anna. Texas became an independent country with the signing of the Treaty of Velasco on May 15, 1836. Sam Houston was named the first president of the Republic of Texas.

Republic of Texas and Statehood

After being moved five times, the capital of the Republic of Texas was established at Austin in 1839. Texas's decade as an independent country was marked by division between those who wished to remain independent and expand Texas's borders, and those, like Houston, who wished to become part of the United States. Houston's vision won out, and in 1845, Texas was annexed to the United States and made a state. In 1850, as part of the Compromise of 1850 that ended the Mexican–American War, Texas's borders were adjusted to the present boundaries, and the United States assumed the debts Texas incurred while fighting against Mexico.

> After being moved five times, the capital of the Republic of Texas was established at Austin in 1839.

Approximately a decade later, in 1861, Texas would secede from the United States as part of the Confederacy. Sam Houston, then governor of the State of Texas, refused to swear allegiance to the Confederacy and was replaced. The final battle of the Civil War was fought in Texas at Palmito Ranch on May 12, 1865. One month later, federal troops landed at Galveston to enforce the Emancipation Proclamation, which abolished slavery. Texas was readmitted into the Union in 1870.

Development of Texas

Cattle and livestock and agriculture were important factors in the development of Texas with its open spaces. Many of the cities began as trading posts and then developed. Railroads and other modes of transportation aided the growth of the cities. Dallas became a focal point for grain and cotton trade and was a stop-off point for western migration. Houston was a center for the sugar trade.

Beginning of Twentieth Century

The twentieth century began with disaster for Texas when, in 1900, a category 4 hurricane struck the coast at Galveston, completely destroying the city and killing approximately 8,000 people. The century also started with prosperity, however, when the Spindletop oil range was discovered in early 1901, starting the Texas oil boom. Texas became a major oil-producing state, which resulted in the creation of many jobs and the infrastructure to support such an industry. In the 1940s major companies began to relocate to Texas providing even more jobs.

Houston is a major port and is a center for the oil and aeronautics industry.

See also Skill 21.1

> **SKILL 21.3** **Demonstrates an understanding of similarities and differences among Native American groups in Texas, the United States and the Western Hemisphere before European colonization.**

Archaeologists have discovered evidence of Native American civilization in Texas dating back to the Upper Paleolithic period (at least 9200 BCE, in the late Ice Age). For the most part, these ancient peoples lived in temporary camps along riverbanks. Their subsistence was based on hunting and gathering. As the resources of an area were exhausted, they moved to another area. Some of those Native American tribes were "just passing through"; others stayed, in some cases for many years. Among the major settled tribes were the Caddo, Cherokee, Chickasaw, Choctaw, Comanche, Karankawa, Kickapoo, and Tonkawa.

These first known inhabitants of the state were connected with the Clovis complex. The Folsom complex dates from around 8800–8200 BCE. The Archaic period of Texas history extended from about 6000 BCE to about 700 CE. Little is known about the Early Archaic period (6000–2500 BCE). Hunting was accomplished by spear throwing. The groups that populated the region were small and nomadic. There are indications that there were some relationships across the regions. The Middle Archaic period (2500–1000 BCE) was a time of great population increase and proliferation of the number of occupied sites. Regional differences between the groups began to appear during this period. There is also evidence of some trading of artifacts, sometimes over great distances. The Late Archaic period (1000–300 BCE) continued to be a time of hunting societies. There is abundant evidence that bison became a vital source of food. The transitional Archaic period (300 BCE–700 CE) was a time of some development in tool making as well as the time of the first appearance of settled villages. The settlement of villages marks the emergence of agriculture and the beginning of social and political systems.

The Late Prehistoric period extends from 700 CE to historic times. It is during this period that the bow and arrow first appeared, as well as new types of stone tools, pottery, and the creation and trade of ornamental items. During this period, as well, the early Caddoan culture began to emerge and mound building began. Agriculture spread and became more complex and in some areas pithouse dwellings appeared. In particular, the presence of obsidian artifacts demonstrates the participation of these peoples in a north-south system of trade that extended to the Great Plains and to Wyoming and Idaho, in particular.

The Caddo, in the east, were good at farming, trading, and making pottery. The Cherokee and Choctaw had advanced political structures, with an elected chief. The Chickasaw didn't stay in Texas long but were known as good hunters and farmers. The Choctaw were also good farmers, hunters, tool makers, and house builders. The Comanche were famous horsemen and hunters. The Karankawa were good jewelers and shell makers. The Tonkawa were famous for hunting bison and gathering fruits and nuts.

Some of the Native American tribes that have inhabited the area include the Apache, Comanche, Cherokee, and Wichita tribes, among others.

> ### SKILL 21.4 Demonstrates an understanding of the causes and effects of European exploration and colonization of Texas, the United States and the Western Hemisphere.

For a summary of the early settlement of Texas, see Skill 21.1.

Early exploration and attempts to establish a settlement by the French were ostensibly for the purpose of opening trade opportunities and discovering a direct route from Texas into Louisiana to the Mississippi River. Although their settlement was short-lived, French claims to the territory were maintained for the next seventy years as part of the efforts to expand the French empire in North America.

French and Spanish explorers reached Texas in the sixteenth century, and settlers soon followed. The first important Frenchman to arrive was Sieur de La Salle, as part of his overall exploration of what became the Mississippi Territory. Other French explorers and settlers also arrived, but a combination of meager resources and a surge in Spanish explorers eliminated the French from further influence in the majority of Texas. The Spanish were far more successful in colonizing Texas. Spain had a whole colony called the Kingdom of Texas, which was administered by forces of varying sizes. Conflict erupted over Louisiana but the Spanish missions provided a strong base for settlement and defense and French influence ended for good with the Louisiana Purchase.

Spanish exploration began with the search for the cities of gold. The failure of the French colony in Texas had become known throughout the world and Spain was quick in moving to destroy the ruins of it and to establish a Spanish presence in the area. Spain's interests were both in the resources of Texas, the

Catholic missionary zeal to convert the native peoples, and expansion of the Spanish empire.

See also Skill 21.2

The colonization of Texas by Europeans affected the Native Americans in many ways, some of which were undesirable. The Spanish approach to occupation of a new region was to plant Catholic missions, which would convert the natives, bring them into conformity with Spanish beliefs and ideas, and teach them subsistence agriculture. One of the negative effects of the arrival of the Spanish was the introduction of a number of diseases to which the native people had not been exposed and to which they had no natural immunities.

The Spanish colonists and missionaries introduced a number of European crops as well as methods of irrigation that greatly improved the agricultural output of the Native Americans. They also introduced methods of animal husbandry. But throughout the early years of European occupation, Texas was primarily a buffer zone between the French, Spanish, English, and Americans as each country sought to expand its empire and exploit the native land and people. The greatest influence during this period, however, was that of the Spanish missions and presidios. These colonial institutions had been very successful in Hispanicizing the native people.

Mexican independence from Spain resulted in Mexican control over much of Texas. This control was harsh and dictatorial. In the 1820s, Mexico reached an agreement with Stephen Austin to allow several hundred U.S. settlers, called Texians, to move to the area. Mexico wanted to populate and develop the region. In a short period of time, thousands of settlers arrived to populate Texas. Mexico abolished slavery, a move with which many settlers refused to comply, and the Mexican government tried to tighten its control over the political and economic life of the settlers. Further, the government expected good citizens to be members of the Catholic Church. Most of the settlers were Protestant. Emotions were aroused among the settlers and the local Tejanos, which led to the Texas Revolution.

Spanish influence continued into the nineteenth century but ended with Mexican independence in 1821. Texas passed into Mexican hands until the end of the Mexican–American War, which handed Texas over to the United States.

One major result of the European occupation was a lasting dedication to Spanish culture, especially in the names of towns and foods, which is still reflected in the state. The French influence has by and large disappeared.

One of the negative effects of the arrival of the Spanish was the introduction of a number of diseases to which the native people had not been exposed and to which they had no natural immunities.

In the 1820s, Mexico reached an agreement with Stephen Austin to allow several hundred U.S. settlers, called Texians, to move to the area.

Analyzes the influence of various factors (e.g., *geographic contexts, processes of spatial exchange, science, technology*) **on the development of societies.**

See also Skills 22.1, 22.3, and 22.5

A way to describe where people live is by the geography and topography around them. The vast majority of people on the planet live in areas that are very hospitable. Some people do live in the Himalayas and in the Sahara, but the populations in those areas are small indeed when compared to the plains of China, India, Europe, and the United States. People naturally want to live where they won't have to work hard just to survive, and world population patterns reflect this.

We can examine the spatial organization of the places where people live. For example, in a city, where are the factories and heavy industry buildings? Are they near airports or train stations? Are they on the edge of town, near major roads? What about housing developments? Are they near these industries, or are they far away? Where are the other industrial buildings? Where are the schools and hospitals and parks? What about the police and fire stations? How close are the homes to these other facilities? Towns and especially cities are routinely organized into neighborhoods, so that each house is near most things that its residents might need on a regular basis. This means that large cities have multiple schools, hospitals, grocery stores, fire stations, etc.

Related to this is the distance between cities, towns, villages, or settlements. In certain parts of the United States and in many countries in Europe, the population settlement patterns achieve megalopolis standards, with no clear boundaries from one town to the next. Other, more sparsely populated areas have towns that are few and far between and have relatively few people in them. Some exceptions to this exist, of course, like oases in the deserts; for the most part, however, population centers tend to be relatively near one another or at least near smaller towns.

Most places in the world are close to agricultural land as well. Food makes the world go round and some cities are more agriculturally inclined than others. Rare is the city, however, that grows absolutely no crops. The kind of food grown is almost entirely dependent on the kind of land available and the climate where that land is. Rice doesn't grow well in the desert, for example, and bananas don't grow well in snowy lands. Certain crops are easier to transport than others and the ones that aren't easy to transport are usually grown near ports or other areas of export.

The one thing that changed all of this, of course, is the airplane. Flight has made possible global commerce and the exchange of goods on a level never before seen. Foods from all around the world can be flown literally around the world and, with the aid of refrigeration techniques, be kept fresh enough to sell in markets nearly everywhere. The same is true of medicine and, unfortunately, weapons.

> **SKILL 21.6** **Understands common characteristics of communities past and present, including reasons people have formed communities** (e.g., need for security, religious freedom, law and material well-being)**, ways in which different communities meet their needs** (e.g., government, education, communication, transportation, recreation) **and how historical figures, patriots and good citizens helped shape communities, states and nations.**

Communities, past and present, share common characteristics. People who gather to form communities usually share common goals and ideals. They want to live and work where they feel safe and where they have resources available to sustain themselves. Geography is a factor in where people locate. For example, New England became an industrial center because of its rivers. The rivers supplied water to power machinery that was needed to produce textiles and other equipment. People have settled close to trade routes throughout the centuries. Whether the routes were caravan routes in Africa where products were carried by camels or highway corridors where today's products are carried by trucks, people have established communities to be near sources of food and other products needed for survival. In addition to forming communities for security and material well-being, people also form communities for various purposes, such as religious, educational, and recreational.

In addition to forming communities for security and material well-being, people also form communities for various purposes, such as religious, educational, and recreational.

Communities meet the needs of their residents in various ways. Governments are established; schools and educational systems are created; and interest groups are organized. A community can also, for example, develop a transportation system, industrial complexes, and recreational areas to meet its needs.

People shape communities, states, and nations. Individuals who are elected to office contribute to the betterment of communities. State leaders, such as governors and judges contribute to the economic, cultural, and legal growth of their states. Presidents, leaders of nations throughout the world, and members of world organizations shape trade and monetary policy as well as formulate security measures and agreements that promote stability and peace.

SKILL 21.7 Demonstrates an understanding of basic concepts of culture and the processes of cultural adaptation, diffusion and exchange.

CULTURE: the way of life that includes knowledge, beliefs, values, law, custom, and other human-made elements of a group's environment that the group transmits to the next generation

CULTURAL ADAPTATION: the way a group, as a whole, adapts to a situation or event in the group's environment

CULTURAL DIFFUSION: what happens when an idea, value, or belief of one culture is transmitted to and adopted by other cultures

CULTURAL EXCHANGE: the exchanging of ideas between cultures

CULTURE is the way of life that includes knowledge, beliefs, values, law, custom, and other human-made elements of a group's environment that the group transmits to the next generation.

CULTURAL ADAPTATION is the way a group, as a whole, adapts to a situation or event in the group's environment. The event may be an epidemic, the loss of industry, or a dust storm that ruins crops. The group, or society, uses its knowledge and information to overcome the change that occurred to alter their lives. Cultural adaptation can also result from changes in the family. For example, immigrant children will learn English in school while their parents may retain their native language. Adaptation to a new environment, in various ways, is what occurs when there is cultural adaptation.

CULTURAL DIFFUSION is what happens when an idea, value, or belief of one culture is transmitted to and adopted by other cultures. For example, filling a piñata and having guests break it to obtain candies at a birthday party has become a popular tradition in many homes outside the Mexican culture. Soccer is another example of a game that has been diffused culturally. Once, popular in locations in other countries, the sport is now very popular in the United States.

CULTURAL EXCHANGE refers to the exchanging of ideas between cultures. High school exchange programs where students from other countries live in the homes of Americans are an excellent example of cultural exchange where ideas of one culture are shared with another culture. Cities may sponsor an annual event to share tastes of the different cultures living in the city. When a city has a "Tastes of the City," restaurants prepare ethnic foods for people to purchase. Schools may have a cultural exchange event where students of different cultures bring foods and other items or information about their countries to share with other students and families.

See also Skill 22.9

> **SKILL 21.8** Applies knowledge and analyzes the effects of scientific, mathematical, and technological innovations on political, economic, social and environmental developments as they relate to daily life in Texas, the United States and the world.

Historic Causation

HISTORIC CAUSATION is the concept that events in history are linked to one another by an endless chain of cause and effect. The root causes of major historical events cannot always be seen immediately, and are only apparent when looking back many years later.

> **HISTORIC CAUSATION:** the concept that events in history are linked to one another by an endless chain of cause and effect

When Columbus landed in the New World in 1492, the full effect of his discovery could not have been measured at that time. By opening the Western Hemisphere to economic and political development by Europeans, Columbus changed the face of the world. The Native American populations that had existed before Columbus arrived were fairly quickly decimated by disease and warfare. Over the following century, the Spanish conquered most of South and Central America, and English and French settlers arrived in North America, eventually displacing the Native Americans. This gradual displacement took place over many years and could not have been foreseen by those early explorers. Nevertheless, looking back it is clear that Columbus caused a series of events that had a great impact on world history.

In some cases, individual events can have an immediate, clear effect. In 1941, Europe was embroiled in war. On the Pacific Rim, Japan was engaged in the military occupation of Korea and other Asian countries. The United States took a position of isolation, choosing not to become directly involved in the conflicts. This position changed rapidly, however, on the morning of December 7, 1941, when Japanese forces launched a surprise attack on a U.S. naval base at Pearl Harbor in Hawaii. The United States immediately declared war on Japan and became involved in the European theater shortly afterwards. The U.S. entry into the Second World War undoubtedly contributed to the eventual victory of the Allied forces in Europe and the defeat of Japan after the U.S. dropped two atomic bombs there. The surprise attack on Pearl Harbor affected the outcome of the war and the shape of the modern world.

Agricultural Revolution

The Agricultural Revolution, initiated by the invention of the plow six thousand years ago in Mesopotamia, led to a thorough transformation of human society by making large-scale agricultural production possible and facilitating the development of agrarian societies. During the period in which the plow was invented, the wheel, numbers, and writing were also invented. Coinciding with the shift from hunting wild game to the domestication of animals, this period was one of dramatic social and economic change.

Numerous changes in lifestyle and thinking accompanied the development of stable agricultural communities. Instead of people gathering a wide variety of plants as hunter-gatherers, agricultural communities become dependent on a limited number of harvested plants or crops. Subsistence became vulnerable to the weather and dependent upon planting and harvesting times. Agriculture also required a great deal of physical labor and the development of a sense of discipline. Agricultural communities became stable in terms of location; people were now tied to the land. This made the construction of dwellings appropriate. Dwellings tended to be built relatively close together, creating villages or towns.

Stable communities also freed people from the need to carry everything with them and the moving from hunting ground to hunting ground. This facilitated the invention of larger, more complex tools. As new tools were developed it began to make sense to have some specialization within the society. Skills began to have greater value, and people began to do work on behalf of the community that utilized their particular skills and abilities. Settled community life also gave rise to the notion of wealth. It was now possible to keep possessions.

Settled communities that produce the necessities of life are self-supporting. Advances in agricultural technology and the ability to produce a surplus of produce created two opportunities: first, the opportunity to trade the surplus goods for other desired goods, and second, vulnerability to others who might steal those goods. Protecting domesticated livestock and surplus as well as stored crops became an issue for agricultural communities. This, in turn, led to the construction of walls and other fortifications around communities. The ability to produce surplus crops created the opportunity to trade or barter with other communities in exchange for desired goods. Traders and trade routes began to develop between villages and cities. The domestication of animals expanded the range of trade and facilitated an exchange of ideas and knowledge.

Scientific Revolution

The Scientific Revolution and the Enlightenment were two of the most important movements in the history of civilization, resulting in a new sense of self-examination and a wider view of the world than ever before. The Scientific Revolution was, above all, a shift in focus from belief to evidence. Scientists and philosophers wanted to see the proof, not just believe what other people told them. It was an exciting time, if you were a forward-looking thinker.

Information Revolution

The **INFORMATION REVOLUTION** refers to the sweeping changes in the latter half of the twentieth century that were a result of technological advances and a new respect for the information provided by trained, skilled, and experienced professionals in a variety of fields. This approach to understanding a number of social and economic changes in global society arose from the ability to make computer technology both accessible and affordable. In particular, the development of the computer chip has led to such technological advances as the Internet, the cell phone, cybernetics, wireless communication, and the related ability to disseminate and access a massive amount of information quite readily.

In terms of economic theory and segmentation, it is now the norm to distinguish three basic economic sectors: agriculture and mining, manufacturing, and services. Indeed, labor is now often subdivided into manual labor and informational labor. According to some, the fact that businesses are involved in the production and distribution, processing, and transmission of information has created a new business sector.

> **INFORMATION REVOLUTION:** the sweeping changes in the latter half of the twentieth century that were a result of technological advances and a new respect for the information provided by trained, skilled, and experienced professionals in a variety of fields

> **SKILL** Demonstrates an understanding of historical information and ideas
> **21.9** in relation to other disciplines.

Major Disciplines in the Social Sciences

The disciplines within the social sciences, sometimes referred to as social studies, include anthropology, geography, history, sociology, economics, and political science. Some programs include psychology, archaeology, philosophy, religion, law, and criminology. Also, the subjects of civics and government may be a part of an educational curriculum.

Anthropology

ANTHROPOLOGY is the scientific study of human culture and humanity and the relationship between humanity and culture. Anthropologists study different groups and how they relate to other cultures, patterns of behavior, similarities, and differences. Their research is twofold: cross-cultural and comparative. The major method of study is referred to as participant observation. The anthropologist studies and learns about people by living among them and participating with them in their daily lives. Other methods may be used, but this is the most characteristic method used.

> **ANTHROPOLOGY:** the scientific study of human culture and humanity and the relationship between humanity and culture

Archaeology

ARCHAEOLOGY is the scientific study of past human cultures by examining the remains they left behind—objects such as pottery, bones, buildings, tools, and artwork. Archaeologists locate and examine evidence to help explain the way people lived in the past. They use special equipment and techniques to gather the evidence and keep detailed records of their findings because much of their research causes destruction of the remains being studied.

The first step is to locate an archaeological site, using various methods. Next, surveying the site starts with a detailed description of the site through notes, maps, photographs, and artifacts collected from the surface. Excavating follows, either by digging for buried objects or by diving and working in submersible decompression chambers when underwater. Archaeologists record and preserve the evidence for eventual classification, dating, and evaluation.

Civics

CIVICS is the study of the responsibilities and rights of citizens with emphasis on such subjects as freedom, democracy, and individual rights. Students study local, state, national, and international government structures, functions, and problems. Related to this topic are other social, political, and economic institutions. As a method of study, students gain experience and understanding through direct participation in student government, school publications, and other such involvements. They also participate in community activities such as conservation projects and voter registration drives.

Economics

ECONOMICS is the study of how goods and services are produced and distributed. It also includes the ways people and nations choose what and from whom they buy. Some of the methods of study include research, case studies, analysis, statistics, and mathematics.

Geography

GEOGRAPHY is the study of places and the way living things and Earth's features are distributed throughout the Earth. It includes where animals, people, and plants live and the effects of their relationship with Earth's physical features. Geographers also explore the locations of Earth's features, how they got there, and why it is so important.

History

HISTORY is the study of the past, especially the human past, its important political and economic events, and its cultural and social conditions. Students study history through textbooks, research, field trips to museums and historical sites, and other methods. Most nations establish requirements that history students study the country's heritage, usually to develop an awareness and feeling of loyalty and patriotism. History is generally divided into three main categories: time periods, nations, and specialized topics. Study is accomplished through research, reading, and writing.

> **HISTORY:** the study of the past, especially the human past, its important political and economic events, and its cultural and social conditions

Political Science

POLITICAL SCIENCE is the study of political life and various aspects of government, including elections, political parties, and public administration. In addition, political science examines values such as justice, freedom, power, and equality. There are six main fields of political study in the United States:

> **POLITICAL SCIENCE:** the study of political life and various aspects of government

1. Political theory and philosophy

2. Comparative governments

3. International relations

4. Political behavior

5. Public administration

6. American government and politics

Psychology

PSYCHOLOGY involves scientifically studying behavior and mental processes by observing and recording the ways people and animals relate to each other. Psychologists scrutinize specific patterns, enabling them to discern and predict certain behaviors, using scientific methods to verify their ideas. In this way, they have been able to learn how to help people fulfill their individual human potential and to strengthen understanding between individuals as well as between groups, nations, and cultures. The results of psychological research have deepened our understanding of the reasons for people's behavior.

> **PSYCHOLOGY:** involves scientifically studying behavior and mental processes by observing and recording the ways people and animals relate to each other

Sociology

SOCIOLOGY is the study of human society: the individuals, groups, and institutions that make up human society. It includes every feature of the human social condition. It deals with the predominant behaviors, attitudes, and types of relationships

> **SOCIOLOGY:** the study of human society: the individuals, groups, and institutions that make up human society

within a society, a group of people with a similar cultural background living in a specific geographical area.

Formulating meaningful questions is a primary part of any research process. Providing students with a wide variety of resources promotes this ability by making students aware of a wide array of social studies issues. Encouraging the use of multiple resources also introduces diverse viewpoints and different methods of communicating research results. This promotes the ability to judge the value of a resource and the appropriate ways to interpret it, which supports the development of meaningful inquiry skills.

A clearly presented description of research results spells out the question the researchers hoped to answer. Analyzing research results includes relating the information obtained to this initial question. One must also consider the methods used to gather the data and whether they truly measure what the researchers claim they do.

A research project that sets out to measure the effect of a change in average temperature on the feeding habits of birds, for instance, should use appropriate measurements such as weather observations and observations of the birds in question. Measuring rainfall would not be an appropriate method for this research, because it is not related to the primary area of research. If, during the experiment, it appeared that rainfall might be affecting the research, a researcher could design another experiment to investigate this additional question.

Making a decision based on particular information requires careful interpretation of that information to determine the strength of the evidence supplied and what it means. A chart showing that the number of foreign-born citizens living in the United States has increased annually over the last ten years might allow one to make conclusions about population growth and changes in the relative sizes of ethnic groups in the United States. The chart would not give information about the reason the number of foreign-born citizens increased or address matters of immigration status. Conclusions in these areas would be invalid based on this information.

> ## SKILL 21.11 Demonstrates an understanding of historical research and knows how historians locate, gather, organize, analyze and report information by using standard research methodologies.

Social studies is a broad field that incorporates many kinds of research and results. A historian's job is to locate, research, analyze, and interpret artifacts, oral records, and written records from the past. These different types of research lend themselves to varying types of communication.

Historians have created an organized system of time periods within which to classify information. Depending on the area of social science, time is classified in different ways. For example, historians may refer to the Egyptian period or the Roman period. However, one of the main classification systems is the geologic time scale used by geologists, paleontologists, and other Earth scientists. The largest time period in this system is the super eon, which is composed of eons (half a billion or more years). Eons are divided into eras, which comprise several hundred million years. The eras are broken down into periods (much longer than a casual discussion of periods such as the Greek period), which are then further broken down into epochs (tens of millions of years). Finally, epochs are divided into ages, which refer to millions of years.

Archaeologists use existing knowledge of cultures to help them locate resources including fossils, artifacts, and primary documents (such as letters, diaries, speeches, etc.) to find historical information. They sometimes incorporate secondary sources such as books, paintings, and media reports, but they rely more on primary resources. In the event that a culture had no written records, historians attempt to utilize the culture's oral history from resources such as legends, songs, folklore, and traditions.

For more information on primary and secondary resources, see Skills 21.12 and 21.19.

Historians use the resources they can to confirm and/or project theories about ideas, events, and people in the past. To report information, geographic material might be best communicated with a map, for instance, while historical material might be best conveyed through writing. Population changes might be displayed in a chart or graph. It is important to make students familiar with appropriate ways to communicate various types of information and to give them several options to keep their interest level high.

> **SKILL 21.12** Knows the characteristics and uses of primary and secondary sources used for historical research (e.g., databases, maps, photographs, media services, the Internet, biographies, interviews, questionnaires, artifacts); analyzes historical information from primary and secondary sources; understands and evaluates information in relation to bias, propaganda, point of view and frame of reference.

Primary Sources

Primary sources include the following kinds of materials:

- Documents created during the time period being studied, including diaries, letters, newspapers, books, magazines, legal papers, the manuscript census, etc.

- Objects made and/or used during the time period being studied

Guidelines for the use of primary sources:

- Be certain that you understand both explicit and implicit references.

- Read the entire text you are reviewing; do not simply extract a few sentences.

- Although anthologies of materials may help you identify primary source materials, the full original text should be consulted.

Secondary Sources

Secondary sources include the following kinds of materials:

- Books about the period of time, based on primary materials

- Books written on the basis of primary materials about persons who played a major role in the events under consideration

- Books and articles written on the basis of primary materials about the culture, the social norms, the language, and the values of the period

- Quotations from primary sources

- Statistical data on the period

- The conclusions and inferences of other historians

- Multiple interpretations of the ethos of the time

Guidelines for the use of secondary sources:

- Do not rely on only a single secondary source.

- Check facts and interpretations against primary sources whenever possible.

- Do not accept the conclusions of other historians uncritically.

- Place greatest reliance on secondary sources created by the best and most respected scholars.

- Do not use the inferences of other scholars as if they were facts.

- Ensure that you recognize any bias the writer brings to his or her interpretation of history.

- Understand the primary point of the book as a basis for evaluating the value of the material to your questions.

Evaluating Sources

Especially with written or oral resources, historians must consider the point of view, context, and time frame of each resource. This is important because the resource may lack objectivity if it was generated by someone who existed during the time period being studied and may present information the author's point of view.

Challenges with evaluating sources include:

- Understanding the vocabulary and specific terms in the context of the time frame

- Understanding the tone, intended audience, and purpose of publication

- Being aware of the education/position of the author as well as his or her assumptions

This is where secondary sources become valuable. Other accounts found by historians may corroborate, disprove, or provide an alternative explanation to one found in a primary source. This is why historians study a number of resources to analyze historical data.

See also Skill 22.21

> SKILL 21.13 **Applies and evaluates the use of problem-solving processes, gathering of information, listing and considering options, considering advantages and disadvantages, choosing and implementing solutions and assessing the effectiveness of solutions.**

For information about posing questions, see Skill 21.10.

For information about sources, see Skill 21.12.

Social studies provides an opportunity for students to broaden their general academic skills in many areas. By encouraging students to ask and investigate questions, teachers help students learn to make meaningful inquiries into social issues. Providing them with a range of sources requires students to make judgments about the best sources for investigating a line of inquiry and develops the ability to determine authenticity among those sources. Collaboration develops the ability to work as part of a team and to respect the viewpoints of others.

Historic events and social issues cannot be considered only in isolation. People and their actions are connected in many ways, and events are often linked through cause and effect over time. Identifying and analyzing these social and historic links is a primary goal of the social sciences.

> Historic events and social issues cannot be considered only in isolation.

The methods used to analyze social phenomena borrow from several of the social sciences. Interviews, statistical evaluation, observation, and experimentation are just some of the ways to measure people's opinions and motivations. From analysis of people's opinions and motivations, larger social beliefs and movements can be interpreted, and events, issues, and social problems can be placed in context, which provides a fuller view of their importance.

SKILL 21.14 **Applies and evaluates the use of decision-making processes to identify situations that require decisions: by gathering information, identifying options, predicting consequences and taking action to implement the decisions.**

Decision making can be broken down into methodical steps that result in sound decisions based on the relevant facts.

The first step in decision making is to identify situations that require decisions. These situations often present themselves in daily life. One decision that many people face is whether to buy a home or rent an apartment.

Before making a decision to buy or rent, one should gather information (the second step), including information on the availability of apartments and homes for sale and the relative monthly costs of each option. The third step—identifying options—organizes the facts gathered in the second step into clear potential decisions.

Predicting the consequence of a decision is an important step in the process. In this example, forecasting the effect of buying vs. renting on one's monthly income would be a crucial step. One choice might be less expensive but might be farther from work, increasing commuting expenses, for example. Predicting how a decision will affect other areas of one's life is essential before arriving at a final decision, which is the last step in the process.

> ### SKILL 21.15 Communicates and interprets historical information in written, oral and visual forms and translates information from one medium to another (e.g., written to visual, statistical to written or visual).

It is important to present information in a way that students retain the material being presented. It has been said that "a picture is worth a thousand words." For example, a lesson plan that focuses on the Great Depression can identify the "alphabet" agencies that were created to put people back into the workforce. Written lists of the agencies and brief descriptions of their work can be used to present the activity. However, pictures of the workers or types of work that was done translate written information into visual information, which is more interesting, more meaningful, and more lasting for the student.

See also Skills 21.10 and 21.11

> ### SKILL 21.16 Analyzes historical information by categorizing, comparing and contrasting, making generalizations and predictions and drawing inferences and conclusions (e.g., regarding population statistics, patterns of migration, voting trends and patterns).

One way to analyze historical events, patterns, and relationships is to focus on specific elements of history. Some of these are described below.

- **Politics and political institutions** can provide information about the prevailing opinions and beliefs of a group of people and how they change over time. Historically, Texas has been a traditional supporter of the Democratic Party. Looking at the political history, population statistics, and voting trends in the state can reveal the popular social ideals that have developed in Texas and how they have changed over time.

- **Race and ethnicity** is another historical lens. Researching the history of how people of different races have treated one another reflects on many other social aspects of a society, and can be a fruitful line of historical interpretation. Patterns of migration and statistics relating to locations of ethnic communities also are ways to analyze historical information.

- Gender is a lens that focuses on the relative positions men and women hold in a society, and is connected to many other themes such as politics and economics. In the United States, for many years, women were not allowed to vote, for example. Married women were not expected to hold jobs. For women who did work, only certain types of work were available. Investigating gender issues reveals changes in public attitudes, economic changes, and shifting political attitudes, among other things.

- Economic factors drive many social activities, such as where people live and work and the relative wealth of nations. As a historical lens, economic factors can connect events to their economic causes. The Great Migration of African Americans from the South to Texas in the early decades of the twentieth century can be interpreted along economic themes, for example: Many blacks were searching for better-paying jobs. One reason more jobs were available in the North was World War I, which took many northern men into the armed forces and away from the workforce. Thus, economic factors were related to political factors and had repercussions in race relations. Historical themes are often connected in this way and can provide a framework upon which to build a fuller interpretation of history.

Historical Concepts

HISTORICAL CONCEPTS are movements, belief systems, or other phenomena that can be identified and examined individually or as part of a historical theme. Capitalism, communism, democracy, racism, and globalization are all examples of historical concepts. Historical concepts can be interpreted as part of larger historical themes and provide insight into historical events by placing them in a larger historical context.

> **HISTORICAL CONCEPTS:** movements, belief systems, or other phenomena that can be identified and examined individually or as part of a historical theme

The historical concept of colonialism, for example, has a connection to the history of Texas. COLONIALISM is the concept that a nation should seek to control areas outside of its borders for economic and political gain by establishing settlements and controlling the native inhabitants. Beginning in the seventeenth century, the nations of France and Britain were both actively colonizing North America, with the Spanish initially controlling the area that is now Texas. These colonial powers eventually clashed, and Texas came under Mexican control. This is an example of how a historical concept can connect local history with larger national and worldwide movements.

> **COLONIALISM:** the concept that a nation should seek to control areas outside of its borders for economic and political gain by establishing settlements and controlling the native inhabitants

SKILL 21.17 Applies knowledge of the concept of chronology and its use in understanding history and historical events.

As part of the discipline of history, chronology locates events in time. It can also be the arrangement of the time line itself, such as moving from earliest to latest or latest to earliest.

RELATIVE CHRONOLOGY is locating events in relation to each other; for example, the Revolutionary War came before the Civil War. ABSOLUTE CHRONOLOGY is attaching events to specific dates; for example, the Revolutionary War began in 1776 and ended in 1783, or the Civil War began in 1861 and ended in 1865. Dates in an absolute chronology may vary depending on the type of chronological calendar being used. The Julian calendar and the Gregorian calendar are two of many examples.

Although the abstract concept of chronology is difficult for elementary students to understand, they can begin by learning about the passing of time with concepts such as "before," "after," and "a long time ago." They can sort events in chronological order and be aware of a time beyond their memory. Later, they can sort events into periods and use dates and terms to describe the past. Eventually, they can write about events in chronological order and understand terminology such as *CE, BCE, century,* and *decade.*

By understanding chronology, students get a sense of the past; learn to understand causes and effects; learn about people, events, and periods in history; and can understand their own relationship with the world.

> **RELATIVE CHRONOLOGY:** locating events in relation to each other

> **ABSOLUTE CHRONOLOGY:** attaching events to specific dates

SKILL 21.18 Applies different methods of interpreting the past to understand, evaluate and support multiple points of view, frames of reference and the historical context of events and issues.

Interpreting the past is more than examining past experience. It is a way to establish a connection and provide context to modern life. As teachers, you will use a wide variety of methods to help your students understand past events and their connections to our lives. Through your guidance and structured activities, students can compare and contrast cultures, examine continuity and change over time, and explore cause-and-effect relationships.

At a basic level, elementary students can tell and write stories that show their understanding of past events and they can connect these events to episodes in their own lives to demonstrate an understanding of cause and effect. Sometimes having them summarize an event is sufficient to determine their comprehension.

Give students a short primary or secondary document and ask them to discuss the point of view of the writer or speaker. Have students create their own document, such as a letter or journal from an historical figure.

The National Center for Restructuring Education, Schools, and Teaching (NCREST) advocates role-playing and simulation activities to help students understand historical time and place. By engaging them in creative activities, teachers help students become active learners who can identify and elaborate on their roles. Not only do they study significant events, they examine issues from a personal perspective.

One activity that provides a broad perspective is a time line that examines the art, literature, religion, inventions, politics, issues, events, and people of a certain period. What was going on around the country and around the world at the time of a particular event?

Visiting a museum is an important way for students to experience history. According to the Texas Education Agency Social Studies Center, there are "ten things every social studies teacher ought to know about using museums and historic sites to teach the social studies":

1. Museums are a significant TEKS teaching resource.

2. Museums and historic sites inspire students.

3. There are many types of museums.

4. Museums offer students informal opportunities to learn and can help you to design rich experiences for your students.

5. Museums and historic sites have good curriculum support materials.

6. Virtual trips to a museum or historic site are almost as good as real trips.

7. A successful museum trip involves the three P's: preparation, participation, and post-visit reflection.

8. You and your students can make a museum together.

9. Museum educators and curators are both resources and role models.

10. Texas has many excellent museums with unlimited learning opportunities.

Demonstrates an understanding of the foundations of representative government in the United States, significant individuals, events and issues of the Revolutionary era and challenges confronting the United States government in the early years of the Republic.

Causes of the American Revolution

The earliest sign of the coming American Revolution was conflict over the issue of trade and taxation. Tensions between the colonists and England arose over the Quartering Act, the Sugar Act, and the Stamp Act, and were expressed in the Boston Massacre and the Boston Tea Party.

Before 1763, except for trade and supplying raw materials, the colonies had been left pretty much to themselves. England viewed the colonies as part of its economic empire. Little consideration was given to how the colonists were to conduct their daily affairs, so they became independent and extremely skillful at handling those daily affairs.

The colonists' protest of no taxation without representation was meaningless to the English. The colonists considered their colonial legislative assemblies to be equal to Parliament, which was an unacceptable idea in England. By 1763, Britain had changed its perception of its American colonies to a "territorial" empire. The stage was set and the conditions right for a showdown.

In 1763 Parliament decided it needed a standing army in North America to reinforce British control. In 1765, the Quartering Act was passed, requiring the colonists to provide supplies and living quarters for the British troops. In addition, the British attempted to keep the peace by establishing good relations with the Native Americans. They issued a proclamation prohibiting any American colonists from making any settlements west of the Appalachians until treaties had been established with the Native Americans.

The Sugar Act of 1764 required the efficient collection of taxes on molasses brought into the colonies and gave British officials free license to conduct searches of the premises of anyone suspected of violating the law. The colonists were taxed on newspapers, legal documents, and other printed matter under the Stamp Act of 1765. Although a stamp tax was already in effect in England, the colonists would have none of it. After a violent protest, Parliament repealed the tax.

In Boston, mob violence provoked retaliation by British troops, bringing about the deaths of five people and the wounding of eight others. The Boston Massacre shocked Americans and British alike. Subsequently, in 1770, Parliament voted to repeal all of the provisions of the Townshend Acts, with the exception of the tea tax. In 1773, the tax on tea sold by the British East India Company was substantially reduced.

This fueled colonial anger once more because it gave the company an unfair trade advantage and forcibly reminded the colonists of the British right to tax them. Merchants refused to sell the tea; colonists refused to buy and drink it; and a shipload of tea was dumped into Boston Harbor—an incident remembered as the Boston Tea Party.

The American Revolution began when the British and colonial soldiers met at Lexington and Concord in April 1775.

The American Revolution began when the British and colonial soldiers met at Lexington and Concord in April 1775. George Washington was named commander-in-chief of the American forces. The American victory at the Battle of Saratoga was the turning point of the war for the Americans, and the British forces led by Cornwallis later surrendered at Yorktown. European military personnel who assisted the Americans included Kosciusko, Pulaski, and Lafayette.

Articles of Confederation

THE ARTICLES OF CONFEDERATION: the first political system under which the newly independent colonies organized themselves

THE ARTICLES OF CONFEDERATION were the first political system under which the newly independent colonies organized themselves. They were drafted after the Declaration of Independence in 1776, passed by the Continental Congress on November 15, 1777, ratified by the thirteen states, and took effect on March 1, 1781.

The Articles gave Congress the power to declare war, appoint military officers, and coin money. The Congress was also responsible for foreign affairs. The Articles of Confederation limited the powers of Congress by giving the states final authority. Although Congress could pass laws, at least nine of the thirteen states had to approve a law before it went into effect. Congress could not pass any laws regarding taxes. To get money, Congress had to ask each state for it; no state could be forced to pay.

The serious weaknesses of the Articles were:

- lack of power to regulate finances over interstate trade
- lack of power to regulate finances over foreign trade
- lack of power to enforce treaties
- lack of power to maintain the military

Within a few months from the adoption of the Articles of Confederation, it became apparent that there were serious defects in the system of government established for the new republic. There was a need for change that would create a national government with adequate powers to replace the Confederation, which was actually only a league of sovereign states.

In 1786, an effort to regulate interstate commerce ended in what is known as the Annapolis Convention. Because only five states were represented, this Convention was not able to accomplish definitive results. The debates, however, made it clear that a government with as little authority could not regulate foreign and interstate commerce as the government established by the Confederation. Congress was, therefore, asked to call a convention to provide a constitution that would address the emerging needs of the new nation. The convention met under the presidency of George Washington, with 55 of the 65 appointed members present. A constitution was written in four months.

Constitutional Convention

In May 1787, delegates from all states (except Rhode Island) met in Philadelphia. At first, they met to revise the Articles of Confederation as instructed by Congress, but they soon realized that much more was needed. Abandoning their instructions, they set out to write a new CONSTITUTION, the foundation of government in the United States and a model for representative government throughout the world.

> CONSTITUTION: the foundation of government in the United States and a model for representative government throughout the world

Patrick Henry was one well-known person who was concerned that creation of a powerful central government would subvert the authority of the state legislatures. Between the official notes kept and the complete notes of future president James Madison, an accurate picture of the events of the Constitutional Convention is part of the historical record. The delegates went to Philadelphia representing different areas and different interests. They all agreed on a strong central government but not one with unlimited powers. They also agreed that no one part of government should control the rest.

The delegates settled on a republican form of government (sometimes referred to as representative democracy) in which the supreme power was in the hands of the voters who would elect the people who would govern for them.

Controversies and compromises

One of the first serious controversies involved the small states versus the large states over representation in Congress. After much argument and debate, the Great Compromise, or Connecticut Compromise, was proposed by Roger Sherman. It was agreed that Congress would have two houses: the Senate would have two senators from each state, giving equal powers to the states in the Senate. The House of Representatives would have its members elected based on each state's population. Both houses could draft bills to debate and vote on, with the exception of bills pertaining to money, which must originate in the House of Representatives.

Another controversy involved economic differences between North and South, specifically, the counting of African slaves for purposes of determining representation in the House of Representatives. The Southern delegates were in favor of this but did not want it to determine the amount of taxes to be paid. The Northern delegates argued the opposite: Count the slaves for tax purposes but not for representation. The resulting agreement was known as the three-fifths compromise. Three-fifths of the slaves would be counted for both tax purposes and determining representation in the House.

The last major compromise, also between North and South, was the Commerce Compromise. The economic interests of the North were related to industry and business whereas the economic interests of the South were primarily in farming. The northern merchants wanted government to regulate and control commerce with foreign nations and with the states. Southern planters opposed this idea because they felt that any tariff laws passed would be unfavorable to them.

The compromise to this dispute was that Congress was given the power to regulate commerce with other nations and the states, including levying tariffs on imports. However, Congress was not given the power to levy tariffs on exports. This increased concern in the South about the effect it would have on the slave trade. The delegates finally agreed that the importation of slaves could continue for twenty more years with no interference from Congress. Any import tax could not exceed ten dollars per person. After 1808, Congress would be able to decide whether to prohibit or regulate any further importation of slaves.

The fourth major area of conflict was how the President would be chosen. One side of the disagreement argued for election by direct vote of the people. The other side thought Congress should choose the President. One group feared the ignorance of the people; the other feared the power of a small group of people. The compromise was the Electoral College.

Ratification of the Constitution

Eleven states finally ratified the Constitution, and the new national government went into effect. It was no small feat that the delegates were able to produce a workable, satisfactory document.

The separation of powers into three branches of government was a built-in system of checks and balances and a stroke of genius. It provided individual and states' rights as well as an organized central authority to keep a new, inexperienced young nation on track. The system of government was so flexible that it has continued in its basic form to this day—through civil war, foreign wars, economic depression, and social revolution for over two hundred years.

As a living document, the Constitution remains strong while allowing itself to be changed with changing times. As Benjamin Franklin said, "Though it may not be the best there is," he "wasn't sure that it could be possible to create one better." In 1789, the Electoral College unanimously elected George Washington as the country's first president, and the new nation was on its way.

See Skill 24.3 on the three branches of government.

War of 1812

The new nation faced an international crisis in the War of 1812. This resulted from political and economic struggles between France and Great Britain. Napoleon's goal was complete conquest and control of Europe, including Great Britain. Although British troops were temporarily driven off the mainland of Europe, the British navy still controlled the seas, which France had to cross to carry the products it traded. The United States traded with both nations, especially with France and its colonies.

The British decided to destroy the U.S. trade with France, for two main reasons:

- Products and goods from the United States gave Napoleon what he needed to continue his struggle with Britain. The British argued that the Americans were aiding Britain's enemy.

- Britain felt threatened by the increasing strength and success of the U.S. merchant fleet who were becoming major competitors with the ship owners and merchants in Britain.

The British issued the ORDERS IN COUNCIL, which was a series of measures prohibiting American ships from entering French ports, not only in Europe but also in India and the West Indies. At the same time, Napoleon began efforts for a coastal blockade of the British Isles. He issued a series of orders prohibiting all nations, including the United States, from trading with the British. He threatened to seize every ship entering French ports after it stopped at a British port or colony, even threatening to seize every ship inspected by a British cruiser or that paid any duties to the British government. The British were stopping American ships and pressing American seamen into service on British ships. Americans were outraged.

In 1807, Congress passed the Embargo Act, forbidding American ships from sailing to foreign ports. It could not be completely enforced and it hurt business and trade in the United States so it was repealed in 1809. Two additional acts passed by Congress after James Madison became president attempted to regulate trade with other nations and to get Britain and France to remove the restrictions they had imposed on American shipping. The catch was that, whichever nation removed restrictions, the United States agreed not to trade with the other one.

> **ORDERS IN COUNCIL:** a series of measures prohibiting American ships from entering French ports, not only in Europe but also in India and the West Indies

Napoleon was the first to agree, prompting Madison to issue orders prohibiting trade with Britain. This did not work either, and although Britain eventually rescinded the Orders in Council, war came in June 1812.

During this war, Americans were divided over whether it was necessary to fight as well as over which territories should be fought for and taken. The nation was still young and not prepared for war. The primary U.S. objective was to conquer Canada, but it failed.

The war ended on Christmas Eve, 1814, with the signing of the Treaty of Ghent. The treaty brought peace, released prisoners of war, restored all occupied territory, and set up a commission to settle boundary disputes with Canada.

Monroe Doctrine

The war proved to be a turning point in American history. European events had profoundly shaped U.S. policies, especially foreign policies. Thus, in President Monroe's message to Congress on December 2, 1823, he delivered a speech now known as the Monroe Doctrine. The United States was informing the powers of the Old World that the American continent was no longer open to European colonization and that any effort to extend European political influence into the New World would be considered by the United States "as dangerous to our peace and safety." The United States would not interfere in European wars or internal affairs and expected Europe to stay out of American affairs.

> SKILL 21.20 Demonstrates an understanding of westward expansion and analyzes its effects on the political, economic and social development of the United States and Texas, including its effects on American Indian life.

In the United States, territorial expansion occurred in the expansion westward under the banner of Manifest Destiny. In addition, the United States was involved in the war with Mexico, the Spanish–American War, and support of the Latin American colonies of Spain in their revolt for independence. In Latin America, the Spanish colonies were successful in their fight for independence and self-government.

After the United States purchased the Louisiana Territory, Jefferson appointed Captains Meriwether Lewis and William Clark to explore it, to find out exactly what had been purchased. The expedition went all the way to the Pacific Ocean, returning two years later with maps, journals, and artifacts. This led the way for future explorers to learn more about the territory and resulted in the westward movement and the later belief in the doctrine of Manifest Destiny.

The United States and Britain had shared the Oregon country. By the 1840s, with the increase in the free and slave populations and the settlers' demand for U.S. control and government, the conflict had to be resolved. In a treaty signed in 1846 by both nations, there was a peaceful resolution with Britain giving up its claims south of the 49th parallel.

In the American Southwest, the results were exactly the opposite. Spain had claimed this area since the 1540s, had spread northward from Mexico City, and, in the 1700s, had established missions, forts, villages, towns, and large ranches. After the purchase of the Louisiana Territory in 1803, Americans began moving into Spanish territory. A few hundred American families in what is now Texas were allowed to live there but had to agree to become loyal subjects to Spain. In 1821, Mexico successfully revolted against Spanish rule, won independence, and chose to be more tolerant toward the American settlers and traders. The Mexican government encouraged and allowed extensive trade and settlement, especially in Texas. Many of the new settlers were southerners who brought their slaves with them. Slavery was outlawed in Mexico and technically illegal in Texas, although the Mexican government looked the other way.

Friction increased between land-hungry Americans swarming into western lands and the Mexican government, which controlled these lands. The clash was not only political but also cultural and economic. The Spanish influence permeated all parts of southwestern life: law, language, architecture, and customs. By this time, the doctrine of Manifest Destiny was in the hearts and on the lips of those seeking new areas to settle and a new life. Americans were demanding U.S. control of not only the Mexican territory but also Oregon. Peaceful negotiations with Great Britain secured Oregon but it took two years of war to gain control of the southwestern United States.

In addition, the Mexican government owed debts to U.S. citizens whose property was damaged or destroyed during its struggle for independence from Spain. By the time war broke out in 1845, Mexico had not paid its war debts. The government was weak, corrupt, irresponsible, torn by revolution, and in poor financial condition. Mexico was also bitter over American expansion into Texas and the 1836 revolution, which resulted in Texas's independence. In the 1844 presidential election, the Democrats pushed for annexation of Texas and Oregon and, after winning, started the procedure to admit Texas to the Union.

When statehood occurred, diplomatic relations between the United States and Mexico ended. President Polk wanted U.S. control of the entire Southwest, from Texas to the Pacific Ocean. He sent a diplomatic mission with an offer to purchase New Mexico and Upper California but the Mexican government refused to even receive the diplomat. Consequently, in 1846, each nation claimed aggression on the part of the other and war was declared. The treaty signed in 1848 and a subsequent one in 1853 completed the southwestern boundary of the United States, reaching to the Pacific Ocean, as President Polk wished.

The impact of the westward movement resulted in the completion of the borders of the present-day conterminous United States. Contributing factors included the bloody war with Mexico, the ever-growing controversy over slave versus free states affecting the balance of power or influence in the U.S. Congress (especially the Senate), and finally, the Civil War itself.

For information about expansion in the Southwest, see Skill 21.1.

> ## SKILL 21.21 Analyzes ways that political, economic and social factors led to the growth of sectionalism and the Civil War.

> *Slavery in the English colonies began in 1619 when twenty Africans arrived in the colony of Virginia at Jamestown.*

Slavery in the English colonies began in 1619 when twenty Africans arrived in the colony of Virginia at Jamestown. From then on, slavery had a foothold, especially in the agricultural South, where a large amount of labor was needed for the extensive plantations. Free men refused to work for wages on the plantations when land was available for settling on the frontier.

This period of U.S. history was a period of compromises, breakdowns of the compromises, desperate attempts to restore and retain harmony, short-lived intervals of the uneasy balance of interests, and ever-increasing conflict.

For a brief period after 1815, the nation enjoyed the "era of good feelings." People were moving into the West; industry and agriculture were growing; and a feeling of national pride united Americans in their efforts and determination to strengthen the country. However, tensions mounted and it appeared to the South that the federal government was siding with northern industrial interests over the South's agricultural concerns. Over-speculation in stocks and land for quick profits backfired. Cotton prices were rising, and many southerners bought land for cultivation at inflated prices. Manufacturers in the industrial North purchased land to build more plants and factories as an attempt to have a part of this prosperity.

Settlers in the West rushed to buy land to reap the benefits of the increasing prices of meat and grain. To have the money for all of these economic activities, all of these groups were borrowing heavily from the banks, and the banks themselves encouraged this by giving loans on insubstantial security.

In late 1818, the Bank of the United States and its branches stopped renewing personal mortgages and required state banks to immediately pay their bank notes in gold, silver, or national bank notes. The state banks were unable to do this so they closed their doors and were unable to do any business at all. Since mortgages could not be renewed, people lost their properties, and foreclosures were rampant throughout the country.

At the same time, cotton prices collapsed in the English market. The high price of cotton had caused the British manufacturers to seek cheaper cotton from India for their textile mills. With the fall of cotton prices, the demand for American manufactured goods declined, revealing how fragile the economic prosperity had been.

In 1824, Congress, favoring the financial interests of the manufacturers in New England and the Middle Atlantic states, passed a higher tariff. Proposed by Henry Clay and called the American System, the purpose of the tariff was to fund road building and other infrastructure as well as to create the national bank. The 1824 tariff was also closely tied to the presidential election of that year. Before it became law, John C. Calhoun had proposed the very high tariffs in an effort to get Eastern business interests to vote with the agricultural interests in the South (who were against it). Supporters of candidate Andrew Jackson sided with whichever side served their best interests.

The bill became law, to Calhoun's surprise, due mainly to the political maneuvering of Martin van Buren and Daniel Webster. By the time the higher 1828 tariff was passed, feelings were extremely bitter in the South, where many believed that the New England manufacturers greatly benefited from it. Vice President Calhoun, speaking for his home state of South Carolina, promptly declared that if any state felt that a federal law was unconstitutional, that state could nullify it.

In 1832, Congress lowered the tariff slightly but not enough to please South Carolina, which promptly declared it null and void, threatening to secede from the Union.

In 1833, Congress lowered the tariff again, this time to a level acceptable to South Carolina. Although President Jackson believed in states' rights, he also firmly believed in and was determined to preserve the Union. A constitutional crisis had been averted, but sectional divisions were getting deeper and more pronounced. Meanwhile, the abolition movement was growing rapidly, becoming an important issue in the North. The issue of slavery, in addition to the tariff issue, resulted in sectional division. People were moving into western lands and the issue of slavery moved with them. In addition to whether slavery would be permitted in the territories, Congress had to decide whether to admit slaves and free states and how to maintain a balance between the two.

Understands individuals, issues and events involved in the Civil War and analyzes the effects of Reconstruction on the political, economic and social life of the United States and Texas.

At the Constitutional Convention, one of the slavery compromises concerned counting slaves to determine the number of representatives each state would have in the House of Representatives and the amount of taxes to be paid. Southerners pushed for counting the slaves for representation but not for taxes. Northerners pushed for the opposite. The resulting compromise, sometimes referred to as the three-fifths compromise, was that both groups agreed that three-fifths of the slaves would be counted for both taxes and representation.

The other compromise over slavery was part of the disputes over how much regulation the central government would impose on commercial activities such as trade with other nations and the slave trade. It was agreed that Congress would regulate commerce with other nations, including taxing imports. Southerners were worried about the taxing of slaves coming into the country and the possibility of Congress prohibiting the slave trade altogether. The agreement reached allowed the states to continue importing slaves for the next twenty years, until 1808, at which time Congress would make a decision about the future of the slave trade. During the twenty-year period, no more than ten dollars per person could be levied on slaves coming into the country.

An additional provision of this compromise was that with the admission of Missouri, slavery would not be allowed in the rest of the Louisiana Purchase territory north of latitude 36°30'. This was acceptable to the southern congressmen since it was not profitable to grow cotton on land north of this latitude anyway.

The crisis was thought to have been resolved, but the next year it was discovered that in its state constitution, the Missouri Territory allowed slavery. Admitting Missouri as a state was the first serious clash between North and South. In 1819, the United States consisted of twenty-one states: eleven free states and ten slave states. The Missouri Territory allowed slavery, and if Missouri were admitted, it would cause an imbalance in the number of U.S. senators. Alabama had already been admitted as a slave state and that had balanced the Senate, with the North and South each having twenty-two senators.

The first Missouri Compromise resolved the conflict by approving admission of Maine as a free state along with Missouri as a slave state, thus maintaining a balance of power in the Senate with the same number of free and slave states. Henry Clay, known as the Great Compromiser, then proposed a second Missouri Compromise, which was acceptable to everyone. His proposal was that the U.S. Constitution guaranteed protections and privileges to citizens of states, and

Missouri's proposed constitution could not deny these to any of its citizens. The acceptance in 1820 of this second compromise opened the way for Missouri's statehood—a temporary reprieve only—and brought Maine into the Union as a free state, while Missouri was a slave state.

The DOCTRINE OF NULLIFICATION stated that the states had the right to nullify (declare invalid) any act of Congress they believed to be unjust or unconstitutional. The nullification crisis of the mid-nineteenth century climaxed over a new tariff on imported manufactured goods that was enacted by the Congress in 1828. While this tariff protected the manufacturing and industrial interests of the North, it placed an additional burden of cost on southerners, who were only affected by the tariff as consumers of manufactured goods. The North had become increasingly economically dependent on industry and manufacturing, while the South had become increasingly agricultural. Despite the fact that the tariff was primarily intended to protect northern manufacturing interests in the face of imports from other countries, the effect on the South was to simply raise the prices of needed goods.

> **DOCTRINE OF NULLIFICATION:** the states had the right to nullify (declare invalid) any act of Congress they believed to be unjust or unconstitutional

Lincoln–Douglas Debates

In 1858, Abraham Lincoln and Stephen A. Douglas were running for the office of U.S. Senator from Illinois and participated in a series of debates, which directly affected the outcome of the 1860 presidential election. Douglas, a Democrat, was up for reelection and knew that if he won this race, he had a good chance of becoming president in 1860. Lincoln, a Republican, was not an abolitionist but he believed that slavery was morally wrong, and he firmly supported the Republican Party principle that slavery must not be allowed to extend any further.

The slavery issue flared up again, not to be done away with until the end of the Civil War. It was obvious that newly acquired territory would be divided up into territories and would later become states. In addition to the northerners who advocated the prohibition of slavery and the southerners who favored slavery, a third faction arose supporting the doctrine of POPULAR SOVEREIGNTY. This doctrine stated that people living in territories and states should be allowed to decide for themselves whether slavery should be permitted. In 1849, California applied for admission to the Union and the furor began.

> **POPULAR SOVEREIGNTY:** people living in territories and states should be allowed to decide for themselves whether slavery should be permitted

The result was the Compromise of 1850, a series of laws designed as a final solution to the issue. Concessions made to the North included the admission of California as a free state and the abolition of slave trading in Washington, DC. The laws also provided for the creation of the New Mexico and Utah territories. As a concession to southerners, the residents there would decide whether to permit slavery when these two territories became states. In addition, Congress authorized implementation of stricter measures to capture runaway slaves.

In the course of the debates, Lincoln challenged Douglas to show that popular sovereignty reconciled with the Dred Scott decision (in which the Supreme Court ruled that Congress had no authority to prohibit slavery in federal territories). Either way he answered Lincoln, Douglas would lose crucial support from one group or the other. If he supported the Dred Scott decision, southerners would support him but he would lose Northern support. If he supported popular sovereignty, he would have Northern support, but Southern support would be lost. His reply to Lincoln, stating that territorial legislatures could exclude slavery by refusing to pass laws supporting it, gave him enough support and approval to be reelected to the Senate. But it cost him the Democratic nomination for president in 1860.

Civil War

It is ironic that South Carolina was the first state to secede from the Union and that the first shots of the war were fired on Fort Sumter in Charleston harbor. Both sides quickly prepared for war. The North had more in its favor: a larger population; superiority in finances and transportation facilities; and manufacturing, agricultural, and natural resources. The North possessed most of the nation's gold, had about 92 percent of all industries, and almost all known supplies of copper, coal, iron, and various other minerals. Since most of the nation's railroads were in the North and Midwest, men and supplies could be moved wherever needed and food could be transported from the farms of the Midwest to workers in the East and soldiers on the battlefields. Trade with nations overseas could go on as usual due to control of the navy and the merchant fleet. There were twenty-four Northern states, including western (California and Oregon) and border states (Maryland, Delaware, Kentucky, Missouri, and West Virginia).

The Southern states numbered eleven and included South Carolina, Georgia, Florida, Alabama, Mississippi, Louisiana, Texas, Virginia, North Carolina, Tennessee, and Arkansas to make up the Confederacy. Although outnumbered in population, the South was completely confident of victory. The southerners knew that all they had to do was fight a defensive war, protecting their own territory until the North, who had to invade and defeat an area almost the size of Western Europe, tired of the struggle and gave up. Another advantage of the South was that a number of its best officers had graduated from the U.S. Military Academy at West Point and had had long years of army experience, some even exercising varying degrees of command in the Indian Wars and the war with Mexico.

Men from the South were conditioned to living outdoors and were more familiar with horses and firearms than many men from northeastern cities. Since cotton was such an important crop, southerners felt that British and French textile mills were so dependent on raw cotton that they would be forced to help the Confederacy in the war.

The South had specific reasons and goals for fighting the war. The major aim of the Confederacy never wavered: to win independence, the right to govern themselves as they wished, and to preserve slavery. The northerners were not as clear in their reasons for conducting war. At the beginning, most believed, along with Lincoln, that preservation of the Union was paramount. Only a few extremely fanatical abolitionists looked on the war as a way to end slavery. However, by war's end, more and more northerners had come to believe that freeing the slaves was just as important as restoring the Union.

The Civil War took more American lives than any other war in history, with the South losing one-third of its soldiers in battle compared to about one-sixth for the North. More than half of the total deaths were caused by disease and the horrendous conditions of field hospitals. Both sides paid a tremendous economic price, but the South suffered more severely from direct damages. Destruction was widespread, with towns, farms, trade, industry, lives, and homes of men, women, and children all destroyed. An entire Southern way of life was lost.

Effects of the Civil War

The Civil War has been called the first modern war, and its effects were far-reaching. It changed the methods of waging war: It introduced weapons and tactics that, after later improvements, were used extensively in wars of the late 1800s and 1900s. Civil War soldiers were the first to fight in trenches, the first to fight under a unified command, and the first to wage a defense called "major cordon defense," a strategy of advance on all fronts. They were also the first to use repeating and breech-loading weapons. Observation balloons were first used during the Civil War along with submarines, ironclad ships, and mines. Telegraphy and railroads were first put to use in the Civil War.

The Civil War was considered a modern war because of the vast destruction it created, and it was a "total war," involving the use of all of the resources of the opposing sides. There was probably no way it could have ended other than in the total defeat and unconditional surrender of one side or the other.

By executive proclamation and constitutional amendment, slavery was officially and finally ended, although there remained deep prejudice and racism, which still exist today. Also, the Union was preserved, and the states were finally truly united. Sectionalism, especially in the area of politics, remained strong for another hundred years, but not to the degree and with the violence that existed before 1861.

The Civil War was considered a modern war because of the vast destruction it created, and it was a "total war," involving the use of all of the resources of the opposing sides.

The victory of the North established that no state has the right to end or leave the Union. Because of its newfound unity, the United States became a major global power. Lincoln never proposed to punish the South. He was most concerned with restoring the South to the Union in a program that was flexible and practical rather than rigid and unbending. In fact, he never really felt that the states had succeeded in leaving the Union, but rather that they had left the "family circle" for a short time. His plans consisted of two major steps:

1. All Southerners must swear an oath of allegiance to the Union, promising to accept all federal laws and proclamations dealing with slavery in order to receive a full pardon. The only people excluded from this were men who had resigned from civil and military positions in the federal government to serve in the Confederacy, those who were part of the Confederate government, those in the Confederate army above the rank of lieutenant, and Confederates who were guilty of mistreating prisoners of war and blacks.

2. A state would be able to write a new constitution, elect new officials, and return to the Union fully equal to all other states on certain conditions: a minimum number of persons (at least 10 percent of those who were qualified voters in their states before secession from the Union who had voted in the 1860 election) must take an oath of allegiance.

Reconstruction

Following the Civil War, the nation was faced with repairing the torn Union and readmitting the Confederate states. Reconstruction refers to the period between 1865 and 1877 when the federal and state governments debated and implemented plans to provide civil rights to freed slaves and to set the terms under which the former Confederate states might once again join the Union.

In 1865, Abraham Lincoln was assassinated, leaving Vice President Andrew Johnson to oversee the beginning of the actual implementation of Reconstruction. Johnson assumed a moderate position and was willing to allow former Confederates to keep control of their state governments. These governments quickly enacted Black Codes that denied the vote to blacks and granted them only limited civil rights.

The radical Republicans in Congress responded to the Black Codes by continuing their hard line on allowing former rebel states back into the Union. In addition, they sought to override the Black Codes by granting U.S. citizenship to blacks by passing a civil rights bill. Johnson, supported by Democrats, vetoed the bill, but Congress had the necessary votes to override it, and the bill became law.

In 1866, the radical Republicans won control of Congress and passed the Reconstruction Acts, which placed the governments of the southern states under the control of the federal military. With this backing, the Republicans began to implement their policies such as granting all black men the vote and denying the vote to former Confederate soldiers. Congress had passed the Thirteenth, Fourteenth, and Fifteenth Amendments granting citizenship and civil rights to blacks. Ratification of these amendments was a condition of readmission into the Union by the rebel states. The Republicans found support in the South among freedmen (former slaves), white southerners who had not supported the Confederacy (SCALAWAGS), and northerners who had moved to the South (CARPETBAGGERS).

Federal troops were stationed throughout the South and protected Republicans who took control of southern governments. Bitterly resentful, white southerners fought the new political system by joining a secret society called the Ku Klux Klan (KKK). It used violence to keep black Americans from voting and was a loose group made up mainly of former Confederate soldiers who opposed the Reconstruction government and espoused a doctrine of white supremacy. KKK members intimidated and sometimes killed their proclaimed enemies. The first KKK was never completely organized, despite having nominal leadership. In 1871, President Ulysses S. Grant took action to use federal troops to halt the activities of the KKK and actively prosecuted them in federal court.

> **SCALAWAGS:** white southerners who had not supported the Confederacy

> **CARPETBAGGERS:** northerners who had moved to the South

However, before being allowed to rejoin the Union, the Confederate states were required to agree to all federal laws. Between 1866 and 1870, all of the states had returned to the Union, but northern interest in Reconstruction was fading.

Reconstruction was a limited success. Its goals had been both the reunification of the South and the North and the granting of civil rights to freed slaves. In the eyes of blacks it was considered a failure. Its limited success included the establishment of public school systems and expanded legal rights of black Americans; however, many former Confederates and slave owners regained power so whites came to be in control again.

Life after Reconstruction

The Emancipation Proclamation in 1863 and the Thirteenth Amendment in 1865 ended slavery in the United States, but these measures did not erase the centuries of racial prejudice among whites that held blacks to be inferior in intelligence and morality. The rise of the Redeemer governments (Democrats that took control after federal troops and Republicans left at the end of Reconstruction) marked the beginning of the Jim Crow laws and official segregation. Blacks were still allowed to vote, but ways were found to make it difficult for them to do so, such as literacy tests and poll taxes.

The Jim Crow laws were upheld in 1896 when the Supreme Court handed down its decision in the case *Plessy v. Ferguson*. In 1890, Louisiana had passed a law requiring separate train cars for blacks and whites. In 1892, Homer Plessy, a man who had a black great grandparent and so was considered legally black in that state, challenged this law by purchasing a ticket in the white section. Upon informing the conductor that he was black, he was told to move to the black car. He refused and was arrested. His case was eventually decided by the Supreme Court.

> The Jim Crow laws were upheld in 1896 when the Supreme Court handed down its decision in the case Plessy v. Ferguson.

The Court ruled against Plessy, thereby ensuring that the Jim Crow laws would continue to be enforced. The Court held that segregating races was not unconstitutional as long as the facilities for each were identical. This became known as the separate but equal principle. In practice, facilities were seldom equal. Black schools were not funded at the same level, for instance. Streets and parks in black neighborhoods were not maintained.

> **SKILL 21.23** Demonstrates an understanding of major United States and Texas reform movements of the nineteenth and twentieth centuries (e.g., abolitionism, women's suffrage, civil rights, temperance).

Abolition Movement

Antislavery sentiment increased in the first half of the 1800s, and numerous organizations took up the cause. The American Colonization Society was founded in 1816 with the goal of sending free black people to Africa. Reformers' motives varied; some wanted to abolish slavery, while others believed that there was no place in American society for free blacks. The society created the colony of Liberia.

> The American Colonization Society was founded in 1816 with the goal of sending free black people to Africa.

The American Anti-Slavery Society was founded by Quaker William Lloyd Garrison, who also started a newspaper called *The Liberator*. The newspaper was an important voice for the abolitionist movement, and Garrison was a controversial figure with both supporters and enemies around the country.

Women also formed some abolitionist organizations when they were denied full access to existing groups. Margaretta Forten, for example, cofounded the Philadelphia Female Anti-Slavery Society, a group of black and white women, because the American Anti-Slavery Society would not grant women full membership.

The Anti-Slavery Convention of American Women held its first meeting in Philadelphia in 1838. Pennsylvania Hall, the building they had raised money for to be the site of their meetings, was burned down by a proslavery mob, but the fire did not stop the women. They continued meeting at Sarah Pugh's school-house. Many women joined the Female Vigilant Society, a group that raised money for food, transportation, and other assistance for refugee slaves.

The abolitionist movement was not significant in Texas. Many of the settlers were from other southern areas who has moved west. There were few Union settlers, and even fewer abolitionists.

Education Reform

A new understanding of education led to major efforts for public education for all children. In Massachusetts, Horace Mann published the *Common School Journal,* so the public could become more familiar with the importance of education. He and other members of the common school movement argued that free public schools were essential for educating citizens who would be capable of sustaining American democracy. Further, they believed that common schools would help create a more unified American society and increase the wealth of individuals, communities, and the nation.

As public schools were established, more people became literate. This meant that there was more participation in literature and the arts. The more literate society broadly appreciated newspapers and works of literature, art, and live entertain-ment. Education also helped people become more informed about previously unknown areas, including the West. By the end of the nineteenth century, free public elementary school was available for all children in America.

Early Labor Movement

Before 1800, most manufacturing activities took place in small shops or in homes. However, starting in the early 1800s, the ability to build machines resulted in factories that made it easier to produce goods faster. More industries required more labor. Women, children, and, at times, entire families worked long hours and days in mills and factories, and employers began hiring immigrants who were coming to America in huge numbers.

As the nature of work changed in the nineteenth century, workers began their efforts for reform. By the 1830s, many labor organizations began a struggle for a ten-hour workday. In 1844, in Lowell, Massachusetts, female textile employees organized the Lowell Female Labor Reform Association to get shorter hours, higher wages, and better working conditions.

As the nature of work changed in the nineteenth century, workers began their efforts for reform. By the 1830s, many labor organiza-tions began a struggle for a ten-hour workday.

In the 1890s, an economic recession called the Panic of 1893 struck the industrial areas of cities. The Knights of Labor had been formed in 1869 under Uriah

Stephens and then Terrence Powderly, and its goal remained to organize all workers—whether they were skilled or unskilled, black or white, male or female—into one big union united for the rights of workers. Their goals included:

- an eight-hour workday

- equal pay for women

- the elimination of child labor

- cooperative ownership of factories and mines

The Second Great Awakening

Religious beliefs also fueled the spirit of reform. The First Great Awakening had taken place in the 1730s and 1740s, and the Second Great Awakening took place about sixty years later, between 1790 and 1830. The Second Great Awakening was an evangelical Protestant revival that preached about how salvation was available to everyone, not just a chosen few. Inspired by the idea that it was possible to gain salvation, adherents subscribed to a strong work ethic, avoided being wasteful, and abstained from drinking. Further, the idea of creating a more godly society inspired reform efforts aimed at improving conditions in the United States.

Preachers traveled the country spreading the gospel of social responsibility. This point of view then extended to mainline Protestant adherents, who began to believe that the Christian faith should be expressed for the good of society. Preachers argued that people should see God as one who looks after and cares for the individual and for society. They preached that sin is selfishness, behavior should be benevolent, and people needed to purify for the arrival of the coming Kingdom when Jesus would return to Earth.

Temperance Movement

Closely allied to the Second Great Awakening was the temperance movement. The largest and most influential temperance organization was the Women's Christian Temperance Union (WCTU), founded in 1874. Under the banner of "home protection," WCTU members advocated not just temperance, but all kinds of reform that would protect women and children from the effects of men who drank alcohol.

The Eighteenth Amendment, known as the Prohibition Amendment, was ratified in 1917 and prohibited the sale of alcoholic beverages throughout the United States. This led to a rise in bootlegging, organized crime, and the creation of speakeasies.

In Texas, the Constitution of 1876 included a "local option" clause. Methodist and Baptist ministers led a movement for complete prohibition. In 1887, the legislature decided to allow the people to vote on the issue and placed a constitutional amendment on the ballot. The voters decided not to ban liquor sales.

Women's Suffrage Movement

The first American women's rights movement began in the 1840s. Among the early leaders of the movement were Elizabeth Cady Stanton, Lucretia Mott, and Ernestine Rose. At the time, very few states recognized women's rights to vote, own property, sue for divorce, or execute contracts.

The SENECA FALLS CONVENTION, held in the New York mill town of Seneca Falls in 1848, was the first women's rights convention in the United States. Lucretia Mott had attended the World Anti-Slavery Society in Britain in 1840, but she was not allowed to speak from the floor or be seated as a delegate. This led to a discussion of how women could neither vote nor hold important positions in American government. Abigail Adams had even addressed this subject with her husband John Adams many years before when the Constitution was being written.

> SENECA FALLS CONVENTION: the first women's rights convention in the United States

Some 300 people attended the convention, which culminated in the publication of a Declaration of Sentiments, largely written by Stanton and signed by sixty-eight women and thirty-two men. Frederick Douglass described it as the "grand basis for attaining the civil, social, political, and religious rights of women." Others thoroughly objected. The structure of the document was based on the Declaration of Independence: "We hold these truths to be self-evident: that all men and women are created equal."

In 1869, Susan B. Anthony, Ernestine Rose, and Elizabeth Cady Stanton founded the National Women's Suffrage Association.

In 1920, the Nineteenth Amendment, which guaranteed women the right to vote, was ratified. Roles and opportunities for women grew, and more women sought careers outside the home. Jeanette Rankin was a pacifist, politician, and social activist who helped ensure the amendment passed.

Civil Rights

African Americans and Hispanics were the two largest racial minorities in Texas. Most African Americans were sharecroppers, and they formed the Colored Farmers' Alliance in the 1880s to deal with their economic problems. Segregation existed throughout the state.

Hispanics composed the majority of people south of San Antonio and along the Rio Grande River. They retained their culture, owned businesses, herded cattle, and performed manual labor. Conflicts arose with other Texans over cattle and land.

State politics and political parties were shaped as the result of the racial and other issues of the time period. After the Civil War, Democrats supported white supremacy and states' rights on issues involving race. The Republican Party had African American members and favored the expansion of civil rights.

> SKILL
> 21.24
> **Demonstrates knowledge of boom and bust cycles of leading Texas industries** (e.g., railroads, the cattle industry, oil and gas production, cotton, real estate, banking, computer technology).

Railroads

In 1836, approximately ten years after the first railroad came into existence, the Texas Congress authorized a charter for the first building of a railroad in Texas. The state government offered land grants to companies interested in adding rail transportation. By the late 1870s, significant amounts of rail mileage had been added. In the late 1880s, railroads had become powerful and several lawsuits were filed against the railroads to curb abuses, such as pooling. A rail regulatory commission was created to regulate the growth of the rail industry.

The growth of railroads resulted from the oil boom. There was much optimism about the possible growth of rail traffic and after World War II, new equipment was purchased to meet the anticipated needs. With the growth of interstate highways and better roads, the rail passenger traffic did not increase to meet expectations. Chemicals and coal are mainly transported by rail today and many of the rail companies in the state have merged or are no longer operating in the state.

Cattle Industry

The cattle industry has been important in Texas for nearly three hundred years.

The cattle industry has been important in Texas for nearly three hundred years. The Spanish brought cattle with them when settling the area. When the number of Spanish missions declined, ranching became a private enterprise.

Early ranching efforts were concentrated in southeast Texas, being closer to the New Orleans market. Before the Civil War, the cattle industry shifted to north central Texas. The Panic of 1873 had a limited effect on the industry but within ten years, in the 1880s, there was "boom" for the cattle industry. In the late 1880s, conflict developed between small and large ranchers and the need for grazing land that was sometimes limited by barbed-wire fenced areas. By the end of the century open area grazing had almost ended, with closed-range ranching.

Another boom occurred before World War I, but prices declined and a slump occurred in the 1920s. Because the market was depressed, the government, in the mid-1930s, intervened with a program to purchase and kill cattle to bring better prices and stability to the industry.

Major ranching areas focused on cattle again in the 1950s. Small-herd stock farming also became important for the cattle industry. Beef cattle raising increased and dairy farming declined during the 1960s and 1970s. Prices for beef rose in the 1980s and declined in the 1990s.

Today the cattle industry is recognized for its commercial feedlots and meat-packing industries. Computers are now an important part of the industry. Some ranches have replaced the cattle raising industry with the raising of other animals such as the ostrich. Other ranches have shifted the use of their property to leased hunting grounds.

Oil and Gas Production

The first oil field opened in Texas in the last nineteenth century. The discovery of oil changed the growth and development of the state. The "oil boom" was also called the "gusher age" and led to Texas's becoming a leading oil-producing state. In the 1920s many small towns became "boom towns" but by the late 1930s many of the small town economies had collapsed. Some of the larger cities that had grown because of large oil reserves weathered the Depression because of the oil boom.

By 1940, Texas led the United States in oil production. Larger oil-reserve areas and major refineries continued to be successful until after World War II. There were wide swings in the prices of oil but they began to stabilize in the 1940s when Texas transitioned into an industrial state. Petroleum prices rose again in the 1970s and 1980s during the energy crisis. Stagnant prices and rising costs resulted in downsizing of the petroleum sites. State and local revenue also decreased considerably.

Gas reserves in Texas total between 20 percent and 25 percent of the reserves in the United States. Gas production began as a by-product of oil production and production peaked in the early 1970s. The largest natural gas field is located in north central Texas. Approximately 3 percent of the state's population is employed in the oil and gas industry today.

Cotton

The Spanish were the first to grow cotton in Texas. The Americans continued growing the crop when they arrived in the 1820s. New areas were opened up for cotton production in the 1850s and 1860s when the Native Americans were removed from land. During the Civil War, cotton production decreased.

In the later part of the nineteenth century, the cotton industry was stimulated by an influx of immigrants into central Texas, the improvement of rail transportation, and the development of the plow and the cotton gin. Much of the cotton growing during this time period was done by tenant farmers and sharecroppers. The arrival of the boll weevil caused much devastation to the industry.

The demand for cotton grew during the World War I era but after the war, prices for cotton decreased. Production continued to decline and during World War II many sharecroppers and tenant farmers moved to cities to work in wartime industries.

Today, there are fewer farms producing cotton but the cotton-producing farms are larger than before. Improvements have made the harvesting easier, and there are better, and more, weed and pest control methods.

Real Estate

The real estate market responds to economic conditions and to the need for land. Cotton production and cattle ranching require larger areas of land. The old boom brought people into Texas to live and work; these people required housing as well as areas to establish production facilities. The real estate boom occurred during the oil boom. When oil prices skyrocketed and cause a decline in the oil industry, the housing market was also affected. When people moved from Texas, houses became vacant, unable to be resold, and real estate sales and prices declined. When Texas became a center for banking and computer technology, the larger cities were revitalized and real estate sales and prices again increased.

Banking

The first bank, which was the first chartered bank west of the Mississippi River, was established in Texas in 1822, shortly after Mexico became independent from Spain. The first commercial bank in Texas was established in 1835 and provided loans for the Texas Revolution.

The state's 1845 constitution prohibited the incorporation of banks but many merchants performed banking functions and there were many moneylenders throughout the state. The only chartered bank in the state before the Civil War was established in 1847 in the city of Galveston.

After Reconstruction, banks were established by special acts of the legislature. As industry and commerce developed, the state constitution was amended to permit state banks. By 1920, there were more than 1,000 state banks and about 500 national banks in Texas.

The economic downturns in Texas before World War II and the chartering of too many banks contributed to the failure of many banks. After the war, the banking system in Texas expanded. The 1980s saw a downturn in the Texas banking industry. Lending practices, overextension of credit, decline petroleum prices, problems in the savings and loan industry, and speculation in the real estate sector caused damage to the banking industry. Some banks failed and others were unable to shift financing to long-term projects. As a whole, the commercial banking industry suffered losses for about four years, until 1990.

Banking reform laws were put into place to help the distressed industry. Banks tightened their lending policies and the problems within the industry lessened.

Computer Technology

Information technology is playing an increasing role in the Texas economy. Computer technology services accounts for approximately 70 percent of the employment in the information technology sector. Computer systems design companies have increased and many well-known companies are located in major cities such as Dallas, Fort Worth, San Antonio, Austin, and Houston. In 2012, Texas was ranked No. 3 in the United States for employment in the computer systems sector.

Information technology is playing an increasing role in the Texas economy.

> **SKILL 21.25** **Demonstrates an understanding of important individuals, issues and events of the twentieth and twenty-first centuries in Texas, the United States and the world** (e.g., urbanization, Great Depression, the Dust Bowl, the Second World War, growth of the oil and gas industry).

The time from 1830 to 1914 was characterized by the extraordinary growth of patriotism in the United States along with intense, widespread imperialism.

For more information on westward expansion, see Skill 21.19.

For information on the Civil War and Reconstruction, see Skills 21.20 and 21.21.

World War I: 1914 to 1918

The origins of World War I are complex, and drawn mainly along the lines of various alliances and treaties that existed between the world powers. Imperialism, nationalism, and economic conditions of the time led to a series of sometimes shaky alliances among the powerful nations, each wishing to protect its holdings and provide mutual defense against smaller powers.

On June 28, 1914, Serbian Gavrilo Princip assassinated Archduke Ferdinand of Austria-Hungary while on a visit to Sarajevo, Serbia. Serbian nationalism had led the country to seek dominance of the Balkan peninsula, a move that had been opposed by Austria-Hungary.

Seeing an opportunity to move on Serbia, Austria-Hungary issued an ultimatum after the assassination, demanding they be allowed to perform a complete investigation. Serbia refused, and in July, Austria-Hungary, with the backing of its ally Germany, declared war on Serbia. Serbia called on its ally Russia to come to its defense, and Russia began to move troops into the area.

Germany, allied with Austria-Hungary, viewed the Russian mobilization as an act of war, and declared war on Russia. A few days afterwards, Germany declared war on France, which was allied with Russia by treaty. Germany invaded Belgium, a neutral country, so as to be closer to Paris. Britain, bound by treaty to defend both Belgium and France, subsequently declared war on Germany.

The United States, under President Woodrow Wilson, declared neutrality and did not enter the war immediately. Not until Germany threatened commercial shipping with submarine warfare did the United State get involved, in 1917. Fighting continued until November 1918, when Germany petitioned for armistice. Peace negotiations began in early 1919, and the Treaty of Versailles was signed in June of that year. One result of the peace negotiations was the establishment of the League of Nations (the precursor to the United Nations), a group of countries that agreed to avoid armed conflict through disarmament and diplomacy.

World War II: 1939 to 1945

The Treaty of Versailles that ended the First World War was in part the cause of the second. Severely limited by the treaty, Germany grew to resent its terms, which required reparations and limited the size of its army, and worked constantly to revise them. This was done through diplomacy and negotiation through the 1920s. In 1933, Adolf Hitler became chancellor of Germany and shortly thereafter was granted dictatorial powers. Hitler was determined to remove all restrictions imposed by the treaty and to unify the German-speaking people of the surrounding countries into a single country. Toward this end, Hitler marched into Austria in 1938 and was welcomed. He later made a claim on the Sudetenland, a German-speaking area of Czechoslovakia, a claim that was supported internationally. However, Hitler continued to march into the rest of Czechoslovakia, to which he had no claim.

France and Britain, which had followed a policy of appeasing Hitler in the hopes he would be content with Austria, were now concerned, as Germany looked next to Poland. They pledged to fight Germany if Hitler invaded Poland, which he did in September 1939, after signing a pact with the Soviet Union. Days later, France and Britain declared war on Germany, and the fighting began.

Again, the United States stayed out of the conflict at first. Only when Japan, an ally of Germany, attacked a U.S. naval base in Pearl Harbor, Hawaii, did the U.S. enter the war.

The European theater of WWII ended in 1945, when Allied troops invaded Germany and Hitler committed suicide. In the Pacific, the U.S. dropped two atomic bombs on Japan in August of that year, forcing the Japanese to surrender.

WWII left the British and European economies in ruins, and established the United States and the Soviet Union as the two major powers of the world, laying the foundation for the Cold War. After the failure of the League of Nations to prevent war, a stronger organization was created, the United Nations, with the ability to raise peacekeeping forces. Under the Marshall plan, the United States helped rebuild Europe into an industrial, reliable economy again.

> *WWII left the British and European economies in ruins, and established the United States and the Soviet Union as the two major powers of the world, laying the foundation for the Cold War.*

Korean War: 1950 to 1953

With the surrender of Japan at the end of WWII, its thirty-five-year occupation of Korea came to an end. The Soviet Union and the United States assumed trustee-ship of the country, with the Soviets occupying the northern half and the United States controlling the south. Elections were ordered by the United Nations to establish a unified government, but with each occupying country backing differ-ent candidates, the result was the formation of two separate states divided along the thirty-eighth parallel of latitude, and each claimed sovereignty over the whole country. These conflicting claims led to occasional military skirmishes along the common border throughout 1949, with each side aiming to unify the country under its own government. In June 1950, North Korea mounted a major attack across the thirty-eighth parallel, marking what is considered the beginning of the war.

The North Koreans received military aid and backing from the Soviet Union, which aroused fear in the United States that communism and Soviet influence might spread. In August 1950, American troops arrived in South Korea to join the fight, along with British, Australian, and UN forces.

Control of the peninsula see-sawed over the next year, with North Korea captur-ing the South Korean capital of Seoul but then being pushed back to the north, with southern forces eventually capturing the North Korean capital, Pyongyang, and driving to the border of China. China had already announced its intention to get involved should forces enter North Korea, and the Chinese army mounted a push that reclaimed the North.

In 1953, peace negotiations resulted in a cease-fire and created a buffer zone between the two countries along the thirty-eighth parallel. This cease-fire has been in effect for more than fifty years. The Korean War has never officially ended. Since the cease-fire, North Korea has become an increasingly isolated communist dictatorship, while South Korea has grown into a major world economy.

The Korean War has never officially ended. Since the cease-fire, North Korea has become an increasingly isolated communist dictatorship, while South Korea has grown into a major world economy.

U.S. Involvement in the Vietnam War: 1957 to 1973

Like Korea, Vietnam became a divided country after WWII, with a Soviet- and Chinese-backed communist government in the north, led by Ho Chi Minh, and a western-backed government in the south. As the communist-backed north drove out the occupying French and maintained more and more insurgency in the south, the larger powers became increasingly involved, with the United States sending advisors and small numbers of troops between 1955 and 1964.

In 1964, following an attack on U.S. ships by North Vietnamese forces in the Gulf of Tonkin, the United States escalated its military involvement, sending more and more troops over the next four years. As fighting continued with no decisive progress, opposition to the war began to grow among the American public. President Richard Nixon began to make reductions in troops while trying to assist the South Vietnamese army in building enough strength to fight on its own. In January 1973, the Paris Peace Accords were signed, ending offensive action by the United States in Vietnam. Nixon promised defensive assistance, but in 1974 Congress cut off all funding to the South Vietnamese government after Nixon had resigned the presidency following the Watergate scandal.

The withdrawal of the United States left South Vietnam without economic or military support, and the North Vietnamese army was able to overrun and control the entire country. North Vietnamese forces took Saigon, the southern capital, in April 1975. North and South were unified under one socialist government.

The social impact of the Vietnam War was considerable in the United States. Opposition to the draft and to U.S. involvement in the war led to large protests, particularly among young people, and returning veterans found they were not treated as heroes, as veterans of other wars had been.

The beginning of the modern civil rights movement is usually identified as the Montgomery (Alabama) bus boycott in 1955.

Civil Rights

The beginning of the modern civil rights movement is usually identified as the Montgomery (Alabama) bus boycott in 1955. The movement used nonviolence to end segregation in public places. Supreme Court rulings, like *Brown v. Board of Education*, contributed to integrating the South, while laws like the Voting Rights Act of 1965 helped African Americans exercise the rights that the Constitution had guaranteed them one hundred years before. In the late 1960s and the 1970s, the movement grew to include more radical organizations like the Black Panthers.

In 1957, the formation of the Southern Christian Leadership Conference by Martin Luther King, Jr., John Duffy, Rev. C. D. Steele, Rev. T. J. Jemison, Rev. Fred Shuttlesworth, Ella Baker, A. Philip Randolph, Bayard Rustin, and Stanley Levison provided training and assistance to many local efforts to fight segregation. Nonviolence was its central doctrine and its major method of fighting segregation and racism.

Communications Revolution

At the turn of the twenty-first century, the world witnessed unprecedented strides in communications, a major expansion of international trade, and significant international diplomatic and military activity.

The Internet and World Wide Web continued to grow and connect people all over the world, opening new routes of communication and providing commercial opportunities. The expansion of cell phone usage and Internet access led to a worldwide society that is interconnected as never before.

In Asia, new economies matured and the previously tightly controlled Chinese market became more open to foreign investment, increasing China's influence as a major economic power. The European Union made a bold move to a common currency, the euro, in a successful effort to consolidate the region's economic strength. African nations, many struggling under international debt, appealed to the international community to assist them in building their economies. In South America, countries such as Brazil and Venezuela showed growth despite political unrest, as Argentina suffered a near complete collapse of its economy. As the technology sector expanded, so did the economy of India, where high-tech companies found a highly educated workforce.

Conflict between the Muslim world and the United States increased during the last decade of the twentieth century, culminating in a terrorist attack on New York City and Washington, DC, in 2001. These attacks, sponsored by the radical group Al-Qaeda, prompted a military invasion by the United States of Afghanistan, where the group is based. Shortly afterwards, the United States, the UK, and several smaller countries addressed further instability in the region by ousting Iraqi dictator Saddam Hussein in a military campaign. In the eastern Mediterranean, tension between Israelis and Palestinians continued to build, regularly erupting into violence.

The threat of the spread of nuclear weapons, largely diminished after the fall of the Soviet Union and the end of the Cold War, reared its head again with North Korea's nuclear missile test launces and ongoing suspicion that Iran is working toward the creation of weapons-grade nuclear material, despite agreements in 2015 between Iran and the international community. As international conflict and tension increased, the role of international alliances such as NATO and the United Nations grew in importance.

Texas

During the twentieth and twenty-first centuries, Texas, as well as the United States, was affected by urbanization, the Great Depression, the Second World War, and the growth of the oil and gas industry. In addition, it was affected by the Dust Bowl.

In the early 1900s, Texas had a population of approximately 3 million. Of that number, more than 80 percent worked in the farming sector. After oil was discovered, rail transportation increased and the economy grew. In 1929, Texans felt the effects of the Great Depression as did others throughout the country. Unemployment increased and eventually government public works programs helped to return the economy to a more stable level.

In the 1930s, a severe drought extended across the Panhandle of the state. Topsoil was blown off the dry lands and storms of dust swept across the region. The dusts of storm resulted in the area being referred to as the Dust Bowl. There were weeks of storms and in one year alone, more than 100 million acres of farm land had lost topsoil. The effects of the storms led Congress to pass soil conservation legislation.

Urbanization in Texas began to take place rapidly after the discovery of oil. In the 1990s, more than 80 percent of the state's population lives in cities of various sizes. Ships began plying the waterways to bring people and products to Texas. Cities grew up along the coast, and population moved from east to west. Railroads provided quicker access to remote areas in the state, and towns sprang up along the rail routes. Dallas and Fort Worth grew, even during the Depression. As automobiles became more popular, they influenced the growth of metropolitan areas. After World War II ended, Houston became the fastest growing city in the nation. Austin developed as a center of higher education, and San Antonio grew after serving as a military base during the Second World War.

Urban areas in Texas have experienced problems that are similar to problems in other metropolitan areas but major effects have been undertaken to dissipate pollution and to provide solutions to the rapid population growth and other urban issues of modern-day Texas.

In the 1930s, a severe drought extended across the Panhandle of the state. Topsoil was blown off the dry lands and storms of dust swept across the region. The dusts of storm resulted in the area being referred to as the Dust Bowl.

Individuals who have played an instrumental role in the development of Texas in the twentieth and twenty-first centuries include Lyndon B. Johnson and George H. W. Bush, presidents of the United States; Walter Cronkite, new commentator who grew up in Houston and Dan Rather, news correspondent; Kay Bailey Hutchinson, the first woman to represent Texas in the U.S. Senate; Scott Joplin, the "King of Ragtime"; Chester Nimitz, naval commander who led forces in the Pacific during World War II; and Sam Rayburn, Speaker of the U.S. House of Representatives.

See also Skill 21.24

SKILL 21.26 Analyzes ways that particular contemporary societies reflect historical events *(e.g., invasion, conquests, colonization, immigration)*.

Contemporary societies reflect upon past historical events to learn from the mistakes and benefits of those events to take action in future similar events. The reasons for the Second World War can be a lesson in determining a need to combat the growth of groups invading and attempting to conquer areas of the Middle East. Diseases such as ebola and problems such as AIDS need to be eradicated. By analyzing how diseases such as polio and smallpox were eradicated, medical science can hopefully bring about the end to new and dangerous health problems throughout the world.

At the beginning of the twentieth century, countries were racing to establish colonies and claim areas with untapped resources. Contemporary societies need to analyze the problems, in addition to the benefits, brought on by such land acquisition and avoid the results of war that resulted because of such action.

Immigration issues are reoccurring. During the westward expansion period of the United States and during the Industrial Revolution immigrants from Asian and European nations came to the United States to obtain work and establish homes. Congress passed legislation to prohibit some of the immigration. Congress also limited immigration by placing quotas on the number of people from various countries that want to enter the United States. Today's societies are facing immigration problems because of the numbers of undocumented immigrants that are in the United States. Throughout the world, there are "boat people" who leave their homelands to seek better conditions of life in other countries. Contemporary societies must learn ways to resolve those immigration issues.

See also Skill 21.1

For information on westward expansion in the United States, see Skill 21.20.

COMPETENCY 22
GEOGRAPHY AND CULTURE

> **SKILL 22.1** **Analyzes and applies knowledge of key concepts in geography** *(e.g., location, distance, region, grid systems)* **and knows the locations and the human and physical characteristics** *(e.g., culture, diversity)* **of places and regions in Texas, the United States and the world.**

> *Geography involves studying places and the way living things and the Earth's features are distributed.*

Geography involves studying places and the way living things and the Earth's features are distributed. It includes where animals, people, and plants live and the effects of their relationship with Earth's physical features. Geographers also explore the locations of Earth's features, how they got there, and why it is so important.

Themes of Geography
The five themes of geography are:

1. **Location:** Location includes relative and absolute location. A relative location refers to the surrounding geography, e.g., "on the banks of the Mississippi River." Absolute location refers to a specific point, such as "41 degrees north latitude, 90 degrees west longitude," or "123 Main Street."

2. **Spatial organization:** This is a description of how things are grouped in a given space. In geographical terms, spatial organization can describe people, places, and environments anywhere and everywhere on Earth. The most basic form of spatial organization for people is where they live. The vast majority of people live near other people, in villages and towns and cities and settlements. People live near others in order to take advantage of the goods and services that naturally arise from cooperation. Villages and towns, cities and settlements are, to varying degrees, near bodies of water. Water is a staple of survival for every person on the planet, and is a good source of energy for various industries as well as a form of transportation for people and goods.

3. **Place:** A place has both human and physical characteristics. Physical characteristics include features such as mountains, rivers, and deserts. Human characteristics are the features created by humans' interaction with their environment such as canals and roads.

4. **Human-environmental interaction:** The theme of human-environmental interaction has three main concepts: humans adapt to the environment (e.g., wearing warm clothing in a cold climate); humans modify the environment (e.g., planting trees to block a prevailing wind); and humans depend on the environment (for food, water, and raw materials).

5. **Movement:** Movement refers to the way humans interact with one another through trade, communications, emigration, and other forms of interaction.

Regions

A region is an area that has some kind of unifying characteristic such as a common language or a common government. There are three main types of regions:

- **Formal regions** are areas defined by actual political boundaries, such as cities, counties, or states.

- **Functional regions** are areas defined by a common function, such as the areas covered by a telephone service.

- **Vernacular regions** are less formally defined areas that are formed by people's perception, e.g., the Middle East or the South.

Absolute vs. relative locations

An **ABSOLUTE LOCATION** is the exact whereabouts of a person, place, or thing, according to any kind of geographical indicators. One could be talking about latitude and longitude or GPS or any other kind of indicators. For example, Paris is at 48 degrees north longitude and 2 degrees east latitude. One can't get much more exact than that. If you had a map that showed every degree of latitude and longitude, you could pinpoint exactly where Paris was and be absolutely certain that your geographical depiction was accurate.

> **ABSOLUTE LOCATION:** the exact whereabouts of a person, place, or thing, according to any kind of geographical indicators

A **RELATIVE LOCATION**, in contrast, is *always* a description that involves more than one thing. When you describe a relative location, you indicate where something is by describing what is around it. A description of where the nearest post office is in terms of relative location might be: "It's down the street from the supermarket, on the right side of the street, next to the dentist's office."

> **RELATIVE LOCATION:** a description that involves more than one thing

Geography of Texas

The state of Texas has varied geographical features, which have changed over time, depending on who was living where at the time. Among the known settlers have been Native Americans, French, Spanish, and Americans.

Geographically, most of Texas is flat farmland, particularly West Texas, where the dominant crops are cotton, wheat, and sorghum. The land is semiarid and, for the most part, flat, with the exception of some hills and a mountain range, the Davis Mountains. Oil can be found in West Texas as well, near the Midland-Odessa corridor. The antebellum and Civil War–era civilizations in East Texas depended almost entirely on King Cotton, with the various hills and swamps dominated by vast plantations. Cotton's influence can still be felt there, but the dominant crop now is rice. The vast majority of the state's rice comes from this region. Lumber can be found here as well. As in nearly every other part of the state, however, oil is the new king of East Texas.

The Gulf Coast is dominated by Houston, the fourth-largest city in the United States. Houston is very much a port city, capitalizing on an early-twentieth-century canal to the Gulf of Mexico as a way to ship goods to the world. Indeed, only New York ships more than Houston. The lower Rio Grande area has citrus fruits and winter vegetables in abundance. The rest of the Rio Grande valley is dotted with cattle ranches, some of which are very large.

Further north are the backland prairies, a large range of agricultural and ranch land, where large quantities of cotton and grain are grown and there are a lot of cattle. The large cities of Dallas and Fort Worth are in this area. These two cities together form one of the most burgeoning metropolitan areas, with big business in oil refining, grain milling, and cotton processing. The high plains have a somewhat varied landscape, although the semiarid climate falls mostly on flat land. Of note is a dry-farming area near Lubbock, one of the larger cities of the region. Oil, grain, wheat, and cotton are the major industries. All major cities in Texas play a role in the advancement of modern technology, although Houston, Dallas, and Fort Worth are the leaders in the high-tech arena, as they were during World War II in weapons production.

The people who live and have lived in Texas have made the land their own, turning flat, sometimes water-starved lands into vast plantations, ranches, and fields.

The people who live and have lived in Texas have made the land their own, turning flat, sometimes water-starved lands into vast plantations, ranches, and fields. Large cities have not been confined to those on waterways (although the state's largest city, Houston, is on the Gulf Coast). Dirt roads, railroads, and then paved roads have connected the large state's many towns and cities.

The most drastic change to the environment wrought by people has been the sheer number of square miles devoted to living space. Texas still maintains vast areas of agricultural and ranch land, but that area is shrinking by the year, as more and more people claim land exclusively to be lived on. The farmers of the past lived on their land but also lived off it. Their houses were part of their farms and their jobs were working the land. These days, skyscrapers dot the skylines of large cities along with high-rise apartment buildings, which serve no function other than to provide living areas for the people who work in those large cities.

Geography of the United States

The continental United States is bordered by the Pacific Ocean on the west and the Atlantic Ocean on the east. The country is divided into two main sections by the Rocky Mountains, which extend from New Mexico in the south through the Canadian border in the north. The western portion of the country contains forested, mountainous areas in the Pacific Northwest and northern California, including Mt. St. Helens, an active volcano in the Cascade Range. Dryer, warmer regions in the south include the Mojave Desert in the Southwest. The Great Salt Lake in Utah is at the foot of the Wasatch Mountains.

The Rocky Mountains slope down in the east to the Great Plains, a large, grassy region drained by the Mississippi River, the nation's largest river, and one of the largest rivers in the world. The Great Plains give way in the east to hilly, forested regions. The Appalachian Mountain chain runs along the eastern coast of the United States. Along the border with Canada between Minnesota and New York are Lake Huron, Lake Ontario, Lake Michigan, Lake Erie, and Lake Superior, known as the Great Lakes.

Alaska is located in northwestern North America and contains Mt. McKinley, also called Denali, which is the highest mountain on the continent. Hawaii is a series of volcanic islands in the South Pacific.

Geographical Features of the Earth

The Earth's surface is made up of 70 percent water and 30 percent land. Physical features of the land surface include mountains, hills, plateaus, valleys, and plains. Other minor landforms include deserts, deltas, canyons, mesas, basins, foothills, marshes, and swamps. The Earth's water features include oceans, seas, lakes, rivers, and canals.

MOUNTAINS are landforms with steep slopes at least 2,000 feet or more above sea level. Mountains are found in groups called mountain chains or mountain ranges. At least one range can be found on six of the Earth's seven continents. North America has the Appalachian and Rocky Mountains; South America, the Andes; Asia, the Himalayas; Australia, the Great Dividing Range; Europe, the Alps; and Africa, the Atlas, Ahaggar, and Drakensburg Mountains.

HILLS are elevated landforms rising to an elevation of about 500 to 2,000 feet. They are found everywhere on Earth including Antarctica, where they are covered by ice.

PLATEAUS are elevated landforms that usually are level on top. Depending on their location, they range from being an area that is very cold to one that is cool and healthful. Some plateaus are dry because they are surrounded by mountains that

> **MOUNTAINS:** landforms with steep slopes at least 2,000 feet or more above sea level

> **HILLS:** elevated landforms rising to an elevation of about 500 to 2,000 feet

> **PLATEAUS:** elevated landforms that usually are level on top

keep moisture out. Examples include the Kenya Plateau in East Africa, which is very cool. The plateau extending north from the Himalayas is extremely dry while those in Antarctica and Greenland are covered with ice and snow.

PLAINS: areas of flat or slightly rolling land, usually lower than the landforms next to them

PLAINS are areas of flat or slightly rolling land, usually lower than the landforms next to them. Sometimes called lowlands (and sometimes located along seacoasts), they support the majority of the world's people. Some are found inland, and many were formed by large rivers. This resulted in extremely fertile soil, which allowed for the successful cultivation of crops and large settlements of people. In North America, the vast plains extend from the Gulf of Mexico north to the Arctic Ocean and between the Appalachian and Rocky Mountains. In Europe, rich plains extend east from Great Britain into central Europe on into the Siberian region of Russia. Plains in river valleys are found in China (the Yangtze River valley), India (the Ganges River valley), and Southeast Asia (the Mekong River valley).

VALLEYS: land areas found between hills and mountains

VALLEYS are land areas found between hills and mountains. Some have gentle slopes with trees and plants; others have very steep walls and are referred to as canyons. One famous example is Arizona's Grand Canyon of the Colorado River.

DESERTS: large, dry areas of land receiving ten inches or less of rainfall each year

DESERTS are large, dry areas of land receiving ten inches or less of rainfall each year. Among the better-known deserts are Africa's large Sahara Desert, the Arabian Desert on the Arabian peninsula, and the Outback desert covering roughly one third of Australia.

DELTAS: areas of low-lands formed by soil and sediment deposited at the mouths of rivers

DELTAS are areas of lowlands formed by soil and sediment deposited at the mouths of rivers. The soil is generally very fertile, and most fertile river deltas are important crop-growing areas. One well-known example is the delta of Egypt's Nile River, known for its production of cotton.

MESAS: the flat tops of hills or mountains, usually with steep sides

MESAS are the flat tops of hills or mountains, usually with steep sides. Sometimes plateaus are also called mesas. Basins are considered to be low areas drained by rivers or low spots in mountains. Foothills are generally considered a low series of hills found between a plain and a mountain range. Marshes and swamps are wet lowlands where plants such as rushes and reeds grow.

Water features

Water features include:

- Oceans: The largest bodies of water on the planet. The four oceans of the Earth are the Atlantic Ocean, the Pacific Ocean, the Indian Ocean, and the ice-filled Arctic Ocean, extending from North America and Europe to the North Pole. The waters of the Atlantic, Pacific, and Indian oceans also touch the shores of Antarctica.

- **Seas:** Smaller than oceans and surrounded by land. Some examples include the Mediterranean Sea, found between Europe, Asia, and Africa; and the Caribbean Sea, touching the West Indies and South and Central America. A **LAKE** is a body of water surrounded by land. The Great Lakes in North America are a good example.

- **Rivers:** Considered a nation's lifeblood, rivers usually begin as very small streams, formed by melting snow and rainfall, flowing from higher to lower land, emptying into a larger body of water, usually a sea or an ocean. Examples of important rivers for the people and countries affected by and/ or dependent on them include: the Nile, Niger, and Zaire rivers of Africa; the Rhine, Danube, and Thames rivers of Europe; the Yangtze, Ganges, Mekong, Hwang He, and Irrawaddy rivers of Asia; the Murray-Darling in Australia; and the Orinoco in South America. River systems are made up of large rivers and numerous smaller rivers or tributaries flowing into them. Examples include the vast Amazon River system in South America and the Mississippi River system in the United States.

- **Canals:** Human-made water passages constructed to connect two larger bodies of water. Famous examples include the Panama Canal across Panama's isthmus, connecting the Atlantic and Pacific oceans and the Suez Canal in the Middle East between Africa and the Arabian peninsula, connecting the Red and Mediterranean seas.

Weather

WEATHER is the condition of the atmosphere, including temperature, air pressure, wind, and moisture or precipitation, which includes rain, snow, hail, or sleet.

> **WEATHER:** the condition of the atmosphere, including temperature, air pressure, wind, and moisture or precipitation

> **SKILL 22.2** **Analyzes ways that location (absolute and relative) affects people, places and environments** *(e.g., the location of renewable and nonrenewable natural resources such as fresh water, fossil fuels, fertile soils and timber).*

See Skills 22.1 and 22.5

> SKILL
> 22.3
>
> **Analyzes how geographic factors have influenced the settlement patterns, economic development, political relationships and historical and contemporary societies, including those of Texas, the United States and the world.**

See Skill 22.1

The varied geography of Texas has produced some vastly different settlement patterns, economic developments, and political conflicts over the hundreds of years that people have been migrating to the area. The vast plains of central and western Texas are perfect for agricultural and ranch land, and that's what they have become. Among the areas inhabited and/or controlled by humans, wheat, cotton, sorghum, and cattle are the top-producing industries. The farms are big and the ranches bigger. The relative flatness of the land contributes to a sense of shared hardship, since ranchers can usually see the land of their neighbors, even if it is far away. This also means, of course, that the potential for land disputes is high, even today.

East Texas is similar, in a way, in that huge rice fields dot the landscape, with towns built up around them. Although the crop is different, the interests and concerns are the same. The Gulf Coast is known for its oil and its ports. However, it's not just oil that goes out of those ports: Nearly all of the state's myriad products flow out through one or a handful of the state's Gulf Coast ports. Oil can be found in many parts of the state, not just on the Gulf Coast. Texas is known for its oil production and its oil exports, particularly in the western part of the state.

The larger cities of Texas—Houston, Austin, Dallas, and Fort Worth, most notably—are known for their dedication to high tech. Many Internet and computer companies make their home in Texas, and the state is a leader in scientific development efforts as well.

Politics in Texas

Politics throughout the history of the state have been contentious. In the early days, there was conflict between Mexicans and Americans as American settlers encroached on Mexican-owned territories and settled in for the long haul. After Mexico gave up all claims to Texas, a reverse immigration took place. This movement of people is still taking place. The vast agricultural lands of Texas cry out for cheap labor, and many Mexican residents are only too happy to cross the border to supply it. The question of documented versus undocumented workers continues to be a controversial issue today. (This is the case in other states as well, but it is a major issue in Texas because the state shares such a long border with Mexico.)

Another source of contention is the struggle between the ranch politics of yesterday and the high-tech politics of today. Farmers and ranchers obviously have different interests than atomic scientists, and these interests often clash in the halls of Austin policy makers. Geography contributes to this since farmers' and ranchers' concerns are related to their locations, and urbanites' perspectives are influenced by their environments, which are more metropolitan. Oil companies and their lobbyists must be heard from as well. Oil continues to be a staggeringly large business in Texas, and oil interests often clash with those of other industries.

The carpetbaggers of yesterday are the high-tech mavens of today and the visionaries of tomorrow. They vie for political time and will with the farmers and ranchers of yesterday, today, and tomorrow. While some people reinvent themselves every few years, others stay the same. So it is in Texas.

Settlement Patterns

Humans subsisted initially as gatherers—gathering berries, leaves, and roots, using many resources lightly rather than depending heavily on just a few. With the invention of tools it became possible to dig for roots, hunt small animals, and catch fish in rivers and oceans. Humans observed their environments and soon learned to plant seeds and harvest crops. As people migrated to areas in which game and fertile soil were abundant, communities began to develop. When people acquired the knowledge to grow crops and the skills to hunt game, they began to understand division of labor. Some of the people in the community tended to agricultural needs while others hunted game.

Settlements began in areas that offered natural resources to support life—food and water. With the ability to manage the environment, populations began to concentrate. The ability to transport raw materials and finished products brought mobility. With increasing technology and the rise of industrial centers came a migration of the workforce.

As habitats attracted larger numbers of people, environments became crowded, and there was competition. The concept of division of labor and sharing of food soon took hold in more heavily populated areas. Groups of people focused on growing crops while others concentrated on hunting. Experience led to the development of skills and knowledge that made the work easier. Farmers began to develop new plant species, and hunters began to protect animal species from other predators for their own use. This ability to manage the environment led people to settle down, to guard their resources, and to manage those resources.

Camps soon became villages. Villages became year-round settlements. Animals were domesticated and gathered into herds that met the needs of the village. With the settled life, it was no longer necessary to "travel light." Pottery was developed for storing and cooking food.

By 8000 BCE, culture was beginning to evolve in these villages. Agriculture was developed for the production of grain crops, which led to a decreased reliance on wild plants. Domesticating animals for various purposes decreased the need to hunt wild game. Life became more settled. It was then possible to turn attention to such matters as managing water supplies, producing tools, and making cloth. There was both social interaction and the opportunity to reflect upon existence. Mythologies arose, as did various belief systems. Rituals arose that reenacted the mythologies that sought to explain the meaning of life.

As farming and animal husbandry skills increased, the dependence upon wild game and food gathering declined. With this change came the realization that a larger number of people could be supported by farming and animal husbandry.

> *Two things seem to have come together to produce cultures and civilizations: a society/culture based on agriculture and the development of social centers populated with a literate minority and religious organizations.*

Two things seem to have come together to produce cultures and civilizations: a society/culture based on agriculture and the development of social centers populated with a literate minority and religious organizations. The members of these elite groups managed the functional aspects of society, such as the water supply and irrigation, as well as the religious aspects of society, such as rituals and religious life. They asserted their own right to use a portion of the goods produced by the community in return for their management of the community.

Further division of labor and community development resulted from:

- sharpened skills

- development of more sophisticated tools

- commerce with other communities and increasing knowledge of the environment

- resources available

- responses to the needs to share goods, order community life, and protect possessions from outsiders

As trade routes developed and travel between cities became easier, trade led to specialization. Trade enables people to obtain the goods they desire in exchange for the goods they are able to produce. This, in turn, leads to increased attention to refinements of technique and the sharing of ideas. The knowledge of a new discovery or invention provides knowledge and technology that increases the ability to produce goods for trade. As each community learns the value of the goods it produces and improves its ability to produce the goods in greater quantity, industry is born.

Cities and rural areas

Cities are the major hubs of human settlement. Almost half of the population of the world now lives in cities. These percentages are much higher in developed regions. Established cities continue to grow. The fastest growth, however, is occurring in developing areas. In some regions there are "metropolitan areas" made up of urban and suburban areas. In some places cities and urban areas have become interconnected into "megalopoli" (e.g., Tokyo-Kawasaki-Yokohama).

The concentration of populations varies widely from place to place. North American cities are different from European cities in terms of shape, size, population density, and modes of transportation. Whereas in North America, the wealthiest economic groups tend to live outside the cities, the opposite is true in Latin America.

Rural areas tend to be less densely populated due to the needs of agriculture. More land is needed to produce crops or for animal husbandry than is required for manufacturing. Rural areas, however, must be connected via communication and transportation in order to provide food and raw materials to urban areas. Social policy addresses basic human needs for the sustainability of the individual and the society. The concerns of social policy, then, include food, clean water, shelter, clothing, education, health, and social security.

Spatial organization

We can examine the spatial organization of the places where people live. For example, in a city, where are the factories and buildings for heavy industry? Are they near airports or train stations? Are they on the edge of town, near major roads? What about housing developments? Are they near these industries, or are they far away? Where are the other industrial buildings? Where are the schools and hospitals and parks? What about the police and fire stations? How close are homes to each of these things? Towns, and especially cities, are routinely organized into neighborhoods, so that each house or home is close to most things its residents might need on a regular basis. This means that large cities have multiple schools, hospitals, grocery stores, fire stations, and other services.

Related to this is the distance between cities, towns, villages, or settlements. In certain parts of the United States and definitely in many countries in Europe, the population settlement patterns achieve megalopolis standards, with no clear boundaries from one town to the next. Other, more sparsely populated areas have towns that are few and far between and have relatively few people in them. Some exceptions to this exist, of course, like oases in the deserts; for the most part, however, population centers tend to be relatively near one another with small towns nearby.

Patterns of Urban Development

Environmental and geographic factors have affected the pattern of urban development in Texas and the rest of the United States. In turn, urban infrastructure and development patterns are interrelated factors, which affect one another.

The growth of an urban area is often linked to the advantages provided by its geographic location.

The growth of an urban area is often linked to the advantages provided by its geographic location. Before the advent of efficient overland routes of commerce, i.e., railroads and highways, water provided the primary means of transportation of commercial goods. Most large American cities are situated along bodies of water.

As transportation technology advanced, the supporting infrastructure was built to connect cities with one another and to connect remote areas to larger communities. The railroad, for example, allowed for the quick transport of agricultural products from rural areas to urban centers. This newfound efficiency not only further fueled the growth of urban centers, but it changed the economy of rural America. When once farmers had practiced only subsistence farming—growing enough to support one's own family—the new infrastructure meant that farmers could convert agricultural products into cash by selling them at market.

For urban dwellers, improvements in building technology and advances in transportation allowed for larger cities to develop. Growth brought a new set of problems, unique to each location. The bodies of water that had made the development of cities possible in their early days also formed natural barriers to growth. Further infrastructure in the form of bridges, tunnels, and ferry routes were needed to connect central urban areas with outlying communities.

As cities grew in population, living conditions became more crowded. As roads and bridges became better, and transportation technology improved, many people began to look outside the city for living space. Along with the development of new suburbs came the infrastructure to connect them to the city in the form of commuter railroads and highways. In the case of New York City, which is spread out over several islands, a mass transit system became crucial early on to bring essential workers from outlying areas into the commercial centers.

The growth of suburbs had the effect in many cities of creating a type of economic segregation. Working-class people who could not afford new suburban homes and perhaps an automobile to carry them to and from work were relegated to closer, more densely populated areas. Frequently, these areas had to be passed through by those on their way to the suburbs, and rail lines and freeways sometimes bisected these urban communities.

In the modern age, advancements in telecommunications infrastructure may have an impact on urban growth patterns as information can now pass instantly and freely between almost any two points on the globe, providing access to some aspects of urban life to those in remote areas. Flight has made possible global commerce and goods exchange on a level never before seen. Foods from all around the world can be flown literally around the world, and, with the aid of refrigeration techniques, be kept fresh enough to sell in markets nearly everywhere. The same is true of medicine, and, unfortunately, weapons.

For more information on settlement patterns, see Skills 22.5 and 22.24.

> **SKILL 22.4** **Demonstrates an understanding of physical processes** *(e.g., erosion, deposition, weathering; plate tectonics; sediment transfer; flows and exchanges of energy and matter in the atmosphere that produce weather and climate; weather patterns)* **and their effects on environmental patterns.**

World weather patterns are greatly influenced by ocean surface currents in the upper layer of the ocean. These currents continuously move along the ocean surface in specific directions. Ocean currents that flow deep below the surface are called subsurface currents and are influenced by such factors as the location of landmasses in the current's path and the Earth's rotation.

The Gulf Stream and the California Current are the two main surface currents that flow along the coastlines of the United States. The **GULF STREAM** is a warm current in the Atlantic Ocean that carries warm water from the equator to the northern parts of the Atlantic Ocean. Benjamin Franklin studied and named the Gulf Stream. The California Current is a cold current that originates in the Arctic regions and flows southward along the west coast of the United States.

CLIMATE is the average weather or daily weather conditions for a specific region or location over an extended period of time. Studying the climate of an area includes gathering information on the area's monthly and yearly temperatures and amounts of precipitation. Another characteristic of an area's climate is the length of its growing season.

Natural changes can occur that alter habitats—floods, volcanoes, storms, and earthquakes. These changes can affect the species that exist within the habitat, either by causing extinction or by changing the environment such that it no longer supports the life systems. Climate changes can have similar effects. Inhabiting species can also alter habitats, particularly through migration.

Plate tectonics is a geological theory that explains **CONTINENTAL DRIFT**, which refers to the large movements of the solid portions of the Earth's crust floating on the molten mantle. There are ten major tectonic plates and several smaller plates. There are three types of plate boundaries: convergent, divergent, and transform.

GULF STREAM: a warm current in the Atlantic Ocean that carries warm water from the equator to the northern parts of the Atlantic Ocean

CLIMATE: the average weather or daily weather conditions for a specific region or location over an extended period of time

CONTINENTAL DRIFT: the large movements of the solid portions of the Earth's crust floating on the molten mantle

Convergent boundaries exist where plates are moving toward one another. When this happens, the two plates collide and fold up against one another, called continental collision, or one plate slides under the other, called subduction. Continental collision can create high mountain ranges, such as the Andes and the Himalayas. Subduction often results in volcanic activity along the boundary, as in the horseshoe-shaped "Ring of Fire" that encircles the basin of the Pacific Ocean.

EROSION: the displacement of solid earth surfaces such as rock and soil

EROSION is the displacement of solid earth surfaces such as rock and soil. Erosion is often a result of wind, water, or ice acting on surfaces with loose particles, such as sand, loose soils, or decomposing rock. Gravity can also cause erosion on loose surfaces. Factors such as slope, soil and rock composition, plant cover, and human activity all affect erosion.

WEATHERING: the natural decomposition of the Earth's surface from contact with the atmosphere

WEATHERING is the natural decomposition of the Earth's surface from contact with the atmosphere. It is not the same as erosion but can be a factor in it. Heat, water, ice, and pressure are all factors that can lead to weathering. Chemicals in the atmosphere can also contribute to weathering.

TRANSPORTATION: the movement of eroded material from one place to another by wind, water, or ice

TRANSPORTATION is the movement of eroded material from one place to another by wind, water, or ice. Examples of transportation include pebbles rolling down a streambed and boulders being carried by moving glaciers.

DEPOSITION: the result of transportation, and occurs when the material being carried settles on the surface and is deposited

DEPOSITION is the result of transportation, and occurs when the material being carried settles on the surface and is deposited. Sand dunes and moraines are formed by transportation and deposition of glacial material.

See also Skill 39.1 in Domain IV, Science.

SKILL 22.5 Analyzes how humans adapt to, use, and modify the physical environment and how the physical characteristics of places and human modifications to the environment affect human activities and settlement patterns.

Influences on Land Use

The greatest influence on land use is population and population growth. A burgeoning population demands a considerable amount from the land it surrounds and eventually incorporates—for food, living, and industrial use. The more people who want to live in a certain area, the more the land in that area will have to be transformed to meet that population's needs. In some cases, land is simply appropriated. Naturally aerated land is perfect for farms and ranches, with an abundance of water and natural food for the crops and animals; in other cases however, the land is transformed—agricultural land becoming industrial land, for example, or farmland being plowed over in favor of living space. In all cases, the land is being used to support the population, which is growing and expanding its needs and demands at the expense of the land.

Geography also influences land use, sometimes limiting it and sometimes inviting it. Inhospitable lands are usually not well populated because of the inherently harsh living conditions. We just don't see large cities built into the sides of the world's tallest mountains. (The population situation is not that desperate yet; perhaps, in the future, such cities will exist out of necessity.) Similarly, settlements in the middle of the desert may become a growing concern (Las Vegas is the exception to this rule).

Land that is easy to fortify is naturally inhabited by people looking to defend themselves from invasion. The presence of a large body of water routinely results in the human use of that water in some way, as a source of drinking water for people and animals or as a source of nourishment for crops. Rare, indeed, is the body of water that has not been appropriated in some form by human hands.

Geography can also form natural boundaries for settlements and civilizations. Mountain ranges and large bodies of water make effective borders between states and countries. If a civilization that has a mountain range, a river, or an ocean as a boundary wants to grow, it might be forced to grow upward rather than outward. Prime examples of this are New York City and San Francisco, both of which have limited land on which to build but use that land to the fullest by building tall skyscrapers that house large numbers of people and businesses.

Geography can also form natural boundaries for settlements and civilizations. Mountain ranges and large bodies of water make effective borders between states and countries.

Types of Land Use

Land-use patterns vary substantially by region. Factors that influence the use of land include: differences in climate, soil makeup, and topography and population dispersal. There are several different types of land use:

- **Cropland:** Makes up 20 percent of U.S. land use. This category includes land that is actively being used to grow crops as well as idle cropland. Cropland is roughly concentrated in the central regions of the contiguous United States. Cropland accounts for the majority of land use in the northern plains and the corn belt. The southern plains, lake states, and delta states also have cropland shares above the national average.

- **Grassland pasture and range:** Makes up 26 percent of U.S. land use. This category includes land used for grazing livestock, ranching, and animal husbandry. Lower levels of precipitation make land in the West more suitable for grazing. Most of the land in the mountain region and southern plains falls in this category. The northern plains and the Pacific region also have relatively large amounts of grazing land.

- **Forestland:** Makes up 29 percent of U.S. land use. This category includes land used to grow timber for building and fuel. This type of land use is most prevalent in the eastern regions such as the Northeast, Appalachian, Southeast, and delta states. The lake states and the Pacific region also have a large share of forestland because the topography and climate of these regions are conductive to growing trees.

- **Urban uses:** Make up 3 percent of U.S. land use. The Northeast and Southeast have the highest percentage of urban-use land.

- **Special uses:** Make up 13 percent of U.S. land use. Special uses include land used for national and state parks, roads, and recreational areas.

- **Miscellaneous uses:** Make up 10 percent of U.S. land use. This category includes most other types of land such as swamps, tundras, bare rock areas, and marshes.

Land-Use Models

LAND-USE AND DEVELOPMENT MODELS: theories that attempt to explain the layout of urban areas, primarily in more economically developed countries or less economically developed countries

LAND-USE AND DEVELOPMENT MODELS are theories that attempt to explain the layout of urban areas, primarily in more economically developed countries or less economically developed countries.

Two primary land-use models are generally applied to urban regions. These are:

1. **The Burgess model (also called the concentric model):** In this model cities are seen to develop in a series of concentric circles, with the central business district at the center, ringed by the factories and industrial usage area, ringed by the lower-class residential area, then the middle-class residential area, and finally the higher-class residential area (often suburbs).

2. **The Hoyt model (also called the sector model):** In this model the central business district occupies the central area of a circle, with factories and industry occupying an elongated area that abuts the city center and the lower-class residential area surrounding the industrial area, the middle-class residential area forming a semicircle toward the other side of the city center, and a small upper-class residential sector extending from the city center out through the middle of the middle-class residential area.

In rural areas, land use usually includes agriculture, forestry, and sometimes fishing. In the Von Thunen model, a city is the center of a state or region, from which a series of concentric circles emanates, each devoted to particular rural land-use patterns: The first ring from the city is devoted to dairy farming and intensive farming, which allows produce to reach the market quickly. The second zone focuses on forestland, which, because of its weight, needs to be relatively close to the city. The third zone is dedicated to extensive field cropland. The fourth zone is dedicated to grassland. Beyond this is miscellaneous land.

Consequences of Various Types of Land Use

There are many environmental, cultural, and economic consequences of various types of land use. Human beings have long been altering their surroundings in order to provide water, food, fiber, and shelter for billions of people. However, changes to our natural landscape to create croplands, pastures, plantations, and urban areas have had a significant impact on the Earth's natural resources and biodiversity. Some of the consequences of various types of land use are:

- Loss of natural landscape: The conversion of the world's natural landscape (forest, wetlands, waterways, etc.) for agriculture, settlement, and other human uses may soon undermine the capacity of the Earth's ecosystems to sustain an ever-growing population. This is because in order to create profitable production, unsustainable agricultural practices have become the norm. Humans have changed the natural landscape through the use of chemical fertilizers, diverting water, deforestation, and in many other ways.

- Loss of natural resources: By making changes to our natural landscape, humans have been able to allocate a huge portion of Earth's natural resources. In many ways this use of natural resources has been unchecked; if human society does not successfully regulate the use of resources, the world will face problems with sustaining food production and maintaining soil conditions and the water supply.

- Loss of biodiversity: By altering the Earth's natural makeup, humans have vastly changed the plant and animal diversity on the Earth. By destroying the natural habitat of these life forms, humans have put many of them in peril.

- Climate change: Land-cover change has been a major source of greenhouse gases, gases that accumulate in the atmosphere and increase global temperature. Increased levels of carbon dioxide (deforestation), methane (rice paddies, landfills, biomass burning, cattle), and nitrous oxide (fertilizer) are of primary concern. Climate change is also a regional issue. Economic sectors related to land use—agriculture, livestock, timber production, and fisheries— are the most sensitive to climate change. The more a region depends on these industries and the more land they use to support them, the more vulnerable a region is to climate change.

> *Human civilization has disrupted the ecological balance, contributed to the extinction of animal and plant species, and destroyed ecosystems through uncontrolled harvesting.*

For centuries, social, economic, and political policies have ignored the impact of human civilization on the environment. Human civilization has disrupted the ecological balance, contributed to the extinction of animal and plant species, and destroyed ecosystems through uncontrolled harvesting. If modern societies have no understanding of the limits on natural resources or how their actions affect the environment, it will become impossible for the Earth to sustain human existence. We face the task of balancing immediate human needs with maintaining the ability of the Earth to provide natural resources in the long term.

Strategies for maintaining this balance include making agricultural production more efficient, increasing open spaces in urban areas, and using forestry techniques that provide food and fiber yet sustain habitats for threatened plant and animal species. The main concerns in nonrenewable resource management are conservation, allocation, and environmental mitigation. Policymakers, corporations, and governments must determine how to use and distribute scarce resources. Decision makers must balance the immediate demand for resources with the need for resources in the future. Finally, scientists attempt to minimize and mitigate the environmental damage caused by resource extraction. Scientists can devise methods of harvesting and using resources that do not unnecessarily affect the environment. After the extraction of resources from a location, scientists can devise plans and methods to restore the environment to as close to its original state as possible.

See also Skill 22.3

SKILL 22.6 Demonstrates an understanding of the physical environmental characteristics of Texas, the United States and the world, past and present, and analyzes how humans have adapted to and modified the environment.

See Skills 21.8 and 22.1

SKILL 22.7 Examines how developments in science and technology affect the physical environment; the growth of economies and societies; and definitions of, access to and the use of physical and human resources.

See Skills 21.8 and 23.9 and Skills 39.4 and 40.4 in Domain IV, Science.

SKILL
22.8 **Creates and interprets maps of places and regions that contain map elements, draws sketch maps that illustrate various places and regions, and uses the compass rose, grid system and symbols to locate places on maps and globes.**

Maps present information about part of the Earth's surface, as seen from above. The representation is drawn to scale and includes symbols to show various features. Maps show locations of places and features, routes of travel, terrain, and natural features.

Symbols are used on maps to represent real objects. Shapes and colors are used as symbols. Blue is often used to show water, and a triangle may show elevation. A legend is similar to a dictionary because it explains the symbols that are shown on the map. The COMPASS ROSE is a drawing on a map, in the shape of a compass, which shows the orientation of the directions of North, South, West, and East. A GRID SYSTEM, or plan, is a series of lines placed at equal distances from each other on a map and cross each other at right angles to pinpoint exact locations.

> **COMPASS ROSE:** a drawing on a map, in the shape of a compass, which shows the orientation of the directions of North, South, West, and East

> **GRID SYSTEM:** a series of lines placed at equal distances from each other on a map and cross each other at right angles to pinpoint exact locations

SKILL
22.9 **Demonstrates an understanding of basic concepts of culture; processes of cultural adaptation, diffusion, and exchange; and positive and negative qualities of a multicultural society.**

Ethnocentrism

Humans are social animals who naturally form groups based on familial, cultural, national, and other lines. Conflicts and differences of opinion are just as natural between these groups.

One source of differing views among groups is ethnocentrism, the belief that one's own culture is the central and usually superior culture. An ethnocentric view usually considers different practices in other cultures inferior.

A variety of factors differentiate cultures: language, customs, dress, food, religious beliefs, and ethnicity. It is these attributes that define a culture and emphasize the differences between cultures. For example, citizens of the United States share a common language, English, whereas in Europe a multitude of languages and dialects are spoken by people from a variety of cultures, including Spanish, French, German, Italian, and Swedish. If you visit various regions of the United States, you will find a variety of accents and cadences from the slang of the ghettos of New York City or Los Angeles to the soft, drawl of Southern Texas to the flat, nasal tones of a Bostonian.

Psychologists have suggested that ethnocentrism is a naturally occurring attitude. People tend to be most comfortable among other people who have had a similar upbringing and who share their language and cultural background.

Historical developments are likely to affect different groups in different ways, some positively and some negatively. These effects can strengthen the ties an individual feels to the group he or she belongs to and solidify differences between groups.

Belief Systems

Belief systems, like other cultural elements or institutions, spread through human interaction.

Belief systems, like other cultural elements or institutions, spread through human interaction. Thus it is natural that religions and belief systems have regional or cultural markers that are transmitted across regions. Religions and belief systems in general originate in a particular region, with elements that are culturally or regionally defined or influenced. As they are introduced to new groups or societies, some of those regional and cultural markers penetrate the new society. By the same token, as interaction between the originating society and the new society continues and the belief system finds new expression, some regional or cultural elements introduced by the new society are carried back to the originating culture.

Belief systems are introduced to new societies in a variety of ways. One method is military and political conquest. As the originating society conquers a new territory and incorporates it into the political entity, belief systems are frequently either peaceably spread to the conquered people or forced upon them in the name of cultural unity. This has occurred frequently in human history. The rise and spread of the Islamic empire both converted and forced the conversion of conquered peoples to Islam. Another example can be seen in the conversion of the Emperor Constantine to Christianity and his imposition of Christianity upon Rome as the national religion.

Belief systems are also introduced through other types of human interaction, such as commercial interaction or the identification of common or similar primitive mythologies (e.g., similar creation and great flood myths). Educational interaction and cultural sharing frequently spread religious belief systems as well.

INNOVATION: the introduction of new ways of performing work or organizing societies

INNOVATION is the introduction of new ways of performing work or organizing societies, and can spur drastic changes in a culture. Prior to the innovation of agriculture, for instance, human cultures were largely nomadic and survived by hunting and gathering their food. Agriculture led directly to the development of permanent settlements and a radical change in social organization. Similarly, technological innovations in the Industrial Revolution of the nineteenth century changed the way work was performed and transformed the economic institutions of western cultures. Recent innovations in communications are changing the way cultures interact today.

CULTURAL DIFFUSION is the movement of cultural ideas or materials between populations independent of the movement of those populations. Cultural diffusion can take place when two populations are close to one another, through direct interaction, or across great distances, through mass media and other routes. American movies are popular all over the world, for instance. Within the United States, hockey, traditionally a Canadian pastime, has become a popular sport. These are both examples of cultural diffusion.

ADAPTATION is the process that individuals and societies go through in changing their behavior and organization to cope with social, economic, and environmental pressures.

ACCULTURATION is an exchange or adoption of cultural features when two cultures come into regular direct contact. An example of acculturation is the adoption of Christianity and western dress by many Native Americans in the United States.

ASSIMILATION is the process of a minority ethnic group adopting the culture of the larger group in which it exists. Immigrants moving to a new country typically assimilate into the larger culture.

EXTINCTION is the complete disappearance of a culture. Extinction can occur suddenly, from disease, famine, or war when the culture is completely destroyed, or slowly over time as a culture adapts, acculturates, or assimilates to the point where its original characteristic features are lost.

See also Skill 21.7

> **CULTURAL DIFFUSION:** the movement of cultural ideas or materials between populations independent of the movement of those populations

> **ADAPTATION:** the process that individuals and societies go through in changing their behavior and organization to cope with social, economic, and environmental pressures

> **ACCULTURATION:** an exchange or adoption of cultural features when two cultures come into regular direct contact

> **ASSIMILATION:** the process of a minority ethnic group adopting the culture of the larger group in which it exists

> **EXTINCTION:** the complete disappearance of a culture

SKILL 22.10 Demonstrates an understanding of the contributions made by people of various racial, ethnic, and religious groups.

Race, Ethnicity, and Cultural Identity

RACE is a term used most generally to describe a population of people from a common geographic area who share certain common physical traits. Skin color and facial features have traditionally been used to categorize individuals by race. The term has generated some controversy among sociologists, anthropologists, and biologists regarding what race and racial variation mean. Biologically speaking, a race of people shares a common genetic lineage. Socially, race can be more complicated to define, with many people identifying themselves as members of a racial group that others might not. This self-perception of racial identity, and the

> **RACE:** a term used most generally to describe a population of people from a common geographic area who share certain common physical traits

perception of race by others, is perhaps more crucial than any genetic variation when trying to understand the social implications of variations in race.

An ETHNIC GROUP is a group of people who identify themselves as having a common social background and set of behaviors and who perpetuate their culture by traditions of marriage within their own group. Ethnic groups often share a common language and ancestral background and frequently exist within larger populations. Ethnicity and race are sometimes interlinked but differ in that many ethnic groups can exist within a population of people thought to be of the same race. Ethnicity is based more on common cultural behaviors and institutions than common physical traits.

CULTURAL IDENTITY is the identification of individuals or groups as belonging to a particular group or culture. This refers to the sense of who one is, what values are important, and what racial or ethnic characteristics are important in one's self-understanding and manner of interacting with the world and with others. In a nation with a well-deserved reputation as a "melting pot," people's attachment to various cultural identities can become a divisive factor in communities and societies. Cosmopolitanism, its alternative, tends to blur those cultural differences in the creation of a shared new culture.

Throughout the history of the nation, groups have defined themselves and/or assimilated into the larger population to varying degrees. In order for a society to function as a cohesive and unifying force, there must be some degree of enculturation of all groups. The alternative is a competing, and often conflicting, collection of subgroups that are not able to cohere into a society. The failure to assimilate often results in culture wars as values and lifestyles come into conflict.

> **ETHNIC GROUP:** a group of people who identify themselves as having a common social background and set of behaviors and who perpetuate their culture by traditions of marriage within their own group

> **CULTURAL IDENTITY:** the identification of individuals or groups as belonging to a particular group or culture

> **SKILL 22.11** Analyzes the effects of race, gender, socioeconomic class, status and stratification on ways of life in Texas, in the United States and the world.

Texas, the Melting Pot

The story of Texas is replete with people of varying nationalities competing for a slice of life in what one relatively recent ad campaign called "a whole other country." At various times, the residents of what is now Texas have included Native Americans, French, Spanish, British, Mexicans, and Americans. The current population is a melting pot, just like the United States.

Among the Native American tribes who made their home in Texas were the Apache, Cherokee, and Comanche. These were by no means the only tribes;

numerous tribes roamed the great plains of Texas for many, many years before white explorers and settlers appeared.

French and Spanish explorers reached the area in the sixteenth century, and settlers soon followed. The Rio Grande and other rivers provided avenues for transportation, of both goods and people. Americans came in during the late eighteenth and early nineteenth centuries and were an established presence after the Louisiana Purchase.

The nineteenth century saw tremendous change in Texas. At the urging of the Mexican government, which wanted to expand the population of the newly independent territory, Stephen F. Austin and other Americans moved into the area to stay. Austin soon led a movement to colonize the area as American. This conflict escalated for several years until the United States annexed Texas. This, in part, brought on the Mexican–American War.

The American victory in that war brought a tremendous influx of American settlers into Texas. The state's population continued to grow at a rapid rate throughout the rest of the nineteenth century and into the twentieth century. Not even the deadly Civil War could stop the tide of new Texas residents. They came for economic and settlement opportunities, working at oil fields and on farms and ranches. They came to start new businesses and new lives. The latter half of the twentieth century saw a boom in high-tech companies and jobs, with Houston, San Antonio, and Dallas leading the way. These cities—and the state in general—continue to be a driving force in high technology.

In a reverse trend, the number of Mexicans moving into Texas began to grow in the twentieth century, reaching a staggering rate in the latter half of the century and into the twenty-first century (with the exception of the 1930s, when the Dust Bowl drove Texans away from Texas in large numbers). The proximity of the American state and the promise of new opportunity drove immigration to an all-time high. Texas to this day is made up mostly of Americans and Mexican Americans.

Stretching back through the history of the Mexican Territory, the number of Mexican residents who have migrated to Texas to seek their fortunes is very large indeed. Mexican Americans work in a variety of capacities throughout the state—in agriculture, at oil fields, on ranches, and in hundreds of other white-collar and professional capacities.

> Stretching back through the history of the Mexican Territory, the number of Mexican residents who have migrated to Texas to seek their fortunes is very large indeed.

African Americans were brought to Texas first as slaves of the early white settlers. They worked both on cattle ranches and in cotton fields. After the Civil War, many African Americans migrated from Southern states in search of greater opportunity. In 1966, Curtis Graves and Barbara Jordan became the first African

Americans elected to the state legislature since 1898. The Mansfield School Desegregation Incident in 1956 was a notable turning point in school desegregation in Texas.

Throughout its history from the time of the first European contact, Texas has been home to a diverse population in terms of race, ethnicity, and religion. The current culture of the state reflects the numerous influences that have shaped the people and institutions of Texas.

Major Cultural Regions of the World

North America includes the countries of the United States and Canada. Mexico, while geographically part of North America, is often considered to be closer to Latin and South America culturally. English is the primary language of North America, with large numbers of French speakers in Quebec, Canada, and Spanish speakers in the southwestern United States. Because of its history of immigration from wide areas, North America contains people of many cultures, with people of western European descent in the majority. Christianity is the primary religion, with significant populations practicing other religions such as Judaism and Islam.

Latin America includes the mainly Spanish- and Portuguese-speaking countries of Mexico, Central America, and South America.

Europe is a diverse collection of independent countries that have banded together economically.

The Middle East and North Africa includes the countries of Saudi Arabia, Egypt, Libya, Iran, Iraq, Israel, Lebanon, Jordan, and Syria.

Sub-Saharan Africa is that portion of Africa located south of the great Sahara desert and includes the countries of South Africa, Kenya, Rwanda, and Ghana as well as thirty-eight other nations.

The region of Russia and Central Asia is made up of many of the former states of the Soviet Union.

East Asia includes China, North and South Korea, and Japan.

South Asia includes the countries of India, Pakistan, Bangladesh, Nepal, and Sri Lanka.

Southeast Asia includes the countries of Thailand, Vietnam, Cambodia, and Laos on the mainland of Asia, and Indonesia, the Philippines, Malaysia, and Singapore off the shore of Asia.

Australia and New Zealand are two former British colonies that have much in common with western European and American cultures.

Major Cultural Regions of the United States

New England is located in the northeastern part of the United States and includes the states of Maine, New Hampshire, Vermont, Massachusetts, Rhode Island, and Connecticut. It was the first region of the United States to be heavily settled by Europeans, beginning in the seventeenth century. The largest city in the region is Boston. New Englanders, or "Yankees" as they are often called, share a tradition of direct involvement in government through small town meetings where local decisions are made. The Democratic Party is the dominant political group in the region. Education is highly regarded, and several of the nation's top universities are located in New England.

The Mid-Atlantic region is located in the central part of the east coast of the United States, and includes the states of New York, New Jersey, Pennsylvania, Delaware, and Maryland.

The South is one of the country's most distinctive cultural regions, and includes the states of North Carolina, South Carolina, Tennessee, Georgia, Florida, Alabama, Mississippi, Louisiana, Texas, and Arkansas. Also sometimes considered part of the South are the states of Oklahoma, Missouri, Kentucky, Virginia and West Virginia.

The Midwest is located in the northern central part of the United States, and traditionally includes the states of Minnesota, Wisconsin, Iowa, Illinois, Indiana, Ohio and Michigan. North Dakota, South Dakota, Nebraska, Kansas and Missouri are also sometimes thought of as being midwestern states.

The Southwest region of the United States is an area where Native American and Latin American culture has had the most influence. Arizona and New Mexico are the two states that make up the main part of the Southwest, with some of the surrounding states of California, Nevada, Utah, Colorado, Oklahoma and Texas extending into the region.

The West extends from the Pacific Coast of the United States eastward to the Rocky Mountain states, and includes the states of California, Colorado, Idaho, Montana, Nevada, Oregon, Utah, Washington, and Wyoming.

See also Skill 22.13

SKILL
22.12 **Identifies, explains and compares various ethnic and/or cultural customs, celebrations and traditions.**

Ethnic traditions often involve holidays, religion, and family events such as weddings. Ethnic customs, celebrations, and traditions can be found throughout the United States and Texas.

Texas has a Mexican heritage and many of the Mexican traditions are followed. Cinco de Mayo is one example. Germans settled Texas in the mid-1800s, and Oktoberfest and Wurstfest events are examples of German celebrations. The Czech religious Feast of the Assumption of the Virigin each August has historical and religious importance, and the Westfest is also popular. Irish celebrations may turn rivers green in celebration of St. Patrick's Day or include music at events such as the North Texas Irish Festival in Dallas. Texans of Italian heritage celebrate St. Joseph's Day in March, and African Americans celebrate the end of slavery in Texas on June 19, which is known as Juneteenth. Among other Native America celebrations is the Fiesta de San Antonio, held yearly in San Anontio to honor the patron saint of the Tigua Indians.

Cultural customs, celebrations, and traditions range from music to athletics to folklore. The American cowboy culture has had an influence on Texas because of the state's ranching history. Associated with cowboys is the rodeo, which is considered an official sport of Texas. The ranching and cowboy cultures are described in folklore, which includes famous individuals like Davy Crockett, Pecos Bill, and "Bigfoot" Wallace.

> Texas has a Mexican heritage and many of the Mexican traditions are followed.

SKILL
22.13 **Demonstrates an understanding of relationships among cultures of people from various groups, including racial, ethnic and religious groups, in the United States and throughout the world** *(e.g., conflict and cooperation among cultures; factors that influence cultural change, such as improved communication, transportation and economic development).*

Cross-cultural exchanges can enrich every involved group of persons with the discovery of shared values and needs, as well as an appreciation for the unique cultural characteristics of each group. For the most part, the history of the nation has been the story of successful enculturation and cultural enrichment. The notable failures, usually resulting from prejudice and intolerance of one form or another, include oppression of Chinese, Japanese, and African Americans.

In the United States, many diverse cultures came together in a steady stream of immigration to the New World. These cultures were mainly Western European, and the immigrants who came to the United States usually assimilated into

American culture within two generations although the cultural practices and traditions they brought with them often survived in an Americanized form. While somewhat tolerant of other European immigrants and cultural practices, Americans treated most nonwhite cultures as inferior. African Americans were enslaved for centuries, and even after the end of slavery were officially segregated from European-American society in some parts of the country.

In recent years, a respect for cultural diversity has grown in the United States and worldwide. Texas, with its history of shifting dominant cultures and immigration, has been a leader in promoting cultural diversity in the United States.

The Hispanic heritage of many Texas citizens is officially honored by the preservation of early settlements and artifacts such as Ceremonial Cave, Espiritu Santo, and Morhiss Mound, and ethnic and cultural concentrations of people currently thrive.

See also Skill 22.10

> *Texas, with its history of shifting dominant cultures and immigration, has been a leader in promoting cultural diversity in the United States.*

SKILL 22.14 Compares and analyzes similarities and differences in the ways various peoples at different times in history have lived and have met basic human needs, including the various roles of men, women, children and families in past and present cultures.

Food, clothing, and shelter are the three basic needs of human beings. As early humans increased in number and moved into new parts of the world, they had to adapt to their new environments by finding new ways to satisfy these needs.

Early humans hunted animals and gathered food from wild sources. Taking their basic support from nature required them to move with their food sources. Game animals might migrate, and seasonal food sources might require groups to travel to the regions where they could find food. To facilitate moving around to different areas, portable methods of shelter were developed such as the Native American teepee or the Mongolian yurt. These shelters could be carried from place to place, allowing a greater range.

Clothing allowed humans to adapt to the wider range of climates they discovered as they moved from place to place, both in their annual circuit and as they moved into new wilderness areas that had lower average temperatures. Clothing protects the body from cold, sun exposure, and the elements. In very hot climates, early humans wore little or no clothing. The advantages of having an extra layer of protection were soon realized, however, and basic coverings were fashioned from animal skin. Foot coverings were developed to protect the feet from rough ground and sharp rocks. In colder climates, clothing was crucial for survival. Animal pelts with the fur attached provided warmth. Foot coverings could also be lined with fur or stuffed with grass. Mittens or gloves kept vulnerable fingers warm and protected.

As humans moved away from hunting and gathering into agricultural pursuits, other materials for clothing became available. Wool-bearing animals were domesticated and plant fibers were woven into cloth. During the Industrial Revolution, weaving methods took a great stride forward, greatly expanding the use of garments made from woven cloth.

Agriculture also expanded the types of food that were available. Grains and fruits could be grown in place and meat could be obtained from domesticated animals. Not all climates are suitable for all crops, however, and humans have had to adapt plant varieties and agricultural methods to successfully produce food.

For information on early human history, see Skill 21.3.

For information on families, see Skill 22.16.

For additional information, see Skill 23.1.

> **SKILL 22.15** **Compares similarities and differences among Native American groups in Texas, the United States and the Western Hemisphere before European colonization.**

The first documented history of Texas originates in 1519, when the first European explorers discovered that the province was occupied by a number of Indian tribes. During the period from 1519 to 1865, sections of Texas were claimed by six countries: Mexico, Spain, France, the Republic of Texas, the United States of America, and the Confederate States of America.

Texas lies at the intersection of two major cultural areas of pre-Columbian North America, the Southwest and the Plains areas. The area now covered by the state of Texas encompassed three major native civilizations that reached their developmental peak prior to the arrival of European explorers and that are known from archaeological findings. This area was home to the Pueblo from the upper Rio Grande region, centered west of Texas; the Mound Builder culture of the Mississippi Valley region, centered east of Texas, ancestral to the Caddo nation; and the civilizations of Mesoamerica, centered south of Texas.

Native Americans determined the destiny of European explorers and settlers depending on whether a tribe was welcoming or aggressive. Friendly tribes taught the newcomers how to grow native crops, prepare foods, and organize hunting trips for wild game. Warlike tribes made life disagreeable, dangerous, and difficult for the settlers through their attacks and resistance to European invasion and occupation.

There was not one dominant civilization in the present-day Texas region; many diverse tribes populated the area. Native American tribes that lived within the boundaries of present-day Texas include the Alabama, Apache, Atakapan, Bidai, Caddo, Coahuiltecan, Comanche, Cherokee, Choctaw, Coushatta, Hasinai, Jumano, Karankawa, Kickapoo, Kiowa, Tonkawa, and Wichita.

Currently, there are three federally recognized Native American tribes located in Texas: the Alabama-Coushatta Tribe of Texas, the Kickapoo Traditional Tribe of Texas, and the Ysleta Del Sur Pueblo of Texas.

See also Skill 21.3

Currently, there are three federally recognized Native American tribes located in Texas: the Alabama-Coushatta Tribe of Texas, the Kickapoo Traditional Tribe of Texas, and the Ysleta Del Sur Pueblo of Texas.

SKILL 22.16 Applies knowledge of the role of families in meeting basic human needs and how families and cultures develop and use customs, traditions and beliefs to define themselves.

The traditions and behaviors of a culture are based on the prevailing beliefs and values of that culture. Beliefs and values are similar and interrelated systems. Beliefs are those things that are thought to be true. Beliefs are often associated with religion but they can also be based on political or ideological philosophies. "All men are created equal" is an example of an ideological belief.

Values are what a society thinks is right and wrong, and are often based on and shaped by beliefs. The value that every member of the society has a right to participate in his or her government might be considered to be based on the belief that "All men are created equal," for instance.

A culture's beliefs and values are reflected in its cultural products, such as literature, the arts, media, and architecture. These products last from generation to generation, becoming one way that culture is transmitted through time. A common language among all members of a culture makes this transmission possible.

Sociologists have identified five different types of institutions around which societies are structured: family, education, government, religion, and economy. These institutions provide a framework for members of a society to learn about and participate in the society, and allow the society to perpetuate its beliefs and values to succeeding generations.

Sociologists have identified five different types of institutions around which societies are structured: family, education, government, religion, and economy.

The family is the primary social unit in most societies. It is through the family that children learn the most essential skills for functioning in their society such as language and appropriate forms of interaction. The family is connected to ethnicity, which is partly defined by a person's heritage.

Education is an important institution in a society, as it allows for the formal passing on of a culture's collected knowledge. Education is connected to the family, as that is where a child's earliest education takes place. The United States has a public school system administered by the states that ensures a basic education and provides a common experience for most children.

A society's governmental institutions often embody its beliefs and values. Laws, for instance, reflect a society's values by enforcing its ideas of right and wrong. The structure of a society's government can reflect a society's ideals about the role of an individual in society. The American form of democracy emphasizes the rights of the individual but in return expects individuals to respect the rights of others, including those of ethnic or political minorities.

Religion is frequently the institution from which a society's primary beliefs and values stem, and can be closely related to other social institutions. Many religions have definitive teachings on the structure and importance of the family, for instance. The U.S. Constitution guarantees the free practice of religion, which has given rise to a large number of denominations in the United States today. Most Americans identify with Christian faiths.

A society's economic institutions define how an individual can contribute and receive economic reward from his or her society. The United States has a capitalist economy motivated by free enterprise. While this system allows for economic advancement for the individual, it can also create poverty and economic depression.

SKILL 22.17 Understands and applies the concept of diversity within unity.

The teaching of diversity is a quest for equality, social justice, and the pursuit of democracy. The foremost goal of diversity education is to reorganize schools so that all students gain an understanding of the attitudes and skills needed to function in a culturally and ethnically diverse nation and world. Diversity education is consistent with the principles outlined in the Declaration of Independence, the U.S. Constitution, and the Bill of Rights. These documents guarantee basic human rights, civil liberties, and equality, democracy, freedom, and justice to individuals from all cultural, language, and social groups.

Integration of diversity content material allows teachers to illustrate key concepts, cultural values, and theories in their subject areas from a variety of cultures and groups. Diversity theories assert that the values, personal histories, and attitudes of various cultural groups are an integral part of diversity learning. This content material includes teaching activities that enable students to investigate, comprehend, and synthesize this new material into already assimilated knowledge.

Research has proven that the use of ethnically diverse textbooks and other supplementary teaching materials can assist students from diverse cultural and ethnic groups to develop a more self-determining cultural attitude and awareness of other groups. Curriculum activities can include: cultural plays, folk dances, ethnic music, and dramatic role-playing.

> *Integration of diversity content material allows teachers to illustrate key concepts, cultural values, and theories in their subject areas from a variety of cultures and groups.*

SKILL 22.18 Relates geographic and cultural information and ideas to information and ideas in other social sciences and other disciplines.

For information on the disciplines that make up the social sciences, see Skill 21.9.

The study of social phenomena can draw on the methods and theories of several disciplines. The field of anthropology is largely concerned with the institutions of a society and intercultural comparisons. Anthropologists observe people of a particular culture acting within their culture and interacting with people of other cultures, and interpret social phenomena. Anthropology relies on qualitative research, such as examining the types of rituals a culture has, as well as quantitative research, such as measuring the relative sizes of ethnic groups.

Psychology is mainly focused on the study of the individual and his or her behavior. Because humans are social animals, the methods of psychology can be used to study society and culture by asking questions about how individuals behave within these groups, what motivates them, and the ways they find to express themselves.

Sociology is the study of how humans act as a society and within a society, and involves examining the rules and mechanisms people follow as a society. Sociology also looks at groups within a society and how they interact. The field relies on research methods from several disciplines, including anthropology and psychology.

SKILL 22.19 Formulates geographic and cultural research questions and uses appropriate procedures to reach supportable judgments and conclusions.

Analyzing an event or issue from multiple perspectives involves seeking out sources that advocate or express those perspectives and comparing them with one another. For example, listening to the speeches of Martin Luther King, Jr. provides insight into the perspective of one group of people concerning the issue of civil rights in the United States in the 1950s and 1960s. Listening to the public statements of George Wallace, an American governor opposed to desegregation, provides another perspective from the same time period. Looking at the legislation that was proposed at the time and how it came into effect offers a window onto the political thinking of the day. Comparing these perspectives on the matter of civil rights provides information on the key issues that each group was concerned about, and gives a fuller picture of the societal changes that were occurring at that time. Analysis of any social event, issue, problem, or phenomenon requires that various perspectives be taken into account in this way.

See also Skill 22.20

SKILL 22.20 Demonstrates an understanding of research related to geography and culture and knows how social scientists in those fields locate, gather, organize, analyze and report information by using standard research methodologies.

According to the TEKS glossary, "An hypothesis is an explanation or a theory which can be tested by further investigation. It derives from comprehending a relationship between a cause and an effect and developing a theory linking the two. Researchers develop hypotheses from these 'best-guess theories,' and base their ideas on observed data with the supposition that the informed 'guess' (hypothesis) will stand up to further analysis based on additional data.

Cause-and-Effect Hypothesis

"Hypotheses can also be generated by predicting a different result emanating from some type of change (intervention) in the input (stimulus), which would be phrased as an "if-then" statement. The Russian physiologist Ivan Pavlov tested his theory that a repeated stimulation or conditioning could cause a specific response and won the Nobel Prize in 1904 for his work. B. F. Skinner, an American psychologist, expanded on the theory by researching human behavior and the relationship of positive reinforcement to human behavior. Systems of controlled reward and punishment developed from Skinner's cause-and-effect hypothesis."

Correlational Analyses

According to the TEKS glossary, "The degree to which two sets of data are related is the correlation. Correlational analyses result from the analysis of sets of data to determine relationships. By studying the IQ scores of good students, researchers determine that IQ scores do have a relationship to academic achievement. A positive correlation between two sets of data means that both sets of data increase (or decrease) together, or in equal proportions. A negative correlation means the two sets of data will move in opposite directions from each other (one increases and the other decreases relative to each other). CAUTION: A positive or negative correlation between two sets of data does NOT necessarily imply a relationship or causality. An example would be that an increase in both crime rate and church construction is coincidence—not a positive correlation!"

Ethical Standards of Survey Information

According to the TEKS glossary, "Researchers who study people and their behavior must understand that confidentiality and privacy often limit the use of information. The rights of subjects in any research project are protected by an ethical agreement between the researcher and the subject. It is similar to doctor/patient confidentiality. Researchers who are ethical, that is, they have a high moral standard and conform with professional codes of behavior, must respect the confidentiality of information, must not identify informants unless the subject approved the release of information, preferably in writing or on tape in the case of an oral interview, prior to and after the collection of the information, and must satisfy any special restrictions placed on the information by the subject. If researchers promise anonymity they must abide by it. Example: a parent admitting on a confidential survey that they participated in the counter culture in the 1960s could suffer if the information leaked to his/her boss, community organizations, or relatives. The person surveyed could respond with legal action against the researcher who initially guaranteed anonymity."

> **SKILL 22.21** Demonstrates an understanding of the characteristics and uses of various primary and secondary sources *(e.g., databases, maps, photographs, media services, the Internet, biographies, interviews, questionnaires, artifacts)*; utilizes information from a variety of sources to acquire social science information; answers social science questions; and evaluates information in relation to bias, propaganda, point of view and frame of reference.

Primary Sources

According to the TEKS glossary, "Primary sources consist of evidence produced by someone who participated in an event or lived during the time being studied. A letter written to a friend or a map to a friend's house are both primary sources."

> *Primary sources consist of evidence produced by someone who participated in an event or lived during the time being studied.*

Secondary Sources

According to the TEKS glossary, "Secondary sources are descriptions or interpretations prepared by people who were not involved in the events described. Researchers often use primary sources to understand past events but they produce secondary sources. Secondary sources provide useful background material and context for information gained from primary sources."

Bias Related to Various Points of View

According to the TEKS glossary, "Participants in events view the action from different points of view, physically and psychologically. Those favoring one side over another tend to be biased in their reporting of the events. Their interests, opinions, and attitudes appear in their descriptions. For instance, the viewpoints of a person driving a car which runs a red light may be different from those of the pedestrian who observes the resulting accident. Prior experience also contributes to bias. People may feel certain ways due to their treatment, responses to, or opinion of incidents previously experienced."

Multiple Sources of Evidence

According to the TEKS glossary, "Geographers, historians, archaeologists, and others rarely rely on one source of evidence to formulate their theories of the social studies. Instead they look for multiple sources of evidence, study them, and search for patterns within the evidence. Sources might include letters, diaries, books published during a particular period, and other qualitative sources which express people's concerns and attitudes. Quantitative sources such as census returns, responses to questionnaires, and prices and amounts sold recorded in account books provide less subjective information but can still reflect biases of the recorder. For instance, determining something as ordinary as the foods people ate for supper requires a survey of period cookbooks, examination of cooking utensils and fireplaces or stoves used in the era, and an understanding of the crops farmers grew."

Frames of Reference

According to the TEKS glossary, "People experience life from a variety of vantage points (frames of reference). Peasants in third-world countries perceive the world from their small villages. Business people negotiating trade deals in the board-rooms of international corporations perceive the world differently. The experience of the coffee bean picker who helps procure the product rarely influences the deci-sions of the trader. People involved in each part of the process from coffee picking through curing, roasting, grinding, brewing, and drinking all engage the bean at different stages and express their involvement in the coffee business differently. By understanding how the frame of reference of different participants involved in growing, marketing, and purchasing coffee may affect the evidence they produce documenting their involvement, students gain a greater understanding of what happened and how it relates to current international events. Historians and other social scientists also have a frame of reference, one based in the present. Their job is to sort through the evidence, prioritize it, distinguish important information from the less important, and interpret it. Those who study society reflect their times, and as a result, the interpretations of events change over time. Throughout the process, historians, geographers, sociologists, economists, and others must be aware that they view the events from the present, but they must avoid 'present-mindedness,' judging the past or other cultures in relation to accepted behavior today within their society."

See also Skill 21.12

> **SKILL 22.22** Applies evaluative, problem-solving and decision-making skills to geographic and cultural information, ideas and issues by identifying problems, gathering information, listing and considering options, considering advantages and disadvantages, choosing and implementing solutions, and assessing the solutions' effectiveness.

Geography lends itself to many other disciplines. Geographical factors have a bearing on problems and solutions in a number of other fields of study. One of the foremost examples of this is geography's application to economics. Business owners seeking the best location for a manufacturing plant will naturally consider geographic factors when making their final decision. Will the plant depend on hydroelectric power? If so, should the plant be located near a natural water source like a river or lake or dam? Will the plant be exporting or importing a large number of products? If so, then where is the nearest airport and how far away are the nearest highways and residential areas? If the plant owners will depend heavily on land-based transportation, what is the surrounding terrain like? Can heavy trucks easily connect from plant to highway, and vice versa? Is privacy a concern? How will what the company is doing affect the local community? Strip mining of local hills and mountains could be a source of much friction. If the plant is manufacturing secret products, then the owners will want to situate that plant as far away from the rest of civilization as possible, within the guidelines already mentioned.

Simpler decisions must be made when a group of people is looking to open a new business or shopping mall. Practical considerations such as the locations of nearby homes and possible competitors factor into the decision of where to locate that new business or shopping mall. Is the city an urban hub, with shoppers already coming from nearby towns? If so, the new business can count on more than just the local population for business. If the business is a grocery store, can the owners count on a steady supply of varied foods and beverages to keep customers keeping back? If the business is a niche market, is the local population large enough to sustain such a niche?

Geography's influence extends to politics also. The way an industry or organization treats the land around them can be the source of political debate. So can the treatment of nearby wildlife. Some of the most caustic debates these days are between animal rights activists and proponents of technological growth at all costs. On a more traditional note, the closer a city or town is to a major airport and the more population that city has, the more often political candidates will visit that city in search of support from voters who live there.

> **SKILL 22.23** Communicates and interprets geographic and cultural information in written, oral, and visual form (e.g., maps and other graphics) and translates the information from one medium to another (e.g., written to visual, statistical to written or visual).

Maps

A map can provide information that might take hundreds of words to explain. Maps can be used to convey a wide variety of information and can be made in many different ways. It is important for students to understand how to use them. Once they do, maps can provide a solid foundation for social science studies.

Graphs

To apply information obtained from graphs, one must understand the two major reasons why graphs are used:

1. To present a model or theory visually to show how two or more variables interrelate

2. To present real-world data visually to show how two or more variables interrelate

Bar graphs and line graphs are the types of graphs used most often. (Charts are often used for similar reasons and are explained in the next section.)

Graphs are most useful when one wishes to demonstrate the sequential increase or decrease of a variable or to show specific correlations between two or more variables in a given circumstance. Most common is the bar graph, because it is easy to read and a clear way to show the difference in a given set of variables. However it is limited in that it cannot show an actual proportional increase or decrease of one given variable to another.

Line graphs

To show a proportional increase or decrease, one must use a line graph. There are two types of line graphs: linear and nonlinear. A linear line graph uses a series of straight lines; a nonlinear line graph uses a curved line. Although the lines can be either straight or curved, all of the lines are called curves.

> To show a proportional increase or decrease, one must use a line graph.

A line graph uses a number line, or axis. The numbers are generally placed in order, equal distances from one another. The number line is used to represent a number, degree, or other such variable at an appropriate point on the line. Two lines are used, intersecting at a specific point. They are referred to as the x-axis and the y-axis.

The y-axis is a vertical line; the x-axis is a horizontal line. Together they form a coordinate system. The difference between a point on the line of the x-axis and a point on the y-axis is called the SLOPE of the line, or the change in the value on the vertical axis divided by the change in the value on the horizontal axis. The y-axis number is called the rise and the x-axis number is called the run, thus the equation for slope is:

> **SLOPE:** The difference between a point on the line of the x-axis and a point on the y-axis

$$\text{SLOPE} = \frac{\text{RISE (Change in value on the vertical axis)}}{\text{RUN (Change in value on the horizontal axis)}}$$

The slope indicates the amount of increase or decrease of a given specific variable. When using two or more variables, one can plot the difference between them in any given situation. This makes presenting information on a line graph more involved. It also makes it more informative and accurate than a simple bar graph. Understanding what the slope is and how it is measured helps us describe verbally the pictures we are seeing visually. For example, if a curve is said to have a slope of zero, you should picture a flat line. If a curve has a slope of one, you should picture a rising line that makes a 45-degree angle with the horizontal and vertical axis lines.

With nonlinear curves (the ones that really do curve) the slope of the curve is constantly changing, so we must understand that the slope of the nonlinear curved line will be at a specific point. How is this done? The slope of a nonlinear curve is determined by the slope of a straight line that intersects the curve at that specific point.

In all graphs, an upward sloping line represents a direct relationship between the two variables. A downward sloping line represents an inverse relationship between the two variables. In reading any graph, one must always be very careful to understand exactly what is being measured.

Charts

Charts are similar to graphs. It depends on the type of information you want to illustrate whether you choose to use a chart or a graph. One of the most common types of chart is the pie chart because it is the easiest to read and understand. Pie charts are used often, especially when one is trying to illustrate the differences in percentages among various items, or when one is demonstrating a whole divided into parts.

See also Skill 22.24

SKILL 22.24 **Analyzes geographic and cultural data using geographical tools and basic mathematical and statistical concepts and analytic methods.**

Qualitative Methods of Inquiry

According to the TEKS glossary, "Research based on qualitative methods of inquiry uses selected writings or actions which best represent the point to be proven or disproven. A sociologist who uses a qualitative approach to a study of the factors motivating high school students to join gangs could ask certain gang members a series of questions and use the personal responses as evidence in the study. Other strategies to gather qualitative data include in-depth interviews, open-ended surveys, key informants, and anecdotal-data collection."

Quantitative Methods of Inquiry

According to the TEKS glossary, "Research based on quantitative methods of inquiry uses data which was systematically collected to prove or disprove a hypothesis. A sociologist who uses a quantitative approach to study factors motivating high school students to join gangs could develop a standard questionnaire to distribute to gang members, collect the results, and perform statistical analysis to arrive at a conclusion. Other sources of quantifiable data include census reports, statistics collected by schools or districts, or other evidence gathered using standardized procedures."

See also Skill 22.23

SKILL 22.25 Understands and analyzes the characteristics, distribution and migration of populations and the interactions between people and the physical environment, including the effects of those interactions on the development of Texas, the United States and the world.

See also Skill 22.1

Migration

According to the TEKS glossary, "Migration is the process of moving from one place to another place intending to stay permanently or at least for a long period of time. Pull factors draw migrants from their original location. These include social, economic, and environmental attractions. Push factors are the social, economic, and environmental forces which drive people from their original location and cause them to seek a new one."

Physical and Human Factors

According to the TEKS glossary, "Several factors may influence ongoing development and events in history. Physical factors relate to the physical characteristics of a place such as climate, weather, and landforms. These lead to events, such as tornadoes, hurricanes, or droughts, which influence the chain of events constituting Texas history. Physical factors also influence development. Most early settlement in Texas concentrated in the eastern portion of the state because the soils, climate, and vegetation compared favorably to other parts of the South from which most settlers migrated. Transportation routes developed to link settlements which evolved into cities. Human factors relate to the human characteristics of a place. These also play a role in Texas history. As population pressures in the eastern portion of the state increased, settlement moved west. As technology improved, settlers in the western plains began to irrigate their crop land and the area's economy developed around cotton-based agriculture. This is one way human factors influence development by modifying the environment."

See also Skills 22.3 and 22.5

> **SKILL 22.26** Demonstrates knowledge of the institutions that exist in all societies and how the characteristics of those institutions may vary among societies.

Societal Values

According to the TEKS glossary, "Each society identifies values that everyone within the society is expected to uphold. Societal values vary among cultures within nations and among nations. These influence public behavior including business dealings. For instance, some cultures expect to barter as a part of normal business transactions while others may view bartering as insulting. Business people must understand the societal values of all trading partners to be most effective."

See also Skills 22.1, 22.10, 22.11, and 22.13

> **SKILL 22.27** Demonstrates an understanding of how people use oral tradition, stories, real and mythical heroes, music, paintings and sculpture to represent culture in communities in Texas, the United States and the world *(e.g., importance of individual writers and artists to the cultural heritage of communities; significant examples of art, music and literature from various periods).*

Oral Tradition and Mythology

Before the time of the written word, cultures transmitted their stories, laws, history, beliefs, and knowledge through the spoken word. This could take the form of ballads, stories, poems, speeches, or chants. The purpose of maintaining an oral tradition is to transmit cultural knowledge from one generation to the next, thus reinforcing cultural norms and cultural identity.

Before the time of the written word, cultures transmitted their stories, laws, history, beliefs, and knowledge through the spoken word.

Although each culture has developed its own unique oral traditions, many similarities exist between them. Oral traditions, or the mythologies they may include, often seek to explain the world and our relation to the world. They provide insight into the order and ethics of life and provide explanations for the origin of the universe, the workings of natural phenomena, and the unique story of one's own people. Myths often depict heroes overcoming challenges or modeling exemplary behavior or deeds worthy of recognition and homage.

Oral traditions continue to thrive even in the modern world, because they reinforce and express cultural identity. Passing along stories, songs, and art has helped to create and maintain the distinct culture in Texas. The legend of Gregorio Cortez Lira, the stories of Sam Houston, myths from the Alabama-Coushatta Indians, lyrics to songs like "Weevily Wheat," and the craft of quilting in the Texas Star pattern have been passed down from one generation to the next. Some deer hunters in East Texas still blow horn signals that can be traced back to the Middle Ages, and cowboys have customs from the vaqueros, Mexican horsemen with exceptional cattle-herding skills.

Cultural heritage and history are expressed in music, literature, and art. Historical events from the ages of the Native Americans to the oil and gas "booms" are described in works of nonfiction and fiction. Western art, with links to the days of the cowboy and ranching play a dominant role in the collections by state writers.

J. Frank Dobie became a spokesman of Southwestern culture with the publication of his book, *Vaquero of the Brush Country*, in 1929. Katherine Ann Porter published a best-selling novel, *Ship of Fools*, in 1962. Porter's *Collected Stories of Katherine Ann Porter* received several awards, including the Pulitzer Prize. Eugene Roddenberry produced the first Star Trek movie, co-authored *The Making of Star Trek* and wrote *The Questor Tapes*.

Famous Texan musicians include Gene Autry (cowboy singer), Kris Kristofferson (singer and songwriter), Trini Lopez (singer), Willie Nelson (country singer), Kenny Rogers (country singer), and Stevie Ray Vaughn (Blues guitarist).

Robert Rauschenberg, painter and sculptor, is known for his collaged multimedia works, called "combines," that denote the combination of dimensional space of everyday art and life. Harlem Renaissance writer Gwendolyn Bennett was also a visual artist who furthered educational programs for local African American communities.

> ### SKILL 22.28
> Understands the relationship between the arts and the times and societies in which they are produced, including how past and contemporary issues influence creative expressions, and identifies examples of art, music and literature that have transcended the boundaries of societies and convey universal themes such as religion, justice and the passage of time.

Traditional themes such as religion, justice, and the passage of time are prevalent in literature, art, and music. Christianity was an important power that shaped European culture after the Dark and Middle Ages. During the Renaissance, artists used various mediums to express the nature of religion. Religious art in the American colonies was sparse but the Spanish who settled in the American southwest contributed religious art to the area. Paintings of saints and religious subjects were crafted to demonstrate the importance of religion in the Spanish settlements. During the Great Awakening, after the American Revolution, religious paintings appealed to Americans. Thomas Cole, a great American painter, was inspired by the Great Awakening to create works depicting spirituality.

Music has been an important part of religious services since the days of the Catholic settlement of Maryland and the Spanish settlement of the American southwest. "God Bless America" is a patriotic and religious song that was written by Irving Berlin in 1918 and revised in 1938 as a song of peace when Adolph Hitler was gaining power in Germany. The song continues to be sung today.

Religious-themed literature includes books such as *The Da Vinci Code* by Dan Brown, *The Silver Chalice* by Thomas Bertram Costain, and *Pilgrim's Progress* by John Bunyan.

Homer's *Odyssey*; Agatha Christie's *And Then There Were None*; and Harper Lee's *To Kill a Mockingbird* have themes about justice.

Songs such as "9 to 5" and "We Shall Overcome" have lyrics that are about social justice.

> ### SKILL 22.29
> Analyzes relationships among religion, philosophy and culture and their effect on ways of life in Texas, the United States and the world.

See Skills 21.1 and 21.4

Religious and Philosophical Ideas and Cultures

According to the TEKS glossary, "To believe means to accept the truth or actuality of something. When people believe in a number of related truths or tenets, the body of knowledge is a belief system. These beliefs come from and are affected by religious and philosophical ideas, and are difficult to change. Belief systems also prescribe appropriate behavior in a society, regulating such social behavior as dating and marriage customs and the role of women. Other belief systems regulate attitudes toward government and authority. Belief systems affect how groups of people view and use the environment. Some people believe that humans have dominion over nature (Maoris of New Zealand, most adherents of Judeo-Christian religions). Humans, they believe, are not part of nature but separate. Further, they believe that Earth was given to humans by God for their use. Other groups (Hindus, Buddhists, Confucianists) see people as part of, and at harmony with, nature."

SKILL 22.30 Understands and analyzes how changes in science and technology relate to political, economic, social and cultural issues and events.

Technological Innovations

According to the TEKS glossary, "Technological innovations are new ways of doing things which are based in a technology. An example is the telephone which revolutionized the way people communicated because it allowed people to hear the voices of friends and family living miles away. Travel became easier due to improvements in transportation which began with systems of canals and railroads and expanded to include automobiles, interstate roadway systems, and airlines with international flights. Computers and software revolutionized the ways people process information and communicate. Computers connected to the Internet allow people to share information and conduct personal and professional business nearly instantaneously and relatively inexpensively. The demands of new technologies and their applications promote further innovation to meet changing needs."

See also Skills 20.5, 21.5, and 21.8

COMPETENCY 23
ECONOMICS

> **SKILL 23.1** Compares and contrasts similarities and differences in how various peoples at different times in history have lived and met basic human needs, including the various roles of men, women, children and families in past and present cultures.

See Skill 22.14

> **SKILL 23.2** Understands and applies knowledge of basic economic concepts *(e.g., economic system, goods and services, free enterprise, interdependence, needs and wants, scarcity, roles of producers and consumers, factors of production, specialization and trade, entrepreneurship)*; **knows that basic human needs are met in many ways; and understands the value and importance of work and of spending, saving and budgeting money.**

> **OPPORTUNITY COST:** the value of the sacrificed alternative

> **DEMAND:** the quantities of a good or service that buyers are willing and able to buy at different prices during a given period of time

> **SUPPLY:** the quantities that sellers are willing and able to sell at different prices during a given period of time

> **FREE ENTERPRISE:** when business is conducted based on the laws of supply and demand rather than governmental regulations

Basic Economic Concepts

Economics is the study of how a society allocates its scarce resources to satisfy what are basically unlimited and competing wants. A fundamental fact of economics is that resources are scarce and that wants are infinite. The fact that scarce resources have to satisfy unlimited wants means choices have to be made. If a society uses its resources to produce good A then it doesn't have those resources to produce good B. More of good A means less of good B. This trade-off is referred to as the OPPORTUNITY COST, or the value of the sacrificed alternative.

A market economy answers these questions in terms of demand and supply and the use of markets. DEMAND is based on consumer preferences and satisfaction and refers to the quantities of a good or service that buyers are willing and able to buy at different prices during a given period of time. SUPPLY is based on costs of production and refers to the quantities that sellers are willing and able to sell at different prices during a given period of time. The determination of market equilibrium price is where the buying decisions of buyers coincide with the selling decisions of sellers. FREE ENTERPRISE is when business is conducted based on the laws of supply and demand rather than governmental regulations.

For more information on free enterprise, see Skills 23.4 and 23.5.

Economic systems refer to the arrangements a society has made to answer what are known as the three questions: what goods to produce, how to produce them, and for whom they are being produced, or how the allocation of the output is determined.

The economic term GOODS refers to the physical products that can be delivered to, purchased by, owned by, and/or sold to a consumer. SERVICES, in contrast, are intangible goods, i.e., things someone can do for someone else, that are exchanged for money. The factors of production refer to the resources people and businesses use to create goods and supply services.

> **GOODS:** the physical products that can be delivered to, purchased by, owned by, and/or sold to a consumer

> **SERVICES:** intangible goods, i.e., things someone can do for someone else, that are exchanged for money

Consumer economics

Consumers vote for the products they want with their dollar spending. Goods acquiring enough dollar votes are profitable, signaling to the producers that society wants their scarce resources used in this way. This is how the "what" question is answered. The producer then hires inputs in accordance with the goods consumers want, looking for the most efficient or lowest-cost method of production. The lower a firm's costs for any given level of revenue, the higher the firm's profits. This is the way the "how" question is answered in a market economy. The "for whom" question is answered by the determination of the equilibrium price. Price serves to ration the goods to those who can and will transact at the market price or higher. Those who can't or won't are excluded from the market. This mechanism results in market efficiency, or obtaining the most output from the available inputs that are consistent with the preferences of consumers. Society's scarce resources are being used the way society wants them to be used.

The interdependence of households and businesses is illustrated by a circular flow diagram. In the two markets, inputs and outputs are exchanged and paid for by households and businesses. Factor owners sell their factors to employers in the input market. Firms use those factors to produce outputs that are sold in the output market. This is where factor owners spend their incomes on goods and services. Receipts for goods and services flow from households to businesses, and factor incomes flow from businesses to households.

Consumer economics refers to the way consumers make their decisions and the role that consumer decision making plays in a capitalist economy. Consumers buy the goods and services that give them satisfaction, or utility. They want to obtain the most utility they can for their dollar. The quantity of goods and services that consumers are willing and able to purchase at different prices during a given period of time is referred to as demand. Aggregating all of the individual demands yields the market demand for a good or service. Since consumers buy the goods and services that give them satisfaction, this means that, for the most part, they don't buy the goods and services that they don't want, that don't give them satisfaction.

Consumers do not have enough time and money to do everything they want and to buy everything they want. Time and money are scarce resources. If a consumer spends time doing one activity, he or she is sacrificing another activity. For example, if the consumer spends the afternoon playing golf, he is sacrificing doing the garden work. If the consumer decides to enroll in evening classes, she has less time to spend with family and friends. Devoting time to one activity means that there is another activity that has to be sacrificed. There are only twenty-four hours in the day and people can only be in one place at a time.

Scarcity is evident in personal financial management. Scarcity here refers to dollars and paying bills. Buying one good means sacrificing another good. This is the concept of opportunity cost. This is why consumers have to make choices. The consumer has to decide which goods offer the most satisfaction for his or her dollars. There are only so many dollars available. This is why responsible people don't go on wild spending sprees. Their paycheck has to cover the bills or they find themselves in the position of paying one bill and not another bill. There aren't enough dollars to buy both a diamond ring and a new car, so which one does the consumer want? Just as consumers have to choose how to spend their time, they also have to choose how to spend their dollars. Scarcity means that consumers can't have all of the goods that they want and do all of the activities that they want to do. This is true on both a micro and a macro level.

Scarcity affects the decision making of all economic agents. Scarcity means that choices have to be made by all. No economic agent can have more of all goods. Producing more of one good means that there aren't enough resources to produce other goods. That is the constraint of a fixed supply of resources. This is the relationship shown in a production possibilities curve. Every point on the curve represents the different combinations the economy can have of the two goods, given their supply of resources and that they are producing efficiently. The curve shows the trade-off between the two goods, or the opportunity cost imposed by the fact that resources are scarce. Having more of both goods isn't feasible. It would put society at a point beyond the curve, a point that is unattainable given the supply of resources.

This means that households, businesses, and governments, as well as society as a whole, must make decisions and choices within this framework. There are only so many resources that can be devoted to the production of consumer goods for households. Households have to decide which goods they want within those parameters. A limited budget means they can't afford to buy both a new car and a new house. So which do they buy? Whichever provides them with the most satisfaction.

In the two markets, inputs and outputs are exchanged and paid for by households and businesses. Factor owners sell their factors to employers in the input market.

Firms use those factors to produce outputs that are sold in the output market. This is where factor owners spend their incomes on goods and services. Receipts for goods and services flow from households to businesses, and factor incomes flow from businesses to households.

The means of payment, whether it is barter, currency, or credit, do not affect the income flows; they are just different ways in which the money can flow through the economy. BARTER refers to the exchange of one good for another good. An example of a barter transaction would be a painter painting a mechanic's house in exchange for the mechanic repairing the painter's car. The monetary value of these transactions would be represented by the flows through the circular flow diagram. The goods are the painting and the repair work done on the car; the factor flows are the labor services of the painter and the mechanic. The value of the labor services represents the factor incomes, and the value of the painting and repairs represents the receipts for goods and services. If currency were used instead of barter, there would be actual dollars flowing through the input and output markets between the households and the businesses, as described above.

Payment by use of credit does not alter any of the relationships either. Credit cards just allow consumers to spend beyond their incomes. So there is more output purchased and there are more dollars flowing to producers from credit card companies, with households making their payments to credit card companies. The credit card companies are more or less acting as an intermediary facilitating the flow of money through the economy.

BARTER: the exchange of one good for another good

Loans

All markets function to effect an efficient allocation of resources, even financial markets. They also function on the basis of supply and demand and loan funds to those who are willing to transact at the market price. The market price of loans is the interest rate. The supply of loanable funds comes from savings. Since savings represent dollars of postponed spending, households have to have some form of inducement to save. They have to be compensated in some way to postpone their spending and hold dollars in the form of savings. This inducement or payment for saving dollars is the interest rate. The higher the interest rate is, the more dollars households will be willing to save. The interest rate is an opportunity cost. At higher interest rates, the opportunity cost of not saving dollars is higher than at lower interest rates. Thus, the supply of loanable funds curve slopes upward.

All markets function to effect an efficient allocation of resources, even financial markets.

Loans are needed for investment purposes by businesses and by individuals. Borrowers are willing to pay a price for the funds they borrow. This price is the interest rate. Borrowers want more funds at lower interest rates than they do at higher interest rates. This means that the demand for loanable funds curve slopes downward. We now have the downward-sloping demand for loanable funds curve and the upward-sloping supply of loanable funds curve. If we put the two curves together then we have the market equilibrium at the point of intersection of demand and supply.

This gives the equilibrium rate of interest that equates the quantity demanded and quantity supplied of loanable funds. Lenders and borrowers willing and able to transact at that interest rate are included in the market. Lenders and borrowers who can't or won't transact at that interest rate are excluded from the market. The market interest rate performs a locative function just as a market price does. The interest rate will adjust to guarantee the equality of quantity demanded and quantity supplied, keeping the market in equilibrium.

Economic growth

Since investment is a component of gross domestic product (GDP), the financial markets and their stability are an important part of the economy. Economies need investment funds in order to grow. Economies with higher rates of savings have higher rates of investment and therefore higher growth rates. When households save and delay consumption, they are freeing resources for other uses, principally for investment. This is what leads to economic growth. Economies with low rates of savings are economies that don't domestically supply enough funds for investment purposes. These are economies that have lower growth rates because they don't have the investment funds required for growth. The banking sector with its financial markets is very important for economies. Without a well-developed banking center there is no mechanism for savings and therefore investment funds that are required for economic growth.

> SKILL 23.3 **Demonstrates knowledge of the ways people organize economic systems and of the similarities and differences among various economic systems around the world.**

ECONOMIC SYSTEM: a plan for how goods and services will be produced, utilized, and consumed

An ECONOMIC SYSTEM, in general, is a plan for how goods and services will be produced, utilized, and consumed. According to the TEKS glossary, "Five major economic activities are producing, exchanging, consuming, saving, and investing. Patterns of production, distribution, and use develop as the economic activities become concentrated in urban, industrial, or agricultural areas. Geographic and human factors also influence patterns of economic activity. Ski resorts develop in the mountains, farming in the valleys, and mining where there are ore deposits.

Saving and investment also follow patterns, becoming concentrated in areas of potential growth."

Economists identify three types of economic systems:

- Traditional (known as subsistence)

- Command (also known as planned)

- Market (commercial)

In a **TRADITIONAL ECONOMY**, goods and services are produced by a family for the family's personal consumption. There is little surplus and little exchange of goods. There is only a limited need for markets (places to buy and sell goods and services). This is the type of economy found in less developed nations, usually in rural areas. The economy reflects the customs, habits, laws, and religious beliefs of the area, and these control decisions. Most less developed nations today are a mix of traditional and either market or command economies. In a command economy, the government regulates economic activity, making decisions about what and how much to produce, where to locate economic activities, and what prices to charge for goods and services. These economic decisions are often made to further social goals.

> **TRADITIONAL ECONOMY:** goods and services are produced by a family for the family's personal consumption

Communism is one example of a command economy; socialism is another. In a **COMMAND ECONOMY**, the price of goods, including agricultural products, is controlled by the government, not market forces. Production costs are not reflected in prices. For example, it may cost $1.00 to produce a loaf of bread, but the price may be set at $.25 to ensure that customers are able to afford adequate provisions. The price also may be set over production costs given demand. In a market economy, elements of which may be considered a free enterprise economic system, the laws of supply and demand and the market determine decisions about what and how much to produce, where to locate economic activities, and what prices to charge for goods and services. Profit drives decisions in a market economy. A mixed economy combines elements of these three systems."

> **COMMAND ECONOMY:** price of goods, including agricultural products, is controlled by the government, not market forces

> *Profit drives decisions in a market economy.*

SKILL 23.4 **Understands and applies the knowledge of the characteristics, benefits and development of the free-enterprise system in Texas and the United States and how businesses operate in the United States free-enterprise system** (e.g., importance of morality and ethics in maintaining a functional free-enterprise system and the impact of past and present entrepreneurs).

The Free-Enterprise System

The free-enterprise system in Texas developed as it did in the rest of the United States. In a market economy the markets function on the basis of supply and demand and, if markets are free, the result is an efficient allocation of resources.

The seller's supply curve represents the different quantities of a good or service the seller is willing and able to bring to market at different prices during a given period of time. The seller has to have the good and be willing to sell it in order to be a part of the relevant market supply. The supply curve represents the selling and production decisions of the seller and is based on the costs of production. A product's production costs are based on the costs of the resources used to produce it. The resource costs are based on the scarcity of the resource. The scarcer a resource is, relatively speaking, the higher its price. A diamond costs more than paper because diamonds are scarcer than paper is. All of these concepts are embodied in the seller's supply curve.

The same is true on the buying side of the market. The buyer's preferences, tastes, income, etc.—all buying decisions—are embodied in the demand curve. The demand curve represents the various quantities of a good or service that the buyer is willing and able to buy at different prices during a given period of time.

The buyer has to want the good and be willing and able to purchase it. The buyer may want a Ferrari but cannot afford one; if this is the case, he or she is not a part of the relevant market demand.

The demand side of the market shows us what buyers are willing and able to purchase, and the supply side shows us what sellers are willing and able to supply. But we don't know anything about what buyers and sellers actually do buy and sell without putting the two sides together. If we compare the buying decisions of buyers with the selling decisions of sellers, the place where they coincide represents the **MARKET EQUILIBRIUM**. This is where the demand and supply curves intersect. At this point of intersection, the quantity that buyers want to buy at a particular price is equal to the quantity that sellers want to sell at that particular price. The quantity demanded is equal to the quantity supplied. This price-quantity combination represents an efficient allocation of resources.

> **MARKET EQUILIBRIUM:** where the demand and supply curves intersect

Consumers basically vote for the goods and services they want with their dollar spending. When a good accumulates enough dollar votes, the producer earns a profit. Profits are the way the market signals the seller that he or she is using society's resources in a way that society wants them used. Consumers are obtaining the most satisfaction they can from the way their society's scarce resources are being used. When consumers don't want a good or service, they don't purchase it, and the producer doesn't accumulate enough dollar votes to have profits. Losses are the market's way of signaling that consumers don't want their scarce resources used in the production of that particular good or service. Firms that incur losses eventually go out of business. They either have a product that consumers don't want or they have an inefficient production process that results in higher costs and therefore higher prices. Higher costs than a competitor's costs means that there is inefficiency in production. All of this occurs naturally in markets in a market economy.

The U.S. Economic System

The fundamental characteristics of the U.S. economic system are competition and markets. Profit and competition go together in the U.S. economic system. Competition is determined by market structure. Since the cost curves are the same for all firms, the only difference comes on the revenue side. The most competitive of all market structures is perfect competition, characterized by numerous buyers and sellers, all with perfect knowledge. No one seller is big enough to influence price. Products are homogenous so buyers are indifferent about which companies they buy from. The absence of barriers to entry makes it easy for firms to enter and leave an industry. At the other end of the spectrum is monopoly, in which there is only one seller of a particular product or commodity. Barriers to entry are significant enough to keep firms from entering or leaving an industry.

In monopolistic competition, firms sell similar products in an industry with low barriers to entry, making it easy for firms to enter and leave the industry. Oligopoly is a market structure in which a few large firms sell heterogeneous or homogenous products in a market structure with varying barriers to entry. Each firm maximizes profits by producing at the point where marginal costs equal marginal revenue. The existence of economic profits, an above-normal rate of return, attracts capital to an industry and results in expansion. Whether or not new firms can enter depends on barriers to entry. Firms can enter easily in perfect competition, and expansion will continue until economic profits are eliminated and firms earn a normal rate of return. The significant barriers to entry in a monopoly serve to keep firms out so the monopolist continues to earn an above-normal rate of return. Some firms will be able to enter in monopolistic competition but won't have a monopoly over the existing firm's brand name. The competitiveness of the market structure determines whether new firms or capital can enter in response to profits.

Profit functions as a financial incentive for individuals and firms. The possibility of earning profit is why individuals are willing to undertake entrepreneurial ventures and why firms are willing to spend money on research and development and innovation. Without these kinds of financial incentives, there would be no new product development or technological advancement.

SKILL 23.5 Applies knowledge of the effects of supply and demand on consumers and producers in a free-enterprise system.

See Skills 23.2 and 23.4

SKILL 23.6 Demonstrates knowledge of patterns of work and economic activities in Texas and the United States, past and present, including the roles of consumers and producers, and the impact of geographic factors, immigration, migration, limited resources, mass production, specialization and division of labor, and American ideas about progress and equal opportunity.

Economic activities are closely tied to the availability of resources required to support them. Resources include the raw materials required to make a product, the communications and transportation infrastructure needed to provide a service, and a supply of people to work at the activity with the essential skills needed to do it efficiently.

Historically, many towns and cities grew up around a single economic activity. A mill town, for instance, usually located along a river to harness its waterpower, was a central place for grain farmers from the surrounding regions to bring their products for processing. Mining towns and logging towns were organized in a similar way, with most of the economic survival of the community reliant on a local natural resource.

This kind of reliance could result in economic catastrophe if the central resource was depleted or not managed properly. Mines were abandoned after they failed to continue to produce enough ore. Too much logging in some areas led to the collapse of logging towns.

The failure of an economically active community places a strain on the entire economy, and many governments have taken action to manage key natural resources and prevent their depletion. Fishing is an example of an industry the government has become involved in, monitoring populations of fish and passing regulations limiting where and when commercial fishing can take place.

Modern transportation means that economic activities are not as closely tied to particular locations as they were in the past. Oil, for instance, is sometimes transported for thousands of miles to the refineries where it is processed. The technological improvements in transporting materials cheaply allow production facilities to draw natural resources from a wider area. This presents new challenges in managing natural resources, however, as new sources must constantly be sought.

See also Skill 22.3

SKILL 23.7 Demonstrates knowledge of categories of economic activities, economic indicators and how a society's economic level is measured.

According to the TEKS glossary, "Economic development occurs in stages. Countries do not necessarily move through these stages in any order. The first stage is called 'primitive equilibrium' and applies to nations with no monetary system or other formal economic organization. Rules pass from generation to generation and the economy exists in equilibrium based on tradition. The second state is one of transition when cultural traditions begin to crumble and people adopt new patterns of living. The third state is 'takeoff' and occurs when primitive equilibrium breaks down. During takeoff a nation spends more of its national income, new industries grow, and profits are reinvested. Both the agricultural and the industrial sectors expand. The fourth stage is 'semidevelopment,' a time when a nation's economy expands significantly. Core industries develop and the rates of technological development and capital investment increase. The nation enters the international economy, making goods and services for other nations. The final stage is 'highly developed' in which the basic human needs are met easily and economic efforts turn toward production of consumer goods and public services. The service and manufacturing sectors of the economy mature during this stage."

The size of an economy is typically measured as the gross domestic product, or GDP. Economic activities can also be measured through one or more of the following methods: gross national product (GNP), GDP per capita, gross domestic income (GDI), consumer spending, stock markets, interest rates, rate of inflation, national debt, and unemployment. All of these measures shed light on the economic state of a nation.

The size of an economy is typically measured as the gross domestic product, or GDP.

SKILL 23.8 Understands the effects of government regulation and taxation on consumers, economic development and business planning.

The purpose of a government's economic regulation of private enterprise is to control prices. Legislation, in the form of anti-trust laws, is enacted to prohibit mergers and predatory practices that monopolize and restrict competition.

Government regulation can also focus on improving the environment and protecting health and safety. The degree of regulation has increased or decreased at various times throughout the history of the United States. For example, in the1970s and 1980s, telecommunication companies, thought to be natural monopolies, were broken into smaller units. During the 1980s, under President Reagan, government lessened regulation to promote more free enterprise.

Taxation also has effects on consumers, economic development, and business planning. Those who favor tax cuts argue that reducing the tax rate will lead to increased economic growth because the consumers will make more purchases. Some economists argue that consumers will only increase spending if they believe tax cuts are permanent. Tax changes can encourage or discourage economic growth. A reduction in tax revenue can result in government budget deficits and cause interest rates to rise. The impact of tax cuts on economic growth is uncertain but is a factor that must be considered in maintaining a stable economy, improving a sagging economy, or lessening an inflationary economy.

> **SKILL 23.9 Demonstrates an understanding of major events, trends and issues in economic history** *(e.g., factors leading societies to change from rural to urban or agrarian to industrial, economic reasons for exploration and colonization, economic forces leading to the Industrial Revolution, processes of economic development in different areas of the world, factors leading to the emergence of different patterns of economic activity in the various regions of the United States).*

A preindustrial society has several distinguishing features, including:

- primarily an agricultural society (mainly rural)

- limited division of labor

- limited specialized skills and craftsmanship

- limited production of goods

- limited variation in social classes

When a society transforms from preindustrial to more organized and mechanized labor, skills, trades, and mass production, it is said to have become industrialized. Typically, this occurs when a country or society 1) expands its territory (therefore gaining access to more trade); 2) enhances transportation systems which help ensure trade (such as roads, railroads, steamboats, airplanes); 3) develops technological innovations that increase availability of machines or improve the production of goods, services, and communication (e.g., cotton gin, telephone, textile machines); and 4) experiences population growth (for example, immigration into the United States in the nineteenth and early twentieth centuries).

The Industrial Revolution

In the United States, the Industrial Revolution of the eighteenth and nineteenth centuries resulted in many changes in human civilization and greater opportunities for trade, increased production, and the exchange of ideas and knowledge. The first phase of the Industrial Revolution (1750–1830), which took place in Great Britain and Europe, saw the mechanization of the textile industry, vast improvements in mining, with the invention of the steam engine, and numerous improvements in transportation, with the development and improvement of turnpikes and canals and the invention of the railroad.

The second phase (1830–1910) resulted in vast improvements in a number of industries that had already been mechanized through such inventions as the Bessemer steel process and the invention of steamships. New industries arose as a result of the technological advances such as photography, electricity, and various chemical processes. New sources of power were harnessed and applied, including petroleum and hydroelectric power. Precision instruments were developed and engineering was launched. It was during this second phase that the Industrial Revolution spread to other European countries, Japan, and the United States.

Results of the Industrial Revolution

The direct results of the Industrial Revolution, particularly as they affected industry, commerce, and agriculture, included the following:

- Enormous increases in productivity

- Huge increases in world trade

- Specialization and division of labor

- Standardization of parts and mass production

- Growth of giant business conglomerates and monopolies

- A new revolution in agriculture facilitated by the steam engine, machinery, chemical fertilizers, processing, canning, and refrigeration

The political results included the following:

- Growth of complex government by technical experts

- Centralization of government, including regulatory administrative agencies

- Advantages of democratic development, including extension of franchise to the middle class, and later to all elements of the population; mass education to meet the needs of an industrial society; the development of media of public communication, including radio, television, and inexpensive newspapers

- Dangers to democracy, including the risk of manipulation of the media of mass communication; facilitation of dictatorial centralization and totalitarian control; subordination of the legislative function to administrative directives; efforts to achieve uniformity and conformity; and social impersonalization

The economic results were numerous:

- Conflict between free trade and low tariffs and protectionism
- Issue of free enterprise against government regulation
- Struggles between labor and capital, including the trade-union movement
- Rise of socialism
- Rise of the utopian socialists
- Rise of Marxian or scientific socialism

The social results of the Industrial Revolution included the following:

- Increase of population, especially in industrial centers
- Advances in science applied to agriculture, sanitation, and medicine
- Growth of great cities
- Disappearance of the difference between city dwellers and farmers
- Faster tempo of life and increased stress from the monotony of the work routine
- Emancipation of women
- Decline of religion
- Rise of scientific materialism
- Darwin's theory of evolution

SKILL 23.10 Analyzes the interdependence of the Texas economy with those of the United States and the world.

Texas, like all of the other states, is a part of the U.S. economy. Texas engages in trade and commerce with other states and the national government. In today's world, markets are international. All nations are part of a global economy; no nation exists in isolation or can be totally independent of other nations.

Isolationism is referred to as autarky or a closed economy. Participation in a global economy means that what one nation does affects other nations because economies are linked through international trade, commerce, and finance. All nations have open economies. International transactions affect the levels of income, employment, and prices in each of the trading economies.

Trade and Trade Barriers

The relative importance of trade is based on what percentage of a country's gross domestic product trade constitutes. In a country like the United States, trade represents only a few percent of GDP. In other nations, trade may represent over 50 percent of GDP. For those countries, changes in international transactions can cause many economic fluctuations and problems.

Trade barriers can cause economic problems in other countries. Suppose a domestic government is confronted with rising unemployment in a domestic industry due to cheap foreign imports. Consumers are buying the cheaper foreign import instead of the higher-priced domestic good. In order to protect domestic labor, the government imposes a tariff, thus raising the price of the more-efficiently-produced foreign good. The result of the tariff is that consumers buy more of the domestic good and less of the foreign good. However, the foreign good is the product of the foreign nation's labor. A decrease in the demand for the foreign good means that foreign producers don't need as much labor, so they lay off workers in the foreign country.

Thus the result of the trade barrier is that unemployment has been exported to the foreign country. Treaties like the North American Free Trade Agreement (NAFTA) are a way of lowering or eliminating trade barriers on a regional basis. As they are lowered or eliminated, it causes changes in labor and output markets: Some grow; some shrink. These adjustments are taking place now for Canada, the United States, and Mexico. Membership in a global economy adds another dimension to economics, in terms of aiding developing countries and implementing national policies.

Treaties like the North American Free Trade Agreement (NAFTA) are a way of lowering or eliminating trade barriers on a regional basis.

U.S. Economy after World War I

The United States engaged in trade but remained basically isolationist until World War I. The end of the war began a period of prosperity that lasted until 1929. The Roaring Twenties wasn't just a period of speakeasies and bootleggers. The economy, freed from its wartime restraints, had to satisfy the pent-up demand caused by the war. Mass production satisfied the mass demand and supplied the wages for the people to buy the output. Manufacturing output doubled during this period. The building sector experienced a boom that eventually faded. The financial sector was making loans for all of the building. The stock market was booming with almost unlimited buying and selling on margin. When stock prices fell, many speculators could not meet their margin calls. This led to the onset of the Great Depression. The New Deal policies of public spending and the onset of World War II brought the economy slowly out of the Great Depression.

See Skill 20.23 for information on the effects of the international economy in the first decades of the twentieth century.

Bretton Woods System (Post–World War II)

The United States, along with the Soviet Union, emerged as the new world powers after World War II. The European economies were shattered by the war, as were their infrastructures. America embarked on a program of massive aid called the Marshall Plan to help the war-devastated economies rebuild. The Bretton Woods system was established to provide stable exchange rates. The General Agreement on Tariffs and Trade (GATT) and other trade organizations were established to help lower trade barriers. This system worked well and the world economies recovered from the war.

Under the Bretton Woods system, the U.S. dollar was expressed in terms of gold, at $35.00 per ounce, and all other world currencies were expressed in terms of the dollar. Nations were required to keep their currency values within specified ranges and nations would settle their balance of payments imbalances at the end of the year. This system worked well until the 1960s, when the world kept experiencing exchange-rate crises that resulted in the exchange markets closing. The situation continued until 1973 when world exchange rates began to float. This eliminated the need for the settlement of payment imbalances because the exchange rate adjusts to eliminate any payment disequilibrium. A deficit results in currency depreciation and a surplus results in currency appreciation. As firms and traders became more adept at hedging, currency problems were eliminated and international trade continued to grow.

After this time, many industries began to relocate to Texas and the oil and aeronautics industries as well as other industries developed. Houston remains a major international shipping center.

The Global Economy

In today's world, all nations have a national economy. What happens in one nation affects other nations because they are all related through international trade and finance. For example, if one nation lowers its interest rates to stimulate its domestic economy, the lower interest rates cause an outflow of dollars to a foreign country with higher interest rates. This results in dollar depreciation and an appreciation of the foreign currency. The cheaper dollar makes U.S. exports more attractive to foreigners because they are cheaper due to the lower-priced dollar.

The result is that foreigners buy more U.S. exports. The higher value of the foreign currency makes foreign imports more expensive to U.S. citizens so they buy fewer foreign imports. The result is higher employment levels in the United States and more unemployment in the foreign country. A nation cannot act in isolation in today's world.

COMPETENCY 24
GOVERNMENT AND CITIZENSHIP

> **SKILL 24.1** Demonstrates knowledge of historical origins of democratic forms of government, such as ancient Greece.

The classical civilization of Greece reached the highest levels of human achievement based on the foundations already laid by ancient groups such as the Egyptians, Phoenicians, Minoans, and Mycenaeans. Ancient Greece is often called the cradle of Western civilization because of the enormous influence it had, not only on the time in which it flourished, but on Western culture ever since.

Early Greek institutions have survived for thousands of years and have influenced the entire world. The Athenian form of democracy, with all citizens having an equal vote in their own government, is a philosophy upon which all modern democracies are based. In the United States, the Greek tradition of democracy was honored in the choice of Greek architectural styles for the nation's government buildings.

The Greek civilization served as an inspiration to the Roman Republic, which followed in the Greek tradition of democracy and was directly influenced by the Greeks' achievements in art and science.

> **SKILL 24.2** Understands and applies the purpose of rules and laws; the relationship between rules, rights and responsibilities; the fundamental rights of American citizens guaranteed in the Bill of Rights and other amendments to the U.S. Constitution; and the individual's role in making and enforcing rules and ensuring the welfare of society.

How a Bill Becomes Law

Federal laws are passed by the Congress, and can originate in either the House of Representatives or the Senate, with the exception of bills for raising revenue. Revenue bills must originate in the House of Representatives. The first step in the passing of a law is for the proposed law to be introduced in one of the houses of Congress. A proposed law is called a bill while it is under consideration by Congress.

> A proposed law is called a bill while it is under consideration by Congress.

✗

Once a bill is introduced, it is assigned to one of several standing committees of the house in which it was introduced. The committee studies the bill and researches the issues it covers. The committee may gather public comments and call experts to testify about a bill. The committee may revise the bill. Finally, the committee votes on whether to release the bill for a vote by the full body. A committee may also lay aside a bill to eliminate the voting opportunity. Once a bill is released, it can be debated and amended by the full body before the vote occurs. If it passes by a simple majority vote, the bill is sent to the other house of Congress, where the process begins again.

Once a bill has passed both the House of Representatives and the Senate, it is assigned to a conference committee made up of members of both houses. The conference committee resolves differences between the House and Senate versions of a bill, if any, and then sends it back to both houses for final approval. Once a bill receives final approval, it is signed by the Speaker of the House and the vice president, who is also the president of the Senate, and sent to the president for consideration. The president can either sign the bill or veto it. If the bill is vetoed, the veto can be overruled if two-thirds of both the Senate and the House vote to do so. Once signed by the president, the bill becomes a law.

Federal laws are enforced by the executive branch and its departments. The Department of Justice, led by the U.S. attorney general, is the primary law enforcement department of the federal government. The Justice Department is aided by other investigative and enforcement departments such as the Federal Bureau of Investigation (FBI) and the U.S. Postal Inspection Service.

Rights and Responsibilities of Citizenship

Citizenship in a democracy bestows on an individual certain rights, the most important of which is the right to participate in one's own government. Along with these rights come responsibilities, including the responsibility of a citizen to participate in his or her government.

Citizenship in a democracy bestows on an individual certain rights, the most important of which is the right to participate in one's own government.

The most basic form of participation is voting. Citizens who have reached the age of 18 in the United States are eligible to vote in public elections. With this right comes the responsibility to be informed before voting, and not to sell or otherwise give away one's vote. Citizens are also eligible to run for public office. Along with the right to run for office comes the responsibility to represent the voters as fairly as possible and to perform the duties expected of a representative of the government.

In the United States, citizens are guaranteed the right to free speech, the right to express an opinion on public issues. In turn, citizens have the responsibility to allow others to speak freely. At the community level, this might mean speaking at a city council hearing while allowing others with opposing viewpoints to have their say without interruption or comment.

The U.S. Constitution also guarantees freedom of religion. This means that the government cannot impose an official religion on its citizens, and that people are free to practice any religion they choose. Citizens are also responsible for allowing those of other religions to practice freely without obstruction. Occasionally, religious issues are put before the public at the state level in the form of ballot measures or initiatives. To what extent it should be acceptable for people to express religious beliefs in a public setting such as a public school is an issue that has been debated recently.

In making decisions on matters like these, citizens are expected to inform themselves regarding the issues and to vote based on their own opinions. Being informed about how one's government works and what the effects of new legislation will be is an essential part of being a good citizen.

The U.S. Constitution guarantees that all citizens be treated equally by the law. In addition, federal and state laws make it a crime to discriminate against citizens based on their sex, race, religion, and other factors. To ensure that all people are treated equally, citizens have the responsibility to follow these laws.

These rights and responsibilities are essentially the same whether one is voting in a local school board election, for the passage of a new state law, or for the president of the United States. Being a good citizen means exercising one's own rights while allowing others to do the same.

Almost all representative democracies in the world guarantee similar rights to their citizens and expect them to respect the rights of others. As a citizen of the world one is expected to respect the rights of other nations, and the people of those nations, in the same way.

Citizens of the state of Texas have a host of rights and responsibilities. The state constitution protects them from harm, from unfair government and laws, and from violence from outside sources. The state government protects their right to a legal job at a fair wage, as well.

Texas residents are expected to obey their state, local, and national laws and to pay their taxes and vote in elections at all three levels of government. They are expected to represent their state well when they travel outside its borders.

Bill of Rights

The first ten amendments to the U.S. Constitution, written mostly by James Madison, constitute the Bill of Rights and deal with civil liberties and civil rights. They are, in brief:

1. Freedom of religion

2. Right to bear arms

3. Security from the quartering of troops in homes

4. Right against unreasonable search and seizures

5. Right against self-incrimination

6. Right to trial by jury, right to legal council

7. Right to jury trial for civil actions

8. No cruel or unusual punishment allowed

9. These rights shall not deny other rights the people enjoy

10. Powers not mentioned in the Constitution shall be retained by the states or the people

> SKILL 24.3 **Understands the basic structure and functions of the United States government, the Texas government and local governments (including the roles of public officials); the relationships among national, state and local governments; and how local, state and national government services are financed.**

Texas Government

The government of Texas is like a miniature U.S. government. Texas has three branches of government: executive, legislative, and judicial. The governor is the head of the executive branch, vetoes or signs bills into law, commands the state militia, and can call special sessions of the state legislature. That legislature has two houses, a House of Representatives with 150 members and a Senate with 31, and meets in regular session every two years. The judicial branch has many, sometimes overlapping courts, of which the Supreme Court (civil cases) and the Texas Court of Criminal Appeals are the highest. Judges are elected, as are many members of the executive branch.

State and Local Governments

State governments are mirror images of the federal government, with a few important exceptions: governors are not technically commanders-in-chief of armed forces; state supreme court decisions can be appealed to federal courts; terms of state representatives and senators vary; judges, even of the state supreme courts, are elected by popular vote; and governors and legislators have term limits that vary by state.

Local governments vary widely across the country, although none of them has a judicial branch per se. Some local governments consist of a city council with limited powers, of which the mayor is a member and in other cities, the mayor is the head of the government and the city council are the chief lawmakers. Local governments also have less strict requirements for people running for office than do the state and federal governments.

U.S. Government

There are three branches of government at the U.S. federal level: legislative, executive, and judicial.

Legislative branch

Article I of the Constitution established the legislative or law-making branch of the government called the Congress. It is made up of two houses, the House of Representatives and the Senate. Voters in each state elect the members who represent them in each respective house of Congress. The legislative branch is responsible for making laws, raising and printing money, regulating trade, establishing the postal service and federal courts, approving the president's appointments, declaring war, and supporting the armed forces. The Congress also has the power to change the Constitution itself, and to impeach (bring charges against) the president. Charges for impeachment are brought by the House of Representatives and then tried in the Senate.

Executive branch

Article II of the Constitution created the executive branch of the government, headed by the president, who leads the country, recommends new laws, and can veto bills passed by the legislative branch. As the chief of state, the president is responsible for carrying out the laws of the country and the treaties and declarations of war passed by the legislative branch. The president also appoints federal judges and is commander-in-chief of the military when it is called into service. Other members of the executive branch include the vice president, also elected, and various officials appointed by the president: cabinet members, ambassadors, presidential advisors, members of the armed forces, and other civil servants of government agencies, departments, and bureaus. Although the president appoints them, they must be approved by the legislative branch.

Judicial branch

Article III of the Constitution established the judicial branch of government, headed by the Supreme Court. The Supreme Court has the power to declare a law passed by the legislature or an act of the executive branch illegal and unconstitutional. Citizens, businesses, and government officials can appeal to the Supreme Court to review a decision made in a lower court if they believe the ruling by a judge is unconstitutional. The judicial branch also includes lower federal courts known as federal district courts that have been established by the Congress. These courts try and review cases referred from other courts.

Powers of the federal government

1. To tax

2. To borrow and coin money

3. To establish postal service

4. To grant patents and copyrights

5. To regulate interstate and foreign commerce

6. To establish courts

7. To declare war

8. To raise and support the armed forces

9. To govern territories

10. To define and punish felonies and piracy on the high seas

11. To fix standards of weights and measures

12. To conduct foreign affairs

Powers of the states

1. To regulate intrastate trade

2. To establish local governments

3. To protect general welfare

4. To protect life and property

5. To ratify amendments

6. To conduct elections

7. To make state and local laws

Concurrent powers of the federal government and states

1. Both Congress and the states may tax

2. Both may borrow money

3. Both may charter banks and corporations

4. Both may establish courts

5. Both may make and enforce laws

6. Both may take property for public purposes

7. Both may spend money to provide for the public welfare

Implied powers of the federal government

1. To establish banks or other corporations implied from delegated powers to tax, borrow, and to regulate commerce

2. To spend money for roads, schools, health, insurance, etc., implied from powers, to establish post roads, to tax to provide for general welfare and defense, and to regulate commerce

3. To create military academies, implied from powers to raise and support an armed force

4. To locate and generate sources of power and sell surplus implied from powers to dispose of government property, commerce, and war powers

5. To assist and regulate agriculture implied from power to tax and spend for general welfare and regulate commerce

Financing government services

Taxes are a major source of funding for government services at all levels—federal, state, and local. Income taxes, property taxes, and sales taxes are examples.

Taxes are a major source of funding for government services at all levels—federal, state, and local. Income taxes, property taxes, and sales taxes are examples. Property taxes are a primary source of local government funding. Federal grants fund state governments, and money from licenses and business fees provide revenue to states. Several states receive income from inheritance taxes that are imposed when a person dies. States also receive money from taxes places on liquor, automobiles, cigarettes, and gasoline. In the past few years, state funding has also come from lotteries. In addition to income from the federal income tax and payroll taxes, federal estate taxes provide income to the federal government in instances where a decedent's assets are above a certain level. Tariffs, or import duties, provide another source of revenue for the federal government.

Demonstrates knowledge of key principles and ideas contained in major political documents of Texas and the United States (e.g., the Declaration of Independence, United States Constitution, Texas Constitution) **and of relationships among political documents.**

Declaration of Independence and U.S. Constitution

Many of the core values in the U.S. democratic system can be found in the opening words of the Declaration of Independence, including the belief in equality, and the rights of citizens to "life, liberty and the pursuit of happiness." The Declaration was a condemnation of the British king's tyrannical government, and these words emphasized the American colonists' belief that a government received its authority to rule from the people, and its function should not be to suppress the governed, but to protect the rights of the governed, including protection from the government itself. These two ideals, popular sovereignty and the rule of law, are basic core values.

POPULAR SOVEREIGNTY is the idea that citizens should have the ability to directly participate in their own government by voting and running for public office. This ideal is based on the right of all citizens to engage in their own governance, established in the U.S. Constitution. The Constitution also contains a list of specific rights of citizens, which the government cannot infringe upon. Popular sovereignty also includes the idea that citizens can change their government if they feel it is necessary. This was the driving ideal behind the Declaration of Independence and is embodied in the governmental structure laid out in the Constitution.

The RULE OF LAW is the ideal that the law applies not only to the governed but also to the government. This core value gives authority to the justice system, which grants citizens protection from the government by requiring that any accusation of a crime be proved by the government before a person is punished. This principle, called DUE PROCESS, ensures that any accused person has an opportunity to confront his or her accusers and provide a defense. Due process follows from the core value of a right to liberty. The government cannot take away a citizen's liberty without reason or proof. The correlating ideal is also a core value: that someone who harms another or breaks a law will receive justice under the democratic system. The ideal of justice holds that a punishment will fit the crime, and that any citizen can appeal to the judicial system if the citizen feels that he or she has been wronged.

> **POPULAR SOVEREIGNTY:** the idea that citizens should have the ability to directly participate in their own government by voting and running for public office

> **RULE OF LAW:** the ideal that the law applies not only to the governed but also to the government

> **DUE PROCESS:** ensures that any accused person has an opportunity to confront his or her accusers and provide a defense

Bill of Rights

The first ten amendments to the U.S. Constitution, called the Bill of Rights, deal with civil liberties and civil rights. James Madison was credited with writing a majority of them.

See Skill 24.2 for further review.

Texas Constitution

From its earliest days, Texas was governed by a document of some sort. The Republic of Texas had a constitution that very much resembled the U.S. Constitution, with a government that had three branches, a tradition of checks and balances, a stipulation for the democratic election of officials, and a bill of rights.

The Texas constitution also reflected certain Spanish and Mexican traditions, such as provisions for community property and debt relief. Those traditions have carried over to the present day.

The state has had a number of constitutions. Texas was, of course, a Confederate state and had a separate constitution during that period in its history. A flurry of governmental activity followed the end of the Civil War, and no fewer than three constitutions came into existence between 1866 and 1876. The last one stuck, however. The Texas Constitution of 1876 continues in force today.

SKILL 24.5 **Demonstrates an understanding of how people organized governments in colonial America and during the early development of Texas.**

See also Skills 21.1 and 21.19

The original thirteen colonies announced their independence from Great Britain in 1776. The colonies then formed a government under the Articles of Confederation in 1781, adopting a new constitution that went into effect after 1789. After this, the nation soon began to expand westward.

The first European base in the Texas Territory was established in 1682. Numerous missions were built in East Texas but were eventually abandoned in 1691. Concerned with the French presence in neighboring Louisiana, Spanish authorities began to colonize Texas. Over the next 110 years, Spain established numerous villages and missions in the province. However, disputes arose and Texas became angry with the government in Mexico City. Texans revolted, fought and ultimately won the Texas Revolution in 1835–1836. Texas became the Republic of Texas, an independent nation.

Internal conflict over the politics of the Republic was between two factions. There was a nationalist faction, led by Mirabeau B. Lamar, who promoted the sustained independence of Texas, the removal of the Native Americans, and the continued westward expansion of Texas. The other side, led by Sam Houston, supported the annexation of Texas to the United States and peaceful coexistence with Native Americans.

Texas seceded from the union on February 1, 1861, and joined the Confederate States of America on March 2, 1861. Sam Houston, who was governor at the time, was against seceding. He cautioned that it would be the worst error that Texas ever made and promptly left office.

The Texas Constitution, adopted in 1876, is the second oldest state constitution still in effect. Like most state and local constitutions, it clearly provides for the division of powers and incorporates a bill of rights directly into the constitution.

On February 28, 1845, the U.S. Congress approved a bill that would authorize the United States to annex the Republic of Texas. On March 1, President John Tyler signed the bill.

SKILL 24.6 Understands the political processes in the United States and Texas and how the United States political system works.

One of the most famous words in the Declaration of Independence is liberty. The idea that people should be free to pursue their own paths, even to the extent of making their own mistakes, has dominated political thought in the 200-plus years of the American republic.

Representation, the idea that a people can vote, and even vote to replace their lawmakers, was not a new idea, except in the American colonies. Residents of other British colonies did not have these rights, of course, and the American colonies were only colonies, according to the conventional wisdom of the British government at the time. What the Sons of Liberty and other revolutionaries were asking for was to stand on an equal footing with the mother country.

Along with the idea of representation came the notion that key ideas and concepts could be deliberated and discussed, with everyone having a chance to voice his or her views. This applied to both lawmakers and the people who elected them. Lawmakers wouldn't just pass bills that became laws; rather, they would debate the particulars and go back and forth on the strengths and weaknesses of proposed laws before voting on them. Members of both houses of Congress had the opportunity to speak out on the issues, as did the people at large, who could contact their lawmakers and express their views. This idea ran very much counter to the experience the Founding Fathers had before the revolution—that of taxation without representation.

Another key concept in the American ideal is **equality**, the idea that every person has the same rights and responsibilities under the law. The Great Britain that the American colonists knew was a stratified society, with distinct social classes. The goal of the Declaration of Independence and the Constitution was to provide equality for all. The reality, though, was vastly different for large sectors of society, including women and nonwhite Americans. The so-called American dream is that every individual has an equal chance to make his or her fortune and that the United States will welcome and even encourage that initiative. The history of the country is filled with stories of people who came here and made their fortunes in the land of opportunity. Unfortunately, for anyone who wasn't a white male, however, that basic opportunity was sometimes a difficult thing to take advantage of.

> **LAW:** the set of established rules or accepted norms of conduct in people's relationships with other individuals, organizations, and institutions

The **LAW** is the set of established rules or accepted norms of conduct in people's relationships with other individuals, organizations, and institutions. The rule of law recognizes that the authority of the government is to be exercised only within the context and boundaries established by laws that are enacted according to established procedure and publicly disclosed. Since our government is a constitutional government and political system, the basis of all laws, all decisions, and the enforcement of laws is the U.S. Constitution. The Constitution establishes the process by which laws can be written and enacted, the basis of their legitimacy within the context of the principles documented in the Constitution, and the means of interpretation and enforcement of those laws by the police and the courts.

All federal law begins in the Constitution, which grants the U.S. Congress the power to enact laws for certain purposes. The statutes are published in the United States Code. Since ratification of the Constitution, laws have been enacted that give agencies of the executive branch of government the power to create regulations that carry the force of law. If those regulations are challenged or questioned, the courts determine their meaning; the courts' decisions then assume the force of law.

The process by which laws and regulations can be enacted is defined by the Constitution, with the protection of the balance of powers. Laws are introduced, debated, and passed by the U.S. Congress, with both houses passing the same version of the law. Laws must then be signed by the president. Once signed, a law is considered enacted and is enforced. Challenges to the constitutionality of the law and questions of interpretation of the law are handled by the federal court system. Each state has the authority to make laws covering anything not controlled by the federal government. State laws cannot negate federal laws.

In order to maintain the structure and functioning of a society and the safety of its people, adherence to the law is required for all who live within the jurisdiction of the law. Failure to adhere to the laws of the state or the nation is punishable under the legal code.

CIVIL DISOBEDIENCE is the refusal to obey certain laws, regulations, or requirements of a government because one believes those laws to be detrimental to the freedom or right of the people to exercise government-guaranteed personal and civil liberties. Civil disobedience, in principle, is nonviolent in the steps taken to resist or refuse to obey the law.

Notable examples of civil disobedience in U.S. history include Henry David Thoreau's refusal to pay taxes in protest against slavery and against the Mexican–American War and Dr. Martin Luther King, Jr.'s nonviolent protests against racial segregation during the civil rights movement of the 1960s.

> **CIVIL DISOBEDIENCE:** the refusal to obey certain laws, regulations, or requirements of a government because one believes those laws to be detrimental to the freedom or right of the people to exercise government-guaranteed personal and civil liberties

---

SKILL 24.7 **Demonstrates knowledge of types of government** (e.g., democratic, totalitarian, monarchical) **and their respective levels of effectiveness in meeting citizens' needs** (e.g., reasons for limiting the power of government, record of human rights abuses by limited and unlimited governments).

Systems of government vary throughout the world, and the way the government of a society rules the citizen body is called the form, or type, of government. Below is a look at some of the most common forms of government.

FORM OF GOVERNMENT	DESCRIPTION
Anarchism	Political movement advocating the elimination of all government and its replacement by a cooperative community of individuals. Sometimes it has involved political violence such as assassinations of important political or governmental figures. The historical banner of the movement is a black flag.
Communism	A belief as well as a political system, characterized by the ideology of a classless system and commonly controlled property. Communism encourages a one-party state/dictatorship and government ownership of the means of production and the distribution of goods and services. This revolutionary ideology preaches the eventual overthrow of all other political orders and the establishment of one world communist government. The historical banner of the movement is a red flag and a variation of stars, hammer, and sickle, representing various types of workers.

Continued on next page

Dictatorship	The rule by an individual or small group of individuals (oligarchy) that centralizes all political control in itself and enforces its will with a terrorist police force.
Fascism	A belief as well as a political system, opposed ideologically to communism, though similar in basic structure, with a one-party state, centralized political control, and a repressive police system. Fascism, however, tolerates private ownership of the means of production, though it maintains tight overall control. Central to its belief is the idolization of the leader, a "cult of personality," and most often an expansionist ideology. Examples have been German Nazism and Italian Fascism.
Monarchy	The rule of a nation by a monarch, (a nonelected, usually hereditary leader), most often a king or queen. Monarchy may or may not be accompanied by some measure of democratic open institutions and elections at various levels. A modern example is Great Britain, which is called a constitutional monarchy.
Democracy	A familiar system to most, the system under which we live in the United States. The term comes from the Greek "for the rule of the people," and that is just what it is. The two most prevalent types are direct and indirect democracy. Direct democracy usually involves all of the people in a given area coming together to vote and decide on issues that will affect them. It is used only when the population involved is relatively small, for example, a local town meeting. An indirect democracy involves much larger areas and populations and involves sending representatives to a legislative body to vote on issues affecting the people. Such a system can be a presidential or parliamentary system. In the United States, we have an indirect, or representative, democracy of the presidential type.
Parliamentary system	A system of government with a legislature, usually involving a number of political parties and often coalition politics. There is a distinction between the head of state and the head of government. The head of government is usually known as a prime minister, who is also usually the head of the largest party. The head of government and the cabinet usually both sit and vote in the parliament. The head of state is most often an elected president (although in the case of a constitutional monarchy, like Great Britain, the sovereign may take the place of a president as head of state). A government may fall when a majority in parliament votes "no confidence" in the government.
Presidential system	A system of government with a legislature, which can involve few or many political parties, with no distinction between head of state and head of government. The president serves in both capacities. The president is elected either by direct or indirect election. A president and cabinet usually do not sit or vote in the legislature and the president may or may not be the head of the largest political party. A president can thus rule even without a majority in the legislature. He or she can only be removed from office before an election for major infractions of the law.
Socialism	Political belief and system in which the state takes a guiding role in the national economy and provides extensive social services to its population. The state does not own the means of production, but it exercises some control over them. It usually promotes democracy (democratic socialism), although the heavy state involvement can produce excessive bureaucracy and inefficiency. Taken to an extreme, it may lead to communism as government control increases and democratic practice decreases. Socialism is considered a variant of Marxism. It also has used a red flag as a symbol.

Difference between Totalitarianism and Authoritarianism

On the political spectrum, democracy is on one side and totalitarianism and authoritarianism are both on the other. However, there is a great difference between totalitarianism and authoritarianism.

Consider the two terms. Totalitarianism is derived from the word *total*, while authoritarianism is derived from the word *authority*. Although some people use the two terms interchangeably in regard to political movements such as fascism and communism and governments ruled by dictators, there are really two different ideas behind these terms. The difference is that a *totalitarian* system doesn't view any aspect of society as outside the influence of the state. A totalitarian government sees itself as having a legitimate concern with all levels of human existence. Not only in relation to freedom of speech or freedom of the press but even in relation to social and religious institutions, it tries to enforce complete conformity to its ideals. Thus, those ideologies that presume to speak to all of society's ills, such as communism and fascism, look to this model for what they attempt to create in society. As Benito Mussolini said, "Nothing outside of the state, nothing instead of the state."

Those regimes that conform to the authoritarian model never presume to seek such a complete reordering of society. They do usually leave some autonomous institutions, such as the Church, alone as long as they do not interfere with the state authority. The authoritarian model can be seen throughout the history of Central and South America, where a number of regimes, usually representing the interests of the upper classes, have come to power and instituted dictatorships that seek to concentrate all political power in a few hands.

> **SKILL 24.8** Understands the formal and informal processes of changing the United States and Texas Constitutions and the impact of changes on society.

Amendments to the U.S. Constitution

An amendment is a change or addition to the U.S. Constitution. Two-thirds of both houses of Congress must propose and then pass an amendment. Or two-thirds of the state legislatures must call a convention to propose one and then it must be ratified by three-fourths of the state legislatures. To date, only twenty-seven amendments to the Constitution have passed. An amendment can be used to cancel out a previous one; for example, the Eighteenth Amendment (1919), known as Prohibition, was canceled by the Twenty-First Amendment (1933). Amending the U.S. Constitution is an extremely difficult thing to accomplish.

To date, only twenty-seven amendments to the Constitution have passed. An amendment can be used to cancel out a previous one; for example, the Eighteenth Amendment (1919), known as Prohibition, was canceled by the Twenty-First Amendment (1933).

The final and most difficult step for an amendment is the ratification by the state legislatures. A total of three-fourths of those must approve an amendment. Approvals in the state legislatures only need to be a simple majority, but the number of states that must approve the amendment is thirty-eight. Hundreds of amendments have been proposed through the years, but only twenty-seven have become part of the Constitution.

A key element in some of those failures has been the time limit Congress has the option to put on amendment proposals. A famous example of an amendment that got close but didn't reach the threshold before the deadline expired was the Equal Rights Amendment (ERA), which was proposed in 1972. It couldn't muster enough support for passage, even though the deadline was extended from seven to ten years.

The first ten amendments are called the Bill of Rights and were approved at the same time, shortly after the Constitution was ratified. The Eleventh and Twelfth Amendments were ratified around the turn of the nineteenth century and, respectively, voided foreign suits against states and revised the method of presidential election. The Thirteenth, Fourteenth, and Fifteenth Amendments were passed in succession after the end of the Civil War. The Thirteenth Amendment outlawed slavery. The Fourteenth and Fifteenth Amendments provided for equal protection and for voting rights, respectively, without consideration of skin color.

The first twentieth-century amendment was the Sixteenth Amendment, which provided for a federal income tax. Providing for direct election to the Senate was the Seventeenth Amendment. Until then, Senators were appointed by state leaders, not elected by the public at large.

The Eighteenth Amendment prohibited the use or sale of alcohol across the country. The long battle for voting rights for women ended in success with the passage of the Nineteenth Amendment. The Twentieth Amendment changed the date for the beginning of terms from March to January for the president and the Congress. With the Twenty-First Amendment came the only instance in which an Amendment was repealed. In this case, it was the Eighteenth Amendment and its prohibition of the sale or consumption of alcohol.

The Twenty-Second Amendment limited the number of terms a president could serve to two. Presidents since George Washington had followed Washington's practice of not running for a third term; this changed when Franklin D. Roosevelt ran for reelection a third time, in 1940. He was reelected that time and a fourth time, too, four years later. He didn't live out his fourth term, but he did convince Congress and most of the state legislatures that some sort of term limit should be put in place.

The little-known Twenty-Third Amendment provided for representation of Washington, DC, in the Electoral College. The Twenty-Fourth Amendment prohibited poll taxes, which some people—usually African Americans—had been required to pay in order to vote.

Presidential succession is the focus of the Twenty-Fifth Amendment, which provides a blueprint of who will serve as president if the president is incapacitated or killed. The Twenty-Sixth Amendment lowered the legal voting age for Americans from twenty-one to eighteen. The Twenty-Seventh, and final, Amendment, prohibits members of Congress from substantially raising their own salaries. This amendment was one of twelve originally proposed in the late eighteenth century. Ten of those twelve became the Bill of Rights, and one has yet to become law.

A host of potential amendments have made news headlines in recent years. A total of six have been proposed by Congress and passed muster in both houses but have not been ratified by enough state legislatures. The aforementioned equal rights amendment is one. Another one, which would grant the District of Columbia full voting rights equivalent to the states, has not passed; like the equal rights amendment, its deadline has expired. A handful of others remain on the books without expiration dates, including an amendment to regulate child labor.

The Texas Constitution

The Texas constitution is an extremely long document, full of details for nearly every imaginable eventuality. It also has several long blank stretches, since wholesale sections of it have been repealed. State and local statutes range from the vital to the trivial, from land sales to road construction, from parks administration to dueling. Seemingly everything is covered by a statute in the Texas constitution. The constitution also has an exceedingly large number of amendments, including a Bill of Rights, just like the federal document.

The overriding idea behind the Texas constitution is the protection of individual rights. Texas was a frontier society for much of its existence. (Indeed, many would argue it is still that today.) The constitution, as vibrant today as when it was created in 1876, goes out of its way to protect the individual—the person or the corporation—against encroachment from the government.

Amending the Texas Constitution requires two-thirds approval by the Texas House and Senate, followed by a majority vote of the people approving the amendment.

See also Skills 24.2 and 24.4

Understands and promotes students' understanding of the impact of landmark Supreme Court cases.

Key Supreme Court cases include the following:

Marbury v. Madison (1803) held that the Supreme Court could strike down an act of Congress that was in conflict with the Constitution.

McCulloch v. Maryland (1819) established the doctrine of implied powers. The federal government can use any means not forbidden by the Constitution; the states cannot hinder legal actions by the federal government.

Dred Scott v. Sanford (1857) ruled that African Americans were not U.S. citizens and could not sue in federal courts. Slavery could not be outlawed in western territories before they became states.

Plessy v. Ferguson (1896) ruled that "separate but equal" facilities were constitutional; lasted for sixty years; overturned by Brown v. Board of Education.

Korematsu v. United States (1944) held that citizens of Japanese ancestry could be interned and would forfeit constitutional rights.

Brown v. Board of Education (1954) ruled that segregated schools were unconstitutional; that separate facilities were not equal facilities and overturned *Plessey v. Ferguson*.

Mapp v. Ohio (1961) ruled that evidence obtained illegally is inadmissible at trial.

Gideon v. Wainwright (1963) ruled that anyone charged with a serious criminal offense has the right to an attorney and the state must provide one if the individual charged cannot afford legal counsel.

Miranda v. Arizona (1966) ruled that police must advise suspects of their rights to remain silent, to consult with a lawyer and to have one appointed; police must stop interrogation if suspect asks for an attorney.

Tinker v. Des Moines (1969) held that wearing armbands is protected under the First Amendment.

Roe v. Wade (1973) ruled that laws restricting abortion were unconstitutional.

United States v. Nixon (1974) ruled that the president of the United States is not above the law.

Regents of CA v. Bakke (1978) ruled that race-based admissions in education did not violate the Equal Protection Clause of the Constitution.

Hazelwood v. Kuhlmeier (1983) ruled that public school newspapers have a lower level of protection under the First Amendment rights of free speech.

Texas v. Johnson (1989) ruled that a law prohibiting burning of the American flag is unconstitutional and a violation of the First Amendment.

> **SKILL 24.10** **Understands the components of the democratic process** *(e.g., voluntary individual participation, effective leadership, expression of different points of view, the selection of public officials)* **and their significance in a democratic society.**

See also Skills 24.1 and 24.2

The essential meaning of democracy derives from two Greek words: *demos* and *kratos*. *Demos* signifies the common people and *kratos* signifies rule. Therefore, the word democracy fundamentally means the *rule* of the *common people*.

> *The word democracy fundamentally means the rule of the common people.*

Democracy as defined by Abraham Lincoln is government for the people by the people and of the people. This definition includes the voluntary individual participation of all citizens, government that is a product of effective leadership, and the importance of each citizen's significant contribution to a democratic society. This form of government stems from a popular sovereignty in which the general public is endowed with the ability and the right to govern themselves.

The major components of democratic process include: freedom of speech, opportunity for individual participation, tolerance of public opinion, respect for individual rights, and a degree of decentralized political power. The democratic process is a way for the people to elect their leaders and hold them responsible for their conduct in office as well as their governmental policies.

Elected officials at the national, state, and local levels are required to pay attention to the citizens of their districts and take action in response to their needs and suggestions. Citizens, on the other hand, have a responsibility to stay informed about public issues, to carefully monitor the actions of their political leaders and how they use their powers. Voting in elections is another significant contribution and civic duty of all citizens in a democratic society.

SKILL 24.11 Understands the importance of effective leadership in a constitutional republic and identifies past and present leaders in state, local and national governments and their leadership qualities and contributions.

Leaders in the national government from Texas include: President Lyndon Johnson; President George H. W. Bush; Lady Bird Johnson and Laura Bush, First Ladies; John Connally, Jr., governor of Texas and Secretary of the Treasury; Kay Hutchinson, the first woman from Texas to be elected to the U.S. Senate; Speakers of the House of Representatives Sam Rayburn and John Nance Garner; Barbara Jordan, the first black Texan to be elected to Congress; and Sarah Ragle Weddington, general counsel for the Department of Agriculture, advisor to the president on women's issues, and member of the White House senior staff.

Important leaders in Texas state government include: Irma Rangel, the first Mexican American woman elected to the Texas House of Representatives; Ann Richards, the second woman to be elected as governor of Texas; and John Connally, governor.

SKILL 24.12 Demonstrates knowledge of important customs, symbols, landmarks and celebrations that represent American and Texan beliefs and principles and contribute to national unity.

Customs

Customs in the United States include a wide variety of traditions and beliefs that date back to before European exploration. With Native Americans, explorers, colonists, and immigrants all contributing to our culture, the United States has developed a unique culture of its own. As a whole, Americans have a strong sense of pride in their holidays, customs, principles, pastimes, and artistic contributions.

Symbols

The United States has a variety of symbols that represent the country, including the American bald eagle, the Great Seal, the American flag (and, in general, the colors red, white, and blue), the Statue of Liberty, the national anthem and "America, the Beautiful" (musical symbols), the Liberty Bell, the Pledge of Allegiance, and Uncle Sam. Teachers can utilize these symbols in a variety of lesson plans with students.

Celebrations

The United States observes many holidays throughout the calendar year. These include Martin Luther King, Jr. Day, the Fourth of July, Presidents' Day, Labor Day, Memorial Day, Columbus Day, Veterans Day, Flag Day, and Thanksgiving. Some religious holidays are also celebrated, such as Easter, Christmas, Rosh Hashanah, Yom Kippur, and Kwanza. Other days of note that many people celebrate include Mother's Day, Father's Day, Valentine's Day, Groundhog Day, Earth Day, Halloween, Cinch de Mayo, and of course, Super Bowl Sunday.

SKILL 24.13 **Analyzes the relationships between individual rights, responsibilities and freedoms in democratic societies.**

Civil Rights and Civil Liberties

Citizens of the United States recognize their responsibilities to the country and know that the surest way to protect their rights is to exercise them, which also entails a responsibility. Examples of this include the *right* to vote and the *responsibility* to be well informed on various issues, the *right* to a trial by jury and the *responsibility* to ensure the proper working of the justice system by serving on a jury if summoned for jury duty (rather than avoiding it). It is only recognition of the fact that an individual has both rights and responsibilities in society that enables the society to function in order to protect those very rights.

The term *civil rights* refers to rights that can be described as guarantees against the state authority interfering with citizens' liberties. Although the term *civil rights* has thus been identified with the ideal of equality and the term *civil liberties* with the idea of freedom, the two concepts are really inseparable. Equality implies liberty in a society such that one individual's freedom does not infringe on the rights of others.

Bill of Rights

All of these ideas found their final expression in the U.S. Constitution's first ten amendments, known as the Bill of Rights. In 1789, the first Congress passed these amendments and by December 1791 three-fourths of the states had ratified them. The Bill of Rights protects certain liberties and basic rights of citizens. James Madison, who wrote the amendments, said that the Bill of Rights does not give Americans these rights; people already have these rights. The Bill of Rights simply prevents the governments from taking them away.

The Bill of Rights reflects the fears and concerns of the people that the power and authority of the government be restricted from denying or limiting the rights of the people. The experiences of the Founding Fathers as colonists formed the foundation of these concerns.

The Bill of Rights has been interpreted in different ways at different times. The terms of the amendments can be defined in different ways to enfranchise or disenfranchise individuals or groups of people. For example, during and after Reconstruction, the interpretation of the Bill of Rights did not include blacks in the definition of a citizen, necessitating the passage of the Fourteenth and Fifteenth Amendments. The amendments were broadly interpreted by the Supreme Court in the *Plessy v. Ferguson* case, resulting in the establishment of the doctrine of "separate but equal." It was not until fifty years later, in the case of Brown v. Board of Education, that a narrower interpretation of the amendment resulted in a Supreme Court decision that reversed the previous interpretation.

The First Amendment guarantees the basic rights of freedom of religion, freedom of speech, freedom of the press, and freedom of assembly. The next three amendments came out of the colonists' struggle with Great Britain. For example, the Third Amendment prevents Congress from forcing citizens to keep troops in their homes. Before the Revolution, Great Britain tried to coerce the colonists to house soldiers.

Amendments five through eight protect citizens who are accused of crimes and brought to trial. Every citizen has the right to due process of law, including the right to a trial by an impartial jury, the right to be defended by a lawyer, and the right to a speedy trial. The last two amendments limit the powers of the federal government to those expressly granted in the Constitution; any rights not expressly mentioned in the Constitution therefore belong to the states or to the people.

Freedom of Religion

Religious freedom has not been seriously threatened in the United States historically. The policy of the government has been guided by the premise that church and state should be separate. However, when religious practices have been at cross purposes with prevailing attitudes in the nation at particular times, restrictions have been placed on these practices. For example, there have been restrictions against the practices of polygamy, animal sacrifice, and the use of mind-altering illegal substances that are supported by various religious groups or used in religious rituals.

Freedom of Speech, Press, and Assembly

These rights historically have been given wide latitude in their practice although there have been instances when one or the other has been limited for various reasons. In regard to freedom of speech, for example, individuals are prohibited from yelling "fire!" in a crowded theater. Thus the state decrees that freedom of speech does not extend to speech that might endanger other people. There is also a prohibition against slander, or knowingly stating a deliberate falsehood about someone. There are many regulations regarding freedom of the press; the most common examples are the various laws against libel (a written or printed falsehood). In times of national emergency, various restrictions have been placed on the rights of freedom of speech, press, and sometimes assembly.

See Skill 24.2 for information on rights and responsibilities.

See also Skills 24.14 and 24.15

SKILL 24.14 Applies knowledge of the rights and responsibilities of citizens and nonprofit and civic groups in Texas and the United States, past and present, and understands characteristics of good citizenship *(e.g., community service)* as exemplified by historical and contemporary figures.

See Skill 24.2

Civic Responsibilities

According to the TEKS guidelines, civic responsibilities are "the obligations of citizens to be active, peaceful, loyal, and supportive to the community (local, state, or nation) in which they live. Citizens in a democratic society such as the United States, governed by a constitution, should understand and obey the law, be knowledgeable about public issues, be concerned about the performance of political leaders, pay taxes, vote, lead fellow citizens, and participate in public service, including the military, as appropriate."

http://ritter.tea.state.tx.us/ssc/teks_and_taas/teks/gloss7.htm#physhumfac

---

SKILL 24.15 Understands how the nature, rights and responsibilities of citizenship vary among societies.

Rights in Democratic Societies

According to the TEKS glossary, "The liberal democratic tradition seeks to protect individual rights, the unalienable rights to life, liberty, and the pursuit of happiness listed in the Declaration of Independence. Personal rights in democratic societies include the freedom to travel, to live where one chooses, to marry and have children, and to have freedom of thought. Political rights include the right to vote, petition, assemble, and speak or publish freely. Economic rights include the ability to own property, change employment, join a union, or start a business. Democratic governments protect all three types of rights but limit those which may harm or endanger members of the democracy. Documents governing democracies must be flexible to adapt to changing public opinion and to continually protect personal and public rights."

Responsibilities in Democratic Societies

According to the TEKS glossary, "Citizens in a democratic society have a responsibility to all other citizens to ensure that the enjoyment of their individual rights does not impede the development of the common good of society. For American democracy to flourish, citizens must be aware of their rights and must exercise them responsibly. They must fulfill those responsibilities necessary to a self-governing, free, and just society. There are two categories of responsibilities: Personal responsibilities, e.g., taking care of themselves, accepting responsibility for the consequences of their actions, taking advantage of the opportunity to be educated, and supporting their families; Civic responsibilities, e.g., obeying the law; respecting the rights of others; being informed and attentive to the needs of their community; staying informed about issues impacting the decisions of elected leaders; paying attention to how well their elected leaders are doing their jobs; communicating with their representatives in their school, local, state, and national governments; voting; paying taxes; serving on juries; and serving in the armed forces."

Citizenship

According to the TEKS glossary, "A person with citizenship is legally recognized as a citizen of a nation. Citizens may have equal rights under the law and have certain privileges and responsibilities as citizens. These differ from nation to nation. A citizen owes allegiance to his or her country and expects to be protected by his or her government and from unfair use of governmental power. The term citizen can have broader meanings. Students can be citizens of their classroom. Citizens can be natural born or naturalized. When naturalized, they vow their allegiance to their adopted country and sometimes cease being legal citizens of their homeland."

DOMAIN IV
SCIENCE

PERSONALIZED STUDY PLAN

✗ KNOWN MATERIAL/ SKIP IT

PAGE	COMPETENCY AND SKILL	
391	**25: Safe and proper laboratory process**	☐
	25.1: Understands safety regulations and guidelines for science facilities and science instruction.	☐
	25.2: Knows procedures for and sources of information regarding the appropriate handling, use, disposal, care, and maintenance of chemicals, materials, specimens, and equipment.	☐
	25.3: Knows procedures for the safe handling and ethical care and treatment of organisms and specimens.	☐
	25.4: Selects and safely uses appropriate tools, technologies, materials and equipment needed for instructional activities.	☐
	25.5: Understands concepts of precision, accuracy, and error with regard to reading and recording numerical data from a scientific instrument.	☐
	25.6: Understands how to gather, organize, display and communicate data in a variety of ways (e.g., charts, tables, graphs, diagrams, written reports, oral presentations).	☐
	25.7: Understands the international system of measurement (i.e., metric system) and performs unit conversions within measurement systems, including the use of nonstandard units.	☐
401	**26: History and nature of science**	☐
	26.1: Understands, plans, designs and implements instruction that provides opportunities for all students to engage in nonexperimental- and experimental-inquiry investigations.	☐
	26.2: Focuses inquiry-based instruction on questions and issues relevant to students and uses strategies to assist students with generating, refining and focusing scientific questions and hypotheses.	☐
	26.3: Understands and instructs students in the safe and proper use of a variety of grade-appropriate tools, equipment, resources, technology and techniques to access, gather, store, retrieve, organize and analyze data.	☐
	26.4: Knows how to guide students in making systematic observations and measurements and posing questions to guide investigations.	☐
	26.5: Knows how to promote the use of critical-thinking skills, logical reasoning and scientific problem solving to reach conclusions based on evidence.	☐
	26.6: Knows how to teach students to develop, analyze, and evaluate different explanations for a given scientific result, including that repeated investigations may increase reliability.	☐
	26.7: Knows how to teach students to demonstrate an understanding of potential sources of error in inquiry-based investigation.	☐
	26.8: Knows how to teach students to demonstrate an understanding of how to communicate and defend the results of an inquiry-based investigation.	☐
	26.9: Understands principles of scientific ethics.	☐

PERSONALIZED STUDY PLAN

KNOWN MATERIAL/ SKIP IT

PAGE	COMPETENCY AND SKILL	

26.10: Understands the roles that logical reasoning, verifiable evidence, prediction and peer review play in the process of generating and evaluating scientific knowledge. ☐

26.11: Understands the historical development of science *(e.g., cell theory, plate tectonics, laws of motion, universal gravity)* and technology and the contributions that diverse cultures and individuals of both genders have made to scientific and technological knowledge. ☐

416   27:   Impact on science ☐ ☐

27.1: Understands that decisions about the use of science are based on factors such as ethical standards, economics, and personal and societal needs.

27.2: Applies scientific principles to analyze the advantages of, disadvantages of or alternatives to a given decision or course of action. ☐

27.3: Applies scientific principles and processes to analyze factors that influence personal choices concerning fitness and health, including physiological and psychological effects and risks associated with the use of substances and substance abuse. ☐

27.4: Understands concepts, characteristics and issues related to changes in populations and human population growth. ☐

27.5: Identifies and understands the types and uses of natural resources and the effects of human consumption on the renewal and depletion of resources. ☐

27.6: Understands the role science and scientists can play in helping resolve personal, societal and global challenges. ☐

423   28:   Concepts and processes ☐ ☐

28.1: Understands how a unifying, explanatory framework across the science disciplines is provided by the concepts and processes of systems, order and organization; evidence, models and explanation; change, constancy and measurements; and form and function.

28.2: Demonstrates an understanding of how patterns in observations and data can be used to make explanations and predictions. ☐

28.3: Analyzes interactions and interrelationships between systems and subsystems. ☐

28.4: Applies unifying concepts to explore similarities in a variety of natural phenomena. ☐

28.5: Understands how properties and patterns of systems can be described in terms of space, time, energy and matter. ☐

28.6: Understands how change and constancy occur in systems. ☐

28.7: Understands the complementary nature of form and function in a given system. ☐

28.8: Understands how models are used to represent the natural world and how to evaluate the strengths and limitations of a variety of scientific models *(e.g., physical, conceptual, mathematical).* ☐

PERSONALIZED STUDY PLAN

KNOWN MATERIAL/ SKIP IT ✗

PAGE	COMPETENCY AND SKILL	
429	**29:** **Theory and practice of science teaching**	☐
	29.1: Understands how developmental characteristics, prior knowledge and experience and students' attitudes influence science learning.	☐
	29.2: Selects and adapts science curricula, content, instructional materials, collaborations, vocabulary and activities to meet the levels of interest, knowledge, and understanding as well as the abilities, experiences and needs of all students, including English-language learners.	☐
	29.3: Understands how to use situations from students' daily lives to develop instructional materials that investigate how science can be used to make informed decisions.	☐
	29.4: Understands common misconceptions in science and has effective ways to address those misconceptions.	☐
	29.5: Understands developmentally appropriate design and implementation of hands-on learning experiences in science and selects effective, appropriate instructional practices, activities, technologies and materials to promote students' scientific knowledge, skills and inquiry processes.	☐
	29.6: Understands questioning strategies designed to elicit higher-level thinking and how to use them to move students from concrete to more abstract understanding.	☐
	29.7: Understands the importance of planning activities that are inclusive and that accommodate the needs of all students.	☐
	29.8: Understands how to sequence learning activities in a way that enables students to build on their prior knowledge and that challenges them to expand their understanding of science.	☐
436	**30:** **Science assessment**	☐
	30.1: Understands the relationships between a science curriculum, assessment and instruction and bases instruction on information gathered through assessment of students' strengths and needs.	☐
	30.2: Understands the importance of monitoring and assessing students' understanding of science concepts and skills on an ongoing basis, including how to use formal and informal assessments of student performance and how to use products *(e.g., projects, lab journals, rubrics, portfolios, student profiles, checklists)* to evaluate students' understanding of and participation in the inquiry process.	☐
	30.3: Selects—or designs—and administers a variety of appropriate assessments *(e.g., performance assessment, self-assessment, formal/informal assessment, formative/summative assessment)* to monitor students' understanding and progress and to plan for instruction.	☐
	30.4: Understands the importance of communicating evaluation criteria and assessment results to students.	☐

PERSONALIZED STUDY PLAN

KNOWN MATERIAL/ SKIP IT

PAGE	COMPETENCY AND SKILL	
441	**31: Forces and motion**	☐
	31.1: Demonstrates an understanding of the properties of universal forces *(e.g., gravitational, electrical, magnetic)*.	☐
	31.2: Understands how to measure, graph and describe changes in motion by using concepts of position, direction of motion and speed.	☐
	31.3: Analyzes the ways unbalanced forces acting on an object cause changes in the position or motion of the object.	☐
	31.4: Analyzes the relationship between force and motion in a variety of situations *(e.g., simple machines, geologic processes)*.	☐
451	**32: Physical and chemical properties**	☐
	32.1: Describes the physical and chemical properties of substances *(e.g., size, shape, temperature, magnetism, hardness, mass, conduction, density)*.	☐
	32.2: Describes the physical properties of solids, liquids and gases.	☐
	32.3: Distinguishes between physical and chemical changes in matter.	☐
	32.4: Applies knowledge of physical and chemical properties (including atomic structure) of and changes in matter to processes and situations that occur in life and in earth and space science.	☐
	32.5: Distinguishes between elements, compounds, mixtures and solutions and describes their properties.	☐
	32.6: Explains the importance of a variety of chemical reactions that occur in daily life *(e.g., rusting, burning of fossil fuels, photosynthesis, cell respiration, chemical batteries, digestion of food)*.	☐
461	**33: Physical science: Energy and interactions between matter and energy**	☐
	33.1: Understands conservation of energy and energy transformations and analyzes how energy is transformed from one form to another *(e.g., potential, kinetic, mechanical, sound, heat, light, chemical, electrical)* in a variety of everyday situations and how increasing or decreasing amounts affect objects.	☐
	33.2: Understands the basic concepts of heat energy and related processes *(e.g., melting, evaporation, boiling, condensation)*.	☐
	33.3: Understands the principles of electricity and magnetism and their applications *(e.g., electric circuits, motors, audio speakers, lightning)*.	☐
	33.4: Applies knowledge of properties of light *(e.g., reflection, refraction)* to describe the functioning of optical systems and phenomena *(e.g., camera, microscope, rainbow, eye)*.	☐
	33.5: Demonstrates an understanding of the properties, production, and transmission of sound.	☐

PERSONALIZED STUDY PLAN

KNOWN MATERIAL/ SKIP IT

PAGE	COMPETENCY AND SKILL	
467	**34: Physical science: Energy transformations and the conservation of matter and energy**	☐
	34.1: Describes sources of electrical energy and processes of energy transformation for human uses *(e.g., fossil fuels, solar panels, hydroelectric plants).*	☐
	34.2: Applies knowledge of transfer of energy in a variety of situations *(e.g., the production of heat, light, sound, and magnetic effects by electrical energy; the process of photosynthesis; weather processes; food webs; food and energy pyramids).*	☐
	34.3: Understands applications of energy transformations and the conservation of matter and energy in life and in earth and space science.	☐
471	**35: Life science: Structure and function of living things**	☐
	35.1: Understands that living systems have different structures that perform different functions.	☐
	35.2: Understands and describes stages in the life cycles of common plants and animals.	☐
	35.3: Understand that organisms have basic needs.	☐
	35.4: Analyzes how structure complements function in cells, tissues, organs, organ systems and organisms.	☐
	35.5: Identifies human body systems and describes their functions.	☐
	35.6: Understands the relationship between characteristics, structures, and functions and corresponding taxonomic classifications.	☐
489	**36: Reproduction and the mechanisms of heredity**	☐
	36.1: Describes the processes by which plants and animals reproduce and explains how hereditary information is passed from one generation to the next.	☐
	36.2: Compares and contrasts inherited traits and learned characteristics.	☐
	36.3: Understands the organization of hereditary material and how an inherited trait can be determined by one or many genes and how more than one trait can be influenced by a single gene.	☐
	36.4: Distinguishes between dominant and recessive traits and predicts the probable outcomes of genetic combinations.	☐
	36.5: Evaluates the influence of environmental and genetic factors on the traits of an organism.	☐
500	**37: Adaptations and evolution**	☐
	37.1: Demonstrates knowledge of adaptive characteristics and explains how adaptations influence the survival of populations or species.	☐
	37.2: Describes how populations and species change through time.	☐
	37.3: Describes processes that enable traits to change through time, including selective breeding, mutation and other natural occurrences.	☐

PERSONALIZED STUDY PLAN

KNOWN MATERIAL/ SKIP IT

PAGE	COMPETENCY AND SKILL	
506	**38: Organisms and the environment**	☐
	38.1: Understands that organisms respond to internal or external stimuli and analyzes the role of internal and external stimuli in the behavior of organisms.	☐
	38.2: Understands relationships between organisms and the environment and describes ways that living organisms depend on each other and on the environment to meet their basic needs.	☐
	38.3: Identifies organisms, populations or species with similar needs and analyzes how they compete with one another for resources.	☐
	38.4: Analyzes the interrelationships and interdependence among producers, consumers and decomposers in an ecosystem (e.g., food webs, food chains, competition, predation).	☐
	38.5: Identifies factors that influence the size and growth of populations in an ecosystem.	☐
	38.6: Analyzes adaptive characteristics that result in a population's or species' unique niche in an ecosystem.	☐
	38.7: Knows how populations and species modify and affect ecosystems.	☐
511	**39: Structure and function of Earth systems**	☐
	39.1: Understands the structure of Earth and analyzes constructive and destructive processes (including plate tectonics, weathering and erosion) that produce geologic change, including how these processes have affected Earth history.	☐
	39.2: Understands the form and function of surface water and groundwater.	☐
	39.3: Applies knowledge of the composition and structure of the atmosphere and its properties.	☐
	39.4: Applies knowledge of how human activity and natural processes, both gradual and catastrophic, can alter Earth systems.	☐
521	**40: Cycles in Earth systems**	☐
	40.1: Understands the rock cycle and how rocks, minerals, and soils are formed, and their respective properties.	☐
	40.2: Understands the water cycle and its relationship to weather processes.	☐
	40.3: Understands the nutrient (e.g., carbon, nitrogen) cycle and its relationship to Earth systems.	☐
	40.4: Applies knowledge of how human and natural processes affect Earth systems.	☐
	40.5: Understands and describes the properties and uses of Earth materials (e.g., rocks, soils, water, atmospheric gases).	☐

PERSONALIZED STUDY PLAN

KNOWN
MATERIAL/
SKIP IT

PAGE	COMPETENCY AND SKILL	
526	**41:** **Energy in weather and climate**	☐
	41.1: Understands the elements of weather *(e.g., humidity, wind speed and direction, air pressure, temperature)* and the tools used for measurement.	☐
	41.2: Compares and contrasts weather and climate.	☐
	41.3: Analyzes weather charts and data to make weather predictions.	☐
	41.4: Applies knowledge of how transfers of energy between Earth systems affect weather and climate.	☐
	41.5: Analyzes how Earth's position, orientation, and surface features affect weather and climate.	☐
529	**42:** **Earth and space science: Characteristics of the solar system and the universe**	☐
	42.1: Understands the properties and characteristics of objects in the sky.	☐
	42.2: Applies knowledge of the Earth-Moon-Sun system and the interactions between them *(e.g., seasons, lunar phases, eclipses)*.	☐
	42.3: Identifies properties of the components of the solar system.	☐

COMPETENCY 25
SAFE AND PROPER LABORATORY PROCESS

Understands safety regulations and guidelines for science facilities and science instruction.

See also Skill 26.3

Safety in the science classroom and laboratory is of great importance to the science educator. One key to maintaining a safe learning environment is proactive training and regular in-service updates for all staff and students who utilize the science laboratory. This training should include how to identify and evaluate potential hazards as well as how to prevent or respond to them.

Right-to-know laws cover science teachers who work with potentially hazardous chemicals. Briefly, the law states that employees must be informed of potentially toxic chemicals. An inventory must be made available, if requested. The inventory must contain information about the hazards and properties of the chemicals. Training must be provided in the safe handling and interpretation of the Material Safety Data Sheet.

Schools should consider the following types of training:

- Right-to-know training (OSHA training on the importance and benefits of properly recognizing and safely working with hazardous materials), along with some basic chemical hygiene as well as instruction in how to read and understand a Material Safety Data Sheet

- Instruction in how to use a fire extinguisher

- Instruction in how to use a chemical fume hood

- General guidance on when and how to use personal protective equipment (e.g., safety glasses or gloves)

- Instruction in how to monitor activities for potential impact on indoor air quality

It is also important for the instructor to use Material Safety Data Sheets (MSDS). MSDSs include information on substances such as physical data (melting point, boiling point, etc.), toxicity, health effects, first aid, reactivity, storage, disposal, protective gear, and spill/leak procedures. They are particularly

MSDSs include information on substances such as physical data (melting point, boiling point, etc.), toxicity, health effects, first aid, reactivity, storage, disposal, protective gear, and spill/ leak procedures.

important to have available if a spill or other accident occurs. You should have an MSDS in the lab for every item in your chemical inventory. This will assist you in determining how to store and handle your materials. In most cases the manufacturer provides recommendations with regard to protective equipment, ventilation, and storage.

In addition to requirements set forth by your place of employment, the National Association of Biology Teachers (NABT) and International Science Education Foundation (ISEF) have set parameters for the science classroom:

All science labs should contain the following items of safety equipment (*required by law*):

- Fire blanket which is visible and accessible
- Ground Fault Circuit Interrupters (GFCIs) within two feet of water supplies
- Emergency shower capable of providing a continuous flow of water
- Signs designating room exits
- Emergency eye-wash station which can be activated by the foot or forearm
- Eye protection for every student and a means of sanitizing equipment
- Emergency exhaust fans providing ventilation to the outside of the building
- Master cut-off switches for gas, electric, and compressed air. Switches must have permanently attached handles. Cut-off switches must be clearly labeled.
- An ABC fire extinguisher
- Storage cabinets for flammable materials

Also recommended, but not required by law:

- Chemical spill control kit
- Fume hood with a motor that is spark proof
- Protective laboratory aprons made of flame-retardant material
- Signs that will alert people to potentially hazardous conditions
- Containers for broken glassware, flammables, corrosives, and waste
- Containers should be labeled

In addition to the safety laws set forth by the government for equipment necessary to the lab, the Occupational Safety and Health Administration (OSHA) has helped to make environments safer by creating signs for the laboratory. Of particular importance are diamond safety signs, prohibitive signs, and triangle danger signs. Each sign encloses a descriptive picture.

It is the teacher's responsibility to provide a safe environment for his or her students. Proper supervision greatly reduces the risk of injury. A teacher should never leave a class for any reason without providing alternate supervision. When an accident occurs, two factors are always considered; foreseeability and negligence. Foreseeability is the anticipation that an event may occur under certain circumstances. Negligence is the failure to exercise ordinary or reasonable care. Safety procedures should be built in to the science curriculum, and a well-managed classroom is critical to avoiding potential problems.

> **SKILL 25.2** Knows procedures for and sources of information regarding the appropriate handling, use, disposal, care, and maintenance of chemicals, materials, specimens, and equipment.

See also Skill 25.1

All laboratory solutions should be prepared as directed in the lab manual. Care should be taken to avoid contamination. All glassware should be rinsed thoroughly with distilled water before using, and cleaned well after use. All solutions should be made with distilled water, as tap water contains dissolved particles that can affect the results of an experiment. Students should wear safety goggles while working with glassware in case of an accident.

Chemicals should not be stored on benches or near heat sources; they should be stored in a secure, dry area. They should be stored in accordance with their reactability. Acids should be locked in a separate area from nonacids.

All containers in the lab must be labeled. Suspected and known carcinogens must be labeled as such and segregated within trays to contain leaks and spills.

Used solutions should be disposed of according to local disposal procedures. Any questions regarding the safe disposal of solutions or chemical safety can be directed to the local fire department.

Chemical waste should be disposed of in properly labeled containers. Waste should be separated based on its reactivity with other chemicals. Biological material should never be stored near food or water used for human consumption.

All biological material should be appropriately labeled. All blood and body fluids should be put in a well-secured container with a secure lid to prevent leaking. All biological waste should be disposed of in biological hazardous waste bags.

The following chemicals are potential carcinogens and are not allowed in school facilities: acrylonitriel, arsenic compounds, asbestos, benzidine, benzene, cadmium compounds, chloroform, chromium compounds, ethylene oxide, ortho-toluidine, nickel powder, and mercury.

SKILL 25.3 Knows procedures for the safe handling and ethical care and treatment of organisms and specimens.

There are many important procedures for handling specimens in the scientific laboratory. First, only animals obtained from recognized sources should be used. Decaying animals or those of unknown origin may harbor pathogens and/or parasites. Specimens should be rinsed before handling, and the teacher and students should wear latex gloves during handling. If gloves are not available, students with sores or scratches should be excused from the activity.

Formaldehyde is a carcinogen and should be avoided or disposed of according to district regulations. Students objecting to dissections for moral reasons should be given an alternative assignment.

No dissections can be performed on living mammalian vertebrates or birds. Lower-order life and invertebrates can be used. Biological experiments can be done with all animals except mammalian vertebrates or birds. No physiological harm can result to the animal. All animals housed and cared for in the school must be handled in a safe and humane manner. Animals are not to remain on school premises during extended vacations unless adequate care is provided. Many laws state that any instructor who intentionally refuses to comply with the laws can be suspended or dismissed. For those students who object to performing dissections, interactive dissections are available online or from software companies. There should be no penalty for those students who refuse to physically perform a dissection.

Selects and safely uses appropriate tools, technologies, materials and equipment needed for instructional activities.

Equipment

If Bunsen burners are used, the following precautions should be followed:

1. Know the location of fire extinguishers and safety blankets and train students in their use.

2. Make sure students secure long hair and long sleeves to keep them out of the way.

3. Turn the gas all the way on and make a spark with the striker. The preferred method of lighting burners is to use strikers rather than matches.

4. Adjust the air valve at the bottom of the Bunsen burner until the flame shows an inner cone.

5. Adjust the flow of gas to the desired flame height by using the adjustment valve.

6. Do not touch the barrel of the burner (it is hot).

7. Use hot plates whenever possible to avoid the risk of burns or fire.

Light microscopes are commonly used in high school laboratory experiments. Total magnification is determined by multiplying the ocular (usually 10X) and the objective (usually 10X on low, 40X on high) lenses. A few steps should be followed to properly care for this equipment:

- Clean all lenses with lens paper only.

- Carry microscopes with two hands, one on the arm and one on the base.

- Always begin focusing on low power, then switch to high power.

- Store microscopes with the low-power objective down.

- Always use a cover slip when viewing wet-mount slides.

- Bring the objective down to its lowest position, then focus by moving up to avoid breaking or scratching the slide.

Life-science studies often use the following equipment and techniques for measuring small quantities:

- Spectrophotometers use the percentage of light absorbance to measure a color change, thus giving qualitative data a quantitative value.

- **Graduated cylinders** are used for precise measurements. They should always be placed on a flat surface. The surface of the liquid forms a meniscus (lens-shaped curve). The measurement is read at the bottom of this curve.

- **Electronic balances** are easy to use but expensive. An electronic balance should always be tarred (returned to zero) before measuring and used on a flat surface. Substances should always be placed on a piece of paper to avoid spills and/or damage to the instrument. Triple-beam balances must be used on a level surface. There are screws located at the bottom of the balance for making adjustments. Start with the largest counterweight first and proceed toward the last notch that does not cause the balance to tip. Do the same with the next largest counterweight, etc., until the pointer remains at zero. The total mass is the total of all of the readings on the beams. Again, use paper under the substance to protect the equipment.

- A **buret** is used to dispense precisely measured volumes of liquid. A stopcock is used to control the volume of liquid dispensed at one time.

Procedures

Common laboratory techniques are dissection, preserving, staining and mounting microscopic specimens, and preparing laboratory solutions.

Staining

Specimens have to be stained because they are mostly transparent (except plant cells, which are green) under the microscope and difficult to see against a white background. The stains work by fixing themselves to various structures on or in the cell, making the components of the specimen much easier to see. The exact structure determines the staining process used.

The variety of stains available is numerous. Stains represent a vital tool for determining cellular components. Starch, protein, and even nucleic acids can be brought out using special stains. Some common stains used in laboratories are methylene blue, chlorazol black, lignin pink, and gentian violet.

Mounting of specimens

In order to observe microscopic specimens or minute parts, mounting them on a microscope slide is essential. Water is a common mounting medium in high school laboratories because it is cheap and well suited for temporary mounting. One problem with water mounting, however, is that the water evaporates.

Glycerin can also be used for mounting. Glycerin is nontoxic and remains stable for years. It provides good contrast to the specimens under microscopic examination. The only problem with glycerin as a medium is that it supports mold formation.

Preparation of laboratory solutions

The correct preparation of laboratory solutions is a critical skill needed for experimental success. The procedure for making solutions must be followed to get maximum accuracy:

1. Weigh out the required amount of each solute.

2. Dissolve the solute in less than the total desired volume (about 75%).

3. Add enough solvent to get the desired volume.

> **SKILL 25.5** Understands concepts of precision, accuracy, and error with regard to reading and recording numerical data from a scientific instrument.

All experimental uncertainty is due to either random errors or systematic errors. Systematic and random errors refer to problems associated with making measurements. Mistakes made in calculations or instrument reading are not considered in error analysis.

RANDOM ERRORS are statistical fluctuations in the measured data due to the precision limitations of the measurement device. Random errors usually result from the experimenter's inability to take the same measurement in exactly the same way to get exactly the same number.

SYSTEMATIC ERRORS, by contrast, are reproducible inaccuracies that are consistently in the same direction. Systematic errors are often due to a problem that persists throughout the entire experiment.

ACCURACY is the degree of conformity of a measured, calculated quantity to its actual (true) value. PRECISION is also called reproducibility or repeatability and is the degree to which further measurements or calculations show the same or similar results.

Accuracy is the degree of veracity while precision is the degree of reproducibility. The best analogy to explain accuracy and precision is the target comparison. Repeated measurements are compared to arrows that are fired at a target. Accuracy describes how close the arrows get to the bull's eye at the center of the target. Arrows that strike closer to the bull's eye than others are considered more accurate.

RANDOM ERRORS: statistical fluctuations in the measured data due to the precision limitations of the measurement device

SYSTEMATIC ERRORS: reproducible inaccuracies that are consistently in the same direction

ACCURACY: the degree of conformity of a measured, calculated quantity to its actual (true) value

PRECISION: the degree to which further measurements or calculations show the same or similar results

In order to obtain accurate results, students need to be able to read an instrument precisely and record experimental data correctly. Some of the factors that affect one's ability to read/record data correctly include the table height, use of laptops, portable data-recording devices, and clean and visible lines on glass or plastic materials (such as beakers).

> **SKILL 25.6** **Understands how to gather, organize, display and communicate data in a variety of ways** *(e.g., charts, tables, graphs, diagrams, written reports, oral presentations).*

See also Skill 26.3

Graphing is an important skill for visually displaying collected data for analysis. The two types of graphs most commonly used are the line graph and the bar graph (histogram).

Line Graphs

INDEPENDENT VARIABLES: variables that would be present independently of the experiment

Line graphs show two variables represented by one point on the graph. The *x*-axis is the horizontal axis and represents the dependent variable. INDEPENDENT VARIABLES are variables that would be present independently of the experiment. A common example of an independent variable is time. Time proceeds regardless of anything else occurring. The *y*-axis is the vertical axis and represents the dependent variable. DEPENDENT VARIABLES are variables manipulated by the experiment, such as the amount of light or the height of a plant.

DEPENDENT VARIABLES: variables manipulated by the experiment

Graphs should be calibrated at equal intervals. If one space represents one day, the next space cannot represent ten days. A best-fit line is drawn to join the points and cannot include all of the points in the data. Axes must always be labeled for the graph to be meaningful. A good title describes both the dependent and the independent variables.

Bar Graphs

In bar graphs, points are not plotted. Instead, the dependent variable is set up as a bar where the *x*-axis intersects the *y*-axis. Each bar is a separate item of data.

SKILL **Understands the international system of measurement** *(i.e., metric*
25.7 *system)* **and performs unit conversions within measurement systems, including the use of nonstandard units.**

See also Skills 17.8 and 17.11 for metric conversions.

The metric system provides units of measurement for distance, volume, mass, time, and temperature. The table below shows the basic unit of measurement for these parameters. The basic unit for distance is the meter, for volume is the liter, for mass is the gram, for time is the second, and for temperature is the degree Celsius.

It's important to remember the prefixes that allow conversion between metric units. For instance, the prefix *kilo-* means one thousand and is equal to one thousand meters. The most common prefixes are shown below and allow for easy conversions along the scale. The nanometer is the smallest unit shown. Proteins in our bodies are on the nanometer scale and only electron microscopes can resolve such small structures.

Prefix	Means:	Power of 10	Prefix	Means:	Power of 10
Giga-	One billion	10^9	Deci-	One tenth	10^{-1}
Mega-	One million	10^6	Centi-	One hundredth	10^{-2}
Kilo-	One thousand	10^3	Milli-	One thousandth	10^{-3}
Hecta-	One hundred	10^2	Micro-	One millionth	10^{-6}
Deca-	Ten	10^1	Nano-	One billionth	10^{-9}

Nonstandard Units

When measuring instruments like rulers or measuring tape are not available, one can estimate the measurable characteristic (e.g., length, weight, temperature, etc.) of an object using another object. If an exact or precise measurement is not needed, then a nonstandard unit can also be used. Typically, the object that is used to estimate the characteristic being measured is comparable in scale to the object being measured. This reference object is called the nonstandard unit.

An example of using a nonstandard unit to measure the length of an object is using paper clips to measure the length of a piece of paper. The length of the paper would be given as the number of paper clips needed to match the length of one of its sides.

Other examples of using nonstandard units include the following:

- Estimating the length of a walkway based on the number of steps one takes from one end of the walkway to the other

- Using paper clips to approximate the length of a sharpened pencil

- Estimating the weight of a jar full of candy based on the weight of tennis ball

It should be noted that nonstandard measurements are not precise and are always estimates since the nonstandard unit is the relative size or weight or an object. Introducing students to the use of nonstandard units is an effective way to convey the importance of precise measurements and explain why an international system of measurement exists.

COMPETENCY 26
HISTORY AND NATURE OF SCIENCE

> **SKILL 26.1** Understands, plans, designs and implements instruction that provides opportunities for all students to engage in nonexperimental- and experimental-inquiry investigations.

See also Skill 29.6

Influence of Developmental Stages on Learning

Teachers must understand that some techniques will only be effective at certain stages during childhood. The following gives examples of inquiry-related activities that are appropriate for each grade level.

Early-childhood students

Plant growth: Students should plant seeds and take care of plants while the teacher models and explains the process and stages of plant growth (germination, sprouting, seedling, and so on).

Elementary students

Study of rocks and porosity: Students can test the porosity of limestone, shale, slate, sandstone, and so on, using droppers filled with water.

Middle-school students

Cells and genetics: Students can learn about their own genetics and cells during this study. One good idea is to include a study of how each student is different in genetic ways; for example, detached/attached earlobes, widow's peak, tongue rolling, swirls in fingerprints, and hair characteristics.

Sequence of presentation

Generally, science textbooks present an approach to science sequenced to allow basic principles to be taught first and advanced principles to be taught later. Even when curricula are oriented toward specific testable outcomes or objectives, the materials included should be sequenced to support educational progress.

The sequence of presentation must be appropriate for the available instructional hours and period. The sequence should also conform to policy guidelines and optimally align with the organization of textbooks and other course materials in use. The sequence may need to conform to mandated educational outcomes.

Teachers must ensure that students understand foundational principles before moving on to derived principles. When students have mastered principles, it is time to move forward with the sequenced material to maintain a challenging educational environment. The sequenced materials should not be pinned to a strict schedule; they should be implemented flexibly to accommodate and challenge students.

> **SKILL 26.2** Focuses inquiry-based instruction on questions and issues relevant to students and uses strategies to assist students with generating, refining and focusing scientific questions and hypotheses.

There are two types of inquiry approaches to teaching: deduction and inquiry. Both are approaches used to answer questions about or to explain phenomena in the natural world. Deductive inquiry takes advantage of prior learning, models, or knowledge to explain new material. Inductive inquiry uses observations and data collection and presentation to reach conclusions about new material.

Deductive Inquiry

The main goal of deductive inquiry is to move students from generalized principles to specific instances.

The main goal of deductive inquiry is to move students from generalized principles to specific instances. The strategy stresses the process of testing general assumptions, applying them, and exploring the relationships between specific elements.

Inductive Inquiry

The information-seeking process of the inductive inquiry method helps students establish facts, determine relevant questions, develop ways to pursue these questions, and build explanations.

The information-seeking process of the inductive inquiry method helps students establish facts, determine relevant questions, develop ways to pursue these questions, and build explanations. Students are encouraged to develop and support their own hypotheses. Through inductive inquiry, students experience the thought processes that require them to move from specific facts and observations to inferences.

Interactive Instruction

Both deductive and inductive inquiry can be interactive. Interactive instruction relies heavily on discussion and sharing among participants. Examples of this type of instruction include debates, brainstorming, discussions, and laboratory groups.

The Scientific Method

The SCIENTIFIC METHOD is the basic process of scientific investigation. It begins by posing a question and ends by drawing a conclusion based on reproducible experimental results. Good scientific investigation should seek to provide a number of plausible hypotheses for any given phenomenon and then identify the correct hypothesis as established by experimental results. It is therefore critical that students approach a given scientific phenomenon with an open mind and a willingness to accept logical conclusions, even when they are unanticipated. Additionally, a variety of explanations may be correct for a given phenomenon if they seek to explain the phenomenon as resulting from different causes.

> SCIENTIFIC METHOD: the basic process of scientific investigation. It begins by posing a question and ends by drawing a conclusion based on reproducible experimental results.

Posing a question: Although many discoveries happen by chance, the standard thought process of a scientist begins with forming a question to research. The more limited the question, the easier it is to set up an experiment to answer it.

Questions are often formulated after a scientist makes some observation for which there is no published answer in scientific literature.

Forming a hypothesis: Once the question is formulated, the researcher makes an educated guess about the answer to the problem or question. This "best educated guess" is the hypothesis. Hypotheses tend to follow an "if/then" format. For example, if a student wanted to know whether exposure to music aided plant growth, her hypothesis could be "if music aids plant growth, then plants exposed to an hour of music per day will grow faster than plants that are not exposed to music."

Once a hypothesis has been formulated, it time to test it and observe and record data.

Conducting the test: The design of an experiment is important since it involves identifying a control, constants, independent variables, and dependent variables. A control is something we compare our results with at the end of the experiment. It is like a reference and is necessary to prove that the results occurred because of the changed conditions and would not have happened otherwise. Constants are the factors that are kept the same in an experiment to get reliable results.

Independent variables are factors we change in an experiment. Dependent variables are the changes that arise from the changes in the independent variable. It is important to bear in mind that there should be more constants than variables to obtain reproducible results in an experiment.

Observing and recording data: Observations and results of the experiment should be recorded. Drawings, graphs, and illustrations should be included to support the gathered information. Observations are objective, whereas analysis and interpretation are subjective. Reporting of the data should include specific information about how the measurements were calculated. For example, a graduated cylinder needs to be read with proper procedures. For beginning students, technique must be part of the instructional process so as to give validity to the data.

> **SKILL 26.3** Understands and instructs students in the safe and proper use of a variety of grade-appropriate tools, equipment, resources, technology and techniques to access, gather, store, retrieve, organize and analyze data.

Laboratory Activities

Many simple but profound experiments can be demonstrated with near-complete safety and little financial outlay; these should always be used because they invite students to engage and interact with the physical world. While some students learn solely from lectures, notes, and reading, most students benefit from personal interaction with scientific processes. According to the National Science Teachers Association, "Problem-solving abilities are refined in the context of laboratory inquiry. Laboratory activities develop a wide variety of investigative, organizational, creative, and communicative skills. The laboratory provides an optimal setting for motivating students while they experience what science is." Laboratory activities enhance student performance in the following domains:

- **Process skills:** Observing, measuring, manipulating physical objects

- **Analytical skills:** Reasoning, deduction, critical thinking

- **Communication skills:** Organizing information, writing

- **Conceptualization** of scientific phenomena

The National Science Teachers Association makes the following recommendations for the preschool and elementary level:

- Classes should include activity-based, hands-on experiences that allow students to discover and construct science concepts; and, after a concept is labeled and developed, activities should allow for application of the concept to the real lives of students. Teachers should also provide activities in which students manipulate one variable while holding others constant and establish experimental and control groups.

- Appropriate hands-on experiences must be provided for children with special needs who are unable to participate in classroom activities.

- A minimum of 60 percent of the science instruction time should be devoted to hands-on activities, in which children are manipulating, observing, exploring, and thinking about science using concrete materials.

- Evaluation and assessment of student performance must reflect hands-on experience.

- Hands-on activities should be revised and adapted to meet student needs and to enhance curricular goals and objectives.

- Enough supplies (e.g., magnets, cells, hand lenses) should be available to allow each child to have hands-on experiences.

- Reasonable and prudent safety precautions should always be taken when teachers and students are interacting with manipulative materials.

- Workspace should include flat, moveable desks or tables/chairs, equipment, and hands-on materials. Computers, software, and other electronic tools should be available.

- Parents, members of the community, and members of parent/teacher organizations should be enlisted to assist.

- There should not be more than twenty-four children assigned to each class.

> ## SKILL 26.4 Knows how to guide students in making systematic observations and measurements and posing questions to guide investigations.

See also Skill 26.2

Once a student has formed a hypothesis, it is important to ensure that the hypothesis

- includes two comparable groups (e.g., a treatment and a control group).

- has a specific and testable outcome.

- answers the initial question that was posed.

- can be tested within the resource and time constraints of the class.

- is scientifically founded and is not based on the student's opinion.

The teacher can advise the student if any of these points are not accounted for with the hypothesis. Similarly, once a student has begun experimentation advice can be provided on the refinement of the hypothesis based on the outcomes of experimentation. For example, a student may not find a difference in plant growth after plants are exposed to music for one hour versus none at all, but after increasing the time of music exposure to twelve hours there, in fact, may be a difference. The hypothesis would then be refined to distinguish the effect of time of music exposure.

Guidance on proper measurement techniques is also necessary to reduce the risk of error in an experiment. If a student is measuring a small plant's growth, it probably would not make sense to use a yardstick, and in the same line of thought, a scale would not be appropriate because length, not weight, is being measured. These considerations should be discussed prior to the start of an experiment so that an inappropriate instrument is not used and invalid data obtained.

Guidance on proper measurement techniques is also necessary to reduce the risk of error in an experiment.

Additionally, the timing of measurements (sampling) is important. If a student is tracking plant growth does she measure once a day, twice a day, once a week, twice a week? It is often optimal to advise students to decide data collection frequency based on what is feasible from a time and resource standpoint and also which method will yield the most informative data. The objective always is to answer the question that was posed at the beginning of the inquiry. If a student can answer his or question *with confidence* by measuring once a day, then that is the method that should be chosen. If the frequency of measurement is only possible once a week, then that method should be chosen. The reason for choosing a given measurement frequency should always be recorded and provided when communicating results. Ultimately, instructing students on these factors is important for yielding valid and reliable results.

SKILL 26.5 Knows how to promote the use of critical-thinking skills, logical reasoning and scientific problem solving to reach conclusions based on evidence.

Recording and Evaluating Data

Whenever scientists begin an experiment or project, they must decide which pieces of data they are going to collect. This data can be qualitative or quantitative. Scientists use a variety of methods to gather and analyze data. These methods include storing the data in a table or analyzing the data using a graph. Scientists also make notes of their observations (what they see, hear, smell, and so on), throughout the experiment.

After recording the data, it is compared with data from other groups. Graphs utilize numbers to demonstrate patterns. The patterns offer a visual representation, making it easier to draw conclusions. A conclusion is the judgment derived from the results. A conclusion should explain why the results of the experiment either prove or disprove the hypothesis.

Students should follow several steps in interpreting and evaluating data:

1. Apply critical analysis and thinking strategies, asking questions about the accuracy of the data and the procedures of the experiment and procurement of the data.

2. Determine the importance of information and its relevance to the essential question. Any experiment may produce a plethora of data, not all of which is necessary to consider when analyzing the hypothesis. The useful information must then be separated into component parts.

3. Make inferences, identify trends, and interpret data.

4. Determine the most appropriate method of communicating these inferences and conclusions to the intended audience.

Making inferences is usually done with statistical methods that are outside the scope of elementary education, but suffice it to say that quantitative data have to show mathematical significance in the proving or disproving of the hypothesis in addition to practical significance.

> ### SKILL 26.6 Knows how to teach students to develop, analyze, and evaluate different explanations for a given scientific result, including that repeated investigations may increase reliability.

When your students are interpreting their data and making inferences, it is important to guide them in considering the following:

- What are other explanations (that I didn't test) that could also explain this result?

- If I changed a parameter in my study (for instance, frequency of measurement), would the result be the same?

- How many times did I repeat the experiment? Is that enough to be able to draw this conclusion?

- Is there evidence from others' experiments that support what I'm claiming?

- Do my results violate any of nature's laws?

Students must be taught not to think that their results are infallible. No experiment is perfect, and every experiment has at least one limitation. Students must always consider alternate scenarios or conditions that could produce the same results. This is why repeated experiments are important to increase the confidence

> *Students must be taught not to think that their results are infallible.*

in a particular trend that is observed. Running an experiment once is never acceptable for professional scientists whose work is under intense scrutiny.

In the same line of thought, if a student has covered her bases, then it is important that she have confidence in her work and avoid doubting it if the proper controls were used in her experiment. Teaching students to have a healthy amount of doubt about their experiments is critical to exposing them to how science is done in real life.

> **SKILL 26.7** **Knows how to teach students to demonstrate an understanding of potential sources of error in inquiry-based investigation.**

See also Skill 25.5

Uncertainty is a factor in everyday life as well as in the experiments conducted in laboratories. In addition, potential sources of error exist with almost every experiment. Teachers and students should be aware of potential errors so they can minimize them during experimentation. Potential sources of error include

- human error (e.g., errors that occur as a result of inexperience).

- use of the wrong chemical.

- instrumental limitations (for instance, a digital balance rounds to three. decimal places, which may not suffice for the measurement).

- external influences (e.g., impure chemical used).

- an unrepresentative sample.

The question stage of scientific inquiry involves repetition. By repeating the experiment you can discover whether or not you have reproducibility. If the results are reproducible, the hypothesis is valid. If the results are not reproducible, one has more questions to ask.

Error Analysis

All scientific reports must contain a section detailing error analysis that serves to show the deviation of measured values from their expected values. One can calculate the percent error observed in an experiment in the following manner:

$$\text{Percent Error} = 100 \times \frac{(\text{Observed} - \text{Expected})}{\text{Expected}}$$

Observed = Average of experimental values observed

Expected = The value that was expected based on the hypothesis

Sources of error should always be specified so that they can be corrected or minimized in future experiments. Additionally, when analyzing data and forming inferences, students should consider how sources of error affect the results.

> **SKILL 26.8** **Knows how to teach students to demonstrate an understanding of how to communicate and defend the results of an inquiry-based investigation.**

See also Skill 25.6

Conclusions must be communicated by clearly describing the information using accurate data, visual presentations, and other appropriate media such as a PowerPoint presentation. Examples of visual presentations are graphs (bar/line/pie), tables and charts, diagrams, and artwork.

Lab Report

Normally, knowledge is integrated in the form of a lab report. A report has many sections. It should include a specific title that tells exactly what is being studied. The abstract is a summary of the report written at the beginning of the paper. The purpose should always be defined to state the problem. The purpose should include the hypothesis (educated guess) of what is expected from the outcome of the experiment. The entire experiment should relate to this problem. It is important to describe exactly what was done to prove or disprove a hypothesis.

Again, a control is necessary to prove that the results occurred from the changed conditions and would not have happened normally. Only one variable should be manipulated at a time. Observations and results of the experiment, including all results from data, should be recorded. Drawings, graphs, and illustrations should be included to support information. Observations are objective, whereas analysis and interpretation are subjective. A conclusion should explain why the results of the experiment either proved or disproved the hypothesis.

Guiding students to have intangibles

You can prepare your students for communicating their scientific results by

- instructing them to practice speaking in front of their family and classmates.

- telling them to think ahead and prepare for the questions they think they will receive.

- instructing them to know their experiment inside and out.

- encouraging them to prepare with their friends and classmates.

- encouraging them to use different forms of media (physical models, digital, visual cues, and so on) to showcase their work and to appeal to people's varying modes of learning.

- instructing them to construct a short explanation of their work that anyone could understand.

- encouraging them to just have confidence and enjoy it.

Concise design of an experiment is the most important defense when presenting experimental results. After considering sources of error and/or problems encountered during the experiment, the researcher should be confident in his or her results. Teachers should aid students in experimental design so that proper sampling, constants, variables, documentation, and materials are all built in to the experimental design.

Beyond the science, people respond viscerally to presentations in which the speaker is passionate and shows command and conviction with whatever he or she is presenting. Engaging students at an early age with science activities that have both the substantive technical side and the creative freedom of presentation is a great way to build their self-confidence.

SKILL 26.9 Understands principles of scientific ethics.

ETHICS: a system of public, general rules for guiding human conduct

To understand scientific ethics, we need to have a clear understanding of ethics in general. ETHICS is defined as a system of public, general rules for guiding human conduct. The rules are general because they are supposed to apply to all people at all times, and they are public because they are not secret codes or practices.

Philosophers have proposed a number of moral theories to justify moral rules, including the following:

- **Utilitarianism:** A theory of ethics that prescribes the quantitative maximization of good consequences for a population. Utilitarianism is a form of consequentialism. This theory was proposed by Mozi, a Chinese philosopher who lived from 471–381 BCE.

- **Kantianism:** A theory proposed by Immanuel Kant, a German philosopher who lived from 1724–1804, which ascribes intrinsic value to rational beings and is the philosophical foundation of contemporary human rights.

- **Social contract theory:** A view of the ancient Greeks that states that a person's moral and/or political obligations depend on a contract or agreement between people to form society.

The guiding principles of scientific ethics include the following:

1. **Scientific honesty:** Not to commit fraud; not to fabricate or misinterpret data for personal gain

2. **Caution:** To avoid errors and sloppiness in all scientific experimentation

3. **Credit:** To give credit where credit is due and not to copy

4. **Responsibility:** To report only reliable information to the public and not to mislead in the name of science

5. **Freedom:** To embrace the freedom to criticize old ideas, to question new research, and to conduct research

Many principles could be added to this list. Although these principles seem straightforward, it is difficult to put them into practice since they can be interpreted in many ways. Nevertheless, it is not an excuse for scientists to overlook these ethical principles.

Scientists are expected to show good conduct in their scientific pursuits. Conduct here refers to all aspects of scientific activity including experimentation, testing, education, data evaluation, data analysis, data storage, peer review, government funding, staff, and so on. At no point should the integrity at any of these stages be compromised, particularly because so much of scientific research is publicly funded.

> **SKILL 26.10** Understands the roles that logical reasoning, verifiable evidence, prediction and peer review play in the process of generating and evaluating scientific knowledge.

Science is tentative. By definition, it is about humans searching for information by making educated guesses. It must be replicable. Another scientist must be able to achieve the same results under the same conditions at a later time. The term empirical means that a phenomenon must be assessed through tests and observations. Science changes over time. Science is limited by available technology. An example of how science evolves is the relationship of the discovery of the cell and the invention of the microscope. As our technology improves, more hypotheses will become theories and possibly laws. Science is also limited by the data that can

Science is tentative. By definition, it is about humans searching for information by making educated guesses.

be collected. Data may be interpreted differently on different occasions. The limitations of science cause explanations to be changed as new technologies emerge. New technologies gather previously unavailable data and enable us to build on current theories with new information.

The Nature of Science

The nature of science consists of the following:

1. **The scientific worldview:** It is possible to understand this highly organized world and its complexities with the help of the latest technology. Scientific ideas are subject to change. After repeated experiments, a theory is established, but this theory can be changed or supported in the future. Only laws that occur naturally do not change. Scientific knowledge may not be discarded but can be modified (for instance, Albert Einstein didn't discard Newtonian principles but modified them in his theory of relativity). Also, science can't answer all of our questions. We can't find answers to questions related to our beliefs, moral values, and norms.

2. **Scientific inquiry:** Scientific inquiry starts with a simple question. This simple question leads to information gathering and an educated guess otherwise known as a hypothesis. To prove the hypothesis, an experiment has to be conducted, which yields data and the conclusion. All experiments must be repeated at least twice to get reliable results. Thus, scientific inquiry leads to new knowledge or the verification of established theories. Science requires proof or evidence. Science depends on accuracy, not on bias or prejudice. In science, there is no place for preconceived ideas or premeditated results. By using their senses and modern technology, scientists get reliable information. Science is a combination of logic and imagination. A scientist needs to think and imagine and be able to reason.

3. **Scientific enterprise:** Science is a complex activity involving various people and places. A scientist may work alone or in a laboratory, in a classroom, or almost anywhere. Most of the time, it is a group activity requiring the social skills of cooperation, communication of results or findings, consultations, and discussions. Science demands a high degree of communication to governments, funding authorities, and the public. Science explains, reasons, and predicts. These three actions are interwoven and inseparable. While reasoning is absolutely important for science, there should be no bias or prejudice. Science is not authoritarian because it has been shown that scientific authority can be wrong. No one can determine or make decisions for others on any issue.

Science is a process of checks and balances. It is expected that scientific findings will be challenged, and in many cases retested through the process of peer review, in which scientists evaluate and critique another scientist's (or group of scientists') work and decide whether it is fit to be published publicly. Peer review is expected to be completely objective.

Often, one experiment will be the beginning point for another. While bias does exist, the use of controlled experiments and an awareness on the role of the scientist can go far to ensure a sound experiment. Even if the science is well done, it may still be questioned. It is through this continual search that hypotheses develop into theories and sometimes become laws. A scientific theory is an explanation of a set of related observations based on a proven hypothesis. A scientific law usually lasts longer than a scientific theory and has more experimental data to support it. It is also through this search that new information is discovered.

> ### SKILL 26.11
> **Understands the historical development of science** (e.g., cell theory, plate tectonics, laws of motion, universal gravity) **and technology and the contributions that diverse cultures and individuals of both genders have made to scientific and technological knowledge.**

Overview of History of Science

Andreas Vesalius (1514–1564) was a Belgian anatomist and physician whose dissections of the human body and descriptions of his findings helped to correct the misconceptions of science.

Anton van Leeuwenhoek is known as the father of microscopy. In the 1650s, Leeuwenhoek began making tiny lenses that gave magnifications up to 300x. He was the first to see and describe bacteria, yeast, and the microscopic life found in water. Anton van Leeuwenhoek is known as the father of microscopy. Over the years, light microscopes have advanced to produce greater clarity and magnification. The scanning electron microscope (SEM) was developed in the 1950s. Instead of light, a beam of electrons passes through the specimen. Scanning electron microscopes have a resolution about one thousand times greater than light microscopes. The disadvantage of the SEM is that the chemical and physical methods used to prepare the sample results in the death of the specimen.

Robert Hooke (1635–1703) was a renowned inventor, natural philosopher, astronomer, experimenter, and cell biologist. He is remembered mainly for Hooke's law, an equation describing elasticity. He devised the compound microscope and illumination system. With it he observed organisms as diverse as insects, sponges, bryozoans, foraminifera, as well as bird feathers.

Carl Von Linnaeus (1707–1778), a Swedish botanist, physician, and zoologist, is well known for his contributions in ecology and taxonomy. Linnaeus is famous for his binomial system of nomenclature in which each living organism has two names, a genus and a species name.

In the late 1800s, Louis Pasteur discovered the role of microorganisms in the cause of disease, invented the process that came to be called pasteurization, and created the rabies vaccine. Robert Koch took Pasteur's observations one step further by formulating the hypothesis that specific diseases are caused by specific pathogens. Koch's postulates are still used as guidelines in the field of microbiology. They state that the same pathogen must be found in every diseased person; that the pathogen must be isolated and grown in culture; that the disease must be induced in experimental animals from the culture; and that the same pathogen must be isolated from the experimental animal.

> In the late 1800s, Louis Pasteur discovered the role of microorganisms in the cause of disease, invented the process that came to be called pasteurization, and created the rabies vaccine.

Matthias Schleiden, a German botanist, is famous for his cell theory. He observed plant cells microscopically and concluded that the cell is the common structural unit of all plants. He proposed the cell theory along with Theodor Schwann, a zoologist, who observed cells in animals.

In the twentieth century, the rediscovery of Gregor Mendel's work led to the rapid development of genetics. In the 1950s, James Watson and Francis Crick discovered that the structure of a DNA molecule is a double helix building off the work of female scientist Rosalind Franklin. The discovery of this structure made it possible to explain DNA's ability to replicate and to control the synthesis of proteins. Following the cracking of the genetic code, biology has largely split between organismal biology (ecology, ethology, systematics, paleontology, evolutionary biology, developmental biology, and other disciplines that deal with whole organisms or groups of organisms) and the disciplines related to molecular biology (cell biology, biophysics, biochemistry, neuroscience, immunology, and many other overlapping subjects).

Other Notable Developments in Science

- Sir Isaac Newton described the laws of motion mathematically in the late seventeenth century.

- The plate tectonics theory was introduced in the twentieth century and describes the movement of plates in the Earth's lithosphere.

- Charles Darwin published his work on the theory of evolution in the nineteenth century, introducing the concept of natural selection and its effect on biological evolution.

Diverse Contributors

It's important to teach students that individuals from many cultures have contributed to scientific advancement over time, particularly women and under-represented minority groups that were often marginalized. Inventors like ex-slave Lewis Latimer (invented the carbon light bulb filament), Hedy Lamarr (created a frequency hopping system in radio transmissions), Marie Curie (the first female Nobel double Laureate in Physics and Chemistry), George Washington Carver (improved farming through crop rotation and nitrogen restoration), and others have contributed greatly to modern science and the world we live in now. Anyone can and should be empowered to do science if they desire.

COMPETENCY 27
IMPACT ON SCIENCE

> **SKILL 27.1** Understands that decisions about the use of science are based on factors such as ethical standards, economics, and personal and societal needs.

The influence of social and cultural factors on science can be profound. Some early societies had trouble accepting science, especially when the science exposed some cultural beliefs as myths. This created a dilemma concerning whether or not to accept the facts provided by scientific investigations or to cling to cultural norms. This struggle went on for centuries. It took a long time for societies to accept scientific facts and to leave some of the cultural beliefs behind or modify them.

It can be extremely difficult for some societies to come to terms with technological advances. Even today, some cultures are not using modern technology, but, at the same time, they are using technology in principle, e.g., using simple machines for farming rather than complex machines like tractors.

Other cultures have so readily adapted to technology that lives are intertwined with it to the extent that individuals utilize the computer, television, microwave, dishwasher, washing machine, cell phone, and so on, on a daily basis. It is surprising to realize that we began with no technology and now are surrounded by it.

The religious beliefs and institutions of a culture can greatly influence scientific research and technological innovation. Political factors affect scientific advancement as well, especially in cultures that partially support scientific research with public money. Warfare has traditionally been a strong driver of technological advancement as cultures strive to outpace their neighbors with better weapons and defenses. Technologies developed for military purposes often find their way into the mainstream. Significant advances in flight technology, for example, were made during the two world wars.

Many cultures have come to value innovation and welcome new products as well as improvements to older products. The desire to always be advancing and obtaining the latest, newest technology creates economic incentives for innovation.

> **SKILL 27.2** Applies scientific principles to analyze the advantages of, disadvantages of or alternatives to a given decision or course of action.

See Skills 24.5, 25.2, 25.4, 25.6, and 25.9

> **SKILL 27.3** Applies scientific principles and processes to analyze factors that influence personal choices concerning fitness and health, including physiological and psychological effects and risks associated with the use of substances and substance abuse.

While genetics plays an important role in health, human behaviors can greatly affect short- and long-term health both positively and negatively. Behaviors that negatively affect health include smoking, excessive alcohol consumption, substance abuse, and poor eating habits. Behaviors that positively affect health include good nutrition and regular exercise.

Smoking negatively affects health in many ways: It decreases lung capacity, causes persistent coughing, and limits one's ability to engage in strenuous physical activity. In addition, the long-term effects are even more damaging. Long-term smoking can cause lung cancer, heart disease, and emphysema (a lung disease).

Alcohol is the most abused legal drug. Excessive alcohol consumption has both short- and long-term negative effects. Drunkenness can lead to reckless behavior and distorted judgment that can cause injury or death. Extreme alcohol abuse can cause alcohol poisoning which can result in immediate death. Long-term alcohol abuse is also extremely hazardous. The potential effects of long-term alcohol abuse include liver cirrhosis, heart problems, high blood pressure, stomach ulcers, and cancer.

The abuse of illegal substances can also negatively affect a person's health. Commonly abused drugs include cocaine, heroin, opiates, and methamphetamines, and, in some states, marijuana. Drug abuse can cause immediate death or injury, and long-term drug abuse can cause many physical and psychological health problems.

A healthy diet and regular exercise are the cornerstones of a healthy lifestyle. A diet rich in whole grains, fruits, vegetables, polyunsaturated fats, lean protein, and low in saturated fat and sugar can have a positive effect on one's overall health. Such diets can reduce cholesterol levels, lower blood pressure, and help manage body weight. Conversely, diets high in saturated fat and sugar can contribute to weight gain, heart disease, strokes, and cancer.

Finally, regular exercise has both short- and long-term health benefits. Exercise increases physical fitness and improves energy levels, overall body function, and mental well-being. Over the long term, exercise helps protect against chronic diseases, maintains healthy bones and muscles, helps one maintain a healthy body weight, and strengthens the body's immune system.

SKILL 27.4 Understands concepts, characteristics and issues related to changes in populations and human population growth.

A population is a group of individuals of one species that live in the same general area. Many factors can affect a population size and growth rate. Population size may depend on the total amount of life a habitat can support, or the carrying capacity of the environment. Once the habitat runs out of food, water, shelter, or space, the carrying capacity decreases and then stabilizes.

Limiting factors can affect population growth. As a population increases, the competition for resources is more intense, and the growth rate declines. This is a density-dependent growth factor. The carrying capacity can be determined by the density-dependent factor. Density-independent factors such as weather and climate affect the individuals in a population regardless of population size. Temperatures that are too hot or too cold may kill many individuals in a population that has not reached its carrying capacity.

The human population increased slowly until 1650. Since 1650, it has grown almost exponentially, reaching the current population of over 6 billion.

The human population increased slowly until 1650. Since 1650, it has grown almost exponentially, reaching the current population of over 6 billion. Factors that have led to this increased growth rate include improved nutrition, sanitation, and health care. In addition, advances in technology, agriculture, and scientific knowledge have made the use of resources more efficient and increased their availability.

While the Earth's ultimate carrying capacity for humans is uncertain, some factors that may limit growth are the availability of food, water, space, and fossil fuels. There is a finite amount of land on Earth available for food production. In addition, providing clean, potable water for a growing human population is a real concern. Finally, fossil fuels, important energy sources for human technology, are scarce. The inevitable shortage of energy in the Earth's future will require the development of alternative energy sources to maintain or increase human population growth.

SKILL 27.5 **Identifies and understands the types and uses of natural resources and the effects of human consumption on the renewal and depletion of resources.**

Water

Humans have a tremendous impact on the world's natural resources. The world's natural water supplies are affected by human use. Waterways are major sources of recreation and freight transportation. Oil and waste from boats and cargo ships pollute the aquatic environment, contaminating plant and animal life. To obtain drinking water, contaminants such as parasites, pollutants, and bacteria must be removed from raw water through a purification process involving various screening, conditioning, and chlorination steps.

Most uses of water, such as drinking water and crop irrigation, require fresh water. Only 2.5 percent of the water on Earth is fresh water, and more than two-thirds of this fresh water is frozen in glaciers and polar ice caps. Consequently, in many parts of the world, water use greatly exceeds supply. This problem is expected to increase in the future.

Only 2.5 percent of the water on Earth is fresh water, and more than two-thirds of this fresh water is frozen in glaciers and polar ice caps. Consequently, in many parts of the world, water use greatly exceeds supply.

Plants

Plant resources also make up a large part of the world's natural resources. Plant resources are renewable and can be regrown and restocked. Plant resources can be used by humans to make clothing, buildings, and medicines, and can also be directly consumed.

Forestry is the study and management of growing forests. This industry provides the wood that is essential for use as construction timber or paper. Cotton is a common plant grown on farms in the southern United States. Cotton is used to make fabric for clothing, sheets, furniture, etc. Another example of a plant resource that is not directly consumed is straw, which is harvested for use in plant growth and farm animal care.

The list of plants grown to provide food for the people of the world is extensive. Major crops include corn, potatoes, wheat, sugar, barley, peas, beans, beets, flax, lentils, sunflowers, soybeans, canola, and rice. These crops can have alternate uses as well. For example, corn is used to manufacture cornstarch, ethanol fuel, high fructose corn syrup, ink, biodegradable plastics, chemicals used in cosmetics and pharmaceuticals, adhesives, and paper products.

Nonrenewable Resources

Other resources used by humans are known as nonrenewable resources. Such resources, including fossil fuels, cannot be regenerated and do not naturally re-form at a rate that could sustain human use. Nonrenewable resources are therefore depleted and not restored. Presently, nonrenewable resources provide the main source of energy for humans.

Common fossil fuels used by humans are coal, petroleum, and natural gas, which all form from the remains of dead plants and animals through natural processes after millions of years. Because of their high carbon content, when burned these substances generate high amounts of energy as well as carbon dioxide, which is released back into the atmosphere and increases global warming.

To create electricity, energy from the burning of fossil fuels is harnessed to power a rotary engine called a turbine. Implementation of the use of fossil fuels as an energy source provided for large-scale industrial development.

Minerals

Mineral resources are concentrations of naturally occurring inorganic elements and compounds located in the Earth's crust that are extracted through mining for human use. Minerals have a definite chemical composition and are stable over a range of temperatures and pressures. Construction and manufacturing rely heavily on metals and industrial mineral resources. These metals may include iron, bronze, lead, zinc, nickel, copper, and tin. Other industrial minerals are divided into two categories: bulk rocks and ore minerals. Bulk rocks, including limestone, clay, shale, and sandstone, are used as aggregate in construction, in ceramics, or in concrete. Common ore minerals include calcite, barite, and gypsum. Energy from some minerals can be utilized to produce electricity, fuel, and industrial materials. Mineral resources are also used as fertilizers and pesticides in the industrial context.

Deforestation

Deforestation because of urban development has resulted in the extinction or relocation of several species of plants and animals. Animals have been forced to leave their forest homes or perish amid the destruction. The number of plant and animal species that have become extinct due to deforestation is unknown. Scientists have only identified a fraction of the species on Earth. If the destruction of natural resources continues, there may be no plants or animals left to success-fully reproduce in the wild.

Energy Crisis

The current energy crisis is largely centered on the uncertain future of fossil fuels. The supplies of fossil fuels are limited and rapidly declining. Also, most oil now comes from a politically volatile area of the world. Finally, continuing to produce energy from fossils fuels is unwise given the disruption to the environment necessary to harvest them and the byproducts of their combustion, which cause pollution.

It is important to recognize that a real energy crisis has vast economic implications. Oil, currently the most important fossil fuel, is needed for heating, electricity, and as a raw material for the manufacture of many items, particularly plastics. The gasoline made from oil is important for transporting people and goods, including food and other items necessary for life. A disruption in the oil supply often causes rising prices in all sectors and may eventually trigger recession. Alternative, sustainable energy sources must be found for both economic and ecological reasons.

SKILL 27.6 Understands the role science and scientists can play in helping resolve personal, societal and global challenges.

As the detrimental effects of pollution have received increasing attention, a number of legislative initiatives have been undertaken to control it and mitigate its effect. The U.S. Environmental Protection Agency (EPA) was established in 1970 to protect human health by reducing damage to the environment. The EPA continues to define and enforce standards for pollution control. The Clean Air Act (1963) and Clean Water Act (1977) were two major milestones in the legal battle against pollutants.

Various technologies have been invented to reduce the number of contaminants released into the environment. The devices typically use filters to trap the pollutants or rely on chemical reactions to neutralize them. Examples of the former include electrostatic air cleaners and fabric air filters. Examples of the latter include catalytic converters and scrubbers. Materials such as activated charcoal have properties of both types, since they trap and partially neutralize many contaminants, but may still require the use of further chemical treatment.

Another key area in which technological advances may help control pollution is the search for alternative fuels. Possible alternative energy sources include biodiesel, nuclear power, biomethanol, hydrogen fuel, and fuel cells. Increasing the efficiency of solar fuel cells, hydroelectricity, and wind energy may also help reduce the dependence on fossil fuels.

Also, there are recycling programs for a variety of materials. Recycling is the reprocessing of materials into new products. Recycling prevents many materials from becoming waste and also avoids the need to harvest new materials. For many materials, recycling requires less energy than virgin production. The most commonly recycled materials are glass, paper, aluminum, asphalt, steel, textiles, and plastic. There are two types of recycling: pre-consumer and post-consumer. Post-consumer recycling is the recycling of materials from residential and individual/consumer waste.

COMPETENCY 28
CONCEPTS AND PROCESSES

> **SKILL 28.1** Understands how a unifying, explanatory framework across the science disciplines is provided by the concepts and processes of systems, order and organization; evidence, models and explanation; change, constancy and measurements; and form and function.

See also Skills 28.6, 28.7, and 28.8

Systems, Order, and Organization

Because the natural world is so complex, the study of science involves organizing items into smaller groups, called systems, based on interactions or interdependence. Examples of such organization are the periodic table of the elements and the five-kingdom classification scheme for living organisms. Examples of systems are the solar system, cardiovascular system, Newton's laws of force and motion, and the laws of conservation.

Order refers to the behavior and measurability of organisms and events in nature. The arrangement of planets in the solar system and the life cycle of bacterial cells are examples of order.

Evidence, Models, and Explanation

Scientists use evidence and models to form explanations of natural events. Models are miniaturized representations of a larger event or system. Evidence is anything that furnishes proof.

Evolution and Equilibrium

Evolution is the process of change over a period of time. While biological evolution is the most common example, one can also classify technological advancement, changes in the universe, and changes in the environment as evolution.

EQUILIBRIUM is the state of balance between opposing forces of change. Homeostasis and ecological balance are examples of equilibrium.

> **EQUILIBRIUM:** the state of balance between opposing forces of change

Demonstrates an understanding of how patterns in observations and data can be used to make explanations and predictions.

See Skills 26.2, 26.5, and 26.6

Analyzes interactions and interrelationships between systems and subsystems.

Groups of related organs are called organ systems. Organ systems consist of organs working together to perform a common function. The commonly recognized organ systems of animals include the reproductive system, the nervous system, the circulatory system, the respiratory system, the lymphatic system (immune system), the endocrine system, the urinary system, the muscular system, the digestive system, the integumentary system, and the skeletal system. Organ systems are interconnected; a single system rarely works alone to complete a task.

One obvious example of the interconnectedness of organ systems is the relationship between the circulatory and respiratory systems. As blood circulates through the organs of the circulatory systems, it is reoxygenated in the lungs of the respiratory system. Another example is the influence of the endocrine system on other organ systems. Hormones released by the endocrine system greatly influence processes of many organ systems, including the nervous and reproductive systems.

The body's response to infection is a coordinated effort of the lymphatic (immune system) and circulatory systems. The lymphatic system produces specialized immune cells, filters out disease-causing organisms, and removes fluid waste from in and around tissue. The lymphatic system utilizes capillary structures of the circulatory system and interacts with blood cells in a coordinated response to infection.

The pituitary gland and hypothalamus respond to varying levels of hormones by increasing or decreasing production and secretion. High levels of a hormone cause down-regulation of the production and secretion pathways, whereas low levels of a hormone cause up-regulation of the production and secretion pathways.

"Fight or flight" refers to the human body's response to stress or danger. As a response to an environmental stressor, the hypothalamus releases a hormone that acts on the pituitary gland, triggering the release of another hormone, adreno-corticotropin (ACTH), into the bloodstream. ACTH then signals the adrenal glands to release the hormones cortisol, epinephrine, and norepinephrine. These three hormones act to prepare the body to respond to a threat by increasing blood pressure and heart rate, speeding reaction time, diverting blood to the muscles, and releasing glucose for use by the muscles and brain. The stress-response hormones also down-regulate growth, development, and other nonessential functions. Cortisol completes the "fight or flight" feedback loop by acting on the hypothalamus to stop hormonal production after the threat has passed.

Finally, the muscular and skeletal systems are closely related. Skeletal muscles attach to the bones of the skeleton and drive movement of the body.

SKILL 28.4 Applies unifying concepts to explore similarities in a variety of natural phenomena.

See Skill 28.1

SKILL 28.5 Understands how properties and patterns of systems can be described in terms of space, time, energy and matter.

Most scientific knowledge derives from observation of or experimentation upon systems in transition through space, time, energy state, or some combination of these. A solid understanding of space, time, and energy transitions is thus fundamental to all science learning. Whereas the natural world is complex and dynamic, scientific experimentation generally seeks to simplify systems so that only a single transition occurs. For example, when space and time can be controlled experimentally, the scientist can focus on the transition of energy in the system. This methodology seeks to limit the variables in an experimental system to one or a very few. Later experimentation builds upon understanding by focusing on another variable. Gradually, comprehensive knowledge of a complex system emerges, and as understanding increases the experimental phase mimics ever more closely the natural world. For the most part, educational science activities must necessarily remain fairly simple. For example, most chemistry demonstrations or experimentations focus on the transformation of energy or matter over a very short period of time.

The most common tool used in science education to explain system properties is a simple graph. Often, the *x*-axis is a plot of time in a common increment—seconds, days, or years—and the *y*-axis is a plot of the variable being examined. For example, fungal culture populations can be estimated by plotting observation points of culture area on the *y*-axis and hours on the *x*-axis, typically yielding a sigmoid population curve given sufficient observation points. Numerous other types of graphs are useful depending upon the system. If audiovisual equipment is readily available, another useful technique to convey the magnitude of change over time involves time-lapse photography of processes.

Most well understood scientific processes demonstrate not only predictable energy or matter transformations over time and through space but also patterns of behavior. Patterns are useful inasmuch as they imply a likely result in a similar paradigm and can thus be used as the basis of a hypothesis. Patterns must not be mistaken for conclusive fact and should not be definitively applied to similar systems unless experimentation demonstrates their broader utility. A thorough understanding of the properties and patterns of scientific systems is critical in any endeavor to instruct others in those systems.

SKILL 28.6 Understands how change and constancy occur in systems.

Constancy and change describe the observable properties of natural organisms and events. Scientists use different systems of measurement to observe change and constancy. For example, the freezing and melting points of given substances and the speed of sound are constant under constant conditions. Growth, decay, and erosion are all examples of natural change.

SKILL 28.7 Understands the complementary nature of form and function in a given system.

Form and function are closely related properties of organisms and systems. The function of an object usually dictates its form, and the form of an object usually facilitates its function.

For example, the form of the heart (e.g., muscle and valves) allows it to perform its function of circulating blood through the body.

For information about the form and function of the human heart and its role in the circulatory system, see Skill 34.5.

Understands how models are used to represent the natural world and how to evaluate the strengths and limitations of a variety of scientific models *(e.g., physical, conceptual, mathematical)*.

The model is a basic element of the scientific method. Many things in science are studied with models. A MODEL is any simplification or substitute for what one is studying, understanding, or predicting. We encounter models at every step of our daily living. The periodic table of the elements is a model chemists use for predicting the properties of the elements. Physicists use Newton's laws to predict how objects will interact, such as planets and spaceships. In geology, the continental drift model suggests the past positions of continents. Samples, ideas, and methods are all examples of models.

> **MODEL:** any simplification or substitute for what one is studying, understanding, or predicting

Types of Models

Types of scientific models include:

- **Scale models:** Some models are basically downsized or enlarged copies of their target systems like the models of protein and DNA.

- **Idealized models:** An idealization is a deliberate simplification of something complicated with the objective of making it easier to understand. Some examples are frictionless planes, point masses, and isolated systems.

- **Analogical models:** Standard examples of analogical models are the billiard model of a gas, the computer model of the mind, and the liquid-drop model of the nucleus.

- **Phenomenological models:** These are usually defined as models that are independent of theories.

- **Data models:** These are corrected, rectified, regimented, and in many instances, idealized versions of the data we gain from immediate observation (raw data).

- **Theory models:** Any structure is a model if it represents an idea, or theory. An example of this is a flow chart, which summarizes a set of ideas.

Uses of Models

Models are crucial for understanding the structure and function of processes in science. They help us visualize the organs or systems they represent, like putting a face to a person. Models are also useful for predicting and foreseeing future events like hurricanes.

Limitations of Models

Although models are very useful, they can never replace the real thing. Caution must be exercised before presenting models to a class, as they may not be accurate. It is the responsibility of the educator to analyze a model critically for proportions, content value, and other important data. One must also be aware of the style of representation used by the creator of the model, which varies from person to person.

COMPETENCY 29
THEORY AND PRACTICE OF SCIENCE TEACHING

| SKILL 29.1 | Understands how developmental characteristics, prior knowledge and experience and students' attitudes influence science learning. |

See also Skills 26.1 and 29.8

Teachers must acknowledge the different stages of students' development and implement various practices into teaching and classroom management. Teachers must understand that some techniques will only be effective at certain stages during childhood. For example, if children have reached the stage in which they have mastered conflict resolution (later adolescence), they should be provided opportunities to engage in scientific debate regarding a scientific topic (e.g., the human genome project). Other examples might include experiments such as the following.

Early-Childhood Students

- **Stages of a butterfly:** Students can observe the process by which a caterpillar changes into a butterfly (larva, pupa, cocoon, butterfly).

Elementary Students

- **Early study of the microscope:** This can be done using magnifying glasses, or hand lenses, and a class review or group study of an actual microscope.

- **Study of rocks and porosity:** Students can test the porosity of limestone, shale, slate, sandstone, etc., using droppers filled with water.

- **Study of animals and their habitats:** Students can experience the importance of animal habitats by building dioramas or personal habitats to which they can better relate.

Middle-School Students

- **Study of energy, oil, fossil fuels, etc.:** Teachers can incorporate the study of oil, fossils, and energy into a unit including the study of how fossil fuels are formed; students can build their own models of drilling rigs and other oil-related tools.

- **Study of matter, energy, protons, neutrons, electrons:** Projects demonstrating static electricity are appropriate for middle-school-age students (balloon/hair experiment).

- This is the appropriate time for an in-depth study of microscope parts and terms, and testing of microscope knowledge. Students should learn to master the microscope not only in group projects but in individual study as well; students should be allowed to view multiple slides under the scope and even develop their own slides with guidance from the instructor.

SKILL 29.2 Selects and adapts science curricula, content, instructional materials, collaborations, vocabulary and activities to meet the levels of interest, knowledge, and understanding as well as the abilities, experiences and needs of all students, including English-language learners.

See also Skill 29.7

It is critical that scientific curricula be selected for the intended audience. Just as one would not use a college-level textbook in preschool education, one should not present science topics beyond the comprehension or preparation level of students. Nearly all educational institutions offer suitable textbooks and materials for science courses, but students approach the materials with disparate backgrounds and knowledge. The educator must therefore adapt the curricula to a broad audience and attempt to meet the needs of all students.

When it becomes apparent that students are struggling with a particular topic, the teacher should take the time to review underlying principles. Generally, it is insufficient to present material solely based on educational grade level. Teachers should use a variety of teaching techniques and methodologies to fully engage students' interest, increase their knowledge, challenge their understanding, and expand their scientific thinking abilities. Activities are particularly useful in science, as simple experimentation or observation can be quite engrossing and instructive.

Teachers should exercise particular care in helping students develop a thorough understanding of scientific language and process. Words with specific scientific meanings must be carefully defined so students do not mistakenly associate them broader, popular meanings. For example, in biology the word *gene* has a specific and fairly exact meaning whereas in the popular media the word has very little meaning beyond indicating an association with inherited traits. Similarly, scientific processes may be foreign to many students, who may lack background training in rigorous experimentation to establish support for hypotheses. Special

Words with specific scientific meanings must be carefully defined so students do not mistakenly associate them broader, popular meanings.

care should be taken in the basic instruction of the scientific method. Again, simple activities in scientific experimentation are helpful and can maintain student interest.

> **SKILL 29.3** Understands how to use situations from students' daily lives to develop instructional materials that investigate how science can be used to make informed decisions.

See Skills 29.1 and 29.5

> **SKILL 29.4** Understands common misconceptions in science and has effective ways to address those misconceptions.

Few things are more damaging to longitudinal student progress than the classroom presentation of erroneous information as fact. Most people who have misconceptions are not aware that their beliefs are erroneous. It is critical that instructors understand common misconceptions in science so they can not only avoid them but also correct them. Perhaps the most common misconceptions derive from imprecise language: Scientific terminology is often not well understood by students. Also, media reporting about science (particularly on politically sensitive or popular science topics) is often inaccurate or speculative. Finally, generally held public opinions of scientific topics are often incorrect or only partially correct.

Instructors must use caution in using science vocabulary during instruction—precise definitions should be elucidated. Scientific theory and process should be presented apart from mass-media presentations, although popular scientific news stories can be used as a springboard to student involvement. Commonly held misconceptions should be directly addressed.

Commonly held misconceptions include the following:

- The average person uses only a small fraction of his or her brain.

- Hair and/or fingernails continue to grow for some time after death.

- Seasons are caused by the Earth's elliptical orbit (hence, its varying distance from the sun).

- Lemmings participate in planned mass suicide events (e.g., by running into the sea to drown).

- The daddy longlegs spider (or some other innocuous animal) is the most venomous animal in the world.

- Evolution explains the origin of life (the theory of evolution presupposes existing life).

- Humans evolved directly from chimpanzees.

- A given human-made object (often, the Great Wall of China) is visible from the moon.

- In toilets and sinks, water swirls downward in one direction in the Northern Hemisphere and in the other direction in the Southern Hemisphere.

> **SKILL 29.5** Understands developmentally appropriate design and implementation of hands-on learning experiences in science and selects effective, appropriate instructional practices, activities, technologies and materials to promote students' scientific knowledge, skills and inquiry processes.

See also Skill 26.1

In every educational setting, a variety of rules and regulations apply that must direct instructor behavior in practices and activities appropriate to the setting. Financial constraints will largely dictate technologies and materials available. Within this framework, instructors should endeavor to provide effective and appropriate educational activities to further students' scientific knowledge and stimulate their inquisitiveness about natural processes.

Many simple but profound experiments can be demonstrated with near complete safety and very little financial outlay; these should always be used as they invite students to engage and interact with the physical world. While some students learn solely from lectures, notes, and reading, most students benefit from personal interaction with scientific processes. For example, the classic states of matter can easily be demonstrated with balloons, wood or plastic blocks, and water. For more advanced lessons, non-Newtonian fluids can be safely and cheaply demonstrated with starch (e.g., cornstarch) and water mixtures. No amount of lecture or reading will ever engage a student's interest as much as a bowl of non-Newtonian fluid.

Various other inexpensive but instructive demonstrations are easy to arrange. Of course, the hands-on experiences must be age-appropriate and designed to conform to student needs. Safety equipment should always be used and instructors should use caution to protect students' clothing and other personal belongings.

> ## SKILL 29.6 Understands questioning strategies designed to elicit higher-level thinking and how to use them to move students from concrete to more abstract understanding.

See also Skill 26.1

Inquiry-based learning provides opportunities for students to experience and acquire thought processes that enable them to gather information about the world. This requires a higher level of interaction among the learner, the teacher, the area of study, the available resources, and the learning environment. Students become actively involved in the learning process as they do the following:

1. Act upon their curiosity and interests

2. Develop questions that are relevant

3. Think their way through controversies or dilemmas

4. Analyze problems

5. Develop, clarify, and test hypotheses

6. Draw conclusions

7. Find possible solutions

The most important element in inquiry-based learning is questioning. Students must ask relevant questions and develop ways to search for answers and generate explanations. Higher-order thinking is encouraged.

> ## SKILL 29.7 Understands the importance of planning activities that are inclusive and that accommodate the needs of all students.

Every student presents a unique educational need. Not all students learn at a similar rate in a given environment. Each student represents a unique fusion of educational needs and learning potential. The need to accommodate disparate student needs is critical to successful education. It is also often exceptionally challenging. Educational presentation often becomes entrenched in established methods that work fairly well most of the time for most students. This is unfortunate inasmuch as it suggests that established methodology is optimal, whereas some beneficial change can nearly always be implemented.

One of the most significant methods of improving educational presentation is the utilization of a variety of teaching methods. These methods allow students with a variety of learning styles to gain from the educational experience. One of the best teaching methods available is the use of activities that encourage direct student involvement. There is clearly a major role for lecture in the classroom, but there is also an obvious need for hands-on, project work to motivate students. Lecture itself can be delivered in a variety of ways to add and maintain interest. Some students respond well to relatively straightforward lecture while others respond to question-and-answer sessions, review sessions, object lessons, or other common types of presentation. Care should be taken to plan a variety of activities that include all students. Activities should also be planned in accordance with law and school policy.

While planning lectures and activities in advance is critical to success, plans should remain flexible enough to adapt to emerging classroom needs. In most structured learning environments, predefined (e.g., by standardized testing or policy) critical outcomes exist and the instruction supporting these outcomes must not be eliminated. Instead, the plan should adequately address these critical outcomes and simultaneously remain flexible in other areas addressing secondary or supplementary outcomes. In this way the plan is adaptable—content can either be added, expanded, eliminated, or reduced—and yet still addresses all areas supporting critical outcomes.

> *One of the most significant methods of improving educational presentation is the utilization of a variety of teaching methods. These methods allow students with a variety of learning styles to gain from the educational experience.*

SKILL 29.8 **Understands how to sequence learning activities in a way that enables students to build on their prior knowledge and that challenges them to expand their understanding of science.**

Science courses and principles should be taught using an ordered methodology that allows students to leverage existing knowledge. Concepts should be sequenced in a manner that allows prior material to support current and future materials. In most of the sciences and most science applications, a structured and sequenced approach is sensible and intuitive. Generally, science textbooks present an approach to science sequenced to allow basic principles to be taught first and advanced principles to be taught later. Even when curricula are oriented toward specific testable outcomes or objectives, the materials included should be sequenced to support educational progress. For example, in a biology course, basic atomic structure should be presented before molecular structure and bonding, which in turn should be presented before DNA manipulation within the cellular environment. This concept of sequential education is fundamental to modern instructional theory and is evident in progressively complex learning during grade advancement in school. It is also evident in higher education's extensive specification of prerequisites for advanced courses.

While there is no single best approach to material scheduling, some sequences are superior to others. The educator should strive to achieve an optimal sequence of presentation for the majority of students. The sequence must be appropriate for the available instructional hours and period. The sequence should also conform to policy guidelines and optimally align with the organization of textbooks and other course materials in use. The sequence may need to conform to mandated educational outcomes. Teachers can be flexible about spending more or less time on particular areas of difficulty or importance while retaining the basic sequence of presenting materials.

Teachers must ensure that students understand foundational principles before moving on to derived principles. When students have mastered principles it is time to move forward with the sequenced material to maintain a challenging education environment. The sequenced materials should not be pinned to a strict schedule but should be implemented flexibly to accommodate and challenge students.

COMPETENCY 30
SCIENCE ASSESSMENT

SKILL 30.1	Understands the relationships between a science curriculum, assessment and instruction and bases instruction on information gathered through assessment of students' strengths and needs.

See Skills 30.2 and 30.3

SKILL 30.2	Understands the importance of monitoring and assessing students' understanding of science concepts and skills on an ongoing basis, including how to use formal and informal assessments of student performance and how to use products *(e.g., projects, lab journals, rubrics, portfolios, student profiles, checklists)* to evaluate students' understanding of and participation in the inquiry process.

See also Skill 30.3

Some assessment methods can be both formal and informal. For example, observation may incorporate structured observation instruments as well as other informal observation procedures, including professional judgment. When evaluating a child's developmental level, a professional may use a formal adaptive rating scale as well as his or her professional judgment to assess the child's motivation and behavior.

Curriculum-Based Assessment

CURRICULUM-BASED ASSESSMENT: assessment of an individual's performance of objectives within a curriculum such as a reading, math, or science program

CURRICULUM-BASED ASSESSMENT is assessment of an individual's performance of objectives within a curriculum such as a reading, math, or science program. The individual's performance is measured in terms of which objectives were mastered. This type of testing can be verbal, written, or demonstration based. Its general structure may include such factors as amount of time to complete, amount to complete, and whether it was group or individual testing. The level of response may be multiple choice, essay, or recall of facts.

Momentary Time Sampling

MOMENTARY TIME SAMPLING is a technique used for measuring behaviors of a group of individuals or several behaviors of the same individual. Time samples are usually brief, and they can be conducted at fixed or variable intervals. The advantage of using variable intervals is increased reliability, as the students will not be able to predict when the time sample will be taken.

> **MOMENTARY TIME SAMPLING:** a technique used for measuring behaviors of a group of individuals or several behaviors of the same individual

Multiple Baseline Design

Multiple baseline design can be used to test the effectiveness of an intervention in the performance of a skill or to determine if the intervention accounted for the observed changes in a target behavior. First, the initial baseline data is collected, followed by the data during the intervention period. To get the second baseline, the intervention is stopped for a period of time and data is collected again. The intervention is then restarted or reapplied, and data collected on the target behavior.

An example of a multiple baseline design might be ignoring a child who calls out in class without raising her hand. Initially, the baseline might involve counting the number of times the child calls out before getting a response (the intervention). During the time the teacher ignores the child's call-outs, data is collected. For the second baseline, the teacher would resume responding to the child's call-outs in the way she did before ignoring the child. The child's call-outs would probably increase again, if ignoring actually accounted for the decrease. If the teacher reapplies the ignoring strategy, the child's call-outs would probably decrease again.

Group Tests and Individual Tests

The obvious distinction between a group test and an individual test is that individual tests must be administered to only one person at a time, whereas group tests are administered to several people simultaneously or can be administered individually. However, there are several other subtle differences.

When administering an individual test, the tester has the opportunity to observe the individual's responses and to determine how such things as problem solving are accomplished. Within limits, the tester is able to control the pace and tempo of the testing session, and to rephrase and probe responses in order to elicit the individual's best performance. If a child becomes tired, the examiner can give the child a break between parts of the test or end the test; if the child loses his or her place on the test, the tester can help the child regain it; if the child dawdles or loses interest, the tester can encourage or redirect him or her. If the child lacks self-confidence, the examiner can reinforce the child's efforts. In short, individual tests allow the examiner to encourage a child's best efforts and to observe how a student uses his or her skills to answer questions. Thus, individual tests provide for the gathering of both quantitative and qualitative information.

On the other hand, with a group test, the examiner can provide oral directions for younger children; beyond the fourth grade, however, directions are usually written. The children write or mark their own responses, and the examiner monitors the progress of several students at the same time. He or she cannot rephrase questions or probe or prompt responses. Even when a group test is administered to only one child, qualitative information is very difficult, if not impossible, to obtain.

Purpose and efficiency should primarily govern the choice between group and individual testing. When testing for program evaluation, screening, and some types of program planning (such as tracking), group tests are appropriate. Individual tests could be used but are impractical in terms of time and expense. Special consideration may need to be given if there are any motivational, personal, linguistic, or physically disabling factors that might impair testing.

> **SKILL 30.3** **Selects—or designs—and administers a variety of appropriate assessments** (e.g., performance assessment, self-assessment, formal/informal assessment, formative/summative assessment) **to monitor students' understanding and progress and to plan for instruction.**

See also Skills 1.2 and 14.8 on types of assessment.

It is vital for teachers to track student performance using a variety of methods. Teachers should be able to assess students on a daily basis using informal assessments such as monitoring during work time, class discussions, and note taking. Often these assessments are an excellent way to determine whether or not students are "on track" and learning selected objectives. Generally, teachers can assess students by their participation in class discussion, and often this is a good way to give students credit for participation, especially those students who have special needs and who participate well in class but may struggle with alternative assignments.

More formal assessments are necessary to ensure that students fully understand selected objectives. Regular grading using selected performance skills is necessary; however teachers should develop personal ways of grading using a variety of assessment tools. For example, students could keep a science journal, tracking the progress of their ongoing assignments, projects, and labs. Other tools for observing and evaluating students are rubrics and checklists. Student profiles and checklists are an excellent way to quickly determine whether students are meeting selected objectives. It is easy for a teacher to check off students who are meeting objectives, using a checklist while monitoring students' work done in class. See the example below:

Student Name	Objective #1	Objective #2	On Task
Joe Student	X	X	X
Jan Student		X	X

Checklists provide an easy way for teachers to quickly see who is behind or who needs to review a lesson or objective.

SKILL
30.4 **Understands the importance of communicating evaluation criteria and assessment results to students.**

Communicating with Students

How can a teacher provide good feedback so students will learn from their assessments? First, the teacher's language should be helpful and constructive. Critical language does not usually help students learn. Language that is constructive and helpful recommendations will guide students to specific actions that will help them improve in the future.

When teachers provide timely feedback, they increase the chances that students will reflect on the thought processes they went through when they originally produced the work. When feedback comes weeks after an assignment was produced, the student may not remember what caused him or her to respond in a particular way.

Specific feedback is particularly important. Comments like, "This should be clearer," and "Your grammar needs work" provide information that students may already know. Students benefit from comments that include specific actions they can take to make something clearer or to improve their grammar.

When teachers provide feedback on a set of assignments, for example, they enhance students' learning by teaching them how to use the feedback. Teachers can ask students to do additional things to work with their original products, or they can ask students to take small sections and rewrite them based on the feedback. While written feedback enhances student learning, having students do something with the feedback encourages even deeper learning and reflection.

Teachers can also show students how to use scoring guides and rubrics to evaluate their own work, particularly before they turn it in. One particularly effective way of doing this is to have students examine models and samples of proficient work. Teachers should collect samples of good work, remove names and other identifying features, and show these to students so that they understand what is expected of them. Often, when teachers do this, they are surprised to see how much students gain in terms of their ability to assess their own performance.

Finally, teachers can help students develop plans to revise and improve their work, even if the teacher does not evaluate it in the preliminary stages. For example, teachers can have students keep track of words they commonly misspell or make their own lists of areas they feel they need to focus on.

COMPETENCY 31
FORCES AND MOTION

SKILL **Demonstrates an understanding of the properties of universal forces**
31.1 *(e.g., gravitational, electrical, magnetic).*

See also Skill 31.3

Electricity and Magnetism

The electromagnetic spectrum consists of frequency (f), measured in hertz, and wavelength (λ), measured in meters. The frequency times the wavelength of every electromagnetic wave equals the speed of light (299,792,458 meters/second).

> The electromagnetic spectrum consists of frequency (f), measured in hertz, and wavelength (λ), measured in meters.

Roughly, the range of wavelengths in the electromagnetic spectrum is as follows:

	f		λ	
Radio waves	10^5 to 10^{-1}	hertz	10^3 to 10^9	meters
Microwaves	10^{-1} to 10^{-3}	hertz	10^9 to 10^{11}	meters
Infrared radiation	10^{-3} to 10^{-6}	hertz	$10^{11.2}$ to $10^{14.3}$	meters
Visible light	$10^{-6.2}$ to $10^{-6.9}$	hertz	$10^{14.3}$ to 10^{15}	meters
Ultraviolet radiation	10^{-7} to 10^{-9}	hertz	10^{15} to $10^{17.2}$	meters
X-rays	10^{-9} to 10^{-11}	hertz	$10^{17.2}$ to 10^{19}	meters
Gamma rays	10^{-11} to 10^{-15}	hertz	10^{19} to $10^{23.25}$	meters

Electricity

Electrostatics is the study of stationary electric charges. A plastic rod that is rubbed with fur or a glass rod that is rubbed with silk will become electrically charged and will attract small pieces of paper. The charge on the plastic rod rubbed with fur is negative, and the charge on the glass rod rubbed with silk is positive.

Electrically charged objects share these characteristics:

1. Like charges repel each other.

2. Opposite charges attract each other.

3. Charge is conserved. A neutral object has no net charge. If the plastic rod and fur are initially neutral, when the rod becomes charged by the fur, a negative charge is transferred from the fur to the rod. The net negative charge on the rod is equal to the net positive charge on the fur.

A simple device used to indicate the existence of a positive or negative charge is called an ELECTROSCOPE. An electroscope is made up of a conducting knob; attached to it are very lightweight conducting leaves usually made of foil (gold or aluminum). When a charged object touches the knob, the leaves push away from each other because like charges repel each other. It is not possible to tell whether the charge is positive or negative.

> **ELECTROSCOPE:** a simple device used to indicate the existence of a positive or negative charge

Charging by induction

If you touch a knob with your finger while a charged rod is nearby, the electrons will be repulsed and flow out of the electroscope through the hand. If the hand is removed while the charged rod remains close, the electroscope will retain the charge.

When an object is rubbed with a charged rod, the object will take on the same charge as the rod. However, charging by induction gives the object the opposite charge from that of the charged rod.

Grounding charge

Charge can be removed from an object by connecting it to the Earth through a conductor. The removal of static electricity by conduction is called GROUNDING.

> **GROUNDING:** the removal of static electricity by conduction

Circuits

An ELECTRIC CIRCUIT is a path along which electrons flow. A simple circuit can be created with a dry cell, wire, and a bell or light bulb. When all are connected, the electrons flow from the negative terminal through the wire to the device and back to the positive terminal of the dry cell. If there are no breaks in the circuit, the device will work; the circuit is closed. Any break in the flow will create an open circuit and cause the device to shut off.

> **ELECTRIC CIRCUIT:** a path along which electrons flow

Load and switch

The device (bell or bulb) is an example of a load. A load is a device that uses energy. Suppose that you also add a buzzer so that the bell rings when you press the buzzer. The buzzer is acting as a switch. A switch is a device that opens or closes a circuit. Pressing the buzzer makes the connection complete and the bell rings. When the buzzer is not engaged, the circuit is open and the bell is silent.

Circuit types

A SERIES CIRCUIT is one in which the electrons have only one path along which they can move. When one load in a series circuit goes out, the circuit is open. An example of this is a set of Christmas tree lights that is missing a bulb. None of the bulbs will work if one bulb is not working.

A PARALLEL CIRCUIT is one in which the electrons have more than one path to travel. If a load goes out in a parallel circuit, the other load will continue to work because the electrons can still find a way to continue moving along the path.

Potential difference, voltage, and current

When an electron goes through a load, it does work and therefore loses some of its energy. The measure of how much energy is lost is called the potential difference. The potential difference between two points is the work needed to move an electron from one point to another.

Potential difference is measured in a unit called a volt. Voltage is potential difference. The higher the voltage, the more energy the electrons have. This energy is measured by a device called a voltmeter. To use a voltmeter, place it in a circuit parallel with the load you are measuring.

CURRENT is the number of electrons per second that flow past a point in a circuit. Current is measured with a device called an ammeter. To use an ammeter, put it in series with the load you are measuring.

As electrons flow through a wire, they lose potential energy. Some of the energy is changed to heat energy because of resistance. RESISTANCE is the ability of the material to oppose the flow of electrons through it. All substances have some resistance, even if they are good conductors, such as copper. This resistance is measured in units called ohms. A thin wire has more resistance than a thick one because it has less room for electrons to travel in. In a thicker wire, there are more possible paths for the electrons to flow in. Resistance also depends upon the length of the wire. The longer the wire, the more resistance it will have.

Ohm's Law

Potential difference, resistance, and current form a relationship known as Ohm's law. Current (I) is measured in amperes and is equal to potential difference (V) divided by resistance (R).

$$I = V \div R$$

SERIES CIRCUIT: one in which the electrons have only one path along which they can move

PARALLEL CIRCUIT: one in which the electrons have more than one path to travel

CURRENT: the number of electrons per second that flow past a point in a circuit

RESISTANCE: the ability of the material to oppose the flow of electrons through it

If you have a wire with resistance of 5 ohms and a potential difference of 75 volts, you can calculate the current by:

I = 75 volts ÷ 5 ohms

I = 15 amperes

A current of 10 or more amperes will cause a wire to get hot. The maximum for a house circuit is about 22 amperes. Current above 25 amperes can start a fire.

Magnetism

Magnetic fields and poles

Magnets have a north pole and a south pole. Like poles repel and opposing poles attract. A MAGNETIC FIELD is the space around a magnet where its force affects objects. The closer you are to a magnet, the stronger its force. As you move away, the force becomes weaker.

Some materials act as magnets and some do not. This is because magnetism is a result of electrons in motion. The most important motion in this case is the spinning of the individual electrons. Electrons spin in pairs in opposite directions in most atoms. The magnetic field that each spinning electron creates is canceled by another electron spinning in the opposite direction.

A bar magnet has a north pole and a south pole. If you divide the magnet in half, it will have a north and a south pole.

The Earth has a magnetic field. In a compass, a tiny, lightweight magnet is suspended and will line its south pole up with the north-pole magnet of the Earth.

Magnetic domains

In an atom of iron, there are four unpaired electrons. The magnetic fields of these electrons are not canceled out. Their fields add up to make a tiny magnet. Their fields exert forces on each other, setting up small areas in the iron called magnetic domains where atomic magnetic fields line up in the same direction.

You can make a magnet out of an iron nail by stroking the nail in the same direction repeatedly with a magnet. This causes poles in the nail to be attracted to the magnet. The tiny magnetic fields in the nail line up in the direction of the magnet. The magnet causes the domains pointing in its direction to grow in the nail. Eventually, one large domain results and the nail becomes a magnet.

> **MAGNETIC FIELD:** the space around a magnet where its force affects objects

Electromagnets

A magnet can be made out of a coil of wire by connecting the ends of the coil to a battery. When the current goes through the wire, the wire acts the same way that a magnet does; it is called an electromagnet. The poles of the electromagnet will depend upon which way the electric current runs.

There are three ways to make an electromagnet more powerful:

1. Make more coils

2. Put an iron core (nail) inside the coils

3. Use more battery power

Common uses of electromagnets

An electric meter, such as the one found on the side of a house, contains an aluminum disk that sits directly in a magnetic field created by electricity flowing through a conductor. The more the electricity flows (current), the stronger the magnetic field. The stronger the magnetic field, the faster the disk turns. The disk is connected to a series of gears that turn a dial. Meter readers record the number from that dial.

Air conditioners, vacuum cleaners, and washing machines use electric motors. An electric motor uses an electromagnet to change electric energy into mechanical energy.

In a motor, electricity is used to create magnetic fields that oppose each other and cause the rotor to move. The wiring loops attached to the rotating shaft have a magnetic field opposing the magnetic field caused by the wiring in the housing of the motor that cannot move. The repelling action of the opposing magnetic fields turns the rotor.

A GENERATOR is a device that turns rotary, mechanical energy into electrical energy. The process is based on the relationship between magnetism and electricity. As a wire, or any other conductor, moves across a magnetic field, an electric current occurs in the wire. The large generators used by electric companies have a stationary conductor; inside a magnet attached to the end of a rotating shaft is positioned inside a stationary conducting ring that is wrapped with a long, continuous piece of wire. When the magnet rotates, it induces a small electric current in each section of wire as it passes. Each section of wire is a small, separate electric conductor. All the small currents of these individual sections add up to one large current, which is used for electric power.

> **GENERATOR:** a device that turns rotary, mechanical energy into electrical energy

> **TRANSFORMER:** an electrical device that changes electricity of one voltage into another voltage, usually from high to low

A **TRANSFORMER** is an electrical device that changes electricity of one voltage into another voltage, usually from high to low. You can see transformers at the top of utility poles. A transformer uses two properties of electricity: First, magnetism surrounds an electric circuit, and second, voltage is made when a magnetic field moves or changes strength. Voltage is a measure of the strength or number of electrons flowing through a wire. If another wire is close to an electric current changing strength, the electric current will also flow into that other wire, as the magnetism changes. A transformer takes in electricity at a higher voltage and lets it run through many coils wound around an iron core. An output wire with fewer coils is also around the core. The changing magnetism makes a current in the output wire. Fewer coils mean less voltage, so the voltage is reduced.

Common sources of electromagnetic fields (EMFs) include power lines, appliances, medical equipment, cellular phones, and computers.

See also Skill 32.1

> **SKILL 31.2** **Understands how to measure, graph and describe changes in motion by using concepts of position, direction of motion and speed.**

The speed of an object cannot change unless it is acted upon by a force. The direction of the motion is determined by the placement or position of the force being applied. **MOTION** generally is any spatial and/or temporal change in a physical system. To measure changes in motion one needs to understand the *frame of reference*. The frame of reference varies with each object: There is no absolute frame of reference. All particles of matter are in a constant state of motion and therefore motion must be measured against a frame or point of reference.

> **MOTION:** any spatial and/or temporal change in a physical system

Speed is a scalar quantity that refers to how fast an object is moving (i.e., the car was traveling 60 mi./hr).

Velocity is a vector quantity that refers to the rate at which an object changes its position. In other words, velocity is speed with direction (i.e., the car was traveling 60 mi./hr east).

Instantaneous speed is speed at any given instant in time.

Average speed is the average of all instantaneous speeds, found simply by a distance/time ratio.

Acceleration is a vector quantity, defined as the rate at which an object changes its velocity, where *f* represents the final velocity and *i* represents the initial velocity.

Since acceleration is a vector quantity, it always has a direction associated with it. The direction of the acceleration vector depends on whether the object is speeding up or slowing down and whether the object is moving in a positive or negative direction.

> SKILL 31.3 **Analyzes the ways unbalanced forces acting on an object cause changes in the position or motion of the object.**

Dynamics and Motion

DYNAMICS is the study of the relationship between motion and the forces affecting motion. Force causes motion.

Mass and weight are not the same qualities. An object's mass gives it a resistance to change its current state of motion. It is also the measure of an object's resistance to acceleration. The force that the Earth's gravity exerts on an object with a specific mass is the object's weight on Earth. Weight is a force that is measured in Newtons.

Weight (W) — mass times acceleration due to gravity ($W = mg$).

> **DYNAMICS:** the study of the relationship between motion and the forces affecting motion

Newton's laws of motion

Newton's first law of motion is also called the law of inertia. It states that an object at rest will remain at rest and an object in motion will remain in motion at a constant velocity unless acted upon by an external force.

Newton's second law of motion states that if a net force acts on an object, it will cause the acceleration of the object. The relationship between force and motion is force equals mass times acceleration ($F = ma$).

Newton's third law of motion states that for every action there is an equal and opposite reaction. Therefore, if an object exerts a force on another object, that second object exerts an equal and opposite force on the first object.

Work and power

Work is done on an object when an applied force moves across a distance.

Power is the work done divided by the amount of time that it took to do it:
(Power — work ÷ time).

Momentum describes how difficult it would be to stop a moving object and it is calculated my multiplying an object's mass by its velocity.

Motion and Resistance to Motion

Surfaces that touch each other have a certain resistance to motion. This resistance is friction. Some principles of motion and resistance to motion include the following:

1. The materials that make up the surfaces determine the magnitude of the frictional force.

2. The frictional force is independent of the area of contact between the two surfaces.

3. The direction of the frictional force is the opposite of the direction of motion.

4. The frictional force is proportional to the normal force between the two surfaces in contact.

Types of friction and resistance

STATIC FRICTION describes the force of friction of two surfaces that are in contact with each other but do not have any motion relative to each other, such as a block sitting on an inclined plane. KINETIC FRICTION describes the force of friction of two surfaces in contact with each other when there is relative motion between the surfaces.

> **STATIC FRICTION:** the force of friction of two surfaces that are in contact with each other but do not have any motion relative to each other

> **KINETIC FRICTION:** the force of friction of two surfaces in contact with each other when there is relative motion between the surfaces

Some examples of friction and resistance include

- **Push and pull:** Pushing a vacuum cleaner or pulling a bowstring applies muscular force when the muscles expand and contract. Elastic force occurs when an object returns to its original shape (for example, when a bow is released).

- **Rubbing:** Friction opposing the motion of one surface past another. Friction is common when slowing down a car or sledding down a hill.

- **Pull of gravity:** The force of attraction between two objects. Gravity exists not only on Earth but also between planets as well as in black holes.

- **Forces on objects at rest:** The formula $F = \frac{m}{a}$ is shorthand for force equals mass over acceleration. An object will not move unless the force is strong enough to move the mass. Also, there can be opposing forces holding the object in place. For instance, a boat can potentially be forced to drift away by underwater currents but an equal and opposite force, a docking rope, keeps it tied to the dock.

- **Forces on a moving object:** Inertia is the tendency of any object to resist a change in motion. An object at rest tends to stay at rest. An object that is moving tends to keep moving.

- **Inertia and circular motion:** Centripetal force is provided by the high banking of a curved road and by friction between the wheels and the road.

Conserving energy

The law of conservation of energy states that energy can neither be created nor destroyed. Therefore, the sum of all energy in a system remains constant.

The law of momentum conservation states that when two objects collide in an isolated system, the total momentum of the two objects before the collision is equal to the total momentum of the two objects after the collision. That is, the momentum lost by object 1 is equal to the momentum gained by object 2.

Straight-Line, Circular, and Periodic Motion

Matter can move in a straight line, in a circular pattern, and in a periodic fashion. The Greeks were the first people on record to think about motion. They thought that matter wanted to be stopped and were under the impression that after an object moved, it would not keep moving. They thought that the object would slow down and stop because its nature was to be at rest. These early scientists considered that matter moves. Galileo was the first to realize the error in the early scientists' thought process. Galileo concluded that an object keeps moving, even against the force of gravity.

Straight-line motion

To make an object move, a force must be applied. Friction must also be taken into account: friction makes moving objects slow down. Galileo was also the first to notice this characteristic. This is Newton's first law of motion, which states that an object at rest stays at rest unless acted upon by force. Force can have varied effects on moving objects. Force makes objects move, slow down, stop, increase their speed, decrease their speed, and so on.

A moving object has speed, velocity, and acceleration. To summarize, when force is applied to an object, it moves in a straight line (Newton's first law), and adding force can make it go faster or slow it down.

Circular motion

Circular motion is defined as acceleration along a circle, a circular path, or a circular orbit. Circular motion involves acceleration of the moving object by a centripetal force that pulls the moving object toward the center of the circular orbit. Without acceleration, the object would move in a straight line, according to Newton's first law of motion. Circular motion is accelerated even though the speed is constant, because the object's velocity is constantly changing direction.

Let's look at some examples of circular motion: an artificial satellite orbiting the Earth in a geosynchronous orbit; a stone that is tied to a rope and being swung in

> The law of conservation of energy states that energy can neither be created nor destroyed.

> The law of momentum conservation states that when two objects collide in an isolated system, the total momentum of the two objects before the collision is equal to the total momentum of the two objects after the collision.

circles; a race car turning a curve in a racetrack; an electron moving perpendicular to a uniform magnetic field; and a gear turning inside a mechanism.

A special kind of circular motion occurs when an object rotates around its own center of mass. The rotation around a fixed axis of a three-dimensional body involves the circular motion of its parts. This can be called spinning (or rotational) motion. When an object moves in a circular path, a force must be directed toward the center of the circle in order to keep the object moving. This constraining force is called centripetal force. Gravity is the centripetal force that keeps a satellite orbiting the Earth.

Periodic motion

Periodic motion occurs when an object moves back and forth in a regular motion. Some examples of periodic motion are a weight on a string swinging back and forth (a pendulum) and a ball bouncing up and down. Periodic motion has three characteristics:

1. Velocity: The rate at which an object changes its position (speed with direction). Both the bouncing ball and the weight on the pendulum have velocity.

2. Period: The time the object takes to go back and forth. The time the ball takes to bounce back can be measured. Sometimes, the word *period* is replaced by the word *frequency*. Frequency is the reciprocal of period.

3. Amplitude: Half the distance the object goes from one side of the period to the other (the height of the pendulum or bouncing ball). When an object is rotating, the amplitude is the radius of the circle (half the diameter).

There are many devices that use the characteristics of periodic motion. A clock is the most common example of periodic motion.

> SKILL 31.4 **Analyzes the relationship between force and motion in a variety of situations** *(e.g., simple machines, geologic processes).*

See also Skill 31.3 and 39.1

Simple machines include inclined planes, levers, wheels and axles, and pulleys.

Compound machines are two or more simple machines working together. A wheelbarrow is an example of a complex machine. It uses a lever and a wheel and axle. Machines of all types ease people's workloads by changing the size or direction of an applied force. The amount of effort saved by using simple or complex machines is called mechanical advantage, or MA.

COMPETENCY 32
PHYSICAL AND CHEMICAL PROPERTIES

> **SKILL** **Describes the physical and chemical properties of substances** *(e.g.,*
> **32.1** *size, shape, temperature, magnetism, hardness, mass, conduction, density).*

Physical and chemical properties of matter describe the appearance or behavior of a substance. A PHYSICAL PROPERTY can be observed without changing the identity of a substance. For instance, you can describe the color, mass, shape, and volume of a book. A CHEMICAL PROPERTY describes the ability of a substance to change into a new substance. Baking powder goes through a chemical change as it changes into carbon dioxide gas during the baking process.

Everything in our world is made up of matter, whether it is a rock, a building, an animal, or a person. Matter is defined by its characteristics: It takes up space and has mass.

MASS is a measure of the amount of matter in an object. Two objects of equal mass will balance each other on a simple balance scale no matter where the scale is located. For example, two rocks with equal mass that are in balance on Earth will also be in balance on the Moon. They will feel heavier on Earth than on the moon because of the gravitational pull of the Earth. So, although the two rocks have the same mass, they will have different weight.

WEIGHT is the measure of the Earth's pull of gravity on an object. It can also be defined as the pull of gravity between bodies. The units of weight measurement commonly used are the pound (English measure) and the kilogram (metric measure).

In addition to mass, matter also has the property of volume. VOLUME is the amount of cubic space an object occupies.

Volume and mass together provide a more exact description of an object. Two objects may have the same volume but different mass or the same mass but different volume. For example, consider two cubes that are each one cubic centimeter: one made from plastic, one from lead. They have the same volume, but the lead cube has more mass. The measure we use to describe the cubes takes into consideration both the mass and the volume. DENSITY is the mass of a substance per unit of volume. If an object is less dense than a liquid, the object will float in the liquid. If the object is denser than the liquid, then the object will sink.

> **PHYSICAL PROPERTY:** can be observed without changing the identity of a substance

> **CHEMICAL PROPERTY:** the ability of a substance to change into a new substance

> **MASS:** a measure of the amount of matter in an object

> **WEIGHT:** the measure of the Earth's pull of gravity on an object

> **VOLUME:** the amount of cubic space an object occupies

> **DENSITY:** the mass of a substance per unit of volume

Density is stated in grams per cubic centimeter (g/cm³), where the gram is the standard unit of mass. To find an object's density, you must measure its mass and its volume. Then divide the mass by the volume ($D = \frac{m}{V}$).

To discover an object's density, first use a balance to find its mass. Then calculate its volume. If the object is a regular shape, you can find the volume by multiplying the length, width, and height together. However, if it is an irregular shape, you can find the volume by seeing how much water it displaces. Measure the water in the container before and after the object is submerged. The difference will be the volume of the object.

SPECIFIC GRAVITY is the ratio of the density of a substance to the density of water. For instance, the specific density of one liter of turpentine is calculated by comparing its mass (0.81 kg) to the mass of one liter of water (1 kg):

$$\frac{\text{Mass of 1 L alcohol}}{\text{Mass of 1 L water}} = \frac{0.81 \text{ kg}}{1.00 \text{ kg}} = 0.81$$

A **CONDUCTOR** is a material that transfers thermal or electrical energy easily. Metals are known for being good thermal and electrical conductors. Touch your hand to a hot piece of metal and you know it is a good conductor: The heat transfers to your hand and you may be burned. Materials through which electric charges can flow easily are called electrical conductors. Metals that are good electric conductors include silicon and boron. An **INSULATOR** is a material through which electric charges do not move easily, if at all. Examples of electrical insulators would be the nonmetal elements of the periodic table.

Hardness describes how difficult it is to scratch or dent a substance. The hardest natural substance is a diamond.

SOLUBILITY is defined as the amount of substance (referred to as solute) that will dissolve into another substance, called the solvent. The amount that will dissolve can vary according to the conditions, most notably, temperature. The process is called solvation.

Melting point refers to the temperature at which a solid becomes a liquid. Melting takes place when there is sufficient energy available to break the intermolecular forces that hold molecules together in a solid.

Boiling point refers to the temperature at which a liquid becomes a gas. Boiling occurs when there is enough energy available to break the intermolecular forces holding molecules together as a liquid.

SPECIFIC GRAVITY: the ratio of the density of a substance to the density of water

CONDUCTOR: a material that transfers thermal or electrical energy easily

INSULATOR: a material through which electric charges do not move easily, if at all

SOLUBILITY: the amount of substance (referred to as solute) that will dissolve into another substance, called the solvent

SKILL 32.2 **Describes the physical properties of solids, liquids and gases.**

See also Skill 34.3

The phase of matter (solid, liquid, or gas) is identified by its shape and volume. Characteristics of each phase are described below.

Solids

- Have a definite shape that can be changed in some way
- Have a definite volume that cannot be changed
- Mass can be changed when the physical shape is diminished, e.g., sawing a board into two pieces
- Can be any color and temperature
- Some will melt under high temperatures, in which case they become liquid
- Are very hard

Liquids

- Take the shape of the container into which they are poured
- When a liquid results from melting a solid, it has the same color as the solid
- Flow
- Cannot be compressed and keep the same volume
- Weight may be lighter than that of a solid because of evaporation
- Are soft

Gases

- Do not keep their shape and fill a container
- Flow very quickly
- Are colorless
- Can be compressed and take on a different volume than that of a solid or liquid
- Are of high temperature
- Are extremely light and do not have weight

SKILL 32.3 Distinguishes between physical and chemical changes in matter.

PHYSICAL CHANGE: a change that does not produce a new substance

A **PHYSICAL CHANGE** is a change that does not produce a new substance. The atoms are not rearranged into different compounds; the material has the same chemical composition that it had before the change. Changes of state such as freezing and melting are examples of physical changes. Frozen water is still water.

CHEMICAL CHANGE: any change of a substance into one or more other substances

A **CHEMICAL CHANGE** (or chemical reaction) is any change of a substance into one or more other substances. Burning materials turn into smoke; a seltzer tablet fizzes into gas bubbles.

SKILL 32.4 Applies knowledge of physical and chemical properties (including atomic structure) of and changes in matter to processes and situations that occur in life and in earth and space science.

See also Skills 32.1, 32.3, and 32.6

Examples of processes that change chemical and physical properties with emphasis on the atomic level

- **Rusting:** An iron nail rusts to form a rusty nail. The rusty nail, however, is not made up of the same iron atoms as a nail that is not rusty. It is now composed of iron (III) oxide molecules that form *when the iron atoms combine with oxygen molecules during oxidation.*

- **Burning of fossil fuels:** Coal, petroleum, and natural gas all form from the remains of dead plants and animals through natural processes over millions of years. Because of their high carbon content, when burned, these substances generate large amounts of energy as well as carbon dioxide *(reaction of carbon atoms with oxygen molecules).*

- **Cellular respiration:** Cellular respiration is the metabolic pathway in which food (glucose, etc.) is broken down to produce energy in the form of ATP. Steps include glycolysis, the Krebs cycle, and the electron transport chain. The net gain from the whole process of respiration is 36 molecules of ATP. Many molecules are involved but it is the high energy phosphate (PO_4^{3-}) whose production is critical to the sustaining the cell's energy supply.

Atomic Structure

An ATOM is the smallest unit of matter that has the properties of a chemical element. Once thought to be the smallest unit of matter, the atom is larger than and composed of subatomic particles like quarks and nucleons.

> **ATOM:** the smallest unit of matter that has the properties of a chemical element

There are three components of an atom's structure: electrons, protons, and neutrons. An atom's protons and neutrons are housed in its nucleus. Protons are positively charged, while neutrons are neutral (net zero charge). Protons weigh 1.67×10^{-24} grams, which is equal to one atomic mass unit. Neutrons weigh approximately one atomic mass unit.

The negatively charged electrons are found in orbitals (concentric shells) that surround the atomic nucleus. Their attraction to the positive charge in the nucleus keeps them in orbit. Electrons are the smallest of the three particles, weighing 9.11×10^{-28} grams.

Elements on the periodic table are numbered according to the number of protons that they have, and elements are differentiated by the number of protons they have. For example, the atomic number for hydrogen is 1. This means that a hydrogen atom has one proton in its nucleus. The atomic number for helium is 2. This means that a helium atom has two protons in its nucleus.

Because the net charge of an atom must be zero, the number of protons in an atom must equal the number of its electrons. The number of protons in an atom does not change. However, the number of electrons that an atom has can change. When an atom has fewer or more electrons than the number that would give the atom a neutral charge, a charged atom called an ION is formed.

> **ION:** a charged atom

The two types of ions are cations and anions. Cations have fewer electrons than the number necessary to give the atom a neutral charge. Cations have a positive charge. Anions have more electrons than the number necessary to give the atom a neutral charge, and they have a negative charge. For example, when a sodium atom is missing one of its electron pairs, it gains a $+1$ charge, which signifies that is has fewer electrons than a neutral sodium atom.

When the number of neutrons in an atom changes and its number of protons stays constant, the new atom is called an isotope. Like ions, the element's identity remains the same. For example, carbon-12 and carbon-14 have different numbers of neutrons in their nuclei, but both are carbon atoms.

SKILL 32.5 Distinguishes between elements, compounds, mixtures and solutions and describes their properties.

ELEMENT: a substance that cannot be broken down into other substances

COMPOUND: made of two or more elements that have been chemically combined

An **ELEMENT** is a substance that cannot be broken down into other substances. To date, scientists have identified 109 elements. Eighty-nine are found in nature, and 20 are synthetic. A **COMPOUND** is made of two or more elements that have been chemically combined. Atoms join together when elements are chemically combined. The result is that the elements lose their individual identities; the compound that they become has different properties.

Substances can combine without a chemical change. A mixture is any combination of two or more substances in which the substances keep their own properties. A fruit salad is a mixture (so is an ice cream sundae, although you might not recognize each part if it is stirred together). Colognes and perfumes are other examples. You may not readily recognize the individual elements; however, they can be separated.

Mixtures are classified into two types:

- **Heterogeneous mixture:** A mixture that consists of physically distinct parts, each with different properties. Example: Sugar and salt stirred together.

- **Homogeneous mixture (solution):** A mixture that is uniform in its properties throughout a given sample.

Colloids, solutions, and suspensions are types of mixtures consisting of two or more components. Solutions are homogenous mixtures. They are uniform throughout; the individual components are evenly distributed throughout the mixture. Colloids and suspensions are heterogeneous mixtures. They are not uniform; they consist of clumps or pockets of the individual components.

SOLUTIONS: homogenous mixtures of two or more components

SOLUTIONS are homogenous mixtures of two or more components. The components of solutions are atoms and molecules, thus the particles are 1 nanometer (nm) or less in diameter. Solutions are transparent and do not usually absorb visible light. An example of a solution is sugar and water.

SUSPENSIONS: heterogeneous mixtures consisting of particles larger than those found in solutions

SUSPENSIONS are heterogeneous mixtures consisting of particles larger than those found in solutions. The diameter of particles found in suspensions is greater than 1,000 nm. Thus, these particles are visible to the naked eye. Suspensions are murky or opaque and not transparent. Machine shaking can evenly distribute suspensions but the components will settle out in time. Examples of suspensions include blood and a mixture of oil and water.

COLLOIDS: heterogeneous mixtures consisting of particles intermediate in size between those found in solutions and suspensions

COLLOIDS are heterogeneous mixtures consisting of particles intermediate in size between those found in solutions and suspensions. The diameter of particles found in colloids is between 1 and 1,000 nm. Colloids appear homogenous to the naked eye and do not settle out into components. Colloids scatter light and are opaque. Milk is an example of a colloid.

The law of definite proportions (law of constant composition) states that a pure compound, whatever its source, always contains definite or constant proportions of the elements by mass. It has a fixed composition.

SKILL 32.6 Explains the importance of a variety of chemical reactions that occur in daily life *(e.g., rusting, burning of fossil fuels, photosynthesis, cell respiration, chemical batteries, digestion of food).*

See also Skills 32.4, 35.1 and 35.5

Glycolysis

Glycolysis is the first step in respiration. It occurs in the cytoplasm of the cell and does not require oxygen. Each of the ten stages of glycolysis is catalyzed by a specific enzyme.

Steps of glycolysis

In the first stage, the reactant is glucose. For energy to be released from glucose, it must be converted to a reactive compound. This conversion occurs through the phosphorylation of a glucose molecule by two molecules of ATP. This is an investment of energy by the cell.

The six-carbon product, called fructose 1,6-bisphosphate, breaks into two three-carbon molecules of sugar. A phosphate group is added to each sugar molecule and hydrogen atoms are removed. Hydrogen is picked up by NAD^+ (a vitamin). Since there are two sugar molecules, two molecules of NADH are formed. The reduction (addition of hydrogen) of NAD allows the potential for energy transfer.

As the phosphate bonds are broken, ATP is produced. Two ATP molecules are generated as each original three-carbon sugar molecule is converted to pyruvic acid (pyruvate). A total of four ATP molecules are made in the four stages. Since two molecules of ATP were needed to start the reaction, there is a net gain of two ATP molecules at the end of glycolysis. This accounts for only 2 percent of the total energy in a molecule of glucose.

Beginning with pyruvate, which was the end product of glycolysis, the following steps occur before entering the Krebs cycle.

1. Pyruvic acid is changed to acetyl-CoA (coenzyme A). This is a three-carbon pyruvic acid molecule which has lost one molecule of carbon dioxide (CO_2) to become a two-carbon acetyl group. Pyruvic acid loses a hydrogen to NAD^+, which is reduced to NADH.

2. Acetyl-CoA enters the Krebs cycle. For each starting molecule of glucose, two molecules of acetyl-CoA enter the Krebs cycle (one for each molecule of pyruvic acid formed in glycolysis).

Krebs Cycle

The Krebs cycle, also known as the citric acid cycle, occurs in four major steps. First, the two-carbon acetyl-CoA combines with a four-carbon molecule to form a six-carbon molecule of citric acid.

Next, two carbons are lost as carbon dioxide and a four-carbon molecule is formed to become available to join with CoA to form citric acid again. Since we started with two molecules of CoA, two turns of the Krebs cycle are necessary to process the original molecule of glucose.

In the third step, eight hydrogen atoms are released and picked up by FAD and NAD (vitamins and electron carriers).

Finally, for each molecule of CoA (remember, there were two to start with), you get:

- 3 molecules of NADH $\times$ 2 cycles
- 1 molecule of $FADH_2$ $\times$ 2 cycles
- 1 molecule of ATP $\times$ 2 cycles

This completes the breakdown of glucose. At this point, a total of four molecules of ATP have been made (two from glycolysis and one from each of the two turns of the Krebs cycle). Six molecules of carbon dioxide have been released (two prior to entering the Krebs cycle and two for each of the two turns of the Krebs cycle). Twelve carrier molecules have been made (ten NADH and two $FADH_2$). These carrier molecules will carry electrons to the electron transport chain. ATP is made by substrate-level phosphorylation in the Krebs cycle. Notice that the Krebs cycle in itself does not produce much ATP but functions mostly in the transfer of electrons to be used in the electron transport chain, where most of the ATP is made.

Electron Transport Chain

In the electron transport chain, NADH transfers electrons from glycolysis and the Krebs cycle to the first molecule in the chain of molecules embedded in the inner membrane of the mitochondrion. Most of the molecules in the electron transport chain are proteins. Nonprotein molecules are also part of the chain and are essential for the catalytic functions of certain enzymes.

The electron transport chain does not make ATP directly. Instead, it breaks up a large free energy drop into a more manageable amount. The chain uses electrons to pump H^+ across the mitochondrion membrane. The H^+ gradient is used to form ATP synthesis in a process called chemiosmosis (oxidative phosphorylation). ATP synthetase and energy generated by the movement of hydrogen ions coming off of NADH and $FADH_2$ builds ATP from ADP on the inner membrane of the mitochondria. Each NADH yields three molecules of ATP (10×3) and each $FADH_2$ yields two molecules of ATP (2×2). Thus, the electron transport chain and oxidative phosphorylation produces 34 ATP.

So, the net gain from the whole process of respiration is 36 molecules of ATP:

- Glycolysis: 4 ATP made, 2 ATP spent = net gain of 2 ATP

- Acetyl-CoA: 2 ATP used

- Krebs cycle: 1 ATP made for each turn of the cycle = net gain of 2 ATP

- Electron transport chain: 34 ATP gained

COMPETENCY 33
PHYSICAL SCIENCE: ENERGY AND INTERACTIONS BETWEEN MATTER AND ENERGY

> **SKILL 33.1** Understands conservation of energy and energy transformations and analyzes how energy is transformed from one form to another *(e.g., potential, kinetic, mechanical, sound, heat, light, chemical, electrical)* in a variety of everyday situations and how increasing or decreasing amounts affect objects.

See also Skills 31.1, 31.3, 33.4, and 33.5

Laws of Thermodynamics

The relationship between heat, energy, and work (e.g., mechanical or electrical) is expressed by the laws of thermodynamics. These laws deal strictly with systems in thermal equilibrium and not those within the process of rapid change or in a state of transition. Systems that are nearly always in a state of equilibrium are called REVERSIBLE SYSTEMS.

> **REVERSIBLE SYSTEMS:** systems that are nearly always in a state of equilibrium

The **first law of thermodynamics** is a restatement of the **conservation of energy**. The change in heat energy supplied to a system (Q) is equal to the sum of the change in the internal energy (U) and the change in the work done by the system against internal forces ($\Delta Q = \Delta U + \Delta W$).

The **second law of thermodynamics** is stated in two parts:

1. No machine is 100 percent efficient. It is impossible to construct a machine that only absorbs heat from a heat source and performs an equal amount of work because some heat will always be lost to the environment.

2. Heat cannot spontaneously pass from a colder to a hotter object. An ice cube sitting on a hot sidewalk will melt into a little puddle but it will never spontaneously cool and form the same ice cube. Certain events have a preferred direction, called the **arrow of time**.

The law of conservation of energy states that energy is neither created nor destroyed. Thus, energy changes form when energy transactions occur in nature. The major forms energy can take are described below:

- **Thermal energy** is the total internal energy of objects created by the vibration and movement of atoms and molecules. Heat is the transfer of thermal energy.

- **Acoustical energy**, or sound energy, is the movement of energy through an object in waves. Energy that forces an object to vibrate creates sound.

- **Radiant energy** is the energy of electromagnetic waves. Light, visible and otherwise, is an example of radiant energy.

- **Electrical energy** is the movement of electrical charges in an electromagnetic field. Examples of electrical energy are electricity and lightning.

- **Chemical energy** is the energy stored in the chemical bonds of molecules. For example, the energy derived from gasoline is chemical energy.

- **Mechanical energy** is the potential and kinetic energy of a mechanical system. Rolling balls, car engines, and body parts in motion demonstrate mechanical energy.

- **Nuclear energy** is the energy present in the nucleus of atoms. Division, combination, or collision of nuclei release nuclear energy.

Because the total energy in the universe is constant, energy continually transitions between forms.

Because the total energy in the universe is constant, energy continually transitions between forms.

Examples of energy transformations

- **Kinetic to electrical:** Hydroelectric power: power produced from falling water

- **Mechanical electrical:** Wind power: windmills harness the energy of the wind by driving a turbine that generates electricity.

- **Heat to electrical:** Geothermal energy: energy is produced from hot igneous rocks within the Earth. Rainwater percolates porous strata near an active magma chamber and flashes to steam. The steam is captured and routed to turbine-powered electrical generators.

- **Light to electrical:** Solar energy: solar power can be utilized directly as a source of heat or to produce electricity. The most common use of solar power is to heat water.

- **Light to chemical:** Photosynthesis: light energy the sun activates sugar production in plants.

- **Chemical to mechanical:** Car engine burning gasoline
- **Chemical to electrical:** A battery powering a device or instrument

> **SKILL 33.2** **Understands the basic concepts of heat energy and related processes** *(e.g., melting, evaporation, boiling, condensation).*

See also Skill 34.3

When an object undergoes a change of phase it goes from one physical state (solid, liquid, or gas) to another. For instance, water can go from liquid to solid (freezing) or from liquid to gas (boiling). The heat that is required to change from one state to the other is called **LATENT HEAT**.

LATENT HEAT: the heat that is required to change from one state to the other

The **heat of fusion** is the amount of heat that it takes to change from a solid to a liquid or the amount of heat released during the change from liquid to solid.

The **heat of vaporization** is the amount of heat that it takes to change from a liquid to a gaseous state.

Melting takes place when there is sufficient energy available to break the intermolecular forces that hold molecules together in a solid. At the melting point, a solid becomes a liquid.

Boiling occurs when there is enough energy available to break the intermolecular forces holding molecules together as a liquid. At the boiling point, a liquid becomes a gas.

EVAPORATION: the change in phase from liquid to gas

EVAPORATION is the change in phase from liquid to gas.

CONDENSATION: the change in phase from gas to liquid

CONDENSATION is the change in phase from gas to liquid.

> **SKILL 33.3** **Understands the principles of electricity and magnetism and their applications** *(e.g., electric circuits, motors, audio speakers, lightning).*

See Skill 31.1

Light

When we refer to light, we are usually talking about a type of electromagnetic wave that stimulates the retina of the eye, or visible light. Each individual wavelength within the spectrum of visible light represents a particular COLOR. When a particular wavelength strikes the retina, we perceive that color. The colors of visible light are sometimes referred to as ROYGBIV (red, orange, yellow, green, blue, indigo, and violet). The visible light spectrum ranges from red (the longest wavelength) to violet (the shortest wavelength), with a range of wavelengths in between. If all of the wavelengths strike your eye at the same time, you will see white. Conversely, when no wavelengths strike your eye, you perceive black.

Shadows illustrate one of the basic properties of light. Light travels in a straight line; if you put your hand between a light source and a wall, you will interrupt the light and produce a shadow.

Reflection, Refraction, Diffraction

When light hits a surface, it is reflected. The angle of the incoming light (angle of incidence) is the same as the angle of the reflected light (angle of reflection). It is this reflected light that allows you to see objects. This happens when the reflected light reaches your eyes.

Different surfaces reflect light differently. Rough surfaces scatter light in many different directions. A smooth surface reflects the light in one direction. If a surface is smooth and shiny (like a mirror), you see your image in it.

When light enters a different medium, it bends. This bending, or change of speed, is called refraction.

Light can be diffracted, or bent around the edges of an object. Diffraction occurs when light goes through a narrow slit. As light passes through the slit, it bends slightly around the edges of it. You can demonstrate this by pressing your thumb and forefinger together, making a very thin slit between them. Hold them about 8 cm from your eye and look at a distant source of light. The pattern you observe is caused by the diffraction of light.

Light and other electromagnetic radiation can be polarized because the waves are transverse. The distinguishing characteristic of transverse waves is that they are perpendicular to the direction of the motion of the wave. Polarized light has vibrations confined to a single plane that is perpendicular to the direction of motion. Light can be polarized by passing it through special filters that block all vibrations except those in a single plane. Polarized sunglasses cut down on glare by blocking out all but one plane of vibration.

Cameras use a convex lens to produce an image on film. A convex lens is thicker in the middle than at the edges. The image size depends upon the focal length (distance from the focus to the lens). The longer the focal length, the larger the image will be. A converging lens produces a real image whenever the object is far enough from the lens that the rays of light from the object can hit the lens and be focused into a real image on the other side of the lens.

Eyeglasses can help correct deficiencies of sight by changing where the image seen is focused on the retina of the eye. If a person is nearsighted, the lens of his or her eye focuses images in front of the retina. In this case, the corrective lens placed in the eyeglasses will be concave so that the image will reach the retina. In the case of farsightedness, the lens of the eye focuses the image behind the retina. The correction will call for a convex lens fitted into the eyeglasses so that the image is brought forward into sharper focus.

> **SKILL 33.5** Demonstrates an understanding of the properties, production, and transmission of sound.

Sound

Sound waves are produced by a vibrating body, which moves forward and compresses the air in front of it. The body then reverses direction, so that the pressure on the air decreases and expansion of the air molecules occurs. One compression and expansion creates one longitudinal wave. Sound can be transmitted through any gas, liquid, or solid. However, it cannot be transmitted through a vacuum (because there are no particles in a vacuum to vibrate and bump into adjacent particles to transmit the wave).

The vibrating air molecules move back and forth parallel to the direction of motion of the wave as they pass the energy from adjacent air molecules (closer to the source) to air molecules farther away from the source.

Levels of sound

The pitch of a sound depends on the frequency that the ear receives. High-pitched sound waves have high frequencies. High notes are produced by an object that is vibrating at a greater rate per second than one that produces a low note.

The intensity of a sound is the amount of energy that crosses a unit of area in a given amount of time. The loudness of the sound is subjective and depends upon the effect on the human ear. Two tones of the same intensity but different pitches may appear to have different loudness. The intensity level of sound is measured in decibels. Normal conversation is approximately 60 decibels, while a power saw is approximately 110 decibels.

Sound waves

The amplitude of a sound wave determines its loudness, with loud sound waves creating larger amplitudes. The larger the sound wave, the more energy is needed to create the wave.

> The amplitude of a sound wave determines its loudness, with loud sound waves creating larger amplitudes.

An oscilloscope is useful in studying waves because it gives a picture of the wave that shows the crest and trough of the wave. INTERFERENCE is the interaction of two or more waves that meet. If the waves interfere constructively, the crest of each one meets the crests of the others. They combine into a crest with greater amplitude, creating a louder sound. If the waves interfere destructively, then the crest of one meets the trough of another. They produce a wave with lower amplitude that produces a softer sound.

> INTERFERENCE: the interaction of two or more waves that meet

If you have two tuning forks that produce different pitches, one will produce sounds of a slightly higher frequency than the other. When you strike the two forks simultaneously, you will hear beats. Beats are a series of loud and soft sounds: When the waves meet, the crests combine at some points and produce loud sounds. At other points, they nearly cancel each other out and produce soft sounds.

A piano tuner tuning a piano only uses one tuning fork, even though there are many strings on the piano. The piano tuner adjusts the first string to the same pitch as that of the tuning fork. Then he or she listens to the beats that occur when both the tuned and untuned strings are struck. The tuner adjusts the untuned string until he or she can hear the correct number of beats per second. This process of striking the untuned and tuned strings together and timing the beats is repeated until all of the piano strings are tuned.

Pleasant sounds have a regular wave pattern that is repeated over and over. Sounds that do not have regular patterns are unpleasant and are called noise.

Doppler effect

The DOPPLER EFFECT is defined as the changes in experienced frequency due to the relative motion of the source of the sound. When a siren approaches, the pitch is high. When it passes, the pitch drops. As a moving sound source approaches a listener, the sound waves are closer together, causing an increase in frequency in

> DOPPLER EFFECT: the changes in experienced frequency due to the relative motion of the source of the sound

the sound that is heard. As the source passes the listener, the waves spread out, and the sound experienced by the listener is lower.

Transverse waves are characterized by the particle motion being perpendicular to the wave motion; **longitudinal waves** are characterized by the particle motion being parallel to the wave motion.

COMPETENCY 34

PHYSICAL SCIENCE: ENERGY TRANSFORMATIONS AND THE CONSERVATION OF MATTER AND ENERGY

> **SKILL 34.1** Describes sources of electrical energy and processes of energy transformation for human uses *(e.g., fossil fuels, solar panels, hydroelectric plants).*

Alternative Energy Resources

Research into alternative energy sources is directed at producing viable renewable energy sources. Some of the sources under consideration include the following:

- **Hydroelectric power:** Power produced from falling water. This is not a new idea as waterwheels have been in use for centuries. The drawback to this energy source lies in the availability of suitable locations for dams and the expense of construction.

- **Wind power:** Windmills harness the energy of the wind by driving a turbine that generates electricity. Wind power represents another ancient technology being revisited by engineers. However, the wind generators produce very little electricity for the expense involved, and suitable locations (areas with steady, high winds) for windfields are limited.

- **Tidal power:** Another concept in use in some areas of the world is generating electricity by deflecting and diverting strong tidal currents through offshore turbines that drive electric generators. Again, the presence of proper conditions is necessary (strong tidal power), and suitable locations are limited.

- **Geothermal energy:** In some areas of the world such as New Zealand, Iceland, and Italy, energy is produced from hot igneous rocks within the Earth. Rainwater percolates porous strata near an active magma chamber and flashes to steam. Some of the steam returns to the surface through natural fissures or is extracted through drilled vents. The steam is captured and routed to turbine-powered electrical generators to produce geothermal power. The steam can also be used to directly heat buildings. Geothermal energy is used in Reykjavik, Iceland, where captured steam heats many buildings.

  The limitations of this alternative energy source are obvious: the majority of metropolitan locations are not situated near active magma chambers. However, New Zealand does manage to gather enough power to meet approximately 5 percent of its electrical needs.

- **Solar energy:** Solar power can be utilized directly as a source of heat or to produce electricity. The most common use of solar power is to heat water. An array of dark-colored piping is placed on the roof of a structure, and as water circulates through the piping, it heats.

Solar cells produce electricity from the solar radiation. Photons striking the junction between two semiconductors (usually selenium) induce an electrical current that is stored in batteries.

Although this source of power is pollution free, there are two main limitations: First, the production of power is limited by the distribution and periods of insolation (exposure to the sun's rays), and atmospheric conditions can easily interfere with collection efforts (i.e., winter months, cloud cover, pollution, and storms). Second, the solar cells individually produce very small amounts of electricity (trickle changes) and must be arrayed in very large banks. For example, a solar power plant with a capacity of 100 megawatts (MW) would cover a surface area of approximately 4 km².

Solar cells have been used successfully in outer space where atmospheric conditions and cell-size restraints are of less concern. Spacecraft and satellites use solar cells to charge batteries that provide electrical power for communications equipment and operating power.

- **Biomass:** Plant and animal waste (decaying or decayed) can be burned to produce heat for steam turbine electrical generators. In most highly developed countries the biomass is first converted to either methane gas (given off by decaying biomass) or alcohol but in some underdeveloped countries the biomass is still burned directly as a fuel source. For example, for centuries, peat bogs were exploited as a traditional source of home heating and cooking fuel.

- **Fusion power:** Although the technology does not currently exist, researchers are actively pursuing the means to make fusion power a reality. Unlike fission, the other form of nuclear energy currently in use, fusion does not rely on splitting the atoms of uranium or other potentially deadly radioactive elements. Instead, fusion energy mimics the process that produces the energy of the Sun.

Energy is produced when small atomic nuclei fuse together to form new atoms. In a fusion reaction, two isotopes of hydrogen, deuterium, and tritium combine to make helium.

The most significant advantage of fusion power, as opposed to fission power, is that no dangerous radioactive isotopes are produced. The reaction produces only harmless helium, which easily diffuses into the atmosphere and escapes into outer space.

Also, the elements required for a fusion reaction are abundant on Earth (i.e., deuterium and tritium are extracted from seawater) and readily renew themselves through natural processes.

> **SKILL 34.2** **Applies knowledge of transfer of energy in a variety of situations** *(e.g., the production of heat, light, sound, and magnetic effects by electrical energy; the process of photosynthesis; weather processes; food webs; food and energy pyramids).*

See also Skill 33.1

Heat Transfer

Heat energy that moves into or out of a system is HEAT TRANSFER. The temperature change is positive for a gain in heat energy and negative when heat is removed from the object or system.

The formula for heat transfer is $Q = mc\Delta T$, where Q is the amount of heat energy transferred, m is the amount of substance (in kilograms), c is the specific heat of the substance, and ΔT is the change in temperature of the substance. It is important to assume that the objects in thermal contact are isolated and insulated from their surroundings. If a substance in a closed container loses heat, then another substance in the container must gain heat.

Heat is transferred in three ways: conduction, convection, and radiation.

CONDUCTION occurs when heat travels through a heated solid. The transfer rate is the ratio of the amount of heat per amount of time it takes to transfer heat from one area of an object to another. For example, if you place an iron pan on a flame, the handle will eventually become hot. How fast the handle gets hot is a function of the amount of heat applied and how long it is applied. Because the change in time is in the denominator of the function, the less time it takes to heat the handle, the greater the transfer rate.

CONVECTION is heat transported by the movement of a heated substance. Warmed air rising from a heat source such as a fire or electric heater is a common example of convection. Convection ovens make use of circulating air to more efficiently cook food.

RADIATION is heat transfer as the result of electromagnetic waves. The Sun warms the Earth by emitting radiant energy.

HEAT TRANSFER: heat energy that moves into or out of a system

CONDUCTION: when heat travels through a heated solid

CONVECTION: heat transported by the movement of a heated substance

RADIATION: heat transfer as the result of electromagnetic waves

SKILL 34.3 Understands applications of energy transformations and the conservation of matter and energy in life and in earth and space science.

The principle of conservation states that certain measurable properties of an isolated system remain constant despite changes in the system. Two important principles of conservation are the conservation of mass and charge.

> The principle of conservation of mass states that the total mass of a system is constant.

The principle of **conservation of mass** states that the total mass of a system is constant. Examples of conservation of mass in nature include the burning of wood, the rusting of iron, and phase changes of matter. When wood burns, the total mass of the products, such as soot, ash, and gases, equals the mass of the wood and the oxygen that reacts with it. When iron reacts with oxygen, rust is formed. The total mass of the iron-rust complex does not change. Finally, when matter changes phase, mass remains constant. Thus, when a glacier melts because of atmospheric warming, the mass of liquid water formed is equal to the mass of the glacier.

> The principle of conservation of charge states that the total electrical charge of a closed system is constant.

The principle of **conservation of charge** states that the total electrical charge of a closed system is constant. Thus, in chemical reactions and interactions of charged objects, the total charge does not change. Chemical reactions and the interaction of charged molecules are essential and common processes in living organisms and systems.

> The kinetic theory states that matter consists of molecules, possessing kinetic energy, in continual random motion.

The **kinetic theory** states that matter consists of molecules, possessing kinetic energy, in continual random motion. The state of matter (solid, liquid, or gas) depends on the speed of the molecules and the amount of kinetic energy the molecules possess. The molecules of solid matter merely vibrate, allowing strong intermolecular forces to hold the molecules in place. The molecules of liquid matter move freely and quickly throughout the body, and the molecules of gaseous matter move randomly and at high speeds.

Matter changes state when energy is added or taken away. The addition of energy, usually in the form of heat, increases the speed and kinetic energy of the component molecules. Faster-moving molecules more readily overcome the intermolecular attractions that maintain the form of solids and liquids. As the speed of molecules increases, matter changes state from solid to liquid to gas (melting and evaporation).

As matter loses heat energy, the speed of the component molecules decreases. Intermolecular forces have greater impact on slower-moving molecules. Thus, as the speed of molecules decreases, matter changes from gas to liquid to solid (condensation and freezing).

COMPETENCY 35
LIFE SCIENCE: STRUCTURE AND FUNCTION OF LIVING THINGS

> **SKILL 35.1** Understands that living systems have different structures that perform different functions.

See also Skill 35.5

Physical Processes of Plants

PHOTOSYNTHESIS is the process by which plants make carbohydrates from the energy of the Sun, carbon dioxide, and water. Oxygen is a waste product. Photosynthesis occurs in the chloroplast where the pigment chlorophyll traps sun energy. It is divided into two major steps:

> PHOTOSYNTHESIS: the process by which plants make carbohydrates from the energy of the Sun, carbon dioxide, and water

- **Light reactions:** Sunlight is trapped, water is split, and oxygen is given off. ATP is made and hydrogens reduce NADP to $NADPH_2$. The light reactions occur in light. The products of the light reactions enter into the dark reactions (Calvin cycle).

- **Dark reactions:** Carbon dioxide enters during the dark reactions that can occur with or without the presence of light. The energy transferred from $NADPH_2$ and ATP allows for the fixation of carbon into glucose.

The formula for photosynthesis is:

$$CO_2 + H_2O + \text{energy (from sunlight)} \quad \textbf{becomes} \quad C_6H_{12}O_6 + O_2$$

During times of decreased light, plants break down the products of photosynthesis through cellular respiration. Glucose, with the help of oxygen, breaks down and produces carbon dioxide and water as waste. Approximately 50 percent of the products of photosynthesis are used by the plant for energy.

Water travels up the xylem of the plant through the process of transpiration. Water sticks to itself (cohesion) and to the walls of the xylem (adhesion). As it evaporates through the stomata of the leaves, the water is pulled up the column from the roots. Environmental factors such as heat and wind increase the rate of transpiration. High humidity decreases the rate of transpiration.

Angiosperms are the largest group in the plant kingdom. They are the flowering plants that produce true seeds for reproduction. They first appeared about seventy million years ago when the dinosaurs were disappearing. The land was drying up and their ability to produce seeds that could remain dormant until conditions became acceptable allowed for their success. When compared to other plants, they also had more advanced vascular tissue and larger leaves for increased photosynthesis. Angiosperms reproduce through a method of double fertilization. An ovum is fertilized by two sperm. One sperm produces the new plant; the other forms the food supply for the developing plant.

The success of plant reproduction depends on seed dispersal, which involves the seed moving away from the parent plant to decrease competition for space, water, and minerals. Seeds can be carried by wind (maple trees), water (palm trees), or animals (burrs), or ingested by animals and released in their feces in another area.

Structures and Functions of Plant Components

Apical meristem: An area of cell division allowing for growth

Plant tissues: Specialization of tissues enabled plants to grow larger

Xylem: Transports water

Phloem: Transports food (glucose)

Cortex: Storage of food and water

Epidermis: Protective covering

Endodermis: Controls movement between the cortex and the cell interior

Pericycle: Meristematic tissue that can divide when necessary

Pith: Storage in stems

Sclerenchyma and **collenchyma:** Support in stems

Stomata: Openings on the underside of leaves that let carbon dioxide in and water out (transpiration)

Guard cells: Control the size of the stomata; if the plant has to conserve water, the stomata will close

Palisade mesophyll: Contain chloroplasts in leaves; site of photosynthesis

Spongy mesophyll: Open spaces in the leaf that allows for gas circulation

Seed coat: Protective covering on a seed

Cotyledon: Small seed leaf that emerges when the seed germinates

Endosperm: Food supply in the seed

Flowers: The reproductive organs of the plant

Pedicel: Supports the weight of the flower

Receptacle: Holds the floral organs at the base of the flower

Sepals: Green leaf-like parts that cover the flower prior to blooming

Petals: Contain coloration by pigments, whose purpose is to attract insects to assist in pollination

Anther: Male part that produces pollen

Filament: Supports the anther; the filament and anther make up the stamen

Stigma: Female part that holds pollen grains that came from the male part

Style: Tube that leads to the ovary (female)

Ovary: Contains the ovules; the stigma, style, and ovary make up the carpel

---

SKILL 35.2 Understands and describes stages in the life cycles of common plants and animals.

Life Cycles of Common Organisms

Bacteria reproduce by binary fission. This asexual process simply divides the bacterium in half. All new organisms are exact clones of the parent. The obvious advantage of asexual reproduction is that it does not require a partner. This is a huge advantage for organisms that do not move around. Not having to move around to reproduce also allows organisms to conserve energy. Asexual reproduction also tends to be faster. As asexual reproduction produces only exact copies of the parent organism, it does not allow for genetic variation, which means that mutations, or weaker qualities, will always be passed on.

Butterflies actually go through four different stages of life, but they only look like butterflies in the final stage. Many other animals also change as they grow. In the first stage, the adult butterfly lays an egg. In the second stage, the egg hatches into a caterpillar, or larva. Next (third stage), the caterpillar forms the chrysalis, or pupa. Finally, the chrysalis matures and the adult butterfly emerges.

Frogs also have multiple stages in their life cycle. Initially, an adult frog lays its eggs in the water (all amphibians require water for reproduction). In the second stage, tadpoles hatch from the eggs. The tadpoles swim in the water and use gills for breathing. Tadpoles have a tail that is used for locomotion but they grow legs as well. Somewhere between two and four months after hatching, the tadpole is known as a froglet. You can recognize a froglet because the rim around its tail, which appeared more fish-like, has disappeared; its tail is shorter, and its four legs have grown to the extent that its rear legs are bent underneath it to allow for a spring-like jump. The final stage of a frog's life is spent as an adult. Its tail has been entirely reabsorbed; it has a chubby frog-like appearance instead of the tadpole's fish-like appearance; and as a mature frog it can lay eggs.

SKILL 35.3 Understand that organisms have basic needs.

Living versus Nonliving Things

Several characteristics can be used to differentiate living from nonliving things:

1. **Living things are made of cells.** They grow, are capable of reproduction, and respond to stimuli.

2. **Living things must adapt to environmental changes or perish.**

3. **Living things carry on metabolic processes.** They use and make energy.

Basic Requirements for Life

All organisms are adapted to life in their unique habitat. The habitat includes all of the components of their physical environment and is a necessity for the species' survival. Below are several key components of a complete habitat that all organisms require.

Food and water

Because all biochemical reactions take place in aqueous environments, all organisms must have access to clean water, even if only infrequently. Organisms also require two types of food: a source of energy (fixed carbon) and a source of nutrients. Autotrophs can fix carbon for themselves, but must have access to certain inorganic precursors. These organisms must also be able to obtain other nutrients, such as nitrogen, from their environment. Heterotrophs, in contrast, must consume other organisms for both energy and nutrients. The species these organisms use as a food source must be present in their habitat.

Sunlight and air

This need is closely related to that for food and water because almost all species derive some needed nutrients from the sun and atmosphere. Plants require carbon dioxide for photosynthesis and oxygen is required for cellular respiration. Sunlight is also necessary for photosynthesis and is used by many animals to synthesize essential nutrients (for example, vitamin D).

Shelter and space

The need for shelter and space vary greatly among species. Many plants do not need shelter, per se, but must have adequate soil to spread their roots and acquire nutrients. Certain invasive species can threaten native plants by competing with them for space. Other types of plants and many animals also require protection from environmental hazards. Some locations may facilitate reproduction (for instance, nesting sites) or provide seasonal shelter (for examples, dens and caves used by hibernating species).

> **SKILL 35.4** Analyzes how structure complements function in cells, tissues, organs, organ systems and organisms.

See also Skill 35.5

Cell Types

Animal cells have a cell membrane, which lets nutrients in and waste materials out; a cytoplasm, which contains the cellular organelles; and a nucleus, which contains the cellular DNA.

Plant cells are similar to animal cells except they also contain a cell wall, which gives a rigid structure to the cell, and a chloroplast, which contains chlorophyll for photosynthesis.

A single-celled organism is called a PROTIST. Animal-like protists are called proto-zoans. They do not have chloroplasts. They are usually classified by the way they move for food. Amoebas engulf other protists by flowing around and over them. The paramecium has a hair-like structure that allows it to move back and forth like tiny oars searching for food. The euglena moves with a tail-like structure called a flagellum.

> **PROTIST:** a single-celled organism

Plant-like protists have cell walls and float in the ocean. Bacteria are the simplest protists. A bacterial cell is surrounded by a cell wall, but there is no nucleus inside the cell. Most bacteria do not contain chlorophyll so they do not make their own food. The classification of bacteria is by shape. Cocci are round; bacilli are rod-shaped; and spirilla are spiral-shaped.

Prokaryotes versus Eukaryotes

The cell is the basic unit of all living things. The two types of cells are prokaryotic and eukaryotic.

PROKARYOTIC CELLS consist only of bacteria and blue-green algae. Bacteria were most likely the first cells and date back in the fossil record to 3.5 billion years ago. The important things that put these cells in their own group are as follows:

1. They have no defined nucleus or nuclear membrane. The DNA and ribosomes float freely within the cell.

2. They have a thick cell wall. This is for protection, to give shape, and to keep the cell from bursting.

3. The cell walls contain amino sugars (glycoproteins). Penicillin works by disrupting the cell wall, which is bad for the bacteria but will not harm the host.

4. Some have a capsule made of polysaccharides, which make the bacteria sticky.

5. Some have pili, which is a strand of protein. This also allows for attachment of the bacteria and can be used for sexual reproduction (conjugation).

6. Some have flagella for movement.

EUKARYOTIC CELLS are found in protists (single-celled organisms), fungi, plants, and animals. Some features of eukaryotic cells include the following:

1. They are usually larger than prokaryotic cells.

2. They contain many organelles, which are membrane-bound areas for specific cell functions.

3. They contain a cytoskeleton that provides a protein framework for the cell.

4. They contain cytoplasm to support the organelles and contain the ions and molecules necessary for cell function.

Cell Organelles and Their Functions

Parts of eukaryotic cells

1. Nucleus: The brain of the cell. The nucleus contains:

   - **Chromosomes:** DNA, RNA, and proteins tightly coiled to conserve space while providing a large surface area.

- **Chromatin:** Loose structure of chromosomes. Chromosomes are called chromatin when the cell is not dividing.

- **Nucleoli:** Where ribosomes are made. These are seen as dark spots in the nucleus.

- **Nuclear membrane:** Contains pores that let RNA out of the nucleus. The nuclear membrane is continuous with the endoplasmic reticulum, which allows the membrane to expand or shrink if needed.

2. Ribosomes: The site of protein synthesis. Ribosomes may be free floating in the cytoplasm or attached to the endoplasmic reticulum. There may be up to a half a million ribosomes in a cell, depending on how much protein is made by the cell.

3. Endoplasmic reticulum: These are folded and provide a large surface area. They are the "roadway" of the cell and allow for transport of materials. The lumen of the endoplasmic reticulum helps to keep materials out of the cytoplasm and headed in the right direction. The endoplasmic reticulum is capable of building new membrane material. There are two types:

- **Smooth endoplasmic reticulum:** Contain no ribosomes on their surface.

- **Rough endoplasmic reticulum:** Contain ribosomes on their surface. This form of endoplasmic reticulum is abundant in cells that make many proteins, e.g., in the pancreas, which produces many digestive enzymes.

4. Golgi complex or Golgi apparatus: This structure is stacked to increase surface area. The Golgi complex functions to sort, modify, and package molecules that are made in other parts of the cell. These molecules are either sent out of the cell or to other organelles within the cell.

5. Lysosomes: Found mainly in animal cells. Lysosomes contain digestive enzymes that break down food, substances not needed, viruses, damaged cell components, and eventually the cell itself. It is believed that lysosomes are responsible for the aging process.

6. Mitochondria: Large organelles that make ATP to supply energy to the cell. Muscle cells have many mitochondria because they use a great deal of energy. The folds inside the mitochondria are called cristae. They provide a large surface where the reactions of cellular respiration occur. Mitochondria have their own DNA and are capable of reproducing themselves if a greater demand is made for additional energy. Mitochondria are found only in animal cells.

7. Plastids: Found in photosynthetic organisms only. They are similar to the mitochondria due to their double membrane structure. They also have their own DNA and can reproduce if increased capture of sunlight becomes necessary. There are several types of plastids:

- **Chloroplasts:** Green; function in photosynthesis. They are capable of trapping sunlight.

- **Chromoplasts:** Make and store yellow and orange pigments; they provide color to leaves, flowers, and fruits.

- **Amyloplasts:** Store starch and are used as a food reserve. They are abundant in roots like potatoes.

8. Cell Wall: Found in plant cells only, composed of cellulose and fibers. The cell wall is thick enough for support and protection yet porous enough to allow water and dissolved substances to enter. Cell walls are cemented to each other.

9. Vacuoles: Hold stored food and pigments. Vacuoles are very large in plants. This allows them to fill with water in order to provide turgor pressure. Lack of turgor pressure causes a plant to wilt.

10. Cytoskeleton: Composed of protein filaments attached to the plasma membrane and organelles. The cytoskeleton provides a framework for the cell and aids in cell movement. It constantly changes shape and moves about. Three types of fibers make up the cytoskeleton:

- **Microtubules:** Largest of the three; makes up cilia and flagella for locomotion. Flagella grow from a basal body. Some examples are sperm cells and tracheal cilia. Centrioles are also composed of microtubules. They form the spindle fibers that pull the cell apart into two cells during cell division. Centrioles are not found in the cells of higher plants.

- **Intermediate filaments:** Smaller than microtubules but larger than microfilaments. They help the cell to keep its shape.

- **Microfilaments:** Smallest of the three, made of actin and small amounts of myosin (as in muscle cells). They function in cell movement such as cytoplasmic streaming, endocytosis, and ameboid movement. This structure pinches the two cells apart after cell division, forming two cells.

> **SKILL 35.5** Identifies human body systems and describes their functions.

See also Skill 36.1

Skeletal System

The function of the skeletal system is to provide support. Vertebrates have an endoskeleton, with muscles attached to bones.

The AXIAL SKELETON consists of the bones of the skull and vertebrae. The APPENDICULAR SKELETON consists of the bones of the legs, arms, tail (in the case of animals), and shoulder girdle.

Bone is a connective tissue. Parts of the bone include compact bone which gives strength, spongy bone which contains red marrow to make blood cells, yellow marrow in the center of long bones to store fat cells, and the periosteum, which is the protective covering on the outside of the bone.

A joint is defined as a place where two bones meet. Joints enable movement. Ligaments attach bone to bone. Tendons attach bones to muscles.

> **AXIAL SKELETON:** the bones of the skull and vertebrae

> **APPENDICULAR SKELETON:** the bones of the legs, arms, tail (in the case of animals), and shoulder girdle

Muscular System

The function of the muscular system is to allow movement.

There are three types of muscle tissue:

- Skeletal muscle is voluntary. Skeletal muscles are attached to bones.

- Smooth muscle is involuntary. It is found in organs and enables functions such as digestion and respiration.

- Cardiac muscle is a specialized type of smooth muscle and is found in the heart.

Muscles can only contract; therefore, they work in antagonistic pairs to allow back-and-forward movement. Muscle fibers are made up of groups of myofibrils, which are made up of groups of sarcomeres. Actin and myosin are proteins that make up the sarcomere.

Physiology of muscle contraction

A nerve impulse strikes a muscle fiber. This causes calcium ions to flood the sarcomere. Calcium ions allow ATP to expend energy. The myosin fibers creep along the actin, causing the muscle to contract. Once the nerve impulse has passed, calcium is pumped out and the contraction ends.

Nervous System

The NEURON is the basic unit of the nervous system. It consists of the cell body, which contains the nucleus; an axon, which carries impulses away from the cell body, and the dendrite, which carries impulses toward the cell body. SYNAPSES are spaces between neurons. Chemicals called neurotransmitters are found close to the synapse. The myelin sheath, composed of Schwann cells, covers the neurons and provides insulation.

> **NEURON:** the basic unit of the nervous system

> **SYNAPSES:** spaces between neurons

Physiology of the nerve impulse

Nerve action depends on depolarization and an imbalance of electrical charges across the neuron. A polarized nerve has a positive charge outside the neuron. A depolarized nerve has a negative charge outside the neuron. Neurotransmitters turn off the sodium pump, which results in depolarization of the membrane. This wave of depolarization (as it moves from neuron to neuron) carries an electrical impulse. This is actually a wave of opening and closing gates that allows for the flow of ions across the synapse. Nerves have an action potential. There is a threshold of the level of chemicals that must be met or exceeded in order for muscles to respond. This is called the "all or none" response.

The reflex arc is the simplest nerve response. The brain is bypassed. When a stimulus (like touching a hot stove) occurs, sensors in the hand send the message directly to the spinal cord. This stimulates motor neurons that contract the muscles to move the hand.

Voluntary nerve responses involve the brain. Receptor cells send the message to sensory neurons, which lead to association neurons. The message is taken to the brain. Motor neurons are stimulated and the message is transmitted to effector cells, which then cause the end effect.

Organization of the nervous system

The somatic nervous system is controlled consciously. It consists of the central nervous system (brain and spinal cord) and the peripheral nervous system (nerves that extend from the spinal cord to the muscles). The autonomic nervous system is unconsciously controlled by the hypothalamus of the brain. Entities and processes controlled by the autonomic nervous system include smooth muscles, the heart, and digestion. The sympathetic nervous system works the opposite way the parasympathetic nervous system works. For example, if the sympathetic nervous system stimulates an action, the parasympathetic nervous system would end that action.

NEUROTRANSMITTERS are chemicals released by exocytosis. Some neurotransmitters stimulate while others inhibit action.

- **Acetylcholine:** The most common neurotransmitter; controls muscle contraction and heartbeat. The enzyme acetylcholinesterase breaks it down to end the transmission.

- **Epinephrine:** Responsible for the "fight or flight" reaction. Epinephrine causes an increase in heart rate and blood flow to prepare the body for action. It is also called adrenaline.

- **Endorphins and enkephalins:** These are natural painkillers released during serious injury and childbirth.

> **NEUROTRANSMITTERS:** chemicals released by exocytosis

Digestive System

The function of the digestive system is to break food down and absorb it into the bloodstream, where it can be delivered to all cells of the body for use in cellular respiration.

The teeth and saliva begin digestion by breaking food down into smaller pieces and lubricating it so it can be swallowed. The lips, cheeks, and tongue form a bolus (ball) of food. This is carried down the pharynx by the process of peristalsis (wave-like contractions) and enters the stomach through the cardiac sphincter, which closes to keep food from going back up.

In the stomach, pepsinogen and hydrochloric acid form pepsin, the enzyme that breaks down proteins. The food is broken down further by this chemical action and is turned into chyme, an acid. The pyloric sphincter muscle opens to allow the food to enter the small intestine. Most nutrient absorption occurs in the small intestine. Its large surface area, a result of its length and protrusions called villi and microvilli, allow for a great absorptive surface. Upon arrival into the small intestine, chyme is neutralized to allow the enzymes there to function. Any food left after the trip through the small intestine enters the large intestine. The large intestine functions to reabsorb water and produce vitamin K. Feces, or remaining waste, are passed out through the anus.

Although not part of the digestive tract, accessory organs function in the production of necessary enzymes and bile. The pancreas makes a number of enzymes to break down food in the small intestine. The liver makes bile, which breaks down and emulsifies fatty acids.

> *The function of the digestive system is to break food down and absorb it into the bloodstream, where it can be delivered to all cells of the body for use in cellular respiration.*

Respiratory System

The respiratory system functions in the gas exchange of oxygen (needed) and carbon dioxide (waste). It delivers oxygen to the bloodstream and picks up carbon dioxide for release out of the body.

Air enters the mouth and nose, where it is warmed, moistened, and filtered of dust and particles. Cilia in the trachea trap unwanted material in mucus, which can be expelled. The trachea splits into two bronchial tubes, and the bronchial tubes divide into smaller and smaller bronchioles in the lungs. The internal surface of the lung is composed of alveoli, which are thin-walled air sacs. These sacs provide a large surface area for gas exchange. The alveoli are lined with capillaries. Oxygen diffuses into the bloodstream and carbon dioxide diffuses out to be exhaled. The oxygenated blood is carried to the heart and delivered to all parts of the body.

The thoracic cavity holds the lungs. A muscle, the diaphragm, below the lungs is an adaptation that makes inhalation possible. As the volume of the thoracic cavity increases, the diaphragm muscle flattens out and inhalation occurs. When the diaphragm relaxes, exhalation occurs.

Circulatory System

The function of the circulatory system is to carry oxygenated blood and nutrients to all cells of the body and return carbon dioxide waste to be expelled from the lungs.

Unoxygenated blood enters the heart through the inferior and superior vena cava. The first chamber it encounters is the right atrium. It goes through the tricuspid valve to the right ventricle, on to the pulmonary arteries, and then to the lungs where it is oxygenated. It returns to the heart through the pulmonary vein into the left atrium. It travels through the bicuspid valve to the left ventricle where it is pumped to all parts of the body through the aorta.

The sinoatrial node (SA node) is the pacemaker of the heart. Located on the right atrium, it is responsible for contraction of the right and left atrium. The atrioventricular node (AV node), located on the left ventricle, is responsible for contraction of the ventricles.

Blood vessels include the following:

- Arteries: Lead away from the heart. All arteries carry oxygenated blood except the pulmonary artery going to the lungs. Arteries are under high pressure.

- Arterioles: Arteries branch off to form these smaller passages.

- **Capillaries:** Arterioles branch off to form tiny capillaries that reach every cell. Blood moves very slowly in capillaries because they are so small; only one red blood cell can pass at a time to allow for diffusion of gases into and out of cells. Nutrients are also absorbed by the cells from the capillaries.

- **Venules:** Capillaries combine to form larger venules. The vessels are now carrying waste products from the cells.

- **Veins:** Venules combine to form larger veins, leading back to the heart. Veins and venules have thinner walls than arteries because they are not under as much pressure. Veins contain valves to prevent the backward flow of blood due to gravity.

The following are components of the blood:

- **Plasma:** Sixty percent of the blood is plasma. Plasma, the liquid part of blood, contains salts called electrolytes, nutrients, and waste.

- **Erythrocytes:** Also called red blood cells, erythrocytes contain hemoglobin that carries oxygen molecules.

- **Leukocytes:** Also called white blood cells. White blood cells are larger than red cells. They are phagocytic and can engulf invaders. White blood cells are not confined to the blood vessels and can enter the interstitial fluid between cells.

- **Platelets:** Assist in blood clotting. Platelets are made in the bone marrow.

> Sixty percent of the blood is plasma. Plasma, the liquid part of blood, contains salts called electrolytes, nutrients, and waste.

The neurotransmitter that initiates blood-vessel constriction following an injury is called serotonin. A material called prothrombin is converted to thrombin with the help of thromboplastin. The thrombin is then used to convert fibrinogen to fibrin, which traps red blood cells to form a scab and stop blood flow.

Human Reproductive System

Development and function of male and female reproductive systems

Hormones regulate sexual maturation in humans. Humans cannot reproduce until puberty, about the age of 8–14, depending on the individual. The hypothalamus begins secreting hormones that help mature the reproductive system and develop the secondary sex characteristics. Reproductive maturity in girls occurs with their first menstruation and in boys with the first ejaculation of viable sperm.

Hormones also regulate reproduction. In males, the primary sex hormones are the androgens, testosterone being the most important. The testes produce androgens that dictate the primary and secondary sex characteristics of the male. Female hormone patterns are cyclic and complex. Most women have a reproductive cycle of approximately twenty-eight days. The menstrual cycle is specific to the changes in the uterus. The ovarian cycle results in ovulation and occurs in parallel with the menstrual cycle. Hormones regulate this parallelism. Five hormones participate in this regulation, most notably estrogen and progesterone. Estrogen and progesterone play an important role in signaling to the uterus and in the development and maintenance of the endometrium. Estrogens also dictate the secondary sex characteristics of females.

Gametogenesis, fertilization, and birth control

GAMETOGENESIS is the production of the sperm and egg cells.

> **GAMETOGENESIS:** the production of the sperm and egg cells

Spermatogenesis begins at puberty in the male. One spermatogonia, the diploid precursor of sperm, produces four sperm. The sperm mature in the seminiferous tubules located in the testes. Oogenesis, the production of egg cells (ova), is usually complete by the birth of a female. Females do not release egg cells until menstruation begins at puberty. Meiosis forms one ovum with all the cytoplasm and three polar bodies that the body reabsorbs. The ovaries store the ovum and release one each month from puberty to menopause.

Seminiferous tubules in the testes house sperm, where they mature. The epididymis, located on top of the testes, contains mature sperm. After ejaculation, the sperm travel up the vas deferens, where they mix with semen made in the prostate and seminal vesicles and travel out the urethra.

Ovulation releases the egg into the fallopian tubes where cilia move it along the length of the tubes. Fertilization of the egg by the sperm normally occurs in the fallopian tube. If pregnancy does not occur, the egg passes through the uterus and is expelled through the vagina during menstruation. Levels of progesterone and estrogen stimulate menstruation. Implantation of a fertilized egg regulates the levels, stopping menstruation.

There are many methods of contraception (birth control) that affect different stages of fertilization. Chemical contraception (birth control pills) prevents ovulation by synthetic estrogen and progesterone. Several barrier methods of contraception are available. Male and female condoms block semen from contacting the egg. Sterilization is another method of birth control. Tubal ligation in women prevents eggs from entering the uterus. A vasectomy in men involves the cutting of the vas deferens. This prevents the sperm from entering the urethra. The most effective method of birth control is abstinence. Programs exist worldwide that promote abstinence, especially among teenagers.

Lymphatic System (Immune System)

Nonspecific defense mechanisms do not target specific pathogens but are a whole-body response. Results of nonspecific mechanisms are seen as symptoms of an infection. These mechanisms include the skin, mucous membranes, and cells of the blood and lymph (i.e., white blood cells, macrophages). Fever is a result of an increase of white blood cells. Pyrogens are released by white blood cells, which set the body's thermostat to a higher temperature. This inhibits the growth of microorganisms. It also increases metabolism to increase phagocytosis and body repair.

Specific defense mechanisms recognize foreign material and respond by destroying the invader. These mechanisms are specific in purpose and diverse in type. They are able to recognize individual pathogens and differentiate between foreign material and self. Memory of the invaders provides immunity upon further exposure.

An **ANTIGEN** is any foreign particle that invades the body. Manufactured by the body, **antibodies** recognize and latch onto antigens, hopefully destroying them.

IMMUNITY is the body's ability to recognize and destroy an antigen before it causes harm. Active immunity develops after recovery from an infectious disease (e.g., chicken pox) or after a vaccination (e.g., mumps, measles, rubella). Passive immunity can be passed from one individual to another. It is not permanent. A good example is when the immunities are passed from mother to nursing child.

> **ANTIGEN:** any foreign particle that invades the body

> **IMMUNITY:** the body's ability to recognize and destroy an antigen before it causes harm

Excretory System

The function of the excretory system is to rid the body of nitrogenous wastes in the form of urea.

The functional units of excretion are the nephrons, which make up the kidneys. Antidiuretic hormone (ADH), which is made in the hypothalamus and stored in the pituitary, is released when differences in osmotic balance occur. This will cause more water to be reabsorbed. As the blood becomes more dilute, ADH release ceases.

The Bowman's capsule contains the glomerulus, a tightly packed group of capillaries. The glomerulus is under high pressure. Waste and fluids leak out due to pressure. Filtration is not selective in this area. Selective secretion by active and passive transport occur in the proximal convoluted tubule. Unwanted molecules are secreted into the filtrate. Selective secretion also occurs in the loop of Henle. Salt is actively pumped out of the tube and much water is lost due to the hyperosmosity of the inner part (medulla) of the kidney. As the fluid enters the distal convoluted tubule, more water is reabsorbed.

Urine forms in the collecting duct that leads to the ureter, then to the bladder where it is stored. Urine is passed from the bladder through the urethra. The amount of water reabsorbed back into the body depends on how much water or fluid an individual has consumed. Urine can be very dilute or very concentrated if a person is dehydrated.

Endocrine System

The function of the endocrine system is to manufacture proteins called hormones. Hormones are released into the bloodstream and carried to a target tissue where they stimulate an action. Hormones can build up over time to cause their effect, as in puberty or the menstrual cycle.

Hormones fit specific receptors on the target tissue cell surface. The receptor activates an enzyme that converts ATP to cyclic AMP. Cyclic AMP (cAMP) is a second messenger from the cell membrane to the nucleus. The genes found in the nucleus turn on or off to cause a specific response.

There are two classes of hormones: steroid hormones and peptide hormones. Steroid hormones, which come from cholesterol, cause sexual characteristics and mating behavior. These hormones include estrogen and progesterone in females and testosterone in males. Peptide hormones are made in the pituitary glands, adrenal glands (kidneys), and the pancreas. They include:

- **Follicle-stimulating hormone (FSH):** production of sperm or egg cells
- **Luteotropic hormone (LTH):** assists in production of progesterone
- **Growth hormone (GH):** stimulates growth
- **Antidiuretic hormone (ADH):** assists in retention of water
- **Oxytocin:** stimulates labor contractions at birth and letdown of milk
- **Melatonin:** regulates circadian rhythms and seasonal changes
- **Epinephrine (adrenaline):** causes fight-or-flight reaction of the nervous system
- **Thyroxin:** increases metabolic rate
- **Calcitonin:** removes calcium from the blood
- **Insulin:** decreases glucose level in blood
- **Glucagon:** increases glucose level in blood

Hormones work on a feedback system. The increase or decrease in one hormone may cause the increase or decrease in another.

Hormones work on a feedback system. The increase or decrease in one hormone may cause the increase or decrease in another. Release of hormones causes a specific response.

> **SKILL 35.6** **Understands the relationship between characteristics, structures, and functions and corresponding taxonomic classifications.**

Form (also structure) follows function is a principle used to characterize and describe biological systems. This principle implies that an organism is designed in such a way that its individual parts and structures each serve specific purposes in the overall functioning of the organism.

For example, plants have the chlorophyll-containing chloroplasts that are the primary sites for photosynthesis. Similarly, the branched network of tubes in the human lung provides efficient gas exchange that is necessary for breathing.

Carl Von Linnaeus (1707–1778), a Swedish botanist, physician, and zoologist, developed the binomial system of nomenclature in which each living organism has two names, one for its genus and the other for its species. His binomial system has been expanded to include more general classifications of organisms so that they can be grouped broadly. Taxonomic classifications are based on the similarities in structure and function between different species of organisms. The labels in the taxonometric naming system describe an organism in a series of classifications that goes from general to specific names. The order of organism classification in increasing specificity is as follows:

> *Taxonomic classifications are based on the similarities in structure and function between different species of organisms.*

- Domain

    - Archaea – prokaryotic organisms with branched hydrocarbon chains in cell membrane

    - Bacteria – prokaryotic organisms with unbranched hydrocarbon chains in cell membrane

    - Eukarya – eukaryotic organisms

- Kingdom (most general classification)

    - Eubacteria

    - Archaebacteria

    - Animalia

    - Plantae

    - Fungi

    - Protista

- Phylum/Division (divisions used for plants and fungi)

- Class

- Order

- Family

- Genus (plural, *genera*)

- Species (most specific)

An example of grouping organisms by shared characteristics and functions is that organisms with photosynthetic properties are categorized into the Plantae (or Plant) kingdom. Organisms that cannot create the food they need to survive and are able to move around are classified into the Animalia (or Animal) kingdom.

COMPETENCY 36
REPRODUCTION AND THE MECHANISMS OF HEREDITY

> SKILL **Describes the processes by which plants and animals reproduce and**
> 36.1 **explains how hereditary information is passed from one generation to the next.**

Reproduction

For more information about human reproduction, see Skill 35.5.

Sexual reproduction greatly increases diversity because of the many combinations possible through meiosis and fertilization. All organisms (except twins or clones) are genetically unique and represent a unique combination of genetic heritable variation.

Variation is generated by mutation and, in sexually reproducing species, sexual recombination. Mutations can be errors in replication or a spontaneous rearrangement of one or more segments of DNA and—ultimately—mutations are responsible for all innovative heritable variation. Mutations contribute a minimal but constant amount of variation in a population. In sexually reproducing species, the unique recombination of existing alleles causes the majority of genetic difference between individuals. Genetic variability is caused by independent assortment during meiosis, random fertilization, and crossing over during meiosis.

> *Variation is generated by mutation and, in sexually reproducing species, sexual recombination.*

Gametogenesis is the production of the sperm and egg cells. Spermatogenesis begins at puberty in the male. One spermatozoa produces four sperm. The sperm mature in the seminiferous tubules located in the testes. Oogenesis, the production of egg cells, is usually complete by the birth of a female. Egg cells are not released until menstruation begins at puberty. Meiosis (division of sex cells) forms one ovum with all the cytoplasm and three polar bodies, which are reabsorbed by the body. The ovum are stored in the ovaries and released each month from puberty to menopause.

Path of the sperm

Sperm are stored in the seminiferous tubules in the testes, where they mature. Mature sperm are found in the epididymis, located on top of the testes. After ejaculation, the sperm travels up the vas deferens, where they mix with semen made in the prostate and seminal vesicles and travel out the urethra.

Path of the egg

Eggs are stored in the ovaries. Ovulation releases an egg into the fallopian tubes, which are ciliated to move the egg along. Fertilization normally occurs in the fallopian tube. If pregnancy does not occur, the egg passes through the uterus and is expelled through the vagina during menstruation. Levels of progesterone and estrogen stimulate menstruation. In the event of pregnancy, hormonal levels are affected by the implantation of a fertilized egg, so menstruation does not occur.

Pregnancy

If fertilization occurs, the zygote implants in about two to three days in the uterus. Implantation promotes secretion of human chorionic gonadotropin (HCG). This is the hormone detected in pregnancy tests. The HCG keeps the level of progesterone elevated to maintain the uterine lining in order to feed the developing embryo until the umbilical cord forms. Labor is initiated by oxytocin, which causes labor contractions and dilation of the cervix. Prolactin and oxytocin cause the production of milk.

Cell Division

The purpose of cell division is to provide growth and repair in body (somatic) cells and to replenish or create sex cells for reproduction. There are two forms of cell division: MITOSIS is the division of somatic cells and MEIOSIS is the division of sex cells (eggs and sperm). The table below summarizes the major differences between the two processes.

> **MITOSIS:** the division of somatic cells

> **MEIOSIS:** the division of sex cells (eggs and sperm)

Mitosis	Meiosis
1. Division of somatic cells	1. Division of sex cells
2. Two cells result from each division	2. Four cells or polar bodies result from each division
3. Chromosome number is identical to parent cells	3. Chromosome number is half the number of parent cells
4. Division occurs for cell growth and repair	4. Recombinations provide genetic diversity

Key terms

- **Gamete:** Sex cell or germ cell; eggs and sperm.

- **Chromatin:** Mass of DNA and associated proteins that condenses to form chromosomes during cell division.

- **Chromosomes:** Strands of coiled DNA and associated proteins. Carries genetic information in a linear sequence.

- **Homologues:** Chromosomes that contain the same information. They are of the same length and contain the same genes.

- **Diploid:** 2n number; diploid chromosomes are a pair of chromosomes (somatic cells).

- **Haploid:** 1n number; haploid chromosomes are half of a pair (sex cells).

Mitosis

The life cycle of a cell is known as the cell cycle. It is divided into two stages: interphase and mitotic division, when the cell is actively dividing.

Interphase is divided into three steps:

1. G1 (growth) period, when the cell is growing and metabolizing

2. S period (synthesis), when new DNA and enzymes are being made

3. G2 phase (growth), when new proteins and organelles are being made to prepare for cell division

The mitotic stage consists of the stages of mitosis and the division of the cytoplasm. The stages of mitosis and their events are as follows. It is important to know the correct order of steps (IPMAT).

1. Interphase: Chromatin is loose; chromosomes are replicated; cell metabolism is occurring. Interphase is technically *not* a stage of mitosis.

2. Prophase: Once the cell enters prophase, it proceeds through the following steps continuously, with no stopping. The chromatin condenses to become visible chromosomes. The nucleolus disappears and the nuclear membrane breaks apart. Mitotic spindles form, which will eventually pull the chromosomes apart. They are composed of microtubules. The cytoskeleton breaks down and the spindles are pushed to the poles or opposite ends of the cell by the action of centrioles.

3. Metaphase: Kinetechore fibers attach to the chromosomes, which causes the chromosomes to line up in the center of the cell (think: **m**iddle for **m**etaphase).

4. Anaphase: Centromeres split in half and homologous chromosomes separate. The chromosomes are pulled to the poles of the cell, with identical sets at either end.

5. **Telophase:** Two nuclei form with a full set of DNA that is identical to the parent cell. The nucleoli become visible and the nuclear membrane reassembles. A cell plate is visible in plant cells, whereas a cleavage furrow is formed in animal cells. The cell is pinched into two cells. Cytokinesis, or division, of the cytoplasm and organelles occurs.

Meiosis

Meiosis has the same five stages as mitosis, but is repeated in order to reduce the chromosome number by one half. This way, when the sperm and egg join during fertilization, the haploid number is reached. The steps of meiosis are as follows:

Major function of meiosis I: Chromosomes are replicated; cells remain diploid

- **Prophase I:** Replicated chromosomes condense and pair with homologues. This forms a tetrad. Crossing over (the exchange of genetic material between homologues to further increase diversity) occurs during Prophase I.

- **Metaphase I:** Homologous sets attach to spindle fibers after lining up in the middle of the cell.

- **Anaphase I:** Sister chromatids remain joined and move to the poles of the cell.

- **Telophase I:** Two new cells are formed; chromosome number is still diploid.

Major function of meiosis II: To reduce the chromosome number in half

- **Prophase II:** Chromosomes condense.

- **Metaphase II:** Spindle fibers form again; sister chromatids line up in center of cell; centromeres divide; and sister chromatids separate.

- **Anaphase II:** Separated chromosomes move to opposite ends of cell.

- **Telophase II:** Four haploid cells form for each original sperm germ cell. One viable egg cell gets all the genetic information and three polar bodies form with no DNA. The nuclear membrane reforms and cytokinesis occurs.

DNA and DNA Replication

The modern definition of a gene is a unit of genetic information. DNA makes up genes, which in turn make up the chromosomes. DNA is wound tightly around proteins in order to conserve space. The DNA/protein combination makes up the chromosome. DNA controls the synthesis of proteins, thereby controlling the total cell activity. DNA is capable of making copies of itself.

DNA structure

DNA is made of nucleotides, which are composed of a five-carbon sugar, phosphate group, and nitrogen base (adenine, guanine, cytosine, or thymine).

It consists of a sugar/phosphate backbone that is covalently bonded. The bases are joined down the center of the molecule and attached by hydrogen bonds that are easily broken during replication.

The amount of adenine equals the amount of thymine, and the amount of cytosine equals the amount of guanine.

The shape of DNA is called a double helix and looks like a twisted ladder. The sugar/phosphates make up the sides of the ladder and the base pairs make up the rungs of the ladder.

> *DNA is made of nucleotides, which are composed of a five-carbon sugar, phosphate group, and nitrogen base (adenine, guanine, cytosine, or thymine).*

DNA replication

Enzymes control each step of the replication of DNA. The DNA molecule untwists. The hydrogen bonds between the bases break and serve as a pattern for replication. Free nucleotides inside the nucleus join on to form a new strand. Two new pieces of DNA are formed that are identical. This is a very accurate process. There is only one mistake for every billion nucleotides added. This is because there are enzymes (polymerases) present that proofread the molecule. In eukaryotes, replication occurs in many places along the DNA at once. The molecule may open up at many places like a broken zipper. In prokaryotic circular plasmids, replication begins at a point on the plasmid and goes in both directions until the circle is complete.

Base-pairing rules are important in determining a new strand of DNA sequence. For example, say our original strand of DNA had the following sequence:

A T C G G C A A T A G C

This can be called our sense strand, as it contains a sequence that makes sense or codes for something. The complementary strand (or other side of the ladder) would follow base-pairing rules (A bonds with T, and C bonds with G) and would read:

T A G C C G T T A T C G

When the molecule opens up and nucleotides join on, the base-pairing rules create two new identical strands of DNA:

A T C G G C A A T A G C   and   A T C G G C A A T A G C
T A G C C G T T A T C G   T A G C C G T T A T C G

Protein Synthesis

It is necessary for cells to manufacture new proteins for growth and repair of the organism. PROTEIN SYNTHESIS is the process that allows the DNA code to be read and carried out of the nucleus into the cytoplasm in the form of RNA. This is where the ribosomes are found, which are the sites of protein synthesis. The protein is then assembled according to the instructions on the DNA. There are several types of RNA:

> **PROTEIN SYNTHESIS:** the process that allows the DNA code to be read and carried out of the nucleus into the cytoplasm in the form of RNA

- **Messenger RNA (mRNA):** Copies the code from DNA in the nucleus and takes it to the ribosomes in the cytoplasm.

- **Transfer RNA (tRNA):** Free floating in the cytoplasm. Its job is to carry and position amino acids for assembly on the ribosome.

- **Ribosomal RNA (rRNA):** Found in the ribosomes. They make a place for the proteins to be made. This type of RNA is believed to have many important functions, so much research is currently being done in this area.

Along with enzymes and amino acids, the RNA's function is to assist in the building of proteins. There are two stages of protein synthesis:

- **Transcription:** This phase allows for the assembly of mRNA and occurs in the nucleus where the DNA is found. The DNA splits open and the mRNA reads the code and "transcribes" the sequence onto a single strand of mRNA. For example, if the code on the DNA is T A C C T C G T A C G A, the mRNA will make a complementary strand reading: A U G G A G C A U G C U (remember that uracil replaces thymine in RNA). Each group of three bases is called a codon. The codon will eventually code for a specific amino acid to be carried to the ribosome. "Start" codons begin the building of the protein and "stop" codons end transcription. When the stop codon is reached, the mRNA separates from the DNA and leaves the nucleus for the cytoplasm.

- **Translation:** This is the assembly of the amino acids to build the protein and occurs in the cytoplasm. The nucleotide sequence is translated to choose the correct amino acid sequence. As the rRNA translates the code at the ribosome, tRNAs that contain an anticodon seek out the correct amino acid and bring it back to the ribosome. For example, using the codon sequence from the example above:

  The mRNA reads: A U G / G A G / C A U / G C U
  The anticodons are: U A C / C U C / G U A / C G A
  The amino acid sequence would be: Methionine (start) - Glu - His - Ala

This whole process is accomplished through the assistance of activating enzymes. Each of the twenty amino acids has its own enzyme. The enzyme binds the amino acid to the tRNA. When the amino acids get close to each other on the ribosome, they bond together using peptide bonds. The start and stop codons are called nonsense codons. There is one start codon (AUG) and three stop codons (UAA, UGA, and UAG). Addition mutations will cause the whole code to shift, thereby producing the wrong protein or, at times, no protein at all.

Irregularities or interruptions of mitosis and meiosis

Since it's not a perfect world, mistakes happen. Inheritable changes in DNA are called MUTATIONS. Mutations can be errors in replication or a spontaneous rearrangement of one or more segments by factors like radioactivity, drugs, or chemicals. The amount of change is not as critical as where the change is.

Mutations can occur on somatic or sex cells. Usually the ones on sex cells are more dangerous since they contain the basis of all information for the developing offspring. Mutations are not always bad. They are the basis of evolution, and if they make a more favorable variation that enhances the organism's survival, then they are beneficial. But mutations can also lead to abnormalities, birth defects, and even death. There are several types of mutations. Let's suppose a normal sequence was as follows:

Normal: A B C D E F

Duplication: One gene is repeated (A B C C D E F).

Inversion: A segment of the sequence is flipped around (A E D C B F).

Deletion: A gene is left out (A B C E F).

Insertion or translocation: A segment from another place on the DNA is inserted in the wrong place (A B C R S D E F).

Breakage: A piece is lost (A B C); DEF is lost.

Nondisjunction: This occurs during meiosis when chromosomes fail to separate properly. One sex cell may get both genes and another may get none. Depending on the chromosomes involved, this may or may not be serious. Offspring end up with either an extra chromosome or a missing one. An example of nondisjunction is Down syndrome, in which there are three copies of chromosome 21 instead of two.

MUTATIONS: inheritable changes in DNA

Mutations can be errors in replication or a spontaneous rearrangement of one or more segments by factors like radioactivity, drugs, or chemicals. The amount of change is not as critical as where the change is.

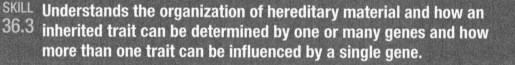

SKILL 36.2 Compares and contrasts inherited traits and learned characteristics.

See also Skill 36.3

Behavior

Animal behavior is responsible for courtship leading to mating, communication between species, territoriality, aggression between animals, and dominance within a group. Animal behaviors may include various body postures, mating calls, display of feathers/fur, coloration, or bearing of teeth and claws.

Innate behavior is behavior that is inborn or instinctual. An environmental stimulus such as the length of day or temperature results in a behavior. Hibernation among some animals is an innate behavior.

Learned behavior is behavior that has been modified based on past experience.

SKILL 36.3 Understands the organization of hereditary material and how an inherited trait can be determined by one or many genes and how more than one trait can be influenced by a single gene.

See also Skill 36.1

Gregor Mendel is recognized as the father of genetics. His work in the late 1800s is the basis of our knowledge of genetics. Although unaware of the presence of DNA or genes, Mendel realized that there were factors (now known as genes) that were transferred from parents to their offspring.

Mendel worked with pea plants and fertilized the plants himself, keeping track of subsequent generations, which led to the Mendelian laws of genetics. Mendel found that two factors governed each trait, one from each parent. Traits or characteristics came in several forms, known as alleles. For example, the trait of flower color had white alleles (*pp*) and purple alleles (*PP*). Mendel formed two laws: the law of segregation and the law of independent assortment.

The Law of Segregation

The LAW OF SEGREGATION states that only one of the two possible alleles from each parent is passed on to the offspring. If the two alleles differ, then one is fully expressed in the organism's appearance (the dominant allele) and the other has no noticeable effect on appearance (the recessive allele).

The two alleles for each trait segregate into different gametes. A Punnett square can be used to show the law of segregation. In a Punnett square, one parent's genes are put at the top of the box and the other parent's on the side. Genes combine in the squares just as numbers are added in addition tables. This Punnett square shows the result of the cross of two F_1 hybrids.

	P	p
P	PP	Pp
p	Pp	pp

$P \quad PP \times pp$

$F_1 \quad Pp \times Pp$

$F_2 \quad \frac{1}{4} + \frac{1}{2} + \frac{1}{4}$

This cross results in a 1:2:1 ratio of F_2 offspring. Here, the P is the dominant allele and the p is the recessive allele. The F_1 cross produces three offspring with the dominant allele expressed (two PP and Pp) and one offspring with the recessive allele expressed (pp).

These are some other important terms to know:

- **Homozygous:** having a pair of identical alleles; for example, PP and pp are homozygous pairs.
- **Heterozygous:** having two different alleles; for example, Pp is a heterozygous pair.
- **Phenotype:** the organism's physical appearance.
- **Genotype:** the organism's genetic makeup; for example, PP and Pp have the same phenotype (purple in color), but different genotypes.

The Law of Independent Assortment

The law of independent assortment states that alleles sort independently of one another. The law of segregation applies for monohybrid crosses (only one character—in this case, flower color—is experimented with). In a dihybrid cross, two characters are being explored.

Two of the seven characters Mendel studied were seed shape and color. Yellow is the dominant seed color (Y) and green is the recessive color (y). The dominant seed shape is round (R) and the recessive shape is wrinkled (r). A cross between a plant with yellow round seeds ($YYRR$) and a plant with green wrinkled seeds ($yyrr$) produces an F_1 generation with the genotype $YyRr$. The production of F_2 offspring results in a 9:3:3:1 phenotypic ratio.

	YR	Yr	yR	yr
YR	YYRR	YYRr	YyRR	YyRr
Yr	YYRr	YYrr	YyRr	Yyrr
yR	YyRR	YyRr	yyRR	yyRr
yr	YyRr	Yyrr	yyRr	yyrr

P $YYRR \times yyrr$

F_1 $YyRr$

F_2

$YYRR$ – 1
$YYRr$ – 2
$YyRR$ – 2
$YyRr$ – 4
} 9 yellow round

$yyRR$ – 1
$yyRr$ – 2
} 3 yellow round

$YYrr$ – 1
$Yyrr$ – 2
} 3 yellow wrinkled

$yyrr$ – 1 } 1 green wrinkled

SKILL 36.4 Distinguishes between dominant and recessive traits and predicts the probable outcomes of genetic combinations.

See also Skill 36.3

Based on Mendelian genetics, the more complex hereditary pattern of **dominance** was discovered. In Mendel's law of segregation, the F_1 generation has either purple or white flowers. This is an example of **complete dominance**.

Incomplete dominance is when the F_1 generation results in an appearance that is a cross between the two parents. For example, red flowers are crossed with white flowers, resulting in an F_1 generation with pink flowers. The red and white traits are still carried by the F_1 generation, resulting in an F_2 generation with a phenotypic ration of 1:2:1.

In **codominance**, the genes may form new phenotypes. The ABO blood grouping is an example of codominance. Types A and B are of equal strength and type O is recessive. Therefore, type A blood may have the genotypes of AA or AO; type B blood may have the genotypes of BB or BO; type AB blood has the genotype A and B; and type O blood has two recessive O genes.

SKILL 36.5 Evaluates the influence of environmental and genetic factors on the traits of an organism.

See also Skills 35.1 and 36.1

BIOTIC FACTORS are living things in an ecosystem: plants, animals, bacteria, fungi, and so on. If one population in a community increases, it affects the ability of another population to succeed by limiting the available amount of food, water, shelter, and space.

ABIOTIC FACTORS are nonliving aspects of an ecosystem: soil quality, rainfall, and temperature. Changes in climate and soil can cause effects at the beginning of the food chain, thus limiting or accelerating the growth of populations.

BIOTIC FACTORS: living things in an ecosystem: plants, animals, bacteria, fungi, and so on

ABIOTIC FACTORS: nonliving aspects of an ecosystem: soil quality, rainfall, and temperature

COMPETENCY 37
ADAPTATIONS AND EVOLUTION

> **SKILL 37.1** Demonstrates knowledge of adaptive characteristics and explains how adaptations influence the survival of populations or species.

Theory of Natural Selection

Darwin defined the theory of natural selection in the mid-1800s. Through the study of finches on the Galapagos Islands, Darwin theorized that nature selects the traits that are advantageous to the organism. Those individuals that do not possess the desirable traits die and do not pass on their genes to future generations. Those more fit to survive reproduce, thus increasing the stronger genes in the population.

> Darwin defined the theory of natural selection in the mid-1800s.

Darwin listed four principles to define natural selection:

1. The individuals in a certain species vary from generation to generation.

2. Some of the variations are determined by the genetic makeup of the species.

3. More individuals are produced than will survive.

4. Some genes allow for better survival of an animal.

Causes of evolution

Certain factors increase the chances of variation in a population, thus leading to evolution. Factors that increase variation include mutations, sexual reproduction, immigration, and large populations. Factors that decrease variation are natural selection, emigration, small populations, and random mating.

Sexual selection

Genes that happen to come together determine the makeup of the gene pool. Animals use mating behaviors that may be successful or unsuccessful. An animal that lacks attractive plumage or has a weak mating call will not attract a female, thereby eventually limiting the gene associated with that feature in the gene pool.

Biological adaptation

Anatomical structures and physiological processes that evolve over geological time to increase the overall reproductive success of an organism in its environment are known as BIOLOGICAL ADAPTATIONS. Such evolutionary changes occur through natural selection, the process by which individual organisms with favorable traits survive to reproduce more frequently than those with unfavorable traits. The heritable component of such favorable traits is passed down to offspring during reproduction, increasing the frequency of the favorable trait in a population over many generations.

Adaptations increase long-term reproductive success by making an organism better suited for survival under particular environmental conditions and pressures. These biological changes can increase an organism's ability to obtain air, water, food, and nutrients, to cope with environmental variables, and to defend themselves. The term adaptation may apply to changes in biological processes that, for example, enable an organism to produce venom or regulate body temperature, and also to structural adaptations, such as organisms' skin color and shape. Adaptations can occur in behavioral traits and survival mechanisms as well.

One well-known structural change that demonstrates the concept of adaptation is the development of the primate and human opposable thumb, the first digit of the hand, which can be moved around to touch other digits and to grasp objects. The history of the opposable thumb is one of complexly linked structural and behavioral adaptations in response to environmental stressors.

Early apes first appearing in the Tertiary Period were mostly tree-dwelling organisms who foraged for food and avoided predators by remaining high above the ground. The apes' need to quickly and effectively navigate among branches led to the eventual development of the opposable thumb through the process of natural selection, as apes with more separated thumbs demonstrated higher survival and reproductive rates. This structural adaptation made the ape better suited for its environment, increasing its dexterity for climbing trees, moving through the canopy, gathering food, and gripping tools such as sticks and branches.

Following the development of the opposable thumb in primates, populations of early human ancestors began to appear in a savanna environment with fewer trees and more open spaces. The need to cross such expanses and to utilize tools led to the development of bipedalism in certain primates and hominids. Bipedalism was both a structural adaptation (in the physical changes that occurred in the skull, spine, and other parts of the body to accommodate upright walking) as well as a behavioral adaptation, which led primates and hominids to walk on only two feet.

> **BIOLOGICAL ADAPTATIONS:** anatomical structures and physiological processes that evolve over geological time to increase the overall reproductive success of an organism in its environment

Freeing of the hands for tool use led, in turn, to other adaptations, and evolutionists attribute the gradual increase in brain size and expansion of motor skills in hominids largely to the appearance of the opposable thumb. Thus, the developments of many of the most important adaptations of primates and humans demonstrate closely connected evolutionary histories.

SKILL 37.2 Describes how populations and species change through time.

See Skill 37.1

A wide range of evidence provides information on the natural processes by which populations and species change through time.

Paleontological Evidence

Paleontology is the study of the life of past geological time periods based on fossil records. When organisms die, they often decompose quickly or are consumed by scavengers, leaving no evidence of their existence. However, occasionally some organisms are preserved. The remains or traces of organisms from a past geological age embedded in rocks by natural processes are called fossils. Fossils are very important for understanding the evolutionary history of life on Earth as they provide evidence of evolution and detailed information on the ancestry of organisms.

Petrification is the process by which a dead animal gets fossilized. For this to happen, a dead organism must be buried quickly to avoid weathering and decomposition. When an organism is buried, the organic matter decays. The mineral salts from the mud (in which the organism is buried) infiltrate the bones and gradually fill up the pores. The bones harden and are preserved as fossils. If dead organisms are covered by windblown sand, and if the sand is subsequently turned into mud by heavy rain or floods, the same process of mineral infiltration may occur. Besides petrification, organisms can be well preserved in ice, in the hardened resin of coniferous trees (amber), in tar, or in anaerobic acidic peat. Fossilization can sometimes be only a trace, an impression of a form, e.g., leaves or footprints.

Horizontal layers of sedimentary rocks (formed by layers of silt or mud) are called strata, and each layer can contain fossils. The oldest layer is the one at the bottom, so the fossils found in this layer are the oldest. This is how paleontologists can determine the relative age of fossils.

Some organisms appear only in certain layers, indicating that they lived only during that period and then became extinct. A succession of animals and plants can also be seen in fossil records, which supports the theory that organisms tend to increase progressively in complexity.

According to fossil records, some modern species of plants and animals are almost identical to the species that lived in ancient geological ages. They have remained unchanged morphologically and maybe physiologically as well. Hence they are called "living fossils." Some examples of living fossils are nautilus, horseshoe crab, gingko, and metasequoia.

Anatomical Evidence

Comparative anatomical studies reveal that some structural features of organisms are basically similar, e.g., flowers generally have sepals, petals, stigma, style, and ovary but the size, color, and number of petals, sepals, etc., may differ from species to species. The degree of resemblance between two organisms indicates how closely they are related in evolution.

Groups with little in common are supposed to have diverged from a common ancestor much earlier in geological history than groups that have more in common. To decide how closely two organisms are related, anatomists look for structures that serve different purposes in the adult, but are basically similar (homologous). In cases where similar structures serve different functions in adults, it is important to trace their origin and embryonic development.

When a group of organisms shares a homologous structure that has been specialized to perform a variety of functions to adapt to different environmental conditions, it is called ADAPTIVE RADIATION. The gradual spreading of organisms with adaptive radiation is known as DIVERGENT EVOLUTION. Examples of divergent evolution are pentadactyl limb and insect mouth parts.

Under similar environmental conditions, fundamentally different structures in different groups of organisms may undergo modifications to serve similar functions. This is called CONVERGENT EVOLUTION. The structures, which have no close phylogenetic links but show adaptation to perform the same functions, are called analogous. Examples include wings of bats, birds and insects, jointed legs of insects and vertebrates, and eyes of vertebrates and cephalopods.

ADAPTIVE RADIATION: when a group of organisms shares a homologous structure that has been specialized to perform a variety of functions to adapt to different environmental conditions

DIVERGENT EVOLUTION: the gradual spreading of organisms with adaptive radiation

CONVERGENT EVOLUTION: under similar environmental conditions, fundamentally different structures in different groups of organisms may undergo modifications to serve similar functions

VESTIGIAL ORGANS:
organs that are smaller and simpler in structure than corresponding parts in the ancestral species

Organs that are smaller and simpler in structure than corresponding parts in the ancestral species are called VESTIGIAL ORGANS. They are usually degenerated or underdeveloped. These organs were functional in the ancestral species but have become nonfunctional, e.g., vestigial hind limbs of whales, vestigial leaves of some xerophytes, and vestigial wings of flightless birds like ostriches.

Geographical Evidence

Continental distribution

All organisms adapt to their environment to a greater or lesser extent. It is generally assumed that the same type of species would be found in a similar habitat in a similar geographic area. Examples: Africa has short-tailed (Old World) monkeys, elephants, lions, and giraffes. South America has long-tailed monkeys, pumas, jaguars, and llamas.

Evidence for migration and isolation

The fossil record shows that the evolution of camels started in North America. Camels then migrated across the Bering Strait into Asia and Africa and through the Isthmus to Panama into South America.

Continental drift

Fossils of ancient amphibians, arthropods, and ferns are found in South America, Africa, India, Australia, and Antarctica which can be dated to the Paleozoic Era, at which time they were all in a single landmass called Gondwana.

Oceanic island distribution

Most small isolated islands only have native species. Plant life in Hawaii could have arrived as airborne spores or as seeds in the droppings of birds. A few large mammals present in remote islands were brought by human settlers.

Comparative Embryological Evidence

Comparative embryology shows that embryos start off looking the same. As they develop, their similarities slowly decrease until they take the form of their particular class.

Example: Adult vertebrates are diverse yet their embryos are quite similar at very early stages. Fishlike structures still form in early embryos of reptiles, birds, and mammals. In fish embryos, a two-chambered heart, some veins, and parts of arteries develop, which persist in adult fish. The same structures form early in human embryos but do not persist in adults.

Physiological and Biochemical Evidence

Evolution of widely distributed proteins and molecules

All organisms make use of DNA and/or RNA. ATP is the metabolic currency. The genetic code is the same for almost every organism. A piece of RNA in a bacterium cell codes for the same protein as in a human cell.

Comparison of the DNA sequence allows organisms to be grouped by sequence similarity, and the resulting phylogenetic trees are typically consistent with traditional taxonomy and are often used to strengthen or correct taxonomic classifications. DNA sequence comparison is considered strong enough to be used to correct erroneous assumptions in the phylogenetic tree in cases where other evidence is missing. The sequence of the 168 rRNA gene, a vital gene encoding a part of the ribosome, was used to find the broad phylogenetic relationships among all life.

The proteomic evidence also supports the universal ancestry of life. Vital proteins such as ribosome, DNA polymerase, and RNA polymerase are found in the most primitive bacteria as well as the most complex mammals. Since metabolic processes do not leave fossils, research into the evolution of the basic cellular processes is done largely by comparison of existing organisms.

SKILL 37.3 Describes processes that enable traits to change through time, including selective breeding, mutation and other natural occurrences.

See Skills 36.1, 36.3, and 37.1

COMPETENCY 38
ORGANISMS AND THE ENVIRONMENT

> ### SKILL 38.1 Understands that organisms respond to internal or external stimuli and analyzes the role of internal and external stimuli in the behavior of organisms.

Response to stimuli is one of the key characteristics of all living things. Any detectable change in the internal or external environment (the stimulus) may trigger a response in an organism. Like physical characteristics, an organism's responses to stimuli are adaptations that allow them to better survive. While these responses may be more noticeable in animals that can move quickly, all organisms are capable of responding to changes.

Single-Celled Organisms

Single-celled organisms are able to respond to basic stimuli such as the presence of light, heat, or food. They typically sense changes in the environment via receptors on the cell surface. These organisms may respond to stimuli by making changes in internal biochemical pathways or initiating reproduction or phagocytosis. Those capable of simple motility, using flagella, for instance, may respond by moving toward food or away from heat.

Plants

Plants typically do not possess sensory organs so individual cells recognize stimuli through a variety of pathways. When many cells respond to stimuli together, a response becomes apparent. Logically then, the responses of plants occur on a rather longer timescale than those of animals. Plants are capable of responding to a few basic stimuli including light, water, and gravity. Some common examples include the way plants turn and grow toward the sun, the sprouting of seeds when exposed to warmth and moisture, and the growth of roots in the direction of gravity.

Animals

Lower members of the animal kingdom have responses similar to those seen in single-celled organisms. However, higher-order animals have developed complex systems to detect and respond to stimuli. The nervous system, sensory organs (eyes, ears, skin, etc.), and muscle tissue all allow animals to sense and quickly respond to changes in their environment.

As with other organisms, many responses to stimuli in animals are involuntary. For example, pupils dilate in response to the reduction of light. Such reactions are typically called reflexes. However, many animals are also capable of voluntary response. In many animal species, voluntary reactions are instinctual. For instance, a zebra's response to a lion is *voluntary* but, *instinctually*, it will flee quickly as soon as it senses the lion's presence. Complex responses, which may or may not be instinctual, are typically termed BEHAVIOR. An example is the annual migration of birds when seasons change. Even more complex social behavior is seen in animals that live in large groups.

> **BEHAVIOR:** complex responses, which may or may not be instinctual

SKILL 38.2 Understands relationships between organisms and the environment and describes ways that living organisms depend on each other and on the environment to meet their basic needs.

See also Skill 35.3

There are many interactions that can occur between different species living together. Predation, parasitism, competition, commensalism, and mutualism are the different types of relationships populations have with each other.

- **Parasitism:** Two species that occupy a similar place. The parasite benefits from the relationship; the host is harmed.

- **Commensalism:** Two species that occupy a similar place; neither species is harmed or benefits from the relationship.

- **Mutualism (symbiosis):** Two species that occupy a similar place; both species benefit from the relationship.

- **Competition:** Two species that occupy the same habitat or eat the same food are said to be in competition with each other.

- **Predation:** Animals that eat other animals are called predators. The animals they feed on are called prey. Population growth depends upon competition for food, water, shelter, and space. The number of predators determines the amount of prey, which in turn affects the number of predators.

> **SKILL 38.3** Identifies organisms, populations or species with similar needs and analyzes how they compete with one another for resources.

See Skills 37.1, 38.2, 38.4, 38.5, and 38.6

> **SKILL 38.4** Analyzes the interrelationships and interdependence among producers, consumers and decomposers in an ecosystem *(e.g., food webs, food chains, competition, predation).*

Tropic levels describe the feeding relationships that determine energy flow and chemical cycling in a food chain. The number of trophic levels is determined by the complexity of the ecosystem. Energy is lost as the trophic levels progress from producer to tertiary consumer. The amount of energy that is transferred between trophic levels is called the ecological efficiency.

Pyramid of Productivity

A pyramid of productivity represents the energy flow through trophic levels. Most food chains are more elaborate, becoming food webs.

Tertiary consumers (eat the secondary consumers)
Secondary consumers (carnivores that eat primary consumers)
Primary consumers (herbivores that eat plants or algae)
Producers (mainly autotrophs/plant life)
Decomposers (consumers that feed off animal waste and dead organisms)

> **SKILL 38.5** Identifies factors that influence the size and growth of populations in an ecosystem.

INTRASPECIFIC COMPETITION: competition among members of the same species

INTERSPECIFIC COMPETITION: competition between individuals of different species

See also Skills 27.4 and 36.5

Competition is one of the many factors that affect the structure of ecologic communities. Competition among members of the same species is known as INTRASPECIFIC COMPETITION, while competition between individuals of different species is known as INTERSPECIFIC COMPETITION.

Once populations reach high densities, density-dependent inhibition is exhibited through intraspecific competition. As resources become limited, the population size can no longer increase within the defined region. Competition between members of the same species may lead certain populations to move to new regions, eventually resulting in speciation, an evolutionary process by which new species arise. Also, natural selection will favor individuals better suited for inter-specific competition. For example, when a tree population becomes dense within a defined area, higher-growing trees will obtain more sunlight and thus contribute more to the population's gene pool. Over time, the taller trees' better fitness will increase the general height of the entire tree population.

SKILL 38.6 Analyzes adaptive characteristics that result in a population's or species' unique niche in an ecosystem.

The term NICHE describes the relational position of a species or population in an ecosystem. A population's niche includes the way it responds to the abundance of its resources and enemies (e.g., by growing when resources are abundant and predators, parasites, and pathogens are scarce).

> **NICHE:** the relational position of a species or population in an ecosystem

Niche also indicates the life history of an organism and its habitat and place in the food chain. According to the competitive exclusion principle, no two species can occupy the same niche in the same environment for a long time. The full range of environmental conditions (biological and physical) under which an organism can exist describes its fundamental niche. Because of the pressure from superior competitors, organisms are driven to occupy a niche much narrower than their previous niche. This is known as the "realized niche."

Examples of Niche

Oak trees:

- Live in forests
- Absorb sunlight by photosynthesis
- Provide shelter for many animals
- Act as support for creeping plants
- Serve as a source of food for animals
- Cover the ground with dead leaves in the autumn

If oak trees were cut down or destroyed by fire or storms they would no longer be doing their job, which would have a disastrous effect on all of the other organisms living in the same habitat.

Hedgehogs:

- Eat a variety of insects and other invertebrates that live underneath the dead leaves and twigs in the garden

- Their spines are a superb environment for fleas and ticks

- Put nitrogen back into the soil when they urinate

- Eat slugs and protect plants from them

If there were no hedgehogs, the population of slugs would increase dramatically and the nutrients in dead leaves and twigs would subsequently not be recycled.

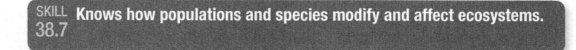

SKILL 38.7 **Knows how populations and species modify and affect ecosystems.**

See Skills 27.4, 27.5, 38.4, 38.5, and 38.6

COMPETENCY 39
STRUCTURE AND FUNCTION OF EARTH SYSTEMS

> **SKILL 39.1** Understands the structure of Earth and analyzes constructive and destructive processes (including plate tectonics, weathering and erosion) that produce geologic change, including how these processes have affected Earth history.

The interior of the Earth is divided into three chemically distinct layers. Starting from the middle and moving toward the surface, these are the core, the mantle, and the crust.

Structure of the Earth

Core

The outer core of the Earth begins about 3,000 km beneath the surface and is a liquid, though far more viscous than that of the mantle. Even deeper, approximately 5,000 km beneath the surface is the solid inner core. The inner core has a radius of about 1,200 km. Temperatures in the core exceed 4,000°C. Scientists agree that the core is extremely dense. This conclusion is based on the fact that the Earth is known to have an average density of 5,515 kg/m^3 even though the material close to the surface has an average density of only 3,000 kg/m^3. Therefore a denser core must exist. Also, it is hypothesized that when the Earth was forming, the densest material sank to the middle of the planet. Thus, it is not surprising that the core is about 80 percent iron. In fact, there is some speculation that the entire inner core is a single iron crystal, while the outer core is a mix of liquid iron and nickel.

Mantle

The Earth's mantle begins about 35 km beneath the surface and stretches all the way to 3,000 km beneath the surface, where the outer core begins. Since the mantle stretches so far into the Earth's center, its temperature varies widely; near the boundary with the crust it is approximately 1,000°C, while near the outer core it may reach nearly 4,000°C. Within the mantle there are silicate rocks, which are rich in iron and magnesium. The silicate rocks exist as solids but the high heat means they are ductile enough to "flow" over long time scales. In general, the mantle is in a state of semisolid plasticity and the viscosity varies as pressures and temperatures change at varying depths.

Crust

It is not clear how long the Earth has actually had a solid crust; most of the rocks are less than 100 million years old, although some are 4.4 billion years old. The crust of the Earth is the outermost layer and continues down for between 5 and 70 km beneath the surface. Thin areas generally exist under ocean basins (oceanic crust) and thicker crust underlies the continents (continental crust). Oceanic crust is composed largely of iron magnesium silicate rocks, while continental crust is less dense and consists mainly of sodium potassium aluminum silicate rocks. The crust is the least dense layer of the Earth and so is rich in those materials that "floated" during Earth's formation. Also, some heavier elements that bound to lighter materials are present in the crust.

Interactions between the layers

It is not the case that these layers exist as separate entities, with little interaction between them. For example, it is generally believed that swirling of the iron-rich liquid in the outer core results in the Earth's magnetic field, which is readily apparent on the surface. Heat also moves out from the core to the mantle and crust. The core still retains heat from the formation of the Earth, and additional heat is generated by the decay of radioactive isotopes. While most of the heat in our atmosphere comes from the Sun, radiant heat from the core does warm oceans and other large bodies of water.

Constructive and Destructive Processes

The Earth has not been static throughout its history. From a geological perspective it is always dynamic. Wind, water, and ice erode and shape the land. Volcanic activity and earthquakes alter the landscape in a dramatic and often violent manner. And on a much longer timescale, the movement of earth's plates slowly reconfigures oceans and continents creating mountains, faults, and other land forms as a result.

Erosion and weathering

EROSION is the inclusion and transportation of surface materials by another moveable material, usually water, wind, or ice. The most important cause of erosion is running water. Streams, rivers, and tides are constantly at work removing weathered fragments of bedrock and carrying them away from their original location. A stream erodes bedrock by the grinding action of the sand, pebbles, and other rock fragments. This grinding is called abrasion. Streams also erode rocks by

EROSION: the inclusion and transportation of surface materials by another moveable material, usually water, wind, or ice

dissolving or absorbing their minerals. Limestone and marble are readily dissolved by streams.

The breaking down of rocks at or near the Earth's surface is known as WEATHERING. Weathering breaks down rocks into smaller and smaller pieces. There are two types of weathering: physical weathering and chemical weathering.

- Physical weathering is the process by which rocks are broken down into smaller fragments without undergoing any change in chemical composition. Physical weathering is mainly caused by the freezing of water, the expansion of rock, and the activities of plants and animals.

- Chemical weathering is the breaking down of rocks through changes in their chemical composition. An example of chemical weathering would be the change of feldspar in granite to clay. Water, oxygen, and carbon dioxide are the main agents of chemical weathering. When water and carbon dioxide combine chemically, they produce a weak acid that breaks down rocks.

> **WEATHERING:** the breaking down of rocks at or near the Earth's surface

Plate tectonics

The theory of plate tectonics is the most current model that explains not only the movement of the continents but also the changes in the Earth's crust caused by internal forces.

Plates are rigid blocks of Earth's crust and upper mantle. These rigid solid blocks make up the lithosphere and are broken into nine large sections and several small ones. The major plates are named after the continents they are "transporting."

The plates float on and move with a layer of hot, plastic-like rock in the upper mantle. Geologists believe that the heat currents circulating within the mantle cause this plastic zone of rock to slowly flow, carrying along the overlying crustal plates.

Movement of these crustal plates creates areas where the plates diverge as well as areas where they converge. A major area of divergence is located in the mid-Atlantic. Currents of hot mantle rock rise and separate at this point of divergence, creating new oceanic crust at the rate of 2 to 10 centimeters per year. Convergence is when the oceanic crust collides with either another oceanic plate or a continental plate. The oceanic crust sinks, forming an enormous trench and generating volcanic activity. Convergence also includes continent-to-continent plate collisions. When two plates slide past one another, a transform fault is created.

These movements produce many major features of the Earth's surface, such as mountain ranges, volcanoes, and earthquake zones. Most of these features are located at plate boundaries, where the plates interact by spreading apart, pressing together, or sliding past each other. These movements are very slow, averaging only a few centimeters a year.

Boundaries form between spreading plates where the crust is forced apart in a process called **rifting**. Rifting generally occurs at mid-ocean ridges. Rifting can also take place within a continent, splitting the continent into smaller landmasses that drift away from each other, thereby forming an ocean basin between them. The Red Sea is a product of rifting. As the seafloor spreading takes place, new material is added to the inner edges of the separating plates. In this way the plates grow larger, and the ocean basin widens. This is the process that broke up the supercontinent Pangaea and created the Atlantic Ocean.

Boundaries between plates that are colliding are zones of intense crustal activity. When a plate of ocean crust collides with a plate of continental crust, the denser oceanic plate slides under the lighter continental plate and they plunge into the mantle. This process is called **subduction**, and the site where it takes place is called a subduction zone. A subduction zone is usually seen on the seafloor as a deep depression called a trench.

The crustal movement that is identified by plates sliding sideways past each other produces a plate boundary characterized by major faults that are capable of unleashing powerful earthquakes. The San Andreas fault forms such a boundary between the Pacific plate and the North American plate.

Earthquakes

An earthquake is the shaking or displacement of the ground at the Earth's surface that results from a sudden release of stored energy in the crust that propagates seismic waves. Earthquakes generally occur along fault lines and are detected by seismometers.

> **EPICENTER:** the point on the Earth's surface located directly above the earthquake's hypocenter

The **EPICENTER** of an earthquake is the point on the Earth's surface located directly above the earthquake's hypocenter. The **HYPOCENTER**, or focus, is the earthquake's point of origin within the Earth. The hypocenter lies along the rupturing geologic fault of an earthquake, and it is from this point that energy is released and seismic waves propagate spherically out.

> **HYPOCENTER:** the earthquake's point of origin within the Earth

Seismic waves

There are two types of simultaneously generated seismic waves that contribute to the characteristic shaking of an earthquake: body waves and surface waves. Body waves, which include P-waves (primary waves) and S-waves (secondary or shear waves), travel through the interior of the Earth along paths bent by the Earth's varying density and composition.

P-waves are longitudinal or compressional waves that alternately dilate and compress the ground in the direction of wave propagation. Such waves can travel through any type of material. P-waves travel 330 meters per second (m/s) in air, 1,450 m/s in water, and 5,000 m/s in granite. S-waves are transverse waves that displace the ground perpendicularly to the direction of wave propagation. For this reason, S-waves are more destructive than P-waves. S-waves can only travel through solids at a speed of approximately 60 percent that of P-waves. Seismic shadowing may occur on the opposite side of the Earth from an earthquake epicenter because S-waves are absorbed by the liquid outer core whereas P-waves are refracted.

Surface waves travel just under the Earth's surface in the same manner as water waves. They are characterized by low frequency, long duration, slow speed, and large amplitude. For these reasons, surface waves are the most destructive type of seismic wave. Surface waves include Rayleigh waves and Love waves.

Distance from a location to the origin of an earthquake less than 200 km away can be determined by calculating the difference in arrival time of an earthquake's P-wave and S-wave in seconds, multiplied by 8 km per second. Recorded distance from an earthquake and observed peak-motion amplitude are the two measurements used by the Richter scale to calculate the magnitude of an earthquake. Richter values range from 0 to 10. For the largest earthquakes, the total distance that the fault plane slips, known as the rupture zone, can be as long as 250 km.

Earthquake damage

Earthquakes occur on a daily basis around the world and, in most cases, cause little to no damage. Large earthquakes, however, can cause severe property damage and loss of life through various agents of damage. These factors include fault rupture, vibratory ground motion, inundation, permanent ground failure, fire, and release of hazardous materials. Historically, the most common and dominant agent of damage is vibratory ground motion (shaking) that is capable of disrupting all infrastructures such as buildings, roads, pipelines, and power lines. Inundation describes numerous earthquake-related phenomena such as tsunamis and dam failures. Earthquakes can cause tsunamis by rapid and massive vertical displacement in a body of water such as an ocean.

Damage caused by an earthquake depends largely on the earthquake's magnitude and duration. These two factors are determined by the amount of stress that accumulates in the Earth's crust and the amount of energy released when this stress causes tectonic plates to slip. Damage at a specific location on the Earth's surface is determined by several factors. As distance from the epicenter increases, seismic wave strength decreases, resulting in less shaking of buildings and other structures. The length of the rupture zone may also affect earthquake magnitude. The smaller the rupture zone, the smaller the displacement of the Earth's surface. Smaller surface displacement leads to less building movement and ocean-water surge.

Mountain formation

OROGENY is the term given to natural mountain building. A MOUNTAIN is terrain that has been raised high above the surrounding landscape by volcanic action or some form of tectonic plate collision.

OROGENY: natural mountain building

MOUNTAIN: terrain that has been raised high above the surrounding landscape by volcanic action or some form of tectonic plate collision

There are many different types of mountains. The physical attributes of a mountain range depend upon the angle at which plate movement thrusts layers of rock to the surface. Many mountains (e.g., the Adirondacks and the Southern Rockies) were formed along high-angle faults.

Folded mountains (e.g., the Alps and the Himalayas) are produced by the folding of rock layers during their formation. The Himalayas are the highest mountains in the world and contain Mount Everest, which rises almost 9 km above sea level. The Himalayas were formed when India collided with Asia. The movement that created this collision is still in process at the rate of a few centimeters per year.

Fault-block mountains (e.g., mountains in Utah, Arizona, and New Mexico) are created when plate movement produces tension forces instead of compression forces. The area under tension produces normal faults and rock along these faults is displaced upward.

Dome mountains are formed as magma tries to push up through the crust but fails to break the surface. Dome mountains resemble a huge blister on the Earth's surface.

Upwarped mountains (e.g., the Black Hills of South Dakota) are created in association with a broad arching of the crust. They can also be formed by rock thrust upward along high-angle faults.

Volcanism

VOLCANISM is the term given to the movement of magma through the crust and its emergence as lava onto the Earth's surface. Volcanic mountains are built up by successive deposits of volcanic materials.

VOLCANISM: the movement of magma through the crust and its emergence as lava onto the Earth's surface

An active volcano is one that is presently erupting or building to an eruption. A dormant volcano is one that is between eruptions but still shows signs of internal activity that might lead to an eruption in the future. An extinct volcano is said to be no longer capable of erupting. Most of the world's active volcanoes are found along the rim of the Pacific Ocean, which is also a major earthquake zone. This curving belt of active faults and volcanoes is often called the Ring of Fire.

The world's best-known volcanic mountains include Mount Etna in Italy and Mount Kilimanjaro in Africa. The Hawaiian Islands are actually the tops of a chain of volcanic mountains that rise from the ocean floor.

There are three types of volcanic mountains: shield volcanoes, cinder cones, and composite volcanoes.

- Shield volcanoes are associated with quiet eruptions. Lava emerges from the vent or opening in the crater and flows freely out over the Earth's surface until it cools and hardens into a layer of igneous rock. A repeated lava flow builds this type of volcano into the largest volcanic mountain. Mauna Loa, a shield volcano in Hawaii, is the largest volcano on earth.

- Cinder-cone volcanoes are associated with explosive eruptions as lava is hurled high into the air in a spray of droplets of various sizes. These droplets cool and harden into cinders and particles of ash before falling to the ground. The ash and cinder pile up around the vent to form a steep, cone-shaped hill called the cinder cone. Cinder-cone volcanoes are relatively small but may form quite rapidly.

- Composite volcanoes are described as being built by both lava flows and layers of ash and cinder. Mount Fuji in Japan, Mount St. Helens in Washington State in the United States, and Mount Vesuvius in Italy arc all famous composite volcanoes.

A caldera is normally formed by the collapse of the top of a volcano. This collapse can be caused by a massive explosion that destroys the cone and empties most if not all of the magma chamber below the volcano.

An inactive volcano may have solidified magma in its pipe. This structure, called a volcanic neck, is resistant to erosion and may be the only visible evidence of the past presence of an active volcano.

Glaciation

About 12,000 years ago, a vast sheet of ice covered a large part of the northern United States. This huge, frozen mass had moved southward from the northern regions of Canada as several large bodies of slow-moving ice, or glaciers. A time period in which glaciers advance over a large portion of a continent is called an ICE AGE. A glacier is a large mass of ice that moves or flows over the land in response to gravity. Glaciers form among high mountains and in other cold regions.

ICE AGE: a time period in which glaciers advance over a large portion of a continent

There are two main types of glaciers: valley glaciers and continental glaciers.

U-shaped erosion is characteristic of erosion by valley glaciers, which produce sharp-peaked mountains such as the Matterhorn in Switzerland. Continental glaciers often ride over mountains in their paths, leaving smoothed, rounded mountains and ridges.

Evidence of the glacier that covered a large part of North America remains as abrasive grooves, large boulders from northern environments dropped in southerly locations, glacial troughs created by the rounding out of steep valleys by glacial scouring, and the remains of glacial sources called cirques that were created by frost wedging the rock at the bottom of the glacier. Remains of plants and animals found in warm climates have been discovered in the moraines and help to support the theory of periods of warmth during the past ice ages.

The ice age began about 2 to 3 million years ago. This age saw the advancement and retreat of glacial ice over millions of years. Theories relating to the origin of glacial activity include the theory of plate tectonics, which proposes that some continental masses now in temperate climates were at one time blanketed by ice and snow. Another theory involves changes in the Earth's orbit around the Sun, changes in the angle of the Earth's axis, and the wobbling of the Earth's axis. Support for the validity of this theory has come from deep-ocean research that indicates a correlation between climate-sensitive microorganisms and the changes in the Earth's orbital status.

SKILL 39.2 Understands the form and function of surface water and groundwater.

See also Skill 40.2

Not all precipitation flows to the streams, rivers, and lakes that constitute the above-ground water supply. Precipitation that soaks into the ground through small pores or openings becomes groundwater. Gravity causes groundwater to move through interconnected porous rock formations from higher to lower elevations. The upper surface of the zone saturated with groundwater is the water table. A swamp is an area where the water table is at the surface. Sometimes the land dips below the water table, and these areas fill with water, forming lakes, ponds, or streams. Groundwater that flows out from underground onto the surface is called a SPRING.

SPRING: groundwater that flows out from underground onto the surface

AQUIFERS: permeable rocks filled with water

Permeable rocks filled with water are called AQUIFERS. An aquifer forms when a layer of permeable rock is trapped between two layers of impermeable rock. Groundwater fills the pore spaces in the permeable rock. Layers of limestone are common aquifers. Confined aquifers are deep in the ground and below the water table. Unconfined aquifers border on the water table.

To visualize the groundwater system, imagine a hole dug in wet sand at the beach and a small pool of water in the hole. The wet sand corresponds to the aquifer, the hole to a well or lake, and the level of water in the hole to the water table.

Groundwater provides drinking water for 53 percent of the population in the United States and is collected in **reservoirs**. Much groundwater is clean enough to drink without any type of treatment. Impurities in the water are filtered out by the rocks and soil through which it flows. However, many groundwater sources are becoming contaminated. Septic tanks, broken pipes, agriculture fertilizers, garbage dumps, rainwater runoff, and leaking underground tanks all pollute groundwater. Toxic chemicals from farmlands mix with groundwater.

Removal of large volumes of groundwater can cause the collapse of soil and rock underground, causing the ground to sink. Along shorelines, excessive depletion of underground water supplies allows the intrusion of saltwater into the freshwater field. The groundwater supply becomes undrinkable.

> **SKILL 39.3** Applies knowledge of the composition and structure of the atmosphere and its properties.

Dry air has three basic components: dry gas, water vapor, and solid particles (e.g., dust from soil).

The most abundant dry gases in the atmosphere are:

(N_2)	Nitrogen	78.09% (makes up about four-fifths of gases in atmosphere)
(O_2)	Oxygen	20.95%
(AR)	Argon	0.93%
(CO_2)	Carbon dioxide	0.03%

The atmosphere is divided into four main layers based on temperature:

1. **Troposphere:** This layer is the closest to the Earth's surface. All weather phenomena occur here as it is the layer with the most water vapor and dust. Air temperature decreases with increasing altitude. The average thickness of the troposphere is 7 miles (11 km).

2. **Stratosphere:** This layer contains very little water; clouds in this layer are extremely rare. The ozone layer is located in the upper portions of the stratosphere. Air temperature is fairly constant but does increase somewhat with height due to the absorption of solar energy and ultraviolet rays from the ozone layer.

3. **Mesosphere:** Air temperature decreases with height again in this layer. This is the coldest layer, with temperatures in the range of –100°C at the top.

4. **Thermosphere:** The thermosphere extends upward into space. Oxygen molecules in this layer absorb energy from the Sun, causing temperatures to increase with height. The lower part of the thermosphere is called the ionosphere. Here, there are charged particles, or ions, and free electrons. When gases in the ionosphere are excited by solar radiation, they give off light and glow in the sky. These glowing lights are called the aurora borealis in the Northern Hemisphere and aurora australis in the Southern Hemisphere. The upper portion of the thermosphere is called the exosphere. Gas molecules are very far apart in this layer. Layers of exosphere are also known as the Van Allen belts and are held together by Earth's magnetic field.

SKILL 39.4 Applies knowledge of how human activity and natural processes, both gradual and catastrophic, can alter Earth systems.

See also Skills 27.5 and 39.1

Natural phenomena affect the makeup and functioning of ecosystems both directly and indirectly. For example, floods and volcanic eruptions can destroy the fixed portions of an ecosystem, such as plants and microbes. Mobile elements, such as animals, must evacuate or risk injury or death. After a catastrophic event, species of microbes and plants begin to repopulate the ecosystem, beginning a line of secondary succession that eventually leads to the return of higher-level species. Often the area affected by the event returns to something like its original state.

Volcanic eruptions produce large amounts of molten lava and expel large amounts of ash and gas. Molten lava kills and destroys any living organisms it contacts. However, when lava cools and hardens, it provides a rich environment for the growth of microbes and plants. Volcanic eruptions also affect ecosystems indirectly. Studies show that the ash and gas released by eruptions can cause a reduction in the area temperature for several years. The volcanic aerosol reflects the Sun's rays and creates clouds that have the same effect. In addition, sulfuric acid released by the volcano suppresses the production of greenhouse gases that damage the ozone layer.

Floods destroy microbes and vegetation and kill or force the evacuation of animals. Only when floodwaters recede can an ecosystem begin to return to normal. Floods, however, also have indirect effects. For example, floods can cause permanent soil erosion and nutrient depletion. Such disruptions of the soil can delay and limit an ecosystem's recovery.

COMPETENCY 40
CYCLES IN EARTH SYSTEMS

SKILL
40.1 **Understands the rock cycle and how rocks, minerals, and soils are formed, and their respective properties.**

Rock Cycle

There is a great deal of interaction between the mantle and the crust. The slow convection of rocks in the mantle is responsible for the shifting of tectonic plates on the crust. Matter can also move between the layers, as occurs during the rock cycle. Within the rock cycle, igneous rocks are formed when magma escapes from the mantle as lava during volcanic eruption. Rocks can also be forced back into the mantle, where the high heat and pressure recreate them as metamorphic rocks.

Rocks

There are three major subdivisions of rocks:

- **Sedimentary rocks:** When fluid sediments are transformed into solid sedimentary rocks, the process is known as lithification. A common process that affects sediments is compaction, when the weight of overlying materials compresses and compacts the deeper sediments. The compaction process leads to cementation. Cementation is when sediments are converted to sedimentary rock.

- **Igneous rocks:** Igneous rocks can be classified according to their texture, their composition, and the way they formed. Molten rock is called magma. When molten rock pours out onto the surface of the Earth, it is called lava. As magma cools, the elements and compounds begin to form crystals. The more slowly the magma cools, the larger the crystals grow. Rocks with large crystals are said to have a coarse-grained texture. Granite is an example of a coarse-grained rock. Rocks that cool rapidly before any crystals can form have a glassy texture like obsidian, also commonly known as volcanic glass.

- **Metamorphic rocks:** Metamorphic rocks are formed by high temperatures and great pressures. The process by which the rocks undergo these changes is called metamorphism. The outcome of metamorphic changes includes deformation by extreme heat and pressure, compaction, destruction of the original characteristics of the parent rock, bending and folding while in a plastic stage, and the emergence of completely new and different minerals due to chemical reactions with heated water and dissolved minerals. Metamorphic rocks are classified into two groups, foliated (leaflike) rocks and unfoliated rocks. Foliated rocks consist of compressed, parallel bands of minerals, which give the rocks a striped appearance. Examples of such rocks include slate, schist, and gneiss. Unfoliated rocks are not banded; examples of unfoliated rocks include quartzite, marble, and anthracite.

Minerals

MINERALS are natural, nonliving solids with a definite chemical composition and a crystalline structure. ORES are mineral or rock deposits that can be mined for profit. ROCKS are earth materials made of one or more minerals.

> **MINERALS:** natural, non-living solids with a definite chemical composition and a crystalline structure

> **ORES:** mineral or rock deposits that can be mined for profit

> **ROCKS:** earth materials made of one or more minerals

Minerals must adhere to five criteria. They must

- be nonliving;
- be formed in nature;
- be solid in form;
- have atoms that form a crystalline pattern; and
- have a chemical composition fixed within narrow limits.

There are more than 3,000 minerals in the Earth's crust. Minerals are classified by composition. The major groups of minerals are silicates, carbonates, oxides, sulfides, sulfates, and halides. The largest group of minerals is the silicates. Silicates are made of silicon, oxygen, and one or more other elements.

Soils

Soils are composed of particles of sand, clay, various minerals, tiny living organisms, and humus, plus the decayed remains of plants and animals. Soils are divided into three classes according to their texture:

- **Sandy soils** are gritty, and their particles do not bind together firmly. Sandy soils are porous: Water passes through them rapidly. Sandy soils do not hold much water.
- **Clay soils** are smooth and greasy; their particles bind together firmly. Clay soils are moist and usually do not allow water to pass through easily.
- **Loamy soils** feel somewhat like velvet and their particles clump together. Loamy soils are made up of sand, clay, and silt. Loamy soils holds water but allow some water to pass through.

In addition to the three main classes, soils are further grouped into three major types based upon their composition:

- **Pedalfers** form in the humid, temperate climate of the eastern United States. Pedalfer soils contain large amounts of iron oxide and aluminum-rich clays, making the soil a brown-to-reddish-brown color. This soil supports forest-type vegetation.

- **Pedocals** are found in the western United States where the climate is dry and temperate. These soils are rich in calcium carbonate. This type of soil supports grasslands and brush vegetation.

- **Laterites** are found where the climate is wet and tropical. Large amounts of water flow through this soil. Laterites are red-orange soils rich in iron and aluminum oxides. There is little humus in this soil, and this soil is not very fertile.

SKILL 40.2 Understands the water cycle and its relationship to weather processes.

Water Cycle

Water that falls to Earth in the form of rain, snow, hail, or sleet is called PRECIPITATION. Precipitation is part of a continuous process in which water at the Earth's surface evaporates, condenses into clouds, and returns to Earth. This process is called the water cycle.

The change of state of surface water from a liquid to a gas is called EVAPORATION.

The change of state of water vapor to a liquid is called CONDENSATION. When water vapor condenses in the atmosphere it forms clouds. Clouds are composed of water vapor or ice crystals and can contain dust and salts, which are known as condensation nuclei. Precipitation is created around these condensation nuclei.

Precipitation includes rain, snow, sleet, and hail. The type of precipitation that falls depends on air temperatures and the height and type of air mass from which it falls. Rain falls from high clouds know as nimbostratus, altostratus, and cumulonimbus clouds. Snow, sleet, and hail are also known as frozen precipitation. The accumulation of ice crystals is snow. Sleet is transparent grains of ice. Hail is created by thunderstorms as ice crystals circulate up and down within the cell, gathering bulk until thrown earthward.

> **PRECIPITATION:** water that falls to Earth in the form of rain, snow, hail, or sleet

> **EVAPORATION:** the change of state of surface water from a liquid to a gas

> **CONDENSATION:** the change of state of water vapor to a liquid

Climate becomes colder and drier at higher altitudes. Solar radiation becomes more severe at higher altitudes and convection forces are minimized. Climate also becomes colder and drier as the distance from the equator increases.

Proximity to land or water masses produces climatic conditions based upon the available moisture. Dry and arid climates prevail where moisture is scarce; lush tropical climates can prevail where moisture is abundant.

> **SKILL 40.3** Understands the nutrient *(e.g., carbon, nitrogen)* cycle and its relationship to Earth systems.

Geochemical Cycles

Essential elements are recycled through an ecosystem. At times, the element needs to be "fixed" in a usable form. Cycles are dependent on plants, algae, and bacteria to fix nutrients for use by animals.

Carbon cycle

Ten percent of all available carbon in the air (from carbon dioxide gas) is fixed by photosynthesis. Plants fix carbon in the form of glucose. Animals eat the plants and are able to obtain the carbon they need. When animals release carbon dioxide through respiration, the plants have a source of carbon to fix again.

Nitrogen cycle

Eighty percent of the atmosphere is in the form of nitrogen gas. Nitrogen must be fixed and taken out of the gaseous form to be incorporated into an organism. Only a few genera of bacteria have the enzymes necessary to break the triple bond between nitrogen atoms. These bacteria live in the roots of legumes (peas, beans, alfalfa) and add bacteria to the soil so the plant can take it up. Nitrogen is necessary to make amino acids and the nitrogenous bases of DNA.

Phosphorus cycle

Phosphorus exists as a mineral and is not found in the atmosphere. Fungi and plant roots have structures called mycorrhizae that are able to fix insoluble phosphates into usable phosphorus. Urine and decayed matter return phosphorus to the earth where it can be fixed in the plant. Phosphorus is needed for the backbone of DNA and for the manufacture of ATP.

SKILL 40.4 Applies knowledge of how human and natural processes affect Earth systems.

See Skills 27.5 and 39.1

SKILL 40.5 Understands and describes the properties and uses of Earth materials *(e.g., rocks, soils, water, atmospheric gases)*.

See Skills 39.2, 39.3, and 40.1

COMPETENCY 41
ENERGY IN WEATHER AND CLIMATE

> **SKILL 41.1** **Understands the elements of weather** *(e.g., humidity, wind speed and direction, air pressure, temperature)* **and the tools used for measurement.**

Wind

Air masses moving toward or away from the Earth's surface are called AIR CURRENTS. Air moving parallel to the Earth's surface is called WIND. Weather conditions are generated by winds and air currents carrying large amounts of heat and moisture from one part of the atmosphere to another. Instruments called anemometers measure wind speeds.

> **AIR CURRENTS:** air masses moving toward or away from the Earth's surface

> **WIND:** air moving parallel to the Earth's surface

The wind belts in each hemisphere consist of convection cells that encircle the Earth like belts. There are three major wind belts on Earth:

1. Trade winds

2. Prevailing westerlies

3. Polar easterlies

Wind-belt formation depends on the differences in air pressure that develop in the Doldrums, the horse latitudes, and the polar regions. The Doldrums surround the equator. Within this belt, heated air usually rises straight up into the Earth's atmosphere. The horse latitudes are regions of high barometric pressure with calm and light winds, and the polar regions contain cold dense air that sinks to the Earth's surface.

Sea breezes are caused by the unequal heating of the land and an adjacent, large body of water. Land heats up faster than water. The movement of cool ocean air toward the land is called a sea breeze. Sea breezes usually begin blowing around midmorning, ending around sunset. A breeze that blows from the land to the ocean or a large lake is called a land breeze.

Monsoons are huge wind systems that cover large geographic areas and reverse direction seasonally. The monsoons of India and Asia are examples of these seasonal winds. They alternate wet and dry seasons. As denser, cooler air over the ocean moves inland, a steady seasonal wind called a summer or wet monsoon is produced.

EL NIÑO refers to a sequence of changes in the ocean and atmospheric circulation across the Pacific Ocean. The water around the equator is unusually hot every two to seven years. Trade winds normally blow east to west across the equatorial latitudes, piling warm water into the western Pacific. A huge mass of heavy thunderstorms usually forms in the area and produces vast currents of rising air that displace heat poleward. This helps create the strong midlatitude jet streams. The world's climate patterns are disrupted by this change in location of thunderstorm activity.

> **EL NIÑO:** a sequence of changes in the ocean and atmospheric circulation across the Pacific Ocean

Storms

A thunderstorm is a brief, local storm produced by the rapid upward movement of warm, moist air within a cumulonimbus cloud. Thunderstorms always produce lightning and thunder, and are accompanied by strong wind gusts and heavy rain or hail.

A severe storm with swirling winds that can reach speeds of hundreds of km per hour is called a tornado. Such a storm is also referred to as a "twister." The sky is covered by large cumulonimbus clouds and violent thunderstorms; a funnel-shaped swirling cloud may extend downward from a cumulonimbus cloud and reach the ground. Tornadoes are storms that leave a narrow path of destruction on the ground. A swirling, funnel-shaped cloud that extends downward and touches a body of water is called a waterspout.

Hurricanes are storms that develop when warm, moist air carried by trade winds rotates around a low-pressure "eye." A large, rotating, low-pressure system accompanied by heavy precipitation and strong winds is called a tropical cyclone (better known as a hurricane). In the Pacific region, a hurricane is called a typhoon.

Storms that occur only in the winter are known as blizzards or ice storms. A blizzard is a storm with strong winds, blowing snow, and frigid temperatures. An ice storm consists of falling rain that freezes when it strikes the ground, covering everything with a layer of ice.

Weather Instruments

Instruments that forecast weather include the aneroid barometer and the mercury barometer (measures air pressure). The air exerts varying pressures on a metal diaphragm that reads air pressure. The mercury barometer operates when atmospheric pressure pushes on a pool of mercury in a glass tube. The higher the pressure, the higher up the tube the mercury rises.

Relative humidity is measured by two kinds of weather instruments: the psychrometer and the hair gygrometer. Relative humidity simply indicates the amount of moisture in the air. Relative humidity is defined as a ratio of existing amounts of water vapor and moisture in the air when compared to the maximum amount of moisture the air can hold at the same given pressure and temperature. Relative humidity is stated as a percentage; so for example, the relative humidity can be as high as 100 percent.

Meteorologists use an anemometer to measure wind speed and a wind vane to measure wind direction.

SKILL 41.2 Compares and contrasts weather and climate.

Unlike the weather, which consists of hourly and daily changes in the atmosphere over a region, climate is the average of all weather conditions in a region over a period of time.

The weather in a region taken over a long period of time is called the climate of that region. Unlike the weather, which consists of hourly and daily changes in the atmosphere over a region, climate is the average of all weather conditions in a region over a period of time. Many factors are used to determine the climate of a region, including temperature and precipitation. Climate varies from one place to another because of the unequal heating of the Earth's surface. This varied heating of the surface is the result of the unequal distribution of landmasses, oceans, and polar ice caps.

Climates are classified into three groups: polar, tropical, and temperate. Climates can be affected by the following events: deforestation, global warming, maritime effect, rain shadow effect, and Chinook winds.

SKILL 41.3 Analyzes weather charts and data to make weather predictions.

See Skill 41.1

SKILL 41.4 Applies knowledge of how transfers of energy between Earth systems affect weather and climate.

See Skill 41.1

SKILL 41.5 Analyzes how Earth's position, orientation, and surface features affect weather and climate.

See Skill 42.2

COMPETENCY 42
EARTH AND SPACE SCIENCE: CHARACTERISTICS OF THE SOLAR SYSTEM AND THE UNIVERSE

> **SKILL 42.1** Understands the properties and characteristics of objects in the sky.

See also Skill 42.3

Sun

The Sun is the nearest star to Earth that produces solar energy. By the process of nuclear fusion, hydrogen gas is converted to helium gas. Energy flows out of the core to the surface then radiation escapes into space.

Parts of the Sun include

- **The core:** The inner portion of the Sun, where fusion takes place.

- **The photosphere:** Considered the surface of the sun, which produces sunspots (cool, dark areas that can be seen on the Sun's surface).

- **The chromosphere:** Hydrogen gas causes this portion to be red in color (also found here are solar flares, or sudden variations in brightness of the chromosphere, and solar prominences, gases that shoot outward from the chromosphere).

- **The corona:** The transparent area of the Sun, visible only during a total eclipse.

SOLAR RADIATION is energy traveling from the Sun that radiates into space. Solar flares produce excited protons and electrons that shoot outward from the chromosphere at great speeds reaching the Earth. These particles disturb radio reception and also affect the magnetic field on the Earth.

> **SOLAR RADIATION:** energy traveling from the Sun that radiates into space

Stars

All stars derive their energy from the thermonuclear fusion of light elements into heavy elements. The minimum temperature required for the fusion of hydrogen is 5 million degrees. Elements with more protons in their nuclei require higher temperatures. For instance, to fuse carbon requires a temperature of about 1 billion degrees.

A star that is composed mostly of hydrogen is a young star. As a star gets older its hydrogen is consumed and tremendous energy and light is released through fusion. This is a three-step process:

1. Two hydrogen nuclei (protons) fuse to form a heavy hydrogen called deuterium and release an electron and 4.04 MeV (milli-electron volt) energy.

2. The deuterium fuses with another hydrogen nucleus (proton) to form a helium-3 and release a neutron and 3.28 MeV energy.

3. The helium-3 fuses with another helium-3 to form a helium-4 and release two hydrogens and 10.28 MeV energy.

In stars with central temperatures greater than 600–700 million degrees, carbon fusion is thought to take over the dominant role rather than hydrogen fusion. Carbon fusions can produce magnesium, sodium, neon, or helium. Some of the reactions release energy and alpha particles or protons.

CONSTELLATIONS: groups or patterns of stars

Astronomers use groups or patterns of stars called CONSTELLATIONS as reference points to locate other stars in the sky. Familiar constellations include Ursa Major (also known as the Great Bear) and Ursa Minor (known as the Little Bear). The Big Dipper is in the Ursa Major, the larger constellation. The Little Dipper is in the Ursa Minor, the smaller constellation. Different constellations appear as the Earth continues its revolution around the Sun with the seasonal changes.

Magnitude stars are twenty-one of the brightest stars that can be seen from the Earth. These are the first stars we notice at night. In the Northern Hemisphere there are fifteen commonly observed first-magnitude stars.

GALAXIES: vast collections of stars

Vast collections of stars are defined as GALAXIES. Galaxies are classified as irregular, elliptical, and spiral. An irregular galaxy has no real structured appearance; most are in their early stages of life. An elliptical galaxy consists of smooth ellipses, containing little dust and gas, but composed of millions or trillions of stars. Spiral galaxies are disk-shaped and have extending arms that rotate around their dense centers. Earth's galaxy is a spiral galaxy, and it is in the Milky Way.

Moon

TIDES: changes in the level of the ocean caused by the varying gravitational pull of the Moon as it orbits the Earth

The planet Earth has just one moon. TIDES are changes in the level of the ocean caused by the varying gravitational pull of the Moon as it orbits the Earth. The Moon's gravitational force coexists with that of the Earth. This interaction produces a common center of gravity between the Earth and the Moon. This center is called the barycenter.

As the barycenter rotates around the Earth it causes high tides and low tides. Neap tides are low tides that occur twice a month when the Sun, Earth, and Moon are positioned at right angles to one another. Spring tides are abnormally high tides that occur twice a month when the Sun, Earth, and Moon are aligned or positioned in a straight line.

> **SKILL 42.2** **Applies knowledge of the Earth-Moon-Sun system and the interactions between them** *(e.g., seasons, lunar phases, eclipses).*

Earth is the third planet away from the Sun in our solar system. Earth's numerous types of motion and states of orientation greatly affect global conditions such as the seasons, tides, and phases of the Moon. The Earth orbits the Sun with a period of 365 days. During this orbit, the average distance between the Earth and Sun is 93 million miles. The shape of the Earth's orbit around the Sun deviates from the shape of a circle only slightly. This deviation, known as the Earth's eccentricity, has a very small effect on the Earth's climate. The Earth is closest to the Sun at perihelion, occurring around January 2 of each year, and farthest from the Sun at aphelion, occurring around July 2. Because the Earth is closest to the Sun in January, the northern winter is slightly warmer than the southern winter.

Seasons

The rotation axis of the Earth is not perpendicular to the orbital (ecliptic) plane. The axis of the Earth is tilted 23.45° from the perpendicular. The tilt of the Earth's axis is known as the obliquity of the ecliptic, and is mainly responsible for the four seasons of the year because it influences the intensity of solar rays received by the Northern and Southern hemispheres. The four seasons—spring, summer, fall and winter—are extended periods of characteristic average temperature, rainfall, storm frequency, and vegetation growth or dormancy.

The effect of the Earth's tilt on climate is best demonstrated at the solstices, the two days of the year when the Sun is farthest from the Earth's equatorial plane. At the summer solstice (June), the Earth's tilt on its axis causes the Northern Hemisphere to lean toward the Sun, while the Southern Hemisphere leans away. Consequently, the Northern Hemisphere receives more intense rays from the Sun and experiences summer during this time, while the Southern Hemisphere experiences winter. At the winter solstice (December), it is the Southern Hemisphere that leans toward the Sun and thus experiences summer. Varying degrees of the same leaning toward or away from the Sun produce spring and fall.

Phases of the Moon

The Earth's orientation with respect to the solar system is also responsible for our perception of the phases of the Moon. As the Earth orbits the Sun with a period of 365 days, the Moon orbits the Earth every twenty-seven days. As the Moon circles the Earth, its shape in the night sky appears to change. The changes in the appearance of the Moon from Earth are known as lunar phases. These phases vary cyclically according to the relative positions of the Moon, the Earth, and the Sun. At all times, half of the Moon is facing the Sun and is thus illuminated by reflecting the Sun's light. As the Moon orbits the Earth and the Earth orbits the Sun, the half of the Moon that faces the Sun changes. However, the Moon is in synchronous rotation around the Earth, meaning that nearly the same side of the Moon faces the Earth at all times. This side is referred to as the near side of the Moon. Lunar phases occur as the Earth and Moon orbit the Sun and the fractional illumination of the Moon's near side changes.

When the Sun and Moon are on opposite sides of the Earth, observers on Earth perceive a "full moon," meaning the Moon appears circular because the entire illuminated half of the Moon is visible. As the Moon orbits the Earth, the Moon "wanes" as the amount of the illuminated half of the Moon that is visible from Earth decreases. A gibbous moon is between a full moon and a half moon, or between a half moon and a full moon. When the Sun and the Moon are on the same side of Earth, the illuminated half of the Moon is facing away from Earth, and the Moon appears invisible. This lunar phase is known as the "new moon." The time between each full moon is approximately 29.53 days.

These are the lunar phases:

- **New moon:** The Moon is invisible or the first signs of a crescent appear
- **Waxing crescent:** The right crescent of the Moon is visible
- **First quarter:** The right quarter of the Moon is visible
- **Waxing gibbous:** Only the left crescent is not illuminated
- **Full moon:** The entire illuminated half of the Moon is visible
- **Waning gibbous:** Only the right crescent of the Moon is not illuminated
- **Last quarter:** The left quarter of the Moon is illuminated
- **Waning crescent:** Only the left crescent of the Moon is illuminated

Viewing the Moon from the Southern Hemisphere would cause these phases to occur in the opposite order.

Eclipses

Eclipses are defined as the passing of one object into the shadow of another object. A LUNAR ECLIPSE occurs when the Moon travels through the shadow of the Earth. A SOLAR ECLIPSE occurs when the Moon positions itself between the Sun and the Earth.

> **LUNAR ECLIPSE:** occurs when the Moon travels through the shadow of the Earth

> **SOLAR ECLIPSE:** occurs when the Moon positions itself between the Sun and the Earth

SKILL 42.3 Identifies properties of the components of the solar system.

There are eight established planets in our solar system: Mercury, Venus, Earth, Mars, Jupiter, Saturn, Uranus, and Neptune. Pluto was considered a planet from its discovery in 1930 until 2006, when it was recategorized as a dwarf planet. The planets are divided into two groups based on their distance from the Sun. The inner planets are Mercury, Venus, Earth, and Mars. The outer planets are Jupiter, Saturn, Uranus, and Neptune.

Planets

- **Mercury:** The closest planet to the Sun. Its surface has craters and rocks. The atmosphere is composed of hydrogen, helium, and sodium. Mercury was named after the Roman messenger god.

- **Venus:** Has a slow rotation when compared to Earth. Venus and Uranus rotate in opposite directions from the other planets. This opposite rotation is called retrograde rotation. The surface of Venus is not visible due to the extensive cloud cover. The atmosphere is composed mostly of carbon dioxide. Sulfuric acid droplets in the dense cloud cover give Venus a yellow appearance. Venus has a greater greenhouse effect than that observed on Earth. The dense clouds combined with the carbon dioxide gas trap heat. Venus was named after the Roman goddess of love.

- **Earth:** Considered a water planet, with 70 percent of its surface covered by water. Gravity holds the water in place. The different temperatures observed on Earth allow for the different states (solid, liquid, gas) of water to exist. The atmosphere is composed mainly of oxygen and nitrogen. Earth is the only planet known to support life.

- **Mars:** The surface of Mars contains numerous craters, active and extinct volcanoes, ridges, and valleys with extremely deep fractures. Iron oxide found in the dusty soil makes the surface seem rust-colored and the skies pink. The atmosphere is composed of carbon dioxide, nitrogen, argon, oxygen, and water vapor. Mars has polar regions with ice caps composed of water. Mars has two satellites. Mars was named after the Roman war god.

- **Jupiter:** Largest planet in the solar system. Jupiter has sixteen moons. The atmosphere is composed of hydrogen, helium, methane, and ammonia. There are white-colored bands of clouds indicating rising gas and dark-colored bands of clouds indicating descending gas. The gas movement is caused by heat resulting from the energy of Jupiter's core. Jupiter has a great red spot that is thought to be a hurricane-type cloud. Jupiter has a strong magnetic field.

- **Saturn:** The second largest planet in the solar system. Saturn has rings of ice, rock, and dust particles circling it. Saturn's atmosphere is composed of hydrogen, helium, methane, and ammonia. Saturn has more than twenty satellites. Saturn was named after the Roman god of agriculture.

- **Uranus:** The second largest planet in the solar system with retrograde revolution. Uranus is a gaseous planet. It has ten dark rings and fifteen satellites. Its atmosphere is composed of hydrogen, helium, and methane. Uranus was named after the Greek god of the heavens.

- **Neptune:** Another gaseous planet with an atmosphere consisting of hydrogen, helium, and methane. Neptune has three rings and two satellites. Neptune was named after the Roman sea god because its atmosphere is the same color as the seas.

Comets, Asteroids, and Meteors

Astronomers believe that rocky fragments may have been the remains of the birth of the solar system that never formed into a planet. Asteroids are found in the region between Mars and Jupiter.

> **COMETS:** masses of frozen gases, cosmic dust, and small rocky particles

COMETS are masses of frozen gases, cosmic dust, and small rocky particles. Astronomers think most comets originate in a dense comet cloud beyond Pluto. Comets consist of a nucleus, a coma, and a tail. A comet's tail always points away from the Sun. The most famous comet, Halley's comet, is named after the person who first discovered it in 240 BCE. It returns to the skies near Earth every seventy-five to seventy-six years.

Meteoroids are composed of particles of rock and metal of various sizes. When a meteoroid travels through the Earth's atmosphere, friction causes its surface to heat up and it begins to burn. The burning meteoroid falling through the Earth's atmosphere is called a meteor (also known as a shooting star).

Meteorites are meteors that strike the Earth's surface. A physical example of a meteorite's impact on the Earth's surface is the Barringer Crater, a huge meteor crater in Arizona. There are many other meteor craters throughout the world.

DOMAIN V
FINE ARTS, HEALTH, AND PHYSICAL EDUCATION

PERSONALIZED STUDY PLAN

KNOWN MATERIAL/ SKIP IT

PAGE	COMPETENCY AND SKILL	
541	**43 Visual arts**	☐

43.1 Knows how to involve students in activities that promote enjoyment and understanding of visual arts by providing students with a wide range of opportunities to create and respond to visual arts so that they develop visual arts literacy. ☐

43.2 Knows and understands how perception is developed through observation, prior knowledge, imaginative and cognitive processes and multisensory experiences. ☐

43.3 Selects and uses instructional strategies, materials and activities to help students deepen and expand their ability to perceive and reflect on the environment. ☐

43.4 Knows and understands how critical thinking and creative problem solving are applied in the perception of artworks. ☐

43.5 Demonstrates knowledge of the elements of art *(i.e., color, texture, shape, form, line, space, value)* and provides instruction that promotes students' understanding of the elements of art as well as students' ability to apply that understanding in creating original artworks. ☐

43.6 Demonstrates knowledge of the principles of art *(e.g., emphasis, contrast, pattern, rhythm, balance, proportion, unity)* and provides instruction that promotes students' understanding of the principles of art as well as students' ability to apply that understanding in creating original artworks. ☐

43.7 Selects appropriate techniques to create art in various media *(e.g., drawing, painting, printmaking, construction, ceramics, fiber art, electronic media)* and promotes students' ability to use those techniques in creating original artworks. ☐

43.8 Understands how different cultures use art elements and principles to create art and convey meaning in different ways. ☐

43.9 Selects and uses instructional strategies, materials and activities to promote students' awareness and appreciation of the characteristics of a variety of art forms of multiple cultures within and outside the Western tradition. ☐

43.10 Provides instruction to develop the skills and knowledge required for visual literacy *(e.g., art elements and principles, art of different areas and cultures, diverse purposes and uses of art).* ☐

43.11 Integrates instruction in the visual arts with instruction in other subject areas. ☐

43.12 Understands how students develop cognitively and artistically and knows how to implement effective art instruction and assessment that are individually, culturally and age appropriate. ☐

43.13 Applies knowledge of visual arts content and curriculum based on the Texas Essential Knowledge and Skills (TEKS) and knowledge of students in early childhood through grade six to plan and implement effective, developmentally appropriate art instruction. ☐

PERSONALIZED STUDY PLAN

PAGE		COMPETENCY AND SKILL	
557	**44**	**Music**	☐
	44.1	Knows how to involve students in activities that promote enjoyment and understanding of music by providing students with a wide range of opportunities to make and respond to music so that they develop music literacy *(e.g., concert attendance, authentic performance opportunities).*	☐
	44.2	Applies knowledge of standard terminology for describing and analyzing musical sound *(e.g., rhythm, melody, form, timbre, tempo, pitch, meter, dynamics, intonation, intervals)* and has a basic understanding of how to read, write, recognize aurally and interpret standard music notation.	☐
	44.3	Knows how to arrange vocal and instrumental music for specific purposes and settings *(e.g., guides students in creating simple song arrangements and accompaniments using voices, classroom percussion, and melody instruments).*	☐
	44.4	Knows and understands music of diverse genres, styles and cultures.	☐
	44.5	Demonstrates an understanding of the purposes and roles of music in society and how music can reflect elements of a specific society or culture.	☐
	44.6	Explains a variety of music and music-related career options.	☐
	44.7	Identifies and describes how music reflects the heritage of the United States and Texas.	☐
	44.8	Applies knowledge of criteria for evaluating and critiquing musical performances and experiences, including using standard terminology in communicating about students' musical skills and performance abilities.	☐
	44.9	Integrates instruction in music with instruction in other subject areas.	☐
	44.10	Knows how to teach students to sing and/or play an instrument with expression, both independently and in small groups.	☐
	44.11	Applies knowledge of music content and curriculum based on the Texas Essential Knowledge and Skills (TEKS) and of students in early childhood through grade six to plan and implement effective, developmentally appropriate instruction, including instruction that promotes students' creativity and performance skills as well as students' ability to use critical-thinking and problem-solving skills in music contexts *(e.g., sequential instruction, music composition, improvisation, concert etiquette).*	☐
	44.12	Manages time, instructional resources and physical space effectively for music education.	☐
572	**45**	**Health**	☐
	45.1	Understands health-related behaviors, ways that personal health decisions and behaviors affect body systems and health and strategies for reducing health risks and enhancing wellness throughout the life span.	☐

PERSONALIZED STUDY PLAN

KNOWN MATERIAL/ SKIP IT

PAGE	COMPETENCY AND SKILL	
45.2	Demonstrates knowledge of major areas in health instruction, including body systems and development *(e.g., structures and functions of various body systems, relationships among body systems, five senses)*; illness and disease *(e.g., types of disease, transmission mechanisms, defense systems, disease prevention)*; nutrition *(e.g., types of foods and nutrients, maintenance of a balanced diet)*; stress *(e.g., effects of stress, stress-reduction techniques)*; and fitness *(e.g., components of fitness, methods for improving fitness, posture)*.	☐
45.3	Knows and understands stages of human growth and development, including physical and emotional changes that occur during adolescence.	☐
45.4	Understands substance use and abuse, including types and characteristics of tobacco, alcohol, other drugs and herbal supplements.	☐
45.5	Understands types of violence and abuse, including causes and effects of violence and abuse and ways to prevent and seek help in dealing with violence and abuse.	☐
45.6	Selects and uses instructional strategies, materials and activities to teach principles and procedures related to safety, accident prevention and response to emergencies.	☐
45.7	Applies critical-thinking, goal-setting, problem-solving and decision-making skills in health-related contexts *(e.g., eating habits, drug use, abstinence)* and understands the use of refusal skills and conflict resolution to avoid unsafe situations *(e.g., bullying, violence, abuse)*.	☐
45.8	Knows and understands strategies for coping with unhealthy behaviors in the family *(e.g., abuse, alcoholism, neglect, anxiety, grief)*.	☐
45.9	Understands types and symptoms of eating disorders.	☐
45.10	Knows how to use various social and communication skills to build and maintain healthy interpersonal relationships *(e.g., tolerance, respect, discussing problems with parents/caregivers, showing empathy)*.	☐
45.11	Understands health care responses to threats to safety, internal injury, early detection and warning signs of illness.	☐
45.12	Selects and uses instructional strategies, materials and activities to help students build healthy interpersonal relationships *(e.g., communication skills)* and demonstrates consideration and respect for self, family, friends and others *(e.g., practicing self-control)*.	☐
45.13	Understands the influence of various factors *(e.g., media, technology, peer and other relationships, environmental hazards)* on individual *(e.g., idealized body images, unhealthy weight-loss plans)*, family and community health.	☐
45.14	Demonstrates knowledge of sources of health information and ways to use information to make health-related decisions.	☐

PERSONALIZED STUDY PLAN

✗✓ **KNOWN MATERIAL/ SKIP IT**

PAGE		COMPETENCY AND SKILL	KNOWN MATERIAL/ SKIP IT
	45.15	Selects and uses instructional strategies, materials and activities to help students understand the roles of health care professionals, the benefits of health maintenance activities and the skills for becoming health-conscious consumers.	☐
	45.16	Applies knowledge of health content and curriculum based on the Texas Essential Knowledge and Skills (TEKS) and of students in early childhood through grade six to plan and implement effective, developmentally appropriate health instruction, including relating the health education curriculum to other content areas.	☐
597	**46**	**Physical education**	☐
	46.1	Applies key principles and concepts in physical education and physical activity (e.g., cardiovascular endurance, muscular strength, flexibility, weight control, conditioning, safety, stress management, nutrition) for the promotion of health and fitness.	☐
	46.2	Knows and helps students understand the benefits of an active lifestyle.	☐
	46.3	Understands appropriate methods, including technological methods, for evaluating, monitoring, and improving fitness levels.	☐
	46.4	Applies knowledge of movement principles and concepts to develop students' motor skills including understanding key elements of mature movement patterns (e.g., throwing, jumping, catching) and various manipulative skills (e.g., volley, dribble, punt, strike).	☐
	46.5	Selects and uses developmentally appropriate learning experiences that enhance students' locomotor, nonlocomotor, body control, manipulative and rhythmic skills.	☐
	46.6	Modifies instruction based on students' individual differences in growth and development.	☐
	46.7	Evaluates movement patterns to help students improve performance of motor skills and to integrate and refine their motor and rhythmic skills.	☐
	46.8	Understands a variety of strategies and tactics designed to improve students' performance, teamwork and skill combinations in games and sports.	☐
	46.9	Selects and uses instructional strategies to promote students' knowledge and application of rules, procedures, etiquette and fair play in developmentally appropriate games and activities.	☐
	46.10	Designs, manages and adapts physical education activities to promote positive interactions and active engagement by all students.	☐
	46.11	Understands areas of diverse needs (e.g., physical and emotional challenges, learning disabilities, sensory difficulties, language differences) and their implications for teaching and learning.	☐
	46.12	Applies knowledge of physical education content and curriculum based on the Texas Essential Knowledge and Skills (TEKS) and knowledge of students in early childhood through grade six to plan, implement and assess effective, developmentally appropriate physical education activities.	☐

✗✓

PERSONALIZED STUDY PLAN

KNOWN MATERIAL/ SKIP IT

PAGE	COMPETENCY AND SKILL	
614	**47 Theatre**	☐
	47.1 Knows and understands how perception is developed through the use of elements of drama and conventions of theatre.	☐
	47.2 Knows how to involve students in activities that promote enjoyment and understanding of theatre arts by selecting and using instructional strategies, materials, and activities to help students interpret creative expression and performance.	☐
	47.3 Demonstrates the knowledge of the elements of theatre (i.e., *dramatic play, expressive movement, voice, characterization*) and theatre occupations, provides instruction that promotes students' understanding of the elements and occupations, and helps them apply that understanding in creating theatrical productions.	☐
	47.4 Integrates instruction in theatre with instruction in other subject areas.	☐
	47.5 Knows how to promote students' ability to identify and use technical elements (e.g., *properties, scenery, sound, costumes, lighting*) to create suitable environments for dramatic play and performance.	☐
	47.6 Knows how to promote students' ability to identify and use technical elements (e.g., *properties, scenery, sound, costumes, lighting*) to define and enhance characterization, mood, theme, and setting.	☐
	47.7 Understands how theatre relates to history, society, and the diverse cultures.	☐
	47.8 Applies knowledge of theatre content and curriculum based on the Texas Essential Knowledge and Skills (TEKS) and knowledge of students in early childhood through grade six to plan and implement effective, developmentally appropriate theatre instruction.	☐
	47.9 Manages time, instructional resources and physical space effectively for theatre education.	☐

COMPETENCY 43
VISUAL ARTS

> **SKILL 43.1** Knows how to involve students in activities that promote enjoyment and understanding of visual arts by providing students with a wide range of opportunities to create and respond to visual arts so that they develop visual arts literacy.

Through art projects, field trips, and theatrical productions, students learn that all forms of art are a way for cultures to communicate with one another and the world at large. By understanding the concepts, techniques, and materials used in the visual arts, music, dance, and literature, students will begin to appreciate the concept of using art to express oneself. They might begin by writing a short story that gets transformed into a play with costumes, music, and movement to experience the relationships among various art forms.

The arts have played a significant role throughout history. In cultures all over the world, people have expressed feelings, told stories, imitated nature, and persuaded others through artistic expression. The arts bring meaning to ceremonies, rituals, celebrations, and recreation. By creating their own art and examining art made by others, children can learn to make sense of and communicate ideas. Through the arts and humanities, students realize that, although people are different, they share common experiences and attitudes. They also learn the power of nonverbal communication.

Benefits of Education in the Arts

Teaching in and through the arts within the context of the total school curriculum, especially during the formative years of a K–6 education, is key to maximizing the benefits of the arts in education.

For students, an education in the arts provides the following:

- The ability to be creative and inventive decision makers
- An enhanced sense of poise and self-esteem
- The confidence to undertake new tasks
- An increased ability to achieve across the curriculum
- A framework that encourages teamwork and fosters leadership skills

- Knowledge of the less-recognized experiences of aesthetic engagement and intuition

- Increased potential for life success

- An enriched quality of life

Guidelines and Strategies for the Classroom

Art-criticism strategies for the classroom include comparing/contrasting works of art and narratives, poetry, and other forms of writing. Literature is the most common means of exposing young students to art, but video and other types of media provide rich art experiences as well. Interpretation of works of art may extend to dramatic presentations through reader's theatre (students write dialogue for the people in an artwork, then perform the parts with different voices), "living paintings" or tableaux, and sound symphonies (students act out the sounds that are suggested by the artwork). A variety of approaches will help students learn to interpret works of art from multiple perspectives.

Example of activities include tasking students to

- experiment using a variety of mediums: drawing, painting, sculpture, ceramics, printmaking, and video.

- produce a collection of artwork (a portfolio) using a variety of mediums, topics, themes, and subject matter.

- convey meaning through their artwork.

- create and evaluate different works of art and types of mediums.

- reflect on their own and others' work.

> **SKILL 43.2** Knows and understands how perception is developed through observation, prior knowledge, imaginative and cognitive processes and multisensory experiences.

Developing Students' Observation Skills

Visual art encompasses many areas. Students are expected to fine-tune their observation skills and be able to identify and recreate their experiences. For example, a group of students may go on a nature hike, and afterward discuss the repetition they see in the leaves on the trees or the bricks in the sidewalk, or the size and shapes of the buildings and how they relate. They may also use such experiences to describe lines, colors, shapes, forms, and textures.

Children begin to notice elements of perspective at an early age. The question of why buildings look smaller at a distance and bigger when they are closer is sure to spark the imagination of early childhood students. Students can then move to a higher level of learning with hands-on activities such as constructing three-dimensional buildings using paper and geometric shapes. Eventually, students should acquire higher-level thinking skills and begin to question artists and analyze many different aspects of visual art.

> **SKILL 43.3** Selects and uses instructional strategies, materials and activities to help students deepen and expand their ability to perceive and reflect on the environment.

Exploring Different Mediums

Students should be able to select and use mediums and processes that actively communicate and express the intended meaning of their artworks and exhibits and prove competence in at least two mediums. For example, students should be able to select a process or medium for their intended work of art and describe the reasons for their selection.

Students should create and experience works of art that explore different types of subject matter, themes, and topics. Students need to understand the sensory elements and organizational principles of art and the expression of images.

Students should also be able to use the computer and electronic media to express their visual ideas and demonstrate a variety of different approaches to their selected medium. An excellent example is for students to produce works using mixed media or a work of art that uses the computer, the camera, the copy machine, or another type of electronic equipment.

Teachers can ask students of any age to compile a variety of their best works of art using different types of media. This is typically referred to as a portfolio. The portfolio should begin with an early sample of the student's work, a rough draft or a sketch. The portfolio shows the student's progress and growth in uses of various mediums and techniques. Progress can be tracked through use of a rubric or simply by observation.

Some of the areas that students should master and that the teacher can model include:

- Experimenting using a variety of mediums: drawing, painting, sculpture, ceramics, printmaking, and video

- Producing a collection of artwork (a portfolio) and using a variety of mediums, topics, themes, and subject matter

- Conveying meaning through artwork

- Creating and evaluating different works of art and types of mediums

- Reflecting on one's own and others' work

> **SKILL 43.4** **Knows and understands how critical thinking and creative problem solving are applied in the perception of artworks.**

Critiquing Artwork

The capacity to critique a work of art is an asset for all teachers, especially in classrooms with integrated curricula, where art is taught in conjunction with other subjects, or in classrooms where there is no separate art program.

Critiquing artwork involves using both objective and subjective approaches. Gathering information is the first step. The next step is analyzing and synthesizing the information. The final step is making an evaluation.

Objective information useful to a thoughtful critique includes the following:

- The artist's name and title of work

- The medium and techniques employed in the work

- The year the work was completed

- Historical information about the work, as well as other aspects of historical relevance

- The period, style, or genre to which the work belongs

- An analysis of the elements of the work, such as color, line, intensity, sense of movement, light, use of space and shape, use of contrast

Subjective information that can contribute to an effective critique includes the following:

- The observer's emotional reaction to the piece

- Others' feelings and reactions to the work (spoken or observed)

- The subject matter (this may be objectively observed in some work)

- Strengths and weaknesses of the work

- Details that draw one's attention

- Elements that seem most important to the work

- The focal point of the piece

- Elements or aspects of the work that elicit excitement or pleasure

Some useful questions that can bring together objective and subjective information include the following:

- How does the title of the work inform the viewer's experience of it?

- What does the work say? What is the artist trying to communicate? How do the colors and lines and textures (and other elements) contribute to the message?

- Is the work original? If it is derivative of others' work, does it contribute something by adding to the genre or the subject?

- What do I like about this work overall?

- Where might this piece be effectively displayed? Why?

- Does this piece of work bring beauty to the world?

- Does it make a statement? If so, what kind of statement?

- Do the choice of media and the craftsmanship enhance the basic message or intent of the artist? Do they detract in any way?

- What would improve this piece, if anything? Why?

Teachers should introduce students to the wide range of opportunities to explore art, including exhibits, galleries, museums, libraries, and personal art collections. Opportunities for research include reproductions, art slides, films, print materials, and electronic media. Once students have learned how to effectively research and use these sources, they should be expected to move on to higher-level thinking skills. Students should begin to reflect on, interpret, evaluate, and explain how works of art and various styles of artwork explain social, psychological, cultural, and environmental aspects of life.

Students should be asked to review, respond to, and analyze various types of art.

> **SKILL 43.5** **Demonstrates knowledge of the elements of art** *(i.e., color, texture, shape, form, line, space, value)* **and provides instruction that promotes students' understanding of the elements of art as well as students' ability to apply that understanding in creating original artworks.**

Elements of Visual Art

Color: An attribute of an object that is visible. When light is emitted, transmitted, or reflected off an object, the retina in our eye perceives color. The primary colors are red, yellow, and blue. The secondary colors are orange (a combination of red and yellow), purple (a combination of red and blue), and green (a combination of yellow and blue).

Texture: The way something feels.

Shape: A shape is a two-dimensional, enclosed space. An example of a shape is a square.

Form: A form is a three-dimensional, enclosed space. An example of a form is a cube.

Line: A mark or point that travels an identifiable path. It has both length and direction. It can be straight, curvy, horizontal, vertical, jagged, or smooth. It can be thin or thick.

Value: The lightness or darkness of a color.

SKILL 43.6 **Demonstrates knowledge of the principles of art** (e.g., emphasis, contrast, pattern, rhythm, balance, proportion, unity) **and provides instruction that promotes students' understanding of the principles of art as well as students' ability to apply that understanding in creating original artworks.**

Principles of Visual Art

Sketch: An image-development strategy; a preliminary drawing

Abstract: An image that reduces a subject to its essential visual elements, such as lines, shapes, and colors

Background: Those areas of composition that are behind the primary, or dominant, subject matter or design areas

Emphasis: Making one or more elements in a work of art stand out in such a way as to appear more significant

Contrast: Juxtaposing one or more elements in opposition to show their differences

Pattern: Also called a motif, a pattern is the repetition of an element. The repeated element can be a shape, line, or color.

Rhythm: The regular repetition of a form or element

Balance: The arrangement of one or more elements in a work of art so that they appear symmetrical or asymmetrical in design and proportion

Proportion: The harmonious relationship of one part to another or of one part to the whole

Unity: The arrangement of one or more elements to create coherence and a feeling of completeness or wholeness

> SKILL **Selects appropriate techniques to create art in various media** *(e.g.,*
> 43.7 *drawing, painting, printmaking, construction, ceramics, fiber art, electronic media)*
> **and promotes students' ability to use those techniques in creating**
> **original artworks.**

In this section, we will briefly go over a few appropriate techniques for various media that teachers can use to promote student ability in these areas.

Drawing

Drawing begins with lines and moves on to shapes. Students need to understand lines, shapes, the space they occupy, and how they relate to one another. Students can complete exercises in blind contouring, where they look at an object or scene and then create the scene on paper, without looking at the paper. The results are often silly, but they teach students to look at detail and shape as they create. This can be an excellent ice-breaker activity. Gesture or movement drawings are another technique. These often are timed. The goal of this activity is not to make a detailed picture, but to capture movement or action. Often, students will use thicker materials, such as chunky pencils or pastels, to create a movement drawing.

Painting

Painting allows students to use many types of supplies, such as watercolors, tempera paint, and acrylics. When teaching painting, include examples from artists you are studying and create a theme around that artist or style. Have students do an underpainting before they complete their actual painting. Underpainting is painting the paper in neutral colors or colors to match the landscape prior to creating the actual painting. This technique adds depth to the final product.

Students can use various materials to create a painting by layering one on top of another. When teachers are instructing students, it's important to allow time for students to learn how to use common art materials such as paintbrushes, pastels, and graphite pencils.

Printmaking

Printmaking involves creating a pattern or object and replicating it to create various patterns or a series of images. Teachers can use Styrofoam plates as materials, because they are inexpensive, easy to obtain, and will allow for students to see the process without a lot of expense.

Construction

When students construct art, they should be given opportunities to use as many tools as possible. Materials can be typical art supplies (paper, glue, scissors) or repurposed items (cardboard boxes, bubble wrap, toilet paper and paper towel rolls). Give children a goal of what to construct but allow them to use whichever materials they find interesting.

Ceramics

Give younger students balls of clay and let them begin their projects. Older students can start with pre-prepared slabs of clay. Younger students can use the "pinch and pull" method to create projects such as pinch pots. Then, as their skills develop, they can change their pinch pots into animals such as turtles. Older students can begin with their rolled slab and create a castle or totem pole using the "slab, slip, and score" method. Initially, the ball will be rolled into a slab. Then, the artist will use scoring instrument to make hash marks in the edge where the second piece of clay will go and use water to seal together the two pieces. Advanced students can create three-dimensional objects such as masks using all the skills they have learned in previous ceramics classes.

Fiber Arts

Fiber arts include techniques such as spinning, weaving, felting, quilting, knitting, braiding, embroidery, applique, and dyeing fabric. Students may not be able to take part in all of these activities due to time or budget constraints. When working with textiles, students should have the opportunity to develop a small project using as many of these techniques as possible.

Electronic Media

Electronic media includes television, radio, and the Internet. Students can develop television spots, blogs, YouTube channels, or social media engagement. Teachers should always obtain parent or guardian permission prior to allowing students to publish anything public online.

- *Line Drawing: A Guide for Art Students*

  http://www.studentartguide.com/articles/line-drawings. Retrieved Aug. 21, 2015.

- *8 Classic Painting Techniques from the Masters to Teach Today*

  http://www.theartofed.com/2015/04/03/8-classic-painting-techniques-from-the-masters-to-teach-today/. Retrieved Aug. 21, 2015.

SKILL 43.8 **Understands how different cultures use art elements and principles to create art and convey meaning in different ways.**

Art in Various Cultures and Periods in History

The greatest works in art, literature, music, theatre, and dance all reflect universal themes. Universal themes reflect the human experience, regardless of time period, location, or social standing. Universal themes tend to fall into broad categories, such as man versus society, man versus himself, man versus God, man versus nature, and good versus evil, to name the most obvious.

The list below provides a brief description of art in some of the important cultures and periods throughout history.

Prehistoric period (ca. 1,000,000–ca. 8000 BCE)

Major themes of this long period center around religious fertility rites and sympathetic magic. Much of the art includes imagery of pregnant animals and faceless, pregnant women.

Mesopotamia (ca. 8000–400 BCE)

The prayer statues and cult deities of this period point to the theme of polytheism in religious worship.

Ancient Egypt (ca. 3000–100 BCE)

The predominance of funerary art from ancient Egypt conveys the importance of the preparation for the afterlife and polytheistic worship. Another dominant theme is the divinity of the pharaohs. In architecture, the themes are monumentality and adherence to ritual.

Ancient Greece (800–100 BCE)

Dominant genres from this period are vase paintings, both black-figure and red-figure, and classical sculpture. The sculpture of ancient Greece is replete with human figures, either nude or draped. Most of the sculptures represent athletes and various gods and goddesses. The predominant theme is that of the ideal human. In architecture, scale is based on the ideal human proportions.

Rome (ca. 480 BCE–476 CE)

Major genres of Roman art include frescoes, classical sculpture, funerary art, state propaganda art, and relief work. The emphasis of the Roman arts is on the realistic depiction of human beings. Another major theme of this period is the glory of serving the Roman state. In architecture, the theme is rugged practicality mixed with Greek proportions and elements.

Middle Ages (300–1400 CE)

Significant genres during the Middle Ages include Byzantine mosaics, illuminated manuscripts, ivory reliefs, altarpieces, cathedral sculptures, and frescoes painted in various styles.

Although the Middle Ages covered a long time span, the major themes of this period remained relatively constant. Since the Roman Catholic Church was the primary patron of the arts, most work was religious in nature. The purpose of much of the art was to educate. Specific themes varied from the illustration of Bible stories, to interpretations of theological allegory, to lives of the saints, to the consequences of good and evil. Depictions of the Holy Family were popular. Themes found in secular art and literature centered on chivalric love and warfare. In architecture, the theme is glorification of God and education of the congregation in religious principles.

Renaissance (ca. 1400–1630 CE)

Important genres from the Renaissance include Florentine fresco painting (mostly religious), High Renaissance painting and sculpture, northern oil painting, Flemish miniature painting, and northern printmaking.

Renaissance themes include Christian religious depiction (see Middle Ages), but tend to reflect a renewed interest in all things classical. Specific themes include Greek and Roman mythological and philosophical figures and ancient battles and legends. Dominant themes reflect the philosophical beliefs of humanism, emphasizing individuality, human reason, and the psychological attributes of individuals. In architecture, scale is based on human proportions.

Baroque period (1630–1700 CE)

Important genres in the baroque era include Mannerism, Italian baroque painting and sculpture, Spanish baroque, Flemish baroque, and Dutch portraiture. Genre paintings in still life and landscape appear prominently in this period.

The predominant themes in the arts of the baroque period include the dramatic climaxes of well-known stories, legends, and battles, and the grand spectacle of mythology. Religious themes are common in the art of this period, but drama and insight are emphasized rather than the medieval "salvation factor." Baroque artists and authors incorporated various types of characters into their works, careful to include minute details. Portraiture focuses on the psychology of the subjects. Architecture is characterized by large-scale grandeur and splendor.

Eighteenth century (1700–1800 CE)

Predominant genres of the eighteenth century include rococo painting, portraiture, social satire, romantic painting, and neoclassical painting and sculpture.

Rococo themes of this century focus on religion, mythology, portraiture of aristocrats, pleasure and escapism, and, occasionally, satire. In architecture, artifice and gaiety prevailed, combined with an organic quality of form. Neoclassical themes centered on examples of virtue and heroism, usually in classical settings and historical stories. Architecture focuses on classical simplicity and utility of design.

Nineteenth century (1800–1900 CE)

Important genres of the nineteenth century include romantic painting, academic painting and sculpture, landscape and realistic painting, Impressionism, and many varieties of post-Impressionism.

Romantic themes include human freedom, equality, and civil rights, a love of nature, and a tendency toward the melancholic and mystic. The underlying theme is that the most important discoveries are made within the self, not in the exterior world. In architecture, the theme is fantasy and whimsy, known as the picturesque style. Realistic themes included social awareness and a focus on society victimizing individuals. The themes behind Impressionism are the constant flux of the universe and the immediacy of the moment. In architecture, the themes are strength, simplicity, and upward thrust as skyscrapers came on the scene.

Twentieth century (1900–2000 CE)

Major genres of the twentieth century include symbolism, art nouveau, fauvism, expressionism, cubism (both analytical and synthetic), futurism, nonobjective art, abstract art, surrealism, social realism, constructivism in sculpture, pop art, op art, and conceptual art.

Diverse artistic themes of the century reflect a parting with traditional religious values and a painful awareness of man's inhumanity to man. Themes also illustrate a growing reliance on science, while simultaneously expressing disillusionment with man's failure to adequately control science. A constant theme is the quest for originality and self-expression, while seeking to express the universal in human experience. In architecture, "form follows function."

See also Skill 43.9

SKILL 43.9 Selects and uses instructional strategies, materials and activities to promote students' awareness and appreciation of the characteristics of a variety of art forms of multiple cultures within and outside the Western tradition.

Art History

Art history has enhanced the study of political history by showing how art interacts with power structures in society.

Art history is a relatively new field in academia. The study of art history relies on the faithful reproduction of artworks as a springboard for discussion and study. The development of new photography techniques after World War II made this possible; however, the appreciation and study of the visual arts has intrigued humanity for hundreds of years. Art history features the study of biographies of individual artists. In the eighteenth century, scholars began arguing that the real emphasis in the study of art should be placed on the views of the learned beholder and not on the unique viewpoint of the charismatic artist.

Art predates history: sculptures, cave paintings, and rock paintings have been found that are roughly 40,000 years old. However, the precise meaning of such art is often disputed because we know so little about the cultures that produced it.

Eastern vs. Western Art

There is an obvious difference in aesthetic principles between works created in Eastern and Western cultures. Eastern works of art are more often based on spiritual concerns, while much Western art is secular in nature. Eastern artists portray the human figure with symbolic meaning and little regard for muscle structure, resulting in a mystical view of the human experience. Western artists use the "principle of ponderation," which requires knowledge of human anatomy.

Eastern artists prefer a diagonal projection of eye movement into the picture plane, and often leave large areas of the surface untouched by detail. The result is the illusion of vast space, an infinite view that coincides with the spiritual philosophies of the East. Western artists rely on several techniques, such as overlapping planes, variation of object size, object position on the picture plane, linear and aerial perspective, color change, and various points of perspective to convey the illusion of depth.

See also Skill 43.8

> SKILL **Provides instruction to develop the skills and knowledge required for**
> 43.10 **visual literacy** *(e.g., art elements and principles, art of different areas and cultures, diverse purposes and uses of art).*

See Skills 43.8 and 43.9

> SKILL **Integrates instruction in the visual arts with instruction in other**
> 43.11 **subject areas.**

Students identify with the arts in their own distinctive way. Because the arts include various forms of expression such as visual arts, music, theatre, and dance, teachers can use this familiarity to reach students and to motivate them to learn material that may seem outdated or irrelevant. But how can a teacher accomplish this?

At first, a teacher may use the art itself to teach the concept. For example, a standardized test may require students to identify the main idea, to identify details, and to analyze a piece of short literature. A teacher can use a song popular among students to help them learn the concept. They will find it enjoyable to dissect a song they hear on the radio and will be motivated to find the answers in subjects they are passionate about. Once the students are familiar with the idea, the teacher can use the material from the lesson as a review. Another example would be to ask students to draw a picture of their understanding of a new concept. Creating a visual can be very helpful for new concepts, especially those that are intangible.

Finally, a teacher can use muscle memory, or simple dance movements, to help teach terms. Instead of asking students to use rote memorization, the teacher can create a movement for each concept and ask students to repeat these movements as they verbalize the concept. Eventually, the children will connect the movement to the words and remember the concept.

The arts can and should be used as foundations and as catalysts to help students connect to new information and concepts.

The arts can and should be used as foundations and as catalysts to help students connect to new information and concepts. Learning styles can be useful here as well. For example, if a student has high musical intelligence or high kinesthetic intelligence, the teacher can use this knowledge to incorporate arts into lessons as often as possible to encourage further understanding.

> **SKILL 43.12** **Understands how students develop cognitively and artistically and knows how to implement effective art instruction and assessment that are individually, culturally and age appropriate.**

According to Jean Piaget, students' cognition changes significantly as they mature. He has labeled four stages: sensorimotor stage, pre-operational stage, concrete operational stage, and formal operational stage. The sensorimotor stage, which is present during infanthood, is recognized based on physical development. Object permanence (knowing an object or person hasn't disappeared forever when it cannot be seen) develops in the second half of the first year.

Teachers will be more concerned with the second two stages: the pre-operational stage and the concrete operational stage. Features of the pre-operational stage (from toddler through preschool age) include using language and imagination. Children still see themselves as the center of the world and have a hard time with empathy. In the concrete operational stage, which is evident in elementary and early teenage years, children become more aware of the world around them, and empathy increases. Concrete thinking also develops.

According to Dr. Viktor Lowenfeld (1947), there are six stages of artistic development in children. They are as follows:

1. **Scribble Stage (age 1–3):** In toddlerhood, a child will draw marks and random lines on a page. He will not connect these to a concept at this point, and he will enjoy the act of drawing.

2. **Preschematic Stage (age 3–4):** Toward preschool age, a child will begin to realize that she can use shapes to represent things she sees. The drawings may not be very "readable" but to the child, but there is a purpose.

3. **Schematic Stage (age 5–6):** In this stage, a child has figured out that shapes can be used to communicate concepts through drawings. At this point, there is also a background schema for creating concepts through art. There may be some detail, including the ground and sky, and a child is starting to understand how objects relate to the space around them.

4. **Dawning Realism (age 7–9):** In this school-age stage, a child may realize that his drawings are not perfect, and he will start to see his errors in spatial relationships or in details.

5. **Pseudo-Naturalistic (age 10–13):** As a child becomes a preteen, she begins to use light and shadows to draw and judges her work based on how realistic it is.

6. **Decision Stage (age 13–16):** In the final stage, a child may feel that he is "not good" at drawing due to his own ability to criticize his work. Some children will enjoy drawing and will continue to get better at it, whereas others will stop because they are convinced they have no skills.

Teachers of the fine arts should be knowledgeable of these stages so they can understand both the limits of their students and how to challenge them appropriately. For example, you wouldn't ask a three-year-old to draw a picture of a landscape with intricate details. The child will not understand the request, and he will not be able to see it through. Instead, reading stories about landscapes, showing pictures, and talking about a few details of a landscape can culminate in a project in which students use a few colors to draw their personal concept. There will be no expectations or criticizing of their work. The teacher should not expect perfectly drawn shapes or any visual spatial detail.

Assessments should match both cognitive and artistic development. For example, grading a fifth grader on his use of color may be appropriate, just as it would be appropriate to grade a second grader on his use of color. However, both rubrics must be developmentally appropriate so students can meet expectations.

- *The Stages of Artistic Development*

  http://thevirtualinstructor.com/blog/the-stages-of-artistic-development. Retrieved Aug. 20, 2015.

> **SKILL 43.13** Applies knowledge of visual arts content and curriculum based on the Texas Essential Knowledge and Skills (TEKS) and knowledge of students in early childhood through grade six to plan and implement effective, developmentally appropriate art instruction.

Educators need to know where they can find the content and curriculum TEKS standards. Standards are laid out at the Texas Education Agency website, at tea. texas.gov. It's imperative for educators to go through their grade level and the content expected and create lesson plans that will match the cognitive development of students.

Students in grades K–6 are advancing in their cognitive and moral development. According to Piaget, these students are in the pre-operational and concrete operational stages. In the pre-operational stage, children are quite egocentric and are engaging in parallel play and pretend play, and they are beginning to play well with one another. Also, children in this stage will focus on one thing at a time. In the next stage, the concrete operational stage, children will become more logical and concrete thinkers. They also will become aware that actions can be reversible, will become less egocentric, and will be able to understand that when something breaks into small pieces, it retains its initial value.

Most students, according to Kohlberg, are in the pre-conventional morality stage. In stage one (younger children), children respond to rules due to fear of punishment. In stage two (older children), they recognize that different authority figures have different rules, and that is acceptable.

When creating lessons to match the content standards, teachers must always take into account the stages of development, the background schema, and the learning styles of the students who are receiving the instruction. This way, the students will be able to relate and engage with the lesson more thoroughly.

COMPETENCY 44
MUSIC

SKILL 44.1 **Knows how to involve students in activities that promote enjoyment and understanding of music by providing students with a wide range of opportunities to make and respond to music so that they develop music literacy** *(e.g., concert attendance, authentic performance opportunities).*

Students can explore creating moods with music and analyzing stories and creating musical compositions that reflect or enhance them. Their daily routines can include exploration and interpretation of musical sound. Immersing them in musical conversations as they sing, speak rhythmically, and walk in step stimulates their awareness of the beauty and structure of musical sound.

As students acquire the skills and knowledge that music brings to their lives, they go through stages similar to the stages of language development. Singing, chanting, and moving; exposing them to many different sources of sound in play, including a variety of styles of music; and reinforcing rhythm through patting, tapping, and moving will enhance students' awareness of musical sound.

See also Skills 44.3 and 44.10

> *Involvement in music is thought to teach basic skills such as concentration, counting, and listening and to promote the understanding of language.*

SKILL 44.2 **Applies knowledge of standard terminology for describing and analyzing musical sound** *(e.g., rhythm, melody, form, timbre, tempo, pitch, meter, dynamics, intonation, intervals)* **and has a basic understanding of how to read, write, recognize aurally and interpret standard music notation.**

Music Notation

When music is written down, the composer includes instructions about what he or she wants listeners to hear and how the musician(s) should perform the music. This is referred to as music notation. Standard present-day music notation is based on a five-line staff called a clef. The upper clef is called the treble clef; the lower clef is called the bass clef. Pitch is shown by placing notes on the staff. These notes are modified by additional symbols called sharps, flats, and naturals. The duration of a note (the length of time it is held) is shown by different note shapes and additional symbols such as ties, dotted notes, and rests. In addition to the notations developed for human performers, there are also computer-generated representations of music designed to either be turned into conventional notation or be read directly by the computer.

MELODIC MUSIC: music that is characterized by a single, strong melody line

MELODIC MUSIC is music that is characterized by a single, strong melody line. The melody line, or tune, is easy to remember and follow. Melodic music can be performed by a singer, an orchestra, a single instrument, or any combination of the three. Opera is considered to be a classical form; the lighter operetta is considered borderline; and the musical is placed in the popular category.

HARMONIC NOTATION: the key in which music is written

HARMONIC NOTATION is commonly referred to as the key in which music is written. Keys can be major or minor, depending on the combination of whole and half steps used in the scale, and are indicated by sharp signs and flat signs after the clef signs in the signature. There are twelve pitches in the musical scale, each of which is a degree of the scale. An interval is the relationship between two separate musical pitches. Harmony is the result of more than one note being played simultaneously (e.g., a chord) and is created by the combination of notes making intervals.

RHYTHMIC NOTATION: the exact rhythm in which the indicated notes or chords are played or sung

RHYTHMIC NOTATION refers to the exact rhythm in which the indicated notes or chords are played or sung. The rhythm key is written above the staff. Rhythms are usually arranged by using a time signature, signifying a meter. The top number of the time signature reflects the number of beats in each measure, whereas the bottom number reflects which type of note uses a single beat (e.g., 1 on the bottom reflects a whole note, 2 on the bottom reflects a half note, 4 reflects a quarter note, etc.). The speed of the underlying beat is the tempo (e.g., allegro, allegretto, presto, moderato, lento, largo).

Musical Terms

- **Accent:** Stress of one tone over others, making it stand out; often it is the first beat of a measure
- **Accompaniment:** Music that goes along with a more important part; often harmony or rhythmic patterns accompanying a melody
- **Adagio:** Slow, leisurely
- **Allegro:** Lively, brisk, rapid
- **Cadence:** The close of a phrase or section of music
- **Chord:** Three or more tones combined and sounded simultaneously
- **Crescendo:** Gradually growing louder

- **Dissonance:** A simultaneous sounding of tones that produces a feeling of tension or unrest

- **Harmony:** The sound resulting from the simultaneous sounding of two or more tones consonant with each other

- **Interval:** The distance between two tones

- **Melody:** An arrangement of single tones in a meaningful sequence

- **Phrase:** A small section of a composition constituting a musical thought

- **Rhythm:** The regular occurrence of accented beats that shape the character of music or dance

- **Scale:** A graduated series of tones arranged in a specified order

- **Staccato:** Separate; sounded in a short, detached manner

- **Syncopation:** The rhythmic result produced when a regularly accented beat is displaced onto an unaccented beat

- **Tempo:** The speed at which a musical composition is performed

- **Theme:** A short musical passage that states an idea; it often provides the basis for variations, development, etc.

- **Timbre:** The quality of a musical tone that distinguishes voices and instruments

- **Tone:** A musical sound or the quality of a musical sound

Musical Instruments

Musical instruments can be divided into four basic categories:

- **Stringed instruments:** Stringed instruments make their sounds through strings. The sound of the instrument depends on the thickness and length of the strings. The more slowly a string vibrates, the lower the resulting pitch. The way the strings are manipulated varies among string instruments. With some string instruments, the strings are plucked (e.g., guitar) while with others the player uses a bow to make the strings vibrate (e.g., violin). Other common string instruments include the viola, double bass, and cello.

- **Percussion instruments:** To play a percussion instrument, the musician hits or shakes it. The sound is created from vibrations as a result of shaking or striking the instrument. Many materials, such as metal or wood, are used to create percussion instruments, and different thicknesses or sizes of the material affect the sound. Thicker, heavier materials like drum membranes make deeper sounds, while thinner materials make higher-pitched sounds.

Common percussion instruments include the cymbals, tambourine, bells, xylophone, and wood block.

- **Wind instruments:** The sound of wind instruments is caused by wind vibrating in a pipe or tube. Air blows into one end of the instrument, and, in many wind instruments, it passes over a reed, which causes the air to vibrate. The pitch depends on the air's frequency as it passes through the tube, and the frequency depends on the tube's length or size. Larger tubes create deeper sounds. The pitch is also controlled by holes or valves. As the musician's fingers cover the holes or press the valves, the pitch changes. Common wind instruments include the pipe organ, oboe, clarinet, and saxophone.

- **Brass instruments:** Brass instruments are similar to wind instruments because music from brass instruments also results from air passing through an air chamber. Brass instruments, however, are made from metal or brass. Pitch on a brass instrument is controlled by the size or length of the air chamber. Many brass instruments are twisted or coiled, which lengthens the air chamber without making the instrument unmanageably long. As with wind instruments, larger air chambers create deeper sounds, and valves on the instrument control the pitch. In addition, in some brass instruments, the position of the musician's mouth on the mouthpiece controls the pitch. Common brass instruments include the French horn, trumpet, trombone, and tuba.

SKILL 44.3 **Knows how to arrange vocal and instrumental music for specific purposes and settings** (e.g., guides students in creating simple song arrangements and accompaniments using voices, classroom percussion, and melody instruments).

Arranging Music

Music is written for many different voices, instruments, uses, and settings. Being able to arrange music for specific purposes—for example, for students in a classroom setting or for a group of students performing in a chorale or band—is a valuable asset for all teachers of music, and is often a necessity when working with older or more accomplished students.

Such work entails familiarity with music notation, basic music theory, the range of musical styles, the key signatures of various instruments, transposition, harmony, and the different abilities of students, among other things. It is also extremely helpful to have access to and the ability to use computer software that scores music. This reduces the amount of time and effort involved in arranging music.

At the elementary level, the arrangement of music is often limited to changing the key to make a song easier for students to sing, adding harmonies to simple or familiar melodies, or incorporating instruments that have different key signatures.

560

Arranging music for use by elementary students should be guided by three factors:

- The content of the instructional activity

- The ability of the student(s)

- The intended outcome

While learning is always the intended outcome to some degree, sometimes there is an additional goal, such as a performance. The audience might be classmates, the whole school, or parents/guardians and the community. Different outcomes may affect how the music is arranged, and should be considered before the musical pieces are selected and arranged.

SKILL 44.4 Knows and understands music of diverse genres, styles and cultures.

Genres of Music

CLASSICAL MUSIC is a type of music based on European secular and religious music from about the ninth century to the present. The term itself is generally understood to refer to the "golden age" of composers from Johann Sebastian Bach (1685–1750) to Ludwig van Beethoven (1770–1827). Classical music often refers to instrumental music in general, although opera is also considered classical.

A BALLAD is a song that contains a story. A ballad usually has simple repeating rhymes and often contains a refrain (or repeating sections) that are played or sung at regular intervals throughout.

FOLK MUSIC is music that has endured and been passed down by oral tradition and that emerges spontaneously from ordinary people. A folk song is usually seen as an expression of a way of life now past or about to disappear.

Call-and-response songs are a form of interaction between a singer and a listener, in which the listener sings a response to the singer. In West African cultures, call-and-response songs were used in religious rituals and gatherings. In certain Native American tribes, call-and-response songs preserve and protect the tribe's cultural heritage and can be seen and heard at modern-day "pow-wows."

The work song is typically a song sung *a cappella* by people working on a physical and often repetitive task. Frequently, the verses of work songs are improvised and sung differently each time.

CLASSICAL MUSIC: a type of music based on European secular and religious music from about the ninth century to the present

BALLAD: a song that contains a story

FOLK MUSIC: music that has endured and been passed down by oral tradition and that emerges spontaneously from ordinary people

Jazz is a form of music that grew out of a combination of folk music, ragtime, and big band music. It has been called the first native art form to develop in the United States.

Blues is a vocal and instrumental music form that came from West African spirituals, work songs, and chants. This musical form has been a major influence on later American popular music, finding expression in jazz, rock and roll, and country music.

Rock and roll, in its broadest sense, refers to almost all pop music recorded since the early 1950s. Its main features include an emphasis on rhythm and the use of percussion and amplified instruments like the bass and guitar.

> **SKILL 44.5** Demonstrates an understanding of the purposes and roles of music in society and how music can reflect elements of a specific society or culture.

See Skills 44.4 and 44.7

> **SKILL 44.6** Explains a variety of music and music-related career options.

Careers in Music

Teachers can inspire students to pursue a career in a music-related field simply by providing information about the kinds of jobs people do that involve music.

Music-based career options are quite varied. The more obvious careers involve music directly, such as performing, composing, teaching, and conducting. Many other music-related careers also exist, such as working as an agent for musicians, making or repairing instruments, and being a disc jockey.

Students who love music may seek out such information and inadvertently discover a satisfying occupation—just because a teacher mentioned it in elementary school.

Music-related career choices:

- Soloist
- Band or orchestra member
- Accompanist
- Background vocalist
- Manager or booking agent
- Composer
- Administrator of a music organization
- Music therapist
- Librettist
- Sound technician or engineer
- Musical librarian or archivist
- Music arranger, orchestrator, or transcriber
- Instrument maker or repairer

- Conductor
- Music teacher (in a school, college, or on an individual basis)
- Choir director
- MIDI engineer or technician
- Music critic
- Disc jockey
- Film scorer
- Music historian
- Recording engineer
- Lyricist
- Music promoter or producer
- Entertainment attorney
- Studio director
- Tour manager

SKILL 44.7 Identifies and describes how music reflects the heritage of the United States and Texas.

Early American Music

Throughout history, American society has used music to pass on traditions, share stories, celebrate, and grieve. Music reflects the heritage of the United States as a whole, and of Texas in particular.

Long before European settlers made it to the United States, Native Americans used song and dance to worship, celebrate the harvest, ward off disease, and pass down stories from one generation to the next. Vocal singing dominated the music of Native Americans, who impressed early explorers with their ability to synchronize large groups of singers into one voice.

Music is a terrific historian. Students can trace the popular music of each decade to observe how it comments on events in American history.

Beginning in the 1700s and throughout the Civil War, slaves contributed to our musical heritage with the singing of spirituals. These spirituals sprang from the tradition of retelling Old Testament stories, but they also highlighted the profound melancholy and sorrow of the life of the slaves. They are the roots of present-day blues and jazz in the United States.

In the 1800s, American folk music took on a distinct sound and again described the history of a new country. Individuals like Stephen C. Foster were instrumental in providing the country with tunes that reflected everyday American life. Some of these songs include "Oh! Susanna," "Camptown Races," "Old Folks at Home," "My Old Kentucky Home," "Jeanie with the Light Brown Hair," and "Beautiful Dreamer."

Nineteenth-Century Music

Music created around the time of the Civil War reflected a time of conflict and uncertainty in the United States. "Amazing Grace," "The Battle Hymn of the Republic," "My Darling Clementine," "Old Black Joe," and "Go Tell it on the Mountain" described events in a torn country and feelings of loss, fear, hope, patriotism, and religious fervor. This time period also saw the growth of American gospel music, which was the first American hymnody. Gospel songs dealt with redemption from sin and were easy and fun to sing in large groups.

Aaron Copeland, one of the best-known American composers of the twentieth century, took many of the cowboy songs popular in the western United States and incorporated them into his classical compositions, which have a uniquely American sound.

Toward the end of the nineteenth century, another American music form was born: ragtime. This new music was the direct result of the combining of diverse cultures—namely, European and African—in the southern United States. Ragtime evolved as an informal experiment in combining music traditions from both cultures. It features syncopated rhythms and the piano.

Around the turn of the century in Texas, another clash of cultures produced the Texas-Mexican music called conjunto. Working-class musicians from German and Mexican backgrounds combined their talents to produce this folk music, which uses the accordion as its main instrument.

Jazz music testifies to the continuous flow of different cultures into a single, uniquely American musical style.

Jazz and Rock 'n' Roll

Gospel and ragtime laid the groundwork for American jazz. It broke down barriers between various groups because the exploration and experimentation involved in the development of jazz pulled from multiple cultural experiences within the United States. Louis Armstrong, Billie Holiday, Duke Ellington, Benny Goodman, and Charlie Parker represent just a few stellar examples of American artists from the golden age of jazz.

One of America's most popular forms of music today–rock 'n' roll–grew out of the roots of jazz and blues in the 1940s. Once icons like Little Richard, Elvis Presley, and Buddy Holly moved it into the mainstream, it caught fire throughout the country and freedom of expression in music took on new dimensions. Rock 'n' roll lyrics have covered everything from personal relationships to war protests to the freedom of dancing without inhibition.

> **SKILL 44.8** Applies knowledge of criteria for evaluating and critiquing musical performances and experiences, including using standard terminology in communicating about students' musical skills and performance abilities.

Critiquing Musical Performances

Teaching basic music terminology is a prerequisite for any critiquing process. Without the necessary language, students will not be able to evaluate a piece of music. Similarly, students must be given the opportunity to develop listening skills so they are able to hear different musical elements, themes, instruments, and tones. They will also benefit from an overview of the sounds of different instruments and a listing of musical styles.

While establishing the fundamental skills noted above, teachers can introduce simple rubrics (often called critique sheets) for critiquing a song. A rubric might include elements like tempo changes, use of specific instruments, rhythms, and loudness and softness, as well as the students' personal responses to the music. Students can also develop their own rubrics for evaluating music, including their own vocal or instrumental performances or their own compositions.

The key steps in critiquing music are: listen, analyze, describe, and evaluate.

Working in pairs or small groups can help students develop the verbal language of critiques and enhance both listening and performance skills. Their peers may point out nuances they have missed or bring a different perspective to a particular piece of music. In a small-group setting, students can discuss likes and dislikes and come to a greater understanding of their own preferences.

Attending live performances by both amateur and professional musicians can be very helpful in enhancing the critiquing skills of all students; it is especially important for older students. There are also a number of online resources for helping students learn to critique music.

As students gain experience and knowledge, they develop more sophisticated critiquing skills. These may involve listening for differences in technique, varied interpretations of the same piece, expressiveness, and the details specific to various musical styles.

When critiquing students' performances, teachers need to be nonjudgmental and respectful when giving feedback. Providing students with the rubric that will be used to assess their performance ahead of time can decrease the sense of judgment that often accompanies critiques. The rubric should describe observable skills with clear parameters, and should be written using standard music terminology. Familiarity with the rubric as well as with the general process of critiquing may decrease students' anxiety about performance evaluations.

> **SKILL 44.9** Integrates instruction in music with instruction in other subject areas.

Integrating Music with Other Subjects

Music lends itself to integration with many subjects in elementary school. Most obviously, reading music involves *reading*. Learning to read music notation generally follows the development of basic literacy skills. Children's first exposure to reading music usually involves reading the words of a song, not the actual musical notes. Therefore, in many cases, basic reading skills are enhanced as music is taught. All of the elements of reading are present when reading music with words, including comprehension, prosody, fluency, and vocabulary development.

In other subject areas, music can be the focus (e.g., discovering the musical styles of a particular culture in a social studies class) or a tool used to facilitate the learning of subject matter (e.g., a song that teaches science concepts). Creative teachers can develop impromptu songs to help students learn lists or details. Engaging students in music-related activities can increase their motivation to study the history and geography of a region more effectively than a "straight" social studies approach.

The same can be said for studying the mathematics of music. By using music as a way "in," students may discover they enjoy math. Music offers many opportunities for counting as well as exploring more complex math concepts. Furthermore, students who do well in music tend to do well in math. Some people believe that music and math strengthen the same neural pathways between the two hemispheres in the brain.

There are a number of writing activities that can be incorporated with music. Concert or album reviews, interviews with musicians, articles about musical styles or upcoming music-related events, and song lyrics are just a few of the writing opportunities that can be included with music education.

Making use of small chunks of time can also benefit the music curriculum. For example, practicing a recently learned song while waiting in line or during a bus ride on a field trip can augment regular music classes. Similarly, bringing rhythm instruments to the gym during an indoor recess period or sharing one's own skill at playing guitar or piano, for example, can facilitate music education without straining resources. These opportunities also help students see music as an integral part of life rather than a separate subject limited to the classroom or the concert hall.

In an integrated curriculum, whether music is the focus or a tool really doesn't matter. As educators and researchers have learned, schools that incorporate the arts into the broader curriculum have better-performing students and more positive school environments. These schools are more effective at narrowing the achievement gap and enhancing students' social development.

> As educators and researchers have learned, schools that incorporate the arts into the broader curriculum have better-performing students and more positive school environments.

SKILL 44.10 **Knows how to teach students to sing and/or play an instrument with expression, both independently and in small groups.**

Teaching Students to Play or Sing with Expression

While some students may display a special talent for expressiveness, it is important for teachers to teach all students to play or sing with expression. As with prosody and fluency in reading, some of the skill in this area emerges naturally once students have mastered basic skills and techniques. It is a developmental process. Learning to read music notation, stringing notes together in phrases, knowing how to use one's voice or an instrument to make different sounds—all of these are essential to expressiveness.

Teachers can engage students in particular activities that help students develop expressiveness. Further, teachers can encourage musical "intelligence" and creativity; some in the field of music believe that these abilities underlie the development of expressiveness.

Activities to foster expression in music

Some activities that teachers can use with students to foster expression in music include the following:

- Introduce the concept of "expression" as a distinct element early in the music curriculum.

- Invite students to experiment with sounds (via voice and/or instruments) and to notice the many ways they can produce sound.

- Provide opportunities for students to compare and contrast recordings of the same piece of music by different artists, ensembles, or orchestras.

- Have students listen to one another play or sing music and notice the differences and similarities.

- Combine music with visual arts: Have students draw pictures of what they feel when they listen to different pieces of music.

- Encourage students to experiment with playing or singing different variations of the same song.

- Help students articulate their understanding of a piece of music, its history, and the meaning and feelings associated with the piece.

- With longer pieces of music, compare and contrast each section with the other sections.

> **SKILL 44.11** Applies knowledge of music content and curriculum based on the Texas Essential Knowledge and Skills (TEKS) and of students in early childhood through grade six to plan and implement effective, developmentally appropriate instruction, including instruction that promotes students' creativity and performance skills as well as students' ability to use critical-thinking and problem-solving skills in music contexts (e.g., sequential instruction, music composition, improvisation, concert etiquette).

Teaching Examples That Incorporate TEKS

The development of music skills not only provides a well-rounded education for students, but it also can be an entertaining and engaging way for students to make strides in a variety of subjects. The following are teaching examples for the classroom that incorporate the TEKS for children in kindergarten through grade 4.

Identify higher, lower, faster, slower music

The teacher brings various musical recordings into the classroom—an example of fast music, such as "The Flight of the Bumblebee" by Nikolai Rimsky-Korsakov, and an example of slow music, like Brahms's "Lullaby"—and plays one after the other. The teacher directs students to move around the room in a way that reflects the music they hear. After playing each excerpt, the teacher asks the students to explain why they moved the way they did and introduces the concept of slow and fast music. The teacher plays several other examples, allowing the students to move with the music quickly and slowly. Then, when students return to their seats, they are asked to close their eyes. The teacher plays the same examples in a different order and asks students to raise their hands when they hear fast music or raise their hands when they hear slow music. The same format can be followed for high-pitch and low-pitch music.

Sing songs from diverse cultures

Singing songs from diverse cultures develops musical skills such as pitch matching and memory of melodic patterns. For older students, it can also incorporate actual identification and reading of musical notes. In addition, students learn about societies from around the world.

Identify musical instruments visually and aurally

Introducing children to musical instruments can be an exercise in creativity and a reinforcement of math concepts. The teacher can start with students in a circle and introduce a percussion instrument such as a tambourine. The teacher demonstrates different ways to play the tambourine (shaking, flicking, banging like a drum, scraping). Then the instrument is passed from student to student, as each one experiments on his or her own. The teacher lets one student play the instrument and then asks the next student to imitate the first student. After three or four different percussion instruments are introduced, the teacher chooses one student to be the conductor and gives instruments to the remaining students. The teacher allows the conductor to choose a card. The cards are numbered from 1 to 10. If the number chosen is 5, then the student gets to conduct five "beats." The conductor gestures to the students in a pulse or beat five times, and the musicians must play on each beat. This can evolve into the conductor choosing two cards and conducting 2 + 2 beats, gesturing to half the class for two beats and the other half of the class for the remaining two beats. As a follow-up, the teacher can ask, "How many total beats did you conduct?"

The conductor game also works with concepts of loud and soft. The teacher asks the conductor to gesture in a way that would encourage students to play loudly and then softly. Teachers may be surprised by the creative ways students direct or conduct their fellow musicians and by the ways the musician students play their instruments. After loud and soft conducting, the teacher can introduce the music terms *forte* (meaning *loud*) and *piano* (meaning *soft*).

In this one short lesson, the teacher has given the students new vocabulary words by introducing the names of instruments, reinforced the math concept of addition, and also introduced basic music terminology such as *conductor*, *beat*, *forte*, and *piano*.

Appropriate behavior during a live performance

- No talking after the lights go down/when the performance begins.

- Clap at the end of the performance to show appreciation.

- No cell phones.

- Sit quietly until the performance ends.

- Actors and musicians perform with a loud voice so they can be heard from the back row of an auditorium.

- Actors and musicians bow at the end of a performance.

SKILL 44.12	Manages time, instructional resources and physical space effectively for music education.

Time on task should begin when students enter the room. Be at the door when class begins and welcome them. Then, direct them to a task to complete. Place the directions for the activity in the same place each day so students know where to look. A beginning activity will soon become a habit for your students, and they will not need reminders to begin learning immediately. Activities could include practicing a scale or playing a few difficult measures of music three to five times. They also could include asking students to write notations on a music sheet, to create a rhythm and write it down, or even to write a few sets of rhyming lyrics. Beginning-of-class activities should be about five minutes in length and be something a student can complete independently. Often, these activities can be review from a previous lesson and can double as a quick assessment to see what students remember.

The rest of the class should be split into review, learning new concepts, and a chance to practice as an ensemble. Giving students a chance to see how the music will come together is very important. If they only see the few measures they are working on and focus on the details instead of the gestalt of the piece, their motivation and morale may be weaker than if the teacher gives the ensemble some time toward the end of the class to practice the piece in its entirety.

In some music classes, such as band or orchestra, each student will have his or her own instrument. In other general music classes, there may not be enough instruments for each student to have an instrument. It is important to use instructional resources effectively. This may mean setting up centers through which students move, especially when dealing with various types of percussion or stringed instruments. Students should not share any mouthpieces or reeds; that is unsanitary.

Music rooms, especially those used for band or orchestra rehearsals, often are spacious. The corners are filled with large instruments such as string basses, drum sets, and xylophones. There are many chairs and music stands for the members of these ensembles and sometimes even lockers to store smaller instruments. The music teacher needs to choose the best student setup so he or she can see all the sections and they can see him or her. Often, teachers choose semicircles, with higher tone instruments in the front circle (such as flutes, clarinets and saxophones) and deeper instruments behind (such as trombones, trumpets, and French horns). The percussion section is in the back because the majority of those students will stand to play their instruments and can see over the other sections. The teacher, or conductor, will stand in the middle to conduct and teach from a place where all can see him or her.

COMPETENCY 45
HEALTH

> **SKILL 45.1** Understands health-related behaviors, ways that personal health decisions and behaviors affect body systems and health and strategies for reducing health risks and enhancing wellness throughout the life span.

Wellness

Wellness has two major components:

- Understanding the basic human body functions and how to care for and maintain personal fitness

- Developing an awareness and knowledge of how certain everyday factors, stresses, and personal decisions can affect one's health

Lifelong fitness and the benefits of a healthy lifestyle need to be part of every physical education teacher's curriculum.

Teaching fitness needs to go along with skill and activity instruction. Cross-discipline teaching and teaching thematically with other subject matter in classrooms is an ideal method to teach health to adolescents.

Positive health behaviors can help decrease the risk of illness and disease. Good nutrition and regular exercise can help prevent everyday illnesses such as colds and flu as well as chronic diseases such as heart disease and cancer. Exercise and a healthy diet help maintain a healthy body composition; reduce cholesterol levels; strengthen the heart, lungs, and musculoskeletal system; and strengthen the body's immune system.

Strategies for Positive Behavior Change

Strategies for positive behavior change in students will relate the teaching of new behaviors to the students' perceptions and frames of reference, and will focus on a series of small, incremental changes. Instructors should link new behaviors to existing behaviors, the goal being to gradually modify behavioral patterns.

Instructors should actively involve students in the process of change. The behavioral change should be the student's own goal, not the teacher's goal for the student. In this way, the process of change becomes intrinsically motivated, making it far more likely the student will seriously commit to the process. The instructor should reinforce positive behavior, but not excessively; behavioral change should, for the most part, be intrinsically motivated.

Supporting positive change

Health and fitness education should include an introduction to research skills so students have access to appropriate and relevant information when they need to make decisions about their health.

Positive health choices and behavior also require a layer of economic support, because healthy lifestyle choices may be more expensive than less-healthy alternatives. It is also important for the student's environment to be conducive to positive choices and behaviors regarding health. For example, the availability of resources (educational and practical) and facilities (medical and fitness) in proximity to the individual can have a positive impact on the decision-making process.

Good resources for research include the Internet, local libraries, and fitness and health-care professionals in the community.

Assessing Behavioral Health Risk Factors

There are various resources available to assess the behavioral-health risk factors of a community. The Centers for Disease Control and Prevention (CDC) annually publishes the Youth Risk Behavior Survey (YRBS). This survey describes national and state-level adolescent health risks. This information is available directly from the CDC. State education agencies compile and maintain statistics on youth health risks. Individual schools or school districts provide data regarding the types of problems seen in the school health room. Individual schools or school districts can also supply information regarding the number of referrals for pregnancy and substance abuse and data on absenteeism, dropouts, and disciplinary actions.

Another source of information is social service agencies, which have data on poverty, unemployment, and child abuse.

Stages of Human Growth and Development

Physical development

Small children (ages 3–5) have a propensity for engaging in periods of intense physical activity, punctuated by a need for a lot of rest. Children at this stage lack fine-motor skills and cannot focus on small objects for very long. Their bones are still developing. At this age, girls tend to be better coordinated and boys tend to be stronger.

The lag in fine-motor skills continues during the early-elementary-school years (ages 6–8).

Preadolescent children (ages 9–11) become stronger, leaner, and taller. Their motor skills improve, and they are able to sit still and focus for longer periods of time. Growth during this period is constant. This is also the time when gender-specific physical predispositions will begin to manifest. Preadolescents are at risk of obesity without proper nutrition and adequate activity.

Young adolescents (ages 12–14) experience dramatic physical growth (girls earlier than boys), and are highly preoccupied with their physical appearance.

As children proceed to the later stages of adolescence (ages 15–17), girls will reach their full height, while boys will continue to grow. The increase in hormone levels may cause acne. At this age, children may begin to initiate sexual activity. There is a risk of teen pregnancy and sexually transmitted diseases.

Cognitive development

Language development is the most important aspect of cognitive development in small children (ages 3–5). Allowing successes, rewarding mature behavior, and allowing the child to explore can improve confidence and self-esteem at this age.

Early-elementary-school children (ages 6–8) are eager to learn and love to talk. Children at this age have a very literal understanding of rules and verbal instructions and must develop strong listening skills.

Language development is the most important aspect of cognitive development in small children (ages 3–5).

Preadolescent children (ages 9–11) display increased logical thought, but their knowledge or beliefs may be unusual or surprising. Differences in cognitive styles develop at this age (e.g., field-dependent or field-independent preferences).

In early adolescence (ages 12–14), boys tend to score higher on mechanical/spatial reasoning, and girls on spelling, language, and clerical tasks. Boys are better with mental imagery, and girls have better access to and retrieval of information from memory. Self-efficacy (the ability to self-evaluate) becomes very important at this stage.

In later adolescence (ages 15–17), children are capable of formal thought but don't always apply it. Conflicts between teens' and parents' opinions and worldviews arise. Children at this age may become interested in advanced political thinking.

Social development

Small children (ages 3–5) are socially flexible. Different children will prefer solitary play, parallel play, or cooperative play. Frequent minor quarrels will occur between children, and boys will tend to be more aggressive (children at these ages are already aware of gender roles).

Early-elementary-school children (ages 6–8) are increasingly selective of friends (usually of the same sex). Children at this age enjoy playing games but are excessively preoccupied by the rules. Verbal aggression becomes more common than physical aggression, and adults should encourage children of this age to solve their own conflicts.

Preadolescent children (ages 9–11) place great importance on the (perceived) opinions of their peers and of their social stature, and will go to great lengths to "fit in." Friendships at this age are very selective, and usually of the same sex.

Young adolescents (ages 12–14) develop greater understanding of the emotions of others, which results in increased emotional sensitivity and affects peer relationships. Children at this age develop an increased need to perform.

In the later stages of adolescence (ages 15–17), peers are still the primary influence on day-to-day decisions, but parents have increasing influence on long-term goals. Girls' friendships tend to be close and intimate whereas boys' friendships are based on competition and similar interests. Many children at this age work part-time, and educators should be alert for signs of potential school dropouts.

Emotional development

Small children (ages 3–5) express emotions freely and have a limited ability to understand how emotions influence behavior. Jealousy at this age is common.

Early-elementary-school children (ages 6–8) have easily bruised feelings and are just beginning to recognize the feelings of others. Children at this age want to please teachers and other adults.

Preadolescent children (ages 9–11) develop a global and stable self-image (self-concept and self-esteem). Comparisons to their peers and the opinions of their peers are important. An unstable home environment at this age contributes to an increased risk of delinquency.

Young adolescence (ages 12–14) can be a stormy and stressful time for children, but, in reality, this is only the case for roughly 20 percent of teens. Boys may have trouble controlling their anger and may display impulsive behavior. Girls may suffer from depression.

In later stages of adolescence (ages 15–17), educators should be alert for signs of surfacing mental health problems (e.g., eating disorders, substance abuse, schizophrenia, depression, and suicide).

> *Young adolescents are very egocentric and concerned with their appearance, and may feel strongly that "adults don't understand."*

Malfunctions of the Body Systems

Respiratory and excretory systems

Emphysema is a chronic obstructive pulmonary disease (COPD), which makes breathing difficult. Partial obstruction of the bronchial tubes limits airflow. The primary cause of emphysema is smoking. There is no cure for emphysema, but there are treatments available. The best prevention against emphysema is to refrain from smoking.

Nephritis usually occurs in children. An antigen-antibody complex that causes inflammation and cell proliferation produces nephritis. Nephritis damages normal kidney tissue and, if left untreated, can lead to kidney failure and death.

Circulatory system

Cardiovascular diseases are the leading cause of death in the United States. Cardiac disease usually results in either a heart attack or a stroke. A heart attack occurs when cardiac muscle tissue dies, usually from coronary artery blockage. A stroke occurs when nervous tissue in the brain dies due to the blockage of arteries in the head.

Atherosclerosis causes many heart attacks and strokes. Plaques form on the inner walls of arteries, narrowing the area in which blood can flow. Atherosclerosis occurs when the arteries harden from the plaque accumulation. A healthy diet low in saturated fats and cholesterol and regular exercise can prevent atherosclerosis. High blood pressure (hypertension) also promotes atherosclerosis.

Diet, medication, and exercise can reduce high blood pressure and prevent atherosclerosis.

Immune system

The immune system attacks both microbes and cells that are foreign to the host. This is the problem with skin grafts, organ transplantations, and blood transfusions. Antibodies to foreign blood and tissue types already exist in the body. Antibodies will destroy the new blood cells in transfused blood that is not compatible with the host. There is a similar reaction with tissue and organ transplants.

Autoimmune disease occurs when the body's immune system destroys its own cells. Lupus, Grave's disease, and rheumatoid arthritis are examples of autoimmune diseases. There is no way to prevent autoimmune diseases. Immunodeficiency is a deficiency in either the humoral or cell-mediated immune defenses. Human immunodeficiency virus (HIV) is an example of an immunodeficiency disease.

> The immune system attacks both microbes and cells that are foreign to the host.

Digestive system

Gastric ulcers are lesions in the stomach lining. Bacteria are the main cause of ulcers, but pepsin and acid can exacerbate the problem if the ulcers do not heal quickly enough.

Appendicitis is the inflammation of the appendix. The appendix has no known function; however, it is open to the intestine and hardened stool or swollen tissue can block it. The blocked appendix can cause bacterial infections and inflammation leading to appendicitis. The swelling cuts off the blood supply, killing the organ tissue. If left untreated, this leads to rupture of the appendix, allowing the stool and the infection to spill out into the abdomen. This condition is life-threatening and requires immediate surgery. Symptoms of appendicitis include lower abdominal pain, nausea, loss of appetite, and fever.

> The blocked appendix can cause bacterial infections and inflammation leading to appendicitis.

Nervous and endocrine systems

Diabetes is the best-known endocrine disorder. A deficiency of insulin resulting in high blood glucose is the primary cause of diabetes. Type I diabetes is an autoimmune disorder. The immune system attacks the cells of the pancreas, ending the ability to produce insulin. Treatment for type I diabetes consists of daily insulin injections. Type II diabetes usually occurs with age and/or obesity.

Hyperthyroidism is another disorder of the endocrine system. Excessive secretion of thyroid hormones is the cause. Symptoms are weight loss, high blood pressure, and high body temperature. The opposite condition, hypothyroidism, causes weight gain, lethargy, and intolerance to cold.

There are many nervous system disorders. The degeneration of the basal ganglia in the brain causes Parkinson's disease. This degeneration causes a decrease in the motor impulses sent to the muscles. Symptoms include tremors, slow movement, and muscle rigidity. Progression of Parkinson's disease occurs in five stages: early, mild, moderate, advanced, and severe. In the severe stage, the person is confined to a bed or chair. There is no cure for Parkinson's disease. Private research with stem cells is currently underway to find a cure.

Types of Disease

Pathogens that enter the body through direct or indirect contact cause communicable, or infectious, diseases. A PATHOGEN is a disease-causing organism. Common communicable diseases include influenza, the common cold, chickenpox, pneumonia, measles, mumps, and mononucleosis. To minimize the circulation of pathogens that cause these illnesses, people can follow simple precautions. Individuals who are ill with these diseases should stay away from others during the contagious period of the infection. All people should avoid sharing items such as towels, toothbrushes, and silverware. At home, thorough clothes washing, dishwashing, and frequent hand washing can decrease pathogen transmission. Keeping immunizations up to date is also important in reducing the spread of communicable diseases.

Sexual activity is the source of transmission for other communicable diseases. The commonly used terms for these diseases are sexually transmitted diseases (STDs) or sexually transmitted infections (STIs). Common STDs include chlamydia, gonorrhea, syphilis, genital herpes, genital warts, bacterial vaginosis, human papillomavirus (HPV), pediculosis pubis (pubic lice), hepatitis B, and HIV. Certain STDs can result in infertility. HPV can result in a deadly form of cervical cancer. HIV may result in Acquired Immunodeficiency Syndrome (AIDS), which can be fatal. Some of these diseases, such as genital herpes, are incurable.

A CHRONIC DISEASE is a disease that is long-lasting. A chronic disease continues for more than three months. Examples of chronic conditions include diseases such as heart disease, cancer, and diabetes. These diseases are currently the leading causes of death and disability in America. Many forms of these widespread and expensive diseases are preventable. Choosing nutritious foods, participating in physical activity, and avoiding tobacco use can prevent or control many of these illnesses.

A DEGENERATIVE DISEASE is a condition in which diseased tissues or organs steadily deteriorate. The deterioration may be due to ordinary wear and tear or to lifestyle choices such as lack of exercise or poor nutrition. In addition, many degenerative diseases are of questionable origin, and may be linked to heredity and

PATHOGEN: a disease-causing organism

CHRONIC DISEASE: a disease that is long-lasting. A chronic disease continues for more than three months

DEGENERATIVE DISEASE: a condition in which diseased tissues or organs steadily deteriorate

environmental factors. Some examples of degenerative diseases include osteoporosis, Alzheimer's disease, ALS (Lou Gehrig's disease), osteoarthritis, inflammatory bowel disease (IBD), and Parkinson's disease.

Public Health

Factors that influence public health include the following:

- Availability of health care in the community

- Pollution levels

- Community resources to promote and facilitate healthy living habits

- Awareness of healthy living habits among adults in the community

Pollution levels in a community can affect public health by exposing the community to toxic and carcinogenic chemicals that negatively affect systems including (but not limited to) the circulatory and respiratory systems.

Community resources are an important influence on public health. When financing is available to support health education and programs that encourage the development of healthy living habits, the health of the community will benefit. Conversely, if the community does not dedicate resources to this cause, the health of the community will suffer.

Related to this is the issue of awareness of healthy living habits among adults in the community. A strong personal commitment among responsible community members sets an important example for others to follow.

Availability of health care in the community that is both accessible and affordable has a critical influence on public health. When health care is not readily available to the community, relatively minor problems will tend to go untreated and develop into bigger problems.

Disease Prevention

Characteristics of disease that must be considered in a discussion of public and family health include the extent to which a disease is contagious and the symptoms that a disease causes. Contagious diseases demand special attention and sensitivity, because the integrative nature of communities (especially among children) provides ample opportunity for diseases to spread. The symptoms of a disease must be considered in order to ensure that members of the community are properly diagnosed and treated.

Education in the community should include the concept of germ theory and the ways in which various diseases can and cannot spread. When community members have a solid understanding of the way diseases "work," they are more likely to respond in an effective manner.

One of the most important principles related to disease prevention and control is hygiene. Community members, especially children, should wash their hands frequently, especially when they are ill or interacting with others who are ill.

Nutrition and Weight Control

Components of nutrition include the following:

- **Carbohydrates:** The main source of energy (glucose) in the human diet. The two types of carbohydrates are **simple** and **complex**. Complex carbohydrates have greater nutritional value because they take longer to digest, contain dietary fiber, and do not excessively elevate blood sugar levels. Common sources of carbohydrates are fruits, vegetables, grains, dairy products, and legumes.

- **Proteins:** Necessary for growth, development, and cellular function. The body breaks down consumed protein into component amino acids for future use. Major sources of protein are meat, poultry, fish, legumes, eggs, dairy products, grains, and legumes.

- **Fats:** A concentrated energy source and important component of the human body. The different types of fats are **saturated, monounsaturated,** and **polyunsaturated**. Polyunsaturated fats are the healthiest because they may lower cholesterol levels, while saturated fats increase cholesterol levels. Common sources of saturated fats include dairy products, meat, coconut oil, and palm oil. Common sources of unsaturated fats include nuts, most vegetable oils, and fish.

- **Vitamins and minerals:** Organic substances that the body requires in small quantities for proper functioning. People acquire vitamins and minerals through their diets and in supplements. Important vitamins include A, B, C, D, E, and K. Important minerals include calcium, phosphorus, magnesium, potassium, sodium, chlorine, and sulfur.

- **Water:** Makes up 55–75 percent of the human body. It is essential for most bodily functions and can be obtained through foods and liquids.

Exercise and diet help maintain proper body weight by equalizing caloric intake and caloric output.

Nutritional requirements vary from person to person. General guidelines for meeting adequate nutritional needs are: no more than 30 percent total caloric intake from fats (preferably 10 percent from saturated fats, 10 percent from monounsaturated fats, 10 percent from polyunsaturated fats), no more than 15 percent total caloric intake from protein (complete), and at least 55 percent of caloric intake from carbohydrates (mainly complex carbohydrates).

Body Composition Management

The only proven method for maintaining a healthy body composition is following a healthy diet and engaging in regular exercise. A healthy diet consists primarily of fruits, vegetables, whole grains, unsaturated fats, and lean protein, and minimizes saturated fat and sugar consumption. Such a program of nutrition and exercise helps balance caloric intake and output and prevents the production of excessive body fat.

Stress

Sources of stress

Stress has many negative effects. It is important that instructors and students recognize the significance of stress to long-term health. To successfully manage it, instructors and students must understand the sources of stress as well as the signs and symptoms of it.

Signs and Symptoms of Stress

Emotional signs of stress: Depression, lethargy, aggressiveness, irritability, anxiety, edginess, fearfulness, impulsiveness, chronic fatigue, hyperexcitability, inability to concentrate, frequent feelings of boredom, feeling overwhelmed, apathy, impatience, pessimism, sarcasm, humorlessness, confusion, helplessness, melancholy, alienation, isolation, numbness, purposelessness, isolation, self-consciousness, and inability to maintain intimate relationships.

Behavioral signs of stress: Elevated use of substances (alcohol, drugs, tobacco), crying, yelling, insomnia or excessive sleep, excessive TV watching, school/job burnout, panic attacks, poor problem-solving capability, avoidance of people, aberrant behavior, procrastination, being accident-prone, restlessness, loss of memory, indecisiveness, aggressiveness, inflexibility, phobic responses, tardiness, disorganization, and sexual problems.

Physical signs of stress: Pounding heart, stuttering, trembling/nervous tics, excessive perspiration, teeth grinding, gastrointestinal problems (constipation, indigestion, diarrhea, queasy stomach), dry mouth, aching lower back, migraine/tension headaches, stiff neck, asthma attacks, allergy attacks, skin problems, frequent colds or low-grade fevers, muscle tension, hyperventilation, high blood pressure, amenorrhea, nightmares, and cold intolerance.

Stress management

General stress management principles include the following:

- Regular physical activity

- Exercise

- Physical play

- Proper nutrition

Proper nutrition is a balanced diet, consisting of adequate amounts of lean protein, complex carbohydrates, fruits, vegetables, and unsaturated fats.

Stress management and good nutrition are cornerstones of healthy living. Physical education instructors can introduce students to these important concepts through development of individualized fitness and wellness plans. Fitness and wellness plans should include a concrete exercise plan and a detailed nutritional plan.

There are five health-related components of physical fitness:

1. **Cardiovascular endurance:** The ability of the body to sustain aerobic activities (activities requiring oxygen utilization) for extended periods

2. **Muscle strength:** The ability of muscle groups to contract and support a given amount of weight

3. **Muscle endurance:** The ability of muscle groups to contract continually over a period of time and support a given amount of weight

4. **Flexibility:** The ability of muscle groups to stretch and bend

5. **Body composition:** Percentage of body fat and ratio of body fat to muscle

Physical activity improves each of the components of physical fitness. Aerobic training improves cardiovascular endurance. Weight training, body support activities, and calisthenics increase muscular strength and endurance. Stretching improves flexibility. Finally, all types of physical activity improve body composition by increasing muscle and decreasing body fat.

> **SKILL 45.3** Knows and understands stages of human growth and development, including physical and emotional changes that occur during adolescence.

See Skill 45.2

SKILL 45.4 **Understands substance use and abuse, including types and characteristics of tobacco, alcohol, other drugs and herbal supplements.**

Substance Abuse

Substance abuse can lead to adverse behaviors and increased risk of injury and disease. All substances affecting the normal functions of the body, illegal or not, are potentially dangerous and students and athletes should avoid them completely.

Substances commonly abused include:

- **Anabolic steroids:** The alleged benefit is an increase in muscle mass and strength. However, this substance is illegal and produces harmful side effects. Premature closure of growth plates in bones can occur if a teenager abuses steroids, limiting adult height. Other effects include bloody cysts in the liver, increased risk of cardiovascular disease, increased blood pressure, and dysfunction of the reproductive system.

- **Alcohol:** Alcohol is legal for adults but is commonly abused. Moderate to excessive consumption can lead to an increased risk of cardiovascular disease, nutritional deficiencies, and dehydration. Alcohol also causes ill effects on various aspects of performance such as reaction time, coordination, accuracy, balance, and strength.

- **Nicotine:** Another legal but often abused substance that can increase the risk of cardiovascular disease, pulmonary disease, and cancers of the mouth and lungs. Nicotine consumption through smoking severely hinders athletic performance by compromising lung function. Smoking especially affects performance in endurance activities.

- **Marijuana:** In the states in which it has not been legalized, this is the most commonly abused illegal substance. Adverse effects include a loss of focus and motivation, decreased coordination, and lack of concentration.

- **Cocaine:** Another illegal and commonly abused substance. Effects of cocaine abuse include increased alertness and excitability. This drug can give the user a sense of overconfidence and invincibility, leading to a false sense of one's ability to perform certain activities. An increased heart rate is associated with the use of cocaine, leading to an increased risk of heart attack, stroke, potentially deadly arrhythmias, and seizures.

Alternatives to substance abuse and aspects of treatment

and control

Alternatives to substance use and abuse include regular participation in stress-relieving activities like meditation, exercise, and therapy, all of which can have a relaxing effect. For example, a healthy alternative would be to train oneself to substitute exercise for a substance abuse problem. More important, the acquisition of longer-term coping strategies (for example, self-empowerment via practice of problem-solving techniques) is key to maintaining a commitment to alternatives to substance use and abuse.

Limiting access to the addictive substance (opportunities for use) is important, because the symptoms of withdrawal and the experiences associated with the substance can provide a strong impetus to return to using it. Finally, recovering addicts should learn strategies of self-control and self-discipline to help them stay off addictive substances.

> **SKILL 45.5** Understands types of violence and abuse, including causes and effects of violence and abuse and ways to prevent and seek help in dealing with violence and abuse.

Violence and Abuse

There is a wide range of hurtful interpersonal behaviors that students may experience from peers or adults in their lives, including ridicule, sexual abuse, exploitation, dating violence, unwanted sexual contact, discrimination, and harassment.

There is a wide range of hurtful interpersonal behaviors that students may experience from peers or adults in their lives, including ridicule, sexual abuse, exploitation, dating violence, unwanted sexual contact, discrimination, and harassment.

Health instructors can teach students ways of avoiding or confronting these behaviors in a proactive manner. For example, students can learn to refuse to accept the hurtful behavior, negotiate to prevent it, or collaborate to change it.

Violence prevention strategies in the home, school, and community

Violence is a primary concern of educators. Assault, rape, suicide, gang violence, and weapons in school are major issues confronting educators in today's schools.

The fear of violence negatively affects students' growth, development, and ability to learn. In order to create learning and healthy growth and development, schools must be violence-free. In order to accomplish this, schools must enact policies and procedures that promote an environment free from crime, drugs, and weapons. For some schools, this may require locker searches, full-time school security officers, and metal detectors. Some school systems may choose to establish separate alternative schools for students proven to be violent or abusive.

Students should be encouraged to have faith in their feelings about people and situations. If their instincts indicate that a person or situation is potentially dangerous, they should trust that feeling and remove themselves from the situation. They should always pay attention and be aware of the actions of people near them. They should avoid situations that increase the chance that something harmful will happen. Finally, adult mentors can play a vital role in helping young people to stay safe. Educators are in a unique position to mentor young people and to act as a resource to help students avoid violence.

Coping with Child Abuse or Neglect

The term neglect is generally defined as deliberately ignoring a child's needs, which causes that child to experience undue harm or stress. There are several types of child neglect, which can include the following:

- Physical neglect

- Emotional neglect

- Mental neglect

- Educational neglect

- Medical neglect

There are several strategies that can be implemented when cases of suspected child abuse are discovered. These include asking various organizations to step in and assist, support of relatives, parental education, housing assistance, and neighborhood advocacy. However, if the abuse is recurring or cannot be halted, more forceful strategies such as the removal of the child from the home, placement in foster care, and, ultimately, criminal prosecution can be implemented to ensure the safety of the child.

> SKILL 45.6 **Selects and uses instructional strategies, materials and activities to teach principles and procedures related to safety, accident prevention and response to emergencies.**

Emergency Action Plans

The first step in establishing a safe physical education environment is creating an emergency action plan (EAP). A good EAP can make a significant difference in the outcome of an injury situation. To ensure the safety of students during physical activities, an EAP should be easily comprehensible yet detailed enough to facilitate prompt, thorough action.

Communication

Instructors should clearly communicate rules and expectations to students. This information should include pre-participation guidelines, emergency procedures, and proper game etiquette. Instructors should collect emergency information sheets from students at the start of each school year. First-aid kits, facility maps, and incident report forms should also be readily available. Open communication between students and teachers is essential.

Creating a positive environment in the classroom allows students to feel comfortable enough to approach an adult/teacher if they feel they have sustained a potential injury.

Teacher education

At the start of each school year, every student should undergo a pre-participation physical examination. This allows a teacher to recognize the "high-risk" students before activity commences. The teacher should also take note of any student who requires any form of medication or special care.

Facilities and equipment

It is the responsibility of the teacher and school district to provide a safe environment, playing area, and equipment for students. Instructors and maintenance staff should regularly inspect school facilities to confirm that the equipment and location are adequate and safe for student use.

First-aid equipment

It is essential to have a properly stocked first-aid kit in an easy-to-reach location. Instructors may need to include asthma inhalers and special-care items to meet the specific needs of certain students. Instructors should clearly mark these special-care items to avoid a potentially harmful mix-up.

Implementing the emergency plan

The main thing to keep in mind when implementing an EAP is to remain calm. Maintaining a sufficient level of control and activating appropriate medical assistance will facilitate the process and leave less room for error.

Strategies for Injury Prevention

- **Participant screenings:** Evaluate injury history, anticipate and prevent potential injuries, watch for hidden injuries and reoccurrence of an injury, and maintain communication

- **Standards and discipline:** Ensure that athletes obey rules of sportsmanship, supervision, and biomechanics

- **Education and knowledge:** Stay current in knowledge of first aid, sports medicine, sport techniques, and injury prevention through clinics, workshops, and communication with staff and trainers

- **Conditioning:** Programs should be yearlong and participants should have access to conditioning facilities in and out of season to produce more fit and knowledgeable athletes who are less prone to injury

- **Equipment:** Perform regular inspections; ensure proper fit and proper use

- **Facilities:** Maintain standards and use safe equipment

- **Field care:** Establish emergency procedures for serious injury

- **Rehabilitation:** Use objective measures such as power output on an isokinetic dynamometer

Injury Follow-up and Reporting

Responding to accidents and injuries is an important responsibility of physical educators. After an injury occurs, instructors should contact an injured student's parents or guardians as soon as possible and notify school administrators. Instructors must also complete an accident report.

> **SKILL 45.7** Applies critical-thinking, goal-setting, problem-solving and decision-making skills in health-related contexts *(e.g., eating habits, drug use, abstinence)* and understands the use of refusal skills and conflict resolution to avoid unsafe situations *(e.g., bullying, violence, abuse)*.

Goal Setting, Problem Solving, and Decision Making

Instructors can give students a clear understanding of the goals they need to attain, problems they need to solve, and decisions they need to make by clearly explaining an entire scenario to them. Instructors should leave students with a clear impression of why they need to take action (analysis/solution/decision) and what the desired outcome should be.

Next, instructors should give students all of the requisite information to take action, including reasonable timelines and the relevant physical and biomechanical principles. For example, if a student is interested in building upper-body strength, the instructor should ensure that he or she understands the biomechanical systems related to upper-body strength development and what actions the student can take to reach his or her goal.

Finally, instructors should emphasize to students that taking action is their responsibility. Whatever their personal training goals may be, it is the role of the physical educator to show students how to achieve their goals but not to force them to take action. The student must provide the motivation. This creates a reciprocal relationship between decision-making and taking action. The more students get accustomed to making decisions and following through, the better equipped they will be to do so in future situations.

Conflict Management and Refusal Skills

Interpersonal conflict is a major source of stress and worry. Common sources of interpersonal conflict include family relationships, competition, and disagreement over values or decisions. Teaching students to successfully manage conflict will help them reduce stress levels throughout their lives, thereby limiting the adverse health effects of stress. The following is a list of conflict resolution principles and techniques:

- **Think before reacting:** In a conflict situation, it is important to resist the temptation to react immediately. Step back, consider the situation, and plan an appropriate response. Also, do not react to petty situations with anger.

- **Listen:** Be sure to listen carefully to the opposing party. Try to understand the other person's point of view.

- **Find common ground:** Try to find some common ground as soon as possible. Early compromise can help ease the tension.

- **Accept responsibility:** In every conflict, there is plenty of blame to go around. Admitting when you are wrong shows you are committed to resolving the conflict.

- **Attack the problem, not the person:** Personal attacks are never beneficial and usually lead to greater conflict and hard feelings.

- **Focus on the future:** Instead of trying to assign blame for past events, focus on what needs to be done differently to avoid future conflict.

- **Key refusal skill:** Don't be afraid to say NO. In any situation, whether it deals with abstinence, drug use, abuse/violence, or bullying, it is always okay to vocalize discomfort with partaking in the activity. As mentioned above, it is good not to provoke others when saying no, but instead to respectfully disagree with their activity/behavior. Saying no requires courage, but having that courage and teaching students to resist peer pressure and wanting to "fit in" will better equip them to handle the world as they get older.

> ## SKILL 45.8 Knows and understands strategies for coping with unhealthy behaviors in the family *(e.g., abuse, alcoholism, neglect, anxiety, grief)*.

Factors That Affect Family Health

The primary factors that affect family health include environmental conditions such as pollution and proximity to industrial areas, smoking and drinking habits of family members, economic conditions that affect nutrition, and level of education of family members related to healthy living habits.

See also Skills 45.4, 45.5, 45.7, and 45.10

> ## SKILL 45.9 Understands types and symptoms of eating disorders.

Types and Symptoms of Eating Disorders

Eating disorders are complex, and often there are genetic, behavioral, and societal disturbances involved that further complicate these illnesses. There are two chief categories of eating disorders: bulimia nervosa and anorexia nervosa. Eating disorders often first occur during adolescence but can develop in later adulthood. Young girls are more likely than boys to develop some type of an eating disorder. However, eating disorders are becoming more common in men and boys.

Anorexia nervosa

Anorexia nervosa is characterized by a persistent quest for a thin body. People who display symptoms of anorexia nervosa have a tremendous fear of gaining weight even when their bodies are severely malnourished. They also tend to have a distorted image of their bodies. They often weigh themselves many times during the course of a day. Some people with anorexia lose weight by doing an extreme amount of exercise combined with an extremely low-calorie diet. Others lose weight by abusing laxatives, inducing vomiting, and using diuretics.

Bulimia nervosa

The symptoms of bulimia nervosa include repeated bouts of consuming abnormally large amounts of food, called binge eating, which causes a feeling of lack of control over the eating. After the episodes of binge eating, the need to get rid of the excess food is expressed as purging in the form of vomiting, excessive use of laxatives, water fasting, or even extreme exercising. This cycle is usually repeated several times a week. Like people with anorexia nervosa, people with bulimia nervosa often also suffer from other disorders such as substance abuse or severe depression, and may even have suicidal thoughts.

> **SKILL 45.10** Knows how to use various social and communication skills to build and maintain healthy interpersonal relationships *(e.g., tolerance, respect, discussing problems with parents/caregivers, showing empathy)*.

Building Healthy Interpersonal Relationships

Teachers' relationships with students and parents

Teachers should develop empathic listening skills, which involve communicating understanding and acceptance of a student's thoughts, feelings, and requests.

Healthy interpersonal relationships are associated with such behaviors as effective communication and empathic listening. By using expressive speaking skills, teachers can discuss their thoughts, emotions, and hopes honestly and respectfully with parents and caregivers without provoking unwanted resentment or hostility.

Strategies to reinforce healthy student-teacher relationships include the following:

- Set clear expectations.
- Praise students for work accomplished.
- Encourage active listening.
- Listen to what students are saying.
- Keep lines of communication open.

Effective communication skills such as controlling facial expressions, maintaining a level tone of voice, using the correct body language, and giving the proper reaction enable teachers to build and maintain strong interpersonal relationships with students and parents/caregivers.

Helping students build healthy relationships

Mutual respect, shared values and interests, and a mutual ability to trust and depend on each other characterize responsible friendship. Genuine respect is vital for a positive and responsible friendship. Shared values are a foundation for mutual respect, and shared interests are necessary for the development of a friendship. Trust and dependability are the cement that holds responsible friendships together.

We can develop positive interpersonal relationships by devoting time to character-building activities to strengthen the traits described above. Individuals can work to become trustworthy and dependable. Specific techniques that one can apply to develop positive interpersonal relationships with others include active listening and considerate respect for the things others value.

Social support systems are the networks that students develop with their peers that provide support when students experience challenges and difficulties. The support offered by these systems is often emotional and sometimes logistical. Financial support is generally inappropriate. Social support systems are vital to students (and individuals, in general), especially students who don't have other support mechanisms in place.

The benefits of maintaining healthy peer relationships include having a social support system to assist one in difficult times and the knowledge that that system exists. This gives students the confidence to take greater risks (within reason) and achieve more because they know the support system is there if they need it.

> We can develop respect for others by actively asking ourselves what others would see as significant in the current scenario we are facing. This is an exercise aimed at placing value and emphasis on the priorities of others.

How Personal Differences Affect Communication

There are many personal differences among students that can affect communication. Instructors should consider cultural, economic, and environmental differences when addressing their students.

Cultural differences that affect communication may include different perceptions of what falls into the category of acceptable behavior. For example, depending on his or her cultural background, a child may believe it is appropriate or inappropriate to speak without having been directly spoken to, look an educator in the eye, or speak out in a classroom setting (some cultures view all of these actions as aggressive behavior).

Economic differences can also affect communication. Children from various socioeconomic backgrounds are likely to have different frames of reference. These may include references to "normal" after-school activities (whether the child spends time in front of a television or computer may depend on whether the family is able to afford the equipment—this can be a significant issue when homework requires a computer) and benchmarks of value (what is seen as valuable, both in dollar amounts and in commodities).

Environmental differences also affect communication. The difference between an urban and rural environment is a major cultural difference (depending on context), and often corresponds to differences in economic means.

Fostering Sensitive Interactions with and among Students

Instructors can foster open communication in the classroom by reminding students that they can and should approach the teacher with issues and concerns. Of course, instructors must make themselves available to students and listen

> An environment conducive to learning has open lines of communication and a clear sense of respect among students and between teachers and students.

respectfully to the issues that they raise. Teachers should also devote classroom time to open, moderated discussions in which students can air their concerns related to issues between classmates. The instructor can serve as a mediator.

Respect is fundamental; otherwise, students will not bring issues to the attention of the teacher more than once. The teacher must be genuinely respectful of the concerns and backgrounds of students, and demand respect in turn. Instructors must also stress that they will not tolerate disrespectful behavior between students.

> **SKILL 45.11** Understands health care responses to threats to safety, internal injury, early detection and warning signs of illness.

See Skill 45.6

> **SKILL 45.12** Selects and uses instructional strategies, materials and activities to help students build healthy interpersonal relationships *(e.g., communication skills)* and demonstrates consideration and respect for self, family, friends and others *(e.g., practicing self-control)*.

See Skill 45.10

> **SKILL 45.13** Understands the influence of various factors *(e.g., media, technology, peer and other relationships, environmental hazards)* on individual *(e.g., idealized body images, unhealthy weight-loss plans)*, family and community health.

Technology

The technology market is rapidly changing. Consumers are progressively turning to technology for a healthier life. Consumer-focused health care information technology helps individuals handle the significant demands of managing their health care.

Health care information technology is a term describing the wide array of digital resources that are available to promote community health and proper health care for consumers. Health care information technology empowers patients to direct their health care and to advocate for themselves and their families as they use health care services. Health care information technology enables consumers, patients, and informal caregivers to gather facts, make choices, communicate with health care providers, control chronic disease, and participate in other health-related activities.

Peer Pressure

Peer pressure can influence children to make both positive and negative decisions. For example, a child who interacts with other children who use drugs is more likely to use drugs. On the other hand, interacting with children who are committed to exercise may encourage a previously inactive child to become physically active.

Media

Media-based expectations influence the development of children's self-concepts. A child's self-concept is a set of statements describing the child's own cognitive, physical, emotional, and social self-assessment.

Media-based role models often become the benchmarks against which students measure their traits.

> **SKILL 45.14** Demonstrates knowledge of sources of health information and ways to use information to make health-related decisions.

Sources of Health Information

State and national initiatives

Important state and national initiatives that influence physical education content and practices include the Texas-based "Eat Smart—Be Active" campaign, and national initiatives like the Centers for Disease Control and Prevention (CDC) National Physical Activity Initiative, programs run by the Office of Safe and Drug-Free Schools (OSDFS) for Health, Mental Health, Environmental Health, and Physical Education, and the National Heart, Lung, and Blood Institute (NHLBI) Obesity Education Initiative (OEI). You can find further information about these initiatives on the following websites:

- "Eat Smart—Be Active"

  http://www.eatsmartbeactivetx.org

- CDC's National Physical Activity Initiative

  http://www.cdc.gov/nccdphp/sgr/npai.htm

- Office of Safe and Drug-Free Schools (OSDFS)

  http://www.ed.gov/about/offices/list/osdfs/programs.html#health

- National Heart, Lung, and Blood Institute

  http://www.nhlbi.nih.gov/about/oei/oei_pd.htm

Consumer education

We can find information related to physical activity at local public and university libraries and online. Educators should regularly inform themselves about updates in the field, and should periodically search for resources that they can use with their students. Instructors should encourage students to make use of free resources like libraries, and especially the Internet, to expand their own knowledge.

> *Most schools maintain relationships with other outside health care agencies in order to offer more extensive health care services to students.*

There are a variety of health care providers, agencies, and organizations involved with the maintenance of student health. On-site, the school nurse assists ill or injured students, maintains health records, and performs health screenings. School nurses also assist students who have chronic illnesses such as diabetes, asthma, epilepsy, or heart conditions. Most schools maintain relationships with other outside health care agencies in order to offer more extensive health care services to students. These community partnerships offer students services such as vaccinations, physical examinations and screenings, eye care, treatment of minor injuries and ailments, dental treatment, and psychological therapy. These community partnerships may include relationships with the following types of health care professionals: physicians, psychiatrists, optometrists, dentists, nurses, audiologists, occupational therapists, physical therapists, dieticians, respiratory therapists, and speech pathologists.

> **SKILL 45.15** Selects and uses instructional strategies, materials and activities to help students understand the roles of health care professionals, the benefits of health maintenance activities and the skills for becoming health-conscious consumers.

From an early age, students can learn what it means to be healthy and health-conscious. Fresh foods, such as fruit and vegetables, are healthier than cookies or ice cream. Young children can draw pictures or make collages that explain the differences between healthy foods and junk foods. Teachers can invite young students to share when they made a healthy choice. Older students can develop healthy food plans for themselves and will understand the differences between healthy and unhealthy choices. Students should be familiar with a variety of health care professionals and their purposes, such as doctors, nurses, nurse practitioners, paramedics, EMTs, and firefighters. They can explore how these professionals are community helpers and when they might encounter them.

Teaching students the importance of being active is a key element of health education. Questions to introduce this topic include the following: What is an active lifestyle? What sorts of activities are health-conscious activities? Brainstorming, setting goals, and working as a team can be excellent and authentic activities to help students create a path to a healthier lifestyle.

> **SKILL 45.16** Applies knowledge of health content and curriculum based on the Texas Essential Knowledge and Skills (TEKS) and of students in early childhood through grade six to plan and implement effective, developmentally appropriate health instruction, including relating the health education curriculum to other content areas.

Relating the Health Curriculum to Other Content Areas

Physical education connects to other subject areas in the following ways:

- **Life and physical sciences:** Teaching students about the life and physical sciences can greatly reinforce their physical education experience. For example, understanding the physics of force and leverage gives children insight into the mechanics of gymnastic activities. The biology of carbohydrates turning into fuel for the muscles and protein rebuilding muscle tissue shows the value of the study of nutrition.

- **Social sciences:** Examining styles of interaction within and between groups in competitive team-based games and sports (e.g., soccer, dodge ball), interaction between children in competitive individual activities (e.g., running a race), and interaction between children engaging in noncompetitive individual activities (e.g., gymnastics training) helps children understand concepts of social organization and interaction and helps them draw parallels with their own experiences in physical education.

- **Health sciences:** Children who are taught the relationship between physical activity and health—not just in a general "exercise is good for you" sort of way, but in a more detailed way (e.g., aerobic fitness training stimulates the cardiovascular system, strengthening the heart)—are much more likely to look to fitness training as a potential response to health problems.

- **Mathematics and language arts:** These two fields are more peripherally connected to physical education. Math and language arts are generally used to quantify and communicate one's achievements.

- **Visual and performing arts:** There is considerable overlap between movement activities and visual and performing arts—whether it is the strenuous work of painting a large canvas or the more obviously artistic elements of gymnastics, dance, figure skating, or martial arts. Helping students to see the connections between these disciplines can stimulate crossovers, helping children to broaden their horizons.

COMPETENCY 46
PHYSICAL EDUCATION

> **SKILL 46.1** **Applies key principles and concepts in physical education and physical activity** *(e.g., cardiovascular endurance, muscular strength, flexibility, weight control, conditioning, safety, stress management, nutrition)* **for the promotion of health and fitness.**

Naturally, variations in levels of health and fitness exist; no two individuals are exactly alike. These variations are apparent in all areas of physical fitness including body composition, cardiovascular endurance, muscular strength and endurance, and flexibility.

Improvement in each of these categories leads to a decreased risk of injury and disease and allows one to perform normal, everyday activities with greater ease. Strategies for enhancing adherence to these fitness programs include appropriately maintaining facilities/equipment, emphasizing short-term goals, minimizing injuries, encouraging group participation, emphasizing variety and enjoyment, and providing support and motivation from family and friends.

Physical Education Standards

The goal of physical education is to give students the knowledge, skills, and confidence to enjoy a lifetime of healthful activity. Following is a list of standards that students of a physical education program should be able to achieve.

- **Standard 1:** Demonstrate competency in motor skills and movement patterns needed to perform a variety of physical activities

- **Standard 2:** Demonstrate understanding of movement concepts, principles, strategies, and tactics as they apply to the learning and performance of physical activities

- **Standard 3:** Participate regularly in physical activity

- **Standard 4:** Achieve and maintain a health-enhancing level of physical fitness

- **Standard 5:** Exhibit responsible personal and social behavior that respects self and others in physical activity settings

- **Standard 6:** Value physical activity for health, enjoyment, challenge, self-expression, and/or social interaction

The goal of physical education is to give students the knowledge, skills, and confidence to enjoy a lifetime of healthful activity.

Basic Training Principles

The overload principle is exercising at an above-normal level to improve physical or physiological capacity.

The progression principle states that once the body adapts to the original load/stress, no further improvement of fitness component will occur without an additional load.

The specificity principle refers to overloading a particular fitness component. In order to improve a particular component of one's fitness, one must isolate and specifically work on a single component. Metabolic and physiological adaptations depend on the type of overload; hence, specific exercise produces specific adaptations, creating specific training effects.

The reversibility-of-training principle refers to the fact that all gains in fitness are lost with the discontinuance of a training program.

> SKILL 46.2 **Knows and helps students understand the benefits of an active lifestyle.**

Benefits of an Active Lifestyle

Students who have been through a good physical education program are better able to care for their own health and use nutrition and exercise to prevent long-term health problems.

Regular physical activity and proper nutrition can help prevent diseases, illnesses, and injuries. In addition, regular exercise and a proper diet help maintain a healthy body composition, which is important physically and psychologically. Physically fit and healthy individuals are generally more productive at work. Finally, preventing disease and avoiding injury through healthy behaviors can reduce health care costs.

Physiological benefits of physical activity include the following:

- Improved cardiovascular fitness
- Improved muscle strength
- Improved muscle endurance
- Improved flexibility
- More lean muscle mass and less body fat
- Quicker rate of recovery from illness and injury
- Improved ability of the body to utilize oxygen
- Lower resting heart rate

- Increased cardiac output

- Improved venous return and peripheral circulation

- Reduced risk of musculoskeletal injuries

- Lower cholesterol levels

- Increased bone mass

- Cardiac hypertrophy and size and strength of blood vessels

- Increased number of red blood cells

- Improved blood-sugar regulation

- Improved efficiency of thyroid gland

- Improved energy regulation

- Increased life expectancy

Psychological benefits of physical activity include the following:

- Relief of stress

- Improved mental health because of better physical health

- Reduced mental tension (relieves depression, improves sleeping patterns)

- More resistance to fatigue

- Better quality of life

- More enjoyment of leisure

- Improved capability to handle some stressors

- Opportunity for successful experiences

- Better self-concept

- Better ability to recognize and accept limitations

- Improved appearance and sense of well-being

- Better ability to meet challenges

- Better sense of accomplishment

Sociological benefits of physical activity include the following:

- The opportunity to spend time with family and friends and make new friends

- The opportunity to be part of a team

- The opportunity to participate in competitive experiences

- The opportunity to experience the thrill of victory

Incorporating physical activity into daily life

One of the most important tasks for physical education instructors is to introduce students to strategies to incorporate physical activity into their everyday lives. For example, instructors can recommend that students walk or ride a bike to school rather than drive or ride the bus. In addition, there are a number of everyday activities that promote fitness, including yard work, sports and games, walking, and climbing stairs.

SKILL 46.3 Understands appropriate methods, including technological methods, for evaluating, monitoring, and improving fitness levels.

All Texas students from grades 3–12 are required to participate in an annual fitness exam. During the 2007–2009 school years, Texas schools were given the selected physical fitness assessment tool, the FITNESSGRAM. Today, it is used as the statewide assessment tool. This technology allows schools to monitor student fitness levels. Fitness tests measure aerobic capacity, body composition, endurance, and strength, among other things. Standards are criterion-referenced, are set by age and gender, and measure "good health" fitness levels. The software has the ability to provide individual fitness reports and personalized goals so that teachers, students, and parents or guardians can be aware of students' fitness ranges and set goals for improvement.

Even young children should be involved in their own fitness levels. Teachers should start with a baseline of activity level and skill, teach that skill, allow time for practice (a few weeks), and then assess growth. Conferencing with the students after instruction but before practice time and allowing them to discuss their perception of their skill and how they can improve will motivate them to achieve the goals they have set for themselves. Younger students can use incentive charts, fundraisers, or stickers to motivate them to reach their fitness goals. Students in high school can even create a fitness plan for themselves that will give them at-home practice strategies. Older students may even be able to record their progress through applications on their cell phones.

Fitnessgram

http://www.austinisd.
org/academics/
physicalhealtheducation/
fitnessgram

- Fitnessgram

  http://www.austinisd.org/academics/physicalhealtheducation/fitnessgram

- Healthy Fitness Zone Standards Overview

  http://www.cooperinstitute.org/healthyfitnesszone. Retrieved Aug. 21, 2015.

- What is Fitnessgram?

  http://everychildstronger.org/?page_id=476. Retrieved Aug. 21 2015.

Applies knowledge of movement principles and concepts to develop students' motor skills including understanding key elements of mature movement patterns *(e.g., throwing, jumping, catching)* **and various manipulative skills** *(e.g., volley, dribble, punt, strike).*

Movement Principles and Concepts

We can use movement concepts and biomechanical principles to analyze movement skills by first examining the movement skill in detail (often with the assistance of recording equipment that allows playback in slow motion), and then breaking down the motions involved. For each motion, we should note the angle through which the joints must move and the direction of force that the muscles must apply. We can then check this information against our knowledge of movement concepts and biomechanical principles. Finally, we can modify the motion to ensure that the joints move and the muscles apply force in the most efficient way.

Concept of body awareness applied to physical education activities

Body awareness is a person's understanding of his or her own body parts and their capacity for movement. Instructors can assess students' body awareness by playing a game of "Simon Says" and asking students to touch different body parts. Instructors can also direct students to make their bodies into various shapes, from straight to round to twisted, and varying sizes, to fit into spaces of different sizes.

In addition, you can instruct children to touch one part of their body to another and to use various body parts to stamp their feet, twist their necks, clap their hands, nod their heads, wiggle their noses, snap their fingers, open their mouths, shrug their shoulders, bend their knees, close their eyes, bend their elbows, or wiggle their toes.

Concept of spatial awareness applied to physical education activities

Spatial awareness is the ability to make decisions about an object's positional changes in space (i.e., awareness of three-dimensional space position changes).

Developing spatial awareness requires

- identifying the location of objects in relation to one's own body in space.

- locating more than one object in relation to each object and independent of one's own body.

Plan activities using different-size balls, boxes, or hoops and have children move toward and away; under and over; in front of and behind; and inside, outside, and beside the objects.

Concepts of space, direction, and speed related to movement concepts

Research shows that the concepts of space, direction, and speed are inter-related with movement concepts. Such concepts are extremely important for students to understand, because they need to relate movement skills to direction in order to move with confidence and avoid collisions.

A student or athlete in motion must take the elements of space, direction, speed, and vision into consideration in order to perform and understand a sport. A player must decide how to handle space as well as numerous other factors that arise on the field.

For an athlete, the concepts are all interlinked. He or she has to understand how to maintain or change pathways with speed. This ability allows the athlete to change motion and perform well in space (or the area that the athletes occupy on the field).

See also Skill 46.5

SKILL 46.5 Selects and uses developmentally appropriate learning experiences that enhance students' locomotor, nonlocomotor, body control, manipulative and rhythmic skills.

Locomotor Skills

Locomotor skills move an individual from one point to another.

- **Crawling:** A form of locomotion in which the person moves in a prone position with the body resting on or close to the ground or on the hands and knees

- **Creeping:** A slightly more advanced form of locomotion in which the person moves on the hands and knees

- **Walking:** With one foot in contact with the surface at all times, walking shifts one's weight from one foot to the other while legs swing alternately in front of the body

- **Running:** An extension of walking that has a phase in which the body is propelled with no base of support (speed is faster, stride is longer, and arms add power)

- **Jumping:** Projectile movements that momentarily suspend the body in midair

- **Vaulting:** Coordinated movements that allow one to spring over an obstacle

- **Leaping:** Similar to running but characterized by greater height, flight, and distance

- **Hopping:** Using the same foot to take off from a surface and land

- **Galloping:** Forward or backward advanced elongation of walking combined and coordinated with a leap

- **Sliding:** Sideward stepping pattern that is uneven, long, or short

- **Body rolling:** Moving across a surface by rocking back and forth, by turning over and over, or by shaping the body into a revolving mass

- **Climbing:** Ascending or descending using the hands and feet, with the upper body exerting the most control

Nonlocomotor Skills

Nonlocomotor skills are stability skills that require little or no movement of one's base of support and do not result in a change of position.

- **Bending:** Movement around a joint where two body parts meet

- **Dodging:** Sharp change of direction from original line of movement, such as away from a person or object

- **Stretching:** Extending/hyperextending joints to make body parts as straight or as long as possible

- **Twisting:** Rotating body/body parts around an axis with a stationary base

- **Turning:** Circular motion of the body through space, releasing the base of support

- **Swinging:** Circular/pendular movements of the body/body parts below an axis

- **Swaying:** Same as swinging, but movement is above an axis

- **Pushing:** Applying force against an object or person to move it away from one's body or to move one's body away from the object or person

- **Pulling:** Executing force to cause objects/people to move toward one's body

Manipulative Skills

Manipulative skills use body parts to propel or receive an object, controlling objects primarily with the hands and feet. Two types of manipulative skills are receptive (catch and trap) and propulsive (throw, strike, kick).

- **Bouncing/dribbling:** Projecting a ball downward
- **Catching:** Stopping momentum of an object using the hands
- **Kicking:** Striking an object with the foot
- **Rolling:** Initiating force to an object to create contact with a surface
- **Striking:** Giving impetus to an object with the use of the hands or an object
- **Throwing:** Using one or both arms to project an object into midair away from the body
- **Trapping:** Receiving and controlling a ball without the use of the hands

Rhythmic Skills

Rhythmic skills include responding and moving the body in time with the beat, tempo, or pitch of music. To develop rhythmic skills, instructors can ask students to clap their hands or stomp their feet to the beat of the music. Dancing and gymnastics require high levels of rhythmic competency. As with all physical skills, development of rhythmic skills is a sequential process.

Skill Development

Motor-development learning theories that pertain to a general skill, activity, or age level are important teacher background information for effective lesson planning. Individuals develop motor skills at different rates, but there is a general sequential pattern of skill development, starting with gross-motor skills and ending with fine-motor skills. Teachers must begin instruction at a level where all children are successful and proceed to the point where frustration for the majority is hindering performance. Students must learn the fundamentals of a skill first, or learning more advanced skills becomes extremely difficult.

Visualizing and breaking a skill down mentally is another way to enhance the learning of motor movements. Instructors can teach students to "picture" the steps involved and see themselves executing the skill. An example is teaching dribbling in basketball. Start teaching the skill with a demonstration of the steps involved in dribbling. Starting with the first skill, introduce key language terms and have students visualize themselves performing the skill. A sample-progression lesson plan to teach dribbling could begin with students practicing while standing still. Next, add movement while dribbling. Finally, teach students how to control dribbling while being guarded by another student.

Instructors must spend enough time on beginning skills that they become second nature. Teaching in small groups with enough equipment for everyone is essential.

Activities for body-management skill development

Locomotor skills

Sequential development = crawl, creep, walk, run, jump, hop, gallop, slide, leap, skip, and step-hop

- **Activities to develop walking skills** include walking slower and faster in place; walking forward, backward, and sideways with slower and faster paces in straight, curving, and zigzag pathways with various lengths of steps; pausing between steps; and changing the height of the body.

- **Activities to develop running skills** include having students pretend they are playing basketball, trying to score a touchdown, trying to catch a bus, finishing a lengthy race, or running on a hot surface.

- **Activities to develop jumping skills** include alternating jumping with feet together and feet apart, taking off and landing on the balls of the feet, clicking the heels together while airborne, and landing with one foot forward and one foot backward.

- **Activities to develop galloping skills** include having students play a game of Fox and Hound, with the lead foot representing the fox and the back foot the hound trying to catch the fox (alternate the lead foot).

- **Activities to develop sliding skills** include having students hold hands in a circle and slide in one direction, then slide in the other direction.

- **Activities to develop hopping skills** include having students hop all the way around a hoop and hop in and out of a hoop, reversing direction. Students can also place ropes in straight lines and hop side to side over the rope from one end to the other and change (reverse) the direction.

- **Activities to develop skipping skills** include having students combine walking and hopping activities leading up to skipping.

- **Activities to develop step-hopping skills** include having students practice stepping and hopping activities while clapping hands to an uneven beat.

Nonlocomotor skills

Sequential development = stretch, bend, sit, shake, turn, rock and sway, swing, twist, dodge, and fall

- **Activities to develop stretching** include lying on the back and stomach and stretching as far as possible; stretching as though one is reaching for a star, picking fruit off a tree, climbing a ladder, shooting a basketball, or placing an item on a high self; waking and yawning.

- **Activities to develop bending** include touching knees and toes, then straightening the entire body and straightening the body halfway; bending as though picking up a coin, tying shoes, picking flowers/vegetables, and petting animals of different sizes.

- **Activities to develop sitting** include practicing sitting from standing, kneeling, and lying positions without the use of hands.

- **Activities to develop falling skills** include first collapsing in one's own space and then pretending to fall like bowling pins, raindrops, snowflakes, a rag doll, or Humpty Dumpty.

Manipulative skills

Sequential development = striking, throwing, kicking, ball rolling, volleying, bouncing, catching, and trapping

- **Activities to develop striking** begin with the striking of stationary objects by a participant in a stationary position. Next, the person remains still while trying to strike a moving object. Then, both the object and the participant are in motion as the participant attempts to strike the moving object.

- **Activities to develop throwing** include throwing yarn/foam balls against a wall, then at a big target, and finally at targets decreasing in size.

- **Activities to develop kicking** include alternating feet to kick balloons/beach balls, then kicking them under and over ropes. Change the type of ball used as proficiency develops.

- **Activities to develop ball rolling** include rolling balls of various sizes to a wall, then to targets decreasing in size.

- **Activities to develop volleying** include using a large balloon and, first, hitting it with both hands, then one hand (alternating hands), and then using different parts of the body. Change the object as students progress (balloon, then beach ball, then foam ball, etc.)

- **Activities to develop bouncing** include starting with large balls, first using both hands to bounce and then using one hand (alternate hands).

- **Activities to develop catching** include using various objects (balloons, beanbags, balls, etc.) to catch; first catching the object the participant has thrown him/herself, then catching objects someone else has thrown, and finally increasing the distance between the catcher and the thrower.

- **Activities to develop trapping** include trapping slow- and fast-rolling balls; trapping balls (or other objects such as beanbags) that are lightly thrown at waist, chest, and stomach levels; trapping balls of various sizes.

Rhythmic skills

Dancing is an excellent activity for the development of rhythmic skills. Any activity that involves moving the body to music can promote rhythmic skill development.

> Dancing is an excellent activity for the development of rhythmic skills. Any activity that involves moving the body to music can promote rhythmic skill development.

SKILL 46.6 Modifies instruction based on students' individual differences in growth and development.

See Skills 46.7 and 46.11

SKILL 46.7 Evaluates movement patterns to help students improve performance of motor skills and to integrate and refine their motor and rhythmic skills.

Integration of Locomotor, Nonlocomotor, and Object-Control Skills in Various Combinations and Activities

Trainers adopt various strategies to incorporate locomotor, nonlocomotor, and object-control skills into their workout schedule. These skills are very effective in making students stronger and healthier.

Combinations of object-control skills

Object-control skills (e.g., run-and-catch, pivot-and-throw) help students remain fit and agile and become better performers. Physical education instructors often combine a number of object-control skills to enhance a child's reflexes.

Catch-and-throw is an ideal example of integrating such skills. This type of skill requires a high level of concentration and nimbleness. A combination of object-control skills is at the heart of all physical activity.

> Object-control skills make all the difference in successful athletic performance. An ideal combination of these skills keeps students healthy and satisfied.

Integration strategies

Physical education instructors should develop innovative strategies to help students learn the nuances of locomotor, nonlocomotor, and object-control skills. Instructors should also present these skills in an entertaining manner for students.

A training schedule with simple activities is more likely to keep students interested. Once students develop interest, the teacher can introduce more complex activities such as running and catching, pivoting and throwing, and running and jumping.

The above progression strategy is a widely accepted method for combining loco-motor, nonlocomotor, and object-control skills. From the moment students start taking interest in physical activities, the job becomes easier for the teacher as well as the students. Finally, traditional sports activities are a perfect way to practice combined skills.

Sports and games

All sports require the application of motor skills in complex forms. For example, the motor skills required to play tennis include running, jumping, striking, and volleying. For example, a tennis player often has to strike the ball while running or jumping. To play any sport at a high level, athletes must master a number of motor skills and develop the ability to combine those skills to master sport-specific movements.

> **SKILL 46.8** Understands a variety of strategies and tactics designed to improve students' performance, teamwork and skill combinations in games and sports.

Improving Students' Performance, Teamwork, and Skills

For most people, the development of social roles and appropriate social behaviors occurs during childhood. Physical play between parents and children, as well as between siblings and peers, serves as a strong regulator in the developmental process. Chasing games, roughhousing, wrestling, or practicing sport skills such as jumping, throwing, catching, and striking, are some examples of childhood play. These activities may be competitive or noncompetitive and are important for promoting the social and moral development of both boys and girls. Unfortunately, fathers often engage in this sort of activity more with their sons than with their daughters. Regardless of the sex of the child, both boys and girls enjoy these types of activities.

Social competence and self-esteem

In addition to the development of social competence, participation in sports can help young people develop self-esteem. Self-esteem is how we judge our worth and indicates the extent to which an individual believes he or she is capable, significant, successful, and worthy. Educators have suggested that one of the biggest barriers to success in the classroom today is low self-esteem.

Children develop self-esteem by evaluating their own abilities and by evaluating the responses of others. Children actively observe their parents' and coaches' responses to their performance, looking for signs of approval or disapproval.

In sports, research shows that the coach is a critical influence on the self-esteem of children.

Children often interpret feedback and criticism as either a negative or a positive response to the behavior.

Little League baseball players whose coaches used a positive approach to coaching (e.g., frequent encouragement; positive reinforcement for effort; and corrective, instructional feedback) had significantly higher self-esteem ratings over the course of a season than children whose coaches used these techniques less frequently. Moreover, studies show that 95 percent of children who played for coaches trained to use the positive approach signed up to play baseball the next year, compared with 75 percent of the children who played for untrained coaches.

Positive social behaviors and traits

Physical education activities can promote positive social behaviors and traits in a number of ways. Instructors can foster improved social relations by making students active partners in the learning process and delegating responsibilities in the classroom environment to students. Giving students leadership positions (e.g., team captain) can give them a heightened understanding of the responsibilities and challenges facing educators.

Team sports promote collaboration and cooperation. Students learn to work together, pooling their talents and minimizing the weaknesses of different team members, in order to achieve a common goal. The experience of functioning as a team can be very productive for the development of loyalty between children, and seeing their peers in stressful situations to which they can relate can promote a more compassionate and considerate attitude among students. Similarly, the need to maximize the strengths of each student on a team (who can complement each other and compensate for weaknesses) is a powerful lesson about valuing and respecting diversity and individual differences. Switching students between leading and following positions in a team hierarchy is a good way to help students become comfortable being both followers and leaders.

Fairness is another trait that physical activities, especially rules-based sports, can foster and strengthen. Children are by nature very rules-oriented, and have a keen sense of what they believe is and isn't fair. Fair play, teamwork, and sportsmanship are all values that should be reinforced in physical education classes.

Finally, communication is another skill that improves enormously through participation in sports and games. Students will come to understand that skill-ful communication contributes to better outcomes, whether winning a game or successfully completing a team project. They will see that effective communication helps one develop and maintain healthy personal relationships, organize and convey information, and reduce or avoid conflict.

SKILL 46.9
Selects and uses instructional strategies to promote students' knowledge and application of rules, procedures, etiquette and fair play in developmentally appropriate games and activities.

Appropriate Behavior in Physical Education Activities

Rules and etiquette are of great importance to sports and physical activities. Rules help ensure fair play, equity, and safety for all participants. Teamwork is another important aspect of sports. Team sports require individual players to come together, merge individual skill sets, and pool individual strengths and weaknesses to achieve team success.

Team sports require individual players to come together, merge individual skill sets, and pool individual strengths and weaknesses to achieve team success.

Appropriate student etiquette and behaviors include: following the rules and accepting the consequences of unfair actions, good sportsmanship, respecting the rights of other students, reporting one's own accidents and mishaps, not engaging in inappropriate behavior as a result of peer pressure, cooperation, paying attention to instructions and demonstrations, moving to assigned places and remaining in one's own space, complying with directions, practicing as instructed, properly using equipment, and not interfering with the practice of others.

See also Skill 46.8

SKILL 46.10
Designs, manages and adapts physical education activities to promote positive interactions and active engagement by all students.

Techniques to Maximize Participation

Curriculum design, group participation, cooperative work, fitness activities, and learning practices work well and instill exciting learning experiences for most, but there may be some students who are left out and need special care.

Instructors must remember to deal with each student as an individual, taking into account his or her capabilities. Although implementing strict management practices may benefit the majority of the class, it can have negative effects, too.

Options for maximizing participation include:

- **Activity modification:** This is simply modifying the type of equipment used or the activity rules. However, the instructor should keep the activity as close to the original as possible (e.g., substitute a yarn ball for a birdie for badminton).

- **Multiactivity designs:** Multiple activities permit greater diversification of equipment and more efficient use of available facilities (and keep all students involved).

- **Homogeneous and heterogeneous grouping:** Groupings can be rearranged for the purpose of individualized instruction, enhancing self-concepts, equalizing competition, and promoting cooperation among classmates.

Furthermore, instructors should plan activities that encourage the greatest amount of participation by utilizing all available facilities and equipment, involving students in planning class work/activities, and being flexible. Instructors can also use tangible rewards and praise.

> **SKILL 46.11** **Understands areas of diverse needs** *(e.g., physical and emotional challenges, learning disabilities, sensory difficulties, language differences)* **and their implications for teaching and learning.**

Factors Influencing Students' Development and Fitness

A variety of factors influence a student's motor development and fitness level.

- **Societal influences:** We cannot separate students from the societies in which they live. The general societal perceptions of the importance of fitness activities will have an effect on their own choices regarding physical activity.

- **Psychological influences:** Psychological influences on motor development and fitness include a student's mental well-being, perception of fitness activities, and level of comfort in a fitness-training environment (both alone and in a group). Students experiencing psychological difficulties, such as depression, tend to be apathetic and lack both the energy and inclination to participate in fitness activities. As a result, their motor development and fitness levels suffer. Factors like the student's confidence level and comfort in a group environment, related to both the student's popularity in the group and the student's own personal insecurities, are also significant.

  It is noteworthy, though, that in the case of psychological influences on motor development and fitness levels, there is a more reciprocal relationship than with other influences. While a student's psychological state may negatively affect his or her fitness level, fitness training has the potential to positively affect the student psychologically, thereby reversing a negative cycle.

- **Cultural influences:** Culture is a significant and sometimes overlooked influence on a student's motor development and fitness, especially in the case of students belonging to minority groups. Students may not feel motivated to participate in certain physical activities, either because the activities are not associated with the student's sense of identity or because the student's culture discourages them. For example, students from cultures with strict dress codes

We should consider the "playground to PlayStation®" phenomenon and the rising levels of obesity among Americans as negative societal influences on motor development and fitness.

may not be comfortable swimming. Some students (especially older children) may be uncomfortable with physical activities in inter-gender situations. Educators must keep such cultural considerations in mind when planning physical education curricula.

- **Economic influences:** The economic circumstances of a student's family can affect his or her motor development and fitness. Lack of resources may impact the parents' ability to provide access to extracurricular activities that promote development, proper fitness-training equipment (ranging from complex exercise machines to team uniforms to something as simple as a basketball hoop), and even adequate nutrition.

- **Familial influences:** Familial factors that can influence motor development and fitness relate to the student's home environment. A student's feelings about physical activity often reflect the degree to which caregivers and role models (like older siblings) are athletically inclined and have a positive attitude toward physical activity. It isn't necessary for the parents to be athletically inclined; however, it is important for them to encourage their child to explore fitness activities that might suit him or her.

- **Environmental and health influences:** Genetic makeup (i.e., age, gender, and ethnicity) has a major influence on growth and development. Various physical and environmental factors directly affect one's personal health and fitness. Poor habits, poor living conditions, and living with a disease or disability can have a negative impact on a person. A healthy lifestyle with adequate living conditions and minimal physical or mental stress will enable a person to develop a positive, healthy existence.

Instructors should provide students with rich learning situations, regardless of students' previous experience or personal issues, which provide plenty of positive opportunities to participate in physical activity. For example, prior to playing a game of softball, instructors might have students practice throwing by tossing the ball to each other, progressing to the underhand toss, and later to the overhand toss.

SKILL 46.12 Applies knowledge of physical education content and curriculum based on the Texas Essential Knowledge and Skills (TEKS) and knowledge of students in early childhood through grade six to plan, implement and assess effective, developmentally appropriate physical education activities.

TEKS for Physical Education

The TEKS for physical education emphasizes core physical education content that instructors must teach students. Instructors must observe educational best practices to educate students in a way that is safe, achieves goals, and ensures students' continued progress and motivation. For example, instructors must tailor the lessons to a variety of learning styles, implement knowledge-based assessment systems to track students' progress over the course of a semester, advance consideration of potential safety hazards in chosen activities, implement compensatory safety procedures, and create a pleasant, fun educational environment that encourages student involvement.

COMPETENCY 47

THEATRE

Knows and understands how perception is developed through the use of elements of drama and conventions of theatre.

Practicing the elements of drama, such as analyzing a character and drawing on personal experiences to make connections to a fictional character, are ways in which students can develop their theatre skills. When students are acting, or using their background schema to create fictional characters, they are relying on their perceptions of who those characters are to decide how to proceed with the exercise.

Elements of drama include "making" and "responding." Making includes "improvising, acting, directing, scripting, practicing, and of course, performing" (*Learning in Drama*). When students are completing any of these actions, they are using their bodies and voices to make connections to a character—to perceive who the character is.

Responding is the second type of critical learning in drama. When students are responding, they are sitting in the audience and "listening to, reflecting or evaluating a live or recorded performance" (*ibid*). In this situation, they are perceiving the performance in an entirely different way than if they were performing it. Both making and responding are important for development of students' theatre skills, and both must be practiced consistently.

For young children, perception is how they view the world through their own narrow lens. A teacher could use kinesthetic exercises to help extend students' perception. There are many exercises that can achieve this goal. For example, playing Simon Says and asking children to act out inanimate objects is a good exercise to teach body control, perception, and spatial relationships. Asking students to be melting ice cream cones, lawnmowers mowing the lawn, boats sailing, or seeds growing into trees will guide them through a process, and they will rely on their own perception to create their movement. Watching other students' ideas for similar concepts will help students understand that not all perceptions are alike.

- *Learning in Drama*

  http://www.australiancurriculum.edu.au/the-arts/drama/learning-in-drama. Retrieved Aug. 20, 2015.

> **SKILL 47.2** Knows how to involve students in activities that promote enjoyment and understanding of theatre arts by selecting and using instructional strategies, materials, and activities to help students interpret creative expression and performance.

The following are examples of activities that will promote students' enjoyment and understanding of the theatre arts:

- Participating in a school play under the direction of teachers and/or parents to be fully immersed in the technical (e.g., scripts and stage directions) and aesthetic (e.g., costumes, makeup, backgrounds, lighting, etc.) elements of the theatre

- Reading a theatre piece aloud in class with each student being assigned specific roles

- Watching film adaptations of plays to compare/contrast works on the stage versus on film

- Taking advantage of digital media to learn about the elements of theatre

- Visiting local children's theatres to meet actors and learn about life in the theatre

- Studying the literary elements of the world's famous plays (e.g., Shakespeare's works)

- Discussing through any of the activities above their feelings about literary works and the theatre and its many features

> **SKILL 47.3** Demonstrates the knowledge of the elements of theatre *(i.e., dramatic play, expressive movement, voice, characterization)* and theatre occupations, provides instruction that promotes students' understanding of the elements and occupations, and helps them apply that understanding in creating theatrical productions.

All of the following are foundational dramatic skills, and though some will be a natural part of a child's play, each skill can be honed and developed in a theatre class. All are necessary for successful theatrical productions; students must be able to project their voice, create a believable character, and express this character through gesture and speech.

- **Dramatic Play:** Particularly important in young childhood, *dramatic play* is another term for pretend play. Children often learn through imagining roles that are real or fictional. Often, pretend play involves using props, mimicking adult behavior, or assigning roles to peers to create a coordinating group. For example, young children may take on various roles in a family.

- **Expressive Movement:** Expressive movement is responding with your body to rhythm, moving your body to music, or using facial expressions or body gestures to communicate. Students can pretend to be inanimate objects, practice showing various emotions on their faces, or practice communicating without words.

- **Voice/Characterization/Theatre Occupations:** Practicing using a clear and loud voice and developing a three-dimensional character are important aspects of the theatre curriculum. Often, warm-up exercises will be voice- or characterization-based to help older students learn basic theatrical skills.

SKILL 47.4 Integrates instruction in theatre with instruction in other subject areas.

Often, students will be able to identify with a concept more easily if they see it performed or if they perform it. That is why it is important to integrate instruction in theatre with instruction in other subject areas. This integration can begin in elementary school. For example, when studying colonial America, students can create costumes and props and then write short skits about life in colonial America to perform for their peers.

In middle and high school, theatre lends itself naturally to English class, where students can discuss characterization, setting, theme and symbolism. Analyzing a play in English class gives students a chance to see literature as dialogue, watching the story unfold as people speak it. Advancing a story using primarily dialogue and very little description is a daunting task, but when done well, such as in Arthur Miller's *Death of a Salesman*, it can be not only a commentary on culture, but also a fantastic story. Students can study the play for its literary value and learn from the techniques the writer uses, such as stage direction, entrances and exits, monologues, satire, symbolism, and imagery. Students can practice these techniques through short writing exercises.

History is a perfect subject in which to incorporate theatre. Because all plays come out of a specific sociocultural context, studying this context and performing or watching a play can give students a more personal and relatable view of a specific historical context that previously may have seemed abstract.

SKILL 47.5 Knows how to promote students' ability to identify and use technical elements *(e.g., properties, scenery, sound, costumes, lighting)* to create suitable environments for dramatic play and performance.

See Skill 47.6

SKILL 47.6 Knows how to promote students' ability to identify and use technical elements *(e.g., properties, scenery, sound, costumes, lighting)* to define and enhance characterization, mood, theme, and setting.

The set (that is, the scenery), costumes, lighting, backgrounds, and sound can greatly influence the mood and setting of a stage.

- The **scenery** is composed of the theatrical equipment, such as curtains, flats, backdrops, or platforms. These are used in a production to communicate the play's environment and bring the audience into the play's world.

- **Costumes** are clothing and accessories worn by actors to portray character and period.

- **Props** (short for properties) are any articles, except costume or scenery, used as part of a production. They also include any moveable object that appears on stage during a performance.

The arrangement and entrance or exit of these elements can change the scene and elicit varied responses from the audience. For example, spotlights are used to focus on a single actor during monologues or soliloquies. Additionally, backgrounds can be used to distinguish between indoors and outdoors within the play's context.

Determining which elements to include when (and for how long) during a production is very much a creative process and is what separates phenomenal directors from others in the theatrical world. However, clues can be gleaned from the literary text that is being adapted into a play. The following are examples of technical questions students can ask when reading a play to gain insights into adapting the text to the stage:

- Is the play set in a specific time period that requires distinct costuming or makeup?

- Is a particular scene central to the storyline and deserving of a change in scenery?

- Are there any long speeches that one character gives that would require intense focus from the audience?

- Are there instances of suspense in the play that would require special effects or manipulation of lighting and sound?

- Which characters are central and which can be cut?

- Is special sound needed for particular scenes (e.g., transitions in weather)?

- What scenes would require more movement than the stage's size can allow?

- What are the play's major moods and how much of an emotional rollercoaster should the audience be taken on?

SKILL 47.7 Understands how theatre relates to history, society, and the diverse cultures.

For centuries, theatre has been a way to escape everyday life. No matter the difficulties faced in day-to-day life, people came to the theatre for relaxation, for escape, and for laughter. Often, writers of plays hide social commentaries inside comedies or use a tragic story to examine a societal flaw. This use of theatre and writing approaches apply across cultures. Often, a playwright will make a political or historical statement through a work of fiction.

The director and the actors interpret the piece using their own perceptions, so the resulting performance becomes a interpretation of both the time in which the play is set and the current culture.

For example, William Shakespeare, famous for plays such as *A Midsummer Night's Dream, Hamlet,* and *Romeo and Juliet,* used his writing to examine the society around him. *A Midsummer Night's Dream* is silly—it is a comedy of four people who are trapped in the woods and trapped in love. In *Hamlet,* Shakespeare examines greediness, and in *Romeo and Juliet,* he depicts unrequited love due to familial conflict.

Theatre is never just a play; even the silliest comedies often have an underlying message meant for the actors, the directors, and the audience to ponder. When students look at a historical theatrical event, it's important for them to consider what was happening in the world at the time the play was written. What was the political, economical, and social climate? Students cannot read a play in a vacuum; they must analyze the surrounding issues from when the play was written. The performance interpretation can use the historical context to evaluate how to adapt the performance.

SKILL 47.8 Applies knowledge of theatre content and curriculum based on the Texas Essential Knowledge and Skills (TEKS) and knowledge of students in early childhood through grade six to plan and implement effective, developmentally appropriate theatre instruction.

Theatre lesson plans should be centered around the content and curriculum for a specific grade level. Play is a young child's most important job, and it is the only time when they can freely explore and develop new concepts in their lives. Young children will play on their own without much direction. They will create dramatic play almost every time they are left to pretend. Some teachers may choose to guide them into a specific setting or specific characters. Lesson plans can include group and partner exercises, team building, Reader's Theatre, and, later, studying scene and character development. Older students may be given monologues to learn and memorize or scenes to discuss and analyze and then perform, or they may read plays to analyze the themes and symbols.

When assessing students, keep their developmental level in mind. For instance, assessments for elementary students may be checkpoints for understanding or participation in a Reader's Theatre. Assessments for older students may include performances and participation in and enthusiasm for the work.

SKILL 47.9 Manages time, instructional resources and physical space effectively for theatre education.

Theatre education is about learning by doing. Students experience, students practice, and students perform. It's important to give students a chance to work as a team, to work independently, to work under pressure, and to rely on others. Each class should allow time for students to practice these skills so that the students can learn and feel comfortable with them. Usually, a teacher will begin with a whole-class warm-up in which students can practice improvisation or team building or perform trust exercises. Next, the teacher may move on to a skill that he or she is working on with her class, such as scene work, a particular type of dramatic ability, or a new skill. Next, there will be time for group or individual practice. Class can close with another group exercise to help students work on teamwork, working under pressure, enthusiasm, or trust.

Instructional resources include items that can spur imagination: for example, props that can be used many ways, pieces of paper with improvisational ideas, mirrors so students can practice facial expressions, scripts, or monologues or dialogues to practice.

A theatre is a three-dimensional classroom. Students will use all of the space to develop their characters or complete the kinesthetic exercise. Movement is a large piece of theatre education, so it's important to allow for it. Sparse furniture usually decorates a theatre classroom—for example, chairs in a wide circle and a moveable board for notes. Sometimes, theatre classes take place on a stage to give students the opportunity to be in the performance environment.

SAMPLE TEST

Questions

English Language Arts

(Average) (Skill 1.1)

1. While standing in line at the grocery store, three-year-old Megan says to her mother in a regular tone of voice, "Mom, why is that woman so fat?" What does this indicate a lack of understanding of?

   A. Syntax

   B. Semantics

   C. Morphology

   D. Pragmatics

(Easy) (Skill 1.4)

2. **Oral language development can be enhanced by which of the following?**

   A. Meaningful conversation

   B. Storytelling

   C. Alphabet songs

   D. All of the above

(Rigorous) (Skill 1.5)

3. Ms. Chomski is presenting a new story to her class of first graders. In the story, a family visits their grandparents, where they all gather around a record player and listen to music. Many students do not understand what a record player is, especially some children for whom English is not their first language. Which of the following would be best for Ms. Chomski to do?

   A. Discuss what a record player is with her students

   B. Compare a record player with a CD player and an mp3 player

   C. Have students look up *record player* in a dictionary

   D. Show the students a picture of a record player

(Rigorous) (Skill 1.7)

4. **Reading aloud correlates with all of the following EXCEPT:**

   A. Reader self-confidence

   B. Better reading comprehension

   C. Literacy development

   D. Overall school success

(Rigorous) (Skill 1.10)

5. Mr. Johns is using an activity that involves having students analyze the public speaking of others. All of the following would be included in the guidelines for this activity EXCEPT:

   A. The speeches to be evaluated are not given by other students

   B. The rubric for evaluating the speeches includes pace, pronunciation, body language, word choice, and visual aids

   C. The speeches to be evaluated are best presented live to give students a more engaging learning experience

   D. One of Mr. Johns's goals with this activity is to help students improve their own public speaking skills

(Average) (Skill 2.1)

6. All of the following are true about phonological awareness EXCEPT:

   A. It may involve print

   B. It is a prerequisite for spelling and phonics

   C. Children can do the activities with their eyes closed

   D. It starts before letter recognition is taught

(Rigorous) (Skill 2.2)

7. Which of the following explains a significant difference between phonics and phonemic awareness?

   A. Phonics involves print, while phonemic awareness involves language

   B. Phonics is harder than phonemic awareness

   C. Phonics involves sounds, while phonemic awareness involves letters

   D. Phonics is the application of sounds to print, while phonemic awareness is oral

(Average) (Skill 2.3)

8. Theorist Marilyn Jager Adams, who researches early reading, has outlined five basic types of phonemic awareness tasks. Which of the following is NOT one of the tasks noted by Jager Adams?

   A. Ability to do oddity tasks

   B. Ability to orally blend words and split syllables

   C. Ability to sound out words when reading aloud

   D. Ability to do phonics manipulation tasks

(Average) (Skill 2.6)

9. Activities that parents can practice at home to improve phonological and phonemic awareness include which of the following?

   A. Play games with words that sound alike as you experience them in everyday home activities

   B. Demonstrate how sounds blend together in familiar words

   C. Play a game in which the goal is to find objects with names that begin with a certain initial sound

   D. All of the above

(Rigorous) (Skill 3.1)

10. **Which of the following statements best describes the alphabetic principle?**

    A. Most reading skills need to be acquired through a regular teaching of the alphabet

    B. Written words are composed of patterns of letters that represent the sounds of spoken words

    C. Written words are composed of patterns that must be memorized to read well

    D. Spoken words (regular and irregular) lead to phonological reading

(Rigorous) (Skill 3.3)

11. **Which of the following is NOT true about multisensory approaches to teaching the alphabetic principle?**

    A. Some children can only learn through multisensory techniques

    B. Multisensory techniques give multiple cues to enhance memory and learning

    C. Quilt book, rhyme time, letter path, and shape game are multisensory strategies

    D. Multisensory techniques require direct teaching and ongoing engagement

(Average) (Skill 3.4)

12. **Activities that facilitate learning the alphabetic principle include:**

    A. Read alouds, alphabet art, concept books, and name sorts

    B. Read alouds, shared reading, concept books, and picture books

    C. Picture books, concept books, and alphabet books

    D. Alphabet art, name sorts, shared reading, and phonics

(Rigorous) (Skill 4.1)

13. **Which of the following is a convention of print that children learn during reading activities?**

    A. The meaning of words

    B. The left-to-right motion

    C. The purpose of print

    D. The identification of letters

(Average) (Skill 4.5)

14. **Alphabet books are classified as:**

    A. Concept books

    B. Easy-to-read books

    C. Board books

    D. Picture books

(Rigorous) (Skill 4.6)

15. **To determine an author's purpose, a reader must:**

    A. Use his or her own judgment

    B. Verify all the facts

    C. Link the causes to the effects

    D. Rely on common sense

(Easy) (Skill 5.1)

16. **To decode is to:**

    A. Construct meaning

    B. Sound out a printed sequence of letters

    C. Use a special code to decipher a message

    D. None of the above

(Rigorous) (Skill 5.2)

17. Contextual redefinition is a strategy that encourages children to use the context more effectively by presenting them with sufficient vocabulary _____ the reading of a text.

    A. after

    B. before

    C. during

    D. None of the above

(Average) (Skill 5.6)

18. What is the best place for students to find appropriate synonyms, antonyms, and other related words to enhance their writing?

    A. Dictionary

    B. Spell check

    C. Encyclopedia

    D. Thesaurus

(Rigorous) (Skill 6.1)

19. Which of the following indicates that a student is a fluent reader?

    A. Reads texts with expression or prosody

    B. Reads word to word and haltingly

    C. Must intentionally decode the majority of the words

    D. Sentences in a writing assignment are poorly organized structurally

(Rigorous) (Skill 6.3)

20. Automaticity refers to all of the following EXCEPT:

    A. Automatic whole-word identification

    B. Automatic recognition of syllable types

    C. Automatic reactions to the content of a paragraph

    D. Automatic identification of graphemes as they relate to four basic word types

(Rigorous) (Skill 6.4)

21. Which of the following activities are likely to improve fluency?

    A. Partner reading and a reader's theater

    B. Phrased reading

    C. Both A and B

    D. None of the above

(Rigorous) (Skill 7.7)

22. A child who has had limited exposure to text is:

    A. More likely to refuse to participate in reading

    B. Likely to be at the same developmental level as his or her peers with reading readiness

    C. Likely to need extra support in the reading classroom

    D. Unlikely to catch up to his or her peers in reading readiness

(Rigorous) (Skill 4.1)

23. Students are about to read a text that contains words that students will need to understand to understand the text. When should the vocabulary be introduced to students?

    A. Before reading

    B. During reading

    C. After reading

    D. It should not be introduced

(Rigorous) (Skill 7.5)

24. A sixth-grade science teacher has given her class a paper to read on the relationship between food and weight gain. The writing contains signal words and phrases such as "because," "consequently," "this is how," and "due to." This paper has which text structure?

    A. Cause and effect

    B. Compare and contrast

    C. Description

    D. Sequencing

(Rigorous) (Skill 7.7)

25. Which of the following is NOT a strategy of teaching reading comprehension?

    A. Asking questions

    B. Utilizing graphic organizers

    C. Focusing on mental images

    D. Manipulating sounds

(Easy) (Skill 7.11)

26. The children's literature genre came into its own in the:

    A. Seventeenth century

    B. Eighteenth century

    C. Nineteenth century

    D. Twentieth century

(Rigorous) (Skill 9.4)

27. When evaluating reference sources, students should do all of the following EXCEPT:

    A. Look for self-published books by the author as evidence of expert status

    B. Examine the level of detail provided by the source

    C. Review the references at the end of the book or article

    D. See if the author presents both sides of an argument or viewpoint

(Average) (Skill 9.2)

28. Graphic organizers:

    A. Primarily are used in grades K–3

    B. Work better with poetry than other forms of writing

    C. Help readers think critically by pulling out the main idea and supporting details

    D. Generally aren't helpful to ELL students

(Average) (Skill 8.4)

29. **Which of the following helps students in a way that is similar to using a glossary?**

    A. Information in the text such as charts, graphs, maps, diagrams, captions, and photos

    B. Prewriting

    C. Classroom discussion of the main idea

    D. Paired reading

(Rigorous) (Skill 5.6)

30. **Which of these describes the best way to teach spelling?**

    A. At the same time that grammar and sentence structure are taught

    B. Within the context of meaningful language experiences

    C. Independently so that students can concentrate on spelling

    D. In short lessons because students pick up spelling almost immediately

(Average) (Skill 10.6)

31. **Which of the following sentences is a compound sentence?**

    A. Elizabeth took Gracie to the dog park but forgot to bring the leash.

    B. We thoroughly enjoyed our trip during Spring Break and will plan to return next year.

    C. We were given two choices: today or tomorrow.

    D. By the end of the evening, we were thoroughly exhausted; we decided to forego the moonlight walk.

(Rigorous) (Skill 10.6)

32. **Which of the following sentences contains an error in agreement?**

    A. Jennifer is one of the women who writes for the magazine.

    B. Each one of their sons plays a different sport.

    C. This band has performed at the Odeum many times.

    D. The data are available online at the listed website.

(Average) (Skill 11.4)

33. **Which of the following is NOT a technique of prewriting?**

    A. Clustering

    B. Listing

    C. Brainstorming

    D. Proofreading

(Easy) (Skill 11.6)

34. **A student has written a paper with the following characteristics: written in first person; characters, setting, and plot; some dialogue; events organized in chronological sequence with some flashbacks. In what genre has the student written?**

    A. Expository writing

    B. Narrative writing

    C. Persuasive writing

    D. Technical writing

(Rigorous) (Skill 9.6)

35. A sentence that contains one independent clause and three dependent clauses is best described as a:

    A. Simple sentence

    B. Compound sentence

    C. Complex sentence

    D. Compound-complex sentence

(Rigorous) (Skill 10.3)

36. Which of the following messages provides the most accessibility to the most learners?

    A. Print message

    B. Audiovisual message

    C. Graphic message

    D. Audiovisual message

(Easy) (Skill 10.5)

37. Which of the following advertising techniques is based on appealing to our desire to think for ourselves?

    A. Celebrity endorsement

    B. Intelligence

    C. Independence

    D. Lifestyle

(Average) (Skill 10.7)

38. Which of the following is NOT useful in creating visual media for the classroom?

    A. Limit your graph to just one idea or concept and keep the content simple

    B. Balance substance and visual appeal

    C. Match the information to the format that will fit it best

    D. Make sure to cite all references to copyrighted material

(Rigorous) (Skill 11.1)

39. All of the following are examples of ongoing informal assessment techniques used to observe student progress EXCEPT:

    A. Analysis of student work product

    B. Collection of data from assessment tests

    C. Effective questioning

    D. Observation of students

(Easy) (Skill 13.2)

40. Which of the following is a formal reading-level assessment?

    A. A standardized reading test

    B. A teacher-made reading test

    C. An interview

    D. A reading diary

(Easy) (Skill 13.8)

41. Which of the following is NOT considered a reading level?

    A. Independent

    B. Instructional

    C. Intentional

    D. Frustrational

(Rigorous) (Skill 11.7)

42. Which of the following should NOT be included in the opening paragraph of an informative essay?

    A. Thesis sentence

    B. Details and examples supporting the main idea

    C. A broad, general introduction to the topic

    D. A style and tone that grabs the reader's attention

(Average) (Skill 11.6)

43. Being competent in _____, a reader is able to understand what the writer is trying to convey to the audience.

    A. semantics

    B. pragmatics

    C. morphemes

    D. phonemes

(Easy) (Skill 9.2)

44. A second-grade teacher explains the steps of the writing process to her learners. For the first step, she demonstrates the use of a Venn diagram to compare and contrast two characters from a story the class recently read. These visual representations of content are known as:

    A. Graphic organizers

    B. Running records

    C. Blogs

    D. Phonemes

(Average) (Skill 7.3)

45. By examining an author's word choice, a reader can determine the:

    A. Author's purpose

    B. Author's tone

    C. Main idea

    D. Inference

DIRECTIONS: Read the following passage and answer the questions that follow.

According to Factmonster.com, the most popular Internet activity is sending and/or reading email. Approximately 92% of Internet users report using the Internet for this purpose. 89% of Internet users report that they use the Internet to search for information. Two popular search engines are Google and Yahoo! The introduction of the Internet has made it easy to gather and research information quickly. Other reasons that Internet users use the Internet is for social media, to search for driving directions, look into a hobby or interest, or research a product or service before buying, just to name a few. Creative <u>enterprises</u> such as remixing songs or lyrics stood at the bottom of reasons people use the Internet. Surprisingly, only 11% of Internet users said they use the Internet for creative purposes. Perhaps people are using specific software to be creative.

(Average) (Skill 7.3)

46. What is the main idea of the passage?

    A. Factmonster has a lot of great facts for people to research

    B. People use the Internet for a variety of reasons

    C. The main reason the Internet is used is to check emails

    D. People aren't as creative as they used to be before the Internet

(Average) (Skill 7.4)

47. **Why did the author write this article?**

    A. To convince the reader to use the Internet

    B. To teach the reader how use the Internet

    C. To encourage the reader to use the Internet

    D. To inform the reader about Internet usage trends

(Average) (Skill 7.4)

48. **How is the passage organized?**

    A. Sequence of events

    B. Cause and effect

    C. Statement support

    D. Compare and contrast

(Rigorous) (Skill 7.5)

49. **What cause and effect relationship exists in this paragraph?**

    A. The U.S. postal service is suffering from the introduction of email

    B. Google and Yahoo! are used most often to search information

    C. The introduction of the Internet has made gathering information easy

    D. People are less creative since they aren't using their computers for this reason

(Rigorous) (Skill 7.2)

50. **By using the word "surprisingly" in the passage, what is the author implying?**

    A. It is thought that the Internet is used more for creative purposes

    B. People are thought to be more creative than they really are

    C. It is thought that fewer than 11% would use the Internet for creative purposes

    D. Software companies are making 11% more creative software

(Average) (Skill 7.2)

51. **Which transition word could the author have used to connect these two sentences?**

    Approximately 92% of Internet users report using the Internet for this purpose. 89% of Internet users report that they use the Internet to search for information.

    A. Additionally,

    B. Therefore,

    C. Next,

    D. Similarly,

(Average) (Skill 7.2)

52. **What does the word "enterprises" mean in the passage?**

    A. People

    B. Endeavors

    C. Businesses

    D. Musicians

DIRECTIONS: Read the following passage and answer the questions that follow.

The poems both use personification to bring the subjects of the poem to life. Both poems were also very entertaining. In "The Subway" the author says that the subway, also known as a dragon, swallows up the people and then spits them out at the next stop. Similarly, in "Steam Shovel," the author says that the steam shovel chews up the dirt that it scoops up and smiles amiably at the people below.

The subjects of the poems are compared to different things. The subway is compared to a dragon with green scales. Dragons breathe fire. The steam shovel is compared to an ancient dinosaur with a long neck and dripping jaws.

(Average) (Skill 7.4)

53. **How is the passage organized?**

    A. Compare and contrast

    B. Cause and effect

    C. Sequence of events

    D. Statement support

(Average) (Skill 7.2)

54. **Which sentence in the passage is irrelevant?**

    A. Both poems were also very entertaining.

    B. The subway is also known as a dragon.

    C. The subway swallows people up and spits them out.

    D. The author says that the steam shovel chews up the dirt.

(Easy) (Skill 7.5)

55. **Each of the comparisons mentioned in the paragraph are known as a:**

    A. Metaphor

    B. Hyperbole

    C. Onomatopoeia

    D. None of the above

DIRECTIONS: Read the following passage and answer the questions that follow.

Have you ever wondered what chewing gum is made from? What is it that allows us to chew it for hours without it ever disintegrating? Chicle is a gum, or sap, that comes from the sapodilla tree. The sapodilla tree is an American tropical evergreen that is native to South Florida. Flavorings, corn syrup, and sugar or artificial sweeteners are other ingredients that go into the production of chewing gum. Legend has it that Native Americans chewed spruce resin to quench their thirst. Today, gum is chewed for many reasons by many different groups of people.

(Rigorous) (Skill 7.5)

56. **What conclusion can be drawn from the passage?**

    A. Everyone in South Florida has heard of the sapodilla tree

    B. Many people have wondered what makes gum chewy

    C. Some type of sweetener is used in gum production

    D. Native Americans invented gum

(Rigorous) (Skill 7.4)

57. **What can be inferred from the passage?**

    A. The gum Chiclets took its name from the ingredient chicle used in gum

    B. Gum is disgusting after it's been chewed for a few hours

    C. Gum is only made in the United States because that's where the sapodilla tree grows

    D. When someone is thirsty they should chew gum

DIRECTIONS: Read the following passage and answer the questions that follow.

The word "cycle" comes from the Greek word *kyklos*, which means "circle" or "wheel." There are many different types of cycles. The word "unicycle" comes from the prefix *uni-*, which means "one," combined with the root "cycle." When the prefix and root word cycle are combined, it creates a word that means "one circle or wheel." Unicycles are often used for entertainment rather than exercise.

A prefix *bi-* means "two," which, when combined with the word "cycle," creates the word "bicycle." How many wheels does a bicycle have? Many young children ride a tricycle because it has three wheels and is easy to ride. The prefix *tri-* means "three," and when it is combined with the root word "cycle," the new word is "three wheels." It is even possible to make the word "motorcycle." Once you know how to use <u>roots</u>, it is easy to figure out the meaning of an unknown word.

(Average) (Skill 7.4)

58. **What is the main idea of the passage?**

    A. There are many types of cycles

    B. The prefix *uni-* means one

    C. Words can be defined by their parts

    D. Unicycles are often used for entertainment

(Easy) (Skill 7.2)

59. **What does the word "roots" mean?**

    A. Stable parts of plants

    B. Where one originated

    C. The base portions of a word

    D. A spelling tool

(Average) (Skill 7.7)

60. **Which is an opinion contained in this passage?**

    A. Once you know how to use roots, it is easy to figure out the meaning of an unknown word

    B. Many young children ride a tricycle

    C. Unicycles are often used for entertainment rather than exercise

    D. The word "cycle" comes from the Greek word *kyklos*

(Rigorous) (Skill 7.7)

61. **From this article you can see that the author thinks:**

    A. Riding a bicycle is good exercise

    B. It is important to know about the English language

    C. "Cycle" is a confusing word

    D. It is more important to understand the prefixes and suffixes

DIRECTIONS: The passage below contains many errors. Read the passage. Then, answer each test item by choosing the option that corrects an error in the underlined portion(s). No more than one underlined error will appear in each item. If no error exists, choose "No change is necessary."

If you give me ten dollars, I'll give you fifty in return. Does this sound too good to be true? Well, anything that sounds too good to be true probably is. That stands true for herbal supplements. Herbal supplements are main targeted toward improving one type of ailment. There is no cure-all herbal supplement so don't believe what he tells you. Herbal supplement can fix more than one thing.

Herbal supplements is great and have a lot of positive things to offer its takers and have become very popular with consumers. Many doctors are even suggesting that they try natural herbal remedies before prescribing an over-the-counter medication. Herbal supplements have given consumers a new power to self-diagnose and consumers can head to the health food store and pick up an herbal supplement rather than heading to the doctor. Herbal supplements take a little long than prescribed medication to clear up any illnesses, but they are a more natural way to go, and some consumers prefer that form of medication.

(Average) (Skill 8.1)

62. Herbal supplements are <u>main</u> targeted <u>toward</u> <u>improving</u> one type of ailment.

    A. mainly

    B. towards

    C. improve

    D. No change is necessary

(Easy) (Skill 8.1)

63. There is <u>no</u> cure-all herbal <u>supplement</u> so don't believe what <u>he tells you</u>.

    A. nothing

    B. supplemental

    C. you hear

    D. No change is necessary

(Rigorous) (Skill 8.1)

64. Many doctors <u>are</u> even suggesting that <u>they</u> try natural herbal remedies before <u>prescribing</u> an over-the-counter medication.

    A. is

    B. their patients

    C. prescribing,

    D. No change is necessary

(Easy) (Skill 8.4)

65. Herbal supplements <u>is</u> great and have <u>a lot</u> of positive things to offer <u>its</u> takers and have become very popular with consumers.

    A. are

    B. alot

    C. it's

    D. No change is necessary

(Average) (Skill 8.4)

66. Herbal supplements take a little <u>long</u> <u>than</u> <u>prescribed</u> medications to clear up any illnesses, but they are a more natural way to go, and some consumers prefer that form of medication.

    A. longer

    B. then

    C. perscribed

    D. No changes necessary

(Rigorous) (Skill 8.1)

67. Herbal <u>supplements</u> take a little long than prescribed <u>medication</u> to clear up any illnesses, but they are a <u>more natural</u> way to go, and some consumers prefer that form of medication.

    A. supplement

    B. medications

    C. more naturally

    D. No change necessary

(Average) (Skill 8.1)

68. Herbal <u>supplement</u> can fix more <u>than</u> one <u>thing</u>.

    A. supplements

    B. then

    C. things

    D. No change is necessary

DIRECTIONS: The passage below contains many errors. Read the passage. Then, answer each test item by choosing the option that corrects an error in the underlined portion(s). No more than one underlined error will appear in each item. If no error exists, choose "No change is necessary."

Bingo has many purposes in the United States. It is used as a learning and entertainment tool for children. Bingo is used as an entertainment tool for parties and picnics to entertain a large number of people easily and quickly. Bingo is also a common game played among elderly and church groups because of its simplistic way of entertaining.

A typical bingo card has the word "bingo" printed across the top with columns of numbers inside boxes underneath. There is a "free" space located directly in the middle. There is usually one person who calls the numbers. For example, a ball or chip may be labeled "B12." Players then look under the "B" column for the number 12 and if it appears on their card, they place a marker on top of it. If there isn't a 12 under the letter "B" on a player's card, then they simply wait for the next number to be called.

(Rigorous) (Skill 1.7)

69. <u>Players</u> then look under the "B" column for the number 12 and if it appears on <u>his</u> card, <u>they</u> place a marker on top of it.

    A. He

    B. their

    C. him

    D. No change is necessary.

(Rigorous) (Skill 2.2)

70. *Bingo is used as a learning and entertainment tool for children.*

    How should this sentence be rewritten?

    A. Bingo is used as a learning tool and entertainment for children.

    B. Bingo is used for learning and entertainment for children.

    C. Bingo is used to both teach and entertain children.

    D. No change is necessary

(Easy) (Skill 11.4)

71. **In this step of the writing process, students examine their work and make changes in wording, details, and ideas.**

    A. Drafting

    B. Prewriting

    C. Revising and editing

    D. Proofreading

DIRECTIONS: Read the following passage and answer the questions.

It is a requirement that all parents volunteer two hours during the course of the season. Or an alternative was to pay $8 so you can have some high school students work a shift for you. Lots of parents liked this idea and will take advantage of the opportunity. Shifts run an hour long, and it is well worth it to pay the money so you don't miss your sons game.

(Average) (Skill 10.1)

72. *It is a requirement that all parents volunteer two hours during the course of the season.*

    How should the above sentence be rewritten?

    A. It is a requirement of all parents volunteering two hours during the course of the season.

    B. It is required of all parents to volunteer for two hours during the course of the season.

    C. They require all parents to volunteer during the season.

    D. Requiring all parents to volunteer for two hours of the season.

(Average) (Skill 10.1)

73. **An alternative <u>was</u> to pay $8 so you can have some <u>high school</u> students work a shift for you.**

    Which of the following options corrects an error in one of the underlined portions above?

    A. is

    B. High School

    C. High school

    D. No change is necessary

(Rigorous) (Skill 10.1)

74. *Many parents liked this idea and will take advantage of the opportunity.*

    How should the sentence be rewritten?

    A. Many parent's liked this idea and took advantage of the opportunity.

    B. Many parents like this idea and take advantage of the opportunity.

    C. Many parents like this idea and took advantage of the opportunity.

    D. Many parents did like this idea and take advantage of the opportunity.

(Rigorous) (Skill 7.3)

75. Which is NOT a true statement concerning an author's literary tone?

    A. Tone is partly revealed through the selection of details

    B. Tone is the expression of the author's attitude towards his or her subject

    C. Tone in literature is usually satiric or angry

    D. Tone in literature corresponds to the tone of voice a speaker uses

Mathematics

(Rigorous) (Skill 17.5)

76. These angles are diagonal angles on the inside of two parallel lines cut by a transversal:

    A. Alternate interior

    B. Alternate exterior

    C. Corresponding

    D. Vertical

(Average) (Skill 17.4)

77. These lines do not intersect and do not lie on the same plane:

    A. Parallel

    B. Perpendicular

    C. Intersecting

    D. Skew

(Easy) (Skill 17.1)

78. When divided by a line through the middle, which letter does not demonstrate symmetry?

    A. **T**

    B. **A**

    C. **O**

    D. **F**

(Rigorous) (Skill 15.4)

79. Select the answer that best represents the prime factorization of 245.

    A. $6^2 \cdot 7$

    B. $5^2 \cdot 7$

    C. $4 \cdot 5 \cdot 6$

    D. $5 \cdot 7^2$

(Average) (Skill 16.2)

80. A function defined by the equation $f(x) = 5mx + b$:

   A. Recursive function

   B. Quadratic function

   C. Linear function

   D. Exponential function

(Average) (Skill 16.7)

81. A _____ is a relationship in which two quantities are proportional to each other.

   A. recursive relationship

   B. linear relationship

   C. quadratic relationship

   D. exponential relationship

(Easy) (Skill 19.8)

82. First-grade students have sorted information to put into a graph. Which developmentally appropriate graph would be best to illustrate the various colors of favorite autumn leaves?

   A. Pictograph

   B. Circle graph

   C. Histogram

   D. Line graph

Use the data below to answer questions 83–85.

The following are the percentages that were earned on a fifth-grade math exam:

78	84	86
90	93	90
87	64	98
74	73	72
98	81	77

(Average) (Skill 18.2)

83. Find the median of the given test scores:

   A. 84

   B. 83

   C. 86

   D. 81

(Average) (Skill 18.2)

84. Find the mean of the given test scores:

   A. 78

   B. 83

   C. 87

   D. None of the above

(Average) (Skill 18.2)

85. Find the mode of the given test scores:

   A. 84

   B. 87

   C. 86

   D. 98

(Average) (Skill 19.10)

86. June is planning a vacation. The hotel costs $872.27, the rental car is $189.78, and she budgeted $250 for food. Estimate how much cash June will need to pay for hotel, car, and food.

   A. $1400

   B. $1325

   C. $1300

   D. $1250

(Average) (Skill 16.8)

87. A car traveled 281 miles in 4 hours 41 minutes. What was the average speed of the car in miles per hour?

   A. 66 miles per hour

   B. 70 miles per hour

   C. 56 miles per hour

   D. 60 miles per hour

(Average) (Skill 18.3)

88. A six-sided die is rolled once. What is the probability that the number rolled is an even number greater than 2?

   A. $\frac{1}{6}$

   B. $\frac{1}{3}$

   C. $\frac{1}{4}$

   D. None of the above

(Average) (Skill 17.14)

89. The length of a rectangle is increased to 2 times its original size and its width is increased to 3 times its original size. If the area of the new rectangle is equal to 1800 square feet, what is the area of the original rectangle?

   A. 300 square feet

   B. 360 square feet

   C. 320 square feet

   D. 400 square feet

(Average) (Skill 16.10)

90. Daniel bought a total of 20 game cards, some of which cost $0.25 each and some of which cost $0.15 each. If Daniel spent $4.20 to buy these cards, how many $0.15 cards did he buy?

   A. 9 cards

   B. 8 cards

   C. 12 cards

   D. 10 cards

(Average) (Skill 18.9)

91. In a group of 120 people, 90 have an age of more 30 years, and the others have an age of less than 20 years. If a person is selected at random from this group, what is the probability the person's age is less than 20?

   A. 45

   B. 0.5

   C. 0.75

   D. 0.25

(Average) (Skill 17.2)

92. If the length of the side of a square is doubled, what is the ratio of the areas of the original square to the area of the new square?

   A. 1:2

   B. 1:8

   C. 1:4

   D. 1:6

(Average) (Skill 16.7)

93. The division of a whole number y by 13 gives a quotient of 15 and a remainder of 2. Find y.

   A. 197

   B. 113

   C. 183

   D. 195

(Easy) (Skill 17.15)

94. Sarah spent $\frac{3}{4}$ of her savings on a TV and the rest on clothes. If the clothes cost her $200, what was her original savings?

   A. $900

   B. $1000

   C. $1200

   D. $800

(Average) (Skill 15.3)

95. Samantha bought a sweater on sale for 30% off the original price and another 25% off the discounted price. If the original price of the sweater was $30, what was the final price of the sweater?

   A. $15.75

   B. $16.25

   C. $17.50

   D. $14.90

(Easy) (Skill 19.6)

96. Mr. Michaels begins teaching his students the principles of addition. Before beginning his lessons, he must ensure that:

   A. His students can count

   B. His students have a concrete understanding of one-to-one correspondence

   C. His students can recognize written numbers

   D. All of the above

(Average) (Skill 14.4)

97. Which of the following is a true statement regarding manipulatives in mathematics instruction?

   A. Manipulatives are materials that students can physically handle

   B. Manipulatives help students make concrete concepts abstract

   C. Manipulatives include fingers, tiles, paper folding, and ice cream sticks

   D. Manipulatives help students make abstract concepts concrete

(Easy) (Skill 14.5)

98. In order to create a motivating learning environment in mathematics, Ms. Anders, a kindergarten teacher, should do which of the following?

    A. Utilize large posters with text mathematical definitions

    B. Provide hands-on mathematical learning centers and visuals

    C. Allow the students to only work one on one

    D. Work with all students as a whole group each day

(Easy) (Skill 14.6)

99. All of the following are tools that can strengthen students' mathematical understanding EXCEPT:

    A. Rulers, scales, and protractors

    B. Calculators, counters, and measuring containers

    C. Software and hardware

    D. Money and software

(Average) (Skill 14.9)

100. Which of the following is NOT a good example of helping students make connections between the real world and mathematics?

    A. Studying a presidential election from the perspective of the math involved

    B. Using weather concepts to teach math

    C. Having student helpers take attendance

    D. Reviewing major mathematical theorems on a regular basis

(Easy) (Skill 14.10)

101. While teaching his class, Mr. Diaz asks Rebecca, a first grader, to answer a math question. After about 10 seconds, Rebecca answers the question correctly. Mr. Diaz has done a good job of:

    A. Reminding his students that he expects them to get the correct answer every time

    B. Employing a wait time strategy

    C. Hoping she will come up with the right answer eventually

    D. Utilizing the prompt and wait technique

(Rigorous) (Skill 15.2)

102. Which of the following is an example of the associative property?

    A. $a(b + c) = ab + bc$

    B. $a + b = 2a$

    C. $(a + b) + c = a + (b + c)$

    D. $a + b = b + a$

(Rigorous) (Skill 17.13)

103. Given similar polygons with corresponding sides measuring 6 inches and 8 inches, what is the area of the smaller polygon if the area of the larger is 64 in²?

    A. 48 in²

    B. 36 in²

    C. 144 in²

    D. 78 in²

(Rigorous) (Skill 19.1)

104. Mary did comparison shopping on her favorite brand of coffee. Over half of the stores priced the coffee at $1.70. Most of the remaining stores priced the coffee at $1.80, except for a few that charged $1.90.

    Which of the following statements is true about the distribution of prices?

    A. The mean and the mode are the same

    B. The mean is greater than the mode

    C. The mean is less than the mode

    D. The mean is less than the median

(Easy) (Skill 15.4)

105. What is the mode of the data in the following sample?

    9, 10, 11, 9, 10, 11, 9, 13

    A. 9

    B. 9.5

    C. 10

    D. 11

(Easy) (Skill 15.5)

106. Which of the following is correct?

    A. $2,365 > 2,340$

    B. $0.75 > 1.25$

    C. $\frac{3}{4} < \frac{1}{16}$

    D. $-5 < -6$

(Average) (Skill 16.10)

107. Choose the set in which the members are NOT equivalent.

    A. $\frac{1}{2}$, 0.5, 50%

    B. $\frac{10}{5}$, 2.0, 200%

    C. $\frac{3}{8}$, 0.385, 38.5%

    D. $\frac{7}{10}$, 0.7, 70%

(Easy) (Skill 15.3)

108. The digit 8 in the number 975.086 is in the:

    A. Tenths place

    B. Ones place

    C. Hundredths place

    D. Hundreds place

(Easy) (Skill 15.1)

109. The relations given below demonstrate the following addition and multiplication property of real numbers:

    $a + b = b + a$
    $ab = ba$

    A. Commutative

    B. Associative

    C. Identity

    D. Inverse

(Rigorous) (Skill 15.1)

110. $(3 \times 9)^4 =$

    A. $(3 \times 9)(3 \times 9)(27 \times 27)$

    B. $(3 \times 9) + (3 \times 9)$

    C. (12×36)

    D. $(3 \times 9) + (3 \times 9) + (3 \times 9) + (3 \times 9)$

(Average) (Skill 16.1)

111. Jason can run a distance of 50 yards in 6.5 seconds. At this rate, how many feet can he run in a time of 26 seconds?

    A. 200

    B. 400

    C. 600

    D. 800

(Rigorous) (Skill 16.1)

112. You are helping students list the steps needed to solve the word problem:

    "Mr. Jones is 5 times as old as his son. Two years later he will be 4 times as old as his son. How old is Mr. Jones?"

    One of the students makes the following list:

    1. Assume Mr. Jones' son is x years old. Express Mr. Jones' age in terms of x.

    2. Write how old they will be two years later in terms of x.

    3. Solve the equation for x.

    4. Multiply the answer by 5 to get Mr. Jones' age.

    What step is missing between steps 2 and 3?

    A. Write an equation setting Mr. Jones' age equal to 5 times his son's age

    B. Write an equation setting Mr. Jones' age two years later equal to 5 times his son's age two years later

    C. Write an equation setting Mr. Jones' age equal to 4 times his son's age

    D. Write an equation setting Mr. Jones' age two years later equal to 4 times his son's age two years later

(Easy) (Skill 15.1)

113. What is the next term in the following sequence?

    {0.005, 0.03, 0.18, 1.08...}

    A. 1.96

    B. 2.16

    C. 3.32

    D. 6.48

(Rigorous) (Skill 15.1)

114. A student has taken three tests in his algebra class for which the mean score is 88. He will take one more test and his final grade will be the mean of all four tests. He wants to achieve a final grade of 90. Which one of the following is the correct procedure to determine the score he needs on the fourth test?

    A. He needs a score 92 since $(88 + 92) \div 2 = 90$

    B. He needs a score of 89.5 since $(88 + 90 + 90 + 90) \div 4 = 89.5$

    C. He needs a score of 96 since $(88 + 88 + 88 + 96) \div 4 = 90$

    D. He cannot achieve a final grade of 90 since each of his scores on the first three tests is less than 90

(Average) (Skill 17.6)

115. Given similar polygons with corresponding sides of lengths 9 and 15, find the perimeter of the smaller polygon if the perimeter of the larger polygon is 150 units.

    A. 54

    B. 135

    C. 90

    D. 126

(Average) (Skill 19.1)

116. Which of the following statements best characterizes the meaning of "absolute value of x"?

    A. The square root of x

    B. The square of x

    C. The distance on a number line between x and $-x$

    D. The distance on a number line between 0 and x

(Average) (Skill 19.1)

117. Which of the following terms most accurately describes the set of numbers below?

    $$\{3, \sqrt{16}, \pi^0, 6, \tfrac{28}{4}\}$$

    A. Rationals

    B. Irrationals

    C. Complex

    D. Whole numbers

(Rigorous) (Skill 16.1)

118. What is the GCF of 12, 30, 56, and 144?

    A. 2

    B. 3

    C. 5

    D. 7

(Average) (Skill 16.6)

119. The final cost of an item (with sales tax) is $8.35. If the sales tax is 7%, what was the pre-tax price of the item?

    A. $7.80

    B. $8.00

    C. $8.28

    D. $8.93

(Rigorous) (Skill 16.7)

120. A burning candle loses $\frac{1}{2}$ inch in height every hour. If the original height of the candle was 6 inches, which of the following equations describes the relationship between the height h of the candle and the number of hours t since it was lit?

    A. $2h + t = 12$

    B. $2h - t = 12$

    C. $h = 6 - t$

    D. $h = 0.5t + 6$

(Rigorous) (Skill 16.10)

121. Which set cannot be considered "dense"?

    A. Integers

    B. Rationals

    C. Irrationals

    D. Reals

(Rigorous) (Skill 19.1)

122. In probability, the sample space represents:

    A. An outcome of an experiment

    B. A list of all possible outcomes of an experiment

    C. The number of times you must flip a coin

    D. The amount of room needed to conduct an experiment

Social Studies

(Average) (Skill 20.4)

123. **What is socialization?**

    A. The broad knowledge and thorough understanding of students' development

    B. The contribution of the family to a person's sense of self-importance and identity

    C. A person's sense of belonging developed through common ideals and behaviors

    D. The process by which humans learn the expectations society has for their behavior for them to function successfully within that society

(Rigorous) (Skill 20.5)

124. **All of the following are key elements in planning a child-centered curriculum EXCEPT:**

    A. Referring students who need special tutoring

    B. Identifying students' prior knowledge and skills

    C. Sequencing learning activities

    D. Specifying behavioral objectives

(Average) (Skill 20.6)

125. **Which of the following resources is required to make social studies more interesting to students and to appeal to different learning styles?**

    A. Audiovisual aids

    B. A good textbook

    C. Computers

    D. Library books and magazines

(Easy) (Skill 20.7)

126. **Which of the following is important for preparing resources and collecting data for research projects?**

    A. Identify the purpose of the research

    B. Specify the thesis

    C. Create folders for sorting the information

    D. Prepare visuals, such as poster boards

(Average) (Skill 20.8)

127. **Which of the following is the purpose of social participation in using social science skills and research tools?**

    A. Acquiring information

    B. Communicating information

    C. Tying together major themes

    D. Learning research methods

(Average) (Skill 20.11)

128. **The Texas Assessment of Knowledge and Skills (TAKS) test is an example of:**

    A. Criterion-referenced assessment

    B. Norm-referenced assessment

    C. Performance-based assessment

    D. Another type of assessment

(Average) (Skill 21.1)

129. **Which country established a fort at Matagorda Bay, providing the basis for that country's claim to the Texas territory?**

    A. France

    B. Spain

    C. United States

    D. Mexico

(Average) (Skill 21.2)

130. In what year was Texas annexed to the United States and made a state?

A. 1836

B. 1845

C. 1850

D. 1861

(Rigorous) (Skill 21.3)

131. Which was the earliest period that shows evidence of Native American civilization in Texas?

A. Early Archaic

B. Late Prehistoric

C. Upper Paleolithic

D. Late Archaic

(Easy) (Skill 21.4)

132. Which of the following statements about French settlement of Texas is INCORRECT?

A. The French wanted to open trade opportunities in the area

B. The French wanted to discover a route to the Mississippi River

C. The French wanted to expand the French empire in North America

D. The French settlement in Texas was long-lived

(Average) (Skill 21.5)

133. Which of the following statements about population centers is correct?

A. They tend to be away from agricultural areas

B. They tend to be relatively near one another

C. They tend to be far from smaller towns

D. They tend to achieve megalopolis standards

(Average) (Skill 21.8)

134. Which of the following statements about historic causation is INCORRECT?

A. Its root causes can be seen immediately

B. It is a concept about the events in history

C. Its premise is that events in history are linked

D. Events are linked by cause and effect

(Average) (Skill 21.9)

135. What is the study of the social behavior of groups of humans?

A. Anthropology

B. Psychology

C. Sociology

D. Cultural geography

(Rigorous) (Skills 21.10 and 21.11)

136. **For a historian studying ancient Egypt, which of the following would be LEAST useful?**

    A. The record of an ancient Greek historian on Greek–Egyptian interaction

    B. Letters from an Egyptian ruler to his or her regional governors

    C. Inscriptions on stele of the Fourteenth Dynasty of Egypt

    D. Letters from a nineteenth-century Egyptologist to his wife

(Easy) (Skill 21.12)

137. **Which of the following is a secondary source?**

    A. Objects made during the period being studied

    B. Objects used during the period being studied

    C. Statistical data on the period being studied

    D. Books created during the period being studied.

(Average) (Skill 21.13)

138. **Which statement is true about the problem-solving process?**

    A. The process provides limited opportunity for determining authenticity

    B. Collaboration develops the ability to work as part of a team

    C. Collaboration limits the viewpoints of others

    D. Statistical evaluation is not part of the problem-solving process

(Average) (Skill 21.14)

139. **Which of the following statements about the decision-making process is INCORRECT?**

    A. The first step in the decision-making process is to identify options

    B. Decision-making can be broken down into steps

    C. Using methodical steps results in sound decisions based on relevant facts

    D. Predicting consequences of a decision is an important step in the process

(Average) (Skill 21.16)

140. **African Americans moving to Texas during the Great Migration to search for better-paying jobs is an example of which element of history?**

    A. Politics

    B. Geography

    C. Gender

    D. Economic

(Average) (Skill 22.1)

141. **Which of the following is an example of the human characteristic of "place" in geography?**

    A. Mountains

    B. Canals

    C. Rivers

    D. Deserts

(Average) (Skills 22.1 and 22.2)

142. Which of the following oceans does NOT touch the shores of Antarctica?

A. Atlantic

B. Pacific

C. Indian

D. Arctic

(Average) (Skill 22.3)

143. Where are the vast plains of Texas located?

A. In the northern and western parts of the state

B. In the southern and eastern parts of the state

C. In the central and eastern parts of the state

D. In the central and western parts of the state

(Rigorous) (Skill 22.4)

144. Which of the following statements about the Gulf Stream is INCORRECT?

A. It is a cold current

B. It is a warm current

C. It is in the Atlantic Ocean

D. It was named by Benjamin Franklin

(Average) (Skill 22.5)

145. What is the greatest influence on land use?

A. Geography

B. Industries

C. Population

D. Agriculture

(Easy) (Skill 22.9)

146. What is the term for the introduction of new ways of performing work or organizing societies?

A. Cultural diffusion

B. Innovation

C. Adaptation

D. Acculturation

(Average) (Skill 22.10)

147. Which of the following statements about ethnicity is INCORRECT?

A. An ethnic group is a population of people from a common geographic area who share certain physical traits

B. Ethnic groups often have a common language and ancestral background and frequently exist within larger populations

C. Ethnicity is based more on common cultural behaviors and institutions than on common physical traits

D. Ethnicity and race sometimes are linked, but they differ because many ethnic groups can exist within a population of people considered to be of the same race

(Easy) (Skill 22.11)

148. Which of the following individuals led the movement to colonize the area of Texas as American?

A. Sam Houston

B. Curtis Graves

C. Stephen F. Austin

D. James Bowie

(Average) (Skill 22.13)

149. Which heritage is honored by the preservation of Ceremonial Cave in Texas?

    A. Asian

    B. Western European

    C. Eastern European

    D. Hispanic

(Average) (Skill 22.14)

150. All of the following terms describe characteristics of early human civilizations EXCEPT:

    A. Gatherers

    B. Agricultural

    C. Adaptable

    D. Hunters

(Rigorous) (Skill 22.15)

151. When did the pre-Columbian cultures reach their developmental peak in Texas?

    A. Before the arrival of European explorers

    B. After the arrival of European explorers

    C. Pre-Columbian cultures did not live in the area of present-day Texas

    D. After the groups became recognized by the federal government

(Average) (Skill 22.16)

152. Which of the following statements is true about beliefs and values?

    A. Values are things that are thought to be true

    B. Beliefs are what a society thinks is right and wrong

    C. A culture's beliefs and values are reflected in its cultural products

    D. Beliefs and values are unrelated

(Average) (Skill 22.17)

153. Which of the following statements is true about the concept of diversity?

    A. Diversity content discourages the use of ethnically diverse textbooks

    B. Diversity content discourages the use of curriculum activities

    C. One goal for teachers in teaching diversity is the pursuit of democracy

    D. Supplementary teaching materials diminish the importance of diversity teaching

(Average) (Skill 23.2)

154. Which economic term is defined as the value of the sacrificed alternative?

    A. Demand

    B. Opportunity cost

    C. Supply

    D. Free enterprise

(Rigorous) (Skill 23.3)

155. Which is NOT one of the five major economic activities identified in the TEKS glossary?

    A. Exchanging

    B. Saving

    C. Investing

    D. Marketing

(Easy) (Skill 23.4)

156. What is the basis for the cost of a resource?

    A. The scarcity of the resource

    B. The cost of production

    C. Consumer demand

    D. All of the above

(Average) (Skill 23.6)

157. **Why are economic activities less closely tied to particular locations as they were in the past?**

    A. There are fewer resources

    B. Towns that developed around a single economic activity no longer exist

    C. Modern transportation enables resources to be drawn from a wider area

    D. Economic activities continue to be as closely tied to particular locations as they were in the past

(Average) (Skill 24.2)

158. **What is the purpose of the conference committee?**

    A. It studies the bills presented in Congress

    B. It resolves differences between the House and Senate versions of bills

    C. It researches issues the bills present

    D. It sends bills to the president for the president's signature

(Easy) (Skill 24.2)

159. **What is the most basic form of participation in government?**

    A. Serving as an elected official

    B. Campaigning for candidates

    C. Serving on a jury

    D. Voting

(Rigorous) (Skill 24.3)

160. **Which Amendment to the U.S. Constitution prohibits cruel and unusual punishment?**

    A. Eighth

    B. Sixth

    C. Fifth

    D. First

(Average) (Skill 24.4)

161. **"Life, liberty, and the pursuit of happiness" are referred to in which document?**

    A. Magna Carta

    B. Bill of Rights

    C. Declaration of Independence

    D. Constitution

(Average) (Skill 24.5)

162. **Why did the Spanish begin to colonize Texas?**

    A. They wanted to build missions

    B. They wanted a route to the Mississippi River

    C. They were concerned about the French presence in Louisiana

    D. They wanted to remove the Native Americans from the area

(Average) (Skill 24.6)

163. **What is the basis of all laws in the United States?**

    A. The Supreme Court

    B. The Constitution

    C. Congress

    D. The president

Science

(Rigorous) (Skill 25.7)

164. Which of the following is equivalent to 200nm?

    A. 2 millimeters

    B. 2×10^{-7} meters

    C. 2×10^{-9} meters

    D. 20 centimeters

(Rigorous) (Skill 25.5)

165. Which of the following is NOT true about error?

    A. Systematic error can never be eliminated

    B. Percent error is calculated as the $100 \times$ (Observed − Expected)

    C. Random error can be due to the limitations in the precision of the measuring instrument

    D. An experiment can have a zero error

(Average) (Skill 26.1)

166. The scientific method relies on all but _____.

    A. gathering empirical evidence through testing

    B. manipulating logic and the experimental results

    C. reproducible experiments

    D. testing that relies on observation and measurement

(Average) (Skill 26.2)

167. Your student notices that two of his classmates arrive at school late every morning. He makes an educated guess and tells you that his classmates may oversleep. Which steps of the scientific method has your student completed?

    A. Forming a hypothesis and collecting data

    B. Asking a question and forming a hypothesis

    C. Asking and question and stating a conclusion

    D. Forming a hypothesis and stating a conclusion

(Rigorous) (Skill 26.2)

168. An experiment is performed to determine how the surface area of a liquid affects how long it takes for the liquid to evaporate. One hundred milliliters of water is put in containers with surface areas of 10 cm², 30 cm², 50 cm², 70 cm², and 90 cm². The time it took for each container to evaporate is recorded. Which of the following is a controlled variable?

    A. The time required for each evaporation

    B. The area of the surfaces

    C. The amount of water

    D. The temperature of the water

(Rigorous) (Skill 26.5)

169. Stars near Earth can be seen to move relative to fixed stars. In observing the motion of a nearby star over a period of decades, an astronomer notices that the path is not a straight line but wobbles about a straight line. The astronomer reports in a peer-reviewed journal that a planet is rotating around the star, causing it to wobble. Which of the following statements best describes the proposition that the star has a planet?

   A. Observation

   B. Hypothesis

   C. Theory

   D. Inference

(Rigorous) (Skill 26.4)

170. Your student is studying the effect of soda on plant growth and wants to run an experiment for one week. How should you advise your student to measure plant growth?

   A. Eyeball the growth over the course of the study

   B. Measure the height of the plant before the study starts and every day until the study's end

   C. Measure the height of the plant before adding soda and after one week

   D. Both B and C

(Easy) (Skill 26.5)

171. Your student runs an experiment and finds that a hair growth product increases the length of hair by one inch in a month. Assume that all control and treatment groups were created appropriately. What can you advise him to conclude?

   A. The experiment needs to be repeated

   B. The hair growth product doesn't work

   C. The hair growth product works

   D. There isn't enough information to form a conclusion

(Rigorous) (Skill 26.6)

172. Your student performs a survey to find out why some students excel on your quizzes. She finds that most successful students state that they study more, but she also considers that some students also have tutors or get good sleep before quiz days. How do you advise your student to evaluate these possibilities?

   A. Have her randomly select students and assign them to either study more, get a tutor, or get a good night's sleep before quiz day. Then measure quiz performance.

   B. Have her randomly select students and assign them to either study more, get a tutor, get a good night's sleep before quiz day, or not do any of these three things. Then measure quiz performance.

   C. Have her evaluate according to her opinions.

   D. She doesn't need to evaluate these possibilities.

(Average) (Skill 26.5)

173. A determination reached on the basis of one experiment's evidence and reasoning is a/an _____.

   A. theory

   B. justification

   C. inference

   D. law

(Easy) (Skill 26.8)

174. How can students communicate their experiments?

   A. PowerPoint presentation

   B. Poster

   C. Reports

   D. All of the above

(Average) (Skill 26.9)

175. Which of the following is NOT an unethical action?

   A. Letting one's biases affect the inclusion of human participants in a study

   B. "Fudging" data to make it fit the desired result

   C. Making up experimental results

   D. Sharing an established experimental protocol with a labmate

(Rigorous) (Skill 26.10)

176. Which of the following is true when a new theory is developed regarding a topic?

   A. The existing theories on the topic could be altered/adjusted upon proof

   B. The new theory should just be accepted

   C. The new theory should not be even considered

   D. Both the new and old theories should be debated and a vote taken on which one to accept

(Average) (Skill 26.11)

177. Which famous scientist is NOT matched with his work?

   A. Galileo Galilei—discovered Jupiter's four largest satellites

   B. Isaac Newton—created calculus

   C. Thomas Edison—improved carbon light bulb filament

   D. Albert Einstein—created theory of relativity

(Rigorous) (Skill 27.5)

178. Which of the following is the most accurate definition of a nonrenewable resource?

   A. A nonrenewable resource is never replaced once used

   B. A nonrenewable resource is replaced on a time scale that is very long relative to human life spans

   C. A nonrenewable resource is a resource that can only be manufactured by humans

   D. A nonrenewable resource is a species that has already become extinct

(Average) (Skill 28.3)

179. All of the following are hormones in the human body EXCEPT:

    A. Cortisol

    B. Testosterone

    C. Norepinephrine

    D. Hemoglobin

(Rigorous) (Skill 29.4)

180. There are a number of common misconceptions that claim to be based in science. All of the following are misconceptions EXCEPT:

    A. Evolution is a process that does not address the origins of life

    B. The average person uses only a small fraction of his or her brain

    C. Raw sugar causes hyperactive behavior in children

    D. Seasons are caused by the Earth's elliptical orbit

(Rigorous) (Skill 31.1)

181. Which of the following does NOT determine the frictional force of a box sliding down a ramp?

    A. The weight of the box

    B. The area of the box

    C. The angle the ramp makes with the horizontal

    D. The chemical properties of the two surfaces

(Average) (Skill 31.3)

182. Force is measured in _____.

    A. watts

    B. amperes

    C. newtons

    D. meters/second

(Rigorous) (Skill 31.3)

183. An object's _____ indicates how hard it would be to stop its motion.

    A. momentum

    B. potential energy

    C. kinetic energy

    D. mass

(Rigorous) (Skill 32.1)

184. Which of the following statements about the density of a substance is true?

    A. It is a chemical property

    B. It has no units

    C. It is an intensive property

    D. It is ten times the specific gravity of a substance

(Average) (Skill 32.3)

185. The electrons in a neutral atom that are not in an excited energy state are in various energy shells. For example, there are two electrons in the lowest energy shell and eight in the next shell if the atom contains more than 10 electrons. How many electrons are in the shell with the maximum number of electrons?

    A. 8

    B. 18

    C. 32

    D. 44

(Rigorous) (Skill 32.5)

186. Which of the following is NOT an example of a mixture?

    A. Soil

    B. Air

    C. Ocean water

    D. H_2O

(Rigorous) (Skill 32.1)

187. Which statement best explains why a balance scale is used to measure both weight and mass?

    A. The weight and mass of an object are identical concepts

    B. The force of gravity between two objects depends on the mass of the two objects

    C. Inertial mass and gravitational mass are identical

    D. A balance scale compares the weight of two objects

(Average) (Skill 33.2)

188. Which statement is true about temperature?

    A. Temperature is a measurement of heat

    B. Temperature is how hot or cold an object is

    C. The coldest temperature ever measured is zero degrees Kelvin

    D. The temperature of a molecule is its kinetic energy

(Rigorous) (Skill 33.2)

189. When glass is heated, it becomes softer and softer until it becomes a liquid. Which of the following statements best describes this phenomenon?

    A. Glass has no heat of vaporization

    B. Glass has no heat of fusion

    C. The latent heat of glass is zero calories per gram

    D. Glass is made up of crystals

(Easy) (Skill 33.1)

190. Which statement could be described as the first law of thermodynamics?

    A. No machine can convert heat energy to work with 100 percent efficiency

    B. Energy is neither created nor destroyed

    C. Thermometers can be used to measure temperatures

    D. Heat flows from hot objects to cold objects

(Average) (Skill 34.1)

191. What kind of chemical reaction is the burning of coal?

    A. Exothermic and composition

    B. Exothermic and decomposition

    C. Endothermic and composition

    D. Exothermic and decomposition

(Average) (Skill 34.3)

192. Which of the following is a result of a nuclear reaction called fusion?

A. Sunlight

B. Cosmic radiation

C. Supernova

D. Existence of the elements in the periodic table

(Easy) (Skill 35.4)

193. Which of the following processes and packages macromolecules?

A. Lysosome

B. Cytosol

C. Golgi apparatus

D. Plastid

(Average) (Skill 35.1)

194. Which of the following is a property of both eukaryotes and prokaryotes?

A. Nucleus

B. Ribosomes

C. Chromosomes

D. Mitochondria

(Average) (Skill 35.4)

195. At what stage in mitosis does the chromatin become chromosomes?

A. Telophase

B. Anaphase

C. Prophase

D. Metaphase

(Average) (Skill 35.6)

196. Which of the following is not the correct match of an Animalia phylum with examples of organisms found within the phylum?

A. Arthropoda—spiders and insects

B. Echinodermata—sea urchins and starfish

C. Mollusca—clams and octopi

D. Annelida—crustaceans

(Average) (Skill 35.6)

197. Taxonomy classifies species into genera (plural of genus) based on similarities. Species are subordinate to genera. The most general or highest taxonomical group is the kingdom. Which of the following is the correct order of the other groups from highest to lowest?

A. Class $\Rightarrow$ order $\Rightarrow$ family $\Rightarrow$ phylum

B. Phylum $\Rightarrow$ class $\Rightarrow$ family $\Rightarrow$ order

C. Phylum $\Rightarrow$ class $\Rightarrow$ order $\Rightarrow$ family

D. Order $\Rightarrow$ phylum $\Rightarrow$ class $\Rightarrow$ family

(Average) (Skill 36.3)

198. Meiosis starts with two cells ends with which of the following?

A. Four diploid cells

B. Four haploid cells

C. Eight diploid cells

D. Eight haploid cells

(Rigorous) (Skill 37.1)

199. Which of the following is NOT part of Darwinian evolution?

   A. Survival of the fittest

   B. Random mutations

   C. Heritability of acquired traits

   D. Natural selection

(Easy) (Skill 37.3)

200. In _____, advantageous traits lead to species survival and reproduction over time.

   A. natural selection

   B. sexual selection

   C. codominance

   D. artificial selection

(Easy) (Skill 38.2)

201. Which of the following describes the interaction between community members when one species feeds on another species but does not kill it immediately?

   A. Parasitism

   B. Predation

   C. Commensalism

   D. Mutualism

(Average) (Skill 38.4)

202. Which of the following is NOT a type of organismal behavior?

   A. Competition

   B. Mating

   C. Territoriality

   D. Phototrophism

(Easy) (Skill 39.1)

203. Which is the correct order for the layers of Earth's atmosphere, from lowest to highest?

   A. Troposphere, stratosphere, mesosphere, and thermosphere

   B. Mesosphere, stratosphere, troposphere, and thermosphere

   C. Troposphere, stratosphere, thermosphere, and mesosphere

   D. Thermosphere, troposphere, stratosphere, mesosphere

(Rigorous) (Skill 39.1)

204. Which of the following is NOT true about the lithosphere's plates?

   A. When two plates move towards each other, the process is called convergence

   B. When two plates move away from each other, the process is called divergence

   C. Plates move meters per year on average

   D. Subduction is the process in which an oceanic plate slides under a continental plate, resulting in the formation of an oceanic trench

(Easy) (Skill 16.1)

205. What type of rock can be classified by the size of its crystals?

   A. Metamorphic

   B. Igneous

   C. Minerals

   D. Sedimentary

(Average) (Skill 40.1)

206. What are solids with a definite chemical composition and a tendency to split along planes of weakness?

   A. Ores

   B. Rocks

   C. Minerals

   D. Salts

(Easy) (Skill 40.1)

207. In which of the following eras did life first appear?

   A. Paleozoic

   B. Mesozoic

   C. Cenozoic

   D. Precambrian

(Rigorous) (Skill 40.1)

208. Which of the following is NOT true about dating techniques?

   A. When using the principle of superposition, a bed of sedimentary rock is considered older than the bed below it

   B. Fossils found in the same bed of sedimentary rock can be assumed to have lived in the same time period

   C. Absolute dating measures the amount of radioactive material in a specimen

   D. Index fossils are used to identify geologic periods

(Average) (Skill 40.4)

209. _____ is the transport of a rock's surface materials by another moveable material.

   A. Erosion

   B. Weathering

   C. Deposition

   D. Wearing

(Average) (Skill 40.4)

210. When continental plates move as a result of sudden energy release and seismic wave formation in the Earth's crust, _____ occurs.

   A. volcano formation

   B. mountain building

   C. cementation

   D. an earthquake

(Easy) (Skill 42.2)

211. There are _____ established planets in the solar system.

   A. ten

   B. nine

   C. eight

   D. seven

(Average) (Skill 42.1)

212. Interactions between _____ and _____ are responsible for the ocean tides.

   A. the Earth; the moon

   B. the Earth; the sun

   C. the moon; the sun

   D. the moon; Mercury

(Rigorous) (Skills 41.5)

213. **Why is the winter in the Southern Hemisphere colder than winter in the Northern Hemisphere?**

    A. Earth's axis of 24-hour rotation tilts at an angle of $23\frac{1}{2}°$

    B. The elliptical orbit of Earth around the sun changes the distance of the sun from Earth

    C. The Southern Hemisphere has more water than the Northern Hemisphere

    D. The greenhouse effect is greater for the Northern Hemisphere

(Rigorous) (Skill 42.3)

214. **Which of the following astronomical entities is NOT part of the galaxy the sun is located in?**

    A. Nebulae

    B. Quasars

    C. Pulsars

    D. Neutron stars

(Rigorous) (Skill 42.2)

215. **Which of the following facts of physics does NOT explain the cause of tides?**

    A. The density of water is less than the density of rock

    B. The force of gravity follows the inverse square law

    C. Centripetal acceleration causes water on Earth to bulge

    D. The gravitational force of the moon on Earth's oceans

Fine Arts, Health, and Physical Education

(Easy) (Skill 43.1)

216. **You want to expose your students to the visual arts as a profession. Which is the best example of an appropriate activity?**

    A. Spoken word concert

    B. A visit to the orchestra

    C. A live painting session

    D. A Shakespeare play

(Rigorous) (Skill 43.2)

217. **Which of the following is true about linear perspective?**

    A. Objects appear smaller the closer they are

    B. Objects appear larger the farther away they are

    C. There is a convergence point along the horizon of the drawing

    D. Only the space and distance of objects relative to the reference point are shown

(Easy) (Skill 43.4)

218. **The process of critiquing artwork is _____.**

    A. an asset for all teachers

    B. beyond the scope of the elementary teacher

    C. fairly complex and requires specific training

    D. limited to art historians and professional artists

(Easy) (Skill 43.5)

219. _____ is a mark that follows an identifiable path.

A. An impression

B. A line

C. A point

D. A shape

(Rigorous) (Skill 43.7)

220. **All of the following are examples of useful art tools for early childhood students EXCEPT:**

A. A color wheel

B. Oversized crayons and pencils

C. Fine-tipped brushes

D. Clay

(Average) (Skill 43.8)

221. **The Renaissance period was concerned with the rediscovery of the works of _____.**

A. Italy

B. Japan

C. Germany

D. classical Greece and Rome

(Rigorous) (Skill 43.9)

222. **Which of the following correctly describes Western and Eastern art?**

A. Western art is more spiritual; Eastern is more secular in nature

B. Western art focuses on accurately portraying human anatomy

C. Eastern art focuses on muscle tone in depictions of the human body

D. Eastern art requires a horizontal projection of eye movement

(Rigorous) (Skill 43.15)

223. **Which of the following statements is most accurate?**

A. Most artists work alone and are rarely affected by the work of other artists

B. Artists in every field are influenced and inspired by the works of others in the various disciplines in the humanities

C. It is rare for visual arts to be influenced by literature or poetry

D. The political climate of an era affects the art of the period only on specific occasions throughout history

(Average) (Skill 43.8)

224. **Which theme or style is NOT matched with its correct century?**

A. Impressionism—19th century

B. Baroque—17th century

C. Futurism—19th century

D. Expressionism—20th century

(Easy) (Skill 44.1)

225. **You want to expose your students to music. What are potential in-class activities?**

A. A lesson using a digital music-making platform (e.g., PBS, LiveBinders)

B. A kids-themed concert

C. A field trip to the orchestra

D. Both B and C

(Rigorous) (Skill 44.2)

226. **Which of the following is true about music notation?**

  A. The lower clef is the treble

  B. The clef is a four-line staff

  C. The pitch of note is how long it is held

  D. Dotted ties indicate the duration of a note

(Average) (Skill 44.2)

227. **A combination of three or more tones sounded at the same time is called a** _____.

  A. harmony

  B. consonance

  C. chord

  D. dissonance

(Easy) (Skill 44.3)

228. **Which pair is correct?**

  A. Drum—string instrument

  B. Tuba—brass instrument

  C. Trumpet—percussion instrument

  D. Cello—woodwind instrument

(Rigorous) (Skill 44.3)

229. **A piano is a** _____ **instrument.**

  A. percussion and brass

  B. brass and string

  C. string

  D. percussion and string

(Rigorous) (Skill 44.3)

230. **Music arrangement can be taught to elementary students in all of the following ways except** _____.

  A. incorporating instruments with different key signatures

  B. adding harmonies to simple melodies

  C. deep study of musical theory

  D. changing the key of the song

(Average) (Skill 44.7)

231. **The term** *conjunto* **in music refers to:**

  A. Two instruments playing at the same time

  B. A tempo a little faster than allegro

  C. A musical style that involves playing with great feeling

  D. A type of Texas-Mexican music

(Rigorous) (Skill 44.8)

232. **All of the following apply to critiquing music EXCEPT:**

  A. Listening, analyzing, describing, and evaluating

  B. Avoiding the use of musical terminology in order to facilitate students' enjoyment of music

  C. Having students develop their own rubrics for critiques

  D. Encouraging students to work in pairs

(Average) (Skill 45.1)

233. **Behavioral change should be** _____.

  A. externally motivated

  B. internally motivated

  C. both internally and externally motivated

  D. None of the above

(Average) (Skill 45.1)

234. **Behavioral changes _____.**

   A. take time to take effect

   B. should have a positive impact

   C. have to be sustained by the student

   D. All of the above

(Easy) (Skill 45.2)

235. **Which of the following is NOT a type of muscle tissue?**

   A. Skeletal

   B. Cardiac

   C. Smooth

   D. Fiber

(Rigorous) (Skill 45.2)

236. **Which of the following does NOT describe atherosclerosis?**

   A. Plaques form in blood vessels

   B. Red blood cells change shape and "stick" to blood vessel walls

   C. Strokes can occur as a result of plaque formation

   D. Arteries harden as a result of plaque formation

(Average) (Skill 45.2)

237. **Which is NOT a characteristic of veins?**

   A. They have valves that ensure unidirectional flow of blood

   B. They have thin walls

   C. As they approach the heart, their size increases

   D. They have very elastic walls

(Rigorous) (Skill 45.2)

238. **Which of the following produces the least amount of energy in the body?**

   A. Carbohydrates

   B. Oils

   C. Proteins

   D. Fats

(Rigorous) (Skill 45.2)

239. **Which of the following substances is one least likely to find in urine?**

   A. Uric acid

   B. Ammonia

   C. Glucose

   D. Sodium chloride

(Rigorous) (Skill 45.2)

240. **What is the main reason that humans cannot digest cellulose?**

   A. It does not contain sugars and thus cannot be digested by humans

   B. Its protein chains are too long

   C. It is made up of monosaccharides and thus cannot be digested by humans

   D. Humans lack the proper enzymes to digest cellulose

(Rigorous) (Skill 45.2)

241. **Which of the following statements is true about joints?**

   A. They occur where bones intersect

   B. They occur where organs begin

   C. They occur where muscles attach to the skeleton

   D. They occur where ligaments meet tendons

(Average) (Skill 45.2)

242. **Which disease is NOT correctly matched with the body system it primarily affects?**

    A. Diabetes—nervous system

    B. Heart disease—circulatory system

    C. Appendicitis—digestive system

    D. Hyperthyroidism—endocrine system

(Average) (Skill 45.2)

243. **What is the importance of roughage in a balanced diet?**

    A. It promotes peristalsis in the gut

    B. It enhances food absorption in the body

    C. It promotes bile production

    D. It activates enzymes in the gut

(Rigorous) (Skill 45.4)

244. **Of the following, which is the leading cause of preventable death in the United States?**

    A. Distracted driving

    B. Infectious disease

    C. Sedentary lifestyle

    D. Tobacco use

(Rigorous) (Skill 45.4)

245. **HIV/AIDS is a viral disease that has rocked many nations. Which of the following factors has NOT contributed to the persistence of the viral infection?**

    A. Evading immune responses

    B. Irresponsible sex behavior

    C. Lack of education about HIV/AIDS

    D. Sharing the same living quarters

(Average) (Skill 45.6)

246. **A physical education instructor anticipates and prevents potential injuries, watches for hidden injuries, and takes an injury evaluation of the entire class. Which of the following strategies to prevent injuries is the teacher demonstrating?**

    A. Maintaining hiring standards

    B. Proper use of equipment

    C. Proper procedures for emergencies

    D. Participant screening

(Average) (Skill 45.9)

247. **All of the following are signs of anorexia nervosa EXCEPT:**

    A. Malnutrition

    B. Behavior regression

    C. No outward signs

    D. Recognizable weight loss

(Average) (Skill 45.14)

248. **By displaying food product labels and discussing how to choose common healthy foods, Mrs. Watkins is helping her students to _____.**

    A. make positive health-related decisions

    B. understand how real-world concepts apply to health choices

    C. be active learners in their decision-making processes

    D. All of the above

(Rigorous) (Skill 46.1)

249. Which of the following refers to a muscle's ability to contract over a period of time and maintain strength?

   A. Cardiovascular fitness

   B. Muscle endurance

   C. Muscle fitness

   D. Muscle force

(Average) (Skill 46.4)

250. A game of "Simon Says" is an opportunity for the teacher to assess students' _____.

   A. concept of body awareness

   B. concept of spatial awareness

   C. concept of direction and movement

   D. concept of speed and movement

(Average) (Skill 46.5)

251. Bending, stretching, and turning are examples of which type of skill?

   A. Locomotor skills

   B. Nonlocomotor skills

   C. Manipulative skills

   D. Rhythmic skills

(Rigorous) (Skill 46.5)

252. Which of the following is NOT true about physical skills?

   A. An activity to develop galloping skill is playing Fox and Hound

   B. Run-and-catch is an object-control skill

   C. Manipulative skills only propel an object

   D. Rhythmic skills involve motion that follows a beat

(Average) (Skill 46.7)

253. What is the proper sequential order of development for the acquisition of nonlocomotor skills?

   A. Stretch, sit, bend, turn, swing, twist, shake, rock and sway, dodge, fall

   B. Bend, stretch, turn, twist, swing, sit, rock and sway, shake, dodge, fall

   C. Stretch, bend, sit, shake, turn, rock and sway, swing, twist, dodge, fall

   D. Bend, stretch, sit, turn, twist, swing, sway, rock and sway, dodge, fall

(Average) (Skill 46.10)

254. _____ grouping can increase student participation and engagement.

   A. Student-led

   B. Heterogeneous

   C. Homogeneous

   D. Both B and C

(Rigorous) (Skill 46.11)

255. Which of the following statements is NOT true?

   A. Children's motor development and physical fitness are affected by a range of factors, including social, psychological, familial, genetic, and cultural factors

   B. Motor development is complete by the time a student reaches sixth grade

   C. A family's economic status can affect a student's motor development

   D. A physical education program can have a positive impact on a student's level of physical fitness

(Easy) (Skill 47.1)

256. In a play, these performers often have a few lines, but perform as one complete group:

    A. Choir

    B. Chorus

    C. Grand opera

    D. Theatrical band

(Rigorous) (Skill 47.4)

257. As a way to incorporate other subjects into the area of theatre, a teacher should choose to _____.

    A. direct a play related to the students' current interests

    B. collaborate with the principal to find a script to use

    C. plan to create a play using a Social Studies topic that was taught last year

    D. create a unit plan based on reading, math, Social Studies, and theatre concepts that focuses on the story of the first Thanksgiving

(Average) (Skill 47.5)

258. A goal of theatre is to _____.

    A. promote confidence

    B. promote expression

    C. deliver entertainment

    D. All of the above

(Rigorous) (Skill 47.9)

259. A teacher planning a preschool class production should _____.

    A. use any available space

    B. ensure that there is an adequate amount of time to practice

    C. allow the students to run the entire show

    D. ask each student if he or she wants to participate or not

(Easy) (Skill 47.2)

260. Which materials would help your students connect with the characters in a play?

    A. Costumes

    B. Props

    C. Music

    D. All of the above

(Average) (Skill 47.3)

261. Which pair is incorrect?

    A. Chorus—character or group that says the prologue

    B. Soliloquy—extended speech

    C. Epilogue—opening words for play

    D. All of the above

(Average) (Skill 47.3)

262. Which of the following stage elements is correct?

    A. Down-stage—area furthest from audience

    B. Stage left—audience's right

    C. Stage right—actor's (when facing audience) left

    D. Travelers—curtains on the wings of the stage

(Rigorous) (Skill 47.3)

263. **Which of the following is incorrect about these elements of theater?**

    A. Actors never break the "Fourth Wall"

    B. Intermissions give the audience a break

    C. The audience employs suspension of disbelief.

    D. Gaffers operate lighting for the production

(Easy) (Skill 47.3)

264. **To _____ is to deliver lines with feelings appropriate to the scene.**

    A. engage

    B. speak

    C. emote

    D. recite

(Easy) (Skill 47.7)

265. **The Shakespeare play based on the tragic circumstances for two young lovers is _____.**

    A. *Taming of the Shrew*

    B. *Othello*

    C. *The Merchant of Venice*

    D. *Romeo and Juliet*

(Average) (Skill 47.7)

266. **Which pair is incorrect?**

    A. Exposition—straightforward speech or discussion

    B. Irony—a contradiction between what the character thinks and what the audience knows to be the truth

    C. Tragedy—death of a main character

    D. Comedy—appeals to audience's humor

Answer Key

1. D	31. D	61. B	91. D	121. A	151. A	181. B	211. C	241. A
2. D	32. A	62. A	92. C	122. B	152. C	182. C	212. A	242. A
3. D	33. D	63. C	93. A	123. D	153. C	183. A	213. B	243. A
4. A	34. B	64. B	94. D	124. A	154. B	184. C	214. B	244. D
5. C	35. C	65. A	95. A	125. B	155. D	185. C	215. A	245. D
6. A	36. B	66. A	96. D	126. C	156. D	186. D	216. C	246. D
7. D	37. C	67. B	97. D	127. C	157. C	187. C	217. C	247. C
8. C	38. D	68. A	98. B	128. B	158. B	188. B	218. A	248. D
9. D	39. B	69. B	99. C	129. A	159. D	189. B	219. B	249. B
10. B	40. A	70. C	100. D	130. B	160. A	190. B	220. C	250. A
11. A	41. C	71. C	101. B	131. C	161. C	191. A	221. D	251. B
12. A	42. B	72. B	102. C	132. D	162. C	192. D	222. B	252. C
13. B	43. A	73. A	103. B	133. B	163. B	193. C	223. B	253. C
14. A	44. A	74. B	104. B	134. A	164. B	194. B	224. C	254. D
15. A	45. B	75. C	105. A	135. C	165. C	195. C	225. A	255. B
16. A	46. B	76. A	106. A	136. D	166. B	196. D	226. D	256. B
17. B	47. D	77. D	107. C	137. C	167. B	197. C	227. C	257. D
18. D	48. C	78. D	108. C	138. B	168. C	198. D	228. B	258. D
19. A	49. C	79. C	109. A	139. A	169. D	199. C	229. D	259. B
20. C	50. A	80. C	110. A	140. D	170. D	200. A	230. C	260. D
21. C	51. A	81. B	111. C	141. B	171. C	201. A	231. D	261. C
22. C	52. B	82. A	112. D	142. D	172. B	202. D	232. B	262. B
23. A	53. A	83. A	113. D	143. D	173. C	203. A	233. C	263. A
24. A	54. A	84. B	114. C	144. A	174. D	204. C	234. D	264. C
25. D	55. A	85. D	115. C	145. C	175. D	205. B	235. D	265. D
26. B	56. C	86. D	116. D	146. B	176. A	206. C	236. B	266. B
27. A	57. A	87. D	117. D	147. A	177. C	207. D	237. D	
28. C	58. C	88. B	118. A	148. C	178. B	208. A	238. C	
29. A	59. C	89. A	119. A	149. D	179. D	209. A	239. C	
30. B	60. A	90. B	120. A	150. B	180. A	210. D	240. D	

Rigor Table

RIGOR	QUESTIONS
Easy 20%	2, 16, 26, 34, 37, 40, 41, 44, 55, 59, 63, 65, 71, 78, 82, 94, 96, 98, 99, 101, 105, 106, 108, 109, 113, 126, 132, 137, 146, 148, 156, 159, 171, 174, 190, 193, 200, 201, 203, 205, 207, 211, 216, 218, 219, 225, 228, 235, 256, 260, 264, 265
Average 45%	1, 6, 8, 9, 12, 14, 18, 28, 29, 31, 33, 38, 43, 45, 46, 47, 48, 51, 52, 53, 54, 58, 60, 62, 66, 68, 72, 73, 77, 80, 81, 83, 84, 85, 86, 87, 88, 89, 90, 91, 92, 93, 95, 97, 100, 107, 111, 115, 116, 117, 119, 123, 125, 127, 128, 129, 130, 133, 134, 135, 138, 139, 140, 141, 142, 143, 145, 147, 149, 150, 152, 153, 154, 157, 158, 161, 162, 163, 166, 167, 173, 175, 177, 179, 182, 185, 188, 191, 192, 194, 195, 196, 197, 198, 202, 206, 209, 210, 212, 221, 224, 227, 231, 233, 234, 237, 242, 243, 246, 247, 248, 250, 251, 253, 254, 258, 261, 262, 266
Rigorous 35%	3, 4, 5, 7, 10, 11, 13, 15, 17, 19, 20, 21, 22, 23, 24, 25, 27, 30, 32, 35, 36, 39, 42, 49, 50, 56, 57, 61, 64, 67, 69, 70, 74, 75, 76, 79, 102, 103, 104, 110, 112, 114, 118, 120, 121, 122, 124, 131, 136, 144, 151, 155, 160, 164, 165, 168, 169, 170, 172, 176, 178, 180, 181, 183, 184, 186, 187, 189, 199, 204, 208, 213, 214, 215, 217, 220, 222, 223, 226, 229, 230, 232, 236, 238, 239, 240, 241, 244, 245, 249, 252, 255, 257, 259, 263

Questions with Rationales

English Language Arts

(Average) (Skill 1.1)

1. While standing in line at the grocery store, three-year-old Megan says to her mother in a regular tone of voice, "Mom, why is that woman so fat?" What does this indicate a lack of understanding of?

   A. Syntax

   B. Semantics

   C. Morphology

   D. Pragmatics

   Answer: D. Pragmatics

   Pragmatics is the development and understanding of social relevance to conversations and topics. It develops as children age. In this situation, Megan simply does not understand, as an adult would, how that question could be viewed as offensive.

(Easy) (Skill 1.4)

2. Oral language development can be enhanced by which of the following?

   A. Meaningful conversation

   B. Storytelling

   C. Alphabet songs

   D. All of the above

   Answer: D. All of the above

Effective oral language development can be encouraged by many different activities including storytelling, rhyming books, meaningful conversation, alphabet songs, dramatic playtime, listening games, and more.

(Rigorous) (Skill 1.5)

3. Ms. Chomski is presenting a new story to her class of first graders. In the story, a family visits their grandparents, where they all gather around a record player and listen to music. Many students do not understand what a record player is, especially some children for whom English is not their first language. Which of the following would be best for Ms. Chomski to do?

   A. Discuss what a record player is with her students

   B. Compare a record player with a CD player and an mp3 player

   C. Have students look up *record player* in a dictionary

   D. Show the students a picture of a record player

   Answer: D. Show the students a picture of a record player

The most effective method for ensuring adequate comprehension is through direct experience. Sometimes this cannot be accomplished; therefore, it is necessary to utilize pictures or other visual aids to provide students with experience in a mode other than oral language.

(Rigorous) (Skill 1.7)

4. **Reading aloud correlates with all of the following EXCEPT:**

   A. Reader self-confidence

   B. Better reading comprehension

   C. Literacy development

   D. Overall school success

Answer: A. Reader self-confidence

Reading aloud promotes language acquisition and correlates with literacy development, better reading comprehension, and overall success in school. It may or may not promote reader self-confidence, depending on the reader and his or her skills and personality.

(Rigorous) (Skill 1.10)

5. **Mr. Johns is using an activity that involves having students analyze the public speaking of others. All of the following would be included in the guidelines for this activity EXCEPT:**

   A. The speeches to be evaluated are not given by other students

   B. The rubric for evaluating the speeches includes pace, pronunciation, body language, word choice, and visual aids

   C. The speeches to be evaluated are best presented live to give students a more engaging learning experience

   D. One of Mr. Johns's goals with this activity is to help students improve their own public speaking skills

Answer: C. The speeches to be evaluated are best presented live to give students a more engaging learning experience

Analyzing the speech of others is an excellent technique for helping students improve their own public speaking abilities. In most circumstances, students cannot view themselves as they give speeches and presentations, so when they get the opportunity to critique, question, and analyze others' speeches, they begin to learn what works and what doesn't work in effective public speaking. However, an important word of warning: do not have students critique one another's public speaking skills. It could be very damaging to a student to have his or her peers point out what did not work in a speech. Instead, video is a great tool teachers can use. Any appropriate source of public speaking can be used in the classroom for students to analyze and critique.

(Average) (Skill 2.1)

6. **All of the following are true about phonological awareness EXCEPT:**

   A. It may involve print

   B. It is a prerequisite for spelling and phonics

   C. Children can do the activities with their eyes closed

   D. It starts before letter recognition is taught

Answer: A. It may involve print

All of the options are aspects of phonological awareness except A, because phonological awareness does not involve print.

(Rigorous) (Skill 2.2)

7. **Which of the following explains a significant difference between phonics and phonemic awareness?**

    A. Phonics involves print, while phonemic awareness involves language

    B. Phonics is harder than phonemic awareness

    C. Phonics involves sounds, while phonemic awareness involves letters

    D. Phonics is the application of sounds to print, while phonemic awareness is oral

    Answer: D. Phonics is the application of sounds to print, while phonemic awareness is oral

    Both phonics and phonemic awareness involve sounds, but phonics applies these sounds to print. Phonemic awareness is an oral activity.

(Average) (Skill 2.3)

8. **Theorist Marilyn Jager Adams, who researches early reading, has outlined five basic types of phonemic awareness tasks. Which of the following is NOT one of the tasks noted by Jager Adams?**

    A. Ability to do oddity tasks

    B. Ability to orally blend words and split syllables

    C. Ability to sound out words when reading aloud

    D. Ability to do phonics manipulation tasks

Answer: C. Ability to sound out words when reading aloud

The tasks Jager Adams has outlined do not include the ability to sound out words when reading aloud. Her five tasks are: 1) The ability to hear rhymes and alliteration; 2) The ability to do oddity tasks (recognize the member of a set that is different, or odd, among the group); 3) The ability to orally blend words and split syllables; 4) The ability to orally segment words; and 5) The ability to do phonics manipulation tasks.

(Average) (Skill 2.6)

9. **Activities that parents can practice at home to improve phonological and phonemic awareness include which of the following?**

    A. Play games with words that sound alike as you experience them in everyday home activities

    B. Demonstrate how sounds blend together in familiar words

    C. Play a game in which the goal is to find objects with names that begin with a certain initial sound

    D. All of the above

    Answer: D. All of the above

    Games and demonstrations that help children focus on distinguishing sounds are all useful in improving phonological and phonemic awareness.

(Rigorous) (Skill 3.1)

10. **Which of the following statements best describes the alphabetic principle?**

    A. Most reading skills need to be acquired through a regular teaching of the alphabet

    B. Written words are composed of patterns of letters that represent the sounds of spoken words

    C. Written words are composed of patterns that must be memorized to read well

    D. Spoken words (regular and irregular) lead to phonological reading

    Answer: B. Written words are composed of patterns of letters that represent the sounds of spoken words

    The alphabetic principle is sometimes called graphophonemic awareness. This technical reading foundation term describes the understanding that written words are composed of patterns of letters that represent the sounds of spoken words. There are two parts to the alphabetic principle: 1) An understanding that words are made up of letters and that each letter has a specific sound, and 2) The correspondence between sounds and letters leads to phonological reading. This consists of reading regular and irregular words and doing advanced analysis of words.

(Rigorous) (Skill 3.3)

11. **Which of the following is NOT true about multisensory approaches to teaching the alphabetic principle?**

    A. Some children can only learn through multisensory techniques

    B. Multisensory techniques give multiple cues to enhance memory and learning

    C. Quilt book, rhyme time, letter path, and shape game are multisensory strategies

    D. Multisensory techniques require direct teaching and ongoing engagement

    Answer: A. Some children can only learn through multisensory techniques

    Although some children may learn more effectively when multiple senses are involved, there is no evidence to suggest that this is the only way some students can learn. Multisensory techniques enhance learning and memory and provide solid grounding for when students later learn to apply phonics skills to print. Such activities demand teacher engagement with students to directly teach the concepts related to the alphabetic principle.

(Average) (Skill 3.4)

12. **Activities that facilitate learning the alphabetic principle include:**

    A. Read alouds, alphabet art, concept books, and name sorts

    B. Read alouds, shared reading, concept books, and picture books

    C. Picture books, concept books, and alphabet books

    D. Alphabet art, name sorts, shared reading, and phonics

Answer: A. Read alouds, alphabet art, concept books, and name sorts

Read alouds, alphabet art, concept books, name sorts, and shared reading are all activities that help young children learn the alphabetic principle. Picture books and phonics develop other aspects of reading skills and literacy development.

(Rigorous) (Skill 4.1)
13. **Which of the following is a convention of print that children learn during reading activities?**
    A. The meaning of words
    B. The left-to-right motion
    C. The purpose of print
    D. The identification of letters

Answer: B. The left-to-right motion

During reading activities, children learn conventions of print. Children learn the way to hold a book, where to begin to read, the left-to-right motion, and how to continue from one line to the next.

(Average) (Skill 4.5)
14. **Alphabet books are classified as:**
    A. Concept books
    B. Easy-to-read books
    C. Board books
    D. Picture books

Answer: A. Concept books

Concept books combine language and pictures to show concrete examples of abstract concepts. One category of concept books is alphabet books, which

are popular with children from preschool through grade 2.

(Rigorous) (Skill 4.6)
15. **To determine an author's purpose, a reader must:**
    A. Use his or her own judgment
    B. Verify all the facts
    C. Link the causes to the effects
    D. Rely on common sense

Answer: A. Use his or her own judgment

An author may have more than one purpose in writing. Verifying all the facts, linking causes to effects, and relying on common sense all can help a reader in judging the author's purpose, but the reader must use his or her own judgment to determine the author's purpose for writing.

(Easy) (Skill 5.1)
16. **To decode is to:**
    A. Construct meaning
    B. Sound out a printed sequence of letters
    C. Use a special code to decipher a message
    D. None of the above

Answer: A. construct meaning.

Word analysis (phonics or decoding) is the process readers use to figure out unfamiliar words based on written patterns. Decoding is the process of constructing the meaning of an unknown word.

(Rigorous) (Skill 5.2)

17. Contextual redefinition is a strategy that encourages children to use the context more effectively by presenting them with sufficient vocabulary _____ the reading of a text.

    A. after

    B. before

    C. during

    D. None of the above

Answer: B. before

Contextual redefinition is a strategy that encourages children to use the context more effectively by presenting them with sufficient vocabulary *before* they begin reading. To apply this strategy, the teacher should first select unfamiliar words for teaching. No more than two or three words should be selected for direct teaching.

(Average) (Skill 5.6)

18. What is the best place for students to find appropriate synonyms, antonyms, and other related words to enhance their writing?

    A. Dictionary

    B. Spell check

    C. Encyclopedia

    D. Thesaurus

Answer: D. Thesaurus

Students need plenty of exposure to new words. A thesaurus is an excellent resource to use when writing. Students can use a thesaurus to find appropriate synonyms, antonyms, and other related words to enhance their writing.

(Rigorous) (Skill 6.1)

19. Which of the following indicates that a student is a fluent reader?

    A. Reads texts with expression or prosody

    B. Reads word to word and haltingly

    C. Must intentionally decode the majority of the words

    D. Sentences in a writing assignment are poorly organized structurally

Answer: A. Reads texts with expression or prosody

The teacher should listen to the children read aloud, but there are also clues to reading levels in their writing.

(Rigorous) (Skill 6.3)

20. Automaticity refers to all of the following EXCEPT:

    A. Automatic whole-word identification

    B. Automatic recognition of syllable types

    C. Automatic reactions to the content of a paragraph

    D. Automatic identification of graphemes as they relate to four basic word types

Answer: C. Automatic reactions to the content of a paragraph.

Automaticity is the ability to automatically recognize words, graphemes, word types, and syllables. This ability progresses through various stages and facilitates reading fluency and prosody. Automaticity is not related to the content of a paragraph or the student's reactions to the content.

(Rigorous) (Skill 6.4)

21. Which of the following activities are likely to improve fluency?

    A. Partner reading and a reader's theater

    B. Phrased reading

    C. Both A and B

    D. None of the above

Answer: C. Both A and B

Partner reading, tutors, a reader's theater, modeling fluent reading, and opportunities for phrased reading are all strategies designed to enhance fluency.

(Rigorous) (Skill 7.7)

22. A child who has had limited exposure to text is:

    A. More likely to refuse to participate in reading

    B. Likely to be at the same developmental level as his or her peers with reading readiness

    C. Likely to need extra support in the reading classroom

    D. Unlikely to catch up to his or her peers in reading readiness

Answer: C. Likely to need extra support in the reading classroom

Children who are not exposed to text and reading opportunities at a very young age are more likely to need extra support at first to catch up to their peers. Skills like book handling, characters, setting, and plot are skills with which a student might be unfamiliar.

(Rigorous) (Skill 4.1)

23. Students are about to read a text that contains words that students will need to understand to understand the text. When should the vocabulary be introduced to students?

    A. Before reading

    B. During reading

    C. After reading

    D. It should not be introduced

Answer: A. Before reading

Vocabulary should be introduced before reading if there are words in the text that are necessary for reading comprehension.

(Rigorous) (Skill 7.5)

24. A sixth-grade science teacher has given her class a paper to read on the relationship between food and weight gain. The writing contains signal words and phrases such as "because," "consequently," "this is how," and "due to." This paper has which text structure?

    A. Cause and effect

    B. Compare and contrast

    C. Description

    D. Sequencing

Answer: A. Cause and effect

Cause and effect is the relationship between two things when one thing makes something else happen. Writers use this text structure to show order, inform, speculate, and change behavior. This text structure identifies potential causes of a problem or issue in an orderly way.

(Rigorous) (Skill 7.7)

25. Which of the following is NOT a strategy of teaching reading comprehension?

    A. Asking questions

    B. Utilizing graphic organizers

    C. Focusing on mental images

    D. Manipulating sounds

Answer: D. Manipulating sounds

Comprehension means that the reader can ascribe meaning to text. Teachers can use many strategies to teach comprehension, including questioning, asking students to paraphrase or summarize, utilizing graphic organizers, and focusing on mental images.

(Easy) (Skill 7.11)

26. **The children's literature genre came into its own in the:**

    A. Seventeenth century

    B. Eighteenth century

    C. Nineteenth century

    D. Twentieth century

Answer: B. Eighteenth century

Children's literature emerged as a distinct genre in the second half of the eighteenth century. *The Visible World in Pictures* by John Amos Comenius, a Czech educator, was one of the first printed works and the first picture book.

(Rigorous) (Skill 9.4)

27. **When evaluating reference sources, students should do all of the following EXCEPT:**

    A. Look for self-published books by the author as evidence of expert status

    B. Examine the level of detail provided by the source

    C. Review the references at the end of the book or article

    D. See if the author presents both sides of an argument or viewpoint

Answer: A. Look for self-published books by the author as evidence of expert status

Anyone can self-publish a book or pamphlet. Experience and background in the subject area have not been reviewed by anyone in many cases. Therefore, more research needs to be done to determine whether a source document is based on reliable, expert information when it has been published by the author.

(Average) (Skill 9.2)

28. **Graphic organizers:**

    A. Primarily are used in grades K–3

    B. Work better with poetry than other forms of writing

    C. Help readers think critically by pulling out the main idea and supporting details

    D. Generally aren't helpful to ELL students

Answer: C. Help readers think critically by pulling out the main idea and supporting details

Graphic organizers help readers think critically about an idea, concept, or story by pulling out the main idea and supporting details. These pieces of information can then be depicted graphically through the use of connected geometric shapes. Readers who develop this skill can use it to increase their reading comprehension. Graphic organizers are useful for all ages and types of students and for many forms of literature and writing.

(Average) (Skill 8.4)

29. **Which of the following helps students in a way that is similar to using a glossary?**

    A. Information in the text such as charts, graphs, maps, diagrams, captions, and photos

    B. Prewriting

    C. Classroom discussion of the main idea

    D. Paired reading

Answer: A. Information in the text such as charts, graphs, maps, diagrams, captions, and photos

Charts, graphs, maps, diagrams, captions, and photos in text can work in the same way as looking up unknown words in the glossary. They can provide insight into and clarification of concepts and ideas the author is conveying. Students may need to develop these skills to interpret the information accurately, which makes a natural cross-subject opportunity.

(Rigorous) (Skill 5.6)

30. **Which of these describes the best way to teach spelling?**

    A. At the same time that grammar and sentence structure are taught

    B. Within the context of meaningful language experiences

    C. Independently so that students can concentrate on spelling

    D. In short lessons because students pick up spelling almost immediately

Answer: B. Within the context of meaningful language experiences

Spelling should be taught within the context of meaningful language experiences. Giving a child a list of words to learn to spell and then testing the child on the words every Friday will not aid in the development of spelling. The child must be able to use the words in context, and the words must have meaning for the child. The assessment of how well a child can spell or where there are problems also has to be done within a meaningful environment.

(Average) (Skill 10.6)

31. **Which of the following sentences is a compound sentence?**

    A. Elizabeth took Gracie to the dog park but forgot to bring the leash.

    B. We thoroughly enjoyed our trip during Spring Break and will plan to return next year.

    C. We were given two choices: today or tomorrow.

    D. By the end of the evening, we were thoroughly exhausted; we decided to forego the moonlight walk.

    Answer: D. By the end of the evening, we were thoroughly exhausted; we decided to forego the moonlight walk.

    A compound sentence is two independent clauses joined by a coordinating conjunction or a semicolon. The sentences in choices A, B, and C have coordinating conjunctions, but they do not connect two clauses. Sentences A and B have compound verb phrases. Sentence C has a compound object.

(Rigorous) (Skill 10.6)

32. **Which of the following sentences contains an error in agreement?**

    A. Jennifer is one of the women who writes for the magazine.

    B. Each one of their sons plays a different sport.

    C. This band has performed at the Odeum many times.

    D. The data are available online at the listed website.

    Answer: A. Jennifer is one of the women who writes for the magazine.

    Women is the plural subject of the verb. The verb should be *write*.

(Average) (Skill 11.4)

33. **Which of the following is NOT a technique of prewriting?**

    A. Clustering

    B. Listing

    C. Brainstorming

    D. Proofreading

    Answer: D. Proofreading

    Proofreading is not a method of pre-writing because it is done on texts that already have been written.

(Easy) (Skill 11.6)

34. **A student has written a paper with the following characteristics: written in first person; characters, setting, and plot; some dialogue; events organized in chronological sequence with some flashbacks. In what genre has the student written?**

    A. Expository writing

    B. Narrative writing

    C. Persuasive writing

    D. Technical writing

    Answer: B. Narrative writing

    These are all characteristics of narrative writing. Expository writing is intended to give information such as an explanation or directions, and the information is logically organized. Persuasive writing gives an opinion in an attempt to convince the reader that a point of view is valid or tries to persuade the reader to take a specific action. The goal of technical writing is to clearly communicate particular information to a targeted reader or group of readers.

(Rigorous) (Skill 9.6)

35. A sentence that contains one independent clause and three dependent clauses is best described as a:

A. Simple sentence

B. Compound sentence

C. Complex sentence

D. Compound-complex sentence

Answer: C. Complex sentence

A complex sentence is made up of one independent clause and at least one dependent clause. This type of sentence can have multiple dependent clauses. Simple and compound sentences do not have any dependent clauses, and a compound-complex sentence has more than one independent clause as well as one or more dependent clauses.

(Rigorous) (Skill 10.3)

36. Which of the following messages provides the most accessibility to the most learners?

A. Print message

B. Audiovisual message

C. Graphic message

D. Audiovisual message

Answer: B. Audiovisual message

An audiovisual message is the most accessible for learners. It has the advantages of both mediums, the graphic and the audio. Learners' eyes and ears are engaged. Nonreaders get significant access to content. However, viewing an audiovisual presentation is an even more passive activity than listening to an audio message because information is coming to learners effortlessly through two senses.

(Easy) (Skill 10.5)

37. Which of the following advertising techniques is based on appealing to our desire to think for ourselves?

A. Celebrity endorsement

B. Intelligence

C. Independence

D. Lifestyle

Answer: C. Independence

Celebrity endorsements associate product use with a well-known person. Intelligence techniques are based on making consumers feel smart and as if they cannot be fooled. Lifestyle approaches are designed to make us feel we are part of a particular way of living.

(Average) (Skill 10.7)

38. Which of the following is NOT useful in creating visual media for the classroom?

A. Limit your graph to just one idea or concept and keep the content simple

B. Balance substance and visual appeal

C. Match the information to the format that will fit it best

D. Make sure to cite all references to copyrighted material

Answer: D. Make sure to cite all references to copyrighted material

Although it may be important to acknowledge copyright and intellectual property ownership of some materials used in visual media, this factor is not a guideline for creating useful visual media for the classroom.

(Rigorous) (Skill 11.1)

39. All of the following are examples of ongoing informal assessment techniques used to observe student progress EXCEPT:

   A. Analysis of student work product

   B. Collection of data from assessment tests

   C. Effective questioning

   D. Observation of students

Answer: B. Collection of data from assessment tests

Assessment tests are formal progress monitoring measures.

(Easy) (Skill 13.2)

40. Which of the following is a formal reading-level assessment?

   A. A standardized reading test

   B. A teacher-made reading test

   C. An interview

   D. A reading diary

Answer: A. A standardized reading test

If the assessment is standardized, it has to be objective, whereas B, C, and D are all subjective assessments.

(Easy) (Skill 13.8)

41. Which of the following is NOT considered a reading level?

   A. Independent

   B. Instructional

   C. Intentional

   D. Frustrational

Answer: C. Intentional

Intentional is not a reading level. Reading levels for the purpose of assessment and planning instruction are as follows: *Independent.* This is the level at which the child can read text totally on his or her own. When reading books at the independent level, students will be able to decode between 95 and 100 percent of the words and comprehend the text with 90 percent or better accuracy. *Instructional.* This is the level at which the student should be taught because it provides enough difficulty to increase his or her reading skills without providing so much that it becomes too cumbersome to finish the selection. Typically, the acceptable range of accuracy is between 85 and 94 percent, with 75 percent or greater comprehension. *Frustrational.* Books at a student's frustrational level are too difficult for the child and should not be used. The frustrational level is any text with less than 85 percent word accuracy and/or less than 75 percent comprehension.

(Rigorous) (Skill 11.7)

42. Which of the following should NOT be included in the opening paragraph of an informative essay?

   A. Thesis sentence

   B. Details and examples supporting the main idea

   C. A broad, general introduction to the topic

   D. A style and tone that grabs the reader's attention

Answer: B. Details and examples supporting the main idea

The introductory paragraph should introduce the topic, capture the reader's interest, state the thesis, and prepare the reader for the main points in the essay. Details and examples should be given in the second part of the essay to help develop the thesis.

(Average) (Skill 11.6)

43. **Being competent in _____, a reader is able to understand what the writer is trying to convey to the audience.**

    A. semantics

    B. pragmatics

    C. morphemes

    D. phonemes

    Answer: A. semantics

    Semantics concerns the difference between the writer's meaning and the literal meaning of the text based on social context.

(Easy) (Skill 9.2)

44. **A second-grade teacher explains the steps of the writing process to her learners. For the first step, she demonstrates the use of a Venn diagram to compare and contrast two characters from a story the class recently read. These visual representations of content are known as:**

    A. Graphic organizers

    B. Running records

    C. Blogs

    D. Phonemes

    Answer: A. Graphic organizers

Graphic organizers can be used to visually represent text. Examples include Venn diagrams, flowcharts, and webs.

(Average) (Skill 7.3)

45. **By examining an author's word choice, a reader can determine the:**

    A. Author's purpose

    B. Author's tone

    C. Main idea

    D. Inference

    Answer: B. Author's tone

    A reader can determine the overall tone of a statement or passage through the author's word choice.

DIRECTIONS: Read the following passage and answer the questions that follow.

According to Factmonster.com, the most popular Internet activity is sending and/or reading email. Approximately 92% of Internet users report using the Internet for this purpose. 89% of Internet users report that they use the Internet to search for information. Two popular search engines are Google and Yahoo! The introduction of the Internet has made it easy to gather and research information quickly. Other reasons that Internet users use the Internet is for social media, to search for driving directions, look into a hobby or interest, or research a product or service before buying, just to name a few. Creative <u>enterprises</u> such as remixing songs or lyrics stood at the bottom of reasons people use the Internet. Surprisingly, only 11% of Internet users said they use the Internet for creative purposes. Perhaps people are using specific software to be creative.

(Average) (Skill 7.3)

46. **What is the main idea of the passage?**

    A. Factmonster has a lot of great facts for people to research

    B. People use the Internet for a variety of reasons

    C. The main reason the Internet is used is to check emails

    D. People aren't as creative as they used to be before the Internet

    Answer: B. People use the Internet for a variety of reasons

    The passage lists the top reasons why people use the Internet. Therefore, the best choice is B.

(Average) (Skill 7.4)

47. **Why did the author write this article?**

    A. To convince the reader to use the Internet

    B. To teach the reader how use the Internet

    C. To encourage the reader to use the Internet

    D. To inform the reader about Internet usage trends

    Answer: D. To inform the reader about Internet usage trends

    The author wants to let the reader know what the Internet is mostly being used for. The statistics offered are synonymous of Internet usage trends.

(Average) (Skill 7.4)

48. **How is the passage organized?**

    A. Sequence of events

    B. Cause and effect

    C. Statement support

    D. Compare and contrast

    Answer: C. Statement support

    The passage makes a statement at the beginning and then supports it with details in the rest of the passage.

(Rigorous) (Skill 7.5)

49. **What cause and effect relationship exists in this paragraph?**

    A. The U.S. postal service is suffering from the introduction of email

    B. Google and Yahoo! are used most often to search information

    C. The introduction of the Internet has made gathering information easy

    D. People are less creative since they aren't using their computers for this reason

    Answer: C. The introduction of the Internet has made gathering information easy

    Because the Internet was introduced, people are able to search for information easier than they used to be able to. This is a cause and effect relationship.

(Rigorous) (Skill 7.2)

50. **By using the word "surprisingly" in the passage, what is the author implying?**

    A. It is thought that the Internet is used more for creative purposes

    B. People are thought to be more creative than they really are

    C. It is thought that fewer than 11% would use the Internet for creative purposes

    D. Software companies are making 11% more creative software

    Answer: A. It is thought that the Internet is used more for creative purposes

    By using the word "surprisingly," the author is saying that she is surprised that only 11% of Internet users use the Internet for creative purposes. The author would expect that number to be higher.

(Average) (Skill 7.2)

51. **Which transition word could the author have used to connect these two sentences?**

    Approximately 92% of Internet users report using the Internet for this purpose. 89% of Internet users report that they use the Internet to search for information.

    A. Additionally,

    B. Therefore,

    C. Next,

    D. Similarly,

    Answer: A. Additionally,

The author wants to add more information about Internet usage, so "additionally" is the best choice for a transition word.

(Average) (Skill 7.2)

52. **What does the word "enterprises" mean in the passage?**

    A. People

    B. Endeavors

    C. Businesses

    D. Musicians

    Answer: B. Endeavors

    The words "endeavors" and "enterprises" are synonymous, and either word could be used in the passage.

DIRECTIONS: Read the following passage and answer the questions that follow.

The poems both use personification to bring the subjects of the poem to life. Both poems were also very entertaining. In "The Subway" the author says that the subway, also known as a dragon, swallows up the people and then spits them out at the next stop. Similarly, in "Steam Shovel," the author says that the steam shovel chews up the dirt that it scoops up and smiles amiably at the people below.

The subjects of the poems are compared to different things. The subway is compared to a dragon with green scales. Dragons breathe fire. The steam shovel is compared to an ancient dinosaur with a long neck and dripping jaws.

(Average) (Skill 7.4)

53. **How is the passage organized?**

    A. Compare and contrast

    B. Cause and effect

    C. Sequence of events

    D. Statement support

    Answer: A. Compare and contrast

    This passage compares (gives similarities) and contrasts (shows differences) between two poems.

(Average) (Skill 7.2)

54. **Which sentence in the passage is irrelevant?**

    A. Both poems were also very entertaining.

    B. The subway is also known as a dragon.

    C. The subway swallows people up and spits them out.

    D. The author says that the steam shovel chews up the dirt.

    Answer: A. Both poems were also very entertaining.

    Although this may be a similarity between the two poems, it is an opinion that is not necessary to include within the passage, since the focus of the first paragraph is personification.

(Easy) (Skill 7.5)

55. **Each of the comparisons mentioned in the paragraph are known as a:**

    A. Metaphor

    B. Hyperbole

    C. Onomatopoeia

    D. None of the above

Answer: A. Metaphor

Metaphors compare two or more things to one another. The examples listed above are considered metaphors.

DIRECTIONS: Read the following passage and answer the questions that follow.

Have you ever wondered what chewing gum is made from? What is it that allows us to chew it for hours without it ever disintegrating? Chicle is a gum, or sap, that comes from the sapodilla tree. The sapodilla tree is an American tropical evergreen that is native to South Florida. Flavorings, corn syrup, and sugar or artificial sweeteners are other ingredients that go into the production of chewing gum. Legend has it that Native Americans chewed spruce resin to quench their thirst. Today, gum is chewed for many reasons by many different groups of people.

(Rigorous) (Skill 7.5)

56. **What conclusion can be drawn from the passage?**

    A. Everyone in South Florida has heard of the sapodilla tree

    B. Many people have wondered what makes gum chewy

    C. Some type of sweetener is used in gum production

    D. Native Americans invented gum

Answer: C. Some type of sweetener is used in gum production

It is defined in the passage that sugar or artificial sweeteners are used in gum production.

(Rigorous) (Skill 7.4)

57. **What can be inferred from the passage?**

   A. The gum Chiclets took its name from the ingredient chicle used in gum

   B. Gum is disgusting after it's been chewed for a few hours

   C. Gum is only made in the United States because that's where the sapodilla tree grows

   D. When someone is thirsty they should chew gum

   Answer: A. The gum Chiclets took its name from the ingredient chicle used in gum

   It can be inferred from the passage that the brand of gum called Chiclets most likely took its name from the ingredient chicle, or sap, that is found in gum.

   DIRECTIONS: Read the following passage and answer the questions that follow.

   The word "cycle" comes from the Greek word *kyklos*, which means "circle" or "wheel." There are many different types of cycles. The word "unicycle" comes from the prefix *uni-*, which means "one," combined with the root "cycle." When the prefix and root word cycle are combined, it creates a word that means "one circle or wheel." Unicycles are often used for entertainment rather than exercise.

   A prefix *bi-* means "two," which, when combined with the word "cycle," creates the word "bicycle." How many wheels does a bicycle have? Many young children ride a tricycle because it has three wheels and is easy to ride. The prefix *tri-* means "three," and when it is combined with the root word "cycle," the new word is "three wheels." It is even possible to

   make the word "motorcycle." Once you know how to use <u>roots</u>, it is easy to figure out the meaning of an unknown word.

(Average) (Skill 7.4)

58. **What is the main idea of the passage?**

   A. There are many types of cycles

   B. The prefix *uni-* means one

   C. Words can be defined by their parts

   D. Unicycles are often used for entertainment

   Answer: C. Words can be defined by their parts

   Only Option C covers the whole passage and not just one small detail contained within it.

(Easy) (Skill 7.2)

59. **What does the word "roots" mean?**

   A. Stable parts of plants

   B. Where one originated

   C. The base portions of a word

   D. A spelling tool

   Answer: C. The base portions of a word

   "Roots" is a multiple-meaning word, but in the context of the passage, it means the base portions of a word.

(Average) (Skill 7.7)

60. Which is an opinion contained in this passage?

   A. Once you know how to use roots, it is easy to figure out the meaning of an unknown word

   B. Many young children ride a tricycle

   C. Unicycles are often used for entertainment rather than exercise

   D. The word "cycle" comes from the Greek word *kyklos*

   Answer: A. Once you know how to use roots, it is easy to figure out the meaning of an unknown word

   Options B and C could be opinions, but they both have clarifying words like "many" and "often," which makes them facts.

(Rigorous) (Skill 7.7)

61. From this article you can see that the author thinks:

   A. Riding a bicycle is good exercise

   B. It is important to know about the English language

   C. "Cycle" is a confusing word

   D. It is more important to understand the prefixes and suffixes

   Answer: B. It is important to know about the English language

   The author wrote this passage to teach readers about the English language. Therefore, we know that the author thinks it is important to understand the English language.

DIRECTIONS: The passage below contains many errors. Read the passage. Then, answer each test item by choosing the option that corrects an error in the underlined portion(s). No more than one underlined error will appear in each item. If no error exists, choose "No change is necessary."

If you give me ten dollars, I'll give you fifty in return. Does this sound too good to be true? Well, anything that sounds too good to be true probably is. That stands true for herbal supplements. Herbal supplements are main targeted toward improving one type of ailment. There is no cure-all herbal supplement so don't believe what he tells you. Herbal supplement can fix more than one thing.

Herbal supplements is great and have a lot of positive things to offer its takers and have become very popular with consumers. Many doctors are even suggesting that they try natural herbal remedies before prescribing an over-the-counter medication. Herbal supplements have given consumers a new power to self-diagnose and consumers can head to the health food store and pick up an herbal supplement rather than heading to the doctor. Herbal supplements take a little long than prescribed medication to clear up any illnesses, but they are a more natural way to go, and some consumers prefer that form of medication.

(Average) (Skill 8.1)

62. Herbal supplements are <u>main</u> targeted <u>toward</u> <u>improving</u> one type of ailment.

   A. mainly

   B. towards

   C. improve

   D. No change is necessary

Answer: A. mainly

Option B doesn't work because the correct form of the word is indeed "toward." The gerund "improving" is necessary in the sentence. Therefore, Option A, "mainly," is the correct adverb needed.

(Easy) (Skill 8.1)

63. There is <u>no</u> cure-all herbal <u>supplement</u> so don't believe what <u>he tells you</u>.

    A. nothing

    B. supplemental

    C. you hear

    D. No change is necessary

Answer: C. you hear

As the sentence reads now, "he" is a pronoun that doesn't refer to anyone. Therefore, it shouldn't be used at all.

(Rigorous) (Skill 8.1)

64. Many doctors <u>are</u> even suggesting that <u>they</u> try natural herbal remedies before <u>prescribing</u> an over-the-counter medication.

    A. is

    B. their patients

    C. prescribing,

    D. No change is necessary

Answer: B. their patients

The pronoun "they" is used incorrectly because it implies that the doctors should try natural herbal remedies. However, "they" is being used to take the place of their patients but has not been introduced prior to this point in the passage.

(Easy) (Skill 8.4)

65. Herbal supplements <u>is</u> great and have <u>a lot</u> of positive things to offer <u>its</u> takers and have become very popular with consumers.

    A. are

    B. alot

    C. it's

    D. No change is necessary

Answer: A. are

The linking verb must agree with the word supplements which is plural. Therefore, the correct verb must be "are," not "is."

(Average) (Skill 8.4)

66. Herbal supplements take a little <u>long than prescribed</u> medications to clear up any illnesses, but they are a more natural way to go, and some consumers prefer that form of medication.

    A. longer

    B. then

    C. perscribed

    D. No changes necessary

Answer: A. longer

The sentence is comparing two things— herbal supplements to prescribed medications. The comparative form of the adjective "long" needs to be used and should be "longer."

(Rigorous) (Skill 8.1)

67. Herbal <u>supplements</u> take a little long than prescribed <u>medication</u> to clear up any illnesses, but they are a <u>more natural</u> way to go, and some consumers prefer that form of medication.

    A. supplement

    B. medications

    C. more naturally

    D. No change necessary

Answer: B. medications

Since the sentence begins talking about herbal supplements—plural—the comparison, prescribe medications, must be the same and be a plural too.

(Average) (Skill 8.1)

68. Herbal <u>supplement</u> can fix more <u>than</u> one <u>thing.</u>

    A. supplements

    B. then

    C. things

    D. No change is necessary

Answer: A. supplements

The article talks about herbal supplements and therefore must agree at all times throughout the article. Option B is incorrect because then indicates that something happens next. "Than" is the correct word used in comparisons.

DIRECTIONS: The passage below contains many errors. Read the passage. Then, answer each test item by choosing the option that corrects an error in the underlined portion(s). No more than one underlined error will appear in each item. If no error exists, choose "No change is necessary."

Bingo has many purposes in the United States. It is used as a learning and entertainment tool for children. Bingo is used as an entertainment tool for parties and picnics to entertain a large number of people easily and quickly. Bingo is also a common game played among elderly and church groups because of its simplistic way of entertaining.

A typical bingo card has the word "bingo" printed across the top with columns of numbers inside boxes underneath. There is a "free" space located directly in the middle. There is usually one person who calls the numbers. For example, a ball or chip may be labeled "B12." Players then look under the "B" column for the number 12 and if it appears on their card, they place a marker on top of it. If there isn't a 12 under the letter "B" on a player's card, then they simply wait for the next number to be called.

(Rigorous) (Skill 1.7)

69. <u>Players</u> then look under the "B" column for the number 12 and if it appears on <u>his</u> card, <u>they</u> place a marker on top of it.

    A. He

    B. their

    C. him

    D. No change is necessary.

Answer: B. their

The sentence begins with the plural word "player" and is followed by the plural word "they." Therefore, the possessive word "their" is needed rather than the singular word "he" or "him."

(Rigorous) (Skill 2.2)

70. *Bingo is used as a learning and entertainment tool for children.*

    How should this sentence be rewritten?

    A. Bingo is used as a learning tool and entertainment for children.

    B. Bingo is used for learning and entertainment for children.

    C. Bingo is used to both teach and entertain children.

    D. No change is necessary

    Answer: C. Bingo is used to both teach and entertain children.

    The best answer is Option C because the correlative conjunction "both" is used, and there is a similar sentence structure on both sides of the word. In both options A and B, the words being compared do not have the same structure.

(Easy) (Skill 11.4)

71. **In this step of the writing process, students examine their work and make changes in wording, details, and ideas.**

    A. Drafting

    B. Prewriting

    C. Revising and editing

    D. Proofreading

    Answer: C. Revising and editing

    Revision is probably the most important step in the writing process. In this step,

students examine their work and make changes in wording, details, and ideas.

DIRECTIONS: Read the following passage and answer the questions.

It is a requirement that all parents volunteer two hours during the course of the season. Or an alternative was to pay $8 so you can have some high school students work a shift for you. Lots of parents liked this idea and will take advantage of the opportunity. Shifts run an hour long, and it is well worth it to pay the money so you don't miss your sons game.

(Average) (Skill 10.1)

72. *It is a requirement that all parents volunteer two hours during the course of the season.*

    How should the above sentence be rewritten?

    A. It is a requirement of all parents volunteering two hours during the course of the season.

    B. It is required of all parents to volunteer for two hours during the course of the season.

    C. They require all parents to volunteer during the season.

    D. Requiring all parents to volunteer for two hours of the season.

    Answer: B. It is required of all parents to volunteer for two hours during the course of the season.

    This is the only choice that works. Option C makes sense, but the pronoun "they" is not established and cannot be used in the first sentence of the paragraph.

(Average) (Skill 10.1)

73. An alternative <u>was</u> to pay $8 so you can have some <u>high school</u> students work a shift for you.

    Which of the following options corrects an error in one of the underlined portions above?

    A. is

    B. High School

    C. High school

    D. No change is necessary

    Answer: A. is

    The first sentence puts this passage in the present tense. Therefore, the verb tense must remain the same throughout the passage and "was" is a past tense verb.

(Rigorous) (Skill 10.1)

74. *Many parents liked this idea and will take advantage of the opportunity.*

    How should the sentence be rewritten?

    A. Many parent's liked this idea and took advantage of the opportunity.

    B. Many parents like this idea and take advantage of the opportunity.

    C. Many parents like this idea and took advantage of the opportunity.

    D. Many parents did like this idea and take advantage of the opportunity.

    Answer: B. Many parents like this idea and take advantage of the opportunity.

    The verb tense between "like" and "take" must remain consistent in the sentence and consistent with the verb tense of the paragraph.

(Rigorous) (Skill 7.3)

75. Which is NOT a true statement concerning an author's literary tone?

    A. Tone is partly revealed through the selection of details

    B. Tone is the expression of the author's attitude towards his or her subject

    C. Tone in literature is usually satiric or angry

    D. Tone in literature corresponds to the tone of voice a speaker uses

    Answer: C. Tone in literature is usually satiric or angry

    Tone in literature conveys a mood and can be as varied as the tone of voice of a speaker (see D), e.g., sad, nostalgic, whimsical, angry, formal, intimate, satirical, sentimental.

Mathematics

(Rigorous) (Skill 17.5)

76. These angles are diagonal angles on the inside of two parallel lines cut by a transversal:

    A. Alternate interior

    B. Alternate exterior

    C. Corresponding

    D. Vertical

    Answer: A. Alternate interior

    Angles can be classified in a number of ways. Alternate interior angles are diagonal angles on the inside of two parallel lines cut by a transversal.

(Average) (Skill 17.4)

77. **These lines do not intersect and do not lie on the same plane:**

    A. Parallel

    B. Perpendicular

    C. Intersecting

    D. Skew

    Answer: D. Skew

    Angles can be classified in a number of ways. Skew lines do not intersect and do not lie on the same plane.

(Easy) (Skill 17.1)

78. **When divided by a line through the middle, which letter does not demonstrate symmetry?**

    A. **T**

    B. **A**

    C. **O**

    D. **F**

    Answer: D. F

    If printed on a piece of paper, each of the other letters could be folded in half, and each half would be identical.

(Rigorous) (Skill 15.4)

79. **Select the answer that best represents the prime factorization of 245.**

    A. $6^2 \cdot 7$

    B. $5^2 \cdot 7$

    C. $4 \cdot 5 \cdot 6$

    D. $5 \cdot 7^2$

    Answer: D. $5 \cdot 7^2$

Break 245 into its factors, and continue to break into factors until only prime numbers remain.

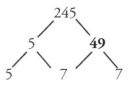

Since 7 is multiplied twice, square it. The prime factorization is written as D: $5 \cdot 7^2$.

(Average) (Skill 16.2)

80. **A function defined by the equation $f(x) = 5mx + b$:**

    A. Recursive function

    B. Quadratic function

    C. Linear function

    D. Exponential function

    Answer: C. Linear function

    A linear function is a function defined by the equation $f(x) = 5mx + b$. This equation can be used to represent patterns in animals, people, and technology.

(Average) (Skill 16.7)

81. **A _____ is a relationship in which two quantities are proportional to each other.**

    A. recursive relationship

    B. linear relationship

    C. quadratic relationship

    D. exponential relationship

    Answer: B. linear relationship

    A linear relationship is a relationship in which two quantities are proportional to each other. Doubling x also doubles y. On a graph, a straight line depicts a linear relationship.

(Easy) (Skill 19.8)

82. **First-grade students have sorted information to put into a graph. Which developmentally appropriate graph would be best to illustrate the various colors of favorite autumn leaves?**

    A. Pictograph

    B. Circle graph

    C. Histogram

    D. Line graph

    Answer: A. Pictograph

    The best way to represent the information is through a pictograph. A pictograph shows comparison of quantities using symbols. Each symbol represents a number of items.

Use the data below to answer questions 83–85.

The following are the percentages that were earned on a fifth-grade math exam:

78	84	86
90	93	90
87	64	98
74	73	72
98	81	77

(Average) (Skill 18.2)

83. **Find the median of the given test scores:**

    A. 84

    B. 83

    C. 86

    D. 81

Answer: A. 84

To determine the median, the numbers need to be placed in numerical order, like this:

64 72 73 74 77 78 81 84 86 87 90 90 93 98 98

The middle number determines the median. The median in this example is 84.

(Average) (Skill 18.2)

84. **Find the mean of the given test scores:**

    A. 78

    B. 83

    C. 87

    D. None of the above

Answer: B. 83

The mean is the sum of all scores divided by the number of scores. In this case, the sum equals 1,245. There are 15 scores. 1,245 divided by 15 equals 83. The mean (average) of the fifteen scores is 83.

(Average) (Skill 18.2)

85. **Find the mode of the given test scores:**

    A. 84

    B. 87

    C. 86

    D. 98

Answer: D. 98

The mode is the most frequent number. In this example, the mode is 98.

(Average) (Skill 19.10)

86. June is planning a vacation. The hotel costs $872.27, the rental car is $189.78, and she budgeted $250 for food. Estimate how much cash June will need to pay for hotel, car, and food.

    A. $1400

    B. $1325

    C. $1300

    D. $1250

    Answer: B. $1325

    Round each cost to a number that is easier to do mental math with, but don't round down, or June will not have enough money. $872.27 becomes $875 and $189.78 becomes $200. $875 + 200 + 250 = 1325$; that is a reasonable amount of cash that is closest to the actual cost of $1312.05.

(Average) (Skill 16.8)

87. A car traveled 281 miles in 4 hours 41 minutes. What was the average speed of the car in miles per hour?

    A. 66 miles per hour

    B. 70 miles per hour

    C. 56 miles per hour

    D. 60 miles per hour

    Answer: D. 60 miles per hour

    To solve, first convert the time of 4 hours 41 minutes in minutes.

    $$4 \text{ hours } 41 \text{ minutes} = 4 \times 60 + 41$$
    $$= 281 \text{ minutes}$$

    Average speed S is given by distance divided by time.

$$S = 281 \text{ miles} \div 281 \text{ minutes}$$
$$= 1 \frac{\text{mile}}{\text{minute}}$$
$$= 60 \text{ miles per hour}$$

(Average) (Skill 18.3)

88. A six-sided die is rolled once. What is the probability that the number rolled is an even number greater than 2?

    A. $\frac{1}{6}$

    B. $\frac{1}{3}$

    C. $\frac{1}{4}$

    D. None of the above

    Answer: B. $\frac{1}{3}$

    Out of the 6 possible numbers that may rolled, 3 are even: 2, 4, and 6 BUT only 4 and 6 are greater than 2. Therefore, the probability that the number rolled is an even number greater than 2 is given by: number of even numbers greater than 2 divided by $6 = \frac{2}{6} = \frac{1}{3}$.

(Average) (Skill 17.14)

89. The length of a rectangle is increased to 2 times its original size and its width is increased to 3 times its original size. If the area of the new rectangle is equal to 1800 square feet, what is the area of the original rectangle?

    A. 300 square feet

    B. 360 square feet

    C. 320 square feet

    D. 400 square feet

    Answer: A. 300 square feet

L and W represent the original length and width of the rectangle, and its area equals $L \times W$.

After the increase, the length becomes $2L$ and the width becomes $3W$.

The area is then given by $(2L) \times (3W)$ and is known.

Therefore:

$(2L) \times (3W) = 1800$ square feet

Solve the above equation to find
$L \times W = 6L \times W = 1800$ square feet

$L \times W = 1800 \div 6 = 300$ square feet

300 square feet is the area of the original rectangle.

(Average) (Skill 16.10)

90. **Daniel bought a total of 20 game cards, some of which cost \$0.25 each and some of which cost \$0.15 each. If Daniel spent \$4.20 to buy these cards, how many \$0.15 cards did he buy?**

   A. 9 cards

   B. 8 cards

   C. 12 cards

   D. 10 cards

Answer: B. 8 cards

Let x be the number of cards that cost \$0.25 each and y the number of cards that cost \$0.15 each. The total number of cards is 20. Therefore: $x + y = 20$.

If x is the number of cards at \$0.25, then the x cards cost $0.25x$

If y is the number of cards at \$0.15, then the y cards cost $0.15y$

The total cost of the x cards and the y cards is known to be \$4.20 and also given by $0.25x + 0.15y = 4.2$

Then you must solve the system of equations:

$x + y = 20$
$0.25x + 0.15y = 4.2$

The first equation gives $y = 20 - x$.

Substitute y by $20 - x$ in the second equation and solve:

$0.25x + 0.15(20 - x) = 4.2$
$x(0.25 - 0.15) + 3 = 4.2$
$x = 1.2$
$x = 12$ and $y = 20 - 12 = 8$

He bought 8 cards that were \$0.15 each.

(Average) (Skill 18.9)

91. **In a group of 120 people, 90 have an age of more 30 years, and the others have an age of less than 20 years. If a person is selected at random from this group, what is the probability the person's age is less than 20?**

   A. 45

   B. 0.5

   C. 0.75

   D. 0.25

Answer: D. 0.25

Number of people whose age is less than 20 is given by: $120 - 90 = 30$

Probability P that a person selected at random from the group is less than 20 is given by:

$30 \div 120 = 0.25$

(Average) (Skill 17.2)

92. If the length of the side of a square is doubled, what is the ratio of the areas of the original square to the area of the new square?

    A. 1:2

    B. 1:8

    C. 1:4

    D. 1:6

    Answer: C. 1:4

    If x is the side of the original square, then its area is equal to: x^2

    If x is doubled to $2x$, then the new area is equal to: $(2x)^2 = 4x^2$

    The ratio of the areas of the original square to the area of the new square: $x^2 \div (4x^2) = \frac{1}{4}$ or 1:4

(Average) (Skill 16.7)

93. The division of a whole number y by 13 gives a quotient of 15 and a remainder of 2. Find y.

    A. 197

    B. 113

    C. 183

    D. 195

    Answer: A. 197

    According to the division process of whole numbers, n can be written, using multiplication, as follows:

    n = quotient × divisor + remainder = $15 \times 13 + 2 = 197$

(Easy) (Skill 17.15)

94. Sarah spent $\frac{3}{4}$ of her savings on a TV and the rest on clothes. If the clothes cost her $200, what was her original savings?

    A. $900

    B. $1000

    C. $1200

    D. $800

    Answer: D. $800

    If Linda spent $\frac{3}{4}$ of her savings on a TV, the rest: $\frac{4}{4} - \frac{3}{4} = \frac{1}{4}$ on clothes, but the clothes cost her $200. So $\frac{1}{4}$ of her savings is $200. So her original savings is 4 times $200, which = $800.

(Average) (Skill 15.3)

95. Samantha bought a sweater on sale for 30% off the original price and another 25% off the discounted price. If the original price of the sweater was $30, what was the final price of the sweater?

    A. $15.75

    B. $16.25

    C. $17.50

    D. $14.90

    Answer: A. $15.75

    The price with 30% off:

    30 − 30% of 30
    = 30 − (30 ÷ 100) × 30
    = 30 − 9 = $21

    The price with another 25% off:

    21 − 25% of 21
    = 21 − (25 ÷ 100) × 21
    = 21 − (525 ÷ 100)
    = 21 − 5.25 = $15.75

(Easy) (Skill 19.6)

96. **Mr. Michaels begins teaching his students the principles of addition. Before beginning his lessons, he must ensure that:**

    A. His students can count

    B. His students have a concrete understanding of one-to-one correspondence

    C. His students can recognize written numbers

    D. All of the above

Answer: D. All of the above

In order for students to be successful with the concept of addition, they must be able to use the concept of one-to-one correspondence to be able to correctly count. Students should also be able to recognize and identify written numbers and understand what each one represents.

(Average) (Skill 14.4)

97. **Which of the following is a true statement regarding manipulatives in mathematics instruction?**

    A. Manipulatives are materials that students can physically handle

    B. Manipulatives help students make concrete concepts abstract

    C. Manipulatives include fingers, tiles, paper folding, and ice cream sticks

    D. Manipulatives help students make abstract concepts concrete

Answer: D. Manipulatives help students make abstract concepts concrete

Manipulatives are materials that students can physically handle and move, such as fingers and tiles. Manipulatives allow students to understand mathematic concepts by allowing them to see concrete examples of abstract processes. Manipulatives are attractive to students because they appeal to their visual and tactile senses.

(Easy) (Skill 14.5)

98. **In order to create a motivating learning environment in mathematics, Ms. Anders, a kindergarten teacher, should do which of the following?**

    A. Utilize large posters with text mathematical definitions

    B. Provide hands-on mathematical learning centers and visuals

    C. Allow the students to only work one on one

    D. Work with all students as a whole group each day

Answer: B Provide hands-on mathematical learning centers and visuals

In order for the teacher to provide students with a motivating environment, young learners need access to hands-on and appropriate learning opportunities, including learning centers and visuals with appropriate amounts of text with corresponding pictures.

(Easy) (Skill 14.6)

99. **All of the following are tools that can strengthen students' mathematical understanding EXCEPT:**

    A. Rulers, scales, and protractors

    B. Calculators, counters, and measuring containers

    C. Software and hardware

    D. Money and software

Answer: C. Software and hardware

Students' understanding of mathematical concepts is strengthened when they use tools to help make the abstract concepts become concrete realities. Teachers have a wide variety of tools available to help students learn mathematics. These include all of the above except for hardware. Hardware technically is not a tool but part of the infrastructure of the classroom.

(Average) (Skill 14.9)

100. **Which of the following is NOT a good example of helping students make connections between the real world and mathematics?**

    A. Studying a presidential election from the perspective of the math involved

    B. Using weather concepts to teach math

    C. Having student helpers take attendance

    D. Reviewing major mathematical theorems on a regular basis

Answer: D. Reviewing major mathematical theorems on a regular basis

Theorems are abstract math concepts, and reviews, while valuable, are not an example of using everyday events to teach math. Teachers can increase student interest in math by relating mathematical concepts to familiar events in their lives and using real-world examples and data whenever possible. Instead of presenting only abstract concepts and examples, teachers should relate concepts to everyday situations to shift the emphasis from memorization and abstract application to understanding and applied problem

solving. This will not only improve students' grasp of math ideas and keep them engaged, it will also help answer the perennial question, "Why do we have to learn math?"

(Easy) (Skill 14.10)

101. **While teaching his class, Mr. Diaz asks Rebecca, a first grader, to answer a math question. After about 10 seconds, Rebecca answers the question correctly. Mr. Diaz has done a good job of:**

    A. Reminding his students that he expects them to get the correct answer every time

    B. Employing a wait time strategy

    C. Hoping she will come up with the right answer eventually

    D. Utilizing the prompt and wait technique

Answer: B. Employing a wait time strategy

Mr. Diaz is aware that learners need time to process information and comprehend questions. By allowing this student time to answer the question, she not only was able to come up with the correct answer, but she has also gained confidence in doing so.

(Rigorous) (Skill 15.2)

102. **Which of the following is an example of the associative property?**

    A. $a(b + c) = ab + bc$

    B. $a + b = 2a$

    C. $(a + b) + c = a + (b + c)$

    D. $a + b = b + a$

    Answer: C. $(a + b) + c = a + (b + c)$

    The associative property is when the parentheses of a problem are switched.

(Rigorous) (Skill 17.13)

103. **Given similar polygons with corresponding sides measuring 6 inches and 8 inches, what is the area of the smaller polygon if the area of the larger is 64 in²?**

    A. 48 in²

    B. 36 in²

    C. 144 in²

    D. 78 in²

    Answer: B. 36 in²

    For similar polygons, the areas are proportional to the squares of the sides. We can set up the proportion $\frac{6^2}{8^2} = \frac{36}{64} = \frac{x}{64}$. Therefore, $x = 36$.

(Rigorous) (Skill 19.1)

104. **Mary did comparison shopping on her favorite brand of coffee. Over half of the stores priced the coffee at $1.70. Most of the remaining stores priced the coffee at $1.80, except for a few that charged $1.90.**

    Which of the following statements is true about the distribution of prices?

    A. The mean and the mode are the same

    B. The mean is greater than the mode

    C. The mean is less than the mode

    D. The mean is less than the median

    Answer: B. The mean is greater than the mode

    Over half the stores priced the coffee at $1.70 per pound, which means that this price is the mode. The mean would be slightly over $1.70 because other stores priced the coffee at over $1.70 per pound.

(Easy) (Skill 15.4)

105. **What is the mode of the data in the following sample?**

    9, 10, 11, 9, 10, 11, 9, 13

    A. 9

    B. 9.5

    C. 10

    D. 11

    Answer: A. 9

    The mode is the number that appears most frequently. The number 9 appears three times, which is more often than any of the other numbers.

(Easy) (Skill 15.5)

106. **Which of the following is correct?**

    A. $2,365 > 2,340$

    B. $0.75 > 1.25$

    C. $\frac{3}{4} < \frac{1}{16}$

    D. $-5 < -6$

    Answer: A. $2,365 > 2,340$

2,365 is greater than 2,340. None of the other comparisons are correct.

(Average) (Skill 16.10)

107. **Choose the set in which the members are NOT equivalent.**

 A. $\frac{1}{2}$, 0.5, 50%

 B. $\frac{10}{5}$, 2.0, 200%

 C. $\frac{3}{8}$, 0.385, 38.5%

 D. $\frac{7}{10}$, 0.7, 70%

Answer: C. $\frac{3}{8}$, 0.385, 38.5%

$\frac{3}{8}$ is equivalent to 0.375 and 37.5%.

(Easy) (Skill 15.3)

108. **The digit 8 in the number 975.086 is in the:**

 A. Tenths place

 B. Ones place

 C. Hundredths place

 D. Hundreds place

Answer: C. Hundredths place

The digit 8 is in the hundredths place; the digit 0 is in the tenths place.

(Easy) (Skill 15.1)

109. **The relations given below demonstrate the following addition and multiplication property of real numbers:**

 $a + b = b + a$
 $ab = ba$

 A. Commutative

 B. Associative

 C. Identity

 D. Inverse

Answer: A. Commutative

Both addition and multiplication of real numbers satisfy the commutative property according to which changing the order of the operands does not change the result of the operation

(Rigorous) (Skill 15.1)

110. $(3 \times 9)^4 =$

 A. $(3 \times 9)\,(3 \times 9)\,(27 \times 27)$

 B. $(3 \times 9) + (3 \times 9)$

 C. (12×36)

 D. $(3 \times 9) + (3 \times 9) + (3 \times 9) + (3 \times 9)$

Answer: A. $(3 \times 9)\,(3 \times 9)\,(27 \times 27)$

$(3 \times 9)^4 = (3 \times 9)\,(3 \times 9)\,(3 \times 9)\,(3 \times 9)$, which, when solving two of the parentheses, is $(3 \times 9)\,(3 \times 9)\,(27 \times 27)$.

(Average) (Skill 16.1)

111. **Jason can run a distance of 50 yards in 6.5 seconds. At this rate, how many feet can he run in a time of 26 seconds?**

 A. 200

 B. 400

 C. 600

 D. 800

Answer: C. 600

$\frac{26}{6.5} = 4$, so Jason can run a distance of $(4)(50) = 200$ yards in 26 seconds. Since 1 yard is equivalent to 3 feet, 200 yards is equivalent to $(200)(3) = 600$ feet.

(Rigorous) (Skill 16.1)

112. **You are helping students list the steps needed to solve the word problem:**

     "Mr. Jones is 5 times as old as his son. Two years later he will be 4 times as old as his son. How old is Mr. Jones?"

     One of the students makes the following list:

     1. Assume Mr. Jones' son is x years old. Express Mr. Jones' age in terms of x.

     2. Write how old they will be two years later in terms of x.

     3. Solve the equation for x.

     4. Multiply the answer by 5 to get Mr. Jones' age.

     What step is missing between steps 2 and 3?

     A. Write an equation setting Mr. Jones' age equal to 5 times his son's age

     B. Write an equation setting Mr. Jones' age two years later equal to 5 times his son's age two years later

     C. Write an equation setting Mr. Jones' age equal to 4 times his son's age

     D. Write an equation setting Mr. Jones' age two years later equal to 4 times his son's age two years later

     Answer: D. Write an equation setting Mr. Jones' age two years later equal to 4 times his son's age two years later

     For step 2, we can represent Mr. Jones' age in two years as $5x + 2$ and his son's age in two years as $x + 2$. But before we can solve an equation for x, we need to state that Mr. Jones' age in two years will be 4 times his son's age in two years. This will show the relationship between father and son in two years. The actual equation becomes $5x + 2 = 4(x + 2)$, which will lead to $x = 6$ (the son's current age).

Note that Mr. Jones' current age must be $(5)(6) = 30$. As a check, we observe that in two years the son will be 8 years old and Mr. Jones will be 32 years old.

(Easy) (Skill 15.1)

113. **What is the next term in the following sequence?**

     $\{0.005, 0.03, 0.18, 1.08 \ldots\}$

     A. 1.96

     B. 2.16

     C. 3.32

     D. 6.48

     Answer: D. 6.48

     This is a geometric sequence where each term is obtained by multiplying the preceding term by the common ratio 6. Thus, the next term in the sequence is $1.08 \times 6 = 6.48$.

(Rigorous) (Skill 15.1)

114. **A student has taken three tests in his algebra class for which the mean score is 88. He will take one more test and his final grade will be the mean of all four tests. He wants to achieve a final grade of 90. Which one of the following is the correct procedure to determine the score he needs on the fourth test?**

     A. He needs a score 92 since $(88 + 92) \div 2 = 90$

     B. He needs a score of 89.5 since $(88 + 90 + 90 + 90) \div 4 = 89.5$

     C. He needs a score of 96 since $(88 + 88 + 88 + 96) \div 4 = 90$

     D. He cannot achieve a final grade of 90 since each of his scores on the first three tests is less than 90

Answer: C. He needs a score of 96 since
$(88 + 88 + 88 + 96) \div 4 = 90$

The sum of all four tests must be $(90)(4) = 360$ in order to achieve a mean score of 90. Since he has averaged 88 on his first three tests, the sum of his scores thus far is $(88)(3) = 264$. Therefore he needs a score of $360 - 264 = 96$ on his fourth test.

(Average) (Skill 17.6)

115. **Given similar polygons with corresponding sides of lengths 9 and 15, find the perimeter of the smaller polygon if the perimeter of the larger polygon is 150 units.**

    A. 54

    B. 135

    C. 90

    D. 126

Answer: C. 90

The perimeters of similar polygons are directly proportional to the lengths of their sides, therefore $\frac{9}{15} = \frac{x}{150}$. Cross-multiply to obtain $1350 = 15x$, then divide by 15 to obtain the perimeter of the smaller polygon.

(Average) (Skill 19.1)

116. **Which of the following statements best characterizes the meaning of "absolute value of x"?**

    A. The square root of x

    B. The square of x

    C. The distance on a number line between x and $-x$

    D. The distance on a number line between 0 and x

Answer: D. The distance on a number line between 0 and x

The absolute value of a number x is best described as the distance on a number line between 0 and x, regardless of whether x is positive or negative. Note that the following expression is valid for $x \geq 0$:

$$|x| = |{-x}|$$

(Average) (Skill 19.1)

117. **Which of the following terms most accurately describes the set of numbers below?**

    $$\{3, \sqrt{16}, \pi^0, 6, \frac{28}{4}\}$$

    A. Rationals

    B. Irrationals

    C. Complex

    D. Whole numbers

Answer: D. Whole numbers

Let's simplify the set of numbers as follows.

$$\{3, 4, 1, 6, 7\}$$

Note that this set of numbers can be described as real numbers, rationals, integers, and whole numbers, but they are best described as whole numbers.

(Rigorous) (Skill 16.1)

118. **What is the GCF of 12, 30, 56, and 144?**

    A. 2

    B. 3

    C. 5

    D. 7

Answer: A. 2

One way to determine the greatest common factor (GCF) is to list the factors for each number. Although this can be tedious, it is a relatively sure method of determining the GCF. Note that you need not determine any factors larger than the smallest number in the list (12, in this case)—12 doesn't have any factors greater than 12.

12:   2, 3, 4, 6, 12
30:   2, 3, 5, 6, 10
56:   2, 4, 7, 8
144: 2, 3, 4, 6, 8, 9, 12

By inspection of these lists, we see that 2 is the greatest common factor.

(Average) (Skill 16.6)

119. **The final cost of an item (with sales tax) is $8.35. If the sales tax is 7%, what was the pre-tax price of the item?**

    A. $7.80

    B. $8.00

    C. $8.28

    D. $8.93

Answer: A. $7.80

We can solve this problem by constructing a proportionality expression. Let's call the pre-tax price of the item x; then, if we add 7% of x to this price, we get a final cost of $8.35.

$$x + 0.07x = \$8.35$$
$$1.07x = \$8.35$$
$$x = \frac{\$8.35}{1.07} = \$7.80$$

Thus, the initial price of the item was $7.80 (answer A). You can also determine this answer by multiplying each option by 1.07; the correct answer is the one that yields a product of $8.35.

(Rigorous) (Skill 16.7)

120. **A burning candle loses $\frac{1}{2}$ inch in height every hour. If the original height of the candle was 6 inches, which of the following equations describes the relationship between the height h of the candle and the number of hours t since it was lit?**

    A. $2h + t = 12$

    B. $2h - t = 12$

    C. $h = 6 - t$

    D. $h = 0.5t + 6$

Answer: A. $2h + t = 12$

Since the height of the candle is falling, the slope $= -\frac{1}{2}$. Thus, the equation in the slope-intercept form is $h = -\left(\frac{1}{2}\right)t + 6$ since $h = 6$ for $t = 0$. Multiplying both sides of the equation by 2, we get $2h = -t + 12$ or $2h + t = 12$.

(Rigorous) (Skill 16.10)

121. **Which set cannot be considered "dense"?**

A. Integers

B. Rationals

C. Irrationals

D. Reals

Answer: A. Integers

A set of numbers is considered dense if between any two arbitrary values from the set, there exists another value from the set that lies between these two values. For instance, between 1 and 3 is the number 2. For integers, however, there is no integer between 1 and 2, for example (or between any two consecutive integers). Thus, the correct answer is choice A. For the other sets (rationals, irrationals, and reals), there is always a value between any two arbitrary values from those sets.

(Rigorous) (Skill 19.1)

122. **In probability, the sample space represents:**

A. An outcome of an experiment

B. A list of all possible outcomes of an experiment

C. The number of times you must flip a coin

D. The amount of room needed to conduct an experiment

Answer: B. A list of all possible outcomes of an experiment

The sample space is the list of all possible outcomes that you can have for an experiment.

Social Studies

(Average) (Skill 20.4)

123. **What is socialization?**

A. The broad knowledge and thorough understanding of students' development

B. The contribution of the family to a person's sense of self-importance and identity

C. A person's sense of belonging developed through common ideals and behaviors

D. The process by which humans learn the expectations society has for their behavior for them to function successfully within that society

Answer: D. The process by which humans learn the expectations society has for their behavior for them to function successfully within that society

Although the teacher has a broad knowledge and thorough understanding of students' development, this is not socialization. The family is the primary influence on a child's socialization, and a person's sense of belonging through common ideals and behaviors results from socialization.

(Rigorous) (Skill 20.5)

124. **All of the following are key elements in planning a child-centered curriculum EXCEPT:**

    A. Referring students who need special tutoring

    B. Identifying students' prior knowledge and skills

    C. Sequencing learning activities

    D. Specifying behavioral objectives

Answer: A. Referring students who need special tutoring

A child-centered curriculum is the result of careful and deliberate planning. Good planning includes specifying behavioral objectives and students' entry behavior (knowledge and skills), selecting and sequencing learning activities to move students from entry behavior to objective, and evaluating the outcomes of instruction to improve planning. Referring a student who needs special tutoring to someone else or to another program is not part of a child-centered curriculum.

(Average) (Skill 20.6)

125. **Which of the following resources is required to make social studies more interesting to students and to appeal to different learning styles?**

    A. Audiovisual aids

    B. A good textbook

    C. Computers

    D. Library books and magazines

Answer: B. A good textbook

Library resources can expand a child's knowledge, and computers offer teaching tools and resources. Audiovisual aids can be beneficial in the classroom environment, but a good textbook is required to make the subject matter more interesting and to appeal to different learning styles because a textbook provides the students with something they can refer to and study.

(Easy) (Skill 20.7)

126. **Which of the following is important for preparing resources and collecting data for research projects?**

    A. Identify the purpose of the research

    B. Specify the thesis

    C. Create folders for sorting the information

    D. Prepare visuals, such as poster boards

Answer: C. Create folders for sorting information

When preparing the resources and collecting data, students should create folders for sorting the data/information. Providing labels for the folders will organize it and make construction of the final project or presentation easier and faster.

(Average) (Skill 20.8)

127. **Which of the following is the purpose of social participation in using social science skills and research tools?**

   A. Acquiring information

   B. Communicating information

   C. Tying together major themes

   D. Learning research methods

Answer: C. Tying together major themes

Acquiring information is accomplished by using a variety of methods. Communicating the information is considered social participating. Learning research methods teaches students to acquire information. The purpose of social participation ties together the major themes that cross the spectrum of the social sciences.

(Average) (Skill 20.11)

128. **The Texas Assessment of Knowledge and Skills (TAKS) test is an example of:**

   A. Criterion-referenced assessment

   B. Norm-referenced assessment

   C. Performance-based assessment

   D. Another type of assessment

Answer: B. Norm-referenced assessment

A criterion-referenced assessment is used to see how well schools are meeting national and state learning standards. The national educational mandate of No Child Left Behind (NCLB) and Adequate Yearly Progress (AYP) use criterion-referenced assessments to measure student learning, school performance, and school improvement goals. Performance-based assessments currently are used in a number of state testing programs to measure the learning outcomes of individual students in subject content areas. Another type of assessment is used for ESL students. Norm-referenced assessments are used to classify student learners in homogenous groupings based on ability level or basic skills into a ranking category. TAKS is an example of a norm-referenced assessment.

(Average) (Skill 21.1)

129. **Which country established a fort at Matagorda Bay, providing the basis for that country's claim to the Texas territory?**

   A. France

   B. Spain

   C. United States

   D. Mexico

Answer: A. France

In 1685, the French explorer Sieur de La Salle established Fort St. Louis at Matagorda Bay, which was the basis of France's claim to the Texas territory.

(Average) (Skill 21.2)

130. In what year was Texas annexed to the United States and made a state?

A. 1836

B. 1845

C. 1850

D. 1861

Answer: B. 1845

Texas became an independent country in 1836. In 1850, Texas's borders were adjusted after the Mexican–American War to comply with the Compromise of 1850. In 1861, Texas seceded from the United States and became part of the Confederacy. In 1845, Texas was annexed to the United States and was granted statehood.

(Rigorous) (Skill 21.3)

131. Which was the earliest period that shows evidence of Native American civilization in Texas?

A. Early Archaic

B. Late Prehistoric

C. Upper Paleolithic

D. Late Archaic

Answer: C. Upper Paleolithic

The Early Archaic period was from 6000 to 2500 BCE. The Late Prehistoric period extends from 700 CE to historic times. The Late Archaic period lasted from 1000 to 300 BCE. Archaeologists have discovered evidence of Native American civilization in Texas dating back to the Upper Paleolithic period in the late Ice Age, approximately 9200 BCE.

(Easy) (Skill 21.4)

132. Which of the following statements about French settlement of Texas is INCORRECT?

A. The French wanted to open trade opportunities in the area

B. The French wanted to discover a route to the Mississippi River

C. The French wanted to expand the French empire in North America

D. The French settlement in Texas was long-lived

Answer: D. The French settlement in Texas was long-lived

The purposes of early French exploration and attempts to establish a settlement were establishing trading opportunities and discovering a direct route into Louisiana to the Mississippi River. The French claimed the territory for approximately 70 years in efforts to expand the French empire in North America. In comparison to other European countries' settlements in Texas, their settlement was short-lived.

(Average) (Skill 21.5)

133. Which of the following statements about population centers is correct?

A. They tend to be away from agricultural areas

B. They tend to be relatively near one another

C. They tend to be far from smaller towns

D. They tend to achieve megalopolis standards

Answer: B. They tend to be relatively near one another

Most places in the world are close to agricultural land, and population centers tend to be relatively near one another. When population centers reach mega-lopolis standards, there often are no clear boundaries between one town and the next.

(Average) (Skill 21.8)

134. **Which of the following statements about historic causation is INCORRECT?**

   A. Its root causes can be seen immediately

   B. It is a concept about the events in history

   C. Its premise is that events in history are linked

   D. Events are linked by cause and effect

   Answer: A. Its root causes can be seen immediately

   Historic causation is the concept that events in history are linked to one another by a chain of cause and effect. The root causes of major historical events cannot always be seen immediately. Usually, they become apparent many years later.

(Average) (Skill 21.9)

135. **What is the study of the social behavior of groups of humans?**

   A. Anthropology

   B. Psychology

   C. Sociology

   D. Cultural geography

   Answer: C. Sociology

The study of social behavior in minority groups would be primarily in the area of sociology, as it is the discipline most concerned with social interaction.

(Rigorous) (Skills 21.10 and 21.11)

136. **For a historian studying ancient Egypt, which of the following would be LEAST useful?**

   A. The record of an ancient Greek historian on Greek–Egyptian interaction

   B. Letters from an Egyptian ruler to his or her regional governors

   C. Inscriptions on stele of the Fourteenth Dynasty of Egypt

   D. Letters from a nineteenth-century Egyptologist to his wife

   Answer: D. Letters from a nineteenth-century Egyptologist to his wife

   Historians use primary sources from the period they are studying whenever possible. Ancient Greek records of interaction with Egypt, letters from an Egyptian ruler to regional governors, and inscriptions from the Fourteenth Dynasty of Egyptian are all primary sources created during or near the period being studied. Letters from a nineteenth-century Egyptologist would not be considered primary sources because they were created thousands of years after the period being studied and may not relate directly to the subject of study.

(Easy) (Skill 21.12)

137. **Which of the following is a secondary source?**

A. Objects made during the period being studied

B. Objects used during the period being studied

C. Statistical data on the period being studied

D. Books created during the period being studied.

Answer: C. Statistical data on the period being studied

Objects made and used during the period being studied are primary sources. Books created during the period being studied also are primary sources. Statistical data on the period being studied is a secondary source because the data was not created during the period being studied.

(Average) (Skill 21.13)

138. **Which statement is true about the problem-solving process?**

A. The process provides limited opportunity for determining authenticity

B. Collaboration develops the ability to work as part of a team

C. Collaboration limits the viewpoints of others

D. Statistical evaluation is not part of the problem-solving process

Answer: B. Collaboration develops the ability to work as part of a team

The problem-solving process provides a good opportunity for investigating a line of inquiry and develops the ability to determine authenticity among sources.

Collaboration develops the ability to determine and respect the viewpoints of others. Statistical evaluation is an important part of the problem-solving process, and collaboration develops the ability to work as part of a team.

(Average) (Skill 21.14)

139. **Which of the following statements about the decision-making process is INCORRECT?**

A. The first step in the decision-making process is to identify options

B. Decision-making can be broken down into steps

C. Using methodical steps results in sound decisions based on relevant facts

D. Predicting consequences of a decision is an important step in the process

Answer: A. The first step in the decision-making process is to identify options

Decision-making can be broken down into steps that result in sound decisions based on relevant facts, and predicting consequences in an important step in the process. The first step in the decision-making process is identifying situations that require decisions.

(Average) (Skill 21.16)

140. **African Americans moving to Texas during the Great Migration to search for better-paying jobs is an example of which element of history?**

A. Politics

B. Geography

C. Gender

D. Economic

Answer: D. Economic

Gender focuses on the relative positions men and women hold in a society and is connected to other themes, such as politics and economics. Politics provides information about opinions and groups of people and how they change over time. As a historical lens, economic factors can connect events to their economic causes. The Great Migration of African Americans to Texas in search of better-paying jobs is an example of an economic factor of history.

(Average) (Skill 22.1)

141. **Which of the following is an example of the human characteristic of "place" in geography?**

    A. Mountains

    B. Canals

    C. Rivers

    D. Deserts

Answer: B. Canals

Place is one theme of geography. Mountains, rivers, and deserts are examples of physical characteristics of place. Canals and roads are examples of human characteristics. Human characteristics are features created by humans' interaction with their environment.

(Average) (Skills 22.1 and 22.2)

142. **Which of the following oceans does NOT touch the shores of Antarctica?**

    A. Atlantic

    B. Pacific

    C. Indian

    D. Arctic

Answer: D. Arctic

The Atlantic, Pacific, and Indian oceans touch the shores of Antarctica. The Arctic Ocean does not touch Antarctica.

(Average) (Skill 22.3)

143. **Where are the vast plains of Texas located?**

    A. In the northern and western parts of the state

    B. In the southern and eastern parts of the state

    C. In the central and eastern parts of the state

    D. In the central and western parts of the state

Answer: D. In the central and western parts of the state

The vast plains of Texas are located in the central and western parts of the state.

(Rigorous) (Skill 22.4)

144. **Which of the following statements about the Gulf Stream is INCORRECT?**

    A. It is a cold current

    B. It is a warm current

    C. It is in the Atlantic Ocean

    D. It was named by Benjamin Franklin

Answer: A. It is a cold current

All of the statements are true about the Gulf Stream except for Choice A. The Gulf Stream is a warm current in the Atlantic Ocean that carries warm water from the equator to the northern parts of the Atlantic Ocean. Benjamin Franklin studied and named the Gulf Stream.

(Average) (Skill 22.5)

145. **What is the greatest influence on land use?**

    A. Geography

    B. Industries

    C. Population

    D. Agriculture

Answer: C. Population

Industries and agriculture are two ways people use land. Although geography influences land use, the greatest influence on land use is population and population growth.

(Easy) (Skill 22.9)

146. **What is the term for the introduction of new ways of performing work or organizing societies?**

    A. Cultural diffusion

    B. Innovation

    C. Adaptation

    D. Acculturation

Answer: B. Innovation

Cultural diffusion is the movement of cultural ideas or materials among populations, independent of the movement of those populations. Adaptation is the process by which individuals and societies change their behavior and organization to cope with social, economic, and environmental pressures. Acculturation is an exchange or adoption of cultural features when two cultures come into regular direct contact. Innovation is the introduction of new ways of performing work or organizing societies. Innovation can spur drastic changes in a culture.

(Average) (Skill 22.10)

147. **Which of the following statements about ethnicity is INCORRECT?**

    A. An ethnic group is a population of people from a common geographic area who share certain physical traits

    B. Ethnic groups often have a common language and ancestral background and frequently exist within larger populations

    C. Ethnicity is based more on common cultural behaviors and institutions than on common physical traits

    D. Ethnicity and race sometimes are linked, but they differ because many ethnic groups can exist within a population of people considered to be of the same race

Answer: A. An ethnic group is a population of people from a common geographic area who share certain physical traits

Choices B, C, and D are correct. Choice A is incorrect because *race,* not *ethnicity,* is the term used to describe a population of people from a common geographic area who share certain physical traits.

(Easy) (Skill 22.11)

148. **Which of the following individuals led the movement to colonize the area of Texas as American?**

    A. Sam Houston

    B. Curtis Graves

    C. Stephen F. Austin

    D. James Bowie

Answer: C. Stephen F. Austin

Sam Houston was president of the Republic of Texas and supported bringing Texas into the United States. Curtis Graves was an African American who was elected as a member of the Texas state legislature in 1966. James Bowie fought in the Texas Revolution. Stephen Austin led a movement to colonize the area of Texas an American.

(Average) (Skill 22.13)

149. **Which heritage is honored by the preservation of Ceremonial Cave in Texas?**

    A. Asian

    B. Western European

    C. Eastern European

    D. Hispanic

Answer: D. Hispanic

Ceremonial Cave, Espiritu Santo, and Morhiss Mound honor the Hispanic heritage of many Texas citizens.

(Average) (Skill 22.14)

150. **All of the following terms describe characteristics of early human civilizations EXCEPT:**

    A. Gatherers

    B. Agricultural

    C. Adaptable

    D. Hunters

Answer: B. Agricultural

Early humans were hunters and gatherers. They needed to be adaptable to find ways to obtain food and shelter and to create clothing for survival in different climates. Later, human civilizations moved from hunting and gathering to agricultural pursuits.

(Rigorous) (Skill 22.15)

151. **When did the pre-Columbian cultures reach their developmental peak in Texas?**

    A. Before the arrival of European explorers

    B. After the arrival of European explorers

    C. Pre-Columbian cultures did not live in the area of present-day Texas

    D. After the groups became recognized by the federal government

Answer: A. Before the arrival of the European explorers

Texas lies at the intersection of the Southwest and the Plains areas, both of which are major cultural areas of pre-Columbian North America. There were three major native civilizations in the area now covered by the state of Texas. They reached their developmental peak before the arrival of European explorers.

(Average) (Skill 22.16)

152. **Which of the following statements is true about beliefs and values?**

    A. Values are things that are thought to be true

    B. Beliefs are what a society thinks is right and wrong

    C. A culture's beliefs and values are reflected in its cultural products

    D. Beliefs and values are unrelated

Answer: C. A culture's beliefs and values are reflected in its cultural products

Beliefs are things that are thought to be true. Values are what a society thinks is right and wrong. Beliefs and values are similar. Choice C is correct because a culture's beliefs and values are reflected in its cultural products, such as literature, art, media, and architecture.

(Average) (Skill 22.17)

153. **Which of the following statements is true about the concept of diversity?**

    A. Diversity content discourages the use of ethnically diverse textbooks

    B. Diversity content discourages the use of curriculum activities

    C. One goal for teachers in teaching diversity is the pursuit of democracy

    D. Supplementary teaching materials diminish the importance of diversity teaching

Answer: C. One goal for teachers in teaching diversity is the pursuit of democracy

The teaching of diversity is a quest for equality, social justice, and the pursuit of democracy. Integration of diversity content material allows teachers to illustrate key concepts, cultural values, and theories from a variety of cultures. Textbooks, curriculum activities, and supplementary teaching materials are all used in teaching the concept of diversity.

(Average) (Skill 23.2)

154. **Which economic term is defined as the value of the sacrificed alternative?**

    A. Demand

    B. Opportunity cost

    C. Supply

    D. Free enterprise

Answer: B. Opportunity cost

Demand refers to the quantity of a good or service that buyers are willing and able to buy at different prices during a given period. Supply refers to the quantity of a good or service that sellers are willing and able to sell at different prices during a given period. In a free enterprise system, business is based on the laws of supply and demand rather than government control. Opportunity cost, also referred to as the value of the sacrificed alternative, is the tradeoff when deciding which goods to produce.

(Rigorous) (Skill 23.3)

155. **Which is NOT one of the five major economic activities identified in the TEKS glossary?**

    A. Exchanging

    B. Saving

    C. Investing

    D. Marketing

Answer: D. Marketing

According to the TEKS glossary, the five major economic activities are producing, exchanging, consuming, saving, and investing. Marketing is the program or method used to provide ways for manufacturers to obtain purchasers for the products they are producing.

(Easy) (Skill 23.4)

156. **What is the basis for the cost of a resource?**

    A. The scarcity of the resource

    B. The cost of production

    C. Consumer demand

    D. All of the above

    Answer: A. The scarcity of the resource

    The free-market economy functions on supply and demand. The cost of production is based on a variety of factors. Consumer demand represents the desires of the consumer for a product. Resource costs are based on the scarcity of the resource. The scarcer a resource is, relatively speaking, the higher its price.

(Average) (Skill 23.6)

157. **Why are economic activities less closely tied to particular locations as they were in the past?**

    A. There are fewer resources

    B. Towns that developed around a single economic activity no longer exist

    C. Modern transportation enables resources to be drawn from a wider area

    D. Economic activities continue to be as closely tied to particular locations as they were in the past

Answer: C. Modern transportation enables resources to be drawn from a wider area

The ability to transport materials cheaply over long distances has freed producers from their previous ties to particular locations. For example, in the past, a town with a river may have harnessed its water power for a mill, and the economic viability of that town would have depended upon the success of the mill. Today, products such as oil can be shipped over long distances. Production facilities therefore can draw natural resources from a wider area.

(Average) (Skill 24.2)

158. **What is the purpose of the conference committee?**

    A. It studies the bills presented in Congress

    B. It resolves differences between the House and Senate versions of bills

    C. It researches issues the bills present

    D. It sends bills to the president for the president's signature

Answer: B. It resolves differences between the House and Senate versions of bills

The standing committees study the bills and the issues raised by the bills after the bills are introduced in Congress. The president receives the bill after the bill has passed both the House and Senate in the same form. The conference committee resolves differences between House and Senate versions of a bill before both houses of Congress approve it.

(Easy) (Skill 24.2)

159. What is the most basic form of participation in government?

    A. Serving as an elected official

    B. Campaigning for candidates

    C. Serving on a jury

    D. Voting

Answer: D. Voting

People can participate in government by serving as an elected official, campaigning for candidates running for office, and serving on a jury, but the most basic form of participation in government is voting.

(Rigorous) (Skill 24.3)

160. Which Amendment to the U.S. Constitution prohibits cruel and unusual punishment?

    A. Eighth

    B. Sixth

    C. Fifth

    D. First

Answer: A. Eighth

The First Amendment guarantees freedom of religion and free speech. The Fifth Amendment guarantees against self-incrimination. The Sixth Amendment provides for a trial by jury and the right to legal counsel. The Eighth Amendment prohibits cruel and unusual punishment.

(Average) (Skill 24.4)

161. "Life, liberty, and the pursuit of happiness" are referred to in which document?

    A. Magna Carta

    B. Bill of Rights

    C. Declaration of Independence

    D. Constitution

Answer: C. Declaration of Independence

The Declaration of Independence identifies life, liberty, and pursuit of happiness as rights of citizens.

(Average) (Skill 24.5)

162. Why did the Spanish begin to colonize Texas?

    A. They wanted to build missions

    B. They wanted a route to the Mississippi River

    C. They were concerned about the French presence in Louisiana

    D. They wanted to remove the Native Americans from the area

Answer: C. They were concerned about the French presence in Louisiana

Spain became concerned with the French presence in Louisiana and began to colonize Texas. The Spanish established numerous villages and missions in the province.

(Average) (Skill 24.6)

163. **What is the basis of all laws in the United States?**

    A. The Supreme Court

    B. The Constitution

    C. Congress

    D. The president

Answer: B. The Constitution

The Supreme Court interprets the laws. The president enforces the laws, and Congress makes the laws. The Constitution provides the basis of all laws in the United States.

Science

(Rigorous) (Skill 25.7)

164. **Which of the following is equivalent to 200nm?**

    A. 2 millimeters

    B. 2×10^{-7} meters

    C. 2×10^{-9} meters

    D. 20 centimeters

Answer: B. 2×10^{-7} meters

There are 10^{-9} nanometers in one meter so 200nm is equal to 2×10^{-7} meters.

(Rigorous) (Skill 25.5)

165. **Which of the following is NOT true about error?**

    A. Systematic error can never be eliminated

    B. Percent error is calculated as the $100 \times$ (Observed − Expected)

    C. Random error can be due to the limitations in the precision of the measuring instrument

    D. An experiment can have a zero error

Answer: C. Random error can be due to limitations in the precision of the measuring instrument

Measurements are always limited by the precision of the measuring instrument. For instance, a ruler can resolve to the millimeter level but not the micrometer or nanometer level.

(Average) (Skill 26.1)

166. The scientific method relies on all but

_____.

A. gathering empirical evidence through testing

B. manipulating logic and the experimental results

C. reproducible experiments

D. testing that relies on observation and measurement

Answer: B. manipulating logic and the experimental results

The scientific method relies on careful and accurate testing of a hypothesis to obtain observable, measurable, and empirical evidence about whether the hypothesis is true. Experiments must be reproducible (can be repeated by others with the same results). Manipulating logic and the experimental results runs counter to the philosophy of the scientific method and is also unethical.

(Average) (Skill 26.2)

167. Your student notices that two of his classmates arrive at school late every morning. He makes an educated guess and tells you that his classmates may oversleep. Which steps of the scientific method has your student completed?

A. Forming a hypothesis and collecting data

B. Asking a question and forming a hypothesis

C. Asking and question and stating a conclusion

D. Forming a hypothesis and stating a conclusion

Answer: B. Asking a question and forming a hypothesis

Your student has asked why his classmates are tardy and has guessed (hypothesized) that they oversleep every morning.

(Rigorous) (Skill 26.2)

168. An experiment is performed to determine how the surface area of a liquid affects how long it takes for the liquid to evaporate. One hundred milliliters of water is put in containers with surface areas of 10 cm^2, 30 cm^2, 50 cm^2, 70 cm^2, and 90 cm^2. The time it took for each container to evaporate is recorded. Which of the following is a controlled variable?

A. The time required for each evaporation

B. The area of the surfaces

C. The amount of water

D. The temperature of the water

Answer: C. The amount of water

The surface area is the independent variable and the time is the dependent variable. The temperature of the water should have been controlled in this experiment.

(Rigorous) (Skill 26.5)

169. Stars near Earth can be seen to move relative to fixed stars. In observing the motion of a nearby star over a period of decades, an astronomer notices that the path is not a straight line but wobbles about a straight line. The astronomer reports in a peer-reviewed journal that a planet is rotating around the star, causing it to wobble. Which of the following statements best describes the proposition that the star has a planet?

   A. Observation

   B. Hypothesis

   C. Theory

   D. Inference

Answer: D. Inference

The observation in the report was the wobbly path of the star. It would be a hypothesis if this was the basis of a further experiment or observation about the existence of the planet. A theory would be less speculative. The astronomer didn't just suggest that the planet was there; the report stated that the star has a planet.

(Rigorous) (Skill 26.4)

170. Your student is studying the effect of soda on plant growth and wants to run an experiment for one week. How should you advise your student to measure plant growth?

   A. Eyeball the growth over the course of the study

   B. Measure the height of the plant before the study starts and every day until the study's end

   C. Measure the height of the plant before adding soda and after one week

   D. Both B and C

Answer: D. Both B and C

Either of the choices are reasonable and depend on how much data your student wants to collect. However, the more data the better so that one does not have to extrapolate between the before and after measurements. For instance, if there's an increase in plant growth, having daily measurements would allow your student to know whether the increase was gradual over the week or rapid during specific days.

(Easy) (Skill 26.5)

171. Your student runs an experiment and finds that a hair growth product increases the length of hair by one inch in a month. Assume that all control and treatment groups were created appropriately. What can you advise him to conclude?

   A. The experiment needs to be repeated

   B. The hair growth product doesn't work

   C. The hair growth product works

   D. There isn't enough information to form a conclusion

Answer: C. The hair growth product works

The results indicate that length of hair increased so the hair growth product worked in your student's particular experiment.

(Rigorous) (Skill 26.6)

172. Your student performs a survey to find out why some students excel on your quizzes. She finds that most successful students state that they study more, but she also considers that some students also have tutors or get good sleep before quiz days. How do you advise your student to evaluate these possibilities?

A. Have her randomly select students and assign them to either study more, get a tutor, or get a good night's sleep before quiz day. Then measure quiz performance.

B. Have her randomly select students and assign them to either study more, get a tutor, get a good night's sleep before quiz day, or not do any of these three things. Then measure quiz performance.

C. Have her evaluate according to her opinions.

D. She doesn't need to evaluate these possibilities.

Answer: B. Have her randomly select students and assign them to either study more, get a tutor, get a good night's sleep before quiz day, or not do any of these three things. Then measure quiz performance.

To evaluate the contribution of each factor to quiz performance she could randomly select and assign students as described in the answer choice. The control group would not do any of the three tasks.

(Average) (Skill 26.5)

173. A determination reached on the basis of one experiment's evidence and reasoning is a/an _____.

A. theory

B. justification

C. inference

D. law

Answer: C. inference

Scientists infer, statistically and with existing knowledge, the meaning and implications of their experimental data. A theory and law are inferences made from many experiments.

(Easy) (Skill 26.8)

174. How can students communicate their experiments?

A. PowerPoint presentation

B. Poster

C. Reports

D. All of the above

Answer: D. All of the above

All the following media are ways in which scientific findings are communicated.

(Average) (Skill 26.9)

175. **Which of the following is NOT an unethical action?**

A. Letting one's biases affect the inclusion of human participants in a study

B. "Fudging" data to make it fit the desired result

C. Making up experimental results

D. Sharing an established experimental protocol with a labmate

Answer: D. Sharing an established experimental protocol with a labmate

It is not considered unethical to share experimental protocols, and it is actually encouraged in the scientific community in order to streamline procedures. It is never acceptable to fudge or make up data.

(Rigorous) (Skill 26.10)

176. **Which of the following is true when a new theory is developed regarding a topic?**

A. The existing theories on the topic could be altered/adjusted upon proof

B. The new theory should just be accepted

C. The new theory should not be even considered

D. Both the new and old theories should be debated and a vote taken on which one to accept

Answer: A. The existing theories on the topic could be altered/adjusted upon proof

The nature of science is such that it is always changing. Therefore, new theories, upon proof, can help adjust/alter currently existing theories. New data and new technologies contribute to different interpretations of observations.

(Average) (Skill 26.11)

177. **Which famous scientist is NOT matched with his work?**

A. Galileo Galilei—discovered Jupiter's four largest satellites

B. Isaac Newton—created calculus

C. Thomas Edison—improved carbon light bulb filament

D. Albert Einstein—created theory of relativity

Answer: C. Thomas Edison—improved carbon light bulb filament

Lewis Latimer, an African American inventor, improved Edison's light bulb filament in the late 1800s, and it was his design that was introduced across society.

(Rigorous) (Skill 27.5)

178. **Which of the following is the most accurate definition of a nonrenewable resource?**

    A. A nonrenewable resource is never replaced once used

    B. A nonrenewable resource is replaced on a time scale that is very long relative to human life spans

    C. A nonrenewable resource is a resource that can only be manufactured by humans

    D. A nonrenewable resource is a species that has already become extinct

Answer: B. A nonrenewable resource is replaced on a time scale that is very long relative to human life spans

Renewable resources are renewed, or replaced, in time for humans to use more of them. Examples include fast-growing plants, animals, and oxygen gas. (Note that while sunlight is often considered a renewable resource, it is actually a nonrenewable but extremely abundant resource.) Nonrenewable resources renew themselves only on very long time scales, usually geologic time scales. Examples include minerals, metals, and fossil fuels.

(Average) (Skill 28.3)

179. **All of the following are hormones in the human body EXCEPT:**

    A. Cortisol

    B. Testosterone

    C. Norepinephrine

    D. Hemoglobin

Answer: D. Hemoglobin

Hemoglobin is a protein molecule that carries oxygen in red blood cells. Cortisol and norepinephrine are stress-related hormones. Testosterone is a sex-related hormone.

(Rigorous) (Skill 29.4)

180. **There are a number of common misconceptions that claim to be based in science. All of the following are misconceptions EXCEPT:**

    A. Evolution is a process that does not address the origins of life

    B. The average person uses only a small fraction of his or her brain

    C. Raw sugar causes hyperactive behavior in children

    D. Seasons are caused by the Earth's elliptical orbit

Answer: A. Evolution is a process that does not address the origins of life

The theory of evolution presupposes existing life, but does not explain the origins of life. This is a good example of a truth that can easily be misconstrued. Most people holding misconceptions are not aware that their beliefs are erroneous. It is critical that instructors understand common misconceptions in science so that they can not only avoid them but also correct them.

(Rigorous) (Skill 31.1)

181. Which of the following does NOT determine the frictional force of a box sliding down a ramp?

    A. The weight of the box

    B. The area of the box

    C. The angle the ramp makes with the horizontal

    D. The chemical properties of the two surfaces

Answer: B. The area of the box

The frictional force is caused by bonding between the molecules of the box with the molecules of the ramp. At a small number of points, there is contact between the molecules. While there may be a small increase in the frictional force as the area increases, it is not noticeable. The main determinant of the frictional force is the weight of the box and the nature of the two surfaces.

(Average) (Skill 31.3)

182. Force is measured in _____.

    A. watts

    B. amperes

    C. newtons

    D. meters/second

Answer: C. newtons

The unit of measurement for force is the newton, named after Sir Isaac Newton.

(Rigorous) (Skill 31.3)

183. An object's _____ indicates how hard it would be to stop its motion.

    A. momentum

    B. potential energy

    C. kinetic energy

    D. mass

Answer: A. momentum

Momentum, an object's mass multiplied by its velocity, indicates the magnitude of a counter object that would be needed to stop the object's motion.

(Rigorous) (Skill 32.1)

184. Which of the following statements about the density of a substance is true?

    A. It is a chemical property

    B. It has no units

    C. It is an intensive property

    D. It is ten times the specific gravity of a substance

Answer: C. It is an intensive property

The density of a substance is the mass of the substance divided by its volume. It is an intensive property as it does not change if the mass of the substance changes.

(Average) (Skill 32.3)

185. The electrons in a neutral atom that are not in an excited energy state are in various energy shells. For example, there are two electrons in the lowest energy shell and eight in the next shell if the atom contains more than 10 electrons. How many electrons are in the shell with the maximum number of electrons?

A. 8

B. 18

C. 32

D. 44

Answer: C. 32

There is no energy level with 44 electrons. There is however, a shell with 18 electrons. The number of electrons in an atom's outer shell determines how the atom chemically interacts with other atoms.

(Rigorous) (Skill 32.5)

186. **Which of the following is NOT an example of a mixture?**

A. Soil

B. Air

C. Ocean water

D. H_2O

Answer: D. H_2O

H_2O is not a mixture but is instead a compound because the two elements, hydrogen and oxygen, are chemically bound.

(Rigorous) (Skill 32.1)

187. **Which statement best explains why a balance scale is used to measure both weight and mass?**

A. The weight and mass of an object are identical concepts

B. The force of gravity between two objects depends on the mass of the two objects

C. Inertial mass and gravitational mass are identical

D. A balance scale compares the weight of two objects

Answer: C. Inertial mass and gravitational mass are identical

The mass of an object is a fundamental property of matter and is measured in kilograms. The weight is the force of gravity between Earth and an object near Earth's surface and is measured in newtons or pounds. Newton's second law

$(F = ma)$ and the universal law of gravity $(F = G\frac{m_{earth}m}{d^2})$ determine the weight of an object. The mass in Newton's second law is called the inertial mass and the mass in the universal law of gravity is called the gravitational mass. The two kinds of masses are identical.

(Average) (Skill 33.2)

188. **Which statement is true about temperature?**

A. Temperature is a measurement of heat

B. Temperature is how hot or cold an object is

C. The coldest temperature ever measured is zero degrees Kelvin

D. The temperature of a molecule is its kinetic energy

Answer: B. Temperature is how hot or cold an object is

Temperature is a physical property of objects relating to how they feel when touched. For example, 0 degrees Celsius or 32 degrees Fahrenheit is defined as the temperature of ice water. Heat is a form of energy that flows from hot objects in thermal contact with cold objects. The greater the temperature of an object, the greater the kinetic energy of the molecules making up the object, but a single molecule does not have a temperature. The third law of thermodynamics is that absolute zero can never be achieved in a laboratory.

(Rigorous) (Skill 33.2)

189. **When glass is heated, it becomes softer and softer until it becomes a liquid. Which of the following statements best describes this phenomenon?**

    A. Glass has no heat of vaporization

    B. Glass has no heat of fusion

    C. The latent heat of glass is zero calories per gram

    D. Glass is made up of crystals

Answer: B. Glass has no heat of fusion

Glass does not have a well-defined melting temperature and latent heat is not required for the completion of its transformation from solid to liquid. The heat of vaporization is the calories of heat needed to change one gram of the liquid into a gas.

(Easy) (Skill 33.1)

190. **Which statement could be described as the first law of thermodynamics?**

    A. No machine can convert heat energy to work with 100 percent efficiency

    B. Energy is neither created nor destroyed

    C. Thermometers can be used to measure temperatures

    D. Heat flows from hot objects to cold objects

Answer: B. Energy is neither created nor destroyed

The first law of thermodynamics is considered to be a statement of the conservation of energy. Choices B and D are statements of the second law of thermodynamics.

(Average) (Skill 34.1)

191. **What kind of chemical reaction is the burning of coal?**

    A. Exothermic and composition

    B. Exothermic and decomposition

    C. Endothermic and composition

    D. Exothermic and decomposition

Answer: A. Exothermic and composition

Burning coal means oxygen is combining with carbon to produce carbon dioxide. Since heat is released, the reaction is exothermic. Since coal and oxygen are combining to form a carbon dioxide, the reaction is a composition.

(Average) (Skill 34.3)

192. **Which of the following is a result of a nuclear reaction called fusion?**

    A. Sunlight

    B. Cosmic radiation

    C. Supernova

    D. Existence of the elements in the periodic table

Answer: D. Existence of the elements in the periodic table

Inside stars, the atoms of hydrogen and helium combined to form the higher elements on the periodic table.

(Easy) (Skill 35.4)

193. **Which of the following processes and packages macromolecules?**

    A. Lysosome

    B. Cytosol

    C. Golgi apparatus

    D. Plastid

Answer: C. Golgi apparatus

Lysosomes contain digestive enzymes. Cytosol is the liquid inside cells. Plastids manufacture chemicals used in plant cells.

(Average) (Skill 35.1)

194. **Which of the following is a property of both eukaryotes and prokaryotes?**

    A. Nucleus

    B. Ribosomes

    C. Chromosomes

    D. Mitochondria

Answer: B. Ribosomes

Prokaryotes do not have a nucleus, and the DNA is not packed into chromosomes. Mitochondria are organelles that produce power and do not exist in the prokaryotes. Ribosomes are the sites of protein assembly.

(Average) (Skill 35.4)

195. **At what stage in mitosis does the chromatin become chromosomes?**

    A. Telophase

    B. Anaphase

    C. Prophase

    D. Metaphase

Answer: C. Prophase

Prophase is the beginning of mitosis and chromatin condense in this stage. In metaphase, fibers attach to chromosomes, and in anaphase, the chromosomes separate. In telophase, the cells divide.

(Average) (Skill 35.6)

196. **Which of the following is not the correct match of an Animalia phylum with examples of organisms found within the phylum?**

    A. Arthropoda—spiders and insects

    B. Echinodermata—sea urchins and starfish

    C. Mollusca—clams and octopi

    D. Annelida—crustaceans

Answer: D. Annelida—crustaceans

Annelida is the phylum of animals that includes segmented worms.

(Average) (Skill 35.6)

197. Taxonomy classifies species into genera (plural of genus) based on similarities. Species are subordinate to genera. The most general or highest taxonomical group is the kingdom. Which of the following is the correct order of the other groups from highest to lowest?

   A. Class ⇒ order ⇒ family ⇒ phylum

   B. Phylum ⇒ class ⇒ family ⇒ order

   C. Phylum ⇒ class ⇒ order ⇒ family

   D. Order ⇒ phylum ⇒ class ⇒ family

Answer: C. Phylum ⇒ class ⇒ order ⇒ family

In the case of the domestic dog, the genus (Canis) includes wolves, the family (Canidae) includes jackals and coyotes, the order (Carnivore) includes lions, the class (Mammals) includes mice, and the phylum (Chordata) includes fish.

(Average) (Skill 36.3)

198. Meiosis starts with two cells ends with which of the following?

   A. Four diploid cells

   B. Four haploid cells

   C. Eight diploid cells

   D. Eight haploid cells

Answer: D. Eight haploid cells

The single cell that begins the creation of a gamete has a full set of chromosomes in matched pairs. This is called a diploid cell. After the first division there are two haploid cells. After the second division, there are four haploid cells. If meiosis starts with two cells then there would be two sets of four haploid cells.

(Rigorous) (Skill 37.1)

199. Which of the following is NOT part of Darwinian evolution?

   A. Survival of the fittest

   B. Random mutations

   C. Heritability of acquired traits

   D. Natural selection

Answer: C. Heritability of acquired traits

Acquired traits change somatic cells but not gametes so they are not passed on to succeeding generations. The idea that acquired traits can be passed on to offspring is called Lamarkism. Natural selection occurs because offspring through random mutations are more fit than others to survive.

(Easy) (Skill 37.3)

200. In _____, advantageous traits lead to species survival and reproduction over time.

   A. natural selection

   B. sexual selection

   C. codominance

   D. artificial selection

Answer: A. natural selection

Darwin's theory of natural selection states that nature selects the traits (genes) that facilitate the survival of a species. The fittest animals survive and their genes will be most prevalent in the environment as a result.

(Easy) (Skill 38.2)

201. Which of the following describes the interaction between community members when one species feeds on another species but does not kill it immediately?

   A. Parasitism

   B. Predation

   C. Commensalism

   D. Mutualism

Answer: A. Parasitism

Predation occurs when one species kills another species. In mutualism, both species benefit. In commensalisms, one species benefits without the other being harmed.

(Average) (Skill 38.4)

202. Which of the following is NOT a type of organismal behavior?

   A. Competition

   B. Mating

   C. Territoriality

   D. Phototrophism

Answer: D. Phototrophism

Organismal behaviors are the ways in which individuals of different or the same species interact within their environments. Organisms can compete for resources or territories, and also can mate with each other. Phototrophism is the behavioral response (growth) of a plant towards light, not another organism.

(Easy) (Skill 39.1)

203. Which is the correct order for the layers of Earth's atmosphere, from lowest to highest?

   A. Troposphere, stratosphere, mesosphere, and thermosphere

   B. Mesosphere, stratosphere, troposphere, and thermosphere

   C. Troposphere, stratosphere, thermosphere, and mesosphere

   D. Thermosphere, troposphere, stratosphere, mesosphere

Answer: A. Troposphere, stratosphere, mesosphere, and thermosphere

All weather occurs in the troposphere. There are few clouds in the stratosphere, but weather balloons can float in this region. Air temperatures start to drop in the mesosphere. The coldest spot on Earth is where the mesosphere meets the thermosphere. The thermosphere extends into outer space.

(Rigorous) (Skill 39.1)

204. Which of the following is NOT true about the lithosphere's plates?

   A. When two plates move towards each other, the process is called convergence

   B. When two plates move away from each other, the process is called divergence

   C. Plates move meters per year on average

   D. Subduction is the process in which an oceanic plate slides under a continental plate, resulting in the formation of an oceanic trench

Answer: C. Plates move meters per year on average

Plates move centimeters per year on average.

(Easy) (Skill 16.1)

205. **What type of rock can be classified by the size of its crystals?**

A. Metamorphic

B. Igneous

C. Minerals

D. Sedimentary

Answer: B. Igneous

Igneous rock is formed when molten rock material cools. It is characterized by its grain size and mineral content. Metamorphic rocks are formed from other rocks as a result of heat and pressure. Sedimentary rocks come from weathering and erosion of preexisting rocks.

(Average) (Skill 40.1)

206. **What are solids with a definite chemical composition and a tendency to split along planes of weakness?**

A. Ores

B. Rocks

C. Minerals

D. Salts

Answer: C. Minerals

Rocks are made up of minerals, and ores are rocks than can be processed for a commercial use. Salts are ionic compounds formed from acids and bases.

(Easy) (Skill 40.1)

207. **In which of the following eras did life first appear?**

A. Paleozoic

B. Mesozoic

C. Cenozoic

D. Precambrian

Answer: D. Precambrian

The first multicellular organisms evolved during the Precambrian. The Cambrian explosion, the rapid appearance of most groups of complex invertebrate organisms, took place in the Cambrian period, which is part of the Paleozoic era. Fish evolved in the Paleozoic era, dinosaurs in the Mesozoic era, and humans in the Cenozoic era.

(Rigorous) (Skill 40.1)

208. **Which of the following is NOT true about dating techniques?**

A. When using the principle of superposition, a bed of sedimentary rock is considered older than the bed below it

B. Fossils found in the same bed of sedimentary rock can be assumed to have lived in the same time period

C. Absolute dating measures the amount of radioactive material in a specimen

D. Index fossils are used to identify geologic periods

Answer: A. When using the principle of superposition a bed of sedimentary rock is considered older than the bed below it

A bed of sedimentary rock is considered younger than the bed below it if, according to the principle of superposition, deposition of sediments and minerals occurs from the bottom and upward. An index fossil is typically a fossil of an organism that is known to have lived in a specific time period in many geographic locations. So if the index fossil is found in a bed of sedimentary rock among other fossils, the other fossils can be dated to that same time period.

(Average) (Skill 40.4)

209. _____ is the transport of a rock's surface materials by another moveable material.

A. Erosion

B. Weathering

C. Deposition

D. Wearing

Answer: A. Erosion

Erosion is a form of weathering in which the surface materials of a rock are transported away by another moveable material, like water or air.

(Average) (Skill 40.4)

210. When continental plates move as a result of sudden energy release and seismic wave formation in the Earth's crust, _____ occurs.

A. volcano formation

B. mountain building

C. cementation

D. an earthquake

Answer: D. an earthquake

An earthquake can occur when quickened plate movement and sudden energy release cause rocks in the plate to break. The seismic wave is created by the break and its size and distance of diffusion reflects the magnitude of the break.

(Easy) (Skill 42.2)

211. There are _____ established planets in the solar system.

A. ten

B. nine

C. eight

D. seven

Answer: C. eight

As of 2006, Pluto is classified as a dwarf planet, not a planet.

(Average) (Skill 42.1)

212. Interactions between _____ and _____ are responsible for the ocean tides.

A. the Earth; the moon

B. the Earth; the sun

C. the moon; the sun

D. the moon; Mercury

Answer: A. the Earth; the moon

Gravitational interactions between the earth and moon are responsible for the ocean's tides.

(Rigorous) (Skills 41.5)

213. **Why is the winter in the Southern Hemisphere colder than winter in the Northern Hemisphere?**

   A. Earth's axis of 24-hour rotation tilts at an angle of $23\frac{1}{2}°$

   B. The elliptical orbit of Earth around the sun changes the distance of the sun from Earth

   C. The Southern Hemisphere has more water than the Northern Hemisphere

   D. The greenhouse effect is greater for the Northern Hemisphere

Answer: B. The elliptical orbit of Earth around the sun changes the distance of the sun from Earth

The tilt of Earth's axis causes the seasons. The Earth is close to the sun during winter in the Northern Hemisphere. Winter in the Southern Hemisphere occurs six months later when Earth is farther from the Sun. The presence of water explains why winters are harsher inland than by the coast.

(Rigorous) (Skill 42.3)

214. **Which of the following astronomical entities is NOT part of the galaxy the sun is located in?**

   A. Nebulae

   B. Quasars

   C. Pulsars

   D. Neutron stars

Answer: B. Quasars

Nebulae are visible in the night sky and are glowing clouds of dust, hydrogen, and plasma. Neutron stars are the remnants of super novae, and pulsars are neutron stars that emit radio waves on a periodic basis. A quasar is a distant galaxy that emits large amounts of visible light and radio waves.

(Rigorous) (Skill 42.2)

215. **Which of the following facts of physics does NOT explain the cause of tides?**

   A. The density of water is less than the density of rock

   B. The force of gravity follows the inverse square law

   C. Centripetal acceleration causes water on Earth to bulge

   D. The gravitational force of the moon on Earth's oceans

Answer: A. The density of water is less than the density of rock

The main cause of lunar tides is that the moon's gravitational force is greater on water near the moon than on the other side of Earth. This causes the bulge of water. Earth's rotation causes the location of the bulge to change. Centripetal acceleration causes Earth's water to bulge and affects tides caused by the sun's gravity, but the effect is minor. The density of water and rock are not a cause of tides.

Fine Arts, Health, and Physical Education

(Easy) (Skill 43.1)

216. **You want to expose your students to the visual arts as a profession. Which is the best example of an appropriate activity?**

    A. Spoken word concert

    B. A visit to the orchestra

    C. A live painting session

    D. A Shakespeare play

    Answer: C. A live painting session

    Local live painting sessions can expose students to not only the finished work of art but also the process by which the artist creates the work.

(Rigorous) (Skill 43.2)

217. **Which of the following is true about linear perspective?**

    A. Objects appear smaller the closer they are

    B. Objects appear larger the farther away they are

    C. There is a convergence point along the horizon of the drawing

    D. Only the space and distance of objects relative to the reference point are shown

    Answer: C. There is a convergence point along the horizon of the drawing

    The vanishing point is the point at which all the lines in the drawing intersect.

(Easy) (Skill 43.4)

218. **The process of critiquing artwork is _____.**

    A. an asset for all teachers

    B. beyond the scope of the elementary teacher

    C. fairly complex and requires specific training

    D. limited to art historians and professional artists

    Answer: A. an asset for all teachers

    The elementary teacher's ability to think critically and problem-solve is reflected in her or his teaching in many ways, including the way art is perceived and discussed in the classroom. The capacity to critique a work of art is an asset for all teachers, especially in classrooms with integrated curricula, where art is taught in conjunction with other subjects, or in classrooms where there is no separate art program. Many people in various settings can learn to critique art.

(Easy) (Skill 43.5)

219. **_____ is a mark that follows an identifiable path.**

    A. An impression

    B. A line

    C. A point

    D. A shape

    Answer: B. A line

    A line is an element of art that starts at one point and has both length and direction.

(Rigorous) (Skill 43.7)

220. **All of the following are examples of useful art tools for early childhood students EXCEPT:**

    A. A color wheel

    B. Oversized crayons and pencils

    C. Fine-tipped brushes

    D. Clay

Answer: C. Fine-tipped brushes

Many prekindergarten and kindergarten students use oversized pencils and crayons for the first semester. Typically, after this first semester children gradually develop the ability to use smaller-sized materials, but they usually do not use fine-tipped brushes until the middle grades due to lack of adequate fine-motor skills. The color wheel is an excellent lesson for young children, and students begin to learn the uses of primary and secondary colors. Clay is also a valuable medium for children; it offers many opportunities for learning about texture, shape, line, and form as well as being creatively expressive.

(Average) (Skill 43.8)

221. **The Renaissance period was concerned with the rediscovery of the works of _____.**

    A. Italy

    B. Japan

    C. Germany

    D. classical Greece and Rome

Answer: D. classical Greece and Rome

The Renaissance period was concerned with the rediscovery of the works of classical Greece and Rome. The art, literature, and architecture of this period (ca. 1400–1630 CE) were inspired by classical order and style, which tended to be formal, simple, and concerned with the ideal human proportions.

(Rigorous) (Skill 43.9)

222. **Which of the following correctly describes Western and Eastern art?**

    A. Western art is more spiritual; Eastern is more secular in nature

    B. Western art focuses on accurately portraying human anatomy

    C. Eastern art focuses on muscle tone in depictions of the human body

    D. Eastern art requires a horizontal projection of eye movement

Answer: B. Western art focuses on accurately portraying human anatomy

In contrast to Eastern art, Western art focuses on accurately portraying the human anatomy, down to the detail of muscle tone, in different art forms.

(Rigorous) (Skill 43.15)

223. **Which of the following statements is most accurate?**

    A. Most artists work alone and are rarely affected by the work of other artists

    B. Artists in every field are influenced and inspired by the works of others in the various disciplines in the humanities

    C. It is rare for visual arts to be influenced by literature or poetry

    D. The political climate of an era affects the art of the period only on specific occasions throughout history

    Answer: B. Artists in every field are influenced and inspired by the works of others in the various disciplines in the humanities

    The history of the humanities is replete with examples of artists in every field being influenced and inspired by specific works of others. Influence and inspiration continuously cross the lines between the various disciplines in the humanities.

(Average) (Skill 43.8)

224. **Which theme or style is NOT matched with its correct century?**

    A. Impressionism—19th century

    B. Baroque—17th century

    C. Futurism—19th century

    D. Expressionism—20th century

    Answer: C. Futurism—19th century

    Futurism emerged as a popular style in the 20th century.

(Easy) (Skill 44.1)

225. **You want to expose your students to music. What are potential in-class activities?**

    A. A lesson using a digital music-making platform (e.g., PBS, LiveBinders)

    B. A kids-themed concert

    C. A field trip to the orchestra

    D. Both B and C

    Answer: A. A lesson with digital music making platforms (e.g., PBS, LiveBinders)

    Only choice A is an in-class activity.

(Rigorous) (Skill 44.2)

226. **Which of the following is true about music notation?**

    A. The lower clef is the treble

    B. The clef is a four-line staff

    C. The pitch of note is how long it is held

    D. Dotted ties indicate the duration of a note

    Answer: D. Dotted ties indicate the duration of a note

    Dotted ties, along with ties and rests, are used to indicate how long a note should be played.

(Average) (Skill 44.2)

227. **A combination of three or more tones sounded at the same time is called a _____.**

    A. harmony

    B. consonance

    C. chord

    D. dissonance

Answer: C. chord

A chord is three or more tones combined and sounded simultaneously. Dissonance is the simultaneous sounding of tones that produce a feeling of tension or unrest and a feeling that further resolution is needed. Harmony is the sound resulting from the simultaneous sounding of two or more tones consonant with one another.

(Easy) (Skill 44.3)

228. **Which pair is correct?**

    A. Drum—string instrument

    B. Tuba—brass instrument

    C. Trumpet—percussion instrument

    D. Cello—woodwind instrument

    Answer: B. Tuba—brass instrument

    A tuba is an instrument made from brass or other metal.

(Rigorous) (Skill 44.3)

229. **A piano is a _____ instrument.**

    A. percussion and brass

    B. brass and string

    C. string

    D. percussion and string

    Answer: D. percussion and string

    A piano is often difficult to categorize because it has strings but its keys are struck by hammers, making it a percussion instrument.

(Rigorous) (Skill 44.3)

230. **Music arrangement can be taught to elementary students in all of the following ways except _____.**

    A. incorporating instruments with different key signatures

    B. adding harmonies to simple melodies

    C. deep study of musical theory

    D. changing the key of the song

    Answer: C. deep study of musical theory

    Deep study of theory would be far too advanced for elementary students.

(Average) (Skill 44.7)

231. **The term *conjunto* in music refers to:**

    A. Two instruments playing at the same time

    B. A tempo a little faster than allegro

    C. A musical style that involves playing with great feeling

    D. A type of Texas-Mexican music

    Answer: D. A type of Texas-Mexican music

    Around the turn of the century in Texas, a clash of cultures produced the Texas-Mexican music called *conjunto*. Working-class musicians from German and Mexican backgrounds combined their talents to produce this folk music, which used the accordion as its main instrument. Musicians could easily transport accordions, making them the perfect accompaniment for dancing, eating, gambling, and other social events.

(Rigorous) (Skill 44.8)

232. **All of the following apply to critiquing music EXCEPT:**

A. Listening, analyzing, describing, and evaluating

B. Avoiding the use of musical terminology in order to facilitate students' enjoyment of music

C. Having students develop their own rubrics for critiques

D. Encouraging students to work in pairs

Answer: B. Avoiding the use of musical terminology in order to facilitate student's enjoyment of music

Teaching basic music terminology is a prerequisite for any critique process. Without the necessary language, it is not effective to try to evaluate a piece of music. Similarly, students must be given the opportunity to develop listening skills so they are able to hear different musical elements, themes, instruments, and tones. They will also benefit from an overview of the sounds of different instruments and a listing of musical styles.

(Average) (Skill 45.1)

233. **Behavioral change should be _____.**

A. externally motivated

B. internally motivated

C. both internally and externally motivated

D. None of the above

Answer: C. both internally and externally motivated

Behavioral change should always be internally motivated first, and then externally motivated by one's support systems.

(Average) (Skill 45.1)

234. **Behavioral changes _____.**

A. take time to take effect

B. should have a positive impact

C. have to be sustained by the student

D. All of the above

Answer: D. All of the above

All are characteristics of behavioral change.

(Easy) (Skill 45.2)

235. **Which of the following is NOT a type of muscle tissue?**

A. Skeletal

B. Cardiac

C. Smooth

D. Fiber

Answer: D. Fiber

The main function of the muscular system is movement. There are three types of muscle tissue: skeletal, cardiac, and smooth. Fiber is unrelated to muscle.

(Rigorous) (Skill 45.2)

236. **Which of the following does NOT describe atherosclerosis?**

    A. Plaques form in blood vessels

    B. Red blood cells change shape and "stick" to blood vessel walls

    C. Strokes can occur as a result of plaque formation

    D. Arteries harden as a result of plaque formation

    Answer: B. Red blood cells change shape and "stick" to blood vessel walls

    Red blood cells changing shape and sticking to blood vessel walls is actually a characteristic of sickle cell disease, another type of vascular disease.

(Average) (Skill 45.2)

237. **Which is NOT a characteristic of veins?**

    A. They have valves that ensure unidirectional flow of blood

    B. They have thin walls

    C. As they approach the heart, their size increases

    D. They have very elastic walls

    Answer: D. They have very elastic walls

    Veins, unlike arteries, do not have very elastic walls. Since veins bring blood back to the heart and much of it travels upward, their valves keep the blood from flowing downward to defy gravity. Arteries have elastic walls because they must withstand the pressure of the heart pumping blood throughout the body.

(Rigorous) (Skill 45.2)

238. **Which of the following produces the least amount of energy in the body?**

    A. Carbohydrates

    B. Oils

    C. Proteins

    D. Fats

    Answer: C. Proteins

    Proteins are body-building molecules that do not release significant energy when broken down in the body. Molecule for molecule, fats and oils release the most energy when metabolized.

(Rigorous) (Skill 45.2)

239. **Which of the following substances is one least likely to find in urine?**

    A. Uric acid

    B. Ammonia

    C. Glucose

    D. Sodium chloride

    Answer: C. Glucose

    It is unlikely to find glucose in urine since it is used as an energy source by the body and is rarely filtered into the urine by the kidney, which is responsible for filtering wastes such as urea and ammonia, from the blood and excreting them in urine.

(Rigorous) (Skill 45.2)

240. **What is the main reason that humans cannot digest cellulose?**

    A. It does not contain sugars and thus cannot be digested by humans

    B. Its protein chains are too long

    C. It is made up of monosaccharides and thus cannot be digested by humans

    D. Humans lack the proper enzymes to digest cellulose

    Answer: D. Humans lack the proper enzymes to digest cellulose

    Cellulose is a very complex carbohydrate. The polysaccharide is composed of more than 3,000 units of glucose strung together, which ruminants like cows can digest over time—with the help of bacteria in their gut. Humans lack the enzymes required to break down the beta-acetal linkages in cellulose.

(Rigorous) (Skill 45.2)

241. **Which of the following statements is true about joints?**

    A. They occur where bones intersect

    B. They occur where organs begin

    C. They occur where muscles attach to the skeleton

    D. They occur where ligaments meet tendons

    Answer: A. They occur where bones intersect

    Joints occur where two bones meet. When ligaments and other tissues join the two bones, they can articulate, allowing movement. Tendons join muscles to bone.

(Average) (Skill 45.2)

242. **Which disease is NOT correctly matched with the body system it primarily affects?**

    A. Diabetes—nervous system

    B. Heart disease—circulatory system

    C. Appendicitis—digestive system

    D. Hyperthyroidism—endocrine system

    Answer: A. Diabetes—nervous system

    Diabetes is a disease of the endocrine system, specifically a dysregulation of the insulin hormone.

(Average) (Skill 45.2)

243. **What is the importance of roughage in a balanced diet?**

    A. It promotes peristalsis in the gut

    B. It enhances food absorption in the body

    C. It promotes bile production

    D. It activates enzymes in the gut

    Answer: A. It promotes peristalsis in the gut

    Roughage, which is not digested, eases movement along the gut, either by binding to fats and excreting them as waste or by creating bulk to move food along and allow absorption of water.

(Rigorous) (Skill 45.4)

244. Of the following, which is the leading cause of preventable death in the United States?

   A. Distracted driving

   B. Infectious disease

   C. Sedentary lifestyle

   D. Tobacco use

Answer: D. Tobacco use

Tobacco use, in particular tobacco smoking, is the leading cause of death in the United States and worldwide. Tobacco use is a major risk factor for heart and lung diseases, including lung cancer.

(Rigorous) (Skill 45.4)

245. HIV/AIDS is a viral disease that has rocked many nations. Which of the following factors has NOT contributed to the persistence of the viral infection?

   A. Evading immune responses

   B. Irresponsible sex behavior

   C. Lack of education about HIV/AIDS

   D. Sharing the same living quarters

Answer: D. Sharing the same living quarters

HIV/AIDS can only be spread through unprotected sexual contact, blood transfusion, or mother to child through pregnancy. It is not spread through casual interaction.

(Average) (Skill 45.6)

246. A physical education instructor anticipates and prevents potential injuries, watches for hidden injuries, and takes an injury evaluation of the entire class. Which of the following strategies to prevent injuries is the teacher demonstrating?

   A. Maintaining hiring standards

   B. Proper use of equipment

   C. Proper procedures for emergencies

   D. Participant screening

Answer: D. Participant screening

In order for the instructor to know each student's physical status, he or she takes an injury evaluation. Such surveys are one way to know the physical status of an individual. Injury evaluations chronicle past injuries, tattoos, activities, and diseases an individual may have or have had. It helps the instructor know the limitations of each individual. Participant screening covers all forms of surveying and anticipation of injuries.

(Average) (Skill 45.9)

247. All of the following are signs of anorexia nervosa EXCEPT:

   A. Malnutrition

   B. Behavior regression

   C. No outward signs

   D. Recognizable weight loss

Answer: C. No outward signs

There are significant outward signs displayed when a person is struggling with anorexia.

(Average) (Skill 45.14)

248. By displaying food product labels and discussing how to choose common healthy foods, Mrs. Watkins is helping her students to _____.

A. make positive health-related decisions

B. understand how real-world concepts apply to health choices

C. be active learners in their decision-making processes

D. All of the above

Answer: D. All of the above

The teacher is helping her students to gain an understanding of the importance of making strong healthy decisions in relation to their food choices. She is doing this in an active way, which will lead to the students gaining further understanding of dietary options. They will then be able to apply this understanding at home.

(Rigorous) (Skill 46.1)

249. Which of the following refers to a muscle's ability to contract over a period of time and maintain strength?

A. Cardiovascular fitness

B. Muscle endurance

C. Muscle fitness

D. Muscle force

Answer: B. Muscle endurance

Cardiovascular fitness relates to the ability to perform moderate-to-high-intensity exercise for a prolonged period. Muscular fitness relates to how much force a muscle group can generate (strength) and how effectively the muscle group can sustain that force over a period of time (endurance).

(Average) (Skill 46.4)

250. A game of "Simon Says" is an opportunity for the teacher to assess students' _____.

A. concept of body awareness

B. concept of spatial awareness

C. concept of direction and movement

D. concept of speed and movement

Answer: A. Concept of body awareness

Instructors can assess body awareness by playing and watching a game of "Simon Says" and asking the students to touch different body parts. You can also instruct students to make their bodies into various shapes, from straight to round to twisted, and varying sizes, to fit into different-sized spaces.

(Average) (Skill 46.5)

251. Bending, stretching, and turning are examples of which type of skill?

A. Locomotor skills

B. Nonlocomotor skills

C. Manipulative skills

D. Rhythmic skills

Answer: B. Nonlocomotor skills

Nonlocomotor skills are stability skills in which the movement requires little or no movement of one's base of support and does not result in a change of position.

(Rigorous) (Skill 46.5)

252. **Which of the following is NOT true about physical skills?**

    A. An activity to develop galloping skill is playing Fox and Hound

    B. Run-and-catch is an object-control skill

    C. Manipulative skills only propel an object

    D. Rhythmic skills involve motion that follows a beat

    Answer: C. Manipulative skills only propel an object

    Manipulative skills use body parts to propel or receive objects, controlling them primarily with the hands and feet.

(Average) (Skill 46.7)

253. **What is the proper sequential order of development for the acquisition of nonlocomotor skills?**

    A. Stretch, sit, bend, turn, swing, twist, shake, rock and sway, dodge, fall

    B. Bend, stretch, turn, twist, swing, sit, rock and sway, shake, dodge, fall

    C. Stretch, bend, sit, shake, turn, rock and sway, swing, twist, dodge, fall

    D. Bend, stretch, sit, turn, twist, swing, sway, rock and sway, dodge, fall

    Answer: C. Stretch, bend, sit, shake, turn, rock and sway, swing, twist, dodge, fall

    Each skill in the progression builds on the previous skills.

(Average) (Skill 46.10)

254. **_____ grouping can increase student participation and engagement.**

    A. Student-led

    B. Heterogeneous

    C. Homogeneous

    D. Both B and C

    Answer: D. Both B and C

    Both heterogeneous and homogeneous grouping can increase student participation and engagement. Student-led grouping may lead to certain students being excluded or picked last.

(Rigorous) (Skill 46.11)

255. **Which of the following statements is NOT true?**

    A. Children's motor development and physical fitness are affected by a range of factors, including social, psychological, familial, genetic, and cultural factors

    B. Motor development is complete by the time a student reaches sixth grade

    C. A family's economic status can affect a student's motor development

    D. A physical education program can have a positive impact on a student's level of physical fitness

    Answer: B. Motor development is complete by the time a student reaches sixth grade

    Motor development continues until adulthood. Furthermore, many factors have an impact on children's motor development and physical fitness.

(Easy) (Skill 47.1)

256. **In a play, these performers often have a few lines, but perform as one complete group:**

    A. Choir

    B. Chorus

    C. Grand opera

    D. Theatrical band

Answer: B. Chorus

The chorus performs in a play or production and may include individuals with certain small speaking parts. The chorus sings numerous songs or recites lines in unison during the production as one complete group.

(Rigorous) (Skill 47.4)

257. **As a way to incorporate other subjects into the area of theatre, a teacher should choose to _____.**

    A. direct a play related to the students' current interests

    B. collaborate with the principal to find a script to use

    C. plan to create a play using a Social Studies topic that was taught last year

    D. create a unit plan based on reading, math, Social Studies, and theatre concepts that focuses on the story of the first Thanksgiving

Answer: D. Create a unit plan based on reading, math, social studies, and theatre concepts that focuses on the story of the first Thanksgiving

The teacher's goal can be to incorporate as many cross-curricular areas as possible into a theatre project. Utilizing concepts from each subject will ensure that he or she does this in an age-appropriate way.

(Average) (Skill 47.5)

258. **A goal of theatre is to _____.**

    A. promote confidence

    B. promote expression

    C. deliver entertainment

    D. All of the above

Answer: D. All of the above

Theatre allows children to gain confidence in front of others through speaking and acting. It also promotes expression and delivers entertainment to a variety of audiences.

(Rigorous) (Skill 47.9)

259. **A teacher planning a preschool class production should _____.**

    A. use any available space

    B. ensure that there is an adequate amount of time to practice

    C. allow the students to run the entire show

    D. ask each student if he or she wants to participate or not

Answer: B. ensure that there is an adequate amount of time to practice

Students will need to feel comfortable with the material they are presenting in a production. In order to do so, the teacher should plan accordingly to make sure that enough practice time has been put into place.

(Easy) (Skill 47.2)

260. **Which materials would help your students connect with the characters in a play?**

    A. Costumes

    B. Props

    C. Music

    D. All of the above

Answer: D. All of the above

Costumes, props, and music (visual or audio cues) may help your students better understand the context and storyline of the play.

(Average) (Skill 47.3)

261. **Which pair is incorrect?**

    A. Chorus—character or group that says the prologue

    B. Soliloquy—extended speech

    C. Epilogue—opening words for play

    D. All of the above

Answer: C. Epilogue—opening words for play

The epilogue contains the closing commentary on the play's events and conclusion.

(Average) (Skill 47.3)

262. **Which of the following stage elements is correct?**

    A. Down-stage—area furthest from audience

    B. Stage left—audience's right

    C. Stage right—actor's (when facing audience) left

    D. Travelers—curtains on the wings of the stage

Answer: B. Stage left—audience's right

Stage directions are always given from the actor's perspective as if she is facing the audience.

(Rigorous) (Skill 47.3)

263. **Which of the following is incorrect about these elements of theater?**

    A. Actors never break the "Fourth Wall"

    B. Intermissions give the audience a break

    C. The audience employs suspension of disbelief.

    D. Gaffers operate lighting for the production

Answer: A. Actors never break the "Fourth Wall"

Actors, in fact, can break the "Fourth Wall," the invisible wall between them and the audience, when they converse with the audience. They are still in character when they break the wall.

(Easy) (Skill 47.3)

264. **To _____ is to deliver lines with feelings appropriate to the scene.**

    A. engage

    B. speak

    C. emote

    D. recite

Answer: C. emote

When an actor emotes, he is not just reciting his lines but also speaking with emotion to reflect the context of the scene.

(Easy) (Skill 47.7)

265. The Shakespeare play based on the tragic circumstances for two young lovers is

   _____.

   A. *Taming of the Shrew*

   B. *Othello*

   C. *The Merchant of Venice*

   D. *Romeo and Juliet*

   Answer: D. *Romeo and Juliet*

   Romeo and Juliet is the classic story of forbidden love between two young people.

(Average) (Skill 47.7)

266. **Which pair is incorrect?**

   A. Exposition—straightforward speech or discussion

   B. Irony—a contradiction between what the character thinks and what the audience knows to be the truth

   C. Tragedy—death of a main character

   D. Comedy—appeals to audience's humor

   Answer: B. Irony—a contradiction between what the character thinks and what the audience knows to be the truth

   This is actually the definition of dramatic irony. Irony is a more general term to reflect amusing or surprising contradictions in literature and by definition does not describe any relationship between characters' and an audience's knowledge.

CPSIA information can be obtained at www.ICGtesting.com
Printed in the USA
BVOW09s0342031215

429024BV00008B/2/P